Intellectual Property and the Internet

A Global Guide to Protecting Intellectual Property Online

Consulting Editor **Neville Cordell**

Consulting editor
Neville Cordell

Managing director
Sian O'Neill

Commissioning editor
Katherine Cowdrey

Editorial services director
Carolyn Boyle

Production manager
Paul Stoneham

Group publishing director
Tony Harriss

Intellectual Property and the Internet: A Global Guide to Protecting Intellectual Property Online
is published by
Globe Law and Business
Globe Business Publishing Ltd
New Hibernia House
Winchester Walk
London SE1 9AG
United Kingdom
Tel +44 20 7234 0606
Fax +44 20 7234 0808
Web www.globelawandbusiness.com

Printed and bound by CPI Group (UK) Ltd, Croydon, CR0 4YY

ISBN 9781905783953

Table of contents

Preface

Neville Cordell
Allen & Overy LLP

When it was created in 1992, one million computers were connected to the Internet worldwide. In 2016, that number will be 10 billion: 10,000 times more! In 1992, we never imagined that one day we would be able to read our favourite newspaper, discover new music or watch a film anytime, anywhere, on any device – a laptop, a tablet or a phone. We could not imagine the opportunities. Or indeed the challenges that would arise.[1]

Today the Internet is all pervasive – it is the principal means through which social, commercial and scientific data content is disseminated, information is searched for, opinions are exchanged and knowledge shared. Huge businesses such as Google, which did not even exist in 1992, have grown with astonishing rapidity to become among the largest global companies, first to help people to navigate their way around the multitude of content, to facilitate sharing of content, and then to aggregate and increase that content. Online, there are new ways of providing, creating and distributing content, and new ways to generate value. Online marketplaces are rapidly outperforming their physical counterparts, and enterprises of all sizes are using the Internet as a tool to locate and secure purchasers for their products and services in a huge global market.

All forms of IP rights are the cornerstone of the new knowledge-based economy, which has been a major driver of growth in the past two decades. Copyright offers protection to the vast array of digitised works, including online traders' immense databases of commercial content, the software enabling the computer to function and the programs that make the digital networks so useful, and user-generated content to name a few. Copyright supports creation, which in turn supports distribution and innovation. Trademarks and service marks are of increasing importance in this virtual environment where consumers rely on strong brand awareness and performance for the confidence to engage in e-commerce, whilst domain names perform a similar identifying function to trademarks. Patents have also migrated to the Internet: the technology-intensive nature of e-commerce means that many of its constituent processes may be patentable subject matter so long as the legal criteria for patentability are met in the jurisdictions concerned.

However, a rapidly developing technology, the continually evolving digital business models, and the growing autonomy of online consumers, are all

---

1 Michel Barnier, in November 2012, in a speech at the launch event of the CEP Digital Forum Taskforce on Copyright in the EU Digital Single Market.

challenging the robustness of these IP rights. There is a call for constant assessment as to whether IP rights are 'fit for purpose' in the internet era; whether they set the right incentives, as well as offering adequate protection and enforcement mechanisms to enable rights holders, users of the rights and consumers to take advantage of the opportunities that modern technologies provide.

The purpose of this book is to provide a comparative view of the protection offered in a wide range of jurisdictions around the world, by the various categories of IP rights to internet-based content, in order to better assess the effectiveness of the level of protection being afforded. In each jurisdiction, it sets out the nature and breadth of IP rights, the defences and remedies available in respect of each right, whilst also dealing with 'news grabbing' issues such as dealing with file-sharing platforms and the liability of internet service providers. It is not prescriptive and does not seek to offer solutions.

It is evident that although there is a level of international and regional harmonisation in relation to some IP rights, diversity remains. So does the question as to whether the current IP rights regimes are exploiting the full potential of the digital economy.

Neville Cordell is a partner in Allen & Overy LLP's London office specialising in IP litigation and advisory work. He has 20 years' experience of acting for some of the world's leading technology companies and brands in patent, trademark, design, breach of confidence and copyright disputes.

Australia

Michael Williams
Gilbert + Tobin

1. Copyright, database rights and design rights

1.1 Overview

Original material that falls within the classification of 'works', under Part III of the Copyright Act 1968 (Cth) ('the Act'), and the classification of 'subject matter other than works', under Part IV of the Act, are capable of recognition and protection under copyright law.

(a) *Literary works and artistic works*

Literary and artistic works are protected under Section 31 of the Act. Software is protected as a species of literary work under Section 10.

(b) *Films, sound recordings, and broadcasts*

Films, sound recordings and broadcasts are protected as 'subject matter other than works' under Part IV of the Act.

(c) *Typographical arrangement of a published edition*

Section 88 protects published editions of works against facsimile copying.

(d) *Protection of the user interface*

There is no specific protection of the user interface of a computer screen or protection of the type described as 'look and feel', under Australian copyright or design law.

(e) *Computer-generated works*

Computer-generated works are not protected under Australian copyright law. Following the decision of the High Court in *IceTV Pty Ltd v Nine Network Australia Pty Ltd*,[1] Australian courts have confirmed that there is no protection over computer-generated works because they lack the necessary element of authorship required for original works under copyright law.

(f) *Websites protected as databases*

There is no separate protection for databases under Australian law, including databases connected with websites. Although the absence of such a form of

1 (2009) 239 CLR 458.

protection has been identified by the highest appellate court, the High Court, no action has been taken by the government to develop or introduce laws that provide database protection.

(g) ***Compilations***

Compilations are protected as literary works under Australian copyright law. The scope of protection of compilations has become less clear after the decision of the High Court in *IceTV Pty Ltd v Nine Network Australia Pty Ltd.*[2] Whilst not expressly overruling prior authority which appeared to recognise copyright protection based on the 'sweat of the brow' doctrine, the Court emphasised the need for there to be a "work [that] originates with an author or joint authors from some independent intellectual effort" and that the skill and labour is directed towards the work produced.

1.2 Infringing acts

There are various types of infringing acts that may be involved in internet activity under Australian law.

(a) ***Copying***

The making of copies of works in a material form or reproductions of other subject matter constitutes an infringement of copyright.

Temporary copies: The making of temporary copies of works or other subject matter is capable of amounting to copyright infringement under Australian law, as long as a substantial part of the original work or other subject matter is involved. See also the requirement of material form below in relation to works.

In any medium: There is no requirement that a copy or reproduction be made in a specific medium. In the case of works, there is a requirement that the copy is reduced to 'material form' which may in some circumstances be met even where a copy is held in RAM or other transient storage device (see Section 10 of the Act).

(b) ***Issuing copies to the public***

The importation and distribution of articles constituting unauthorised (infringing) copies of works or other subject matter is an infringing dealing under Section 102 and Section 103 of the Act, where the importer knew or reasonably ought to have known that the article was infringing or would have been infringing (in the case of importation) had it been made in Australia. The definition of 'article' was amended in 2006, after the decision in *Cooper v Universal Music Australia Pty Ltd,*[3] in which the Court found that there was no infringing dealing in a sound recording for the purposes of Section 103. No Australian court has since considered whether the act of distributing a file over the Internet amounts to an act of dealing or importation under Section 102 or Section 103 under this revised definition of article.

---

2 (2009) 239 CLR 458.
3 (2006) 156 FCR 380.

(c) ***Communicating work to the public***

It is an infringement of copyright to communicate a work or other subject matter to the public. 'Communicate' is defined to include to make available online or to electronically transmit (Section 10). The public is defined to mean the public inside or outside Australia and includes a situation where a file is communicated to the public outside Australia from inside Australia, or the reverse (Section 10).

(d) ***Perform, show or play work in public***

While there is an exclusive right to perform works and other subject matter in public, no Australian court has found that this right is infringed by means of the use of the Internet and it is doubtful that such an act would be found to involve infringement.

(e) ***Rent or lend the work to the public***

There is a lending right in relation to certain works and sound recordings.

(f) ***Authorising another person to do any of the above***

It is an infringement of copyright in Australia to exercise one of the exclusive rights in a work or other subject matter in Australia, or to authorise the doing of such an act (Section 36, Section 101). The court is required by statute to take into account a number of mandatory factors under Section 101(1A) when determining whether or not a person authorised the infringing acts of another. These factors include the extent (if any) of the person's power to prevent the act of infringement, the relationship between the person and the infringer, and whether the person "took any other reasonable steps to prevent or avoid" the act of infringement, including compliance with an industry code. There is no industry code for the purposes of Section 101(1A)(c). While there is established authority on the meaning of 'authorise', a majority of the High Court in *Roadshow Films Pty Ltd v iiNet Ltd*[4] held that the factors under Section 101(1A) supplant the previous case law.

(g) ***Secondary infringement***

While Australian copyright law has no equivalent of contributory or vicarious infringement it does recognise liability for infringement as a joint tortfeasor by reason of participation in a common design. In *Cooper v Universal Music Australia Pty Ltd*,[5] the Court held that liability for common design depends on the participation in conduct with a shared purpose or tacit agreement amongst participants. A participant in a common design is liable to the same extent and to the same remedies as if they had engaged in the primary act of infringement themselves.

1.3 Test for copyright infringement

It is an infringement of copyright to exercise the exclusive rights of the copyright owner in respect of the whole or a substantial part of the work.

In the case of literary, dramatic and musical works (Section 31(1)(a) and (c))

4 (2012) 286 ALR 466.
5 (2006) 156 FCR 380.

exclusive rights include the right to reproduce the work in a material form, to publish the work, to perform the work in public, to communicate the work to the public and to make an adaptation of the work. The exclusive rights in artistic works are more limited (Section 31(1)(b)). The right of communication to the public covers not only the acts of broadcasting, but also the right to make a work 'available online' or 'electronically transmit' a work to the public by means of the Internet (Section 10). In the case of subject matter other than works, such as sound recordings or films, exact copying is required; a soundalike or lookalike would not result in infringement.

Infringement is generally proved by establishing access to the original work, leading to an inference of copying, together with objective similarity of the copy and the original work.

Repeated copying of an insubstantial part will not amount to infringement, as confirmed by the High Court in *IceTV Pty Ltd v Nine Network Australia Pty Ltd*.[6]

1.4 Exemptions/defences to copyright infringement

There are a number of specific exceptions and defences to infringement of copyright. Their scope is currently being reviewed by the Australian Law Reform Commission, which issued its recommendations to the Australian Government at the end of 2013. These recommendations are expected to be made public in early 2014.

(a) Format shifting

There are limited rights to format-shift certain types of works. They include the making of copies of sound recordings for private and domestic use under certain conditions (Section 109A) and the copying of films for use in a different format for private and domestic use (Section 110AA).

(b) Personal copying rights

There are rights to make personal copies of sound recordings for private and domestic use under certain conditions (Section 109A).

(c) Time-shifting

Section 111 permits the making of a film or sound recording of a radio or television broadcast for later hearing or viewing, subject to certain conditions. The defence applies also to works or other subject matter included in a broadcast.

(d) Fair use

There is no 'fair use' defence under Australian copyright law. There are presently specific 'fair dealing' defences for activities that are considered to be in the public interest, including research or study (Section 40 works/Section 103C other subject matter), criticism or review (Section 41 works/Section 103A other subject matter), parody or satire (Section 42 works/Section 103AA other subject matter) and reporting news (Section 43 works/Section 103B other subject matter). There are also fair

6 (2009) 239 CLR 458.

dealing defences for certain activities in relation to computer programs (eg, Sections 47AB to 47H). In *Fairfax Media Publications Pty Ltd v Reed International Books Australia Pty Ltd*,[7] the Federal Court found that the reproduction of headlines and abstracts of articles from a print newspaper for online distribution was fair dealing for the purposes of reporting news under Section 43 of the Copyright Act.

(e) ***Caching/temporary copies as part of communication process***

Temporary copies of works or other subject matter do not infringe copyright where they are made as part of the technical process of making or receiving a communication (Section 43A/Section 111A), or as a necessary part of the technical process of using a work (Section 43B/Section 111B), in each case under certain conditions.

(f) ***Hosting***

The act of 'hosting' copyright works or other subject matter is an infringement of the right of communication to the public, constituting 'making available online' (Section 10). In appropriate factual circumstances, hosting may also amount to authorisation (see 1.2(f) above and *Cooper v Universal Music Australia Pty Ltd*.[8]

There are a number of provisions of the Act that may be available to hosts in this situation, although exactly how they will apply to hosting activities remains untested. Under Section 22(6), a host will not be considered to have made a communication (other than a broadcast) if it can show that it was not 'responsible for determining the content of the communication'. This does not exclude authorisation liability.[9]

Sections 39B and 112E of the Act may be of more use in an authorisation context. These provisions exempt providers of communication facilities from liability for authorisation 'merely because another person uses the facilities so provided' to infringe copyright. While Section 112E was not considered by the High Court in *Roadshow Films Pty Ltd v iiNet Ltd*,[10] the trial judge and the Full Federal Court emphasised that the service provider must have done nothing more than make communication facilities available. Division 2AA of the Act limits the remedies available against 'carriage service providers' for authorising infringements of copyright, provided certain conditions are complied with. While the relevant activities include hosting activities, it is not clear that the definition of 'carriage service provider' includes all internet service providers (ISPs), an issue that has been under consideration by the Australian Government for some time.

(g) ***Back-up copies***

Section 47C provides a fair dealing defence for the making of back-up copies of computer programs from original legitimate software under certain conditions.

---

7 [2010] FCA 984.

8 (2006) 156 FCR 380; cf *Roadshow Films Pty Ltd v iiNet Ltd* (2012) 286 ALR 466).

9 See eg, *Cooper v Universal Music Australia Pty Ltd* (2006) 156 FCR 380.

10 (2012) 286 ALR 466.

(h) ***Reverse engineering***

Section 47D provides the fair dealing defence to 'reverse engineer' computer programs to make an interoperable program (rather than a competing program), under certain conditions.

(i) ***Parody defence***

Section 41A provides a fair dealing defence in the case of works of other subject matter: a fair dealing does not infringe copyright if it is 'for the purpose of parody or satire'.

(j) ***Incidental inclusion***

There is only a defence to incidental inclusion of works in the case of incidental filming or televising of artistic works (Section 67). Otherwise, copyright is not infringed unless either the whole or a substantial part of the work or subject matter is reproduced.

1.5 Remedies available for copyright infringement

Remedies for copyright infringement include injunctions and damages or an account of profits (Section 115(2)). There are well-established authorities detailing the principles upon which monetary relief is capable of being granted under the Act.

Where an infringement was 'innocent', in that the defendant was not aware, and had no reasonable grounds for suspecting, the act was an infringement of the copyright, the monetary relief that may be awarded is limited to an account of profits (Section 115(3)).

Additional damages may be awarded if a court finds that the infringement was flagrant (Section 115(4)), or by reason of a number of other matters including the need to deter similar infringements (Section 115(4)(1a), the conduct of the defendant after the act constituting the infringement and the benefit derived by the infringer.

1.6 Copyright liability

A number of important decisions have provided guidance on the legality of certain activities associated with the operation and hosting of sites and provision of services over the Internet.

(a) ***Hosting/cloud computing where infringing content uploaded by user of service***

Although the act of hosting infringing content has rarely been considered by an Australian court, the decisions that have been given have found that the act of hosting or operating a cloud server on which copies of works or reproductions of other subject matter are made carries with it liability for copyright infringement. In such a case both the user and the service provider may be liable for the acts of infringement.[11]

11 *National Rugby League Investments Pty Limited v Singtel Optus Pty Ltd* [2012] FCAFC 59).

(b) Hypertext linking

To third-party website: The liability of an operator of a website that provides hyperlinks to a website has not yet been determined under Australian law.

To an infringing work: In *Cooper v Universal Music Australia Pty Ltd,*[12] the Court found that the operation in Australia of a website that provided links to infringing sound recording files located on servers outside Australia constituted an act of infringement by authorisation by the operator of the website.

Copying of headlines: In *Fairfax Media Publications Pty Ltd v Reed International Books Australia Pty Ltd,*[13] the Federal Court found that the reproduction of headlines and abstracts of articles from a print newspaper for online distribution was a fair dealing for the purposes of reporting news under Section 43 of the Act. Although the legality of the copying of headlines in the form of hyperlinks has not been separately considered, it is not expected to produce a different result.

(c) P2P network

Supplier of P2P software: The supply of P2P software in Australia may constitute an act of authorisation of copyright infringements carried out by users of the software. In *Universal Music Australia Pty Ltd v Sharman License Holdings Limited,*[14] the Federal Court found the suppliers of the Kazaa file-sharing system liable for the infringing acts of users of the system, both for authorising the acts of infringement and for being in a common design with the users to infringe the copyright of the recording companies in that case.

Uploaders/downloaders: In *Universal Music Australia Pty Ltd v Sharman Networks Ltd*[15] the Full Federal (appeals) Court confirmed the finding at trial that the users of the Kazaa file-sharing systems who uploaded and downloaded files without the licence of the copyright owners infringed the copyright in the relevant works. Similarly, in *Roadshow Films Pty Ltd v iiNet Ltd,*[16] although the Court found that the ISP was not liable for authorising acts of infringement by users, it found that the acts of users who made files available for download by other users infringed the copyright in those works.

(d) Webcasting

The legality of webcasting has not been considered under Australian law. However, there is little reason to doubt that the act of webcasting would amount to a communication to the public. Two recent decisions of the Full Federal Court have

---

12 (2006) 156 FCR 380.
13 [2010] FCA 984.
14 (2005) 220 ALR 1.
15 (2006) 150 FCR 110.
16 (2012) 286 ALR 466

confirmed that internet deliveries of content will be considered as a separate delivery from traditional territorial broadcasts, requiring separate rights.[17]

(e) ***Streaming***

The act of streaming files over the Internet without the authority of the copyright owner may constitute a communication to the public constituted by a transmission. In *Roadshow Films Pty Ltd v iiNet Ltd*,[18] there was insufficient evidence that a substantial part of a file had been transmitted over the Internet to support a finding of infringement by communication.

(f) ***Framing***

The legality of 'framing' has not been determined under Australian copyright law.

(g) ***Transmission of infringing work across a communications network***

In both *Universal Music Australia Pty Ltd v Sharman License Holdings Limited*[19] and *Roadshow Films Pty Ltd v iiNet Ltd*,[20] the acts of infringement by users were found to have occurred over communications networks which were connected to the Internet.

(h) ***Aggregator websites (eg, Google News, price comparison websites)***

The liability of aggregator websites has not been determined under Australian copyright law.

(i) ***Treatment of user-generated content***

The legality of user-generated content has not been determined under Australian copyright law. However, there is no reason to doubt that the act of making a copy of the whole or a substantial part of a work or a reproduction of other subject matter without the licence of the copyright owner would amount to an act of infringement, unless one of the enumerated fair dealing defences applied.

1.7 Joint liability for internet service providers

In *Cooper v Universal Music Australia Pty Ltd*,[21] an ISP and its director were found liable for authorising infringements of copyright by users who accessed a pirate linking website operated by an Australian (www.mp3sforfree). A contrary result occurred in *Roadshow Films Pty Ltd v iiNet Ltd*,[22] which involved an unsuccessful claim for authorisation against an ISP of the copyright infringements engaged in by the ISP's subscribers using BitTorrent P2P software.

1.8 Relief

There is no equivalent in Australia of the no-fault injunction available against an ISP

---

17 *National Rugby League Investments Pty Ltd v Singtel Optus Pty Ltd* (2012) 201 FCR 147; *Phonographic Performance Co of Australia Ltd v Commercial Radio Australia Ltd* (2013) 296 ALR 607).
18 (2012) 286 ALR 466.
19 (2005) 220 ALR 1.
20 (2012) 286 ALR 466.
21 (2006) 156 FCR 380.
22 (2012) 286 ALR 466.

to stop an infringement by its users, such as in Article 11 of Directive 2004/48/EC on the Enforcement of IP Rights or Section 97A of the Copyright, Designs and Patents Act 1988 (UK).

1.9 Issues specific to Australia

(a) *Jurisdiction*

The primary jurisdiction for copyright infringement actions is the Federal Court of Australia (see Section 131C of the Act). Another federal court jurisdiction, the Federal Circuit Court (previously the Federal Magistrates Court) (see Section 131D of the Act), can hear less complex and shorter copyright infringement matters. The Supreme Courts of the Australian states and territories also have jurisdiction to hear copyright infringement matters.

(b) *Claim to infringement of foreign copyright*

It is unclear whether an Australian court will be prepared to hear a case brought in Australia concerning infringements of foreign copyright. Before this could occur, it would be necessary to satisfy a court that the Australian court is not a 'clearly inappropriate forum', applying the test set down by the High Court in *Voth v Manildra Flour Mills Pty Ltd*[23] and for the court to refuse to apply the Moçambique rule, which has traditionally prevented Australian courts from hearing disputes in relation to foreign intellectual property rights. The Moçambique rule has been abolished in at least one state (Jurisdiction of Courts (Foreign Land) Act 1989 (NSW)). An Australian court, particularly one in New South Wales, may follow the decision of the UK Supreme Court in *Lucasfilm v Ainsworth*.[24]

(c) *Emission theory*

In *Cooper v Universal Music Australia Pty Ltd*,[25] the Full Federal Court (an intermediate appellate court) found that copyright is infringed at the location where the infringing work is uploaded (making available online under the right of communication to the public) and where the file is downloaded (reproduction or copy in material form).

1.10 Orphan works

There is currently no regime under Australian copyright law permitting dealings with 'orphan' works without infringing copyright, although a potential limitation of remedies for infringement of orphan works where a 'reasonably diligent search' has been conducted is currently under review.

1.11 Online piracy measures

There are no specific measures against online piracy in Australia. In its decision in *Roadshow Films Pty Ltd v iiNet Ltd*,[26] the High Court of Australia identified the need

23 (1990) 171 CLR 538.
24 [2011] UKSC.
25 (2006) 156 FCR 380.
26 (2012) 286 ALR 466.

for such legislative action to address the issue of online infringements of copyright (in that case BitTorrent).

1.12 Electronic infringement of moral rights

The Act protects the moral rights of creators of certain copyrighted works and performers in live or recorded performances (Part IX). There are three moral rights recognised under the Act: the right of attribution (Section 193), the right not to have authorship falsely attributed (Section 195AC) and the right of integrity of authorship (Section 195AI). The duration of the protection varies according to the right involved (Sections 195AM, 195ANA).

There have only been two cases in which infringement of moral rights have been considered. The most recent of these, *Perez & Ors v Fernandez*,[27] considered whether the editing of a copy of the song "Bon, Bon", and its positing on a website, contravened the moral rights of its composer (the singer Pitbull). The Court found that it did and awarded compensatory damages.

2. Trademarks

2.1 Use of a trademark

Use of a trademark *as a trademark* is an express requirement of trademark infringement under Section 120 of the Trademarks Act 1995. Use of a trademark must involve use as a 'badge of origin' to indicate a connection in the course of trade between goods and the person who applies the mark to the goods.[28]

Where an infringing mark is used on an Australian website or website directed at Australia, in relation to a commercial offering of goods or services covered by a registered mark, the same legal principles apply as for more conventional infringements in the course of trade. In relation to internet-based uses of marks which do not have clear real-world analogies, there is some authority in Australia on what constitutes use of a trademark on the Internet for the purposes of infringement, including the following.

In *Solahart Industries Pty Ltd v Solar Shop Pty Ltd*,[29] trademark use was established in the case of domain names where a person uses an infringing domain name to refer traffic to a non-infringing domain name for the purpose of exploiting the goodwill of a mark, even where the infringed mark did not itself appear in the referred domain name or website. In *Australian Postal Corporation v Digital Post Australia Pty Ltd (No 2)*[30] it was accepted without contest (and not challenged on appeal[31] that the use of a registered mark in connection with a service involving handling of an electronic version of a letter which is stored in the addressee's designated secure digital post box amounted to a use of the mark for the purposes of infringement. The use of the mark in a domain name was also relevant use. In *Edgetec International Pty Ltd v Zippykerb*

---

27 [2012] FMCA 2 (February 10 2012).
28 See, for example, *E & J Gallo Winery v Lion Nathan (Aust) Pty Ltd* (2010) 241 CLR 144 at [41] to [43].
29 (2011) 281 ALR 544.
30 [2012] FCA 862.
31 [2013] FCAFC 153.

(NSW) Pty Ltd[32] the use of a mark in a domain name to redirect internet users to a website which displays goods and services being offered by a company was found to be trademark use. Conversely, in *Complete Technology Integrations Pty Ltd v Green Energy Management Solutions Pty Ltd*[33] it was held that the use of a trademark in a metatag was not 'use as a trademark' so as to infringe, as it could not be seen by the consumer, but this view appears to have been overruled. In *REA Group Ltd v Real Estate 1 Ltd*[34] there was no dispute that the mark 'realestate1.com.au' (both a trading name and a domain name) was used as a trademark on the respondent's websites, in its advertising and promotional activities, in the title of sponsored links and as a domain name address appearing in a URL.

The trademark must be used in Australia. In *Ward Group Pty Ltd v Brodie & Stone plc and Others*[35] it was held the use of a trademark on the Internet, uploaded on a website outside of Australia, without more, is not use by the website proprietor of the mark in each jurisdiction where the mark is downloaded. A clear indication that an overseas website is directed at the Australian market is required to establish use as a trademark *in Australia.*

2.2 Infringement

(a) Metatags

In *Complete Technology Integrations Pty Ltd v Green Energy Management Solutions Pty Ltd,*[36] it was held that the use of a trademark in a metatag was not 'use as a trademark' so as to infringe, as it could not be seen by the consumer. Since then, other cases such as *Solarhart Industries Pty Ltd v Solar Shop Pty Ltd*[37] have concluded that even a trademark reference which is only temporarily visible to a consumer is a trademark use where used for the purpose of exploiting the goodwill of a mark. As *Edgetec International Pty Ltd v Zippykerb (NSW) Pty Ltd*[38] followed *Solarhart, Complete Technology Integrations* may have been superseded.

In *Mantra Group Pty Ltd and Others v Tailly Pty Ltd and Another (No 2),*[39] where other infringing conduct was also involved, excessive use of a trademark in metatags for search engine optimisation was a factor that was inconsistent with the defence of 'good faith' descriptive use which might otherwise have been available to the respondent as a defence to trademark infringement.

(b) Keywords

No cases of trademark infringement have yet been decided based on keywords used by search engines. A recent case brought in the Federal Magistrates Court, by Roses Only against Easyflowers over its use of the keywords 'Roses Only' settled.

32 [2012] FCA 281.
33 [2011] FCA 1319.
34 [2013] FCA 559.
35 (2005) 143 FCR 479.
36 [2011] FCA 1319.
37 (2011) 281 ALR 544.
38 [2012] FCA 281.
39 [2010] 183 FCR 450.

Any keyword being used to serve advertisements using the offending trademark as a trademark in relation to an offer for sale of similar goods or services for which the mark is registered would likely amount to infringement by the advertiser in the absence of any available defence, since this scenario does not differ markedly from conventional trademark infringement based on advertisements. If the keyword served an advertisement which did not include the offending trademark, the offending mark may not be being used as a trademark so as to amount to trademark infringement, but this would depend on the facts of each case.

In the unfair competition context, the leading case is *Google Inc v Australian Competition and Consumer Commission.*[40] The High Court unanimously agreed with the trial judge that Google did not engage in misleading or deceptive conduct by displaying sponsored links in response to search queries. In a finding that was not subsequently challenged on appeal, the trial judge found that the sponsored links conveyed misleading representations to the effect that there was an association between the advertiser and its competitor. Google, however, was not responsible: the advertiser was the author of the sponsored links, which Google merely published and displayed without adopting or endorsing their content. While the Full Federal Court had held Google liable on the basis that the technical operation of the Google search engine meant that Google itself displayed the advertisements, the majority in the High Court emphasised that the technical operation of the Internet should not be used to disturb the analogy between Google and other intermediaries who publish or broadcast the advertisements of others. This conclusion was reinforced by the finding at trial (not disturbed at any stage in the proceedings) that ordinary and reasonable internet users would have understood that the sponsored links were created by advertisers, not Google. In *Specsavers Pty Ltd v Coastal Contacts (Aus) Pty Ltd,*[41] an application for an interlocutory injunction on the basis of misleading and deceptive conduct was granted where Coastal Contacts' advertising campaign included nominating certain keywords and made alleged incorrect price comparisons. The Court found that there was a *prima facie* case that Coastal Contacts' registration of the generic keyword 'contacts' and failure to exclude 'Specsavers' from that keyword (so that a search for 'Specsavers contacts' would serve the Coastal Contacts advertisement) was misleading and deceptive in breach of the Australian Consumer Law (ACL).

(c) *Sponsored links*

Any sponsored link using the offending trademark as a trademark in relation to an offer for sale of similar goods or services for which the mark is registered is likely to amount to trademark infringement on the part of the advertiser in the absence of any available defence, since this does not differ markedly from conventional trademark infringement based on advertisements. In *REA Group Ltd v Real Estate 1 Ltd,*[42] the respondent was found to have infringed the claimant's trademarks

---

40 (2013) 294 ALR 404
41 [2012] FCA 102.
42 [2013] FCA 559.

'realestate.com.au' and 'realcommercial.com.au' by the use of 'realestate1.com.au' and 'realcommercial1.com.au' in, amongst other things, the title of sponsored links. It was relevant to this conclusion that both the claimant and the defendant were using these marks as both domain names and trading names, in which the '.com.au' element was essential.

If the sponsored link does not include the offending trademark, there may be a question as to whether the offending mark is being used as a trademark so as to amount to trademark infringement, but this would depend on the facts of each case.

In the unfair competition context, the key case is *Google Inc v Australian Competition and Consumer Commission*,[43] discussed above.

No Australian case has recognised initial interest confusion as sufficient for trademark infringement. Confusion is not sufficient for trademark infringement, so whether or not an otherwise infringing use also involves initial interest confusion is not relevant in Australia.

(d) *Hidden text*

While there is no direct authority on point, *Solarhart Industries Pty Ltd v Solar Shop Pty Ltd*[44] and *Edgetec International Pty Ltd v Zippykerb (NSW) Pty Ltd*[45] would suggest that use of a trademark in hidden text may be considered to be use as a trademark so as to amount to infringement, at least where that text takes advantage of the goodwill of the original mark (eg, where it has an impact on search ranking results). *Complete Technology Integrations Pty Ltd v Green Energy Management Solutions Pty Ltd* would suggest the contrary,[46] but that case now appears to represent a minority view. Where infringement is found, *Mantra Group Pty Ltd and Others v Tailly Pty Ltd and Another (No 2)*[47] suggests that excessive use of hidden text would preclude a good faith defence.

(e) *Internet domain names*

Mere registration of a domain name which is not in any way associated with a functioning website does not infringe a trademark registration, because there is no use as a trademark in relation to the registered goods or services (*CSR Ltd v Resource Capital (Aust) Pty Ltd*.[48] Infringement was, however, found in both *Solarhart Industries Pty Ltd v Solar Shop Pty Ltd*[49] and *Edgetec International Pty Ltd v Zippykerb (NSW) Pty Ltd*[50] where a domain name was used as a referrer to another commercial website, even where (as in *Solarhart*) that other website did not feature the infringing trademark in the text of the website or the hosting domain name. A commercial offering of goods or services or an exploitation of the goodwill of a trademark for commercial gain is a prerequisite for trademark infringement.

Conversely, in the unfair competition context, CSR followed the UK case of

43 (2013) 294 ALR 404.
44 (2011) 281 ALR 544.
45 [2012] FCA 281.
46 [2011] FCA 1319.
47 [2010] 183 FCR 450.
48 (2003) 128 FCR 408.
49 (2011) 281 ALR 544.
50 [2012] FCA 281.

British Telecommunications plc v One in a Million Ltd,[51] holding that the domain names were an 'instrument of fraud' and therefore likely to mislead or deceive in breach of the Trade Practices Act 1974 (now replaced by the Australian Consumer Law), even though they were not in use.

In *REA Group Ltd v Real Estate 1 Ltd*,[52] the Federal Court held that there was no doubt that a domain name is capable of infringing a trademark: domain names can be used to attract consumers to a site from which goods or services are sold, and this amounts to trademark use. In that case, even though 'realestate1.com.au' did not infringe 'realestate.com.au' when used as a logo (as its generic and descriptive elements would ensure that attention was paid to the '1'), there was trademark infringement when 'realestate1.com.au' was used as a domain name, including on search results pages. In that context, consumers scanning the webpage may miss the '1'.

(f) Search navigation tools

In *REA Group Ltd v Real Estate 1 Ltd*,[53] 'realestate1.com.au' and 'realcommercial1.com.au' were found to infringe the trademarks 'realestate.com.au' and 'realcommercial.com.au' when they appeared as a URL on a search results page.

(g) Hypertext links

No trademark infringement or unfair competition cases have yet been decided in Australia on the basis of hypertext-based practices such as deep linking.

In theory, hypertext links based on use of a trademark, to the website of the trademark owner, may not involve trademark infringement (since the use of the mark may be descriptive in nature and therefore be entitled to a defence even if the offending mark is used as a trademark). However, this may amount to unfair competition where the linking creates the misleading representation that the linker is the source of the linked content. This will be a question of fact in each case.

(h) Framing

No trademark infringement or unfair competition cases have yet been decided in Australia on the basis of framing. Because framing can involve inclusion of a trademark within a frame, suggesting to users that they are at a particular website when they are at another website, this may amount to trademark infringement in Australia, at least where the framer offers similar goods or services to those for which the mark is registered. Framing may also give rise to unfair competition liability where the framing creates a misleading representation as to the source of the framed content.

2.3 Defences

(a) Descriptive (non-trademark) use of the mark

Use as a trademark is a precondition of trademark infringement. Therefore,

---

51 (1998) 42 IPR 289.
52 [2013] FCA 559.
53 [2013] FCA 559.

descriptive (non-trademark use) generally would not amount to use as a trademark so as to infringe in the first place. Where a descriptive use is a trademark use (such as the use in question in *Mantra Group Pty Ltd and Others v Tailly Pty Ltd and Another (No 2)*),[54] there are separate defences under Section 122 of the Trademarks Act for good faith descriptive uses. Unduly prominent use of a mark is not good faith descriptive use (*Mantra*).

(b) Comparative advertising

There is a specific defence to trademark infringement under Section 122(1)(d) of the Trademarks Act for use of a trademark in comparative advertising. Unlike many of the other defences to trademark infringement, this defence does not depend on good faith use or the fairness of the comparison. In any event, many uses of marks in comparative advertising will not involve use as a trademark in the sense required in Australian law, since true comparative advertisements generally draw a distinction between the advertiser and the third party's mark, rather than representing the advertiser as the source of the goods or services offered under the third party's mark.

Use of a trademark in comparative advertising which is not a fair comparison may be actionable under the misleading or deceptive conduct and false representation provisions of the Australian Consumer Law (ACL), even if not trademark infringement.

(c) Parody

There is no defence for parody in relation to trademark infringement under Australian trademark law (Australia also has no constitutional protection for freedom of speech). The only question will be whether the usual requirements of trademark infringement are met, regardless of whether the allegedly infringing use is a parody. In practice, the requirement of use as a trademark operates as a de facto protection for some parodic uses of marks since nominative references to a trademark are not trademark use.

In the unfair competition context, the only question will be whether the parody is likely to mislead or deceive, and there is no set defence for parodic uses of marks (eg, *McIlenny v Blue Yonder Holdings Pty Ltd*,[55] *Pacific Dunlop v Hogan*[56]). A 'successful' parody generally involves a distinction from the original, and depends on consumers recognising that the parody is not the original for its humour, so a successful parody will often not breach the ACL or amount to passing off.

2.4 Parallel imports

Where a website offering parallel import goods is outside Australia, a clear indication that the website is directed at Australia will be required before the mark would be considered to be used in Australia so as potentially to infringe a trademark registration here (*Ward Group Pty Ltd v Brodie & Stone plc and Others*.[57]

---

54 [2010] 183 FCR 450.
55 (1997) 149 ALR 496.
56 (1989) 14 IPR 398.
57 (2005) 143 FCR 479.

Where a website is directed at Australia or based in Australia, Section 123 of the Trademarks Act provides a defence to an action for infringement where "the trademark has been applied to the goods by, or with the consent of, the registered owner of the trademark". Two 2012 decisions have indicated that where parallel import goods have been produced by an overseas licensed manufacturer for sale in breach of a territorial restriction on a licence (ie, the licensed goods were initially sold outside the licensed territory), the trademark owner cannot be deemed to have consented to the application of the mark so the Section 123 defence was not available.[58] Conversely, where the initial sale from the licensed manufacturer is within the terms of the licence (ie, the goods were initially sold within the licensed territory, even if sold outside of it immediately thereafter), Section 123 will apply regardless of subsequent sales outside the territory.[59]

In practice, this has left the question of whether or not parallel imports can be prevented very uncertain and dependent on facts relating to histories of manufacture and dealing which may not be readily apparent to either the trademark owner or to dealers in parallel import goods. However, the position would be the same for parallel import goods offered via a website as for parallel import goods offered through conventional retail channels.

2.5 Remedies

Remedies for trademark infringement include injunctions and either damages or an account of profits. From April 2013, additional damages are available against a trademark infringer. This form of damages has traditionally been available only to copyright, design and patent owners and permits the court to make awards of damages which are non-compensatory or for the purposes of deterring infringements.

2.6 Liability of ISP

The Trademarks Act does not provide for secondary liability for authorising infringing use of a trademark. An ISP (or other party facilitating trademark infringement of third-party rights) would only be liable for trademark infringement for the actions of the third party if they were a joint tortfeasor. While there are no Australian cases directly on point, there are analogous cases including *Louis Vuitton Malletier SA v Toea Pty Ltd*[60] which concerned an action by a trademark owner against the owner and manager of a market where counterfeits were being sold. The Court noted that in order to be liable as joint tortfeasors, the respondents must be linked to the infringers by a 'common design or purpose' or 'act in concert'. The Court held that no such common design was present as there was a distinction between the purposes of the infringers and the respondents. Further, the Court held that the respondents did not have the level of control over the market premises to justify an inference of 'common design'; rather it would have been 'virtually impossible' for

---

58 *Sporte Leisure Pty Ltd v Paul's International Pty Ltd* affirmed on appeal (2012) 95 IPR 151, *Lonsdale Australia Limited v Paul's Retail Pty Ltd* [2012] FCA 584.

59 *Facton Ltd v Toast Sales Group Pty Ltd* [2012] FCA 612.

60 (2006) 156 FCR 158.

the respondents to control stallholders. By analogy, for many if not most ISPs, control over the trademark infringement actions of individual users may not be technically (or commercially) feasible and common design is unlikely to be found.

Google Inc v Australian Competition and Consumer Commission[61] involved a finding that the search engine provider Google was not liable for unfair competition based on keyword advertising, as it merely published and displayed (without adopting or endorsing) advertisements created by the advertiser. ISPs are likely to be considered at a further remove from infringing conduct than search engine providers offering keyword advertising.

There is no provision under Australian law for relief to be granted against an ISP to stop an infringement by its users, in the absence of liability of the ISP as a joint tortfeasor.

2.7 Advertising law and regulation

In Australia there is no dedicated internet advertising regulator. Rather, regulation of advertising is piecemeal and undertaken by both state and federal-based governments.

An Australia-wide legal framework for all forms of advertising is found in Schedule 2 of the Competition and Consumer Act 2010 (Cth), the Australian Consumer Law (ACL) which is designed to protect consumers particularly in relation to internet content, such as advertising and sale of goods and services over the Internet to consumers. The ACL also prohibits misleading or deceptive conduct in trade or commerce, which also applies to online advertising. State-based regulations relate to specific goods and services, including tobacco advertising, advertising of gambling, gaming and lotteries, advertising of auctions, advertising by banks and consumer credit.

Further, the advertising industry operates a self-regulatory regime. The Advertising Standards Bureau (ASB) administers the system through the Advertising Standards Board and Advertising Claims Board which applies a national code of conduct to all forms of advertising, including online advertising. The ASB offers an avenue for consumers to complain to, prior to seeking legal remedy.

The Australian Direct Marketing Association (ADMA) is a self-regulatory industry body which deals with direct advertising such as promotions directed at a consumer by email or through the Internet. The Australian Communications and Media Authority (ACMA) also administers the Spam Act 2003 and registers and monitors compliance with ADMA's code.

The Australian Competition and Consumer Commission and the State/Territory Offices of Fair Trading (and similar agencies; titles vary from state to state) administer consumer protection regimes and may intervene on a consumer's behalf where an internet advertisement is manifestly misleading or deceptive, or likely to mislead or deceive. These agencies are typically unwilling to intervene in disputes concerning competitors.

---

61 (2013) 294 ALR 404.

2.8 Domain name disputes

The .au Dispute Resolution Policy (http://www.auda.org.au/policies/auda-2010-05/) essentially mirrors the Uniform Dispute Resolution Policy and requires the complainant to demonstrate that:

- the domain name is identical or confusingly similar to a name trademark or service mark in which the complainant has rights; and
- the registrant has no rights or legitimate interests in respect of the domain name; and
- the domain name has been registered or subsequently used in bad faith (the use of 'or' instead of 'and' is the only significant difference from the UDRP).

Complaint filing fees are A$2,000, in the case of a single member panel and A$4,500 for a three-member panel. Proceedings are generally resolved in roughly six months.

In addition, trademark owners may be able to rely upon other complaints procedures administered by the central registry, auDA, including the Misspellings Policy (www.auda.org.au/policies/auda-2008-09/) allowing cancellation of domain names involving obvious misspellings of trademarks, and the Complaints (Registrant Eligibility) Policy (www.auda.org.au/policies/auda-2004-01/) which provides for cancellation of domain names owned by fictitious or non-existent registrants (such as deregistered companies). These do not involve any filing fees and are generally resolved in about a calendar month.

2.9 Unfair competition/passing off

Unregistered trademarks are protected under Australian unfair competition law, comprising the misleading or deceptive conduct/false representations provisions of the ACL and the tort of passing off. These actions are based on reputation. Marks in use overseas with a spillover reputation into Australia are also protected, even if they have not been directly used in Australia.[62]

Australian unfair competition law protects the contents of websites in the same manner as it protects the contents of other marketplace communications. Where registered trademark infringement involves different issues to unfair competition, this has been noted above.

3. Patents

3.1 Patentability of 'internet' inventions

An invention may be protected by an Australian patent if it meets the requirements for a 'patentable invention' in Section 18 of the Patents Act, which requires that the patentable invention is 'a manner of manufacture',[63] is novel when compared to the prior art, involves an inventive (or in the case of an innovation patent, an

62 *Conagra Inc v McCain Foods (Aust) Pty Ltd* (1992) 33 FCR 302; *Tivo Inc v Vivo International Corporation Pty Ltd*, [2012] FCA 252; *Knott Investments Pty Ltd v Winnebago Industries, Inc* [2013] FCAFC 59.

63 See *National Research Development Corporation v Commissioner of Patents* [1959] HCA 67).

innovative) step as compared with the prior art, is useful and has not been secretly used in Australia before the priority date by or with the authority of the patent holder. These principles apply equally to 'internet inventions'.

(a) *Computer programs*

The first case to consider whether computer software constituted a 'manner of manufacture', and therefore patentable subject matter, was *International Business Machines Corp v Commissioner of Patents*,[64] which involved an improved method of visually representing curve images in computer graphics displays. The Court upheld the validity of the patent on the basis that it had a commercially useful effect and met the threshold for novelty and non-obviousness. The decision was affirmed by the Full Federal Court.

Two 2013 decisions that reached different conclusions on the patent-eligibility of computer-implemented inventions have been appealed to the Full Federal Court. In *Research Affiliates, LLC v Commissioner of Patents*,[65] a computer-implemented method of constructing and preparing an index for a portfolio of investments weighted according to certain criteria was found not to be a 'manner of manufacture', because the index generated was merely information and did not involve a specific effect being produced by a computer. On the other hand, a computer-implemented method and system 'for the assessment of the competency or qualifications of individuals with respect to recognised standards' was found to be patentable subject matter in *RPL Central v Commissioner or Patents*.[66] At the time of writing, a decision is awaited in the *Research Affiliates* appeal, which was heard at the end of 2013.

(b) *Business methods*

In *Grant v Commissioner of Patents*,[67] the Full Court dismissed an appeal from a finding of a judge upholding a decision of the Deputy Commissioner of Patents revoking a business method innovation patent. The claimed innovation was a method for structuring a financial transaction to protect an individual's assets, such as real property, from legal liability or protecting assets at financial risk. It did not reach the threshold requirement for patentability that it be a method of manufacture according to the test in *N V Philips Gloeilampenfabrieken v Mirabella International Pty Ltd*.[68] In the course of this decision, the Full Court nonetheless expressly approved of earlier cases that allowed for the patenting of business methods in certain circumstances: for example, where the business method was implemented in a computer environment such that performance of the patented method resulted in a 'change in state or information in a part of a machine'.

64 [1991] FCA 625.
65 [2013] FCA 71.
66 [2013] FCA 871.
67 [2006] FCAFC 120.
68 [1995] HCA 15.

(c) *Mathematical methods*

In *Grant v Commissioner of Patents*[69] the Full Court applied, with apparent approval, the reasoning of the United States Court of Appeals in *State Street Bank & Trust Co v Signature Financial Group Inc*[70] and *AT&T Corp v Excel Communications, Inc,*[71] and the reasoning of the Full Federal Court in *CCOM Pty Ltd v Jiejing Pty Ltd*[72] and Heerey J in *Welcome Real-Time SA v Catuity Inc*[73] to the effect that where there is a component that was physically affected or a change in state or information in a part of a machine, there is a physical effect that can be patentable subject matter (cf a mere scheme, an abstract idea, mere intellectual information).

(d) *Presentation of information*

The mere presentation of information is not patentable in Australia. Unless an arrangement serves a 'mechanical purpose', it does not constitute a manner of manufacture and is considered to be analogous to the common law exclusions of mere printed matter and fine arts (as opposed to useful arts).[74] It is more appropriate to consider whether this subject matter is protected by copyright (see section 1 above).

3.2 Bioinformatics

In *Kiren-Amgen Inc v Board of Regents of the University of Washington*[75] an opposition was dismissed because the claims were directed to 'purified and isolated' DNA sequences that were 'an artificially created state of affairs'. More recently, in *Cancer Voices Australia v Myriad Genetics Inc,*[76] the Federal Court held that isolated genetic material as a result of human intervention (ie, an artificial state of affairs) is capable of being patentable as a manner of manufacture, according to the test set out in *National Research Development Corporation v Commissioner of Patents.*[77] This case has been appealed to the Full Federal Court.

IP Australia has previously indicated that subject matter involving "the building blocks of living matter, such as DNA and genes (including human DNA and genes) which have for the first time been identified and copied from their natural source and then manufactured synthetically as unique materials with a definite industrial use" will not be patentable.

3.3 Issues specific to Australia

(a) *Infringement on the Internet*

The infringement of a patent on the Internet has not been considered in Australia.

---

69 [2006] FCAFC 120.
70 [1998] USCAFED 107.
71 [1999] USCAFED 57.
72 [1994] FCA 1168.
73 (2001) 113 FCR 110.
74 See eg, *Fishburn's Application* (1940) 57 RPC 245 and *Moore Business Forms Inc* (1979) 49 AOJP 2521.
75 (1995) 33 IPR 557.
76 [2013] FCA 65.
77 [1959] HCA 67.

(b) ***Process patents***

Australian courts have not considered whether an Australian patent can be infringed by the occurrence of some parts of the process in Australia.

3.4 Remedies available for patent infringement

Injunctions, damages, account of profits and delivery up are available remedies for patent infringement.

4. Disclosure orders against ISPs

4.1 Availability

There is no specific regime in Australia permitting an IPR owner to apply to ISPs to disclose the identity and contact details of a user of their service who is suspected of infringing an IPR. There are, however, general procedural orders that can be sought from Federal and State Courts as part of applications for 'preliminary discovery' which are capable of achieving a similar outcome. In practice these orders are not too difficult to obtain.

4.2 Requirements

There are specific procedural court rules in both the federal and state court systems that provide for the making of disclosure orders for disclosure in applications for 'preliminary discovery'.

4.3 Jurisdictional issues

There are a number of preconditions that must be satisfied before the order is made, including identification of a cause of action that may be available to the IPR holder, proof of attempts to obtain the information and an undertaking to pay the reasonable costs of disclosure.

4.4 'John Doe' injunctions

'John Doe' injunctions are available under Australian law.

The author would like to acknowledge the kind assistance of Rebecca Smith in the preparation of this chapter.

Brazil

Carlos Eduardo Eliziário de Lima
Daniel Avila Failla
Gustavo de Freitas Morais
Dannemann Siemsen Advogados/Dannemann Siemsen Bigler & Ipanema Moreira

---

1. Copyright, database rights and design rights

Copyrights in Brazil are constitutional rights governed by the Copyright Act, Law No 9,610 dated February 19 1998 and, as to software protection, by the Brazilian Software Law, Law No 9,609 also dated February 19 1998. In addition, international conventions such as the Berne and Rome Conventions, ratified and applicable in Brazil, afford broad protection to authors of artistic, literary, scientific and musical works.

The Copyright Act and the Software Law were issued just a couple of years after the Brazilian Industrial Property Law (Law No 9,279/96). This would indicate that, at that time, Brazilian legislators were especially concerned with the protection of intellectual assets. This had a decisive influence in the Copyright Act, and a clear consequence is that the wording of these codes tends to be protective of the interests of authors and copyright owners.

It is also important to note that the Copyright Act and the Software Law pre-date the widespread use of the Internet as a tool for the creation, diffusion and transmission of content; and since their implementation, these laws have not been updated to deal, in a more specific and concrete fashion, with the needs of copyright owners and users in the context of the Internet.

The increasing volume of cultural information and the consequent growth of mechanisms promoting the sharing of content have resulted in an increase in the frequency of copyright infringement cases. Along with a lack of provisions dealing specifically with the Internet, this creates uncertainty in relation to legal issues relating to the Internet.

Therefore, there is an obvious need for the adoption of specific rules relating to online copyright. Against this background, in 2010, the Ministry of Justice issued a draft bill to regulate the internet environment in Brazil, establishing the rights and duties of users, the liability of Internet service providers (ISPs) and limits on acts of the state.

At the time of writing, the bill was still going through public consultation. This chapter, therefore, focuses on the existing law on copyright in the context of the Internet.

1.1 Overview

Under the Copyright Act, every creation of the mind, that is to say, every work originally conceived, whatever its mode of expression or the medium in which it is fixed, tangible or intangible, known or susceptible of invention in the future, may be protected under copyright (Copyright Act, Article 7).

In light of the broad concept of copyrightable creations, the Copyright Act contains two important guidelines to define whether or not a certain work can be protected by copyright.

The first is an open list of copyrightable creations which includes the most common types of content, as follows:

- the texts of literary, artistic or scientific works;
- lectures, addresses, sermons and other works of the same kind;
- dramatic and dramatico-musical works;
- choreographic and mimed works whose stage performance is set down in writing or otherwise;
- musical compositions with or without words;
- audiovisual works, with or without accompanying sounds, including cinematographic works;
- photographic works and other works produced by a process analogous to photography;
- drawings, paintings, engravings, sculptures, lithographs and works of kinetic art;
- illustrations, maps and other works of the same kind;
- drafts, mock-ups and three-dimensional works relating to geography, engineering, topography, architecture, park and garden planning, stage scenery and science;
- adaptations, translations and other transformations of original works, presented as a new intellectual creation;
- computer programs;
- collections or compilations, anthologies, encyclopaedias, dictionaries, databases and other works which, by virtue of the selection, coordination or arrangement of the subject matter, constitute intellectual creations.

The second guideline is a list of creations that are excluded from copyright protection, as follows:

- ideas, normative procedures, systems, methods, projects or mathematical projects or concepts as such;
- diagrams, plans or rules for performing mental acts, playing games or conducting business;
- blank forms intended for completion with all kinds of scientific or other information, and the instruction appearing thereon;
- the texts of treaties or conventions, laws, decrees, regulations, judicial decisions and other official enactments;
- information in common use such as that contained in calendars, diaries, registers or legends;
- names and titles in isolation;
- the industrial or commercial exploitation of the ideas embodied in works.

Hence any creation complying with minimum standards of originality that is not expressly excluded from copyright protection according to the list above is protected by copyright, even if it is created or published on the Internet and/or by any other digital medium. It should also be emphasised that, in Brazil, the protection of copyright is afforded without registration.

As a result of the wide definition of copyrightable work, literary works and artistic works, films, sound recordings, typographical amendments of published editions, user interfaces, websites compilations, uploads to the Internet by e-mail, Flash, PDF, image formats (eg, GIF, JPG, BMP, PNG), video formats (eg, MPEG, MOV, AVI), music and sound formats (eg, MP3, AVI, WAV), etc are all subject to copyright protection.

(a) Computer-generated works

There are three basic types of computer-generated works:

- works where the operator uses the computer program as a tool to create a work;
- works where the operator creates the functions and patterns and inputs the commands, determining the actions of the computer, and ultimately having a decisive influence on the work;
- and works where the operator simply starts the commands and lets the computer work alone, the operator having a minimal or insignificant role in the generated work.

It seems clear that in bullets one and two above, the program operator has an evident influence over the final work, and that the computer performs the function of a tool in the creation process.

As to the third bullet above, there is an indirect human influence on the work. It is not clear, however, whether authorship would be granted to the program operator or to the programmer who established the software logics and, indirectly, determined the final work. To date, there is no case law in relation to computer-generated works to shed light on this issue.

(b) Software

The Brazilian Software Law defines software as the expression of an organised set of instructions in natural or code language, contained in a physical support of any kind, necessarily employed in automatic machines for the manipulation of data, devices, tools, or peripheral equipment, based on digital or analog technique, to enable them to operate in the way and with the purposes determined.

The protection system for software is the same as that granted to literary works by the Copyright Act, with specific rules under the terms of the Brazilian Software Law concerning term of protection, licensing conditions (such as warranties), economic rights appropriation, use, etc.

(c) Broadcasting

The broadcasting of video, music and sound works is a right of the copyright holder. Such broadcasting is, therefore, allowed only if authorised by the copyright owner.

(d) *Websites*

Websites, including their graphics and layouts, electronic databases, content and structure are deemed to be copyrightable work in Brazil.

(e) *Compilations*

Compilations are protected by copyright under Article 7, XIII of the Copyright Act. Even if the compilation consists only of facts, it is the original way of compiling them that will be subject to the copyright protection.

1.2 Infringing acts

Due to the absence of rules harmonising the forms of use brought about by the massive use of the Internet as a medium for content creation and diffusion, and taking into account the protective spirit of the Copyright Act, that establishes few and exhaustive exemptions to copyright (as discussed below), a considerable number of internet practices may be construed as infringing acts.

Moreover, there are few precedents dealing with the interface between copyright and the Internet and, as noted above, this creates uncertainly for content producers, users and intermediaries (such as internet service providers (ISPs)). The Copyright Act states that copyright encompasses two groups of rights: moral rights (see section 1.12 below), and economic rights.

Economic rights relate to rights to use or to allow the use of a work, and can be fully or partially licensed and/or assigned. As a rule, complete or partial reproduction of a work, for any kind of use, depends on express prior authorisation of the author.

In the internet context, among other types of use that exist at present or might be devised in the future, the authorisation of the author will be necessary for the following uses:

- complete or partial reproduction;
- publication;
- adaptation, setting to music or any other transformation;
- translation into any language;
- distribution where it is not provided for in a contract signed by the author with third parties for the use or exploitation of the work;
- distribution for the purpose of offering works or productions by cable, fibre optic, satellite, electromagnetic waves or any other system enabling the user to select a work or production and receive it at the time and place of his/her choice, provided that the access to the works or production is made through any system requiring payment on the part of the user;
- the direct or indirect use of the literary, artistic or scientific work in one of the following forms:
  - performance, recitation or declamation;
  - musical performance;
  - audiovisual, cinematographic or equivalent presentation;
  - use of man-made satellites;
  - use of optical systems, telephone or other lines, cables of all kinds and such comparable means of communication as may be devised in the future;

    - exhibition of works of three-dimensional or figurative art;
- incorporation in databases, storage in a computer, microfilm or any other means of archiving.

There are, however, certain exemptions under the Copyright Act that allow the use or reproduction of a work without the prior consent of the copyright holder. Articles 46 to 48 of the Copyright Act contain an exhaustive list of the exemptions to the economic rights of the copyright owner, and establish that the following acts do not constitute copyright infringement:

- reproduction:
    - in the daily or periodical press of news or informative articles, from newspapers or magazines, with a mention of the name of the author, if they are signed, and of the publications from which they have been taken;
    - in newspapers or magazines of speeches given at public meetings of any kind;
    - of portraits or other forms of representation of a likeness, produced on commission, where the reproduction is done by the owner of the commissioned subject matter and the person represented or his/her heirs have no objection to it;
    - of literary, artistic or scientific works for the exclusive use of the visually handicapped, provided that the reproduction is done without gainful intent, either in Braille or by means of another process using a medium designed for such users;
- the reproduction in one copy of short extracts from a work for the private use of the copier, provided that it is done without gainful intent;
- the quotation in books, newspapers, magazines or any other medium of communication of passages from a work for the purposes of study, criticism or debate, to the extent justified by the purpose, provided that the author is named and the source of the quotation is given;
- notes taken in the course of lessons given in teaching establishments by the persons for whom they are intended, provided that their complete or partial publication is prohibited without the express prior authorisation of the person who gave the lessons;
- the use of literary, artistic or scientific works, phonograms and radio and television broadcasts in commercial establishments for the sole purpose of demonstration to customers, provided that the said establishments market the materials or equipment that make such use possible;
- stage and musical performance, where carried out in the family circle or exclusively for teaching in educational establishments and where there is no profit-making purpose.
- the use of literary, artistic or scientific works as evidence in judicial or administrative proceedings;
- the reproduction in any work of short extracts from existing works, regardless of their nature, or of the whole work in the case of a work of three-

dimensional art, on condition that the reproduction is not itself the main subject matter of the new work and does not jeopardise the normal exploitation of the work reproduced or unjustifiably prejudice the author's legitimate interests;

- paraphrases and parodies that are not actual reproductions of the original work and are not in any way derogatory to it;
- works permanently located in public places – these may be freely represented by painting, drawing, photography and audiovisual processes.

Moreover, paragraph 1 of Article 30 of the Copyright Act states that the right of reproduction is not applicable where the reproduction is temporary and carried out for the sole purposes of making the work, phonogram or performance perceptible by means of an electronic medium, or where it is transitory or incidental, provided that it is done in the course of a use of the work that has been duly authorised by the owner.

The Copyright Act does not limit the medium by which the reproduction is made and, therefore, as a general rule, even if the following acts are carried out on the Internet, they may be construed as copyright infringements: copying in any medium; issuing copies to the public; communicating work to the public; performing, showing or playing a work in public; renting or lending a work to the public; or authorising another person to do any of these acts. Thus, for example, non-authorised video and music streaming, eBooks, text, video or music, and downloading or uploading of images are, in principle, infringing acts in accordance with the Copyright Act.

1.3 Test for copyright infringement

As noted above, the reproduction of a work does not constitute copyright infringement if: (i) a copy of a short extract is done for the private use of the copier without gainful intent; or (ii) the reproduction in any work of short extracts from existing works, regardless of their nature, or of the whole work in the case of a work of three-dimensional art, is not itself the main subject matter of the new work and does not jeopardise the normal exploitation of the work reproduced or unjustifiably prejudice the author's legitimate interests.

The law does not establish objective parameters for defining 'short extracts'. Legal doctrine and jurisprudence tend to view 10% to 15% of the work as being acceptable. However, the precedents are clear in the sense that the purpose of the law is to avoid the main subject matter of the work being reproduced, and this could happen even with reproductions of 15% of the work, for instance. The definition of substantial reproduction will, therefore, depend on the nature of the particular work.

It should be emphasised that the issue of infringement will be judged not in terms of the number of reproductions, but rather the extent of the reproduction. If, however, repeated copies of short extracts constitute a substantial reproduction of a given work, it is arguable that there would be a copyright infringement.

1.4 Exemptions/defences to copyright infringement

The comments under the following headings must be read in light of the exemptions listed in section 1.2, and assuming that the following acts have not been expressly authorised by the copyright owner.

(a) ***Format shifting***

The copyright owner may make the work available to the public in whatever form it considers appropriate, and format shifting may be made only by it, or with its authorisation. Thus, for example, consumers are not allowed to rip a CD they have purchased onto an Mp3 file. Therefore, under the Copyright Act, format shifting is not an exemption/defence to copyright infringement, as only the copyright owner has the right to decide on the format of his/her work.

(b) ***Personal copying rights***

The Copyright Act does not provide an exemption for personal copying rights of entire works. Therefore, copies of entire works are forbidden, even for private purposes. However, as noted above, Articles 46 to 48 of the Brazilian Copyright Act set out certain exemptions, such as for single copies of short extracts (see section 1.3 above) from a work for the private use of the copier, provided the copying is done without gainful intent.

(c) ***Time shifting***

To engage in time shifting, it is necessary to make a copy of the relevant content. Time shifting, therefore, requires the authorisation of the copyright owner. Thus, if a TV viewer records a TV broadcast to watch at a later time, he/she is infringing copyright. Time shifting may be made without the authorisation of the copyright owner, if it comprises only short extracts of the work (see section 1.3 above).

(d) ***Fair use***

The fair use doctrine does not apply in Brazil. Therefore, in order to determine whether the use of a work is allowed under the Copyright Act, it is necessary to ascertain whether it falls under one of the exemptions mentioned in section 1.2 above, irrespective of any consideration of fairness.

For instance, news services are authorised to reproduce news and informative articles with a mention of the name of the author, if they are signed, and of the publications from which they have been taken.

Another important fair use hypothesis in the internet context is the quotation of passages from a work for the purposes of study, criticism or debate.

(e) ***Caching/temporary copies as part of communication process***

Article 30 of the Copyright Act, first paragraph, establishes that the right of reproduction does not apply where the reproduction is temporary and carried out for the sole purposes of making the work, phonogram or performance perceptible by means of an electronic medium, or where it is transitory or incidental, provided that it is done in the course of a use of the work that has been duly authorised by the owner. This provision may be construed as a prohibition on any kind of temporary copying in contexts where there is no authorisation for the use of the work.

On the other hand, internet providers argue that caching and temporary copies are necessary in order to make communications over the Internet technically possible and economically viable, and that it provides them with a tool for identifying users' infringement claims.

In view of a lack of specific provisions relating to the internet environment, however, it is not clear whether caching and temporary copies when made as part of the communication process will constitute a violation of copyright, and, unfortunately, there are no precedents on this issue.

(f) *Hosting*

Hosting a creation without the authorisation of the copyright owner may constitute infringement, as this could be construed as a reproduction or publication (or at least an unauthorised form of use) of the creation.

(g) *Back-up copies*

The Copyright Act does not authorise back-up copies, even though they may be a way to preserve the work as the digital file may be lost.

The Software Law (Law No 9,609/96) stipulates an exemption regarding software back-up copies. The exemption allows for the reproduction of a single copy of legitimately purchased software, provided the copy is intended as a back-up copy or electronic storage. Where the relevant conditions apply, the copy may be used as a back-up copy.

(h) *Reverse engineering*

Reverse engineering for the purpose of analysing software functionalities is allowed.

If the aim of the reverse engineering is to gain an understanding of the functionality of the relevant software, in order to rewrite the software and obtain the same functionality (ie, without using the same source code (ie, so-called 're-engineering')), it will not violate any right.

However, reverse engineering which is carried out to recompile the binary codes of software is not allowed, because the literal expression of the binary code is protected.

(i) *Parody defence*

Paraphrases and parodies that are not actual reproductions of the original work and are not in any way derogatory towards it constitute exemptions under the Copyright Act, as noted above.

(j) *Incidental inclusion*

The Copyright Act does not create an incidental inclusion exemption, and unauthorised inclusion will violate copyright whether it is incidental or not.

1.5 Remedies available for copyright infringement

Copyright infringements are subject to both civil and criminal sanctions, because under Article 184 of the Brazilian Criminal Code, the violation of copyright and related rights is deemed to be a crime, no matter how minor and regardless of commercial intent. In other words, the violating acts the Brazilian Copyright Act treats as civil torts are deemed to be crimes under the Brazilian Criminal Code.

Criminal remedies include:

- search and seizure;
- arrest and possible imprisonment of infringers; and
- costs.

As regards civil sanctions:

- the copyright owner may apply for the seizure of the copies or originals made or the cessation of disclosure, in the event of fraudulent reproduction, disclosure or use;
- the infringer must forfeit to the copyright owner any copies that are seized and must pay it the price of those that have been sold;
- transmission and retransmission by any means or process, and the communication to the public must immediately be discontinued or interrupted by the competent judicial authority, without prejudice to a daily fine for non-observance and such other indemnities as may be applicable.

Regardless of the adopted measure, the copyright owner may claim for compensatory damages. The award of damages will be based on the price of the works sold as noted in the second bullet above, and occasional consequential damages (lost profits) may be complementarily paid if duly proved. As regards infringement of moral rights, Article 108 states that any person who, in the course of using a work by any means, fails to mention or announce the name, pseudonym or conventional mark of the author and performer, apart from having to answer for the moral prejudice, shall be bound to:

- disclose their identity in the case of a broadcasting organisation, at the same time as the identity of those organisation at which the infringement was committed, for three consecutive days;
- disclose their identity in the case of a graphic or phonographic publication, by the inclusion of an *erratum* in the copies not yet distributed, without prejudice to the conspicuous publication of a notice on three consecutive occasions in a major journal at the place of residence of the author, the performer and the publisher or producer;
- disclose their identity in the case of any other form of use, in the press according to the procedure referred to in the foregoing item.

1.6 Joint liability for ISPs

There are no specific regulations regarding the liability of internet service providers (ISPs) in Brazil, and, therefore, the general rules on tortious liability will apply.

In Brazil, a party who by voluntary act or omission, negligence or recklessness, infringes the law and causes harm to others, commits an unlawful act (Article 186 of the Civil Code), and from this there arises a duty to indemnify (Article 927 of the Civil Code).

The courts' prevailing understanding is that the ISP may become liable from the point at which it is notified of the existence of infringing content, as recognised by the Sao Paulo Appellate Court in *Carmen Steffens Franquias Ltda v Google Brasil Internet Ltda*, as follows:[1] "the ISP is only responsible if acquiescent with the illicit activity, retarding the suspension [of the website] or omitting itself from excluding [the website] (...). Scholars argue that an ISP should be held responsible only when it is confirmed that its attitude is typical of a 'negligent controller', passively assuming or affirming the content of the publications posted by users in private spaces (see Demócrito Ramos Reinaldo Filho, *Responsabilidade por publicações na Internet*, Forense, 2005, page 215 and Marcelo J López Mesa and Félix A Trigo Represas, *Responsabilidad civil de los profesionales*, Buenos Aires, Lexis Nexis, 2005, page 727)".

This rationale was followed in the recent decision of the Superior Court of Justice in *Alexandre Magno Silva Marangon v Google Brasil Internet Ltda*.[2] The cause of action concerned indemnification for moral damages in which the defendant claimed to be the target of insults on the Internet on a social network maintained by the provider. The panel upheld the appeal, ruling out responsibility of the provider for harm incurred by the defendant, on the basis that content providers, such as the applicant, that provide network, and information created or developed by providers, and produce information disclosed on the Internet, cannot be required to exercise prior control of the content of the information uploaded to the site by their users. As soon as they are notified of the existence of illegal data on a site, ISPs must remove it immediately, otherwise they will be liable for the relevant damage; and they must maintain a minimally effective system of identification of their users. The effectiveness of such systems will be analysed on a case-by-case basis. In this case, once it was made aware of the existence of offensive material, the provider adopted all the measures for its immediate removal from the site. Moreover, the social network maintained by the provider kept a channel for people whose identity had been violated to apply for the exclusion of false accounts, and also to report abuse of individual profiles or communities. The applicant maintained a reasonably efficient way of tracking users, a security measure that was in line with the expected level of due diligence of a content provider.

1.7 Copyright liability

As a consequence of the doctrine of liability applied by the precedents in cases involving ISPs, it is clear that ISPs will not *prima facie* be held liable for the provision of hosting/cloud computing services where infringing content is uploaded by users of webcasting, streaming, framing services, aggregator websites (eg, Google News, price comparison websites), hypertext linking, or P2P networks.

With regard to the provision of these services, a user who generates, uploads or downloads the infringing work will be held liable for any infringement, given that the ISP will not be aware of such infringing content and will not, therefore, intentionally be committing the infringement.

1 AC 9103068-32.2008.8.26.0000.
2 Special Appeal No 1186616-MG.

1.8 Relief

As noted in section 1.6 above, ISPs may be held liable for online infringement if they do not respond when notified of a violation. If the ISP is notified and refuses to take any action to stop the infringement, it is possible to request an injunction against the ISP and the user.

1.9 Issues specific to Brazil

(a) *Jurisdiction*

The Brazilian courts have jurisdiction to hear copyright infringement claims wherever relevant damage occurs within Brazilian territory.

(b) *Claim to infringement of foreign copyright*

The Brazilian courts will hear claims for infringement of foreign copyrights every time damage occurs within Brazilian territory, as a result of the *lex loci delicti* principle. For instance, if a website is hosted on a server located abroad and is accessed by users in Brazil, and an unauthorised download of a foreign copyright is made, Brazilian courts will have jurisdiction. On the other hand, if an infringer is resident in Brazil but their infringing acts are overseas, the Brazilian courts will not have jurisdiction.

(c) *Emission theory*

The infringing act may be deemed to take place both where the infringing work is downloaded and where it is uploaded.

1.10 Orphan works

The works of deceased authors without heir, and the works of unknown authors, are treated as being in the public domain subject to the legal protection of ethnic and traditional lore.

In the case of an anonymous work, the exercise of the author's economic rights will belong to the person who publishes it.

1.11 Online piracy measures

There are no online piracy measures in Brazil.

1.12 Electronic infringement of moral rights

Article 27 of the Copyright Act provides for moral rights that are inalienable and irrevocable. These grant the author of a work the right:

- to claim authorship of the work at any time;
- to cause his/her name, pseudonym or conventional sign to appear or be announced as that of the author when the work is used;
- to keep the work unpublished;
- to protect the integrity of the work, by objecting to any modifications or any action that may, in any way, have an adverse effect on the work or be prejudicial to the author's reputation or honour;

- to amend the work either before or after it has been used;
- to withdraw the work from circulation or to suspend any kind of use that has already been authorised where the circulation or the use of the work liable to have an adverse effect on the reputation or image of the author;
- to have access to the sole or a rare copy of the work that is lawfully in a third party's possession with a view to preserving the memory thereof by means of a photographic or similar process or an audiovisual process, in such a way that the least possible inconvenience is caused to its possessor who shall in any event be indemnified for any damage or prejudice suffered.

2. Trademarks

2.1 Use of a trademark

If a trademark is used on a website for the purpose of identifying the products or services covered thereby, such use will be considered by the Brazilian Patent and Trademark Office (BPTO) as legitimate evidence against cancellation/forfeiture of the registration for lack of use.

If the website is hosted overseas, the use of the trademark may be considered by the BPTO as evidence to avoid the cancellation/forfeiture of the registration for lack of use if the trademark is being used to identify products and services being commercialised and/or furnished within Brazilian territory.

The use of the trademark must be carried out by the titleholder or by an authorised licensee. If the trademark is used by a licensee, a copy of the licence agreement will probably be requested by the BPTO (the licence agreement does not need to be recorded at the BPTO for this purpose, according to Article 140, Section 2, of the Brazilian IP Law (Law no 9,279/1996)).

It is important to bear in mind that the mere publication of a trademark on a website (without a clear intent of promoting/commercialising the products and services identified thereby), such as on an institutional website, may occasionally not be accepted as proof of use.

It should also be noted that under the Brazilian IP Law (Law no 9,279/1996), a trademark must be used in connection with all products and services claimed and covered thereby, under penalty of partial cancellation of the trademark registration with respect to the products or services not similar to those for which the mark is proven to have been used.

Brazil does not have a specific law harmonising online infringements. Disputes and conflicts on the Internet are resolved under the legal framework that would generally apply to other means of communication or media. In the case of trademark infringement, the most relevant statute is the Brazilian IP Law.

As a rule, any unauthorised use of a trademark in a website is a potential infringement of the exclusive rights granted to the titleholder.

The Brazilian IP Law, however, establishes certain limitations on the exclusive rights of trademark owners. The restrictions are set out in Article 32 of the Brazilian IP Law:

132 The titleholder of a mark may not:

I. prevent merchants or distributors from using their own distinctive signs along with the

mark of the product, in its promotion and commercialisation;
II. prevent manufacturers of accessories from using the mark to indicate the purpose of the product, provided that fair competition practices are followed;
III. prevent the free circulation of the product placed on the domestic market by himself or by another with his consent, except as provided in Paragraphs 3 and 4 of Article 68; and
IV. prevent the mention of the mark in a speech, scientific or literary work, or in any other publication, provided it is done without commercial connotation and without detriment to its distinctive character.

In this sense, if the use of the trademark on a website is construed as a 'fair use' according to the four situations outlined above, the titleholder will probably not be entitled to pursue an infringement claim.

2.2 Infringement

As a rule, the unauthorised use of a trademark as a metatag, keyword, sponsored link, hidden text and within a search/navigation tool may be construed as trademark infringement, provided that the potential infringer is not covered by any of the situations set out in Article 132 of the Brazilian IP Law.

Article 129 of the Brazilian IP Law ensures to the title-holder of trademark registration exclusive rights throughout the country and Article 189 penalises as a crime the reproduction without authorisation of third parties' trademark registrations. In addition, Article 195, III, defines as unfair competition practice any fraudulent act to divert customers from a competitor. Thus, under Brazilian law, the use of metatags, keywords, sponsored links, hidden texts and search/navigation tools tends to be treated as trademark use and, therefore, a violation of industrial property rights.

Brazilian courts have ruled that there was trademark infringement by a company which bought a registered mark as a keyword (eg, *Pistelli Engenharia Ltda v Clovis Alberto Girio E Danilo Moreira,*[3] in which the court ruled that "it is possible to verify, thus, that the links created by the defendant (...) misled consumers, since, when they looked for the company Pistelli, they were directed to (...) the plaintiff's page, promoting, therefore, to its benefit, the diversion of [the plaintiff's] clientele, which characterises the crime of unfair competition"). In the authors' view the same rationale applies to metatags, sponsored links and hidden text.

As to possible liability for search engine sites, the issue remains unsettled before Brazilian courts.

Indeed, in *Coad De Orientação Atualização E Desenvolvimento Profissional Ltda v Google Brasil Internet Ltda*[4] – TJRJ-9CC, the search engine company was held liable for violation by third parties. COAD used the AdWords service, but when the word 'COAD' was searched by Google users, they were redirected to COAD competitors' websites. According to the Rio de Janeiro Appellate Court, this is a typical business risk. Civil and consumer liability was not excluded because risk is part of the activity normally carried out by search engine companies.

---

3 QC 591 – No 591/97 – TJSP-1VCrim.
4 AC 0003615-70.2008.8.19.0209.

By contrast, the Sao Paulo Appellate Court took the view that there was no unfair competition, inasmuch as no evidence on the relationship between the search engine company and the violating party was found *Vegon Corretora De Seguros Ltda v Google Internet Do Brasil Ltda*,[5] in which the court ruled that "in order to avoid any allegation of lack of knowledge and impossibility of content control, serving the supposedly infringing party and/or the search engine with a cease and desist letter should be necessary".

In the authors' experience, search engines usually act positively. Other possible courses of action would be filing a civil court action or even a criminal complaint against all involved parties, in the event that due notice has been served but not acted upon.

As search engine sites profit from advertising, it can be argued that they are also liable for violating activities, when they are put on notice of the infringement and refrain from adopting the appropriate action to take down. The local courts seem to attach considerable weight to the fact that search engines have been put on notice of an infringement and should not then benefit from defences based on a lack of awareness of the infringement.

(a) Internet domain names

Theoretically, the mere unauthorised registration of a trademark as a domain name gives rise to a liability.

Although there is some disagreement, the prevailing position in Brazil is that the mere unauthorised use of a trademark gives rise to losses and damage; in other words, the titleholder does not need to evidence the losses and damage suffered in order to claim for compensation.

In practical terms, however, the person who registers the infringing domain name will usually publish a website or try to sell it in the market. (In some cases, the domain name is offered for sale to the trademark owner.)

As a result, in addition to the mere registration, there are generally additional elements to support a trademark owner who alleges that the domain name was registered in bad faith, that will assist the trademark owner when claiming for losses and damages in a court action.

(b) Search navigation tools

See the general comments on trademark infringement at section 2.2 above.

(c) Hypertext links

The unauthorised use of a trademark as a hypertext link may, theoretically, be construed as a trademark infringement if such use causes any sort of confusion or harm to the legitimate owner of the trademark reproduced in the link.

It is important, however, to consider whether the use falls under the fair use situations set out in Article 132 of the Brazilian IP Law.

In addition, depending on the particular circumstances of the use of the

---

5 AC 0157287-08.2009.8.26.0100 – TJSP – 6CC.

trademark as a hypertext link, the rules against unfair competition practices may also be used by the trademark owner.

(d) ***Framing***

Given that framing may be construed as a particular form of linking, it may also be deemed an infringement in light of the fact that the use of the content of a third party may include its trademarks and other proprietary rights.

In the case of framing, however, the likelihood of confusion and association between the original website and the framed site is even higher in comparison to the practice of linking, given that the user will be exposed to two different websites on the same page.

As a result, therefore, the use of the rules against unfair competition practice may be important in any discussion involving framing.

2.3 Defences

(a) ***Descriptive (non-trademark) use of the mark***

The descriptiveness of a trademark could be used as a defence particularly in cases where the trademark has not been registered by the BPTO (ie, if the unauthorised use of the trademark is challenged based on a trademark application). In such cases, given that the BPTO will not have examined the merits of the trademark application, there could be doubts as to the inherent distinctiveness of the trademark.

If the trademark is already registered, there is a presumption that the trademark is sufficiently distinctive and, therefore, this sort of defence must be linked to a more aggressive strategy on the part of the alleged infringer towards the nullification of the trademark registration.

(b) ***Comparative advertising***

Although comparative advertising is now relatively common in Brazil, there is still uncertainty as to the legality and limits of such campaigns. Moreover, comparative advertising is not specifically regulated by any law in Brazil.

There are, however, certain guidelines established by the National Advertising Self-Regulation Council (CONAR) which, might be used by judges as grounds for a decision in relevant court cases.

In principle, it is possible to use comparative advertising as a defence for the unauthorised use of a trademark on the Internet. See section 2.7 for a fuller treatment of comparative advertising.

(c) ***Parody***

Even though parody is not expressly treated as 'fair use' in Brazilian law, it can be argued that based on freedom of expression, parody should not be construed as a trademark infringement. This will depend, however, on the circumstances of the particular case.

2.4 Parallel imports

If a product identified by a registered trademark in Brazil is offered in the Brazilian territory (regardless of the sales channel) by a party without the consent of the trademark owner, the Brazilian IP Law (Article 132, III) enables the owner to raise a trademark infringement claim on the basis of parallel import.

As a result, therefore, the trademark owner may oppose the commercialisation of its products in Brazil, even if they are offered solely in a web store. In this case, a possible solution to accommodate a trademark owner's rights in Brazil would be to include a shipping restriction on the website to exclude the Brazilian territory.

2.5 Remedies

Under Brazilian law, trademark infringement may constitute both a tort and a crime. Further, parallel importation can be stopped by means of measures taken before a civil court.

Criminal and civil remedies are available in the event of trademark infringement. Criminal remedies include:

- search and seizure;
- arrest and possible imprisonment of infringers; and
- costs.

Civil remedies include:

- search and seizure;
- injunction;
- damages;
- destruction of seized products; and
- costs.

Before adopting any of the measures listed above, however, it is worth considering sending a cease and desist letter as an attempt to put a stop to the infringement. This is a cost-effective way of settling a dispute and avoiding court action. However, cease and desist letters may jeopardise the trademark owner's rights, unless utmost care is taken to follow the appropriate procedures.

A warning letter may be served either through the Registry of Titles and Deeds or by means of a court procedure in which the judge designates a court officer personally to serve the infringing party with the letter. If the infringer does not comply with the terms of the letter, the mark owner must seek judicial measures to stop the infringement within five years of the infringement taking place or risk losing the right to obtain indemnification due to the statute of limitations. Moreover, if the mark owner does not act quickly, it may jeopardise its chances of obtaining a preliminary injunction to stop the infringement based on a provision similar to laches.

Sending a cease and desist letter is not mandatory prior to initiating court procedures.

In short, the decision to serve the infringer with a cease and desist letter is a strategic one and must be carefully considered on a case-by-case basis. In situations where the mark owner is seeking an injunctive order to seize the infringing goods, such a letter could jeopardise the operation because it will alert the infringer to the fact that the mark owner is aware of its illegal activities, giving the infringer time to conceal the infringing products.

2.6 Liability of internet service provider

As noted in section 1.6 above, and based on Brazilian IP law, an ISP can be held liable for online infringement if it fails to respond to notice of a violation. If the ISP is notified and refuses to take any action to stop the infringement, it is possible to request an injunction against the ISP and the user.

2.7 Advertising law and regulation

In Brazil, the guidelines relating to any sort of advertising, including internet advertising, are established and updated by the National Advertising Self-Regulation Council (CONAR). This is a private entity created in 1980 by local advertisers, advertising agencies and media companies.

CONAR's main role is to update the Advertising Code of Ethics and to examine and decide upon any disputes that may arise from violations of the code. The Advertising Code of Ethics regulates virtually every aspect of advertising content, including:

- misleading messages;
- claims of efficiency or superiority;
- testimonials;
- ambush marketing;
- comparative advertising;
- trademark misuse; and
- copyright violation.

The code also has specific rules restricting advertising of certain products, such as alcoholic beverages and products/services targeted at children.

Although CONAR cannot award damages, it does offer a fast and cheap procedure for obtaining a restraining order, making it the best choice for litigators in Brazil. CONAR generally issues preliminary injunctions within a few days of application and a first decision on the merits within three months. Remedies include: a warning; recommendation to amend or correct the relevant announcement; a recommendation to the relevant communication channels to cease the dissemination of the offending announcement; and if these remedies are not accepted, the issuance of a notice through the relevant communication channels in which CONAR states its position regarding the conduct of the advertiser, of the agency and of the communication channels. The costs of this approach represent an advantage, usually ranging from between 2% and 10% of a court action of medium complexity.

As to the jurisdictional requirements, the rules established by CONAR are only applicable to entities which have expressly accepted and adhered to them. Those entities, basically the largest companies in Brazil, adhere to the CONAR rules through associations such as the Brazilian Association of Advertising Agencies (ABAP), the Brazilian Association of Advertisers (ABA), the National Association of Newspaper

(ANJ), the Brazilian Association of Radio and Television (ABERT) and the National Association of Magazine Editors (ANER). In this sense, any advertising developed and published on the Internet by an entity that adheres to the rules of CONAR will be subject to those rules.

2.8 Domain name disputes

The Brazilian alternative dispute resolution system is available for all domain names registered by the local Registrar as from October 1 2010. The dispute resolution system was implemented on that date and must be included in any contracts entered into with the Registrar. Even though this restriction imposes a limit on the scope of the proceeding, the dispute resolution clause might be extended to all domain names when the registrations are renewed, but it still depends on further deliberation from the Registrar.

As regards local disputes, for a complainant to prevail in a dispute involving a '.br' domain name, he/she must prove that the domain name has been registered or is being used in bad faith, and the domain name must:

- be identical or confusingly similar to a mark in which the complainant has rights, which is the object of a granted registration or a prior pending application filed at the Brazilian Patent and Trademark Office (BPTO);
- be identical or confusingly similar to a mark of the complainant which, despite not being the object of a granted registration or a pending application in Brazil, is a well-known mark under the terms of Article 6*bis* of the Paris Convention and Article 126 of the Brazilian Industrial Property Act (Law No 9.279/96);
- be identical or confusingly similar to a trade name, corporate name, civil name, family name or patronymic, well-known pseudonym or nickname, single or collective artistic name, in which the complainant has rights, or even to another domain name registered by the complainant.

The available remedies are limited to the maintenance, transfer or cancellation of the domain name. No damages can be requested. Further, the decision will not be implemented if one of the parties brings a lawsuit or an arbitration proceeding against the other party within 15 days of publication of the decision.

Disputes are handled by one of the dispute resolution service providers authorised by the Registrar. Currently, the Brazil–Canada Chamber of Commerce (CCBC), in Sao Paulo, is the only authorised provider. According to the rules, the provider must provide a decision within 90 days of the filing of the complaint. The deadline may be extended at the provider's request, but the whole proceeding cannot exceed 12 months.

Costs relating to dispute resolution procedures are much lower than those incurred in a traditional lawsuit filed against the infringer.

2.9 Unfair competition/passing off

The Brazilian IP Law stipulates a number of acts that fall within the ambit of unfair competition crimes. These include the following:

Article 195 – A crime of unfair competition is perpetrated by anyone who:
(...)
III. employs fraudulent means to divert the customers of another person to his or another party's advantage;
IV. uses another person's advertising phrase or sign, or imitates it, in order to create confusion among the products or establishments;
V. uses, improperly, another person's trade name, title of establishment, or insignia, or sells, displays, offers for sale, or has in stock a product bearing these references; (...)

In this sense, depending on the specific circumstances of the case, the rules against unfair competition may be raised if the content of a given website is reproduced or imitated without the authorisation of the legitimate owner.

3. Patents

3.1 Patentability of 'internet' inventions

(a) *Computer programs*

According to Brazilian practice, software inventions are considered patentable when they involve a 'technical character'.

Generally, to be patentable in Brazil, an invention must meet the requirements of novelty, inventive activity and industrial application. Further, the invention must not fall within the provisions set out in Article 10 of the Brazilian IP Law, which determines that computer programs per se are not patentable.

It is generally understood that 'computer program per se' means source code. In view of this, computer programs are protected by copyright laws.

On the other hand, computer-implemented inventions involving 'technical character' are allowable in Brazil. The BPTO considers that when the invention is directed to a system that acts on physical data, for instance data representing an image or data that represents parameters and control values of a certain process/method, or it has an effect on the way a computer operates, it can be allowable, provided that it is new and inventive.

Care should be taken if the invention is a mere automation of a business method on a computer or through the Internet, as these applications are commonly rejected by the BPTO.

(b) *Business methods*

The position adopted by the BPTO is that inventions relating to business methods are patentable only if the withdrawal of the business method features from the invention does not affect the patentability of the invention. In other words, the invention must have patentable features even without the method of doing business, which is detached from the invention for examination.

(c) *Mathematical methods*

In view of an express prohibition under the Brazilian IP Law, mathematical methods are not patentable.

(d) ***Presentation of information***

As above, in light of express prohibition under the Brazilian IP Law, presentation of information is not patentable.

3.2 Bioinformatics

In this hypothetical situation, novel sequences/structures are obtained through the use of bioinformatics and research/tests are then carried out to develop a pathway to obtain them synthetically. Such DNA sequences or protein structures may be patented, as long as the patent application describes in sufficient detail how they were obtained (such that a skilled person in the art is able to perform the invention), together with their features.

It should be noted that if such DNA sequence or protein structure is identical to one found in nature, it will be necessary to show how the novel molecule can be differentiated from the natural one. In other words, biological molecules will only merit protection if they are somehow purified or isolated from nature; even a molecule produced by synthetic means (in other words, by human intervention), but containing a nucleotide and/or amino acid sequence identical to one of natural origin will not be accepted by the BPTO according to the logic that the two sequences (the synthetic versus the natural one) cannot be differentiated from one another.

3.3 Issues specific to Brazil

(a) ***Infringement on the Internet***

Before commenting specifically on jurisdiction, it is important to make some observations on patent infringement by means of use of the Internet. There are two main aspects that should be considered when assessing a patent infringement on the Internet:

- all claims must be reproduced in the infringing system/content;
- the patent has territorial effects (ie, it is only valid in the country where it was granted).

In this sense, it is necessary to consider where the infringement really occurs, in view of the location of the ISP and the location of the internet users.

For instance, if a website is hosted on a server located abroad (outside the country where a patent was filed and granted) and is accessed by users of the country in which the patent was granted then, as a result of the use, there is a potential patent infringement (even though the website is hosted outside Brazil). In this situation, the legal scenario is not completely clear in Brazil; but some scholars argue that there may be an infringement given that, although the activities take place outside Brazil, such acts produce economic effects in the country.

From a practical standpoint, if the patent owner files a lawsuit in Brazil in such circumstances, the Brazilian courts will probably determine that they have at least concurrent jurisdiction to decide the case.

(b) *Process patents*

The situation regarding process patents remains unclear in Brazil. In the authors' view, however, there would still be an infringement – particularly if the infringement has a direct economic impact within Brazil.

As mentioned above, Brazilian courts will generally have concurrent jurisdiction to rule on such cases.

3.4 Remedies available for patent infringement

Patent holders in Brazil may seek criminal and civil remedies concurrently in order to put a stop to patent violations. The following remedies are available under local law:

- criminal remedies:
  - *ex parte* search and seizure of the infringing products;
  - criminal prosecution;
  - imprisonment of the infringers;
  - fines.
- civil remedies:
  - search and seizure of the infringing products;
  - *ex parte* preliminary injunctions;
  - recovery of damages;
  - destruction of seized products;
  - recovery of attorney fees and judicial costs.

As noted in section 2.5 above, cease and desist letters are also an option in patent infringement cases.

In both criminal and civil cases it will be necessary to adduce evidence in court that the product manufactured and/sold by the third party or the process applied thereby infringes the patent.

Given that the majority of judges are not very experienced in IP and/or are not particularly qualified to opine on the technical issues involved in discussions of infringement, the opinions issued by technical experts (either by court-appointed experts or by those supported by the parties) tend to play an important role in both civil and criminal spheres.

On the civil side, if the patent owner also raises a claim for loss or damage, the judge may request evidence of the loss or damage suffered – this is not applicable on the criminal side – even though some court decisions hold that proof of an infringing act would be sufficient to entitle the patent owner to raise a claim for loss or damage.

4. Disclosure orders against ISPs

4.1 Availability

Under Brazilian law, it is possible to request a court order to oblige an ISP to disclose the identity and contact details of a user that is infringing an intellectual property right. In practical terms, however, ISPs generally refuse to reveal such details. In most cases, they will only reveal the IP (Internet Protocol) number of the user.

In view of certain crimes allegedly committed through ORKUT – the social network managed by Google – the Brazilian authorities have been requested on a number of occasions to disclose users' information. Google, however, has usually refused to reveal the data on the ground that all users' information is stored outside Brazil, mainly on company servers located in the United States and, therefore, in view of US laws on the protection of personal data, the company is not able to reveal the requested information under penalty of infringing those laws.

If the infringement of the relevant intellectual property rights (IPR) is relatively obvious (ie, if the infringement does not depend on a detailed technical examination, or if it is not subjective), most ISPs will probably agree to remove infringing content upon receipt of written notice from the IPR owner.

4.2 Requirements

As a rule, the IPR owner should show that the content infringes its IPR and that the ISP has refused to disclose the data voluntarily – even though this prior attempt is not a requirement established in Brazilian law.

4.3 Jurisdictional issues

The Brazilian courts will have at least concurrent jurisdiction to rule on the disclosure of the requested information if the activities of the ISP will have a direct impact (ie, publication of content that infringes the IP right of a Brazilian resident), or are generally accessible by Brazilian users.

4.4 'John Doe' injunctions

Under the Brazilian rules, it is not possible to obtain a 'John Doe' injunction to prevent IPR infringements.

On the other hand, it is possible to request an injunction directly against the ISP if, for instance, the content has been published by several different users and the courts have already decided that it does, in fact, infringe the IPR of third parties. In such cases, the court can order the ISP to adopt all (technically possible) measures to prevent any future posts, or the immediate removal of new posts of the infringing content.

Canada

Martin PJ Kratz
Bennett Jones LLP

1. Copyright, database rights and design rights

1.1 Overview

To be protected by copyright in Canada, a work must be original, fixed and appropriately connected to Canada, or to a WTO Agreement, Berne Convention or Universal Copyright Convention member state. Copyright applies to all original literary, dramatic, musical and artistic works. Each of these general categories covers a wide range of creations. The word 'original' is essential in defining a work that qualifies for copyright protection.

Many forms of creative expression that are used on the Internet are therefore protectable under copyright law in Canada. As is set out in more detail below, textual aspects of websites or user-generated textual content are literary works under copyright law. Graphic materials are artistic works, and videos are either artistic works or dramatic works.

The Copyright Act, RSC 1985, c C-42 requires that the work originate from its author, not be copied, be original and involve some intellectual effort.

Equal priority is given to the rights of copyright owners and to the rights of users. The Supreme Court of Canada has held, in *Théberge v Galerie d'Art du Petit Champlain inc*,[1] that copyright law provides a balance between creators and users, namely: "the purpose of copyright law was to balance the public interest in promoting the encouragement and dissemination of works of the arts and intellect and obtaining a just reward for the creator."

Canada has gone through a major copyright reform. The Copyright Modernisation Act, Bill C-11, SC 2012, c 20, received royal assent on June 29 2012, and on November 7 2012 the governor general in council proclaimed into force the majority of the provisions. The 'notice and notice' provisions and provisions regarding implementation of the WIPO Copyright Treaties will be proclaimed at a later date. An objective of Bill C-11 has been to allow Canada to adhere to the WIPO Copyright Treaty) and the WIPO Performances and Phonograms Treaty, together known as the WIPO Internet Treaties. These treaties are considered as updates and supplements of the protection granted by the Berne Convention for the Protection of Literary and Artistic Works (Berne Convention) and the International Convention for the Protection of Performers, Producers of Phonograms and Broadcasting

1 [2002] 2 SCR 336.

Organisations (Rome Convention). References in this chapter to Bill C-11 are to provisions in this recent law.

(a) Literary works and artistic works

Reflecting earlier case law, in Canada software is protected as a literary work and Section 2 of the Copyright Act defines 'literary work' to include tables, computer programs and compilations of literary works.

Section 2 defines 'computer program' to mean a set of instructions or statements, expressed, fixed, embodied or stored in any manner that is to be used directly or indirectly in a computer in order to bring about a specific result.

Section 2 also defines 'artistic work' to include paintings, drawings, maps, charts, plans, photographs, engravings, sculptures, works of artistic craftsmanship, architectural works and compilations of artistic works.

(b) Films, sound recordings, and broadcasts

Section 2 of the Copyright Act defines 'dramatic work' to include any piece for recitation, choreographic work or mime, the scenic arrangement or acting form of which is fixed in writing or otherwise, any cinematographic work and any compilation of dramatic works.

The section defines 'cinematographic work' to include any work expressed by any process analogous to cinematography, whether or not accompanied by a soundtrack.

Section 2 also defines 'sound recording' to mean a recording, fixed in any material form, consisting of sounds, whether or not of a performance of a work, but excludes any soundtrack of a cinematographic work where it accompanies the cinematographic work.

A pre-existing sound recording that is part of a soundtrack cannot be the subject of a tariff when the soundtrack accompanies the cinematographic work.[2]

The Copyright Act provides in Section 18(1) that the maker of a sound recording has a copyright in the sound recording, consisting of the sole right to do the following in relation to the sound recording or any substantial part thereof:

- to publish it for the first time;
- to reproduce it in any material form; and
- to rent it out and to authorise any such acts.

Broadcasts are not defined in the Copyright Act. However, the act provides in Section 21(1) that a broadcaster has a copyright in the communication signals that it broadcasts, consisting of the sole right to do the following in relation to the communication signal or any substantial part thereof:

- to fix it;
- to reproduce any fixation of it that was made without the broadcaster's consent;
- to authorise another broadcaster to retransmit it to the public simultaneously with its broadcast; and

2 See *Re Sound v Motion Picture Theatre Associations of Canada*, 2012 SCC 38.

- in the case of a television communication signal, to perform it in a place open to the public on payment of an entrance fee, and to authorise any act described above.

(c) *Typographical arrangement of a published edition*

Unlike the United Kingdom, Canada does not have a special law regarding 'typographical arrangement', and so any particular engraving or like work would need to be assessed for copyright protection on the same basis as other works.

It is uncertain as to whether a mere change of a font would be sufficient to create a copyright. Such is doubted in *CCH Canadian Ltd v LSUC* where the court, discussing the requirement of originality in Canada, noted "[f]or example, any skill and judgment that might be involved in simply changing the font of a work to produce 'another' work would be too trivial to merit copyright protection as an 'original' work".[3]

(d) *Protection of the user interface*

Canadian copyright law generally protects the graphical user interface of a computer program or of a website as an artistic work under copyright law in respect of copyright in the website).[4]

(e) *Computer-generated works*

While little case law exists on the subject, computer-generated works would be protected if they were original works and the product of skill and judgement. Mere data generated by a machine, however, is unlikely to meet that requirement and so the individual data elements are unlikely to have copyright protection; but a compilation of data may well satisfy the requirements for protection as a compilation.

(f) *Websites protected as databases*

Canada does not have a specific database law.

A website is protected in Canada as a literary or artistic work or as a compilation work.

The WIPO Copyright Treaty and the WIPO Performances and Phonograms Treaty require protection of databases. Canada's position has been that databases are already protected under existing law. Compilations of data are protected under the Copyright Act.

(g) *Compilations*

Section 2 of the Copyright Act defines a 'compilation' as a work resulting "from the selection or arrangement of literary, dramatic, musical, or artistic works of parts thereof or ... a work resulting from the selection or arrangement of data". Merely assembling data and sorting it in an obvious, accepted manner using standards of

3 [2004] 1 SCR 339.
4 See *British Columbia Automobile Association v OPEIU, Local 378* [2001] 3 WWR 95 (SC).

selection commonplace in the industry may not involve 'selection or arrangement', and so may not result in a protectable compilation.

In the *CCH Canadian Ltd v Law Society of Upper Canada*[5] decision, the Supreme Court of Canada commented on what constitutes a compilation and stated that:

> *Copyright protects originality of form or expression. A compilation takes existing material and casts it in a different form. The arranger does not have copyright in the individual components. However, the arranger may have copyright in the form represented by the compilation. It is not the several components that are the subject of the copyright, but the overall arrangement of them which the plaintiff through his industry has produced.*

1.2 Infringing acts

(a) Copying

Temporary copies: Section 2.4(1)(b) of the Copyright Act protects an intermediary on the Internet whose only role is as a conduit. Such protection includes where temporary copies are made solely for technical reasons.[6]

Section 30.71 of Bill C-11 provides that it is not an infringement of copyright to make a reproduction of a work or other subject matter if:

- the reproduction forms an essential part of a technological process;
- the reproduction's only purpose is to facilitate a use that is not an infringement of copyright; and
- the reproduction exists only for the duration of the technological process.

In any medium: Section 3(1) of the Copyright Act states that the sole rights of the copyright owner include making a reproduction in any material form.

The reproduction of a substantial part of a work in which copyright subsists without the authority of the copyright owner is one of the sole rights of the copyright holder. As a result, unless an exemption is available, such an act may infringe the copyright of the owner.

Bill C-11 provides that it is an infringement of copyright for a person, by means of the Internet or another digital network, to provide a service primarily for the purpose of enabling acts of copyright infringement if an actual infringement of copyright occurs by means of the Internet or another digital network as a result of the use of that service. Factors that a court may consider to determine whether such an infringement has occurred include:

- whether the person expressly or implicitly marketed or promoted the service as one that could be used to enable acts of copyright infringement;
- whether the person had knowledge that the service was used to enable a significant number of acts of copyright infringement;
- whether the service has significant uses other than to enable acts of copyright infringement;

---

5 [2004] 1 SCR 339.

6 See *Society of Composers, Authors and Music Publishers of Canada v Canadian Association of Internet Providers* [2004] 2 SCR 427.

- the person's ability, as part of providing the service, to limit acts of copyright infringement, and any action taken by the person to do so;
- any benefits that the person received as a result of enabling the acts of copyright infringement; and
- the economic viability of the provision of the service if it were not used to enable acts of copyright infringement.

Bill C-11 also provides in Section 31.1(1) that a person who, in providing services related to the operation of the Internet or another digital network, provides any means for the telecommunication or reproduction of a work or other subject matter through the Internet or that other network does not, solely by reason of providing those means, infringe copyright in that work or other subject matter. Section 31.1(2) sets out that a person referred to who caches the work or other subject matter, or does any similar act in relation to it, to make the telecommunication more efficient does not, by virtue of that act alone, infringe copyright in the work or other subject matter. However, this provision does not apply unless the person, in respect of the work or other subject matter:

- does not modify it, other than for technical reasons;
- ensures that any directions related to its caching or the doing of any similar act, as the case may be, that are specified in a manner consistent with industry practice by whoever made it available for telecommunication through the Internet or another digital network, and that lend themselves to automated reading and execution, are read and executed; and
- does not interfere with the use of technology that is lawful and consistent with industry practice in order to obtain data on the use of the work or other subject matter.

Section 31.1(4) of Bill C-11 states that a person who, for the purpose of allowing the telecommunication of a work or other subject matter through the Internet or another digital network, provides digital memory in which another person stores the work or other subject matter does not, by virtue of that act alone, infringe copyright in the work or other subject matter.

(b) Issuing copies to the public

The publication of a work in which copyright subsists is one of the sole rights of the copyright holder. As a result, unless an exemption is available, such an act may infringe the copyright of the owner.

(c) Communicating work to the public

The communication of a work in which copyright subsists to the public via telecommunication is one of the sole rights of the copyright holder. The copyright owner has the sole right, in the case of any literary, dramatic, musical or artistic work, to communicate the work to the public by telecommunication. As a result, unless an exemption is available, such an act may infringe the copyright of the owner.

Section 2 of the Copyright Act defines 'telecommunication' to mean any transmission of signs, signals, writing, images or sounds or intelligence of any nature by wire, radio, visual, optical or other electromagnetic system.

The word 'communication' connotes the passing of information from one person to another. The fact that the technology used for the transmission does not permit a person to listen to the music during the transmission does not mean that there is no communication. In the context of a wireless transmission, it is the receipt of the transmission that completes the communication.[7]

The transmission of information over the Internet is a communication once the information is received.[8]

Section 2.4(1)(b) of the Copyright Act protects an intermediary on the Internet whose only role is as a conduit and who provides the means of telecommunication necessary. In such a case, the intermediary does not 'communicate' the work.[9]

A point-to-point email is not a communication to the public.[10]

Similarly, a point-to-point communication such as a fax is not a communication to the public by telecommunication but a series of repeated transmissions may be.[11]

A download of a video game containing a musical work is not a communication of the work to the public within the meaning of Section 3(1)(f) of the Copyright Act. The right to 'communicate' is historically connected to the right to perform a work and not the right to reproduce permanent copies of the work. Therefore, the fundamental nature of the communication right is concerned with performance-based activities.[12]

The communication right may be engaged by internet broadcast to very many parties without restriction, such as if a digital file is available to a large subset of the public even if such individuals download the digital file separately.[13]

Multiple instances of streaming music files may be a communication to the public. A communication is not restricted to a purely non-interactive context. The right to communicate to the public is historically linked to traditional media that operated on a broadcasting, or 'push', model but the right is not limited to this model and also applies in a 'pull' model such as in distribution of numerous instances of streaming music files.[14]

Bill C-11 provides in Section 2(1.1) that the communication of a work or other subject matter to the public by telecommunication includes making it available to the public by telecommunication in a way that allows a member of the public to

---

7 See *Canadian Wireless Telecommunications Association v Society of Composers, Authors and Music Publishers of Canada*, 2008 FCA 6, leave to appeal to SCC refused, September 18 2008.

8 See *Society of Composers, Authors and Music Publishers of Canada v Canadian Association of Internet Providers* [2004] 2 SCR 427.

9 See *Society of Composers, Authors and Music Publishers of Canada v Canadian Association of Internet Providers* [2004] 2 SCR 427.

10 See *Society of Composers, Authors and Music Publishers of Canada v Canadian Assn of Internet Providers* [2004] 2 SCR 427.

11 See *CCH Canadian Ltd v Law Society of Upper Canada* [2004] 1 SCR 339.

12 See *Entertainment Software Association v Society of Composers, Authors and Music Publishers of Canada*, 2012 SCC 34.

13 See *Canadian Wireless Telecommunications Association v Society of Composers, Authors and Music Publishers of Canada*, 2008 FCA 6, leave to appeal to SCC refused, September 18 2008.

14 See *Rogers Communications Inc v Society of Composers, Authors and Music Publishers of Canada*, 2012 SCC 35.

have access to it from a place and at a time individually chosen by that member of the public.

(d) *Perform, show or play work in public*

The performance of a work in which copyright subsists to the public is one of the sole rights of the copyright holder. As a result, unless an exemption is available, such an act may infringe the copyright of the owner.

The same considerations as for a communication to the public arise in the case of a performance in public.

The performance on the Internet occurs upon transmission.[15]

Multiple transmissions of a ringtone over the Internet may be a public performance.[16]

(e) *Rent or lend the work to the public*

Copyright law provides specific rental rights for sound recordings and computer programs as mechanisms to manage the access to these works with adequate compensation to the authors. These provisions give the owner of the copyright control over others providing copies of the computer program or sound recording to others under rental arrangements.

In the case of a musical work, the copyright owner has the right to rent out a sound recording of a musical work.

In the case of a computer program that can be reproduced in the ordinary course of its use, other than by reproduction during its execution in conjunction with a machine, device or computer, the copyright owner has the sole right to rent out the computer program.

(f) *Authorising another person to do any of the above*

Under Section 27(1) of the Copyright Act, it is an infringement of copyright for anyone to do anything that the act only allows owners to do, including authorising the exercise of his own rights.

It does not infringe copyright to authorise a person to do something that would not constitute copyright infringement.[17]

'Authorise' means to "sanction, approve and countenance".[18] 'Countenance' in the context of authorising copyright infringement must be understood in its strongest dictionary meaning, namely, "[g]ive approval to; sanction, permit; favour, encourage".

---

15 See *SOCAN Statement of Royalties, Public Performance of Musical Works 1996, 1997, 1998 (Tariff 22, Internet) (Re)* (1999), 1 CPR (4th) 417 (Copyright Board); *Society of Composers, Authors and Music Publishers of Canada v Canadian Association of Internet Providers*, 2002 FCA 166, 19 CPR (4rth) 289, rev'd in part; *Society of Composers, Authors and Music Publishers of Canada v Canadian Association of Internet Providers* [2004] 2 SCR 427.

16 See *Public Performance of Musical Works (Tariff 24, Ringtones)(Re)* [2006] 52 CPR 375 (Copyright Board), aff'd *Canadian Wireless Telecommunications Association v Society of Composers, Authors and Music Publishers of Canada*, 2008 FCA 6, leave to appeal to SCC refused, September 18 2008.

17 See *Composers, Authors and Publishers Association of Canada Ltd v CTV Television Network Ltd* [1968] SCR 676.

18 See *Muzak Corp v Composers, Authors and Publishers Association of Canada, Ltd* [1953] 2 SCR 182)

Authorisation is a question of fact that depends on the circumstances of each particular case and can be inferred from acts that are less than direct and positive, including a sufficient degree of indifference.

A person does not authorise infringement by authorising the mere use of equipment that could be used to infringe copyright. Courts should presume that a person who authorises an activity does so only insofar as it is in accordance with the law. This presumption may be rebutted if it is shown that a certain relationship or degree of control existed between the alleged authoriser and the persons that committed the copyright infringement.[19]

(g) *Secondary infringement*

Under Section 27(2)(a) of the Copyright Act, it is an infringement of copyright to sell a copy of a work that the person knows or should have known infringes copyright – a practice known as secondary infringement. Section 27(2) provides that it is an infringement of copyright for any person to:

- sell or rent out;
- distribute to such an extent as to affect prejudicially the owner of the copyright;
- by way of trade distribute, expose or offer for sale or rental, or exhibit in public;
- possess for the purpose of doing anything referred to in the bullets above; or
- import into Canada for the purpose of doing anything referred to in the first to third bullets above

a copy of a work, sound recording or fixation of a performer's performance or of a communication signal that the person knows or should have known infringes copyright or would infringe copyright if it had been made in Canada by the person who made it.

Three elements must be proven to ground a claim for secondary infringement:[20]

- The copy must be the product of primary infringement;
- The secondary infringer must have known or should have known that he is dealing with a product of infringement; and
- The secondary dealing must be established; that is, there must have been a sale.

1.3 Test for copyright infringement

(a) *Requirement of substantial reproduction*

Section 27(1) of the Copyright Act provides that it is an infringement of copyright for any person to do, without the consent of the owner of the copyright, anything that by the act only the owner of the copyright has the right to do.

A common type of copyright infringement is copying part or all of a copyrighted

19 See *CCH Canadian Ltd v Law Society of Upper Canada* [2004] 1 SCR 339; *Society of Composers, Authors and Music Publishers of Canada v Canadian Association of Internet Providers* [2004] 2 SCR 427.

20 See *CCH Canadian Ltd v Law Society of Upper Canada* [2004] 1 SCR 339.

work without permission. In determining whether substantial copying has taken place, the court must exclude from consideration any part of the work not properly the subject matter of copyright. For infringement, there must be copying of the work or a substantial part thereof and access to the copyright-protected work. The latter requirement mandates that the plaintiff's work must have been created before the creation of the alleged infringement.

(b) *Repeated copying of insubstantial part*

Infringement may be established where, among other requirements, the evidence shows substantial similarity. Mere similarity is insufficient to find that a work is copied from another. Rather, the copying must be substantial to establish infringement of copyright. Copying may be assessed on the basis of similarity of a quantity of material as well as quality of material. In respect of the threshold needed for infringement, a substantial part of a work may be not merely its collection of words, but its structure and development.

1.4 Exemptions/defences to copyright infringement

(a) *Format shifting*

An exemption provided in Section 29.22 allows a consumer the right to reproduce, for a private purpose, any work or protected subject matter if the source copy was legally obtained (but not onto an 'audio-recording medium' for musical works or sound recordings and not involving circumvention of any technological protection measures). The individual may not give away the recording.

Section 30.6 also permits adaptation of a computer program owned by a person where needed for compatability of the computer program with the person's computer and for the person's own use.

Format shifting may also be covered in some cases under the broader fair dealing exemption.

(b) *Personal copying rights*

There is a subsisting personal copying right in respect of musical works. Canada has a scheme under which blank media are subject to a levy added to all blank audio recording media sold in Canada which is distributed to copyright owners of musical works. The manufacturer or importer of the blank audio recording medium collects the levy. This levy is then remitted to the applicable collective on behalf of the eligible author, performer and makers.

Under the current law, digital audio recorders such as MP3 players and computers with permanently embedded or non-removable memory do not attract private copying royalties as they are not 'audio recording media' themselves and are not subject to the levy.

The personal copying right provides that it is not an infringement of copyright to copy onto an audio recording medium:

- a musical work in a sound recording;
- a performer's performance of a musical work in a sound recording; and

- a sound recording in which a musical work or a performer's performance of a musical work is embodied if it is for private use.

This exemption does not apply if the copying is done for the purpose of doing any of the following:

- selling or renting out, or by way of trade exposing or offering for sale or rental;
- distributing, whether or not for the purpose of trade; or
- communicating to the public by telecommunication.

Uploading a musical work without consent of the copyright owner is an infringement of copyright in Canada. Downloading a musical work for personal use without further distribution or dissemination may be within the personal copying exemption or otherwise subject to the fair dealing right.

A broader personal copying exemption is provided by Bill C-11, which states that it is not an infringement of copyright for an individual to reproduce a work or other subject matter or any substantial part of a work or other subject matter if:

- the copy of the work or other subject matter from which the reproduction is made is not an infringing copy;
- the individual legally obtained the copy of the work or other subject matter from which the reproduction is made, other than by borrowing it or renting it, and owns or is authorised to use the medium or device on which it is reproduced;
- the individual, in order to make the reproduction, did not circumvent a technological protection measure or cause one to be circumvented;
- the individual does not give the reproduction away; and
- the reproduction is used only for private purposes.

(c) ***Time shifting***

A time shifting exemption is provided by Bill C-11 in Section 29.23(1), which provides that it is not an infringement of copyright for an individual to fix a communication signal, to reproduce a work or sound recording that is being broadcast or to fix or reproduce a performer's performance that is being broadcast, in order to record a programme for the purpose of listening to or viewing it later, if:

- the individual receives the programme legally;
- the individual, in order to record the programme, did not circumvent a technological protection measure or cause one to be circumvented;
- the individual makes no more than one recording of the programme;
- the individual keeps the recording no longer than is reasonably necessary in order to listen to or view the programme at a more convenient time;
- the individual does not give the recording away; and
- the recording is used only for private purposes.

Time shifting may also be covered in some cases under the broader fair dealing exemption.

(d) *Fair use*

The fair dealing exception is always available as an integral part of the scheme of copyright law.[21] It is described as a user's right.

In order to show that a dealing was fair under the Copyright Act, a defendant must prove that the dealing was for one of the specified purposes such as research or private study, and that the dealing was fair.

'Research' must be given a wide and liberal interpretation in order to ensure that users' rights are not unduly constrained.

Bill C-11 expanded the permitted purposes for which the fair dealing exemption is available to include education, parody or satire in addition to research and private study.

Fair dealing for the purpose of criticism or review or for the purpose of news reporting or news summary does not infringe copyright if the source and the name of the author, performer or maker, as applicable, are mentioned.

The purpose and fairness of the dealing is assessed from the perspective of the user.

There has been little litigation in Canada regarding the use of the fair dealing exemption for news reporting or news summary in the context of the Internet. It is noted that if news services (eg, Google News) sought to utilise this exemption, they would need to identify and mention the source and the name of the author, performer or maker.

The Copyright Act does not define what will be 'fair'; whether something is fair is a question of fact and depends on the facts of each case.

While there is no set test for fairness, a series of factors could be considered to help assess whether a dealing is fair:

- the purpose of the dealing;
- the character of the dealing;
- the amount of the dealing;
- alternatives to the dealing;
- the nature of the work; and
- the effect of the dealing on the work.

Although these considerations will not all arise in every case of fair dealing, this list of factors provides a useful analytical framework to govern determinations of fairness in individual cases.

Bill C-11 provides a further 'mashup' right as a kind of fair dealing. Section 29.21(1) provides that it is not an infringement of copyright for an individual to use an existing work or other subject matter, or copy of one, which has been published or otherwise made available to the public in the creation of a new work or other subject matter in which copyright subsists and for the individual – or, with the individual's authorisation, a member of his household – to use the new work or other subject matter or to authorise an intermediary to disseminate it, if:

- the use of, or the authorisation to disseminate, the new work or other subject matter is done solely for non-commercial purposes;

21 See *CCH Canadian Ltd v Law Society of Upper Canada* [2004] 1 SCR 339.

- the source – and, if given in the source, the name of the author, performer, maker or broadcaster – of the existing work or other subject matter or copy of it are mentioned, if it is reasonable in the circumstances to do so;
- the individual had reasonable grounds to believe that the existing work or other subject matter or copy of it, as the case may be, was not infringing copyright; and
- the use of, or the authorisation to disseminate, the new work or other subject matter does not have a substantial adverse effect, financial or otherwise, on the exploitation or potential exploitation of the existing work or other subject matter – or copy of it – or on an existing or potential market for it, including that the new work or other subject matter is not a substitute for the existing one.

(e) ***Caching/temporary copies as part of communication process***

As described in section 1.2(a) above, Section 2.4(1)(b) of the Copyright Act protects an intermediary on the Internet whose only role is as a conduit where cache copies are made solely for technical reasons

Bill C-11 adds a statutory right in Section 31.1(1) that would provide that a person who, in providing services related to the operation of the Internet or another digital network, provides any means for the telecommunication or the reproduction of a work or other subject matter through the Internet or that other network does not, solely by reason of providing those means, infringe copyright in that work or other subject matter. Subject to certain exceptions, Section 31.1(3) would provide that such a person (above) who caches the work or other subject matter, or does any similar act in relation to it, to make the telecommunication more efficient does not, by virtue of that act alone, infringe copyright in the work or other subject matter.

Bill C-11, in Section 41.27, provides a limitation on remedies. This provides that the owner of the copyright in a work or other subject matter is not entitled to any remedy other than an injunction against a provider of an information location tool that is found to have infringed copyright by making a reproduction of the work or other subject matter or by communicating that reproduction to the public by telecommunication, provided that the provider in respect of the work or other subject matter:

- makes and caches, or does any act similar to caching, the reproduction in an automated manner for the purpose of providing the information location tool;
- communicates that reproduction to the public by telecommunication for the purpose of providing the information that has been located by the information location tool;
- does not modify the reproduction, other than for technical reasons;
- complies with any conditions relating to the making or caching, or doing of any act similar to caching, of reproductions of the work or other subject matter, or to the communication of the reproductions to the public by telecommunication, that were specified in a manner consistent with industry practice by whoever made the work or other subject matter available through

the Internet or another digital network and that lend themselves to automated reading and execution; and
- does not interfere with the use of technology that is lawful and consistent with industry practice in order to obtain data on the use of the work or other subject matter.

(f) ***Hosting***

The knowledge of an internet service provider (ISP) that a person may be using content-neutral technology in order to infringe copyright is not necessarily sufficient to constitute authorisation which requires that the ISP gave approval to, sanctioned, permitted favoured or encouraged the infringing conduct. Notice of infringing conduct and a failure to respond by taking it down may in some circumstances lead to a finding of authorisation.[22]

Bill C-11 provides, in Section 27(2.3), that it is an infringement of copyright for a person, by means of the Internet or another digital network, to provide a service primarily for the purpose of enabling acts of copyright infringement if an actual infringement of copyright occurs by means of the Internet or another digital network as a result of the use of that service. Factors that a court may consider to determine if such an infringement occurred include:

- whether the person expressly or implicitly marketed or promoted the service as one that could be used to enable acts of copyright infringement;
- whether the person had knowledge that the service was used to enable a significant number of acts of copyright infringement;
- whether the service has significant uses other than to enable acts of copyright infringement;
- the person's ability, as part of providing the service, to limit acts of copyright infringement and any action taken by the person to do so;
- any benefits the person received as a result of enabling the acts of copyright infringement; and
- the economic viability of the provision of the service if it were not used to enable acts of copyright infringement.

Bill C-11 also provides, in Section 31.1(1), that a person who, in providing services related to the operation of the Internet or another digital network, provides any means for the telecommunication or reproduction of a work or other subject matter through the Internet or that other network does not, solely by reason of providing those means, infringe copyright in that work or other subject matter. Section 31.1(2) sets out that a person referred to who caches the work or other subject matter, or does any similar act in relation to it, to make the telecommunication more efficient does not, by virtue of that act alone, infringe copyright in the work or other subject matter. However, this section does not apply unless the person, in respect of the work or other subject matter:

---

22 See *Society of Composers, Authors and Music Publishers of Canada v Canadian Association of Internet Providers* [2004] 2 SCR 427.

- does not modify it, other than for technical reasons;
- ensures that any directions related to its caching or the doing of any similar act, as the case may be, that are specified in a manner consistent with industry practice by whoever made it available for telecommunication through the Internet or another digital network, and that lend themselves to automated reading and execution, are read and executed; and
- does not interfere with the use of technology that is lawful and consistent with industry practice in order to obtain data on the use of the work or other subject matter.

Section 31.1(4) states that a person who, for the purpose of allowing the telecommunication of a work or other subject matter through the Internet or another digital network, provides digital memory in which another person stores the work or other subject matter does not, by virtue of that act alone, infringe copyright in the work or other subject matter.

In addition Section 41.25(1) of Bill C-11 would provide a 'notice and notice' mechanism under which an owner of the copyright in a work or other subject matter may send a notice of claimed infringement to a person who provides:

- the means, in the course of providing services related to the operation of the Internet or another digital network, of telecommunication through which the electronic location that is the subject of the claim of infringement is connected to the Internet or another digital network;
- the digital memory that is used for the electronic location to which the claim of infringement relates; or
- an information location tool. This triggers, among other obligations, an obligation to preserve records of the alleged infringement.

(g) ***Back-up copies***

Section 30.6(b) of the Copyright Act provides that it is not an infringement of copyright in a computer program for a person who owns a copy of the computer program that is authorised by the owner of the copyright to make a single reproduction for back-up purposes of the copy if the person proves that the reproduction for back-up purposes is destroyed immediately when the person ceases to be the owner of the copy of the computer program.

Bill C-11 expands the applicability of this exception to cover licensees. It provides for a specific back-up exemption in Section 29.24(1), which provides that it is not an infringement of copyright in a work or other subject matter for a person who owns – or has a licence to use – a copy of the work or subject matter (in this section referred to as the 'source copy') to reproduce the source copy if:

- the person does so solely for back-up purposes in case the source copy is lost, damaged or otherwise rendered unusable;
- the source copy is not an infringing copy;
- the person, in order to make the reproduction, did not circumvent a technological protection measure, or cause one to be circumvented; and
- the person does not give any of the reproductions away.

(h) ***Reverse engineering***

Copyright law does not extend to ideas. As a result, as a basic principle, the reverse engineering of the ideas that underlie a copyright work is not an infringement of copyright.

Bill C-11 provides for a specific reverse engineering exemption in Section 30.62. This would provide that it is not an infringement of copyright for a person to reproduce a work or other subject matter for the purposes of encryption research if:

- it would not be practical to carry out the research without making the copy;
- the person has lawfully obtained the work or other subject matter; and
- the person has informed the owner of the copyright in the work or other subject matter.

Bill C-11 also provides a right to assess information from a computer program for the purposes of interoperability with another computer program in Section 30.61(1). This sets out that it is not an infringement of copyright in a computer program for a person who owns a copy of the computer program that is authorised by the owner of the copyright, or has a licence to use a copy of the computer program, to reproduce the copy if:

- they reproduce the copy for the sole purpose of obtaining information that would allow the person to make the program and another computer program interoperable; and
- they do not use or disclose that information, except as necessary to make the program and another computer program interoperable or to assess that interoperability.

Subsection (2) goes on to state that in the case where that information is used or disclosed as necessary to make another computer program interoperable with the program, subsection (1) applies even if the other computer program incorporates the information and is then sold, rented or otherwise distributed.

(i) ***Parody defence***

Bill C-11 expands the permitted purposes for which the fair dealing exemption is available to include education, parody or satire in addition to research and private study.

(j) ***Incidental inclusion***

Section 30.7 of the Copyright Act provides that it is not an infringement of copyright incidentally and not deliberately to include a work or other subject matter in another work or other subject matter, or do any act in relation to a work or other subject matter that is incidentally and not deliberately included in another work or other subject matter.

1.5 Remedies available for copyright infringement

A wide range of relief is available for the successful plaintiff in a copyright infringement action, including injunctive relief, damages, delivery up of infringing goods, profits and statutory damages.

1.6 Copyright liability

(a) Hosting/cloud computing where infringing content uploaded by user of service

A user would be liable for his infringing acts.

An ISP is not liable for an infringement by its users where it merely provides infrastructure and does not have knowledge of or promote the infringement. In order for liability to be found, some causality in respect of the ISP is required beyond mere provision of infrastructure.[23]

Bill C-11 adds a further statutory exemption from the liability of ISPs. Bill C-11, Section 31.1(1) provides that a person who, in providing services relating to the operation of the Internet or another digital network, provides any means for the telecommunication or the reproduction of a work or other subject matter through the Internet or that other network does not, solely by reason of providing those means, infringe copyright in that work or other subject matter. Section 31.1(2) sets out that a person referred to who caches the work or other subject matter, or does any similar act in relation to it, to make the telecommunication more efficient does not, by virtue of that act alone, infringe copyright in the work or other subject matter. However, this subsection does not apply unless the person, in respect of the work or other subject matter:

- does not modify it, other than for technical reasons;
- ensures that any directions related to its caching or the doing of any similar act, as the case may be, that are specified in a manner consistent with industry practice by whoever made it available for telecommunication through the Internet or another digital network, and that lend themselves to automated reading and execution, are read and executed; and
- does not interfere with the use of technology that is lawful and consistent with industry practice in order to obtain data on the use of the work or other subject matter.

Section 31.1(4) states that a person who, for the purpose of allowing the telecommunication of a work or other subject matter through the Internet or another digital network, provides digital memory in which another person stores the work or other subject matter does not, by virtue of that act alone, infringe copyright in the work or other subject matter.

(b) Hypertext linking

There has been little consideration of the use of hypertext links in the context of copyright infringement in Canada. The issue for a claim of copyright infringement is where there is a substantial taking by the reproduction of the address of another website, or if such an address is even a work that could be the subject of copyright.

---

23 See *Society of Composers, Authors and Music Publishers of Canada v Canadian Assn of Internet Providers* [2004] 2 SCR 427, 2004 SCC 45.

(c) *P2P network*

The issue of liability for providers of P2P software is whether they have authorised infringements that have arisen out of the use of the software. (See section 1.2(f) above as to the liability of a person who authorises an activity.)

Bill C-11 adds a further statutory exemption from liability of an ISP in Section 31.1, noted above.

See section 1.2(a) above, as to the scope of the statutory protection of certain internet intermediaries under Bill C-11, Section 27(2.3).

The uploading of works without the consent of the copyright owner would violate several rights of the copyright holder and would be an infringement. The downloading of works posted on the Internet without the consent of the copyright owner may be an infringement, unless an exception such as the fair dealing exception or private copying exception were applicable.

See also the discussion of fair dealing and the private copying right above.

(d) *Webcasting*

There has been little consideration of the use of webcasting in the context of copyright infringement in Canada. The uploading of works for the purpose of webcasting without the consent of the copyright owner would violate several rights of the copyright holder and would be an infringement.

(e) *Streaming*

See section 1.2(c) above, for further discussion of streaming.

Streaming a preview of a musical work may be fair dealing and exempt from copyright liability.[24]

(f) *Framing*

There has been little consideration of the use of framing in the context of copyright infringement in Canada. The issue for a claim of copyright infringement would be if there is a taking merely as a result of the framing activity.

(g) *Transmission of infringing work across a communications network*

To the extent to which the transmission of an infringing work across a network is a communication for the purposes of Section 3(1)(f) of the Copyright Act and the conduct is not exempt, such an act may have copyright consequences. (The 'communication' right is discussed at section 1.2(c) above.)

As noted in section 1.2(a) above, Section 2.4(1)(b) of the Copyright Act protects an intermediary on the Internet whose only role is that of a conduit.

The communication to the public right may be engaged by internet broadcast to very many parties without restriction, such as if a digital file is available to a large subset of the public, even if such individuals download the digital file separately.[25]

---

24 See *Society of Composers, Authors and Music Publishers of Canada v Bell Canada*, 2012 SCC 36.

25 See *Canadian Wireless Telecommunications Association v Society of Composers, Authors and Music Publishers of Canada*, 2008 FCA 6, leave to appeal to SCC refused, September 18 2008.

Bill C-11 provides, in Section 2(1.1), that the communication of a work or other subject matter to the public by telecommunication includes making it available to the public by telecommunication in a way that allows a member of the public to have access to it from a place and at a time individually chosen by that member of the public. This provision reflects the earlier case law in *Rogers Communications Inc v Society of Composers, Authors and Music Publishers of Canada.*[26]

Bill C-11 adds a further statutory exemption from liability of an ISP in Section 31.1, noted above.

The scope of the protections provided to certain internet intermediaries under Bill C-11, Section 27(2.3) is described in section 1.2(a) above.

(h) Aggregator websites (eg, Google News, price comparison websites)

There has been little consideration of aggregator websites in the context of copyright infringement in Canada. The issue for a claim of copyright infringement would be if there were a substantial taking that would not be exempt such as, in the case of a news site, under the fair dealing right in relation to news reporting.

(i) Treatment of user-generated content

Bill C-11 provides a 'mashup' right or exemption from a claim of copyright infringement. (Further discussion of the mash up right is found at section 1.2(d) above.)

1.7 Joint liability for ISPs

An ISP is not jointly liable for actions carried out by its users, provided that the ISP is not promoting such infringing acts. Some causality in respect of the ISP is required beyond mere provision of infrastructure.[27]

Bill C-11 adds a further statutory exemption from liability of an internet service provider in Section 31.1 noted above.

The scope of the protections provided to certain internet intermediaries under Bill C-11, Section 27(2.3) is described in section 1.2(a) above.

1.8 Relief

Relief cannot be granted against an ISP to stop an infringement by its users where the ISP is not liable for the copyright infringement. For liability, some causality in respect of the ISP is required beyond mere provision of infrastructure.[28]

Bill C-11 adds a further statutory exemption from liability of an ISP in Section 31.1 noted above.

---

26 2012 SCC 35.

27 See *Society of Composers, Authors and Music Publishers of Canada v Canadian Assn of Internet Providers* [2004] 2 SCR 427, 2004 SCC 45.

28 See *Society of Composers, Authors and Music Publishers of Canada v Canadian Assn of Internet Providers* [2004] 2 SCR 427.

1.9 Issues specific to Canada

(a) *Jurisdiction*

A real and substantial connection with Canada is needed for courts to have jurisdiction to hear a case of copyright infringement.

(b) *Claim to infringement of foreign copyright*

Copyright law is territorial in Canada. The court will hear claims of infringement of copyrights that subsist under the Copyright Act.

(c) *Emission theory*

The upload or download of a work without authorisation or under an exemption may constitute an infringement.

1.10 Orphan works

Section 77 of the Copyright Act provides the ability to obtain approval for dealings with a work in cases where the copyright owner cannot be located. The Copyright Board handles such cases.

1.11 Online piracy measures

Bill C-11 provides for a new category of civil and criminal liability that targets those who enable online piracy in respect of circumvention of, or use of means to defeat, technological protection measures.

Canada has introduced legislation – Bill C-56, the Combating Counterfeit Products Act, First Session, Forty-first Parliament 60-61-62 Elizabeth II, 2011-2012-2013 – to comply with the Anti-counterfeiting Trade Agreement. The objective of this agreement is to put in place international standards for the enforcement of intellectual property rights in order to fight more efficiently the growing problems of counterfeiting and piracy. The agreement covers three areas: improving international cooperation, establishing best practices for enforcement and providing a more effective legal framework.

1.12 Electronic infringement of moral rights

(a) *Right to object to derogatory treatment (eg, of 'mashups')*

Bill C-11 would provide a further 'mashup' right or exemption from a claim of copyright infringement. The new 'mashup' right, however, does not exclude liability for moral rights violation in such a 'mashup'.

Bill C-11 introduces parody and satire as permitted purposes for the fair dealing right.

See section 1.2(d) above for further discussion of the mashup right.

(b) *False attribution – right to guard against impersonation on the Internet*

The paternity right, discussed below, has been used in Canada where another has claimed to be the author of the true author's work. It has not yet been considered in the context of an effort to impersonate the true author.

(c) ***Paternity right***

Section 14.1 of the Copyright Act provides that the author of a work has the right to assert paternity of the work or require the author's name to be associated with the work if reasonable in the circumstances. Where reasonable in the circumstances, the author also has the right to be associated with the work under a pseudonym or the right to remain anonymous.

2. Trademarks

2.1 Use of a trademark

In Canada, use in relation to wares occurs where, at the time of the transfer of the property in or possession of the wares, in the normal course of trade, the trademark is marked on the wares themselves or on the packages in which they are distributed, or is in any other manner so associated with the wares that notice of the association is then given to the person to whom the property or possession is transferred.

Use in relation to services occurs where the trademark is used or displayed in the performance or advertising of those services.

Normal trademark law is applicable in Canada. There must be use in Canada to infringe a Canadian trademark.[29]

2.2 Infringement

Trademark infringement claims may be brought under Sections 19, 20 and 22 of the Trademarks Act (RSC 1985, c T-13).

Section 19 provides protection for a registered trademark holder allowing it the 'exclusive right to the use' of the trademark throughout Canada in respect of the particular wares or services covered by a registration.

Section 20 provides that infringement is perpetrated by a "person not entitled to its use under [the] Act, who sells, distributes, or advertises wares or services in association with a confusing trademark".

Section 22 prohibits "use [of] a trademark registered by another person in a manner that is likely to have the effect of depreciating the value of the goodwill attaching thereto".

(a) ***Metatags***

Normal trademark principles apply in Canada. As a result, use of a metatag that is the same or confusingly similar to a registered trademark or that is used in a manner to pass off on the goods or services of the plaintiff may be an infringement.[30]

(b) ***Keywords***

There has been little consideration of the use of keywords in the context of trademark infringement in Canada. In *Private Career Training Institutions Agency v Vancouver Career College (Burnaby) Inc*,[31] a provincial regulator brought action under

---

29 See *Pro-C Ltd v Computer City Inc* [2001] 55 OR (3d) 577 (Ont CA).

30 See *British Columbia Automobile Association v OPEIU* (2001) BCSC 156 (BC SC).

the Private Career Training Institutions Act, SBC 2003, c 79 against the defendant for keyword advertising on the basis that this caused confusion and was misleading advertising. The court found no violation of Bylaw 29 and noted that the defendants did not hold themselves out in their internet advertisements as anyone other than who they were and, in particular, they did not use the business names or trade names of their competitors to misidentify themselves.

Use of keywords by a union in the context of a labour dispute did not constitute 'use' for trademark purposes.[32]

Use of a keyword by a competitive advertiser that is the same or confusingly similar to a registered trademark, or that is used in a manner to pass off on the goods or services of the plaintiff may be an infringement.

(c) ***Sponsored links***

The normal requirements for a confusion analysis are applicable in Canada. The US concept of initial interest confusion has not been widely accepted in Canada.

(d) ***Hidden text***

There has been little consideration of the use of hidden text in the context of trademark infringement in Canada. Use of hidden text by a competitive defendant that is the same or confusingly similar to a registered trademark or that is used in a manner to pass off on the goods or services of the plaintiff may be an infringement.

(e) ***Internet domain names***

Use of a second level domain name that is the same or confusingly similar to a registered trademark or that is used in a manner to pass off on the goods or services of the plaintiff may be an infringement.

Mere registration of a second-level domain name that is the same or confusingly similar to a registered trademark, without more, is not use of the trademark.

(f) ***Search navigation tools***

There has been little consideration of the use of search/navigation tools in the context of trademark infringement in Canada. Use by a competitive defendant of a search/navigation tool that is the same or confusingly similar to a registered trademark or that is used in a manner to pass off on the goods or services of the plaintiff may be an infringement.

(g) ***Hypertext links***

There has been little consideration of the use of hypertext links in the context of trademark infringement in Canada. Use of a hypertext link by a competitive defendant that is the same or confusingly similar to a registered trademark or that is used in a manner to pass off on the goods or services of the plaintiff may be an infringement.

---

31 2010 BCSC 765.

32 See *British Columbia Automobile Association v OPEIU, Local 378* [2001] 3 WWR 95 (SC).

(h) ***Framing***

There has been little consideration of the use of frames in the context of trademark infringement in Canada. Use of a frame by a competitive defendant that is the same or confusingly similar to a registered trademark or that is used in a manner to pass off on the goods or services of the plaintiff may be an infringement.

2.3 Defences

(a) ***Descriptive (non-trademark) use of the mark***

Descriptive/nominative use or non-trademark use of a trademark does not give rise to trademark infringement, unless captured as dilutive within the meaning of Section 22 of the Trademarks Act.

(b) ***Comparative advertising***

It is trademark infringement under Section 22 to compare trademarks in a manner which constitutes 'use' of the trademarks in Canada.

(c) ***Parody***

Freedom of expression is highly regarded in Canada and is a constitutionally protected right, subject to such limits as can be demonstrated in a free and democratic society. As a result, complaint sites or websites used in labour disputes which use a plaintiff's trademark have not been found infringing where there was no 'use' of the trademark under trademark law.[33]

2.4 Parallel imports

There has been little consideration of the sale of grey market goods from a website in the context of trademark infringement in Canada. Case law in Canada concerning the sale of grey market goods has generally been pro-competitive and this has made it more complex and difficult for the trademark owner to assert trademark rights to preclude the sale of genuine branded goods purchased elsewhere being resold in Canada. Generally, in Canada, once genuine trademarked goods are placed into commerce anywhere by or under the authority of the trademark owner, then that trademark owner or its licensees cannot impose additional restrictions on the sale of those goods using their trademark rights.[34]

2.5 Remedies

A wide range of relief is available for the successful plaintiff in a trademark infringement action, including injunctive relief, damages or a claim to profits, and delivery up or destruction of infringing goods.

---

33 See *British Columbia Automobile Association v OPEIU* (2001) BCSC 156 (BC SC).

34 See *Consumers Distributing Co Ltd v Seiko Time Canada Ltd* (1984), 1 CPR (3d) 1 (SCC); *Smith & Nephew Inc v Glen Oak Inc* (1996), 68 CPR (3d) 153 (FCA); *Coca-Cola v Pardhan* (1999), 85 CPR (3d) 489 (FCA) leave to appeal to SCC dismissed May 3 2000.

2.6 Liability of ISP

Unlike in the United States, there is no right of action for inducing, contributory or indirect trademark infringement in Canada. While there has been no reported case on the point, it is speculated that in an appropriate case, principles of inducement or procurement may be applicable.

2.7 Advertising law and regulation

The general law in Canada regarding misleading advertising is applicable to advertising on the Internet. Such law may be found in the federal Competition Act and in provincial fair trading legislation. Such legislation prohibits false or misleading advertising and provides remedies to parties injured by such false or misleading advertisements. As a result, advertisers on the Internet must, like other advertisers, take precautions to justify the accuracy and veracity of their statements.

See section 2(2)(b) above for further discussion of the impact of the use of business names or trademarks in keyword advertising.

2.8 Domain name disputes

The Canadian Internet Registration Authority manages the '.ca' top level domain. CIRA has adopted a domain name dispute resolution policy which requires a complainant to show that:

- the registrant's domain name is confusingly similar to a mark in which the complainant had rights prior to the date of registration of the domain name and continues to have such rights;
- the registrant has no legitimate interest in the domain name; and
- the registrant has registered the domain name in bad faith.

Compared with conventional litigation options, the CIRA dispute resolution process can be inexpensive. Excluding the costs of preparing the complaint, the cost of initiation of such a complaint will be in the few thousands of dollars.

2.9 Unfair competition/passing off

A passing-off action can be an effective means to protect website content and in particular marks and symbols used on a website in Canada. The Supreme Court of Canada has set out the following requirements for passing-off actions (or of equivalent statutory actions under Section 7(b) of the Trademarks Act):[35]

- goodwill or reputation attached to the plaintiff's goods or services in the mind of the public with the name in question such that the name is identified with the plaintiff's goods or services;
- a misrepresentation by the defendant (whether or not intentional) leading or likely to lead the public to believe that the goods or services are those of or authorised by the plaintiff; and
- the plaintiff has or is likely to have suffered damage.

---

35 See *Ciba-Geigy Canada Ltd v Apotex Inc* [1992] 3 SCR; *Kirkbi AG v Ritvik Holdings Inc* [2005] 3 SCR 302.

The principle in *British Telecom plc v One in a Million Ltd*,[36] as follows, has been considered in Canadian law. "The registration of the distinctive name of another as a business name or a domain name may act as instruments of fraud intended to deceive the public and therefore constitute passing off as an effort to confuse the public as to the source or origin of the applicable wares or services."[37]

3. Patents

3.1 Patentability of 'internet' inventions

(a) Computer programs

Software in the form of an abstract theorem is excluded from patentability under 27(8) of the Patent Act (RSC, 1985, c P-4); however, software that has been integrated with traditionally patentable subject matter may be patentable.

The presence of a programmed computer or a program for such a computer does not lend patentability to, or subtract patentability from, an apparatus or process. Computer-related subject matter is not excluded from patentability if the traditional criteria for patentability are satisfied.

(b) Business methods

The fact that something is a business method does not automatically exclude it from patentability. The proper method to assess patentability is to conduct a purposive construction of the claims. The task of purposive construction of the claims should be undertaken with a mind open to the possibility that a novel business method may be an essential element of a valid patent claim. For a business method to be patentable, the algorithm cannot be the whole invention, but only one aspect of a novel combination.[38]

To be an 'invention' under Section 2, there must be an application of new knowledge to effect a desired result which has an undisputed commercial value and it must fall within the words 'any new and useful art'. The word 'art' in the context of the definition must be given its general connotation of 'learning' or 'knowledge'. 'Art' and 'process' in that definition can include something that is not scientific or technological in nature, something that is merely a business method or something that causes no change to the character or condition of a physical thing.

In order to fall within the definition of 'art':[39]

- it must not be a disembodied idea, but have a method of practical application;
- it must be a new and inventive method of applying skill and knowledge; and
- it must have a commercially useful result.

---

36 [1998] 4 All ER 476 (English CA).
37 See *British Columbia Automobile Association v OPEIU* (2001) BCSC 156 (BC SC).
38 See *Canada (Attorney General) v Amazon.com, Inc*, 2011 FCA 328.
39 See *Progressive Games, Inc v Canada (Commissioner of Patents)*, 177 FTR 241 (TD), aff'd (2000), 9 CPR (4th) 479 (FCA).

(c) ***Mathematical methods***

A claim for a mathematical formula is not patentable subject matter.[40]

A claim may not be made for a 'mere scientific principle or theorem' (Section 27(8) of the Patent Act).

(d) ***Presentation of information***

The presentation of information must be assessed in the context of whether it is an invention, including as discussed in section 3.1(b) above.

3.2 Bioinformatics

The means used to make a discovery do not affect the patentability of the discovery. So if a novel DNA sequence or protein structure is discovered through the use of bioinformatics and the novel DNA sequence or protein structure meets the requirements of an invention, then it should be patentable subject matter.

3.3 Issues specific to Canada

(a) ***Infringement on the Internet***

A real and substantial connection with Canada is needed for courts to have jurisdiction to hear a case of patent infringement.

(b) ***Process patents***

In respect of the use right, all steps of the process would need to be carried out in Canada in order for infringement to take place. However, if a product results from the internet process, there could be infringement in Canada if there were use or sale of the product of the process carried out outside of Canada.

3.4 Remedies available for patent infringement

A wide range of relief is available for the successful plaintiff in a patent infringement action, including injunctive relief, damages or a claim to profits, and delivery up or destruction of infringing goods.

4. Disclosure orders against ISPs

4.1 Availability

An equitable bill of discovery order may be obtained from an innocent ISP to require the ISP to disclose the identity and contact details of a user of their service who is suspected of infringing an intellectual property right. Such an order requires care to satisfy all elements of the test, including the privacy rights of persons whose information may be disclosed.

Once an action has been commenced, such as a John Doe action, the plaintiff would have recourse to the rules of court to seek such discovery from an innocent intermediary.

---

40 See *Schlumberger Canada Ltd v Canada (Commissioner of Patents)* [1982] 1 FC 845 (CA).

4.2 Requirements

The requirements of an equitable bill of discovery are that the potential plaintiff establish:

- a *bona fide* case against the unknown alleged wrongdoer;
- that the person from whom the discovery is sought is in some way involved in the dispute and that is more than an innocent bystander;
- that the person from whom the discovery is sought is the only practical source of information available to the potential plaintiff;
- the person from whom the discovery is sought is reasonably compensated for his expenses arising out of compliance with the discovery order in addition to his legal costs; and
- that the public interest in favour of disclosures outweigh legitimate privacy concerns.[41]

4.3 Jurisdictional issues

A real and substantial connection with Canada is needed for courts to have jurisdiction to hear a case seeking an equitable bill of discovery in respect of a case of IP right infringement conducted on the Internet.

4.4 'John Doe' injunctions

'John Doe' injunctions can be obtained to prevent IP right infringement against persons unknown. Such injunctions are commonly used in anti-counterfeiting enforcement work.

---

41 See *BMI Canada Inc v John Doe,* 2005 FCA 193.

China

Mimiao Hu
Yali Hu
Xiang Wang
Jibo Wu
Carol Yan
Shelley Zhang
Orrick, Herrington & Sutcliffe LLP

1. Copyrights, database rights and design rights

1.1 Overview

In general, the Copyright Law of the People's Republic of China ('Copyright Law')[1] and its corresponding Copyright Law Implementing Regulations of the People's Republic of China ('Implementing Regulations')[2] are the basic controlling legal authorities for the protection of copyrights on the Internet in China. Other laws and regulations specifically governing copyright in cyberspace include the Interpretation of the Supreme People's Court on Certain Issues Related to the Application of Law in the Trial of Civil Dispute Cases involving Infringement of Right of Dissemination via Information Network ('Interpretation')[3] and the Regulations on the Protection of Right of Dissemination via Information Network ('Dissemination Regulations'),[4] which contain safe harbour provisions for internet service providers (ISPs). Also relevant is the first Tort Liability Law of the People's Republic of China ('Tort Law'), which has provisions specifically for torts on the Internet.[5]

Article 3 of the Copyright Law stipulates that protected works include "work(s) of literature, art, natural science, social science, engineering technology" and the like which are created in the forms of: "(1) Written works; (2) Oral works; (3) Musical, dramatic, [oral Chinese folk arts], choreographic, and acrobatic works; (4) Fine art and architectural works; (5) Photographic works; (6) Cinematographic works ... ; (7)

---

1 See Copyright Law (promulgated by the Standing Comm Nat'l People's Cong, February 26 2010, effective April 1 2010), translated in Westlaw China (last visited June 4 2012) (PRC).

2 See Copyright Law Implementing Regulations (promulgated by the St Council, August 2 2002, effective September 15 2002) (amended January 8 2011 and January 30 2013), translated in Westlaw China (last visited November 4 2013) (PRC) [hereinafter 'Implementing Regulations'].

3 See Interpretation of the Supreme People's Court on Certain Issues Related to the Application of Law in the Trial of Civil Dispute Cases Involving Infringement of Right of Dissemination via Information Network (promulgated by the Sup People's Ct, December 17 2012, effective January 1 2013), translated in Westlaw China (last visited November 12 2013) (PRC) [hereinafter 'Interpretation'], replacing the Interpretation of the Supreme People's Court on Certain Issues Related to the Application of Law in the Trial of Cases Involving Computer Network Copyright Disputes (promulgated by the Sup People's Ct, November 22 2006, effective December 8 2006), translated in Westlaw China (last visited November 12 2013) (PRC) [hereinafter 'Old Interpretation'].

4 See Regulations on the Protection of Right of Dissemination via Information Network (promulgated by the St Council, May 18 2006, effective July 1 2006) (amended January 30 2013), translated in Westlaw China (last visited November 4 2013) (PRC) [hereinafter 'Dissemination Regulations'].

5 See Tort Liability Law (promulgated by the Standing Comm Nat'l People's Cong, December 26, 2009, effective July 1 2010), translated in Westlaw China (last visited June 4 2012) (PRC) [hereinafter 'Tort Law'].

Graphic works including engineering design drawings, product design drawings, maps, schematic drawings ... ; (8) Computer software; and (9) Other works specified in laws and administrative regulations."[6]

Article 4 of the Implementing Regulations elaborates on the meanings of the works mentioned in the Copyright Law:

"(1) 'Written works' refer to novels, poems, prose, treatises, and other works that are expressed in word form; (2) 'Oral works' refer to impromptu speeches, lectures, court debates, and other works that are expressed in oral form; (3) 'Musical works' refer to songs, symphonies, and other works, with or without lyrics, that can be sung or played; (4) 'Dramatic works' refer to ... works that are created for stage performance; ... (6) 'Choreographic works' refer to works that express thoughts and feelings through successive movements, postures, facial expressions, etc; ... (8) 'Fine art works' refer to paintings, ... and other two- or three-dimensional aesthetic works of formative arts that are formed by lines, colors, and/or other patterns; ... (11) 'Cinematographic works ... ' refer to works filmed on a certain medium, consisting of images with or without accompanying sounds, and disseminated with the aid of certain appropriate devices or other methods ... ."[7]

Under Article 5 of the Implementing Regulations, " ... (2) 'Sound recording' refers to a recording of the sound of a performance or of another type of sound; [and] (3) 'Visual recording' refers to a recording of successive and related images or pictures with or without accompanying sounds ... ."[8]

(a) *Literary works and artistic works*

Under Article 3(1) and (4) of the Copyright Law, literary works and artistic works are protected, respectively.[9] Software is protected under the Copyright Law as a separate category of work under Article 3(8).[10]

(b) *Films, sound recordings, and broadcasts*

Films are protected as 'cinematographic works' under Article 3(6), while sound recordings and broadcasts are protected as 'oral works' under Article 3(2).[11] Musical elements contained in sound recordings and broadcasts are protected as musical works under Article 3(3).[12]

(c) *Typographical arrangement of published materials*

Under Article 36 of the Copyright Law, publishers of books and periodicals hold the right to prohibit a third party from using the typographical arrangement of published materials.[13] Under Article 26 of the Implementation Regulations, the typographical arrangement is an adjacent right to the original works and belongs to the publisher.[14]

---

6 Copyright Law, above note 1, Article 3.
7 Implementing Regulations, above note 2, Article 4.
8 *Ibid,* Article 5.
9 Copyright Law, above note 1, Articles 3(1), 4.
10 See *Ibid,* Articles 3(1), 4, 8.
11 See *Ibid,* Articles 3(6), 3(2).
12 See *Ibid,* Article 3(3).
13 Copyright Law, above note 1, Article 36.
14 Implementing Regulations, above note 2, Article 26.

There are many reported cases concerning the typographical arrangement of books and other published materials,[15] and all courts have agreed that the typographical arrangement right was an adjacent right owned by the publisher. The typographical arrangement right was not protected under the Dissemination Regulations, which only protect works, performances, and video and sound recordings;[16] however, the publisher had the right to exclude others from using the same typographical arrangement in physical paper books without proper authorisation from the publisher.

(d) Protection of the user interface

China's current Copyright Law and its Implementation Regulations do not have specific provisions protecting software user interfaces, even though software user interfaces are theoretically protected under the Copyright Law as 'artistic works'.[17] The theory of 'artistic works' does not provide ample protection to screen image design works because 'artistic works' have a much higher threshold in terms of the requisite artistic effect.

In *Beijing Jiuqi Software Holdings Co v Shanghai Tianchen Computer Software Co*, ChinaLawInfo (Shanghai High People's Ct, June 21 2005), the defendant developed a web-based user interface similar to the plaintiff's in a very similar application.[18] The court refused the plaintiff's claim that the user interface was protected under the Copyright Law because: the interface's components were not copyrighted; the compilation of the components was not creative enough; and the similarities were due to the application and its client's requirements.[19]

A similar ruling came from *Shenzhen TP-Link Co v Shenzhen Tenda Technology Co*, gdcourts.gov.cn (Guangdong High People's Court, December 15 2006), where the defendant used a similar user interface in its routers.[20] The court found that the components of the interface were not authored by the plaintiff, and the component selection, compilation, and overall arrangement of the components were not creative enough to be copyrighted.[21] Therefore, the plaintiff's user interface was not protected under the Copyright Law.[22]

---

15 See eg, *China Auto-Industry Econ Tech Info Inst v Auto Magazine*, ChinaLawInfo (Sichuan High People's Ct, September 1 2006); *Beijing Univ Publ'g Co Ltd v Beijing Shengshichuangfu Advertisement Co Ltd*, ChinaLawInfo (Beijing Haidian District Court, March 19 2012); *Beijing Univ Publ'g Co Ltd v Shenzhen Tencent Computer Sys Co Ltd*, ChinaLawInfo (Beijing Haidian District Court, November 16 2010); *China Constr Indus Publisher v Beijing Wanfang Data Holdings Co Ltd*, ChinaLawInfo (Beijing No 2 Intermediate People's Court, November 20 2009).

16 See Dissemination Regulations, above note 4, Article 2.

17 Yuying Guan, "The Protection of Screen Images Design – A Comparative Study Between Chinese and Japanese Laws", 12 *Inst Intellectual Prop Bulletin* 124 (2008), www.iip.or.jp/e/e_summary/pdf/detail2007/e19_15.pdf (last visited June 6 2012).

18 See *Beijing Jiuqi Software Holdings Co v Shanghai Tianchen Computer Software Co Ltd*, ChinaLawInfo (Shanghai High People's Court, June 21 2005).

19 *Ibid.*

20 See *Shenzhen TP-Link Co Ltd v Shenzhen Tenda Tech Co Ltd*, gdcourts.gov.cn (Guangdong High People's Ct, December 15 2006).

21 *Ibid.*

22 *Ibid.*

(e) *Computer-generated works*

There are no specific provisions for the protection of computer-generated works under the Copyright Law, nor are there any reported cases on this issue. Currently, there are only academic opinions to provide guidance on this topic.[23]

Basically, copyrights subsist in authors; therefore, a purely computer-generated work is not protected under the Copyright Law if the author is not identifiable.[24] However, most works generated by computers have been conceived by human beings.[25] If the human author is identifiable and the work passes the threshold of creativity required under the Copyright Law, then it is protectable.[26]

(f) *Websites protected as databases and compilations*

There is no separate protection for databases under the Copyright Law. Courts have interpreted databases as compilations of data, which are protected under Article 14 of the Copyright Law and sometimes protected under the provisions of other laws and principles. This is also true for database-backed websites.

Under Article 14 of the Copyright Law:

"Works created through compiling a number of works, segments of works, uncopyrightable data or materials are copyrightable compiled works, provided that the creativity can be reflected through selection or arrangement thereof. The copyright in any such work shall vest in the compiler, provided the compiler's exercise of its rights shall not infringe the copyright in the original work ..."[27]

In China's first 'law and regulation database' infringement case, Hainan Jingtian Information Co compiled a database of uncopyrightable laws and regulations which was copied by the defendant, Haikou Wangwei Technology Co.[28] The court found that the database was protected under Article 14 of the Copyright Law because the compilation itself passed the creativity threshold required by the Copyright Law.[29]

However, the Copyright Law does not protect pure compilation works without passing the threshold of creativity since it does not protect 'sweat of the brow' work. As an alternative, the courts have used the provisions under the Law of the People's Republic of China against Unfair Competition ('Anti-Unfair Competition Law') and the General Principles of the Civil Law of the People's Republic of China ('Civil Law') to prevent unfair profits from other people's work.

Under Article 2 of the Anti-Unfair Competition Law, a 'business operator' shall abide by the principles of "voluntariness, equality, fairness, honesty and credibility", and also observe "generally recognised business ethics".[30] Under Article 4 of the Civil

23 See, eg, *Jungang Li, Ji suan ji zi ti de zhu zuo quan bao hu* [Copyright of Computer Generated Fonts], 110.com (2011), http://www.110.com/ziliao/article-229090.html.

24 *Ibid.*

25 *Ibid.*

26 *Ibid.*

27 See Copyright Law, above note 1, Article 14.

28 2003 *Nian ye jie wei quan da shi ji* [2003 IP Rights Industry Events], gmw.cn (2004), www.gmw.cn/01ds/2004-03/10/content_4688.htm.

29 *Ibid.*

30 See Law Against Unfair Competition (promulgated by the Standing Comm. Nat'l People's Cong, September 2 1993, enacted December 1 1993), Article 2 (amended 2007), translated in Westlaw China (last visited June 4 2012) (PRC) [hereinafter 'Anti-Unfair Competition Law'].

Law, in civil activities, "the principles of voluntariness, fairness, making compensation for equal value, honesty and credibility shall be observed".[31]

In *Guangxi Broadcast TV Newspaper v Guangxi Miner's Newspaper*, ChinaLawInfo, (Liuzhou Dist People's Court, November 25 1994), the defendant published the same TV programme list that was allegedly owned by the plaintiff.[32] The court reiterated that there must be minimal creativity in the work in order to be protected by the Copyright Law, and the TV programme list did not pass this threshold of minimal creativity.[33] However, the court decided that the plaintiff had a civil right to his work pursuant to Article 4 of the Civil Law based on a special regulation on TV programme lists issued by the General Administration of Press and Publication of China.[34]

1.2 Infringing acts

Under the Copyright Law, a copyright comprises a bundle of moral rights and property rights including the right of publication, authorship, alteration, integrity, reproduction, distribution, lease, public display, performance, projection, broadcasting, dissemination via information networks, production, adaptation, translation, compilation, etc.[35] Except as otherwise provided under the Copyright Law, the copyright in a work shall belong to its author.[36]

The Measures of the National Copyright Administration of China and Ministry of Information Industry for the Administrative Protection of Internet Copyright provides specific administrative protections for the right of transmission.[37] The protections apply to service providers that facilitate the "uploading, storage, linking or search of the content of works and audio-visual products, etc without editing, amendment or selection of the stored or disseminated content as instructed by the Internet Content Provider in the course of Internet information service activities".[38] It also applies the Copyright Law whenever internet contents are directly provided through internet information service activities.[39]

(a) Copying

In general, according to the Copyright Law and its Implementation Regulations, all copies, even temporary copies of a copyrighted work without proper authorisation, constitute infringement, unless the copies qualify as exceptions to the general provisions (ie, the copier qualifies as an internet service provider and meets the requirements under the safe harbour provisions).[40]

---

31 See General Principles of the Civil Law (promulgated by the Nat'l People's Cong, April 12 1986, effective January 1 1987), Article 4 (amended 2009), translated in Westlaw China (last visited June 4 2012) (PRC) [hereinafter 'Civil Law'].

32 *Guangxi Broad TV Newspaper v Guangxi Miner's Newspaper,* ChinaLawInfo (Liuzhou Dist People's Court, November 25 1994).

33 *Ibid.*

34 *Ibid.*

35 See Copyright Law, above note 1, Article 10.

36 *Ibid.*

37 See Measures of the National Copyright Administration of China and Ministry of Information Industry for the Administrative Protection of Internet Copyright (promulgated by the Nat'l Copyright Admin; the Ministry Info Indus, April 29 2005, effective May 30 2005), Article 2, translated in Westlaw China (last visited June 4 2012) (PRC).

38 *Ibid.*

Temporary copies: However, neither China's legislature nor its judiciary has ever explicitly treated temporary copies and permanent copies equally. On the contrary, certain local court opinions indicate that China has been leaning towards not recognising temporary copies as copying under the Copyright Law.[41] For example, the Guiding Opinions of the Beijing High People's Court on Certain Issues Related to the Trial of Cases Involving Copyright Dispute in an Internet Environment did not provide that a snapshot copy was copying of the work when it defined a service provider as using a snapshot copy to speed up its indexing service.[42]

Also, under Article 21 of the Dissemination Regulations, it is explicitly provided that ISPs are not liable for infringement for automatically generated temporary copies used for the purpose of improving 'network transmission efficiency', provided certain conditions are met.[43]

In any medium: The copying medium does not constitute a deciding factor for the Copyright Law. However, certain mediums for some popular technologies deserve particular attention.

For example, wireless application protocol (WAP) technology allows ISPs to provide internet service to non-smart cell-phones, which needs a storage ability to allow users to read the web pages. Although the court has yet to decide whether the caching of web pages with WAP technology is an infringement of the web pages, it is not likely an infringement to the owner's copyrights in the sense that, among other reasons, banning this mode of reproduction essentially means banning WAP technology.

(b) Issuing copies to the public

When a copy is issued to the public, there are at least two online players who contribute to the public distribution: the content provider who issues the commands to upload the work to the Internet and the ISP who provides online storage space, an internet connection, data communication, and other services. The content provider directly infringes a copyright holder's right of dissemination via information networks. However, ISPs do not infringe the right of information network dissemination if they meet the requirements for ISP safe harbour protection under the Dissemination Regulations,[44] or are otherwise not at fault.[45]

(c) Communicating work to the public

Under Article 10(12) of the Copyright Law, the author has the right of information network dissemination to make his/her 'work available to the public' in a way that

39 *Ibid.*
40 *Ibid.*
41 See Guiding Opinions of the Beijing High People's Court on Certain Issues Related to the Trial of Cases Involving Copyright Dispute in an Internet Environment (promulgated by the Beijing High People's Court, May 19 2010, effective May 19 2010), Article 12, translated in Westlaw China (last visited June 4 2012) (PRC).
42 *Ibid.*
43 See Dissemination Regulations, above note 4, Article 21.
44 See *Ibid,* Articles 20 to 24.
45 See Interpretation, above note 3, Articles 4 to 14.

members of the public may obtain the work at their own selected times and places.[46] Therefore, communicating work to the public does constitute an infringement of the author's exclusive rights.

In a high-profile case, *Shanghai Busheng Music Culture Media Co v Baidu.com, Inc*, ChinaLawInfo (Beijing Haidian Dist People's Court, September 9 2005), Baidu.com was operating a rapidly growing Chinese search engine powered by its in-house developed software and a "large database of Chinese synonyms and closely associated phrases ... providing access to more than 740 million indexed Chinese websites".[47] Baidu.com's most popular MP3 downloading service allowed a user to perform a keyword search or to browse an index of artists or songs.[48] Its search engine would then return a list of websites containing matching content for the user to download.[49] The trial court ruled that the search engine service provider infringed the plaintiff's right of communication to the public within the scope of the Copyright Law.[50] The case then settled after an appeal by the defendant was filed.[51]

(d) Performing, showing, or playing a work in public

Under the Copyright Law, the right of public performance via any medium, public dissemination of the performance of works by various means, broadcasting via any medium, and information network dissemination are included in the author's copyrights.[52] Therefore, to 'perform, show or play' a copyrighted work in public through the Internet constitutes copyright infringement.

(e) Renting or lending the work to the public

Under the Copyright Law, the 'right of rental', namely the right non-gratuitously to authorise others to "temporarily use a cinematographic work or a work created by means similar to cinematography or computer software ..." belongs to the copyright owner.[53] Therefore, renting to others without permission is an infringement of the owner's exclusive rights under Article 10(7).

(f) Authorising another person to do any of the aforementioned infringing acts

Authorising another person to do any of the above infringing acts will make the authoriser liable for copyright infringement.

Under Article 3 of the Interpretation, an ISP is directly or jointly liable for infringing a copyrighted work if the ISP works in cooperation, instigates, or assists others in the infringing act.[54] The Old Interpretation also had similar provisions.[55]

---

46 Copyright Law, above note 1, Article 10(12).

47 See *Shanghai Busheng Music Culture Media Co Ltd v Baidu.com, Inc,* ChinaLawInfo (Beijing Haidian Dist People's Court, September 9 2005).

48 *Ibid.*

49 *Ibid.*

50 *Ibid.*

51 See *Beijing Baidu.com, Inc v Shanghai Busheng Music Culture Media Co Ltd* (Beijing No 1 Intermediate People's Court, December 19 2006).

52 See Implementing Regulations, above note 2, Article 10.

53 *Ibid.* Article 10(7).

54 See Interpretation, above note 3, Articles 4 and 7.

55 See Old Interpretation, above note 3, Article 3.

One article, citing the Old Interpretation, explicitly points out that a video-sharing website which authorises a user's infringing act shall be held jointly liable, provided that the authoriser made profits from the infringement.[56]

(g) *Secondary infringement*

Since Chinese law does not distinguish between induced infringement, vicarious infringement, and contributory infringement, any liability is a joint liability if it is not a direct liability.[57]

Under Article 130 of the Civil Law, if two or more people jointly infringe a third party's right and their actions result in damages, 'they shall bear joint liability'.[58] Under Article 8 of the Tort Law, "if two or more persons jointly commit a tortious act which results in damages to others, they shall bear joint and several liabilities".[59]

One could be liable for infringement on the Internet under the premises of direct liability and/or joint liability.[60] The Interpretation defines several circumstances under which a service provider shall be held liable for direct and/or joint infringement.[61]

Under Article 4 of the Interpretation, when an ISP "works in cooperation with others to jointly provide works, performance or video/sound recordings", the court shall hold the ISP liable for joint infringement. But the ISP could escape a joint infringement claim if it could demonstrate that it only provides networking services such as automatic access, automatic transmission, information storage space, search, interlinking and document-sharing technologies.[62]

Under Article 5, when an ISP provides works to the public in the forms of snapshots or thumbnail images, etc which can substantially replace other ISPs in providing the works to the public, the court shall hold that the ISP provides the works. However, if such acts do not affect the normal use of relevant works and do not unreasonably harm right holders' legitimate interest to the works, the court shall find no infringement.[63]

Under Article 7, if an ISP 'instigates or assists' another's copyright infringement, the court shall hold the service provider liable for infringement. It constitutes instigation if an ISP induces or encourages users to commit copyright infringement verbally or by promoting technical support or awarding points. In addition, a court shall find assistance in infringement if an ISP did not take necessary measures such as deleting,

---

56 See Xiaofeng Song, *Wang zhan chuan bo ying shi zuo pin de ban quan fa lu wen ti fen xi* [A Legal Analysis Concerning Dissemination of Video Works through Websites], ChinaLawInfo.com (2009), http://article.chinalawinfo.com/Article_Detail.asp?ArticleID=51368.

57 See Qian Wang, *Shi pin fen xiang wang zhan zhu zuo quan qin quan wen ti yan jiu* [Research on Copyright Infringement Issues Concerning Video Sharing Websites], FengXiaopingIP.com (2008), www.fengxiaoqingip.com/ipluntan/lwxd-zz/20090216/3510.html.

58 See General Principles of the Civil Law (promulgated by the Nat'l People's Cong, April 12 1986, effective January 1 1987), Article 130, translated in Westlaw China (last visited June 6 2012) (PRC) [hereinafter 'Civil Law'].

59 See Tort Law, above note 5, Article 8.

60 See Copyright Law, above note 1, Articles 47, 48 (Copyright Law stipulates both direct liability and joint liability for different infringement acts).

61 See Interpretation, above note 3, Articles 3 to 14.

62 See *Ibid,* Article 4.

63 See *Ibid,* Article 5.

blocking or disconnecting, or provided assistance such as technical support with the actual or presumed knowledge that users used its service to infringe copyright.[64]

Article 8 of the Interpretation provides that courts shall decide whether an ISP shall bear responsibility for stipulating or assisting in infringement based on its fault. Whether an ISP is at fault depends on whether it knows or should have known infringing acts of its users. An ISP is not at fault per se by failing actively to inspect infringing acts of users. Courts shall find no fault with an ISP if the ISP establishes that it has taken reasonable and effective technical measures but it is still difficult to discover infringing acts of its users.[65]

Courts will decide whether an ISP should have known infringing acts of its users based on the following elements:

- the ISP's information-management capability based on the nature and the manner of its service and the likelihood of incurring infringement;
- types and popularity of the transmitted works, performance, video and audio recordings, and degree of obviousness of the infringement;
- whether the ISP proactively selects, edits, changes or recommends works, performance, video and audio recordings;
- whether the ISP has actively taken reasonable infringement prevention measures;
- whether the ISP has set up a convenient procedure to accept infringement notices and to take reasonable action in relation to such infringement notices;
- whether the ISP has taken corresponding reasonable measures against repetitive infringing acts of the same users;
- other relevant considerations.[66]

Article 10 of the Interpretation provides that courts shall presume that an ISP knows infringing acts of users if the ISP recommends popular movies or TV shows by ranking, indexing, cataloging them or adding descriptions or brief introductions to them and the public can directly obtain them from its web pages by downloading, browsing or other means.[67]

Under Article 12 of the Interpretation, courts may presume that an ISP of information storage space knows infringing acts of users under the following circumstances:

- the ISP puts popular movies or TV shows on homepage or main pages which can be easily perceived by users;
- the ISP proactively selects, edits, organises, recommends themes and contents of popular movies and TV shows, etc, or ranks them;
- other circumstances where no reasonable measure is taken though it is clear that relevant works, performance, video and audio recordings are provided by users without authorisation from right holders.[68]

---

64 See *Ibid*, Article 7.
65 See *Ibid*, Article 8.
66 See *Ibid*, Article 9.
67 See *Ibid*, Article 10.
68 See *Ibid*, Article 12.

In addition, if an ISP did not take necessary measures such as deleting, blocking, disconnecting in time upon receipt of notifications from right holders in the form of letters, facsimiles, emails, etc, presumed knowledge of infringement shall be found.[69] Whether such necessary measures were taken in time shall be determined based on a consideration of the form of the notice, whether the notice is accurate, whether it is difficult to take the measures, nature of the network services, types/popularity/numbers of works, performance, video and audio recordings involved, etc.[70]

Under Article 11 of the Interpretation, an ISP owes a high level of duty of care to right holders if it receives economic benefits directly from the works, performance, video and audio recordings provided by its users. Direct economic benefits shall be found if an ISP receives benefits by advertising with certain works, performance, video and audio recordings, or there is otherwise a specific connection between the benefits and certain works, performance, video and audio recordings. However, a general advertising fee or service fee for network services does not fall into direct economic benefits.[71]

For ISPs, the safe harbour provisions under the Dissemination Regulations could give them further protection against joint liability provided that they did not know or had no reason to know about the infringing acts and that they took proper measures when receiving proper warning notices.[72]

1.3 Test for copyright infringement

(a) Requirement of substantial reproduction

Although this legal standard is not codified, reported cases have shown that substantial reproduction is required to establish copyright infringement. For example, in *Fujian Weekend TV Co v Music Copyright Society of China*, ChinaLawInfo (Beijing High People's Court, March 2 2004), four pieces of music works were used by the defendant without authorisation in a TV drama series with playing lengths seven seconds, 45 seconds, 45 seconds and 105 seconds respectively.[73] The court held that the defendant was liable for infringing three out of four music works except the song which played only seven seconds.[74] But the court did not explicitly indicate that substantial reproduction was part of the prima facie case for infringement.[75]

(b) Repeated copying of an insubstantial part

There is neither an explicit provision nor any reported case regarding whether repeated copying of an insubstantial part constitutes copyright infringement.

69 See *Ibid,* Article 13.
70 See *Ibid,* Article 14.
71 See *Ibid,* Article 11.
72 See Dissemination Regulations, above note 4, Article 22.
73 See below section 1.4(j); see also *Fujian Weekend TV Co Ltd v Music Copyright Soc'y of China,* ChinaLawInfo (Beijing High People's Court, March 2 2004).
74 See *Ibid.*
75 See *Ibid.*

1.4 Exemptions/defences to copyright infringement

(a) *Format shifting*

There are no clear provisions in any laws or regulations, nor are there are any reported cases regarding whether format shifting constitutes copyright infringement. In general, if it qualifies as personal use, then it might be considered fair use and not liable for infringement; but if it is for commercial use, or if it is assisting another's commercial use, then it might constitute infringement.[76]

(b) *Personal copying rights*

There are no specific provisions in any laws or regulations in China concerning whether personal copying is exempted from copyright infringement. Whether personal copying is fair use or is infringing depends upon whether it falls within any of the fair use exceptions.[77] Article 22 of the Copyright Law provides that it is fair use to use another persons' published works for the purposes of personal 'study, research or enjoyment', but it is unclear if personal copying falls within this exception.[78]

China does not have copyright levies for personal copying.[79] Scholars have suggested that digital document transmission should require authorisation from the rights owner, and payment of a copyright levy.[80]

(c) *Time shifting*

There are no reported cases deciding whether 'time shifting' constitutes an exemption or defence to copyright infringement.[81] However, some defendants in China have raised the 'technology neutral' doctrine as an alternative defence; but the courts have been reluctant to follow the doctrine.

Under *Opinions of the Supreme People's Court on Giving Full Play to the Functional Role of Intellectual Property Trials in Advancing the Great Development and Prosperity of Socialist Culture and Promoting Independent and Coordinated Economic Development* ('IP Opinions'), the Supreme People's Court made clear that the 'technology neutral' concept is not an absolute defence to a copyright infringement claim: a defendant cannot use it as a shield against infringement liabilities, but neither can the plaintiff blame a new technology provider unconditionally.[82] Instead the test should be: if a technology has a substantial non-infringing use, then the court should strictly

---

76 See Copyright Law, above note 1, Article 20 (China's Copyright Law provides only fair use defence).

77 *Ibid.* See also *Wang luo shi dai sir en fu zhi* [Personal Copying in the Internet Era], ChinaLawEdu.com (2009), http://www.chinalawedu.com/new/16900_178/2009_11_10_ji340829424801119002l3867.shtml; *Si ren fu zhi yu he li shi yong yan jiu* [Application Research on 'Personal Copying' and Fair Use], Law.Shangdu.com (2011), http://law.shangdu.com/falvlunwen/falvbiyelunwen/falvzhuanyebiyelunwen/2011/0730/47691.html.

78 See Copyright Law, above note 1, Article 22.

79 See Xiangdong Jiang, *An Analysis of the Present Status of Studies in Digital Library Copyright Problem*, China National Knowledge Infrastructure (2003), http://cpfd.cnki.com.cn/Article/CPFDTOTAL-FJTB200308001040.htm.

80 *Ibid.*

81 See, eg *TCL Group Holdings Co Ltd et al v Beijing Voole Tech Co Ltd*, ChinaLawInfo (Beijing High People's Court, April 20 2011); see also Qing Wang, *Zhongguo ban 'suo ni' an zhi wo jian – TCL MiTV jiu fen an* [China's Version of the 'Sony' Case – The TCL MiTV Dispute], *ZhiShiChanQuanShuFang* (2009), http://blog.sina.com.cn/s/blog_4cb1acf40100eh5k.html.

control the requirements for joint liability of the technology provider; the court cannot presume that the technology provider should have known the existence of the direct infringements, and the provider is liable for joint liability only when it has assisted or incited the infringement.[83] On the other hand, if there is no substantial non-infringing use, the court can presume that the provider should have known of the existence of the direct infringements and he should be liable for joint infringement.[84]

In *National Population and Family Planning Commission v Shanghai Tudou Internet Co*, ChinaLawInfo (Beijing No 1 Intermediate People's Court, June 3 2010), one defendant uploaded the plaintiff's TV series onto its website while a second defendant linked to the TV series to allow its users to watch the copyrighted works.[85] The second defendant, Beijing Baofeng Internet Co, raised the 'technology neutral' defence by claiming it was a linking service provider and linking was a new technology.[86] The court did not give the defence any merit and held that Baofeng was liable for infringement of the works because it was an ISP and it failed its duty to investigate the linked works (ie, should have known about the infringement).[87]

In *Guangzhou Digitnexus Software Technology Co v Beijing Ciwen Video Production Co*, ChinaLawInfo (Guangdong High People's Court, June 23 2008), the defendant Digitnexus, which hosted a P2P service with P2P software that it developed, was found to have infringed a movie that was available through its website.[88] The defendant claimed, and the court recognised, that the P2P software had substantial non-infringing commercial use for its high efficiency in data transmission and broadband utilisation.[89] However, the court applied a different standard than the later promulgated IP Opinions and ruled that Digitnexus was liable for infringement because it failed to fulfil its duty to take measures to eliminate or reduce infringement.[90]

(d) *Fair use*

The Dissemination Regulations define eight fair uses in the area of cyberspace, which is a subset of the fair uses defined under the Copyright Law. The Supreme People's Court also provided additional principles in consideration of fair uses.

Article 22 of the Copyright Law lists 12 uses of a work, under which no permission from and no compensations to the copyright owner are needed to

---

82 See Opinions of the Supreme People's Court on Giving Full Play to the Functional Role of Intellectual Property Trials in Advancing the Great Development and Prosperity of Socialist Culture and Promoting Independent and Coordinated Economic Development (promulgated by the Supreme People's Court, December 16 2011, effective December 16 2011), Article 7, translated in Westlaw China (last visited June 7 2012) (PRC) [hereinafter 'IP Opinions'].

83 *Ibid.*

84 *Ibid.*

85 *Nat'l Population and Family Planning Comm'n v Shanghai Tudou Internet Co*, ChinaLawInfo (Beijing No 1 Intermediate People's Court, June 3, 2010).

86 *Ibid.*

87 *Ibid.*

88 *Guangzhou Digitnexus Software Tech Co Ltd v Beijing Ciwen Video Prod Co Ltd*, ChinaLawInfo (Guangdong High People's Court, June 23 2008).

89 *Ibid.*

90 *Ibid.*

lawfully use the copyrighted work.[91] The Dissemination Regulations emphasise eight out of 12 fair uses defined under Article 22 concerning copyright in cyberspace.[92] Under Article 6 of the Dissemination Regulations, a work may be provided through information networks without permission from and without payment to the copyright owner for the listed uses if it is:[93]

- an appropriate quote of a published work in one's work for the purpose of introducing, or commenting on a particular work, or for elaborating on a particular issue;
- an inevitable display or quote of a published work made available to the public for reporting current news;
- the provision of a small part of a published work, to a small number of teachers or scientific researchers for classroom teaching or scientific research;
- the provision of a published work to the public to an extent that is reasonable for a government agency to fulfil its official duties;
- the translation of a published work into minority languages for publication and distribution in the country;
- the translation of a published work into Braille and publication of the work so translated for a non-profit purpose;
- the provision to the public of articles concerning current political or economic issues which have already been published via the information network; or
- the provision to the public of a speech delivered at a public gathering.

Under the IP Opinions, the Supreme People's Court requested (the lower courts), when applying the fair use exception, to consider: the character and the purpose of the use of the work; the nature of the work being used; the quantity and quality of the portion used in relation to the work; and the effects of the use upon the potential market for, or value of, the work.[94] If the alleged use of the work does not conflict with the normal use of the work and the alleged use does not unreasonably damage the author's fair interest, the alleged use can be taken as fair use of the copyrighted work.[95]

(e) Caching/temporary copies as part of a communication process

In China, service providers with caching/temporary copies, webhosting and back-up copy facilities are all ISPs for the purpose of safe harbour protection rendered by the Dissemination Regulations.

Under Article 21 of the Dissemination Regulations, under the listed circumstances, ISPs that "automatically store works, performances, or audio or visual recordings obtained from other ISPs for the purpose of improving network transmission efficiency", and automatically provide them to "clients according to the technical arrangements", shall not assume liability for infringement.[96]

Even though automatic caching is covered by Article 21, not all temporary copies

91 *See* Copyright Law, above note 1, Article 22.
92 *Ibid.*
93 Dissemination Regulations, above note 4, Article 6.
94 IP Opinions, above note 86, Article 8.
95 *Ibid.*

are free from liability. In *Zhejiang All-Asia Electric Commercial Co v Beijing Baidu Netcom Science and Technology Co*, ChinaLawInfo (Beijing High People's Court, December 19 2008), the defendant, Baidu, stored temporary copies of popular songs as 'snapshots' so its clients could download the songs faster than if they were from the original third-party hosts.[97] Baidu claimed that the 'snapshots' were automatically cached works for the purpose of enhancing transmission efficiency, and should be covered under Article 21.[98] However, the court decided that the 'snapshots' were not covered under Article 21 because the 'snapshot' service practically enabled Baidu's clients to access the songs directly from the defendant's website, which affected the market interest of the third-party music provider.[99] The Interpretation also provides that when an ISP provides works to the public in the forms of snapshots or thumbnail images, etc which can substantially replace other ISPs in providing the works to the public, the court shall hold that the ISP provides the works. However, if such acts do not affect the normal use of relevant works and do not unreasonably harm right holders' legitimate interest to the works, the court shall find no infringement.[100]

(f) ***Hosting***

Web-hosting providers are qualified ISPs under Article 22 of the Dissemination Regulations.

Article 22 of the Dissemination Regulations states, "where an ISP provides information memory space to its clients ... through the information network and conditions are satisfied, he is not required to assume the infringement liabilities ... ."[101] The required conditions include:

> *"(1) The information storage space is clearly indicated as having been provided for use by those who receive its services, accompanied by an announcement on the name, contact person, and Web address of the Web service provider; (2) It has not altered the works ... ; (3) It is unaware of, and has no justified reason to be aware of, the infringement ... ; (4) It has gained no economic benefits directly from [the] works ... ; and (5) It has ... deleted the work[s] ... regarded by the right owner as involving infringement after receiving the right owner's written notice."*[102]

Even though web-hosting services providers are not explicitly mentioned in the above provision, cases have evidenced that they are qualified ISPs covered under Article 22 of the Dissemination Regulations.[103] In *Beijing Sanmianxiang Copyright Agency v Chongqing Lidong Technology Co*, ChinaLawInfo (Chongqing High People's

96 See Dissemination Regulations, above note 4, Article 21 (the listed conditions include: no alterations to the automatically cached works, performances, or audio-visual recordings; no effect on the original network service provider of the works, performances, or audio-visual recordings in managing the relevant works; automatic alteration, deletion, or screening of works, performances, or audio-visual recordings when the original network service provider does the same).

97 *Zhejiang All-Asia Elec Commercial Co Ltd v Beijing Baidu Netcom Sci and Tech Co Ltd*, ChinaLawInfo (Beijing High People's Court, December 19 2008).

98 *Ibid.*

99 *Ibid.*

100 See Interpretation, above note 3, Articles 5.

101 See Dissemination Regulations, above note 4, Article 22.

102 *Ibid.*

103 *Ibid.*

Court, May 15 2009), the defendant was a webhosting company that provided hosting services for its clients' websites.[104] An infringing work owned by the plaintiff was found on one of the defendant's hosted websites, which was later removed by the defendant.[105] The court held that the hosting service provider was a qualified ISP under the Dissemination Regulations because it was a provider of memory space to its clients, and the defendant fulfilled its obligations under the safe harbour provision by clearly indicating themselves as a hosting service provider.[106] Therefore, the defendant was not jointly liable for the infringement.[107]

(g) *Back-up copies*

Under Article 16 of the Computer Software Protection Regulations, the rights of an owner of a lawful copy of software include making back-ups for avoiding damage to the (original) copy.[108] These back-ups may not be provided to other persons for use in any way, and the owner shall be responsible for destroying all back-ups.[109]

There are no internet back-up copy cases reported in China. However, from existing software back-up copy cases, it may be inferred that the core test for whether a back-up copy is protected under Article 16 is whether the back-up copy is for the use of the owner of the lawful copy.[110]

(h) *Reverse engineering*

China applies 'reverse engineering' as a defence only to trade secret violations.[111] In other words, 'reverse engineering' is not recognised as an exception or a defence to copyright infringement in China.[112] Scholars have been advocating the addition of several exceptions including 'reverse engineering' to follow related US law (ie, the Digital Millennium Copyright Act (DMCA)).[113] So far, neither the legislature nor the judiciary have any taken steps to do so.[114]

---

104 See eg *Beijing Sanmianxiang Copyright Agency v Chongqing Lidong Tech Co Ltd*, ChinaLawInfo (Chongqing High People's Court, May 15 2009).

105 *Ibid.*

106 *Ibid.*

107 *Ibid.*

108 See Computer Software Protection Regulations (promulgated by the St Council, December 20 2001, effective January 1 2002), Article 16 (amended January 8 2011 and January 30 2013), translated in Westlaw China (last visited November 4 2013) (PRC).

109 *Ibid.*

110 See, eg, *Autodesk Co v Longfa Co*, ChinaLawInfo (Beijing High People's Court, December 29 2003) (where the defendant bought one copy of the plaintiff's copyrighted software, made copies and installed onto the defendant's subsidiaries, the court ruled the defendant infringed the plaintiff owner's exclusive right to reproduction).

111 See Interpretation of the Supreme People's Court on Certain Issues Concerning the Application of Law in the Trial of Civil Cases Involving Unfair Competition (promulgated by the Sup People's Court, January 12 2007, effective February 1 2007), Article 12, translated in Westlaw China (last visited June 4 2012) (PRC) (under Article 12, acquisition of trade secret by way of self-research or through reverse engineering is not regarded as a violation under the relevant provisions of the Anti-Unfair Competition Law).

112 See, eg, Lu Jing, *Qian tan wo guo ji shu cuo shi lan yong ban quan fa gui zhi xian zhuang ji li fa jian yi* [Introduction to Abuse of China's Copyright Law and Regulations in Technology Protections and Legislature Suggestions], Hnxyzy.ChinaCourt.org (2011), http://hnxyzy.chinacourt.org/public/detail.php?id=3643; see also *Wo guo ji shu cuo shi fa lü zhi du de gai kuang ji wan shan* [Overview to China's Law System on Technology Protection and its Potential Improvements], LuoTuo.net.cn (2012), http://www.luotuo.net.cn/a/lixue/lixueqitaxiangguan/2012/0111/120993_2.html.

113 *Ibid.*

114 *Ibid.*

(i) *Parody defence*

In China, a parody defence is one type of fair use defence because it is a special type of commentary.

A widely reported copyright infringement case concerned a short film 'A Murder Case Caused by a Bun' by Ge Hu, which was based on the film 'The Promise' directed by Kaige Chen.[115] Although the case was settled before filing, several high-profile commentators shared their opinions.[116] They were split on whether the short film should be exempted from copyright infringement; some thought the use was fair because it was a parody of the original work; others thought the use did not qualify for a parody and therefore was not fair use under the Copyright Law.[117] However, all of them agreed that parody is a special form of commentary; quoting a substantial quantity of the original work for the purpose of parody still qualifies as fair use; the author cannot stop others from commenting on his/her work by citing the Copyright Law; and a parody work should not compete with the original work on the market (ie, should not jeopardise the economic interests of the original work).[118]

(j) *Incidental inclusion*

China does not explicitly recognise 'incidental inclusion' or 'de minimis use' as an exception or a defence to copyright infringement. However, some 'incidental inclusion' issues have been covered under the fair use provision of the Copyright Law.

In *Music Copyright Society of China v Fujian Weekend TV Co*, ChinaLawInfo (Beijing High People's Court, March 3 2004), the court affirmed the decision by the lower court, which looked at the length of the playing time of each song in the series.[119] The court then decided that the use of one of the four songs was not an infringement of the owner's copyright because the inclusion was only one line of the lyric lasting seven seconds.[120] When explaining the reason, the court said the defendant's use was obviously minimal which did not result in substantive unfavourable effect or damage to plaintiff's right to the work.[121]

1.5 Remedies available for copyright infringement

In China, remedies for copyright infringement can be categorised into three types: civil remedies, administrative remedies, and criminal remedies. The Copyright Law authorises all three liabilities.

For civil liabilities, under Article 48 of the Copyright Law:

"Those who have committed any of the [listed] infringing actions shall bear civil

---

115 *Qian Wang, Lun ren ding 'mo fang feng ci zuo pin' gou cheng 'he li shi yong' de fa lü gui ze* [Legal Regulations for Deciding 'Parody Works' as 'Fair Use'], ChinaLawInfo (2006), http://article.chinalawinfo.com/article_print.asp?articleid=37105 (last visited May 28 2012).

116 *Ibid.*

117 *Ibid.*

118 *Ibid.*

119 See *Music Copyright Soc'y of China v Fujian Weekend TV Co Ltd*, ChinaLawInfo (Beijing High People's Court, March 3 2004).

120 *Ibid.*

121 *Ibid.*

122 Copyright Law, above note 1, Article 48.

liability such as ceasing the infringement, eliminating the impacts, making an apology, or compensating for the losses ..."[122]

For administrative liabilities, under the same provision of the Copyright Law:

"a copyright administrative department may ... order the infringer to cease the infringing action, confiscate the infringer's illegal gains, confiscate and destroy the infringing reproduction(s), and impose a fine; or may also ... confiscate the materials, tools, equipment, etc., used for producing the infringing reproduction(s) ... ."[123]

With regard to criminal liabilities, under the same provision, (a People's Court may) " ... subject the infringer to criminal liability in accordance with the law, if the infringement constitutes a crime".[124]

Articles 217 and 218 of the Criminal Law of the People's Republic of China provide the test for an infringer to face an imprisonment penalty.[125] As an example, under these provisions, if an infringer knowingly or purposely reproduces and/or distributes a copyrighted work for profit without proper authorisation and the amount involved is substantial, he/she may face up to seven years' imprisonment and a fine.[126]

Normally, when copyright infringement is found, Chinese courts would only order the infringer to cease infringement and pay damages to the copyright holder. However, when the infringement passes the threshold of a criminal violation, the legal sanctions imposed by Chinese courts would be much more serious.

In *Huqiu District Procuratorate, Jiangsu Province v Chengdu Gongruan Network Technology Co*, ChinaLawInfo (Suzhou Huqiu Dist People's Court, August 20 2009), the government filed a lawsuit against the defendant company and four individual defendants.[127] The defendants reproduced many copies of software owned by Microsoft without authorisation, induced users to download the software, and loaded commercial plug-ins with the requested downloads for substantial advertising fees from the company owners of the commercial plug-ins.[128] The court found that the defendant deliberately infringed Microsoft's exclusive rights for the purpose of making substantial profit (over Rmb2.9 million).[129] Pursuant to the Copyright Law and the Criminal Law, the company defendant was fined over Rmb8.7 million and each of the individual defendants was fined between Rmb100,000 and Rmb1 million in addition to a term of imprisonment term from two to three and a half years.[130]

123 *Ibid.*

124 *Ibid.*

125 See Criminal Law (promulgated by the Nat'l People's Cong, March 14 1997, effective October 1 1997), Articles 217, 218 (amended February 25 2011), translated in Westlaw China (last visited June 4 2012) (PRC).

126 *Ibid.*

127 See *Huqiu Dist. Procuratorate of Suzhou City, Jiangsu Province v Chengdu Gongruan Network Tech Co Ltd*, ChinaLawInfo (Suzhou Huqiu Dist. People's Court, August 20, 2009).

128 *Ibid.*

129 *Ibid.*

130 *Ibid.*

1.6 Copyright liability

(a) *Hosting/cloud computing where infringing content uploaded by user of service*

Cloud computing is a relatively new technology in the world, and especially so for China.[131] At this time, only a few scholars have expressed concerns about possible legal issues (eg, how to deal with copyright infringement when the location of the data, governing laws, security, privacy, discovery process, and risk allocation are not certain).[132]

Hosting services have been treated as ISPs in terms of legal responsibilities.[133] As mentioned above, whether hosting service providers will be liable for copyright infringement committed by their users will depend on the relevant provider's knowledge of the infringing act and its involvement in the infringing act; namely, whether the provider knew or should have known of the infringing act, whether the provider assisted the infringing act, and whether the provider profited from the infringing act, etc.[134]

A user's liability remains the same regardless of whether or not he/she uses a hosting service or cloud computing because there are no special provisions concerning the technology medium in the Copyright Law, its related regulations, or judicial interpretations.

(b) *Hypertext linking*

For those that offer hypertext linking services in China, the Dissemination Regulations provide ample protection because they are internet communication service providers.

Under Article 23 of the Dissemination Regulations, when an ISP providing a searching or linking service to its clients cuts off the link to "any infringing works, performance, or audio-visual recording after receiving the rights owner's written notice", it is not jointly liable for infringement unless the provider knew or should have known that any of the works it linked to were infringing.[135]

There are many cases at different levels concerning linking services. All of the decisions rested on whether the defendant had or should have had knowledge of the infringements and whether the defendant fulfilled its duty in protecting the copyrighted works.[136]

Linking to a third-party website: Legitimate linking services to a third-party website provided by an ISP are protected under Chinese law. However, to qualify as a legitimate linking service, the source of the content must be clearly indicated.

In deciding the test for the requirements of a legitimate linking service, the

---

131 See Cloud Computing-China, http://www.cloudcomputing-china.cn (last visited June 4 2012).

132 See *Zhiwen Liang, Yun ji sian, ji shu zhong li yu ju you ban quan de ze ren* [Cloud Computing, Technology Neutral and Copyright Liabilities], ChinaLawInfo (2011), http://article.chinalawinfo.com/Article_Detail.asp?ArticleId=63035.

133 *Ibid.*

134 *Ibid.*

135 See Dissemination Regulations, above note 4, Article 23.

136 See above notes 89 to 91.

Supreme People's Court issued a decision in *Beijing Ciwen Movie Production Co v China Internet Communication Group, Hainan Co*, ChinaLawInfo (Supr People's Court, Civil Div, April 28 2009) with regard to copyright infringement disputes.[137] In *Ciwen v Hainan Co*, the court ruled that if an ISP asserts that it provides content on linked web pages or websites to the public through linking services and if the contents displayed on a web page or website provided by the ISP do not indicate that the linked content was owned by a third party, then the ISP's linking service is not legitimate and the ISP is directly liable for infringement of the linked web pages or websites.[138]

Linking to an infringing work: First, deep linking to a copyrighted work infringes the exclusive rights of the owner because it hides the identity of the source. Second, whether other types of linking to a copyrighted work infringe the right of the owner depends on the knowledge of the user or the service provider. Under the Dissemination Regulations and the Interpretation,[139] if the user or the ISP has known or should have known that the linked contents infringe a copyrighted work, then the user should be liable for the infringement, and/or the service provider should be jointly liable for the infringement.[140]

The Dissemination Regulations do not distinguish between a content provider and a service provider, nor do they distinguish between linking to content and linking to a website.[141]

In cases brought by copyright owners against owners of file sharing indexing sites, courts have ruled based on the nature of the works whose copyrights were allegedly infringed. With regard to movies, courts have unanimously decided that since the production of movies is very costly, website owners should know that it is highly unlikely that copyright owners of movies would share their works on the Internet for free. Courts have also decided that indexing sites, which classify movies and allow users to upload introductions to movies, are liable for copyright infringement as they facilitate copyright infringement that results in additional losses for the copyright owners.[142]

In contrast, in cases involving radio programmes, some courts have decided that unlike movies or TV series, it is relatively cheap to make a radio programme and it is possible that copyright owners may share their radio programmes on the Internet for free. Therefore, a file sharing indexing site did not know and could not have known that the radio programme infringed the copyright owner's copyright.[143]

---

137 See, eg, *Beijing Ciwen Movie Prod Co Ltd v China Internet Commc'n Group, Hainan Co*, ChinaLawInfo (Supr People's Court, Civil Div, April 28 2009).

138 See Kaiji He, *She ji ti gong lian jie fu wu de wang luo fu wu ti gong zhe de zhi jie qin quan ze ren* [Direct Liability of the ISP Providing Linking Service], HeXuanJi.com (2009), www.hexuanji.com/ShowArticle.shtml?ID=20122710582050650.htm.

139 See Interpretation, above note 3, Article 7.

140 See Dissemination Regulations, above note 4, Article 23.

141 *Ibid.*

142 *Beijing Jidong Films Co, Ltd v Shanghai Weixi Network Tech Co, Ltd*, ChinaLawInfo (Shanghai No 1 Intermediate People's Court, July 16 2009).

143 *Cui Yabin v Shanghai Weixi Network Tech Co, Ltd*, ChinaLawInfo (Shanghai Pudong Dist People's Court, November 11 2009).

The Interpretation also stipulates that the type of work will be a consideration in determining whether an ISP should have known that relevant works have been uploaded by users without authorisation from right holders.[144]

In addition to lawsuits, there have been administrative actions against alleged infringers. At the end of 2009, the majority of P2P indexing sites in China were eradicated after the State Administration of Radio Movie and Television of China (SARFT) launched a movement to fight copyright infringement and vulgar content in radio and television. It was reported that SARFT closed down more than 530 audio/video websites, including many P2P file sharing indexing websites, on the grounds that the websites had not been issued a Permit for Dissemination of Audio and Video Programmes on Information Networks by SARFT. According to the Management Provisions on Audio and Video Programmes on the Internet jointly issued by SARFT and the Ministry of Information Industry of China (now the Ministry of Industry and Information Technology (MIIT)) on December 20 2007 (effective January 31 2008), only a state-owned or state-controlled company with at least Rmb10 million registered capital will qualify to apply for such a permit.

During this movement, one of the most popular P2P file sharing indexing websites, btchina.net, was closed down. Another popular website, Verycd.com, removed large amounts of P2P file sharing links to infringing music, movies, and TV series in January 2011. In addition, the Pirate Bay, probably the most popular P2P indexing website in the world, was blocked in China.

Copying of headlines: In China, using headlines as hypertext links is not considered an infringement of a copyrighted work, either because news is not protected under the Copyright Law or because the use of headlines is fair use.[145]

Under Article 5 of the Copyright Law, news is not protected under Copyright Law.[146] Under Article 22(3), the use of a published newspaper for the purpose of reporting current affairs is fair use.[147]

(c) *P2P network*

P2P service providers, who are usually blamed for infringement of copyrights, are protected under the safe harbour provided under the Dissemination Regulations provided that they satisfy the knowledge requirement and fulfil their duties required under the same provision.

Supplier of P2P software: In copyright infringement lawsuits brought against suppliers of P2P file sharing software, plaintiffs have generally based their cases upon the availability of introductions and links to the alleged infringing works on a defendant's websites. Suppliers of P2P software are protected under the safe harbour

144 See Interpretation, above note 3, Article 9.

145 See Lei Jing, *Guan yu wang luo lian jie de fa lü wen ti fen xi* [An Analysis of the Legal Issues of Hypertext Linking], Beijing University Graduate Thesis (2006), http://www.pkunetlaw.cn/uploadfile/862cdb80-223a-4179-b070-3064a5911338.pdf.

146 See Copyright Law, above note 1, Article 5.

147 See *Ibid,* Article 22(3).

provided under the Dissemination Regulations, which makes the main issue of these kinds of claims whether the service providers knew or should have known about the alleged infringement (which can often be proved by whether they were actively involved in the suspected copyright infringement), and whether the defendant fulfilled its duties after receiving proper notice of the existence of the infringing work. For example, one court decided that a supplier of P2P software also hosting a P2P file sharing service infringed an owner's copyrights when it provided background information for the movies that were available over its P2P software network.[148]

Many copyright infringement lawsuits have also been brought against Xunlei (also known as 'Thunder'), one of the most popular P2P file sharing software in China. In most cases, the plaintiffs chose to challenge Xunlei's service provider functionality, and Xunlei usually chose to settle with the plaintiffs.[149]

As an example, in 2008, the Motion Picture Association of America (MPAA) initiated a lawsuit against Xunlei before a court in Shanghai, asking for more than Rmb7 million in damages. After Xunlei successfully raised an objection to the jurisdiction, the case was transferred to a court in Shenzhen, Xunlei's hometown, and the MPAA chose to withdraw its lawsuit.[150]

The Interpretation also provides that whether an ISP (supposedly including suppliers of P2P software) proactively selects, edits, changes or recommends works, performances, videos and audio recordings will be a consideration in determining whether the ISP should have known that the works have been uploaded by users without authorisation from right holders.[151]

Uploaders/downloaders: There is no question that both uploaders and downloaders of a copyrighted work, without proper authorisation, are considered infringers.[152] However, the copyright owners always go after the deeper pocket website service providers when the owners' rights have been infringed because there are too many uploaders and even more downloaders.[153]

So far, there have been no reported cases brought by copyright owners against

148 *Beijing Ciwen Movie & Television Prod Co, Ltd v Guangzhou Shulian Software Tech Co, Ltd*, ChinaLawInfo (Guangdong Guangzhou Intermediate Court, August 14 2006).

149 See, eg, *Anle (Beijing) Movie Distrib Co, Ltd v Shenzhen Xunlei Network Tech Co, Ltd*, ChinaLawInfo (Shanghai No 2 Intermediate Court, October 21 2008); *Shenzhen Xunlei Network Tech Co, Ltd v Shanghai Youdu Broadband Tech Co, Ltd*, ChinaLawInfo (Shanghai No 1 Intermediate Court, June 20 2008); *Beijing Shidaiyingyin Int'l Entm't Co, Ltd v Shenzhen Xunlei Network Tech Co, Ltd*, ChinaLawInfo (Shanghai No 2 Intermediate Court, December 22 2008); Gang Wang, *Ju jue bei di gu xun lei shang shi zai tui chi* [Xunlei Postpones IPO], The Time Weekly (2011), http://tech.163.com/11/0728/07/7A1J9GKV000915BF.html.

150 *Xun lei ban quan an zhuan zhan Shenzhen Nanshan fa yuan: Mei dian ying xie hui che su* [Xunlei Copyright Case Transferred to Shenzhen Nanshan Court: MPA Withdraws the Lawsuit], Southern Metropolis Daily (2008), http://tech.sina.com.cn/i/2008-06-20/09232272429.shtml.

151 See Interpretation, above note 3, Article 12.

152 See Copyright Law, above note 1, Article 10(12) (the author has the right of information network dissemination (ie, the right to provide the public with works by wired or wireless means so as to enable the public to obtain the works at an individually selected time and place; therefore, all unauthorised uploading and downloading of a copyrighted work is an infringement of the author's rights); see also *Ge ren wang shang xia zai yin yue ye qin quan?* [Does the Individual Downloader of Music Infringe?], FaBang.com (2010), http://www.fabang.com/a/20100624/159341.html [hereinafter 'Individual Downloader'].

153 *Ibid.*

internet users in China for uploading or downloading copyrighted materials from content sharing networks.

(d) ***Webcasting***

There are no specific provisions under current Chinese laws regarding webcasting. A reported case evidenced that, under the Copyright Law, if a webcasted performance can be played back or be paused, then it is an infringement of the author's right of information network dissemination; if not, it is not covered under the Copyright Law.[154]

In *CCTV v 21CN Information Network*, the defendant webcasted the ceremony of Passing the Olympic Flame over Everest that was broadcasted by CCTV.[155] The court ruled that the programme broadcasted by CCTV was creative enough to be protected under the Copyright Law because of its planning, selection of historic material, simulation skills, and scheme of interviews, etc, that made it similar to a movie production.[156] The court ruled that the defendant infringed the author's right of information network dissemination under Article 10(12) of the Copyright Law because a viewer could record the programme and play it back later.[157]

(e) ***Streaming***

Streaming makes a work available to the public at an individually selected time and place. Therefore, it infringes the copyright owner's right to information network dissemination under Article 10(12) of the Copyright Law if the work played is copyrighted.[158] Yet, streaming service providers, like other ISPs, might qualify for safe harbour protection depending on their knowledge of the infringement and whether their duties have been fulfilled.

There are several reported cases involving the issue of video streaming; however, video streaming was never the central issue. In *Beijing Star Image Video Culture Dissemination Co v Shanghai Xinhua Information Network Communication Co*, ChinaLawInfo (Shanghai High People's Court, June 6 2009), the defendant was found to have provided streaming services that allegedly infringed a movie.[159] The lower court ruled (and was not challenged on appeal) that 'streaming' made the work accessible to the public at an individually selectable time and place; therefore, streaming of a copyrighted work without proper authorisation constituted infringement of the owner's right to network dissemination.[160]

---

154 See *CCTV Int'l Network Co Ltd v 21CN Info Network Co Ltd*, ChinaLawInfo (Guangdong Guangzhou Intermediate People's Court, January 1 2009).

155 *Ibid.*

156 *Ibid.*

157 *Ibid*; see also Kuiming Ji, *Wang luo guang bo qin quan xing wei de fen xi yu fang fan* [Regulation on Infringements of Copyright in Webcasting], BaiDu.com (2010), http://wenku.baidu.com/view/64f0cadace2f0066f53322f1.html (scholars arguing that if a program was not recordable, the Copyright Law cannot cover webcasting infringement).

158 See Copyright Law, above note 1, Article 10(12).

159 *Beijing Star Image Video Culture Dissemination Co Ltd v Shanghai Xinhua Info Network Commc'n Co Ltd*, ChinaLawInfo (Shanghai High People's Court, June 6 2009) (the defendant challenged the ownership of the right to network dissemination in this case and lost on appeal).

160 *Ibid.*

(f) *Framing*

ISPs using framing to link to a third-party website are protected under a safe harbour provided other conditions have been met.

Furthermore, frame linking to a third party's website has been ruled as 'unfair competition' under Article 2 of the Anti-Unfair Competition Law; where business entities shall abide by the principles of "voluntariness, equality, fairness, honesty and credibility", and also "observe the generally recognised business ethics" in their business transactions.[161] In the first case involving framing, *Beijing Hongyu Haotian Technology Co Ltd v Shen Li*, ChinaLawInfo (Beijing Haidian Dist Court, November 10 2004), the defendant linked four articles from the plaintiff's website with 'iframe' technology, allowing a viewer to perceive the web contents from the plaintiff's website with the impression that the contents were provided by the defendant.[162] Furthermore, the defendant did not remove the link after receiving and acknowledging notice from the plaintiff.[163] The court ruled that the defendant's act was a violation under the Anti-Unfair Competition Law, and damages and fees were awarded to the plaintiff.[164]

(g) *Transmission of infringing work across a communications network*

Chinese laws and regulations do not distinguish service providers who facilitate 'transmission of infringing work across a communications network' or 'user-generated content' from general ISPs, which are protected under safe harbour provisions of the Dissemination Regulations. Under the safe harbour provisions, those service providers without actual or presumed knowledge of the infringement and who have fulfilled their duties imposed under the Dissemination Regulations should not be held liable for the infringing acts of a third-party client.[165]

For 'transmission of infringing work across a communications network', Article 20 of the Dissemination Regulations provides that under listed circumstances, an ISP that provides 'automatic access services according to the instructions' of a client, or provides 'automatic transmission services ... ' shall not be liable for damages.[166]

Possibly because the provision is relatively straightforward, there have been no cases against service providers for their transmission of infringing works across a communication network.

(h) *Aggregator websites (eg, Google News, price comparison websites)*

Most claims against aggregator websites in China have concerned individual copyrighted works. There has yet to be a case in China about a claim against a website with respect to its aggregating functionality.

---

161 See Anti-Unfair Competition Law, above note 30, Article 2.

162 *Beijing Hongyu Haotian Tech. Co Ltd v Shen Li,* ChinaLawInfo (Beijing Haidian Dist Court, November 10, 2004).

163 *Ibid.*

164 *Ibid.*

165 See Dissemination Regulations, above note 4, Article 22 (the ISPs' duty of care includes taking proper measures to stop infringement when they are given notice).

166 See *Ibid,* Article 20 (two conditions must be met for an ISP to avoid liability: not selecting or altering the transmitted content; and providing the content to the designated client while preventing others from having access to the content).

(i) *Treatment of user-generated content*

User-generated content (UGC) is another service where an ISP may be covered under the safe harbour of the Dissemination Regulations. Currently, there are many lawsuits against UGC sharing providers, especially video clip sharing websites such as Tudou.com and Youku.com. Because there are no special provisions in China for UGC sharing websites, they share the same protection and duties as other ISPs. However, most courts have found that sharing websites do not meet the requirements for safe harbour protection.[167]

In *Shanghai Senle Culture Dissemination Co v Shanghai All-Tudou Network Technology Co*, ChinaLawInfo (Shanghai Pudong Dist People's Court, May 13 2010), the defendant's website had an infringing movie owned by the plaintiff.[168] The defendant, Tudou.com, was found jointly liable for infringing the plaintiff's copyright because it failed its duties required by the safe harbour provision.[169] Specifically, the defendant should have known that production of movies is costly and it is unlikely that copyright owners would share them for free.[170] Also, Tudou.com benefited financially from the infringing act and literally assisted the infringement by categorising uploaded contents.[171]

In another similar case, the court decided that Tudou's categorisation of the video works assisted the infringements and Tudou should have known the risk of copyright infringement through the title of its categorisation; therefore, Tudou was liable for infringing the protected works given the fact that it also profited from those acts.[172]

1.7 Joint liability for internet service providers

In China, ISPs are jointly liable for the infringing acts committed by their clients provided that certain conditions are met. Examples of the conditions include: the knowledge of the ISP regarding the infringement, the involvement of the ISP in the infringement, the measures taken after knowing the infringement and so on.

As discussed in section 1.2(g) above, China does not distinguish between secondary liability and joint liability.[173]

1.8 Relief

As stated in section 1.5 above, the Copyright Law and the Dissemination Regulations define the remedies that are available for infringement.[174] As an injured party, a

---

167 See *Beijing Jindian Audio-Video Culture Co Ltd v Shanghai All-Tudou Network Tech Co Ltd,* ChinaLawInfo (Shanghai Pudong Dist People's Court, September 30 2009); see also *Shanghai All-Tudou Network Tech Co Ltd v Guangdong Qianhe Video Dissemination Co Ltd,* ChinaLawInfo (Shanghai No 1 Intermediate People's Court, April 16 2010).

168 See *Shanghai Senle Culture Dissemination Co Ltd v Shanghai All-Tudou Network Tech Co Ltd,* ChinaLawInfo (Shanghai Pudong Dist People's Court, May 13 2010) (the case was later settled after the initial ruling).

169 *Ibid.*

170 *Ibid.*

171 *Ibid.*

172 See *Beijing Sohu New Media Info Tech Co Ltd v Shanghai All-Tudou Network Tech Co Ltd,* ChinaLawInfo (Shanghai No 1 Intermediate People's Court, July 7 2010).

173 See above section 1.2(g).

174 See above section 1.5.

175 See Copyright Law, above note 1, Article 48; see also section 1.5 above.

copyright owner has the right to request certain relief including injunctions, damages, and apologies.[175]

The copyright owner has the right to request the cessation of the infringement, which applies not only to the infringers themselves, but also to all alleged infringers through the ISP, even when the ISP is not liable for the infringements due to safe harbour protection. Under Article 14 of the Dissemination Regulations, a copyright owner can request an ISP to delete the alleged infringing works or to break the link to that work provided the copyright owner satisfied the requirements of the request.[176]

1.9 Issues specific to China

(a) Jurisdiction

Under Article 15 of the Interpretation,

> *"A civil dispute case involving infringement of right of dissemination via information network shall be under the jurisdiction of the people's court at the place of infringement or the place where the defendant is domiciled. The place of infringement shall include the locations of the web server, computer terminal(s), and other equipment used for committing the alleged act of infringement. If it is difficult to determine the place of infringement or the place where the defendant is domiciled, the location of the computer terminal(s) or other equipment in which the plaintiff has discovered the infringing content may be deemed the place of infringement."*[177]

In the first Chinese internet copyright dispute case, *ReadChina (Group) v Yibin City Cuiping District Dongfang Information Services Co*, ChinaLawInfo (Beijing Haidian Dist People's Court, September 9 1999), the plaintiff ran its website in Haidian District, Beijing, where the lawsuit was filed, and the defendant operated and was domiciled in its hometown in Sichuan Province.[178] The defendant claimed that the court in Beijing did not have personal jurisdiction over him because he had no connection with Beijing.[179] The court ruled (and later affirmed on appeal), that Haidian District Court did have personal jurisdiction over the defendant under Chinese law because since the server with its web content copied by the defendant was located in Haidian District, the infringing activity also happened in Haidian District.[180]

(b) Claim to infringement of foreign copyright

Article 2 of the Copyright Law defines two categories of foreigners' works protected under the Copyright Law: works of foreigners "first published in China in accordance with this Law" and works of a foreigner published outside China which are eligible to enjoy copyright "under an agreement concluded between China and the author's

---

176 See below section 4 (certain requirements must be met when a copyright owner makes such a request.

177 See Interpretation, above note 3, Article 15.

178 See *ReadChina (Group) v Yibin City Cuiping Dist Dongfang Info Serv Co Ltd*, ChinaLawInfo (Beijing Haidian Dist People's Court, September 9 1999).

179 *Ibid.*

180 *Ibid.*

country of origin or country of habitual residence ... or under an international treaty" to which both countries are parties.[181]

There are several widely reported cases involving foreign copyrighted works in China. Most of the rights fall under the category involving a treaty.[182] *Sony BMG Music Entertainment v Beijing Alibaba Information Technology Co*, ChinaLawInfo (Beijing No 2 Intermediate People's Court, April 24 2007) is one of a series of lawsuits against Alibaba's online indexing and searching service.[183] One of the issues raised by the defendant was whether the alleged infringing music works, owned by the plaintiff in foreign countries, were protected under Chinese law.[184] The court affirmed the lower court's decision and ruled that Sony, the owner of the alleged infringing music works, was under the protection of the Copyright Law.[185]

However, if a defendant is domiciled in China and commits copyright infringement under a foreign law (eg, he/she has uploaded a copyrighted work outside China to a server located outside China), then technically according to the conflicts of law rules in China, both Chinese courts and the courts where the infringement was committed will have jurisdiction. However, Chinese courts would probably decline to exercise jurisdiction under the *forum non conveniens* doctrine, as it would be difficult for Chinese courts to investigate infringement which occurred outside China. Also, in reality, Chinese courts always apply Chinese IP law in IP infringement suits. In such cases, most scholars incline towards the view that the right of dissemination via information networks does not apply to those cases, because such copyrights are regional to each country.[186]

(c) *Emission theory*

Under Chinese law, "the place where such equipment as the computer terminal on which the plaintiff discovered the infringing content is located may be deemed to be the place where the infringement occurred".[187] Therefore, in China it may be considered that infringing acts take place at the location where the infringing work is uploaded or downloaded.

Even though it is possible to bring lawsuits at the locations where uploading and downloading occur, there are few cases on this issue probably because copyright owners usually choose easy and rich targets, and this will be the company hosting the website where the alleged infringing work was found.

---

181 See Copyright Law, above note 1, Article 2 (China is a member of the Berne Convention; therefore, citizens of signatory countries enjoy the same copyrights as Chinese citizens).

182 For example, the Berne Convention.

183 See, eg, *Sony BMG Music Entm't v Beijing Allibaba Info Tech Co Ltd*, ChinaLawInfo (Beijing No 2 Intermediate People's Court, April 24, 2007).

184 *Ibid.*

185 *Ibid.*

186 See *Guo Peng, Xin Xi Wang Luo Chuan Bo Quan She Wai Qin Quan de Zhong Guo Fa Yuan Guan Xia Quan Fen Xi* [An Analysis of the Chinese Court's jurisdiction for Infringements of Information Dissemination Rights via Internet Related with Foreign Copyrights], doc88.com (2012), www.doc88.com/p-993536351909.html; see also Dai Shaoye, *Qian Xi Hu Lian Wang Zhu Zuo Quan An Jian Guan Xia Wen Ti* [An Introductive Analysis to the Jurisdictions of Copyright Cases in Related to the Internet], lawtime.cn (2011), www.lawtime.cn/info/sunhai/qhccqzzccq/20110713109337.html.

187 See Interpretation, above note 3, Article 15.

1.10 Orphan works

Under Article 13 of the Implementation Regulations, in the case of a work with an unknown author, "copyrights other than right of authorship shall be exercised by the owner of the original version of the work ..."[188]

This provision is not particularly helpful in cyberspace because the 'original works' can be difficult to identify when digital copies of works can easily be produced. Therefore, it is difficult for distributors to acquire legitimate licences from the real owner of the works under the provision provided under Article 13.

The new Copyright Law Revision Draft attempts to address this issue with a new provision for orphan works. Under the Revision Draft, the distributor or user need not identify the owner of the copyright of orphan works. Rather, he/she needs only pay a licence fee to the copyright collective management organisation.[189]

1.11 Online piracy measures

China does not have any law or measure directed specifically against online piracy; however, general laws and regulations may apply.

1.12 Electronic infringement of moral rights

The moral rights of the copyright owner are explicitly protected under the Copyright Law:

(a) Right to object to derogatory treatment

Under Article 10(4) of the Copyright Law, the author of the protected work has the "right of integrity, that is, the right to protect a work from being distorted or falsified".[190] Under Article 20, the protection of 'authorship, alteration and integrity' of an author exists in perpetuity.[191]

(b) False attribution – right to guard against impersonation on the Internet

Pursuant to Article 10(2) of the Copyright Law, the right of authorship, "ie the right to indicate the identity of the author of a work by affixing the author's name thereto ...", is included in the bundle of the author's copyrights.[192] In addition, Article 20 of the Copyright Law provides that the right of authorship exists in perpetuity.[193] Therefore, false attribution would infringe an author's right of authorship.

(c) Paternity right

As indicated above, under Article 10(2), the author of a work has a paternity right to the work because the author has the right to be identified as the author of the work.[194]

---

188 See Implementing Regulations, above note 2, Article 13.

189 *Zhong hua ren min gong he guo zhu zuo quan fa (xiu gai cao an)* [Copyright Law of the People's Republic of China (modified draft)], Law-Lib.com (2012), http://www.law-lib.com/fzdt/newshtml/20/20120331201955.htm.

190 See Copyright Law, above note 1, Article 10(4).

191 See *Ibid*, Article 20.

192 See *Ibid*, Article 10(2).

193 See *Ibid*, Article 20.

194 See *Ibid*, Article 10(2).

2. Trademarks

2.1 Use of a trademark

The evidence of use requirement for the purposes of avoiding revocation of a trademark registration for non-use has been subject to change in recent years. In current practice, whether use of a trademark on a website will be a sufficient defence against a non-use cancellation will also depend upon the goods or services covered by a registered trademark.

Specifically, for registered trademarks covering goods in Classes 1–34 of the Nice Classification,[195] to defeat a non-use cancellation, it is generally required that such goods bearing the registered trademarks are produced and sold (or offered for sale). Therefore, for such trademarks, what is essential is that goods bearing the marks are produced, while the use of the trademark on a website may show that such goods are offered for sale.

On the other hand, for registered trademarks covering services in Classes 35–45 of the Nice Classification,[196] the use of the mark on a website might be sufficient to show that the services are offered under the trademark. In this case, such use may constitute use for the purposes of defeating a non-use cancellation.

Use of a trademark on a website may constitute use for the purposes of an infringement claim if it is clearly in connection with certain goods or services or with the sale of certain goods or services.

If a website is a .com website, the issue of whether the use of a mark on such site will be sufficient to defend against a non-use cancellation will probably depend upon whether consumers in China can actually purchase the goods or use the services provided through that website. Specifically, when goods bearing the trademark are being sold on that website and if consumers in China can place an order on that website and the goods will then be shipped to China, it likely that such use will be adequate to defend against non-use cancellation.

As to services, for many of them, consumers will need to go to service providers' premises to receive the relevant service and in such cases, if the service providers do not run premises in China, the use of the mark on a .com website would probably be insufficient. However, for such internet services, if consumers in China can purchase and use the service on the Internet (such as a domain name registration or search engine), the use of the mark on a .com website will probably be adequate.

2.2 Infringement

(a) Metatags

There are no reported cases regarding metatags. Yet based on various courts' dealings with cases involving keywords and sponsor links, metatags may constitute use for the purposes of an infringement claim if it is clearly in connection with certain goods or services or with the sale of certain goods or services and there is no defence for such use.

---

195 WIPO, International Classification of Goods and Services Under the Nice Agreement, http://web2.wipo.int/nicepub/edition-20130101/taxonomy/?pagination=no&lang=en&mode=flat&explanatory_notes=hide&basic_numbers=show (last visited November 15 2013).

196 *Ibid.*

(b) *Keywords*

Trademark infringement or unfair competition usually arises when the advertiser purchases a keyword which is its competitor's trademark. Recent reported cases show that courts have agreed that advertisers are liable for trademark infringement or unfair competition for making such purchase.[197] Although superficially these cases are different from typical trademark infringement or unfair competition scenarios, they are generally decided pursuant to the classic trademark infringement or unfair competition provisions, including:

- Article 57 of the Trademark Law, which provides, among other things, that it constitutes trademark infringement to use a mark identical or similar to a registered mark on identical or similar goods without authorisation from the owner of the registered mark.[198]
- Article 5 of the Anti-Unfair Competition Law provides, among other things, that a business person or entity shall not counterfeit others' registered trademarks, or use others' trade names or personal names resulting in misidentification of sources of goods.[199]

(c) *Sponsored links*

Similar to keyword advertising, courts have generally decided that the association of another party's registered trademark with sponsored links constitutes trademark infringement.[200]

(d) *Hidden text*

There are no reported cases regarding use in hidden text. Yet based on various courts' dealings with cases involving keywords and sponsor links, such use may constitute use for the purposes of an infringement claim if it is clearly in connection with certain goods or services or with the sale of certain goods or services and there is no defence for such use.

(e) *Internet domain names*

Mere registration of domain names may give rise to liability in that the registrant may lose the domain name if bad faith is found on the part of the registrant by merely registering the domain name.

In China, domain name disputes are generally divided into two groups:

- '.cn'[201] domain names and Chinese character domain names; and
- '.com', '.net', '.org' and other generic top-level domain names.

---

197 See, eg, *Shanghai Meisitaike Biotech Co, Ltd v Wuxi Angusi Constr Tech Co, Ltd*, ChinaLawInfo (Jiangsu Wuxi Intermediate Court, January 18 2009), *Beijing Shangdezhiye Educ Consulting Ctr v Lixiangaofeng Int'l Educ Tech (Beijing) Co, Ltd*, ChinaLawInfo (Beijing Haidian Court, December 16 2011).

198 Trademark Law (promulgated by the Standing Comm Nat'l People's Cong, August 30 2013, and to be effective May 1 2014), Article 57, translated in Westlaw China (last visited November 15 2013) (PRC).

199 Anti-Unfair Competition Law, above note 30, Article 5.

200 See, eg, *Shanghai Meisitaike Biotech Co, Ltd v Wuxi Angusi Constr Tech Co, Ltd*, ChinaLawInfo (Jiangsu Wuxi Intermediate Court, January 18 2009).

201 The country code top-level domain (ccTLD) for mainland China.

Complaints involving the first group of domain names may be submitted to the domain name dispute resolution service providers appointed by the China Internet Network Information Center (CNNIC). Currently, the only two appointed providers are the China International Economic and Trade Arbitration Commission (CIETAC) and the Hong Kong International Arbitration Centre (HKIAC). These domain name disputes are governed by the CNNIC Domain Name Dispute Resolution Policy (CNDRP),[202] and the Procedural Rules for CNNIC Domain Name Dispute Resolution Policy (CNDRP Rules).[203]

The second group of domain name disputes may be submitted to any of the four domain name dispute resolution service providers approved by the Internet Corporation for Assigned Names and Numbers (ICANN).[204] The Asian Domain Name Dispute Resolution Centre (ADNDRC) is the only provider in Asia and has four offices located in Beijing, Hong Kong, Seoul and Kuala Lumpur.[205] The Beijing and Hong Kong offices are respectively operated and managed by CIETAC and HKIAC.[206] ICANN's Uniform Domain Name Dispute Resolution Policy (UDRP, adopted on August 26 1999) governs this group of domain name disputes.[207]

Article 8 of the CNDRP provides that a complaint shall be supported if:[208]

- the disputed domain name is identical with or confusingly similar to the complainant's name or mark in which the complainant has civil rights or interests;
- the holder of the disputed domain name does not have any right or legitimate interest in the domain name or the main part thereof; and
- the holder of the disputed domain name has registered or is using the domain name in bad faith.

Article 9 of the CNDRP provides that any of the following circumstances may constitute evidence of the registration and use of a domain name in bad faith:[209]

- the purpose for registering or acquiring the domain name is to sell, rent or otherwise transfer the domain name registration to the complainant who is the owner of the name or mark or to a competitor of that complainant, and to obtain unjustified benefits;

---

202 *Zhongguo hu lian wang luo xin xi zhong xin yu ming zheng yi jie jue ban fa* [China Internet Network Information Center Domain Name Dispute Resolution Policy] (promulgated by the China Internet Network Info Ctr, February 14 2006, effective March 17 2006 and amended June 28 2012), www.cnnic.cn/ggfw/fwzxxgzcfg/2012/201206/t20120626_30074.htm (last visited November 15 2013) [hereinafter 'CNDRP'].

203 *Zhongguo hu lian wang luo xin xi zhong xin yu ming zheng yi jie jue ban fa cheng xu gui ze* [China Internet Network Information Center Domain Name Dispute Resolution Policy Procedural Rules] (promulgated by the China Internet Network Info Ctr, October 8 2007, effective October 8 2007), http://dndrc.cietac.org/static/cnddr/prodrul.html (last visited June 6 2012) [hereinafter 'CNDRP Rules'].

204 ICANN, List of Approved Dispute Resolution Service Providers, www.icann.org/en/dndr/udrp/approved-providers.htm (last visited June 3 2012).

205 Asian Domain Name Dispute Resolution Centre, https://www.adndrc.org/index.html (last visited June 4 2012).

206 See *Ibid.*

207 ICANN, *Uniform Domain Name Dispute Resolution Policy*, http://www.icann.org/en/help/dndr/udrp/policy (last visited June 4, 2012) [hereinafter 'UDRP'].

208 See CNDRP, above note 207, Article 8.

209 *Ibid.* Article 9.

- the disputed domain name holder repeatedly registers domain names in order to prevent owners of the names or marks from reflecting the names or the marks in corresponding domain names;
- the disputed domain name holder has registered or acquired the domain name for the purpose of damaging the complainant's reputation, disrupting the complainant's normal business or creating confusion with the complainant's name or mark so as to mislead the public; or
- other circumstances which may prove bad faith.

The UDRP contains similar provisions. Paragraph 4(a) of the UDRP provides that: *"(y)ou[, the domain holder,] are required to submit to a mandatory administrative proceeding in the event that a third party (a 'complainant') asserts to the applicable Provider, in compliance with the Rules of Procedure, that*

(i) [Y]our domain name is identical or confusingly similar to a trademark or service mark in which the complainant has rights; and

(ii) [Y]ou have no rights or legitimate interests in respect of the domain name; and

(iii) [Y]our domain name has been registered and is being used in bad faith."[210]

Consequently, paragraph 4(b) of the UDRP provides that:

"the following circumstances, in particular but without limitation, if found by the Panel to be present, shall be evidence of the registration and use of a domain name in bad faith:

(i) [C]ircumstances indicating that you have registered or you have acquired the domain name primarily for the purpose of selling, renting, or otherwise transferring the domain name registration to the complainant who is the owner of the trademark or service mark or to a competitor of that complainant, for valuable consideration in excess of your documented out-of-pocket costs directly related to the domain name; or

(ii) [Y]ou have registered the domain name in order to prevent the owner of the trademark or service mark from reflecting the mark in a corresponding domain name, provided that you have engaged in a pattern of such conduct; or

(iii) [Y]ou have registered the domain name primarily for the purpose of disrupting the business of a competitor; or

(iv) [B]y using the domain name, you have intentionally attempted to attract, for commercial gain, Internet users to your web site or other on-line location, by creating a likelihood of confusion with the complainant's mark as to the source, sponsorship, affiliation, or endorsement of your web site or location or of a product or service on your web site or location."[211]

In addition to administrative domain name dispute resolution proceedings, any party may submit a domain name dispute to arbitration upon the parties' agreement or bring a lawsuit before the courts of competent jurisdiction.[212]

Today, there are only a few reported cases of arbitration over domain name

210 UDRP, above note 207, ¶ 4(a).

211 *Ibid.* ¶ 4(b).

212 See CNDRP, above note 207, Article 15; see also UDRP, above note 211, ¶ 5.

disputes in China, but court proceedings were a popular choice for resolving domain name disputes before the CNDRP was first issued in 2002. The Interpretation of the Supreme People's Court on Certain Issues Concerning the Application of Law in the Trial of Cases Involving Civil Disputes over Computer Network Domain Names was issued on July 17 2001 ('Domain Names Interpretation').[213] Court proceedings will continue to be a choice of resolution due to a two-year time limit and other requirements imposed upon the CNDRP proceedings.

The Domain Names Interpretation provides another version of what constitutes a successful domain name dispute complaint. Article 4 stipulates that the registration or use of a domain name could constitute infringement or unfair competition and four elements must be met:[214]

- the civil rights and interest for which the plaintiff seeks protection are legitimate and valid;
- the defendant's domain name or the major part thereof constitutes a production, imitation, translation or transliteration of the plaintiff's well-known trademark; or is identical or so similar to the plaintiff's registered trademark, domain name, etc that the domain name would cause confusion among the relevant sector of the general public;
- the defendant does not have any right or interest in the domain name or the main part thereof, nor has any justifications for registration or use of the domain name; and
- the defendant has registered or is using the domain name in bad faith.

Article 5 of the Domain Names Interpretation provides that bad faith will be found if the defendant:[215]

- registers another party's well-known trademark as a domain name for commercial purposes;
- registers and uses a domain name identical or similar to the plaintiff's registered trademark or domain name for commercial purposes, and deliberately causes confusion with the plaintiff's products, services or website, or misleads online users to visit its website or other online websites;
- offers for sale at a high price, rents, or otherwise transfers the domain name to obtain unjustified benefits;
- has not used the domain name after registration and does not plan to use it but intends to prevent rights owners from registering the domain name; or
- other circumstances showing bad faith.

Therefore, mere registration of the domain name may give rise to liability when the circumstances provided in the above Articles 8 and 9 of the CNDRP or paragraphs

---

213 Interpretation of the Supreme People's Court on Certain Issues Concerning the Application of Law in the Trial of Cases Involving Civil Disputes over Computer Network Domain Names (promulgated by the Supreme People's Court, June 17 2001, effective June 24 2001), translated in Westlaw China (last visited June 6, 2012) (PRC) [hereinafter 'Domain Names Interpretation'].

214 See *Ibid*, Article 4.

215 See *Ibid*, Article 5.

4(a) and 4(b) of the UDRP or Articles 4 and 5 of the Domain Names Interpretation are found to be present.[216]

(f) *Search navigation tools*

There are no reported cases regarding use as search navigation tools. Yet based on various courts' dealings with cases involving keywords and sponsor links, such use may constitute use for the purposes of an infringement claim if it is clearly in connection with certain goods or services or with the sale of certain goods or services and there is no defence for such use.

(g) *Hypertext links*

All reported cases involving hypertext links are based on copyright infringement or unfair competition, rather than trademark infringement. Yet based on various courts' dealings with cases involving keywords and sponsor links, the use of a trademark in hypertext links may constitute use for the purposes of an infringement claim if it is clearly in connection with certain goods or services or with the sale of certain goods or services and where there is no defence for such use.

(h) *Framing*

There are no reported cases regarding use of a trademark in framing. Again, however, based on various courts' dealings with cases involving keywords and sponsor links, such use may constitute use for the purposes of an infringement claim if it is clearly in connection with certain goods or services or with the sale of certain goods or services and there is no defence for such use.

2.3 Defences

(a) *Descriptive (non trademark) use of the mark*

Neither the Trademark Law nor its implementing regulations provide that descriptive use of a trademark is a potential defence to superficially infringing acts, but courts have confirmed the availability of such a defence.

In *ETS, USA v Beijing Haidian District New Oriental School*, ChinaLawInfo (Beijing High Court, December 27 2003), New Oriental School published TOEFL test forms in China without ETS's authorisation.[217] ETS, as the copyright owner of TOEFL test forms and registrant of the 'TOEFL' trademark in Classes 9, 16, and 41 in China, sued New Oriental School for both copyright and trademark infringement.[218] The Beijing Intermediate Court decided for ETS on both accounts and New Oriental School appealed.[219] The Beijing High Court confirmed the ruling of copyright infringement but reversed that of trademark infringement on the grounds that the use of the word 'TOEFL' on these publications was for the purpose of describing and emphasising

216 See, eg, *Zhou Libo v Hong Yishen*, ADNDRC.org, CN-1100503 (ADNDRC Beijing, December 7 2011), www.adndrc.org/cn/CaseStorage/CN-1100503/Decision/CN-1100503_Decision.pdf.

217 *ETS, USA v Beijing Haidian Dist New Oriental Sch*, ChinaLawInfo (Beijing High Court, December 27 2003).

218 *Ibid.*

219 *Ibid.*

that the content of the publications was relevant to the TOEFL test, but not to identify the source of the publications, and would not mislead or confuse readers as to the source of the publications.[220]

(b) *Comparative advertising*

Article 32 of the Standards for the Examination and Release of Medical Device Advertisements issued by the State Administration for Industry and Commerce of China provides that comparative content in advertising must not involve any specific products or services or otherwise direct form of comparison.[221] Advertising involving indirect comparison with general products or services of the same kind must be supported by a scientific basis and evidence.[222]

Therefore, this provision essentially forbids comparative advertising mentioning a competitor's trademark. In other words, comparative advertising is not available as a defence for the above acts.

(c) *Parody*

In 2001, several famous trademarks including Coca Cola and Bausch & Lomb were satirised in a popular Chinese film 'Big Shot's Funeral'. None of these famous brands filed law suits against the producer of the film, so it remains unclear which side courts would decide for. Scholars are divided as to whether parody constitutes trademark infringement, but the majority view is that it is fair use as it is not for the purpose of identifying the sources of goods or services.

For the above acts, it constitutes trademark infringement if the trademark is used to help sell similar goods or services. For well-known trademarks, trademark infringement occurs even when the goods or services are dissimilar. Therefore, when it is clear that the main purpose is to satirise rather than to sell goods or services, parody may work as a potential defence to the above acts.

2.4 Parallel imports

There is no provision in any laws or regulations of China as to whether parallel importation constitutes trademark infringement. There have been several well-known parallel importation cases in China, but almost all the relevant courts bypassed the question of whether or not parallel importation constitutes trademark infringement and instead based their rulings upon other factors.

In *Shanghai Unilever Co v Guangzhou Import & Export Trading Co*, Guangzhou Intermediate Court (case number not reported), the court decided that the defendant infringed the plaintiff's 'LUX' trademark by importing 'LUX' soap from Thailand on the grounds that the defendant had failed to prove that the 'LUX' soap was genuine.[223]

---

220 *Ibid.*

221 Standards for the Examination and Release of Medical Device Advertisements (promulgated by the Ministry of Health, the State Administration for Industry and Commerce and the State Food and Drug Administration, April 28 2009, effective May 20 2009), Article 32, translated in Westlaw China (last visited June 7 2012) (PRC).

222 *Ibid.*

223 *Shanghai Unilever Co, Ltd v Guangzhou Import & Export Trading Co,* Guangzhou Intermediate Court (case number not reported).

In *Michelin Group v Hu Yaping*, ChinaLawInfo (Changsha Intermediate Court, July 8, 2009), the court decided for the plaintiff on the grounds that the defendant, who imported Michelin tyres from Japan and sold them in China, infringed the plaintiff's Michelin trademark in that the defendant had failed to obtain a China Compulsory Product Certification ('3C Certification') for the imported tyres.[224] As a result, the defendant could not claim the defence provided in the Trademark Law, which states that a seller shall not be subject to damages if he/she does not know that the goods he/she sells infringe any trademarks, can prove that the goods were legally obtained, and can provide the information of the suppliers.[225]

In recent years, it has been very common for Chinese consumers to purchase luxury goods and cosmetics from overseas websites. Yet to date, most discussions focus on tariff evasion rather than the parallel import issue. It is probable that the main reason for this is that in a classic parallel import case, the importer imports large amount of goods and resells them in China, and the lawsuit is filed against the importer. However, in online parallel import scenarios, the majority of goods are sold to individual Chinese consumers and it seems difficult to collect evidence to establish a trademark infringement case in China.

2.5 Remedies

A trademark owner may file a complaint with a local Administration for Industry & Commerce (AIC) office. If trademark infringement is found, an AIC office can order the infringer to cease the infringing acts, confiscate and destroy infringing goods and tools used to manufacture infringing goods or trademark labels, or impose a fine. An AIC office will transfer the case for criminal prosecution if it is found that threshold sales or profits figures are met. The decisions of an AIC office are appealable to the courts.

A trademark owner can also initiate a civil lawsuit against the infringer before a court. Under Article 118 of the Civil Law, a trademark owner may request the infringer to stop infringement, eliminate influence and/or pay damages.[226] In most cases, if trademark infringement is found, the court will order the infringer to stop infringing and pay damages to the trademark owner.

There are no punitive damages for trademark infringement in China. The amount of damages will be equivalent to the infringer's financial gain from the infringement or the trademark owner's financial loss due to the infringement (including reasonable expenditure incurred to stop the infringement, but this amount usually is very limited). If it is difficult to determine either of the above amounts, a court may, at its discretion, grant damages of no more than Rmb3,000,000 to the trademark owner based on the circumstances surrounding the infringement.[227]

224 *Michelin Group v Hu Yaping*, ChinaLawInfo (Changsha Intermediate Court, July 8 2009).

225 *Ibid.*

226 Civil Law, Article 118, above note 31.

227 Trademark Law, Article 63, above note 198.

2.6 Liability of internet service providers

Internet service providers (eg, Google, YouTube, ISPs) may be held jointly liable for online trademark infringement activities, though only in limited scenarios. For example, courts are divided on the issue of whether search engine providers will also be held jointly liable in cases where an advertiser purchases a competitor's trademark as a search keyword associated with its online advertisement.[228] Nevertheless, many courts have stated that search engine providers owe only a duty to exercise reasonable care towards the owners of trademarks.

Specifically, search engine providers can be held liable only when the relevant search keyword is a well-known trademark or a mark of some renown.[229] In such circumstances, by providing keyword advertising services to an advertiser who is not the true owner of the relevant well-known trademark, search engine providers breach their duty to the true owner of the mark.

In another case involving sponsor links of a search engine, the court decided that a search engine provider assisted in the trademark infringement and was, therefore, jointly responsible when it failed to respond and take appropriate action after the rights holder submitted two complaints with supporting materials.[230]

2.7 Advertising law and regulation

The Advertising Law of the People's Republic of China ('Advertising Law') took effect in 1995 and regulates the advertising activities of three categories of entities: advertisers, advertising agencies, and advertising publishers.[231] The Advertising Law is generally considered to apply to online advertisers and advertising agencies, although in trademark infringement or unfair competition cases, plaintiffs usually base their claims upon the Trademark Law and/or the Anti-Unfair Competition Law.

Regarding advertising publishers, Article 2 of the Advertising Law defines advertising publishers as legal persons or other business entities that publish advertisements for advertisers or advertising agencies commissioned by advertisers.[232] Article 27 of the Advertising Law provides that publishers must examine supporting documents and verify the contents of advertisements and must not publish advertisements whose contents are false or insufficiently supported.[233]

Yet reported online advertising cases show that courts have been categorising relevant internet service providers as information search service providers, rather

---

228 See, eg, *Shanghai Yingmai Cultural Communication Co, Ltd v Huagaichuangyi (Beijing) Image Technology Co, Ltd,* ChinaLawInfo, (Beijing No 1 Intermediate Court, October 13, 2011); *Beijing Letao Culture Development Co, Ltd v Google (China) Information Tech Co Ltd,* ChinaLawInfo (Beijing Haidian District Court, November 24 2010); *Dazhong Transportation Group Co, Ltd v Beijing Baidu Netcom Science and Technology Co, Ltd,* ChinaLawInfo (Shanghai No 2 Intermediate Court, June 24 2007).

229 See, eg, *Babaike (Beijing) Software Technology Co, Ltd v Beijing Wolisen Information Technology Co, Ltd,* ChinaLawInfo (Beijing No 1 Intermediate Court, May 14 2010); *Dazhong Transportation Group Co, Ltd v Beijing Baidu Netcom Science and Technology Co, Ltd,* ChinaLawInfo (Shanghai No 2 Intermediate Court, May 24 2008); *Meilipiaopiao (Beijing) E-commerce Co, Ltd v Beijing Baidu Netcom Science and Technology Co, Ltd,* ChinaLawInfo (Beijing Haidian District Court, September 20 2011).

230 *Beijing Guxiang Information Technology Co, Ltd v Guangzhou Lantai Environmental Protection Technology Co, Ltd,* ChinaLawInfo (Beijing No 1 Intermediate Court, May 23 2011).

231 Advertising Law (promulgated by the Standing Comm Nat'l People's Cong, October 27 1994, effective February 1 1995), Article 2, translated in Westlaw China (last visited June 6 2012) (PRC).

232 *Ibid.*

233 *Ibid.* Article 27.

than advertising publishers.[234] Accordingly, internet service providers have only the traditional duty of reasonable care under the Civil Law when well-known or famous trademarks are involved,[235] but not the higher duty of prior examination of verification for advertising publishers.

It was reported in 2011 that the draft revision to the Advertising Law contains detailed provisions concerning online advertising, but at the time of writing it has not been passed.[236]

2.8 Domain name disputes

Complaints involving '.cn'[237] domain names and Chinese character domain names may be submitted to the domain name dispute resolution service providers appointed by the CNNIC. Currently, the only two appointed providers are the CIETAC and the HKIAC.[238]

As the CNDRP Rules provide that panels must make decisions on domain name disputes within 14 days if there are no special circumstances, the whole procedure will usually take no longer than 60 days from the filing of the complaint.[239]

The basic official fee for deciding a dispute involving one domain name is Rmb8,000 for a panel comprising of one panelist, and Rmb14,000 for a panel comprising of three panelists.[240]

Overall, this procedure is much more efficient and cheaper compared to court proceedings.

2.9 Unfair competition/passing off

A claim for unfair competition/passing off can provide protection over and above the protection rendered by registered trademarks if the prior rights upon which the unfair competition/passing off claim is based upon is sufficient to invalidate the registered trademarks under the Trademark Law.

(a) Cancellation of registered trademarks on the basis of prior rights: prior unregistered trademarks, copyrights, design patents, trade names, etc

The second paragraph of Article 13 of the Trademark Law provides that an application for a trademark shall not be approved for registration and the use thereof should be prohibited if the trademark is a copy, imitation or translation of another party's unregistered well-known trademark with respect to identical or similar goods in China and such use would be likely to cause confusion.[241]

---

234 *Meilipiaopiao (Beijing) E-commerce Co, Ltd v Beijing Baidu Netcom Sci and Tech Co, Ltd,* ChinaLawInfo (Beijing Haidian District Court, September 20 2011).

235 See above note 233 and accompanying text.

236 *Gong shang zong ju yi xing cheng guang gao fa xiu ding gao bing bao song guo wu yuan fa zhi ban* [Revision to the Advertising Law Drafted by the State Administration for Industry and Commerce has been Submitted to the Legal Affairs Office of the State Council], Xinhua News Agency (2011), www.gov.cn/jrzg/2011-05/17/content_1865736.htm.

237 The country code top-level domain (ccTLD) for mainland China.

238 See above Part 2.2(e).

239 CNDRP Rules, above note 207, Article 37.

240 CNNIC, *Zhong wen yu ming cheng xu fei yong biao* [Chinese Domain Name Process Fee Schedule], http://dndrc.cietac.org/static/cnddr/prodfee.html (last visited November 15 2013).

241 Trademark Law, above note 198, Article 13.

Article 32 of the Trademark Law stipulates that trademark applications shall not infringe upon another party's existing prior rights.[242] Applicants must not unfairly preemptively register a trademark which has been used by another party and which has acquired a certain reputation.[243]

Under Article 45 of the Trademark Law, the owner of a prior trademark or any interested party may request the China Trademark Review and Adjudication Board (TRAB) to invalidate registered trademarks which violate Articles 13 and 32.[244]

The 'existing prior rights' provided in Article 32 are generally interpreted as covering prior copyrights, design patents, trade names and so on. A claim for infringement of unregistered trademarks (including the first paragraph of Article 13 and the second sentence of Article 32) or trade names would generally be supported when the goods or services are similar, although this is not specifically stated in Article 32. A claim for copyright or design patent infringement could cover dissimilar goods or services.

(b) *Unfair competition/passing off*

Article 5 of the Anti-Unfair Competition Law provides, among other things, that a business entity must not use a name, packaging or decoration identical or similar to the particular name, packaging, or decoration of a famous good without authorisation, thus resulting in confusion of the source of the goods among buyers; nor may it use another party's trade name or personal name without authorisation, and resulting in confusion of the source of the goods among buyers.[245]

Accordingly, together with Article 13 of the Trademark Law, which provides that use of an unregistered well-known trademark with respect to identical or similar goods should be prohibited,[246] Article 5 of the Anti-Unfair Competition Law essentially provides protection for unregistered trademarks on the basis of unfair competition/passing off.

Therefore, the owner of a registered trademark, by registering and using the trademark, may infringe upon an unregistered trademark under the Trademark Law and the Anti-Unfair Competition Law. In this sense, a claim for unfair competition/passing off can provide protection over and above the protection available via registered trademarks.

3. Patents

3.1 Patentability of 'internet' inventions

The rapid development of the Internet has brought about a wave of internet-related patent applications, which are mostly software or business model-related. Such applications may not necessarily be patentable in the perspective of the traditional concept of patentable subject matters under the Patent Law, as this does not protect pure computer software or pure business models.

---

242 *Ibid.* Article 32.

243 *Ibid.*

244 *Ibid.* Article 41.

245 Anti-Unfair Competition Law, above note 30, Article 5.

246 Trademark Law, above note 198, Article 13.

(a) Computer programs and software-related inventions

Protection under the Chinese Patent Law and the Chinese Copyright Law: Computer software refers to computer programs (including source code and object code) and their related documents.[247] Under the current Chinese intellectual property protection system, a piece of computer software can be protected by both a copyright and a patent right. A copyright protects a computer program's 'external' form, or how the program is organised and coded, while a patent right provides protection for the technical solutions involved in a computer program.

Under copyright protection, if a third party modifies or recodes the source code of a computer program but retains the original program functions, the modified/recoded program may not necessarily infringe the copyright of the original program. Fortunately, a patent right on computer software (if applicable) facilitates the protection of the software functions that usually represent the core value of a piece of software and entitles the owner to the exclusive right of exploitation.

Furthermore, among other advantages, an inventor of a computer program is allowed to file a patent application so long as he/she has a practical idea of the innovation in mind. A copyright, on the other hand, would be established only after a piece of the computer program is completely finished.

Patentable subject matter of computer program-related inventions: The general standard for testing patentability of computer program-related subject matter can be summarised as: technical problems; technical means; and technical effects.

Specifically, if a computer program-related patent application involves the execution of computer programs in order to solve technical problems, reflects technical means in conformity with the laws of nature by computers running programs to control and process external or internal objects, and thus obtains technical effects in conformity with the laws of nature, such a solution is subject to patent protection. Such control or process of external objects includes the control of certain external operating processes or external operating devices, the process or exchange of external data etc. This control or process of internal objects includes the improvement of the internal performance of computer systems, the management of internal resources of computer systems, the improvement of data transmission etc.[248]

For instance, computer-implemented solutions aimed at controlling an industrial or measurement process, dealing with a computer's external technical data or improving a computer's internal performance are patentable.

Internet-based companies put emphasis on patent protection: Internet-based companies operating on the same online platform may have a relatively similar

247 See Computer Software Protection Regulations (promulgated by the State Council, December 20 2001, effective January 1 2002; and amended on January 3 2013), Article 2, translated in Westlaw China (last visited November 18 2013) (PRC).

248 See Guidelines for Patent Examination (promulgated by the State Intellectual Property Office, May 24 2006, effective July 1 2006), Part 2, Chapter 9, Section 2 (revised February 1 2010 and September 16 2013), translated in sipo.gov.cn (last visited November 18 2013) (PRC) [hereinafter 'Guidelines'].

business focus, such as instant messaging, search engines, virtual communities, and so on. Internet businesses concentrating on these particular services create intense competition among internet-based companies. In order to gain a better position amid market competition, internet-based companies have used the patent system to protect their competitive advantages.

With a better understanding of the Chinese patent system, Chinese internet-based companies have filed a large number of patent applications mainly involving data processing and communication performance improvements.[249] Some of the applications have been granted, and this has helped the applicants to protect their core businesses more effectively.

One of the top Chinese internet-based companies, Tencent, has filed more than 8,000 patent applications, most of which are invention patent applications with a great portion focusing on Tencent's key service, instant messaging. Until June 2012, over 1,400 of Tencent's patents were granted. Tencent is now planning an increase of its PCT patent applications to extend its business to markets outside of China.[250]

However, foreign internet-based companies, such as Google, may find that they need more time to adapt to the Chinese patent system. Among Google's 566 Chinese patent applications, only 147 have been granted, while most of the other applications are still pending. Of the pending applications, some titles indicate they may be business model applications, which are generally not allowed under the current Chinese patent system.[251]

(b) *Patentability of business models*

China has maintained a cautious approach towards granting business model patents, but may make adaptations with new developments.

Statistical data of business model patents:[252] The definition of a business model may vary in different jurisdictions. The description of a business model widely accepted in China is a method or rule created by human intelligence for handling matters or solving problems in commercial or economic activities. Generally, business model patent applications involve solutions for data processing systems or methods applied to the commercial, financial, administrative, managing, auditing, and forecasting fields.

Based on statistics provided by the China State Intellectual Property Office (SIPO), up to September 2008, SIPO had received approximately 10,000 patent applications regarding the subject of business models. During the past 15 years, the number of business model patent applications has increased annually and experienced a surge from 2000 to 2006. The number of applications from domestic

---

249 Statistics available at the China State Intellectual Property Office's website http://english.sipo.gov.cn/statistics.

250 See Teng xun: *yong zhi shi chan quan wei qi ye chuagn zao jia zhi*, China Intellectual Property News (2013), http://www.iprlawyers.com/ipr_Html/33_08/2013-4/23/20130423110803719.html.

251 Patent search database available at the China State Intellectual Property Office's website http://www.pss-system.gov.cn/sipopublicsearch/search/searchHomeIndex.shtml.

252 Statistics reports available at the China State Intellectual Property Office's website www.sipo.gov.cn/ztzl/ywzt/zlsd/200812/t20081204_428899.html.

companies was almost equivalent to the total number of applicants from beyond mainland China. The top five countries and areas included mainland China, Japan, the United States, Taiwan, and Korea. The applications focused on the fields of 'administration and management', 'commercial area', and 'for particular operating divisions (eg, health care, tourism and legal service)'. However, the granting rate of business model patent applications was only about 15%.

Divergence on business model patentability: The businesses of Internet-based companies usually combine business models with software applications, which means software-related technologies may be involved in and make contributions to their business models. Theoretically, such a combination gives the new business models a good prospect of being granted patent rights in China in view of the patentability test standard (ie, technical problems; technical means; and technical effects as noted above).

With the further development of technologies, it is to be hoped that a trend will emerge which relaxes the requirements for granting patent rights to business models. To prepare for such a potential opportunity, internet-based companies have been filing many patent applications related to business models so that these applications may be granted as soon as the patentability requirements are changed in their favour.

One common mistake Chinese companies often make is that since the Patent Law currently does not protect pure computer software and business models *per se*, especially for internet-related business models, such companies operating in the internet realm simply assume that this also applies for the rest of the world. As a result, many such business model patents have been filed by foreign companies, especially in the United States, and Chinese companies only later find that they are to be sued for alleged infringement upon patents that they could themselves originally have filed.

Such differences on patentable subject matters significantly impact on Chinese companies whose businesses focus on online software or internet applications. Recent patent infringement cases in foreign courts against such Chinese internet service providers, especially online game companies, illustrate this effect. Chinese internet service providers, knowing that software/business models were not eligible for patentability in China, were not aware that they could be protected however by patent rights in certain foreign countries, especially the United States. As a result, their online services over the Internet are then vulnerable to patent infringement claims by foreign patent owners.

(c) Mathematical methods

Under the Patent Law, rules and methods for mental activities are excluded from patentability. Therefore, a pure mathematical method, which is carried out by numbers and provides a result in numerical form (the mathematical method or algorithm therefore being merely an abstract concept prescribing how to operate on the numbers) and thus is usually considered as one type of rule or method for mental activities, will not be patentable under the Patent Law. Typical mathematical methods, such as shortcut arithmetic methods and relevant formulae, mathematical theories and methods for conversion, methods of statistics, accounting or bookkeeping and the like are specifically listed in the Guidelines for Chinese Patent Examination as examples of subject matters that are not patentable.[253]

However, if mathematical methods are used as part of an invention, especially in cases where they are used to calculate/simulate certain physical quantities for solving specific technical problems, this may change the situation. One example is an invention concerning a mathematical method for manipulating data representing an image, leading to an enhanced digital image. Claims to a method of digitally filtering data performed on a conventional general-purpose computer will be rejected, as those claims are held to define an abstract concept undistinguishable from a mathematical method. However, claims to a method of image processing that uses a mathematical method to operate on numbers representing an image can be allowed. The reasoning is that the image processing performed is a technical (ie, non-excluded) process that is related to the technical quality of the image, and a claim directed to a technical process in which the method used does not seek protection for the mathematical method as such. Therefore, the allowable claims go beyond a mathematical method.

In summary, the general patentability tests for an invention related to a mathematical method are similar to a computer program-related patent application. That is, if the invention related to a mathematical method involves the execution of a mathematical method to solve technical problems, reflects technical means, and thus obtains technical effects, such a solution will be subject to patent protection.

(d) Presentation of information

The Patent Law does not state directly whether or not the presentation of information is a patentable subject matter. However, if the representation of information is solely by the content of the information, it may not be patentable as this does not relate to a technical solution, which is defined as an aggregation of technical means applying the laws of nature to solve a technical problem.[254] Obviously, the presentation of information solely by the content of information itself (eg, acoustic signals, optical signals, electrical signals, etc) does not adopt any technical means to solve a technical problem, does not achieve any technical effect in compliance with the laws of nature, and thus does not constitute a patentable technical solution.

If, however, the presentation of information has new technical features, there could be patentable subject matter in the information carrier or in the process or apparatus for presenting the information. The arrangement or manner of representation, as distinct from the information content, may well constitute a patentable technical feature. Examples of where such a technical feature may be present include a telegraph apparatus or communication system using a particular code to represent the characters (eg, pulse code modulation); a measuring instrument

253 Guidelines, above note 248, Part 2, Chapter 1, Section 4.2.

254 Patent Law (promulgated by the Standing Comm Nat'l People's Cong, March 12 1984, effective April 1 1985), Article 2 (amended December 27 2008), translated in Westlaw China (last visited November 18 2013) (PRC).

designed to produce a particular form of graph for representing the measured information; a gramophone record having a particular groove form to allow stereo recordings, etc.

3.2 Bioinformatics

A DNA sequence or protein found in nature and existing in its natural state is merely a discovery and thus falls under 'scientific discoveries', which is unpatentable under the Patent Law.[255]

However, a gene, a DNA fragment, or a protein per se and the process for obtaining these will be subject to patent protection if it is isolated or extracted for the first time from nature using technical means if its sequence is unknown in the prior art and can be definitely characterised, and if it can be exploited industrially.[256]

Therefore, if a novel DNA sequence or protein structure is discovered through the use of bioinformatics (which uses computer tools to store, search, and analyse related bio-information to obtain the DNA sequence or protein structure), it is not a 'scientific discovery' and thus is patentable under the Patent Law. In fact, there are thousands of Chinese-granted patents relating to novel DNA sequences or protein structures which were discovered through the use of bioinformatics methods (eg, gene identification, analysis of gene expression, prediction of protein structure, etc).

3.3 Issues specific to China

(a) Infringement on the Internet

Under the Patent Law, if an entity or an individual exploits an invention/utility model patent without authorisation from a patentee (ie, it makes, uses, offers to sell, sells or imports the patented product, or uses the patented process, and uses, offers to sell, sells or imports the product directly obtained by the patented process), for production or business purposes, such act will constitute an infringement of the Chinese invention/utility model patent. Similarly, if without authorisation from a patentee, an entity or an individual exploits a design patent (ie, it makes, offers to sell, sells or imports the product incorporating the patented design), for production or business, such act shall constitute an infringement of the Chinese invention/utility model patent.[257]

Therefore, in the event that any one of the above acts takes place, then regardless of whether or not it is committed via the Internet, it will constitute patent infringement and Chinese courts will have jurisdiction over such an infringement. For example, if an online system that infringes another's patent is provided on the Internet for business use without the patentee's authorisation, the provider of such an online system may be sued for patent infringement in China. Moreover, there are many products offered for sale and sold through online virtual transaction platforms or e-commerce websites. If the products posted for sale and targeted at Chinese

255 Guidelines, above note 233, Part 2, Chapter 10, Section 9.1.2.2.
256 *Ibid.*
257 Patent Law, above note 239, at Article 11.

customers on the virtual transaction platforms infringe other's Chinese patents, the seller of the products can be sued for patent infringement. Where the posted products are manufactured in China, then the manufacturer can also be sued.

However, this may not apply to online virtual transaction platform providers such as Eachnet (a joint venture with eBay in China), Alibaba, and Taobao. These entities allow sellers and buyers to engage in virtual sales transactions through online channels and to show and review products, negotiate prices, make orders, and eventually confirm delivery entirely by online services without the need for physical shops or traditional cash/check payment processes. Chinese courts have generally taken the view that online virtual transaction platform providers are not liable if they only provide technical services rather than actively participating in providing infringing products. In the case of *Liu Yanfeng v Yuyao Shuangjian Electrical Appliance Co*, ChinaLawInfo (Hangzhou Intermediate Court, August 29 2006), Alibaba was alleged to have helped sell products infringing certain patents, but the court held that Alibaba, as an internet service provider, was not capable of reviewing all the information on its website and that such information was not uploaded by Alibaba but by its registered members.[258] The court further held that since it was not obvious to determine that the alleged products were infringing products and patent infringement analysis would have required special technical knowledge and skills, Alibaba should not have the duty to do so.[259]

Although network service providers, including online virtual transaction platform providers such as Alibaba in the above case, may not be liable for patent infringement if they only provide technical services rather than actively participating in providing infringing products, the patentee is entitled to notify the network service provider of patent infringing acts committed on his/her network service by a network user. The network service provider will be expected to take necessary measures such as deletion, blocking or disconnection of the infringing information/products from its website. If, following receipt of such notification, the network service provider fails to take necessary measures in a timely manner, it shall be jointly and severally liable for the infringement of the network user.[260]

(b) *Process patents*

It is usually difficult to assert direct infringement on a process patent in the event that only a part of the process is carried out in China via the Internet while other parts of the process are carried out outside China, since not all of the technical features of the process patent claim are covered by the act in China. However, there is a possibility to assert indirect infringement.

Although China has not provided formal laws or judicial interpretations to define what constitutes indirect patent infringement, the concept has been acknowledged in Chinese judicial practice according to the general legal provisions on contributory infringement under Chinese Civil Code. There, it is prescribed that

---

258 *Liu Yanfeng v Yuyao Shuangjian Elec Appliance Co, Ltd*, ChinaLawInfo (Hangzhou Intermediate Court, August 29 2006).

259 *Ibid.*

260 Tort Law, above note 5, Article 36.

if two or more persons jointly infringe upon another person's rights and cause damages, they shall bear joint liability, and that a person who instigates or assists others to perform an infringing act will be deemed to be a co-infringer and will face civil liabilities jointly and severally.[261] The *Notice of the Beijing High People's Court on Implementing Opinions on Issues Concerning Patent Infringement Judgment* ('Beijing High People's Court Opinion') had given a detailed standard defining indirect infringement as an act where one intentionally induces or aids and abets others to exploit another person's patent, thus resulting in an act of direct infringement, in which the actor has the subjective intention to induce or aid and abet others to infringe another person's patent right, and objectively creates the necessary conditions for another person's act of direct infringement to take place.[262] The Beijing High People's Court Opinion, however, was replaced by Guidelines for Determination of Patent Infringement newly issued by the Beijing High Court on September 4 2013. This adopts the term of 'contributory infringement' and defines it as an act where two or more persons jointly engage in conduct amounting to patent infringement, or two or more persons work and coordinate with each other jointly to engage in conduct amounting to patent infringement. Such conduct will constitute contributory infringement, and the person who abets or helps others to commit patent infringement will be deemed a contributory infringer with the doer. It further provides several particular examples of contributory infringement: where a product infringing patent right is used as a component to manufacture another product and then put on sale, if the alleged infringers work in cooperation with an element of division of labour, such conduct constitutes contributory infringement; where a party offers, sells or imports materials, special equipment or parts solely for exploiting another's product patent, or offers, sells or imports materials, components or special equipment solely for exploiting another's method patent, this person's conduct constitutes contributory infringement together with the implementing party who exploits another's product patent or method patent; and where one offers a place, warehouse, transportation or other favourable conditions for others to commit patent infringement, such conduct constitutes contributory infringement together with the implementing party.[263] Although the Guidelines for Determination of Patent Infringement are theoretically applicable only in Beijing, many other local courts refer to them in patent trials.

In some specific cases, if the part of a process carried out in China via the Internet produces an intermediate product (which may be a virtual device) specially designed for carrying out the patented process without any other use, and thus the accused

261 See Civil Law, above note 31, Article 132; see also Opinions of the Supreme People's Court on Certain Issues Concerning the Implementation of the "General Principles of the Civil Law of the People's Republic of China" (Trial) (promulgated by the Sup People's Court, January 1 1988, effective January 1 1988), Article 148, translated in Westlaw China (last visited November 18 2013) (PRC).

262 Notice of the Beijing High People's Court on Implementing Opinions on Issues Concerning Patent Infringement Judgment (Trial) (promulgated by the Mun People's Gov't Beijing, September 29 2001, effective September 29 2001, and abolished September 4 2013), Article 73, translated in Westlaw China (last visited November 18 2013) (PRC).

263 Guidelines for Determination of Patent Infringement issued by the Beijing High Court (issued by the Beijing People's High Court, September 4 2013, effective the same day), Articles 105 to 109 (last visited November 18 2013) (PRC).

party has the intention to induce or aid and abet others to exploit the patented process and objectively creates the necessary conditions for direct infringement, it is possible successfully to claim indirect infringement against the accused party, depending on the actual situation.

In practice, however, there have rarely been reported cases supporting indirect infringement, especially for process patent infringement via the Internet.

3.4 Remedies available for patent infringement

China provides both judicial and administrative channels for patent enforcement against infringers.

Administrative and judicial actions provide different remedies and follow different procedures. For instance, administrative actions may be suitable for swift results in some cases but they do not afford a patentee recovery of damages and in most situations, they may be appealed to the judicial system for review. On the other hand, judicial actions may take longer to pursue, but damages may be recovered. Most importantly, judicial actions may provide for the award of a preliminary injunction, which can be essential for an IP holder in many circumstances.

Furthermore, unlike some Western legal systems where a patentee may need to exhaust one approach before taking on another, administrative and judicial systems in China may be taken independently or may interact with each other in most cases. Therefore, a patentee should carefully analyse both systems in order to maximise the chances of prevailing in an administrative action or a judicial action, or both. The administrative and judicial systems discussed below are among those that may be of particular interest when fighting patent infringement.

(a) Administrative disputes at local intellectual property offices

The Patent Law provides an administrative dispute channel at any one of the local intellectual property offices (IPO).[264] A patentee or any interested party may request the local IPO to handle patent dispute matters.[265] Measures that the local IPO may take include ordering an infringer to stop infringing acts and to make a public apology.[266] Also, at the request of the disputing parties, the local IPO may mediate between the parties to reach an amount agreed by all the parties regarding compensation for the damage caused by the infringing act.[267]

(b) Customs protection and raids against patent infringement

Customs protection is also a form of administrative protection available for patentees in China.[268] Unlike many other countries, Chinese Customs has jurisdiction over not only the importation but also the exportation of products suspected of infringing Chinese patents. When a patentee finds suspected infringing goods that are about to

264 Patent Law, Article 60, above note 254.

265 *Ibid.*

266 *Ibid.*

267 *Ibid.*

268 Regulations on Customs Protection of Intellectual Property Rights (promulgated by the St Council, March 24 2010, effective April 1 2010), Article 2 translated in Westlaw China (last visited November 18 2013) (PRC).

be imported or exported, he/she may file an application to the Chinese Customs at the particular place of entry or exit for detainment of such goods. Additionally, if a patent is recorded before the General Administration of Customs of China (GAC), the Customs office may exercise ex officio control over exported and imported products and, at the request of the patentee, detain the suspected patent infringing product.

(c) Judicial channel for patent disputes

In order to curtail rampant patent infringement, the Chinese government has designated many municipal intermediate courts, all provincial or autonomous municipality high courts, as well as the People's Supreme Court to handle patent infringement suits. China uses a two-instance trial system. For patent litigation this will normally be concluded within six months for the first instance trial and three months for appeal. A patent infringement suit in court may be stayed if the alleged infringer or any third party files a request for patent invalidation proceedings before the China Patent Re-examination Board (PRB). If the patent at issue is a Chinese invention patent, the chances are good that the court may not stay the suit.[269] However, the court is likely to stay the suit if the patent at issue is a utility model or design patent, due to the fact that neither patent types are substantively examined by the SIPO.[270]

With the above in mind, the patentee may pursue the following judicial remedies:

Preliminary injunction and evidence preservation: The Patent Law states:

> *"[w]here a patentee or any interested party having evidence to prove that another person is infringing or will soon infringe its or his patent right and that if such infringing act is not checked or prevented from occurring in time, it is likely to cause irreparable harm to it or him, it or he may, before any legal proceedings are instituted, request the people's court to adopt measures for ordering the suspension of relevant acts and the preservation of property."*[271]

Furthermore, in circumstances where evidence could be lost or will be difficult to obtain later, a patentee may apply to a people's court for evidence preservation before initiating legal proceedings.[272] Such evidence preservation can be filed simultaneously when filing for a preliminary injunction, or can be filed separately without filing a preliminary injunction request.

Order for stopping infringement: Under the Patent Law, a people's court has the power to order the cessation of infringing acts at any time during a patent litigation proceeding: before, during, or after the trial. When issued before the trial, it is typically referred to as a preliminary injunction.

---

269 Certain Provisions of the Supreme People's Court on Issues Concerning Application of Law in Trying Cases Involving Patent Disputes (promulgated by the Sup People's Court, June 22 2001, effective July 1 2001), Article 11, translated in Westlaw China (last visited November 18 2013) (PRC).

270 *Ibid.* Article 9.

271 Patent Law, Article 66, above note 254.

272 *Ibid.* Article 67.

Order to pay actual damages – no punitive damages available in China: The Chinese legal system is compensatory rather than punitive in nature. Therefore, no punitive damages or excessive consequential damages are allowed. Under Chinese law, there are several methods to estimate the amount of compensation for a patent infringement suit. These may be summarised as follows:[273]

- loss suffered by the patent owner; or
- profit earned by the infringer; or
- multiples of reasonable royalty under similar situations; or
- when all of the above calculations are not possible, a maximum statutory damage of Rmb1,000,000 (US$154,000) may be awarded.

Unlike some Western legal systems, obtaining large damages awards, or even reasonable awards, in Chinese courts is generally difficult. Therefore, when litigating in China, it is important to remember that the ultimate goal may not necessarily be to seek large damages awards, but rather to secure injunctive relief to put a stop to infringing acts.

4. Disclosure orders against internet service providers

Given the fact that internet violators normally infringe IP owners' copyright, China provides strong measures against copyright infringers. Such remedies may or may not be available for patent and trademark cases.

4.1 Availability

In China, ISPs have legal obligations to submit their client registration information if a copyright administrative agency requests such information to track down a suspected infringer.

Under Article 13 of the Dissemination Regulations, a copyright administrative agency can request an ISP to provide its client's name, contact information, web address etc for the purpose of tracking down infringement of the 'right to internet dissemination'.[274] Under Article 25 of the Regulations, the agency must serve a warning on the ISP if the ISP refuses to provide the suspected infringing client's name, contact information, web address, etc.[275] Depending on the seriousness of the event, the agency can even confiscate the computer equipment used for providing internet services.[276]

The Supreme People's Court once expanded this right to request client information from ISPs to include copyright owners in the Old Interpretation[277] and ISPs frequently satisfied such requests from an alleged copyright owner provided that the owner presented solid information to support their claim(s).[278] However, this provision has been removed from the Interpretation. Although it remains unclear whether copyright owners can still request an ISP to provide such information, given

273 *Ibid.* Article 65.
274 See Dissemination Regulations, above note 4, Article 13.
275 See *Ibid,* Article 25.
276 *Ibid.*
277 See Old Interpretation, above note 3, Article 5.
278 See eg, *Zhiqian (Beijing) Fin Consulting Co Ltd v Zhejiang Taobao Network Co Ltd,* ChinaLawInfo (Beijing No 1 Intermediate People's Court, June 10 2011).

the fact that the Standing Committee of the National People's Congress of China recently promulgated the Decision on Strengthening Network Information Protection[279] and that the Ministry of Industry and Information Technology subsequently promulgated the Provisions on Protecting the Personal Information of Telecommunications and Internet Users,[280] it is likely that ISPs may be ordered only by government agencies or courts to disclose such information.

Although the Dissemination Regulations provide that ISPs have legal obligations to submit their client registration information for copyright infringement, there is no Chinese law, regulation or judicial interpretation that specifies that this is also applicable to patent or trademark infringement. However, in practice, if an ISP is required by a governing administrative authority (eg, a local patent office, a trademark office or by a court in an infringement investigation and evidence collection), the ISP will be responsible for providing information relating to the requested potential infringer, as they will have to comply with the administrative authority or the court's orders regarding evidence production in the infringement investigation and evidence collection procedure.[281]

Because copyright law, regulation and interpretation provide a complete picture (albeit not identical to that of patent's and trademarks) of the Chinese system in relation to the disclosure issue, this section will focus on the field of copyright.

4.2 Requirements

As noted above, under current practice copyright owners may not be able directly to request ISPs to disclose information of suspected infringers. Rather, it is likely that they would have to resort to copyright administrative agencies or courts to issue orders to request such information. The copyright owner will be required to produce his/her own identification, proof of his/her copyright ownership, and proof of the infringement by the suspected infringer.

4.3 Jurisdictional issues

As disclosure orders are issued to ISPs, the copyright administrative agency or the court where the ISP is located is likely to have jurisdiction.

---

279 Decision on Strengthening Network Information Protection (promulgated by the Standing Comm Nat'l People's Cong, December 28 2012, effective December 28 2012), translated in Westlaw China (last visited November 15 2013) (PRC).

280 Provisions on Protecting the Personal Information of Telecommunications and Internet Users (promulgated by the Ministry of Indus and Info Tech, July 16 2013, effective September 1 2013), translated in Westlaw China (last visited November 15 2013) (PRC).

281 See Measures for the Enforcement of the Patent Administrative Law (promulgated by the State Intellectual Prop. Office, December 29 2010, effective February 1 2011), Article 35, translated in Westlaw China (last visited June 7 2012) (PRC); see also Interpretation of Supreme People's Court on Issues Concerning the Application of Law in Pre-Litigation Cessation of Infringement of the Exclusive Right to Use a Registered Trademark and Evidence Preservation (promulgated by the Supreme People's Court, January 9 2002, effective January 22 2002), Articles 2 to 4, translated in Westlaw China (last visited June 7 2012) (PRC); Civil Procedure Law (promulgated by the Standing Comm. Nat'l People's Cong, October 28 2007, effective April 1 2008), Articles 64, 74, translated in Westlaw China (last visited June 1 2012) (PRC); *Zui gao Renmin fa yuan guan yu min shi su song zheng ju de ruo gan gui ding* [Several Provisions of the Supreme People's Court on the Evidence for Civil Actions] (promulgated by the Supreme People's Court, December 21 2001, effective April 1 2002), Article 17, Court.gov.cn (last visited June 7 2012) (PRC).

4.4 'John Doe' injunctions

In China, 'John Doe' cannot be sued as a defendant because of the requirements for service; therefore, 'John Doe' injunctions are not available in China. Under Article 108(2) of the Civil Procedure Law, when a lawsuit is brought, defendants must be identified.[282]

Alternatively, in China, ISPs must cease the identified infringements upon proper warning by the copyright owner, while the infringers remain anonymous.

Under Article 14 of the Dissemination Regulations, a copyright owner can ask an ISP to delete the alleged infringing works or to break the link to the works provided he/she satisfies the requirements for requests.[283] Then, under Article 15, the ISP must remove the works or cut the link to the works immediately and notify the alleged infringing client.[284] Under Articles 16 and 17, if the alleged infringing client submits evidence of non-infringement along with other credentials, then the ISP must restore the deleted works or the broken link to the works.[285]

---

282 See Civil Procedure Law, above note 267, Article 108(2).
283 See Dissemination Regulations, above note 4, Article 14.
284 See *Ibid*, Article 15.
285 See *Ibid*, Articles 16 and 17.

France

Alexandra Néri
Herbert Smith Freehills Paris LLP

1. Copyright, related rights and database rights

1.1 Overview

French copyright law protects any work, based on the fact of its creation alone, provided the work is both original (in the sense that 'it is its author's own intellectual creation', according to the European Court of Justice in *Infopaq*[1]) and expressed in a certain form.

Parts of a work are also protected by copyright, as they share the originality of the work as a whole and contain elements which are the expression of the intellectual creation of the author of the work (*Infopaq*, §38-39).

These criteria also apply to content on the Internet.

As regards software, Article L112-2 of the French Intellectual Property Code (FIPC) lists 'software including the preparatory design material' among the works protected by copyright.

The typographical arrangement of a published edition, as well as the look and feel of a graphical user interface, can also be considered as works protected by copyright.

Under French law, compilations may enjoy copyright protection if the work at issue is an original presentation and arrangement of the information used by the author, even if this information is not protected by copyright in itself. On the other hand, 'sweat of the brow' compilations cannot apply for copyright protection since a mere collection of information is not considered as original, no matter how much work was performed in making the compilation.

French law acknowledges the copyright protection of computer-generated works, provided these works are detached from the software that has contributed to their creation and that the customary prerequisites for copyright protection are fulfilled.

Films, sound recordings and broadcasts are protected under related rights that are divided into three main categories: performers' rights; producers' rights; and the rights of audio-visual communications companies.

Databases, defined as a 'collection of independent works, data or other materials, arranged in a systematic or methodical way, and capable of being individually assessed by electronic or other means' (Article L112-3, §2 FIPC), can be protected both by copyright and by the *sui generis* right of database producers.

The *sui generis* protection results from implementation of Directive 96/9/CE on the legal protection of databases into French law (Articles L341-1 et seq FIPC). The

1 European Court of Justice, July 16 2009, case C-5/08, § 39.

sole criterion for protection is that a substantial investment be made in obtaining, verifying or presenting the content of a database; the courts assess this criterion on a case-by-case basis, taking into consideration the deployment of financial, technical and human resources by the database producer, its commercial and promotional efforts etc.[2] This protection can cover a website (eg, an online database of real estate advertisements from individuals[3]) provided the conditions above are fulfilled. The ECJ has ruled that the rights-holder of sports data protected by database rights can enforce their rights in the 'intended target' country where the sports data is received on the Internet regardless of where the server using those rights is located, and that a company which repackages the sports data can, therefore, be deemed to make the data 'available to the public' by sending it to internet betting websites.[4]

1.2 Infringing acts

Under French law, any act coming within the exclusive rights held by the copyright holder and committed by a person other than the copyright holder without authorisation is regarded as an infringement.

Pursuant to Article L122-4 FIPC, any complete or partial performance or reproduction, as well as any translation, adaptation or transformation, arrangement or reproduction using any technique or process whatsoever carried out without the consent of the copyright holder is unlawful. Moreover, a copyright infringement constitutes a criminal offence (Article L335-2, L335-3 FIPC).

On the Internet, infringing acts may include uploading (communicating a work to the public) or downloading from an illicit source. The digital scanning of works is also considered by French case law as a reproduction that requires the copyright owner's authorisation.[5]

French lawmakers, concerned at the intensification of internet piracy via peer-to-peer software, have inserted a provision into the FIPC – Article L335-2-1 penalises any person who knowingly edits a software programme, or provides or discloses it to the public in any form whatsoever, where such software is clearly intended to make copyrighted works available to the public without the right holder's authorisation, as well as any person who knowingly encourages use of such software through advertising or other means.[6]

This rule is part of a general tendency to take into consideration the difficulties of effectively enforcing copyrights over unidentified individuals who may be infringing them and to give preference to 'secondary copyright liability', which is borne by other parties benefiting from an infringement and who are in a position to control or restrain it.

---

2 Paris *tribunal de grande instance* (TGI – or court of first instance), January 26 2012. The court refused *sui generis* protection to an online database of real estate ads and did not consider the company – editor of the website – as a database producer because of the lack of proof of the substantial investment.

3 Paris TGI, November 14 2001, *Editions Néressis v France Télécom Multimédia Services*.

4 ECJ, October 18 2012.

5 Paris TGI, December 18 2009, *Editions de Seuil v Google* concerning Google Books Search.

6 French Supreme Court, criminal chamber, September 25 2012, No 11-84.224: the French Supreme Court is, for the first time, applying Article L335-2-1 FIPC, to punish Radioblog for providing software applications intended to be used for infringing copyright.

1.3 Test for copyright infringement

Traditionally, the French approach was to consider a reproduction of any part of any copyright-protected original intellectual work as an infringement.

However, European case law (*Infopaq*, mentioned above) has made French courts review their position. Henceforth, to be an infringement an unauthorised reproduction must concern a part of the work that 'contains an element of the work which, as such, expresses the author's own intellectual creation',[7] in other words, that is original in itself.[8]

Under the influence of the aforesaid case law, repeated copying of non-substantial parts of a copyrighted work may also be considered as infringing since 'the cumulative effect of those extracts may lead to the reconstitution of lengthy fragments which are liable to reflect the originality of the work in question'.[9]

1.4 Exemptions/defences to copyright infringement

An exhaustive list of defences to copyright infringement is set out in Article L122-5 FIPC.

These exemptions comprise in particular the family circle defence for private performances carried out free of charge and exclusively within a family circle; the parody defence; the educational exception; the library and archives exemption that allows works to be reproduced for conservation purposes (format shifting), or in order to preserve the conditions of on-site consultation in libraries open to the public, provided there is no economic or commercial purpose; the short quotation defence, provided that the analyses and short quotations at issue are justified by the critical, polemical, educational, scientific or informational nature of the work in which they are incorporated.

French copyright law provides also for a private copying defence that covers copies or reproductions reserved strictly for the private use of the copier. As this exemption is applicable to all formats, including digital, a copyright levy is charged on purchases of recordable media that are used for private individual copying. The private copying defence presumes the copy is made from a lawful source, and therefore does not apply to downloading an infringing work.

Temporary technology-dictated copies as part of technical processes and that are intended to enable the lawful use of a work or its transmission over a network are also exempt, along with back-up copies of software (paragraph II of Article L122-6-1 FIPC) and acts necessary to access the contents of an electronic database for the purposes of and within the limits of the use of that database as set out in a contract.

French law allows press reviews and speeches intended for the public to be published in the press or broadcast, as well as used in public political meetings and at official ceremonies. As for reporting on current events, this exemption concerns only graphic, artistic and architectural works that can be freely reproduced or

---

7 EU Court of Justice, July 16 2009, case C-5/08, *Infopaq*, § 38.
8 Paris TGI, June 8 2010, *Claude Aguttes v Artprice*.
9 EU Court of Justice, July 16 2009, case C-5/08, *Infopaq*, § 50.

represented via the printed or online press, or audiovisual media, for the purpose of providing immediate public information.

The defence of incidental inclusion (either the theory of the background, or the theory of the non-essential) has developed under French case law.

For software, an exemption covering reverse engineering allows software users to reproduce the software code or to translate the form of that code without the copyright owner's authorisation, but only for the purpose of interoperability (Article L122-6-1, IV FIPC).

1.5 Remedies for copyright infringement

First, a copyright holder whose rights have been infringed can claim damages. The rules for calculating such damages were modified under the aegis of the Enforcement Directive (2004/48/EC, transposed into French law via Law No 2007-1544).

Henceforth, when assessing damages, the judge takes into consideration the negative economic consequences of the infringement, including the copyright owner's lost profits, the unfair profits made by the infringer, and the non-financial loss resulting from the breach of the intellectual property right (Article L331-1-3 FIPC).

As an alternative, and where the plaintiff specifically so requests, the calculation of damages may consist in a lump sum fixed by the judge as equal to or greater than the amount of royalties or fees which would have been due if the infringer had requested authorisation to use the work in question.

Additional remedies are set forth in Article L331-1-4 FIPC, and allow a judge, at the plaintiff's request, to order that infringing products and the means of making such products be recalled and withdrawn from commercial networks, destroyed, or confiscated and turned over to the plaintiff. Judges can also order publication of the judgment in appropriate newspapers or on the website of an online public communication service designated by the plaintiff.

Costs relating to such additional measures are borne by the infringer.

1.6 Copyright liability

Under French law, uploading a copyrighted work without authorisation constitutes an infringement because it communicates the work to the public.

As regards downloading, characterisation of any infringement depends on the source used to download from: if the source is lawful, downloading may qualify as private copying provided it was carried out exclusively for the use of the copier. On the other hand, if the source is unlawful (ie, the work was illegally uploaded by another infringer), downloading is considered as a copyright infringement because it reproduces the work without authorisation.

Streaming generally qualifies as communicating a work to the public through a digital medium. Therefore, if the person who organises this communication fails to obtain the copyright owner's authorisation, the distribution of a copyrighted work by way of streaming (webcasting) constitutes an infringement.[10]

10 French Supreme Court, September 25 2012: Radioblog was held liable for communicating works to the public via streaming.

As regards watching a film or other audio-visual work by streaming, this act is permitted without authorisation provided the source of streaming is legitimate. However, if an internet user attempts to download a work communicated to the public by streaming, this act is likely to be illicit since it does not comply with the mode of communication to the public initially authorised by the copyright owner.

Under French law and according to the freedom of 'linking', the mere creation of a hypertext link[11] to a third-party website is allowed and is generally not considered as copyright infringement. The creation of a simple hypertext link generally affects neither the right of reproduction,[12] nor the right of representation.[13] Recently, on the issue of websites specialising in re-broadcasting TV programmes on the Internet, the French Supreme Court[14] ruled that a deep hypertext link directing users to the video broadcast on another website makes the work available but does not communicate the work to the public and consequently does not infringe the copyright. As any such link redirects traffic to the linked website, the link itself could be regarded as a quotation and could be covered by the exemption of short quotation.[15] Although in theory copying and using headlines[16] as hypertext links could be considered as copyright infringement, in practice it would be difficult to apply any protection for this act. Such act should be permitted, provided that the link, just like a real quotation, is incorporated in the text in such a way that its presence in the context is justified. However, the creation of a hypertext link to a website containing infringing content can be considered as a copyright infringement.[17]

When a hypertext link is created, a click on the link must send users directly to the original website, with no modifications. It follows that the practice of 'framing', which is the technique whereby a website contains a page imported from another website, is unlawful. Indeed, if the website protected by copyright is reproduced without any previous consent of the author, it constitutes a copyright infringement.[18]

When users are automatically redirected to a third-party website, the courts tend to take into consideration the specific circumstances of the issue and may hold creators of such hypertext links liable for 'parasitic operation' of domain names[19] on the ground of Article 1382 of the French Civil Code and for trademark infringement on the ground of Article L716-1 FIPC.[20]

Price comparison websites are lawful, provided requirements for advertising are satisfied.[21]

As regards aggregator websites such as Google News, French case law has often

---

11 Two types of hypertext links exist: the simple hypertext link which refers to the main page of the website that is generally allowed; and the deep hypertext link which refers to a secondary page that can be lawful.

12 Article L122-2 FIPC.

13 Article L122-3 FIPC.

14 French Supreme Court, 1st civil chamber, October 31 2012, *Metropole Televisions SDBS*, No 11-20.480.

15 Article L122-5.3° FIPC.

16 Protected by Article L112-4 FIPC.

17 Epinal TGI, ch corr, October 24 2000, *Min Pub and SCPP v Conraud.*

18 Paris TGI, June 25 2009, *Pressvoyages.com.*

19 Paris TGI, November 30 2011, *2xmoinscher.com.*

20 Paris TGI, November 30 2011, *2xmoinscher.com.*

21 French Supreme Court, commercial chamber, November 29 2011, *Kelkoo.*

considered them as search engines specialised in a particular field. Their liability for indexing infringing content hosted by third-party websites is generally assessed on the basis of specific rules[22] set out in the E-Commerce Directive, which was transposed into French law via Law 2004-575 dated June 21 2004, on confidence in the digital economy (*Loi pour la Confiance dans l'Economie Numérique* (LCEN)). But the French Supreme Court has recently applied the civil liability regime to Google Images.[23]

1.7 Joint liability for web service providers

Internet users are liable for any copyright infringement they commit.

However, problems with identifying the original infringer on the Internet have made the question of whether or not technical intermediaries (ie, internet service providers (ISPs) and hosting service providers) can be held liable for such infringements a crucial issue.

Since the adoption of the E-Commerce Directive 2000/31, technical intermediaries have been covered under the specific rules on liability for infringements committed by an internet user via their services. These rules were transposed into French law via Law 2004-575 (LCEN) dated June 21 2004.

According to these rules, as interpreted in the light of European case law, a hosting service provider cannot be liable for content that is transmitted or stored through its service, provided it has not played an active role that has given it any knowledge or control over the information transmitted or stored. Thus, if an intermediary's activity is limited to the technical aspects of providing the service, it cannot be held liable for any copyright infringement committed via its service.

French case law is generally in favour of granting hosting service provider status to video sharing websites such as YouTube,[24] despite the fact that such websites provide specific layout and technical tools for categorising content, adjust content provided by users due to technical constraints (eg, re-encoding, size limits, etc), and sell advertising space.

However, a hosting service provider loses its claim to coverage under these special liability rules once it becomes aware of facts or circumstances that should lead a diligent economic operator to realise that the content at issue is unlawful and if, being so aware, it fails to act expeditiously (Article 6-I-2 LCEN).

According to recent French case law,[25] awareness of unlawful content on a website cannot be presumed; it must be obvious and result from a notice sent by the IPR holder to the hosting service provider. To be admissible, the notice must contain

---

22 Article 6-I-2 of the LCEN. According to this article, once they have been informed of the existence of infringing content, the host providers should remove it from their website. The infringing content is taken to be known by the host provider provided a notification including a certain amount of information provided by article 6-I-5 of the LCEN is sent to the host provider by the copyright owner after the latter has tried to reach the author or publisher of the illicit content.

23 French Supreme Court, civil chamber, July 12 2012, No 11-15.165, *SA Auféminin.com v SARL Google France*.

24 Paris TGI, May 13 2009, *Temps Noir v YouTube and Dailymotion*; Paris TGI, September 22 2009, *Omar et Fred v YouTube*.

25 Eg, Paris TGI, November 14 2008, *Lafesse v YouTube*; Paris TGI, May 13 2009, *Temps Noir v YouTube and Dailymotion*; Paris TGI, September 22 2009, *Omar et Fred v YouTube*.

certain details enabling the content host to locate and remove the infringing content (eg, URL address, screen copies), and state the reasons for having the content removed, including reference to the applicable legal provisions and to the facts at issue (Article 6-I-5 LCEN).[26]

As for ISPs, they cannot be held liable for information transmitted through them provided the ISP does not initiate the transmission, does not select the recipient of the transmission, and does not select or modify the information contained in the transmission (Article 6-I-1 LCEN).

1.8 Relief

LCEN, implementing Article 11 of the IPR Enforcement Directive, provides that a judicial authority can order any measures, either in preliminary proceedings or further to a request filed by the IPR owner, to prevent or terminate a loss caused by content published on a public online communications service (Article 6.8 LCEN).

The question of whether or not such interim relief can include ordering a technical intermediary to engage in filtering – that is, to set up a system to prevent content that has been already notified to and removed by the hosting provider, from being re-posted – has become a hot topic. French case law has so far favoured interim relief that requires hosting providers to prevent the works in question from being re-posted on their internet platform. However, since the most recent European case law (especially, *Scarlet v SABAM*[27] and *Netlog v SABAM*[28]), these measures may be held unlawful because of the prohibition on general monitoring (Article 15 of the E-Commerce Directive) and potential violation of the rights and freedoms of both content service providers (ie, freedom to conduct their business) and users of the services (ie, personal data protections and freedom of information). This line has been followed by the French Supreme Court,[29] which held that the three appellate decisions violated EU and French law by imposing 'a general obligation to monitor' the content that Google stores, as well as actively to 'seek out unlawful uploads'. These decisions would have forced Google to implement a 'blocking mechanism with no limitation in time', which would be 'disproportionate to the pursued aim', according to the court. These rulings against the 'notice-and-staydown' principle will bring clarity to the ongoing debate on the future of the EU E-Commerce Directive and the dangers of blocking measures.

1.9 Issues specific to France

(a) *Jurisdiction*

French courts have jurisdiction to hear copyright infringement claims:

- if the defendant is domiciled or established in France or is a French national

26 French Supreme Court, 1st civil chamber, February 17 2011, *Nord-Ouest Production v Dailymotion*.
27 EU Court of Justice, November 24 2011, case C-70/10.
28 EU Court of Justice, February 16 2012, case C-360/10.
29 French Supreme Court, July 12 2012, *Bach Films v Google France/Google Inc*, No 11-13.669, *André Rau v Google France/auféminin.com*, No 11-15.165; No 11-15.188.

(Article 2, EU Regulation 'Brussels I' no 44/2001 dated December 22 2000);

- if the harmful event occurred or may have occurred in France (the term 'harmful event' comprising both the location of the act that caused the harm and the location where the harm was suffered) (Article 5.3 of said Regulation).

If the defendant is domiciled outside the European Union, it can still be sued in France if the copyright owner is a French national (jurisdiction based on nationality as set out in Articles 14 to 15 of the French Civil Code).

As regards copyright infringements on the Internet, the infringing act is considered to be carried out in France if the website where the infringing content is posted targets the French public.[30] The factors to take into consideration are, in particular, the language of the website and the ability to order products incorporating copyrighted works to be delivered in France.

(b) *Claims to infringement of foreign copyright*

The French courts can hear the claims that a foreign copyright was infringed in the cases listed in (a) above

(c) *Emission theory*

For internet infringements that involve unlawfully uploading/downloading a copyrighted work, the infringing act takes place both at the location where the infringing work is uploaded and at the location where this work is downloaded, since both uploading and downloading can constitute an infringing act. With regard to streaming, the general rules regarding copyright infringement on the Internet apply (see above).

1.10 'Orphan' works

French case law has customarily considered the use of a work without authorisation from the copyright holder as an infringement, even if the 'infringer' had carried out a genuine, but unsuccessful, search for the rights holder.[31] However, these decisions ultimately block any use of works whose copyright holder cannot be identified or located (referred to as 'orphan' works). In this respect, French legal scholars have suggested several solutions to enable good-faith users to use copyrighted works lawfully if they have conducted a diligent search and failed to find the copyright holder.

Preoccupations with large-scale unauthorised uses of photographs circulating on the Internet without any mention of their authors led to a bill on the use of visual 'orphan' works being introduced and passed in the Senate on October 28 2010. However, for the sake of compliance with the coming EU directive on digitisation and online displays of orphan works, the legislative process has been suspended.

However, a law adopted on March 2 2012 on the digital use of out-of-print books has finally given a definition of orphan works. Pursuant to a newly created Article

---

30 French Supreme Court, commercial chamber, March 29 2011, *eBay Europe v Maceo*.

31 Paris Court of Appeal, October 31 2000.

L113-10 FIPC, "An orphan work is a protected and disclosed work whose copyright holder cannot be identified or located, despite a diligent and genuine search."

A European directive on certain permitted uses of orphan works was adopted on October 25 2012. The main purpose of the directive is to provide a legal framework for facilitating the digitisation and dissemination of works protected by copyright or related rights, but of which the author is not known, of if known, cannot be located. The conditions are that the orphan works must be used for the public interest mission of specific cultural institutions[32] using the work, and that the public institutions have carried out a prior 'diligent search' in the member state where the work was first published. It is important to note that rights holders are able to put an end to the orphan status of a work at any time.

1.11 Online piracy measures

As a part of a range of anti-piracy policies, two laws were passed in France in 2009: Law 2009-669 dated June 12 2009 promoting the distribution and protection of creative works on the Internet (HADOPI I) and Law 2009-1311 dated October 28 2009 on the protection of literary and artistic works on the Internet under criminal law (HADOPI II).

The HADOPI laws, which are commonly referred to using the acronym of the independent administrative authority created to implement the newly established mechanisms (*Haute Autorité pour la Diffusion des Oeuvres et la Protection des droits sur Internet* – HADOPI[33]), provide for a 'progressive response' to copyright infringements on the Internet via peer-to-peer software.

First of all, HADOPI laws require each user to ensure that his/her internet access is not used to commit copyright infringements (Article L336-3 FIPC). To enable users to comply with this obligation, ISPs must suggest at least one means of protection for their internet access to their subscribers.

On receipt of a complaint from a copyright holder or a representative thereof, HADOPI may send an e-mail to the user whose internet access was used in copyright infringement, informing him or her of the infringements that have taken place through the internet access, drawing him or her attention to the existence of lawful online sources of copyrighted content, reminding him or her of the obligation to secure one's internet access, including information on the available means for doing so and the penalties that might be incurred for non-compliance with this recommendation.

If the unlawful use of the internet access in question is repeated within six months of the first notice, HADOPI sends the user a registered letter containing the same information as the first e-mail.

If copyright infringements are still taking place one year after receipt of the second notice, the owner of the internet access in question can be charged with 'gross negligence' punishable by a fine (Article L335-7-1 and Article R335-5 FIPC). The

---

32 Libraries, educational establishments, publicly accessible museums, archives, memory and heritage fund institutions.

33 The Ministry of Culture is currently working on a bill intended to abolish the HADOPI and to transfer its mission to the CSA (Conseil Supérieur de l'Audiovisuel – Audiovisual Council). This bill is scheduled to be presented to the Parliament no earlier than April 2014.

original version of the law also provided for an additional penalty of suspended internet access for one month (Article R335-5, III FIPC). However, the respective provision was repealed by Decree No 2013-596 dated July 8 2013. By that date, only one owner of internet access had been subject to suspension of internet access.

Aside from the mechanism described above, which was created to make access owners more responsible, the HADOPI laws stipulate an additional penalty for those persons having carried out copyright infringements over the web. This penalty consists in a suspension of internet access for up to one year and prohibition on subscribing any other contract with another ISP during this time (Article L335-7 FIPC).

Moreover, HADOPI laws have inserted Article L336-2 into FIPC that allows the court, on demand of copyright holders, to order "any measures intended to prevent or terminate a copyright or related rights infringement against any person that is likely to contribute to remedying this infringement".

1.12 Electronic infringements of moral rights

In the internet context, moral rights infringements can take some specific forms.

In the arena of authorship rights, the nature of multimedia works such as online video games and websites that comprise a number of copyrighted works makes it difficult to state the name of the author on each object. Therefore, French case law allows authors' names either to be given in a separate file named 'credits', provided the works created by each author in particular can be clearly identified, or mentioned in a tooltip which appears when putting the cursor on the photo displayed on the screen.[34]

In the name of their right to respect for the integrity of their work, authors can also oppose any treatment that they consider as derogatory. Under French law, digitisation as such is usually not regarded as infringing moral rights. However, any alterations to the work (eg, 'mash-ups') can be prohibited by the court at the author's request. The court's assessment will be made on a case-by-case basis. Moreover, authors can oppose any online use that places the work within a context which is contrary to the spirit of the work.

2. Trademarks

2.1 Use of a trademark

Under French law and in accordance with EU case law, to prevent a trademark registration from being revoked for non-use, the corresponding sign must be used:

- as a trademark, in the sense of indicating the trade origin of the goods and services in question;
- in relation to the goods or services protected by the trademark already marketed or about to be marketed;
- in the course of trade, which presupposes client contact with the sign as opposed to the use thereof within the trademark owner's organisation;

---

34 Paris Court of Appeal, September 26 2007.

- within French territory;
- seriously (ie, the obligation of genuine use), which excludes sporadic use or any artificial use for the sole purpose of avoiding revocation.

Using a trademark on a website constitutes a 'use' for the purposes of an infringement claim if the conditions in the first four bullets above are fulfilled.

All of these requirements apply to the use of a sign on a webpage or online marketplace or as a domain name.

In order to constitute a use within French territory, the website on which the trademark is used must be aimed at French customers.[35] French courts tend to take into account certain criteria to determine whether this is the case, including: the language of the website; the availability in France of the products or services covered by the trademark (delivery conditions);[36] the currency in which customers can pay for the products and/or services covered by the trademark; and the country domain extension of the website (fr.).

2.2 Infringement

According to the most recent French case law, which has been influenced by the EU judgment on the *Google France* cases,[37] the use of a trademark as a metatag cannot constitute a trademark infringement since, insofar as they are used by search engines for the purposes of indexation, metatags remain invisible to internet users and as such are not able to fulfil the function of connecting goods or services to a commercial origin.[38]

The use of a sign that is identical to a trademark as a keyword by a search engine offering referencing services to advertisers does not constitute a trademark infringement as the search engine cannot be construed as using the sign in the course of trade.[39]

However, an advertiser that purchases a keyword that is identical to a trademark to cause its advertisement to display under the heading 'sponsored links' can be said to use the sign in question in the course of trade. When assessing whether or not the advertiser's actions constitute a trademark infringement, the courts must establish whether, based on the specific presentation of the relevant advertisement, customers can reasonably be expected to believe that the advertised goods or services have the same commercial origin as those of the trademark owner or at least that they are provided by an undertaking with economic ties to the trademark owner.[40]

Under French law, merely reserving a domain name that is identical or similar to

---

35 French Supreme Court, 1st civil chamber, January 11 2005, *Hugo Boss*; French Supreme Court, commercial chamber, July 10 2007, *Nutri Rich*.

36 Paris Court of Appeal, September 27 2006.

37 EU Court of Justice, March 23 2010, Cases C-236-08, C-237-08 and C-238-08.

38 Paris TGI, 3rd chamber, 3rd section, October 29 2010; February 18 2011; May 4 2011.

39 French Supreme Court, July 13 2010, three decisions: *Louis Vuitton, Viaticum* and *CNRRH*; and *GIFAM*, issued on the same date.

40 See also, Paris Court of Appeal, November 19 2010, *Google v Syndicat Français de la Literie*; Paris Court of Appeal, February 2 2011, *Google v Auto IES*; Paris TGI, April 29 2011, *Victoires Editions v Seanergic*; Paris TGI, September 22 2011, *LT Services v Com'Online;* Paris Court of Appeal, November 30 2011, *Google v Promovacances*.

a trademark can give rise to liability for trademark infringement if it is possible to ascertain that the person reserving the domain name intends to use it to sell goods or services that are identical or similar to those covered by the trademark.[41]

Nevertheless, given that it can be difficult to ascertain the prospective use of the website, the French courts tend to reserve this type of determination of a trademark infringement to persons who have reserved domain names featuring a well-known trademark that is protected for all types of goods or services.[42]

2.3 Defences

Under French law, the use of a sign that is identical or similar to a trademark for decorative or descriptive purposes[43] or for parody or activism[44] cannot be considered as infringing, as the sign is not used as a trademark in a manner that would be likely to have an adverse effect on its function as a guarantee of origin.

In terms of comparative advertising, this defence can also be invoked by persons using the trademark of a competitor, on the condition that their use of the trademark meets all of the conditions set forth in Article L121-8 *et seq* of the French Consumer Code, which transposes the provisions of Directive 2006/114 on misleading and comparative advertising.

2.4 Parallel imports

Pursuant to Article L713-4 FIPC (and Article 7 of Directive 2008/95/EC on trademarks), trademark owners cannot oppose parallel imports of goods or services if they have been put on the market in the Community under the trademark by the trademark owner or with its consent.

However, the principle of exhaustion of rights is not applicable if the trademark owner can invoke a legitimate reason for opposing any further sale of the goods or services. These include an alteration in the condition of goods after they have been put on the market but also, according to the recent EU case law[45] implemented by French courts,[46] the possibility that selling the goods or services could have an adverse effect on the reputation of the trademark due to the damaging conditions under which they are being sold (in discount and outlet stores or among other items offered as a bulk sale) or to mediocre advertising, damaged packaging, significant discount on the price, etc.

Although the existence of a selective distribution network is often taken into account by courts assessing the adverse effects of parallel imports (or parallel sales

---

41 French Supreme Court, commercial chamber, December 13 2005, *Locatour*. For example, by another functioning website to which the non-functioning website in question redirects internet users: Paris TGI, January 15 2002, *Magique Emile v Secret de Polichinelle;* Paris TGI, injunction, May 14 2010, *Mme Ferrari v Home Sud Service.*

42 Paris TGI, October 29 2010, *SNCF v M Mathieu.*

43 French Supreme Court, commercial chamber, May 10 2011, *Dermo esthétique*; Paris Court of Appeal, February 1 2012, *Le Petit Poucet.*

44 French Supreme Court, commercial chamber, May 8 2010, *Ecco v Greanpeace.*

45 EU Court of Justice, April 23 2009, Case C-59/08, *Dior v Copad.*

46 French Supreme Court, commercial chamber, March 23 2010, three decisions: *Chanel v Caud, Chanel v Land, Chanel v Marm*; French Supreme Court, commercial chamber, May 24 2011, two decisions: *Chanel v Capi; Chanel v Jarnis*; French Supreme Court, commercial chamber, October 4 2011, *Chanel v Vill.*

within the same national territory) on the reputation of a trademark, it is worth noting merely distributing trademarked products outside a selective distribution network will not automatically be considered a trademark infringement.[47] In terms of online sales, the French courts have often held that the fact that goods or services are sold online cannot be considered in and of itself to cause an adverse effect on the reputation of a trademark.[48] The trademark owner must prove that actual damage has been caused to the reputation of its trademark due to the specific circumstances of the sale.

2.5 Remedies

The remedies available to trademark owners in cases of infringement are the same as for copyright holders (see section 1.5 above).

The statutes applicable to patent infringements (Article L716-14 FIPC for rules of assessing damages and Article L716-15 FIPC for alternative measures) are worded in the same way as those applicable to copyright infringements.

2.6 Liability of web services providers

See section 1.7 above.

2.7 Advertising laws and regulations

In France a regulatory body, the Authority of Regulation of Professional Advertising (ARPP),[49] is in charge of regulating advertising and attempts to ensure a balance between freedom of expression and respect for consumers. The rules that apply for advertising mainly appear in the Consumer Code and include online advertising.

In order to protect their rights, some trademark owners file a separate claim for misleading advertising, in addition to a trademark infringement claim. However, in order to succeed, this second claim must be based on different events and losses to those cited in the trademark infringement claim.[50]

Regarding the events that can give rise to liability for misleading advertising, Article L121-1 of the French Consumer Code implementing Directive 2005/29/EC defines a misleading commercial practice as an unfair commercial practice that creates confusion with other goods or services, a trademark, a trade name or with other distinctive signs of a competitor (1°); or a practice that relies on false or misleading allegations, indications or presentations concerning the essential characteristics of goods or services (2°).[51] In more general terms, Article L120-1 of this code sets out two criteria that must be taken into consideration in order to ascertain whether or not a commercial practice is unfair: it must be contrary to the requirements of professional diligence; and it must materially distort the economic behaviour of the average consumer.

---

47 French Supreme Court, commercial chamber, March 23 2010, *Chanel v Béry*.
48 Nanterre TGI, February 11 2010, *Clarins v PMC Distribution*.
49 Replaced the 'BVP' or French Advertising Authority in 2008.
50 Paris TGI, January 25 2011, *Securité privée v Securité Gardiennage*; Paris TGI, July 1 2011, *Cerruti 1881 v Brandalley*; Paris TGI, December 15 2011, *Weston v Shopping Epinions International*.
51 Paris TGI, May 11 2010, *Nature & Emotions*.

The burden of proof in these circumstances has become especially difficult, as the French Supreme Court requires significant evidence of the impact of the practice in question on consumer behaviour.[52]

2.8 Domain name disputes

AFNIC,[53] the agency appointed by the French government to manage the .fr and .re registries, has set up a special alternative dispute resolution procedure known by the acronym SYRELI[54] (from *système de resolution de litiges*, or dispute resolution system) for issues involving domain names using the .fr extension.

In application of Article L45.6 of the Post and Telecommunication Code, this procedure is opened up to anyone demonstrating an interest in acting (referred to as the 'claimant') and who seeks the removal, or the transfer for its benefit, of a domain name falling under the prohibitions defined in Article L45.2 of the Code. The procedure is managed entirely online; trademark owners create an account on the SYRELI website and file a petition with AFNIC to commence the procedure. The petition should be accompanied by all evidence that the claimant intends to use to support its petition. The claimant must demonstrate that he/she has a valid interest in acting, that the domain name involved in the dispute is liable to disrupt public order or morality, to infringe intellectual property rights or personal rights, or is identical to domain names of the French state, local authorities or institutions. Moreover the claimant must prove that the owner of the domain name at stake does not have any legitimate interest and that the owner acted in bad faith.

The claimant pays a non-reimbursable filing fee of €250, before tax, for each petition. AFNIC then has two months in which to rule on the case from the date on which it receives a complete petition.

Under the SYRELI system, the only remedies that can be obtained by trademark owners are the transfer or deletion of the disputed domain name. No damages can be sought or awarded.

2.9 Unfair competition/passing off

In France, it is common for a trademark owner to claim damages for both trademark infringement and unfair competition in the same proceedings.

However, protection can only be afforded via the unfair competition claim if it is based on events that are different to those upon which the trademark infringement claim is based. As a result, since trademark owners tend to rely on the likelihood of confusion to support infringement claims, they cannot use the same argument or rely on any unfair advantages drawn by the perpetrator from confusing the public to support an unfair competition claim.[55]

According to Article 1382 of the French Civil Code, in order to make an unfair

---

52 French Supreme Court, November 29 2011, *Kelkoo*.

53 An association governed by the provisions of the Act of July 1 1901 for assigning and managing certain internet top-level domains corresponding to France and to French territories.

54 Which came into force on November 21 2011.

55 For example: Paris Court of Appeal, October 7 2011, *Victoires Editions v DPE*; Paris TGI, December 15 2011, *Weston v Shopping Epinions International*.

competition claim, the claimant must show that an offence has taken place, that a loss has occurred and that there is a causal link between the two.

The offence may be intentional or non-intentional (ie, the intent to harm does not have to be characterised). Usually, an action for unfair competition linked to a trademark can be based on three types of offence: parasitism,[56] imitation, disparagement.[57] Moreover, the Unfair Commercial Practices Directive of May 11 2005 sets up a common legal framework for three types of unfair commercial practices: misleading practices,[58] aggressive practices,[59] and prohibited practices.[60]

3. Patents

3.1 Patentability of 'internet' inventions

French law provides that patents cannot be filed for 'plans, principles and methods for performing intellectual activities, playing games or doing business, or computer programs' or 'presentations of information' (Article L611-10, (2), (c) and (d) FIPC). These concepts are considered too abstract and not sufficiently technical to be patented.

Nevertheless, it is possible to patent a technical process using mathematical methods to obtain a technical result or a product.

3.2 Bioinformatics

Article L611-18, §1 FIPC provides that "the human body [...] including the mere discovery of one of its elements, including the sequence or partial sequence of a gene" may not be patented.

However, paragraph 2 of the same article provides for an exemption for inventions "constituting a technical application of a function of an element of the human body". It follows that a new DNA sequence or protein structure discovered using bioinformatics cannot be patented as such save "to the extent necessary to the realisation and exploitation of this particular use", which must be set out in the patent application in a specific and precise manner.

3.3 Issues specific to France

(a) Infringements on the Internet

French courts have jurisdiction over patent infringements committed via the Internet in the cases mentioned above in section 1.9.

(b) Process patents

French courts have jurisdiction over infringements of a process patent committed via

56 Fact of unduly appropriating the know-how or reputation of a competitor by creating confusion in the minds of consumers between the trademark and the parasite products.

57 Fact of discrediting a competitor by spreading injurious statements about it, or its services or products.

58 Fact of conveying false information or information likely to deceive the consumer in their overall presentation.

59 Practices that include high pressure sales tactics and demands for payment.

60 Blacklist of practices that are considered unfair in all circumstances.

the Internet, even where only a part of the process is carried out in France, provided the product directly obtained by the patented process is aimed at the French public according the criteria listed in section 1.9 above.

3.4 Remedies available for patent infringement

The remedies available to patent owners in the event of an infringement are the same as for copyright and trademark owners (see section 1.5 above).

The statutes applicable to patent infringements (Article L615-7 FIPC for rules of assessing damages and Article L615-7-1 FIPC for alternative measures) are worded in the same way as those applicable to copyright and trademarks.

4. Disclosure orders against web services providers

4.1 Availability

Pursuant to Article 6.II (3) LCEN, a judicial authority can issue an order to a web services provider (content host or ISP) to disclose personal data relating to the author of a given piece of content. The disclosure is generally ordered at the request of the owner of an intellectual property right who has noticed an infringement of his/her rights and needs such data to identify the author of the illicit content. Decree No 2011-219 dated February 25 2011 sets out the detailed rules that apply for the conservation and disclosure of data allowing the identification of any person who has contributed to the creation of online content. It does not provide any guidelines as to how the request must be made but indicates a limited list of data that must be preserved and that can also be communicated.

Web service providers have an obligation to retain information enabling them to identify those persons who have contributed toward creating the content made available via their services (Article 6.II (1) LCEN). The list of personal data that must be retained was recently established by a decree issued by the French Conseil d'Etat on February 27 2011.

4.2 Requirements

IPR owners must set out all of the facts, circumstances and legal grounds of the alleged infringement that justify the need for the disclosure in the request filed with the court seeking the order.

4.3 Jurisdictional issues

In practice, petitions for disclosure orders are made with requests for an injunction ordering a given web services provider to take all necessary actions to prevent or end any damage caused by the allegedly infringing content (Article 6-I-8 LCEN).

Injunction orders and disclosure orders can be obtained both in urgent proceedings (in the presence of all parties) and by petition (*ex parte*). In practice, IPR owners tend to choose the second method, which is faster and less expensive. However, in this case, they must also provide justification for the need to depart from the usual procedure (ie, in the presence of all parties), failing which the court will not admit the petition.

4.4 'John Doe' injunctions

Under French law, it is impossible to obtain an injunction to prevent IPR infringements against a person whose identity is not known at the time of issue (known as 'John Doe' injunctions).

Germany

David B Adler
Nadine Herrmann
Joachim Lehnhardt
Quinn Emanuel Urquhart & Sullivan LLP

1. Copyright, database rights and design rights

1.1 Overview

The Internet provides access to a variety of content, all of which may enjoy protection under German statutes. While no specific 'internet law' exists, Section 2(1) of the Copyright Act provides a non-exhaustive list of different types of works. Protection can be gained for literary works including speeches and computer programs, musical works, pantomime works including dance, works of fine art including architectural works, photographic works including works created in a similar way to photographic works, cinematographic works including works created in a similar way to cinematographic works, and illustrations of a scientific or technical nature such as drawings, plans, maps, sketches, tables and three-dimensional printouts. As this list is not exhaustive, works that do not fall under one of the above categories may still be protected. Section 2(2) of the Copyright Act provides that "personal intellectual creations alone shall constitute works within the meaning of the German Copyright Act". If the work is not 'individual' enough, but reflects more a routine act or procedure, it cannot be protected. As a consequence, originality of the creation is key.

The Copyright Act grants, in addition, so-called ancillary rights with a slightly different scope of protection if the criteria of a work are not fulfilled. Such ancillary rights exist, for example, in relation to performing artists (Copyright Act, Section 73), organisers of performances (Copyright Act, Section 81), phonogram producers (Copyright Act, Section 85), broadcasting companies (Copyright Act, Section 87), databases (Copyright Act, Section 87a *et seq*), film producers (Copyright Act, Section 88 *et seq*), and moving pictures (Copyright Act, Section 95).

An important difference between a copyright and an ancillary right is their duration. A copyright generally expires 70 years after the author's death (Copyright Act, Section 70(1)), starting with the end of the year in which the author passed away. Most of the ancillary rights fall within the public domain 50 years after the first performance.

With regard to internet content, the following are of particular relevance.

(a) Films, sound recordings and broadcasts

Films of any kind may constitute works that carry copyright protection. The same is true for similar works such as videogames, computer animations and multimedia products. Recordings and broadcasts are not considered a specific type of work. Even though literary or musical works may be the object of sound recordings and broadcasts, they would still be classified as literary or musical works.

(b) *Typographical arrangement of a published edition*

Protection of a typographical arrangement of a published edition under the Copyright Act requires a minimum level of originality and creativity (Copyright Act, Section 2(2), see above). While German courts are reluctant to acknowledge this requirement for mere layouts, graphical arrangements may be capable of being protected under design laws, where the threshold for protection is significantly lower. In contrast to copyright (which automatically subsists upon the creation of a work without any registration being necessary), a design right is registered upon application for new forms addressing the aesthetic perception of the observer without a requirement of a specific originality.

(c) *Protection of the user interface*

As with typographical arrangements, the test as to whether the design of a user interface enjoys protection under the Copyright Act is a question of originality. Again, customary user interfaces are unlikely to pass the required threshold. On the other hand, design rights may be granted where the overall impression generated by the user interface is new and deviates from existing interfaces.

User interfaces may be protected as computer programs. However, it is widely acknowledged that the mere translation of a design into HTML code is not protected under the Copyright Act. This is because HTML is a mere specification language that only causes certain multimedia elements to be displayed, whereas a computer program as protected under the Copyright Act would require a sequence of commands that control the execution of the program. The situation is consequently different where JAVA applets, PHP or Pearl scripts are used for the realisation of the user interface. The interface may then be protected as a computer program. It is worth mentioning, however, that this will not prevent a third party from creating a similar user interface on its own, since the protection extends only to the underlying code which must not be copied but may be reprogrammed.

(d) *Computer-generated works*

Section 2(2) of the Copyright Act requires a personal creation; the work must be created by a human being. Thus, computer-generated works are generally not protected under the Copyright Act. However, licence terms applicable to computer programs may contain (contractual) restrictions for the use of the results created by the computer program.

(e) *Websites protected as databases*

The Copyright Act differentiates between database works (Copyright Act, Section 4) and databases (Copyright Act, Section 87a). Again, a database work needs to show a minimum of creativity and originality. While this may be applicable to specific content, an average website will usually not meet this threshold. The content can nevertheless be protected as a database – that is, a collection of independent works, data or other materials arranged in a systematic or methodical way and individually accessible by electronic or other means (Copyright Act, Section 87a implementing Article 1 of Directive 96/9/EC).

(f) *Compilations*

Compilations can be protected as a literal and/or graphical work where the compilation as such shows a minimum of creativity and originality. In addition, compilations can qualify as a database (see section 1.1(e) above).

1.2 Infringing acts

The Copyright Act details various actions in relation to copyrighted works that must not be committed without the rights holder's consent. Subject to certain exemptions (see section 1.4 below), copyrighted works are, in particular, protected against reproduction, modification, distribution, being made publicly available and retransmission.

(a) *Copying/reproduction*

Sections 15 and 16 of the Copyright Act grant the author of a work the exclusive right of permanent or temporary reproduction (ie, the right to produce copies of the work by any means and in any form, irrespective of the number of copies). A copy under the Copyright Act always requires a physical piece of reproduction. Where copyright-protected content is downloaded from the Internet, a physical copy is generated in the form of the user's data carrier (or, as the case may be, the random access memory of the user's computer). In contrast, the mere presentation of content on a screen is not an act of reproduction.

(b) *Issuing copies to the public*

German law grants authors the exclusive right to distribute the original or copies of their works. Since the right of distribution pertains to physical copies (eg, CDs, DVDs, printed books only, it is predominantly relevant in the 'offline' context where data carriers with software or other works (ordered via the Internet) are physically shipped to the purchaser. Distribution rights are subject to exhaustion if the first sale in the European Economic Area (EEA) was made with the rights holder's consent. That is, copies of copyright-protected works that were legally distributed in the European Union can be resold freely to third parties without the consent of the rights holder (Copyright Act, Section 17(2) with a corresponding provision in Section 69(c)(2) of the act specifically relating to computer software).

With regard to the sale of used software on data carriers, the German Federal Court of Justice has held that, in the interest of marketability, the principle of exhaustion must prevail and that in the absence of a direct contractual arrangement with the end user, the end user is free to resell the software to a third party.[1] The principle of exhaustion in the internet context is subject to an action that was recently referred back to the Munich Court of Appeals by the Federal Court of Justice.

1 Judgment of July 6 2000 – I ZR 244/97– *OEM-Version.*

Before, the Federal Court of Justice had referred certain questions to the European Court of Justice (ECJ),[2] which held in its judgment handed down on July 3 2012 that the distribution right with regard to a computer program downloaded from the rights holder's website would be exhausted and a resale of that copy would consequently be permissible if the rights holder had granted a perpetual licence to the first acquirer in return for payment of a fee intended to enable the rights holder to obtain a remuneration corresponding to the economic value of that copy of his work.

On July 17 2013, the Federal Court of Justice referred the case back to the Munich Court of Appeals to investigate further the underlying facts with a view to the prerequisites of exhaustion stipulated by the ECJ.

(c) Communicating work to the public

Rights holders have the exclusive right to communicate their work to the public (Copyright Act, Section 15(2)). The Copyright Act distinguishes the following categories:

- the right to perform, show or play a work in public (Section 19);
- the right to make a work publicly available (Section 19a);
- the right to broadcast a work (Section 20);
- playback rights by way of picture or sound carriers (Section 21); and
- the right to play broadcasts or works publicly made available (Section 22).

The right to make a work publicly available and the broadcasting right play an important role for internet content. Making a work publicly available means making it available in such a way that members of the public may access it from a place and at a time individually chosen by the user. This right is triggered not only by normal download offerings, but also where content is streamed on demand. In contrast, live streams are subject to the rights holder's broadcasting right.

(d) Authorising another person to do any of the above

The exclusivity of rights also means that the relevant rights holders must authorise third parties that intend to do any of the actions described above. The rights are subject to agreements in the form of licences. Such licences are, as a rule, freely negotiable and can be granted either exclusively or non-exclusively, in perpetuity or temporarily. They can also be limited to certain geographic areas or to specific types of use (Section 32). According to Section 31(5), the scope of the exploitation right is determined in accordance with the purpose envisaged in making the grant, if the types of use to which the exploitation right extends have not been specifically stipulated at the time the right was granted, as German copyright law provides that licences must be construed narrowly so that any type of use must be explicitly mentioned in the licence. Nevertheless, the courts do not accept so-called catch-all clauses under which a licensee is granted any and all use and exploitation rights in a work. They are often ineffective.

---

2 Federal Court of Justice, order of February 3 2011 – I ZR 129/08; ECJ, case C-128/11 – *UsedSoft*.

While no specific form is required to enter into a licence agreement, and while licences can also be granted implicitly, it is notable that if the rights holder makes a work available for free on the Internet, this does not necessarily affect the right to further distribute and/or make that work available to third parties. This is of significance, for example, where free software is downloaded from the Internet. Even though it is made freely accessible to the public by the rights holder, third parties may still be infringing the rights holder's right of reproduction, distribution and/or making the software publicly available by downloading the software and distributing/making available further copies to others.

(e) ***Secondary infringement***

The E-commerce Directive (2000/31/EC), implemented by the German Telemedia Act (*Telemediengesetz* (TMG)), normally absolves host and access providers to a certain extent from liability for third-party content.

Under German case law, however, the privileged liability regime under the TMG (Sections 7 to 10 of the TMG implementing Articles 11 to 14 of the E-commerce Directive) does not in principle apply to claims for cease and desist by third parties. However, it is currently an open question if this is also true for TMG, Section 10 which stipulates that the provider is not liable for the information stored at the request of a recipient of the service under certain conditions. Contrary to the Federal Court of Justice, the ECJ did not hesitate to apply Article 14 of the E-commerce Directive in a case of secondary infringement.[3] However, the ECJ pointed out that the privilege applies only if the provider carries out merely technical services, plays a purely passive role and does not have actual knowledge of the illegal activity. In contrast, if the provider actively supports the users' activities, the limitation of liability is not applicable.

Furthermore, service providers must not formally hide behind a lack of knowledge to the extent that such infringements are obvious and can be anticipated. Various precedents exist where German courts have applied the following principles:

- Third parties who do not themselves infringe a right under the Copyright Act can nevertheless be liable as contributory infringers if they, knowingly and sufficiently causally, contribute to the illegal action.
- The contributory infringer is only liable if he is legally and factually in a position to prevent the infringement.
- The contributory infringer must have violated his duties of care either because he was made aware of the relevant infringement and did not react or because the relevant infringement was easily recognisable. This, for example, may be the case where a contributory infringer has become aware of the fact that his service is used to commit an infringement and he has not taken reasonable measures to make sure that similar infringements are prevented in the future.
- The type and scope of measures are determined on a case-by-case basis. Larger service providers should, however, implement appropriate notice-and-takedown procedures to ensure that complaints are properly handled.

3 ECJ, Case C-324/09, *L'Oreal/eBay*.

Nevertheless, the mere fact that a service may be used to commit unlawful action does not automatically trigger liability for the internet service provider (ISP). On the other hand, the ISP is generally held liable if it advises its customers that the services can be used for unlawful action and uses this as an advertising instrument. Also, where the services are designed in a way that it has to be expected from the very beginning that the services will fundamentally be used unlawfully to share copyright-protected material, there may be an obligation for the relevant ISPs to implement technical protection measures.

1.3 Test for copyright infringement

(a) *Requirement of substantial reproduction*

The reproduction of parts of a work constitutes copyright infringement only if the reproduced parts alone meet the requirements that must be fulfilled to qualify as a work (ie, originality, creativity).

(b) *Repeated copying of insubstantial part*

Since the mere consumption of a work (eg, watching a video) is not infringement, the question arises as to whether the subsequent reproduction of insubstantial parts of a work (each of which would not meet the threshold for protection) constitutes an infringing reproduction if the consecutive download of unprotected parts is used to 'consummate' the work in its entirety. This question has been discussed in the context of streaming services where a ruling of the ECJ suggests that this is not a reproduction in the sense of the relevant European directive (for details see see section 1.6(e) below).

1.4 Exemptions/defences to copyright infringement

The Copyright Act contains some provisions justifying certain types of use even though the rights holder did not consent to that use. In the internet context, the right to make copies for private use is particularly relevant.

(a) *Format shifting*

There is no statutory provision explicitly addressing format shifting. However, format shifting normally also requires that a copy of the corresponding work be made. As a result, format shifting is generally seen as a reproduction of a work (eg, ripping a CD to MP3 files). Should format shifting result in a significant loss of quality, it may be held that this represents a distortion of the work, infringing the moral rights of the author (see section 1.12(a) below).

(b) *Personal copying rights*

Section 53 of the Copyright Act allows third parties to make copies of copyright-protected works for private use. One requirement, however, is that the master from which the copies are made must not have been unlawfully produced or unlawfully made publicly available. This ensures that users cannot legally rely on the right to make copies for private use when downloading (unlawfully offered) music from the Internet (eg, via peer-to-peer networks or other file-sharing services). The right to make private copies also covers capturing publicly available broadcasts. Section 53 of the Copyright Act does not apply to computer programs (where, however, users are allowed to make one single back-up copy) and does not cover the reproduction of music notes and entire books (ie, copying books as a whole).

The copy does not have to be produced by the user who relies on Copyright Act, Section 53. The user is also entitled to instruct third parties to produce the copy. In this case, such third parties must not receive any remuneration for making the copy.

Of specific interest in the online sector is the issue as to whether services offered by providers of online VCRs capturing TV broadcasts from free TV channels received via satellite antennas, and recording and storing such TV broadcasts for their customers, are permissible. While TV channels claim an infringement of their rights in the relevant TV broadcasts, the ISPs rely on their customers' right to make private copies. In an important case where RTL (a German TV channel) sued Save.TV (a provider of a corresponding VCR service), the Federal Court of Justice held that since Save.TV services were not provided free of charge, it needed to be assessed whether Save.TV or the user was the actual producer of the copy. Since this was not properly assessed by the court in this instance (Dresden Court of Appeals), the case was remanded.

The Federal Court of Justice also gave guidance that, in addition, the following principles apply:

- If it turns out that (from a technical perspective) the user is the producer of the copy, the user can rely on the right to make private copies.
- In this case, however, it needed to be assessed whether Save.TV infringed the TV channel's right to transmit TV broadcasts when forwarding the relevant broadcasts from their satellite antennas to the virtual VCRs of the users.
- Whether or not the TV channel's transmission right was infringed depended on whether Save.TV made the relevant broadcast 'publicly available' by forwarding it to several users or whether the relevant broadcast was only forwarded to one user.

On July 12 2011, the Dresden Court of Appeals[4] held that the actual producer of the copies is the user so that the private copying exemption is indeed applicable.

(c) *Time shifting*

Time shifting is an act of reproduction, unless the buffered parts of the work are insignificant so that they are not protected under the Copyright Act (see section 1.2(a)). While no specific exemptions apply, private persons may rely on the private copying exemption (see (b) above).

(d) *Fair use*

The Copyright Act does not provide for a general fair use defence. It does, however, specify certain uses of a third party's work that do not constitute infringement. These uses are subject to the following categories.

---

4 Judgment of July 12 2011 – 14 U 801/07.

While news as such (ie, the content) is not protected under the Copyright Act, it is the prevailing view that news articles normally qualify as literary works and enjoy corresponding protection.[5] Thus, any distribution or making publicly available of such articles generally requires the consent of the rights holder. Section 49 of the Copyright Act allows the reproduction and distribution of single articles in other newspapers to the extent that they pertain to current political, economic or religious topics. The Federal Court of Justice held that this exemption can be applied only in part to electronic press reviews. It must, among other things, be ensured that the review does not allow full-text searches and that the article is made available only within one firm and not distributed to third parties for remuneration.[6]

It is, however, also recognised that the mere linking to third-party content does not constitute a reproduction; nor is the relevant content made publicly available.[7]

With regard to Google's image search services, the Federal Court of Justice held in 2010 that the creation and making publicly available of thumbnails of images is covered by the (implicit) consent of the relevant rights holder that published the content on the Internet.[8]

(e) Caching/temporary copies as part of communication process

Section 44a of the Copyright Act (implementing Article 5(1) of Directive 2001/29/EC) allows the temporary, transient or incidental reproduction of a work if the reproduction forms are an integral and essential part of a technological process. The reproduction is permissible only for the purpose of enabling a transmission in a network between third parties by an intermediary, or lawfully using the work, and the reproduction must have no independent economic significance.

(f) Hosting

Host providers offering only storage space are not deemed to be direct infringers and may rely on privileged liability under TMG, Section 7-10 (Article 14 of the E-commerce Directive) if one of their customers uses the service for an illegal reproduction of copyright-protected content. In this regard, they may be obliged to take certain protection measures if they become aware of illegal behaviour on the part of their customers (see section 1.2(e) above).

(g) Back-up copies

An explicit exemption with regard to back-up copies is foreseen only for computer programs (Copyright Act, Section 69d(2)) to which the personal copying exception does not apply.

(h) Reverse engineering

Reverse engineering of computer programs is permitted only to the extent that this is required to obtain information necessary to achieve the interoperability of an

---

5 See Karlsruhe Court of Appeals, Judgment of August 10 2011 – 6 U 78/10.
6 German Federal Court of Justice, Judgment of July 11 2002 – I ZR 255/00.
7 German Federal Court of Justice, Judgment of July 17 2003 – I ZR 259/00 – *Paperboy*.
8 German Federal Court of Justice, Judgment of April 29 2010 – I ZR 69/08.

independently created computer program with other programs. The German provision (Copyright Act, Section 69e) corresponds to Article 6 of the Computer Program Directive (Directive 2009/24/EC).

(i) *Parody defence*

The parody defence is available under Copyright Act, Section 24 which allows the creation of derivative works. It is a prerequisite that the newly created work meets the requirements of originality and creativity under Copyright Act, Section 2 and that – while an externally similar appearance is permissible – the new work keeps an 'inner distance'.

(j) *Incidental inclusion*

Section 57 of the Copyright Act allows the reproduction, distribution and communication to the public of a work to the extent that it is insignificant and only incidentally reproduced. This applies, for example, where copyright-protected paintings are incidentally visible in a movie.

(k) *Copyright levies*

Under the Copyright Act, copyright levies are imposed on the manufacturers, importers and distributors of devices and storage media that possess (alone or together with other devices) reproduction functionality. Copyright must provide adequate compensation for the exemptions to make copies for personal purposes. The determination of the levies is complex. The process contains self-regulatory elements which encourage the competent collection societies and industry associations to enter into so-called 'overall agreements'.

However, ISPs are not currently (directly) liable for copyright levies.

1.5 Remedies available for copyright infringement

Rights holders whose rights are infringed may request injunctive relief and, where the infringer has acted culpably (ie, intentionally or negligently), claim damages. Host providers are exempt from damages claims for the content of third parties if they take appropriate steps to remove illegal content once they become aware of it (TMG, Section 10).

1.6 Copyright liability

(a) *Hosting/cloud computing where infringing content uploaded by user of service*

Uploading content constitutes an act of reproduction under the Copyright Act. Private users may rely on the private copying exemption (see section 1.4(b) above). This is, however, not the case where the content is made accessible to third parties. The user is then liable not only for making the content publicly available, but also for an unauthorised reproduction through the upload.

The host provider may be liable as a secondary infringer if it is aware of the content and does not take reasonable measures to remove or block access to it (see section 1.2(e) above).

(b) Hypertext linking

To third-party website: Linking to a third-party website is neither an act of reproduction nor an act of making that website's content publicly available.[9]

To an infringing work: Linking to an infringing work may trigger liability where this is done intentionally or if the link is not removed after it has become apparent that it points to illegal content (see section 1.2(e) above).

Copying of headlines (when used as hypertext links): The copying of headlines would, in the first place, qualify as an act of reproduction only where the headline alone is protected as a literary work. While this is generally not the case, certain headlines meet these requirements. It will then be decided on a case-by-case basis whether one of the general exemptions applies and/or whether the rights holder has implicitly declared its consent by making the content publicly available.[10]

(c) P2P network

Supplier of P2P software: It is the general view that the mere supply of peer-to-peer software does not infringe copyrights, because the software can also be used for permissible purposes. However, specific circumstances may trigger cease-and-desist claims of copyright holders against the operators of the underlying platforms (eg, where a platform is predominantly used for infringing actions: see section 1.2(e)).

Uploaders/downloaders: Users making protected content available via a peer-to-peer network infringe the rights holder's right to make their work publicly available. While it was held in the past that the mere download of content (even if it is illegally made available) may fall under the private copying exemption, an amendment to the Copyright Act in 2003 clarified that this exemption applies only where the copy is produced from a legitimate source.

(d) Webcasting

The provision of webcasting services constitutes either an act of broadcast or making the content publicly available.

(e) Streaming

While it is undisputed that a streaming provider who streams a work without the rights holder's consent is either liable for unauthorised broadcasting or making publicly available, the question is whether an internet user accessing (illegally) streamed content infringes the rights holder's right of reproduction.

On October 4 2011, the ECJ held in a judgment relating to the marketing of satellite transmission rights for Premier League matches that:[11]

Article 2(a) of Directive 2001/29/EC (...) must be interpreted as meaning that the

---

9 Federal Court of Justice, Judgment of July 17 2003 – I ZR 259/00 – *Paperboy*.

10 See section 1.4(d) above, Federal Court of Justice, Judgment of April 29 2010 – I ZR 69/08 – Google image search.

11 Joined cases C-403/08 – Football Association Premier League Ltd and C-429/08 – *Murphy*.

reproduction right extends to transient fragments of the works within the memory of a satellite decoder and on a television screen, provided that those fragments contain elements which are the expression of the authors' own intellectual creation, and the unit composed of the fragments reproduced simultaneously must be examined in order to determine whether it contains such elements.

The next question is whether this interpretation is mandatorily applicable to Copyright Act, Section 16 or whether the right granted under German copyright law can go beyond what is foreseen under Directive 2001/29/EC. In this respect the Federal Court of Justice tends to the view that Directive 2001/29/EC not only stipulates minimum requirements, but also sets a limitation for the rights that can be granted to authors and rights holders under national laws.[12]

(f) Framing

Third-party content on an own website by way of frames may represent an act of making the third-party content publicly available.[13]

(g) Transmission of infringing work across a communications network

The transmission of a work across a communications network interferes with the right holder's right to broadcast and/or make its work publicly available (for details see (e) above).

(h) Aggregator websites (eg, Google News, price comparison websites)

To the extent that aggregator websites show content that is protected under the Copyright Act, the provision of such services may interfere with the rights holder's right to make its works publicly available. However, mere price information and/or news headlines generally do not reach the threshold of originality and creativity that is required to qualify as a work under the Copyright Act.

Where the information originates from a third-party database, such websites may infringe corresponding database rights (see section 1.1(e) above).

(i) Treatment of user-generated content

Where users generate protected content (eg, photographs, literary works), they principally enjoy the same protection as other rights holders. Usage rights may explicitly or implicitly be granted to third parties (eg, when uploading that content to forums or other platforms).

1.7 Joint liability for ISPs

ISPs are usually not liable, but benefit from liability privileges under the TMG. However, they can qualify as secondary infringers and should implement appropriate notice and takedown mechanisms to limit their exposure to liability (see section 1.2(e) above).

---

12 German Federal Court of Justice, Judgment of January 22 2009 – I ZR 247/03 – *Le-Corbusier-Möbel II.*
13 District Court of Munich, Judgment of January 10 2007 – 21 O 20028/05.

1.8 Relief

Relief can be granted against ISPs under the prerequisites outlined under section 1.2(e) above.

1.9 Issues specific to Germany

(a) *Jurisdiction*

Under Article 5(3) of EU Regulation 44/2001 (Brussels I) (or Section 32 of the German Code of Civil Procedure, if one of the parties is not based in the European Union), German courts have jurisdiction if Germany is the place where the event which gave rise to the harm occurred or if Germany is the place where the harm arose. In the latter case, German courts have jurisdiction to rule solely with respect to the harm caused on German territory.[14]

The event which gave rise to the harm is defined as any kind of action which goes beyond preparation and constitutes at least a part of the infringing act. This is true for the upload of infringing content which is made available to users. In contrast, as long as the uploaded content remains on the server, the act will qualify as preparatory. Besides, the location of the server may be decisive if it is used knowingly and deliberately by the infringer who has at least the indirect potential to influence it (eg, because of contractual agreements).

The harmful event arises in Germany if the relevant content made available over the Internet has an impact on German territory. General availability of the content for German internet users is not sufficient. The test is rather whether the website or the service in the entire context is also addressed to German users. The factors considered by German courts answering that question include the language, the content and the contact details of the content provider.

(b) *Claim to infringement of foreign copyright*

While, to the extent that protection is sought for the territory of Germany, German copyright law will be applicable (principle of place of protection and territoriality), there may be trans-border cases where an infringement has an impact not just on Germany. In these cases, the general rules of jurisdiction apply regardless of the applicable law. As a consequence, German courts may have to apply foreign IP law once they have jurisdiction. Already in 1956 the Federal Court of Justice had held that German courts have the power to decide over the violation of foreign trademarks.[15] In this decision, the court stressed that the competence of the courts would not lead to any intervention in the sovereignty of other states as the impact of the German judgment was limited to the German territory. Further, the court pointed out that the application of foreign trademark law would not cause more or different difficulties from those already existing in other cases of international private law. This argument has also been used for the application of foreign patent and design patent law. In the absence of a judgment in copyright matters, there is no reason to deviate from these principles.

---

14 ECJ, Case C-68/93 – *Shevill*.

15 German Federal Court of Justice, Judgment of October 2 1956 – I ZR 9/54 – *Flava – Erdgold*.

(c) *Emission theory*

According to the general principles described above, the infringing act takes place at the location where the infringing work is uploaded (place of the event which gave rise to the harm), as well as at the location of the download (place where the harm arose).

1.10 Orphan works

An orphan work is a copyrighted work whose owner cannot be located. Such works are not (yet) regulated under German copyright law. In November 2010 and February 2011, the two German parliamentary groups SPD and DIE LINKE presented bills on orphan works (BT-Drs 17/3991 and BT-Dr 17/4661). The SPD bill suggests the introduction of a new Section 13e to the Copyright Act that would implement a clause to the effect that a licence would be deemed to have been granted to a collection society if careful research does not result in finding the relevant rights holder. The DIE LINKE bill recommends the introduction of a new Section 52c to the Copyright Act according to which it would be legal to make an orphan work publicly available as long as it is for non-commercial purposes only. However, fair remuneration would have to be paid to the collection societies. Both bills were discussed in the Parliament's Legal Committee in September 2011, but no further progress has been made since then.

Moreover, in May 2011, the European Commission issued a proposal for a directive on permitted uses of orphan works (COM (2011) 289 final). In June 2012, an informal deal was reached between the European Parliament and the Council. According to the agreed text, a work would be deemed to be orphan if, after a 'diligent' search made in good faith, it was not possible to identify or locate the copyright holder. The draft legislation lays down criteria for carrying out the search. Works granted orphan status would then be made public, through digitisation and only for non-profit purposes. This would apply to any audiovisual or printed material, including a photograph or an illustration embedded in a book, published or broadcast in any EU country. The rights holder should be entitled to put an end to the orphan status of a work at any time and claim appropriate compensation for the use made of it. At the same time, public institutions would be protected from the risk of having to pay large sums to authors who show up later as compensation would have to be calculated on a case-by-case basis, taking account of the actual damage done to the author's interests and the fact that the use was non-commercial. The outcome of the directive will now need final approval from the Committee on Legal Affairs, Parliament as a whole and the Council.

1.11 Online piracy measures

The Copyright Act has been amended several times to deal specifically with online piracy and in order to keep up with technical changes. For example, the private copying exemption has been clarified (see section 1.4(b) above) and explicit prohibitions to circumvent technical copying protection measures have been introduced (Copyright Act, Sections 95a *et seq*).

After intensive discussions, Germany decided to postpone the execution of the

Anti-counterfeiting Trade Agreement (ACTA). Under ACTA, additional obligations would have been imposed on the internet industry to prevent copyright infringements. The European Commission referred ACTA to the ECJ to clarify compatibility of ACTA with European fundamental rights, and on July 4 2012, the EU Parliament rejected ACTA. This means that neither the European Union nor its individual member states can join the agreement.

1.12 Electronic infringement of moral rights

The following points are important in relation to the electronic infringement of moral rights.

(a) Right to object to derogatory treatment (eg, of 'mashups')

Under the Copyright Act, authors enjoy protection against distortion of their work (Copyright Act, Section 14). In the internet context, the Federal Court of Justice confirmed damage claims in a case pertaining to the conversion of music to ringtones,[16] arguing that ringtones imply that only extracts are played back and consequently peculiarities of the work may be lost (eg, dramaturgy, tension). The same has been discussed with respect to thumbnails of photographs/photographic works. The common view is, however, that a downsizing of photographs and images does not infringe the moral rights of the holder (or is at least covered by the consent to make the work publicly available).

(b) False attribution – right to guard against impersonation on the Internet

Authors have the right to be recognised as the originator of their works (Copyright Act, Section 13). This includes the right to be named as the author, and the author may choose a pseudonym. Moreover, he may claim his function to be mentioned, but no other information (eg, address or telephone number) which could be used for advertising. The exact measures to be taken depend on the publication form of the work. The rules for works available on the Internet principally correspond to those with regard to other kinds of publication. However, some particularities of the Internet have to be taken into account. Use has to be made of the broader technical possibilities offered by the Internet (eg, a hyperlink needs to be placed if the author's designation in the work itself is impossible). Likewise, volatile services (eg, internet radio, web TV) need to make use of meta data. On the other hand, general customs may cause exceptions from the obligation to name the author. Thus, a licence may include such an exemption if the concrete type of use granted by the licence does not customarily go along with the author's designation.

(c) Paternity right

The author has the right to decide whether a work is published (Copyright Act, Section 12), as well as the right to revoke a work under certain prerequisites (Copyright Act, Section 42). Section 12 of the Copyright Act applies to any publication of the work on the Internet. Since publication in the sense of the

---

16 Federal Court of Justice, Judgment of December 18 2008 – ZR 23/06.

Copyright Act, Section 12 requires the availability of the work to an unlimited group of people, the use of FTP servers, P2P systems, mailing lists or news groups may be insufficient. Besides, it is still unclear how paternity rights apply in the case of a work's publication on the Internet subsequent to publication in another medium. Since the right of publication may be exhausted by the first publication or may be refreshed in the case of publication in a different medium, the question arises whether the rights holder still has a right to oppose if the licensee envisages a second publication on the Internet. However, German courts have found that a publication of a work of fine art on TV requires the author's consent, even if the work has previously been presented in an exhibition. This solution may not, however, apply to all kinds of work and licences.

2. Trademarks

2.1 Use of a trademark

As a prerequisite for maintaining a trademark in the register, the Trademark Act requires the genuine use of a trademark. That is, the trademark must be used as a means to distinguish between goods or services.[17] The trademark must be used with the aim of securing or creating an outlet for the relevant products. While an intention to make profits is not decisive, a purely fictitious use does not suffice either. Since a 'physical connection' between the goods and the trademark is not required, a genuine use can also be effectuated by way of advertising/marketing on the Internet.

An infringement requires the use of the trademark in business as an indication of origin. This may be fulfilled where a trademark is used in hyperlinks, metatags, keywords or within domain names (see section 2.2 below).

2.2 Infringement

(a) Metatags

Metatags (ie, the (usually invisible) use of keywords in the source code of a website that are interpreted by search engines) represent a use of a trademark if the result from the search engine is impaired and the user is directed to a third-party website.[18] It is, however, not sufficient if the metatag is used in a descriptive manner and is (incidentally) interpreted by the search engine.[19] Besides, metatagging may constitute an act of unfair competition (eg, deception of origin and exploitation of reputation).

(b) Keywords

Search engine operators sell keywords which may contain trademarks for advertising purposes. If a search based on the keyword is carried out, the advertisement appears as a separate part of the result list. According to the ECJ, the search engine provider

17 German Federal Court of Justice, Judgment of 10 April 2008 – I ZR 167/05.
18 German Federal Court of Justice, Judgment of February 4 2010 – I ZR 51/08 – *Power Ball.*
19 German Federal Court of Justice, Judgment of October 7 2009 – I ZR 109/06.

does not make use of the trademark by selling keywords. The court held that a search engine provider only allows its clients to use signs that are identical or similar to trademarks, without itself using those signs.[20] However, the provider may be liable as contributory infringer. In this case, TMG Section 10 (implementing Article 14 of the E-commerce Directive) applies, which leads to a limitation of liability if the provider carries out merely technical services, plays a purely passive role and does not have actual knowledge of the illegal activity. In contrast, if the provider actively supports the users' activities, the limitation of liability is not applicable.[21]

Further, the sale of keywords of a purely descriptive nature does not constitute trademark infringement.[22]

The ECJ found that the advertiser infringes a trademark only if the design or content of the advertisement, or the homepage linked to it, may hinder the user in clearly differentiating between the advertiser (the third party) and the trademark holder. Therefore, an infringement may be excluded only if users undoubtedly recognise from the advertisement that it is published by a third party.[23] German courts reject liability if the advertisement is graphically separated from the list of results and does not include the keyword or any other reference to the trademark holder or his products.[24]

(c) Sponsored links

Search engine operators further sell keywords in order to distribute the front ranks in the result list. The links placed by the advertiser constitute an integral part of the results list so that users are unable to differentiate between sponsored and unsponsored links. Therefore, German courts reviewed this topic in connection with unfair competition law in the first instance. Since the questions relating to trademark law are comparable to those which arise from metatagging, the same principles are likely to apply with regard to sponsored links.

From the perspective of unfair competition law, the buying of keywords may qualify as concealing the advertising nature of commercial practices (Section 4 lit 3 of the Unfair Competition Act, or as misleading (Unfair Competition Act, Section 5(1)). The qualification depends on the knowledge of an average user regarding possibly manipulated and hazardous results lists. If a search engine clearly informs its users of manipulated results, the risk of unfair competition is eliminated. The same is principally true if the manipulated links are separated from the results list and indicated as such. On the other hand, the threshold of unfair competition is met if the operator manipulates the results list with a multitude of keywords without informing the users (index-spamming).

---

20 ECJ, Case C-236/08 to C-238/08 – *Google and Google France*; ECJ, case C-324/09 – *L'Oreal.*

21 ECJ, Case C-236/08 to C-238/08 – *Google and Google France*; ECJ, case C-324/09 – *L'Oreal.*

22 German Federal Court of Justice, Judgment of January 22 2009 – I ZR 139/07.

23 ECJ, Case C-236/08 to C-238/08 – *Google and Google France.*

24 German Federal Court of Justice, Judgment of January 13 2011 – I ZR 125/07 – *Bananabay I*; Judgment of January 13 2011 – I ZR 46/08 – *Impuls.*

(d) Hidden text

If hidden text which influences the search results is placed on a website, a violation of the Unfair Competition Act is possible. Where there has been a manipulation of the search engine itself (eg, by using text in white on a white background), a deliberate obstruction of competitors (Section 4 lit 10 Unfair Competition Act) has been affirmed by the German courts. With regard to trademark law, the principles set out for metatags apply.

(e) Internet domain names

The mere registration of a trademark as a domain name with the German domain name registry DENIC eG does not constitute the use of a mark as a trademark. Only if every possible use of the domain name would lead to an infringement does the registration qualify as such. Further, registration may cause the so-called danger of first infringement which is necessary to obtain a preliminary injunction.

A domain name used for an active, functioning website which is used in business normally fulfils the function of indicating the origin of the goods and services offered. This does not apply if the user will interpret the domain name not as an indication of origin, but as a mere indication of an address or description.[25] In the event of automatic forwarding to another website, the content of the second website will be attributed to the domain name of the first website.[26] The same is true for advertising links placed on the domain's website.

(f) Search navigation tools

'Breadcrumb trails' can be defined as a navigation aid on websites. As these tools are based on the placement of links, the general rules on links apply.

(g) Hypertext links

Hypertext links constitute electronic cross-references between different websites. The use of a hyperlink may result in a trademark infringement, if the link is identical or similar to a trademark and leads to an identical or similar offer of goods and services. However, the particularities of the Internet must be taken into account. As long as the link serves as a mere connection between websites without infringing the legitimate interests of the trademark holder, an implied consent of the holder is likely. Consequently, the use of the trademark is legal if the link leads to a website where the original products of the trademark holder are sold. However, it is not permitted to use the trademark's graphical representation, as the function of a link may be fulfilled by the simple use of the name.

(h) Framing

Framing constitutes the use of a trademark and is likely to be legally treated like hidden text.

---

25 German Federal Court of Justice, Judgment of November 18 2010 – I ZR 155/09 – *Sedo*.
26 German Federal Court of Justice, Judgment of May 14 2009 – I ZR 231/06 – *AirDsl*.

2.3 Defences

Several defences may come into play.

(a) *Descriptive (non-trademark) use of the mark*

The descriptive use of a mark is legal, and this applies especially when the mark is integrated in the domain of a third party. However, this theory has its limits. The more specifically a mark is presented, the more an infringement is likely. The same applies if the third party gives the impression wrongly of being authorised by the trademark holder.

(b) *Comparative advertising*

The use of a mark on a third party's website is permitted if it constitutes a legal comparative advertisement in the sense of Section 6 of the Unfair Competition Act (see section 2.7).

(c) *Parody*

The defence of parody requires a balancing test between the freedom of property and artistic freedom, rights which are both granted by the Constitution.[27] The courts must decide on a case-by-case basis which right prevails. If artistic freedom dominates, the use of a trademark is justified. The ECJ has held that the need for protection of a trademark must prevail if the user of the trademark seeks to benefit from the power of attraction, the reputation and the prestige of that mark, and to exploit its marketing effort.[28]

2.4 Parallel imports

According to Section 24(1) of the Trademark Act (implementing Article 7(1) of Directive 89/104/EEC), a trademark does not entitle the proprietor to prohibit its use in relation to goods which have been put on the market in the European Union or the European Economic Area (EEA) under that trademark by the proprietor or with its consent. Exhaustion of the rights conferred by a trademark therefore principally occurs once these requirements are met. The principles of exhaustion apply exclusively to goods, but not to services.

Furthermore, some exceptions have to be taken into account. Section 24(2) of the Trademark Act provides that exhaustion does not occur where legitimate reasons for the proprietor to oppose the further commercialisation of the goods exist, especially where the condition of the goods is changed or impaired after they have been put on the market. Legitimate reasons also exist if the trademark's function as an indicator of origin or as a guarantee is affected in other ways. The mere fact of commercialisation via an internet auction platform does not itself constitute impairment if the goods are sold in an unamended form. Moreover, the rights conferred by the trademark are not exhausted if the goods are put on the market in the EU/EEA for the single purpose of being sold outside this territory. The

---

27 German Federal Court of Justice, Judgment of February 3 2005 – I ZR 159/02 – *Lila Postkarte.*

28 ECJ, case C-487/07 – *L'Oréal.*

reimportation of goods (from the EU/EEA into a third country, back into the EU/EEA) is not covered by the trademark holder's original consent.[29]

2.5 Remedies

Remedies which are available for trademark infringement may be demanded by way of a preliminary injunction in case of urgency and if the preliminary decision does not anticipate the final ruling. Otherwise, main proceedings have to be initiated. The following claims may be asserted:

- claims for cease and desist, which require a danger of repetition;
- preventative claims for cease and desist, which require a danger of first infringement;
- damages claims, which presuppose liability for intent or negligence;
- claims for renunciation of a registered domain if the mere registration causes the trademark infringement;
- claims for destruction, recall or permanent removal of the goods owned or held by the infringer that are unlawfully identified (Trademark Act, Section 18);
- claims to be promptly informed of the origin and the sales channels of unlawfully identified goods or services (Trademark Act, Section 19);
- cancellation claims due to revocation (Trademark Act, Sections 49 and 55); and
- cancellation claims due to the existence of earlier rights (Trademark Act, Sections 51 and 55).

2.6 Liability of ISP

ISPs may be liable according to the general rules of perpetration and participation. Perpetration requires the performance of the infringing act, or at least its initiation. Participation, on the other hand, means that someone else has initiated the infringing activity and the participator helped to realise it in some way. However, both forms of liability require intentional acting, which usually cannot be established. Nevertheless, the ISP may be liable as a contributory infringer for a breach of its duty of care. The requirements described in the context of copyright law (see section 1.2(e) above) also apply in trademark law.[30] This is no longer true with regard to unfair competition law.[31]

In trademark law – as in copyright law – ISPs do not have the general obligation to control or actively check the whole content of a website in order to identify infringement.[32] However, special duties of care apply if the ISP becomes aware of a concrete and clearly identifiable infringement.[33] The threshold is met if the trademark owner can indicate that the use of its mark on a third party's website takes place in the course of business. In this case, the ISP not only has to remove the

29 Regional Court of Frankfurt – Judgment of October 23 1997 – 6 U 86/97 – *Reimport from Russia*.

30 German Federal Court of Justice, Judgment of March 11 2004 – I ZR 304/01 – *Internetversteigerung I*; Judgment of April 19 2007 – I ZR 35/04 – *Internetversteigerung II*; Judgment of May 30 2008 – I ZR 73/05 – *Internetversteigerung III*

31 German Federal Court of Justice, Judgment of July 22 2010 – I ZR 139/08 – *Kinderhochstühle im Internet.*

32 German Federal Court of Justice, Judgment of July 12 2007 – I ZR 18/04 – *Jugendgefährenden Medien bei eBay*; German Federal Court of Justice, Judgment of March 11 2004 – I ZR 304/01 – *Internet Versteigerung I.*

33 German Federal Court of Justice, Judgment of March 11 2004 – I ZR 304/01 – *Internet Versteigerung I.*

infringing content and check the existing data in order to identify similar infringements, but also take precautions to prevent further similar infringements.[34] However, the ISP is obliged only to take measures which are technically possible and reasonable. The Federal Court of Justice has held that the use of automatic filter software in order to discover infringements and a subsequent manual verification of the result list is reasonable and adequate. The same is true if the ISP provides such software to the trademark holders to enable them manually to check potential infringements by themselves. On the other hand, it is no longer considered to be reasonable to check the complete content manually.[35]

The liability of an ISP as a contributory infringer will lead to a claim for cease and desist. As in copyright law, the privileges of the TMG do not apply for the most part (see section 1.2(e) above).The principles of contributory infringement, however, do apply (see above).

2.7 Advertising law and regulation

The Unfair Competition Act applies to advertising in general, including internet advertising. This act serves the purpose of protecting competitors, consumers and other market participants against unfair commercial practices. At the same time, it seeks to protect the interests of the public in undistorted competition (Unfair Competition Act, Section 1). Section 4 of the act contains a non-exhaustive list of examples of unfair commercial practices and provides that unfairness occurs, for example, where a person conceals the advertising nature of commercial practices (lit 3) or does not clearly and unambiguously state the conditions for participation in a promotional contest or game of an advertising nature (lit 5). Another non-exhaustive list of misleading commercial practices is provided by Section 5 of the Unfair Competition Act.

Comparative advertising is defined as any advertising which explicitly or by implication identifies a competitor, or goods or services offered by a competitor (Unfair Competition Act, Section 6(1)). While comparative advertising is legal, it must not be unfair. Unfairness occurs, for example, where a person presents goods or services as imitations or replicas of goods or services sold under a protected distinguishing mark (lit 6).

Section 7 of the Unfair Competition Act provides that the commercial practice of unconscionably pestering a market participant is illegal. Unconscionable pestering is assumed in the case of advertising using email without the addressee's prior express consent (Section 7(2) lit 3), unless the following requirements of Section 7(3) are met:

- The entrepreneur has obtained the email address from the customer in connection with the sale of goods or services;
- The entrepreneur uses the address for direct advertising of its own similar goods or services;

---

34 German Federal Court of Justice, Judgment of March 11 2004 – I ZR 304/01 – *Internet Versteigerung I;* German Federal Court of Justice Judgment of July 12 2007 – I ZR 18/04 – *Jugendgefährenden Medien bei eBay.*

35 German Federal Court of Justice, Judgment of July 22 2010 – I ZR 139/08 – *Kinderhochstühle im Internet.*

- The customer has not objected to this use; and
- The customer has been clearly and unequivocally advised, when the address is recorded and each time it is used, that he can object to such use at any time, without costs arising by virtue thereof, other than transmission costs according to the basic rates.

The jurisdictional requirements regarding online advertising in the European Union are regulated under the E-commerce Directive (2000/31/EC), which refers to the 'country of origin principle' (Article 3). The provision has been implemented in TMG, Section 3. With regard to online advertising outside the European Union, German international private law on torts applies. The Federal Court of Justice has found that the law of the country where the competitive interests of the competitors meet was applicable.[36] In the case of advertising, this is the so-called 'marketplace' where the decision of the client is influenced by the competitive behaviour.[37] When advertising is carried out online, the place where the user retrieves the offer as intended is decisive.[38] Consequently, German unfair competition law applies as soon as the online advertisement is directed to German users (at least among others), retrieval by German users has taken place and competitive interests of third parties are affected. The direction of advertising to German users must be established on a case-by-case basis, taking into account indicators such as disclaimers, language or currency.

German courts will have jurisdiction if the harmful event occurred or may occur on the German territory (Article 5(3) of EU Regulation 44/2001 (Brussels I) or Section 32 of the Code of Civil Procedure) (see section 1.9 above). In case of unfair competition, there must be a noticeable impact on the German territory if the German courts are to have jurisdiction.

2.8 Domain name disputes

The dispute resolution procedure on the basis of the Uniform Domain Name Dispute Resolution Policy (UDRP) applies to generic top-level domains (TLDs), as well as to some country-specific TLDs, but not to the German local country extension '.de'. Moreover, no special German dispute resolution procedure has been established.

Domain names with the extension '.eu' are capable of revocation through an alternative dispute resolution (ADR) procedure described in Article 22 of EU Regulation 874/2004.

2.9 Unfair competition/passing off

The Federal Court of Justice has held that trademark law and unfair competition law are mutually exclusive. This means that if the Trademark Act is applicable, unfair competition law is not. This 'theory of priority' has been confirmed in recent

---

36 German Federal Court of Justice, Judgment of November 15 1990 – I ZR 22/89 – *Kauf im Ausland.*

37 German Federal Court of Justice, Judgment of March 30 2006 – I ZR 24/03 – *Arzneimittelwerbung im Internet.*

38 German Federal Court of Justice, Judgment of March 17 1994 – I ZR 304/91 – *Beta.*

decisions.[39] Therefore, protection for registered trademarks is the only protection available within the scope of trademark law.

However, the 'theory of priority' is subject to debate among German scholars. While some support concurring claims of trademark law and unfair competition law in general, others do not apply the 'theory of priority' where an additional element of unfairness occurs.

3. Patents

3.1 Patentability of 'internet' inventions

(a) Computer programs

According to Section 1(3) lit 1, (4) of the Patent Act, computer programs are not considered as inventions. This, however, does not preclude the patentability of inventions interrelated with computer programs. Huge numbers of patent applications use computer programs for the solution of technical problems. While earlier German patent examination practice was very reluctant with regard to such inventions, examination practice nowadays is more consistent with the proceedings of the European Patent Office (EPO).

The EPO focuses on the technical character when examining the patentability of a solution to a problem which uses a computer program. Only if a technical character exists, is patentability possible. In the vast majority of cases, the question as to whether an 'inventive step' exists is examined only in a second step. While examining this step, only the technical substance of the invention counts. In *Computerprogrammprodukt* it was held for the first time that a pure computer program is not necessarily beyond the scope of a patentable invention, as long as it causes a technical effect which goes beyond the ordinary physical interaction between a computer program and a computer.[40]

German jurisdiction was dominated by two questions:

- Does the invention which will solve the problem have a technical character?
- Is there an inventive step?

Technical character of the invention: The Federal Court of Justice initially established strict boundaries regarding the patentability of inventions which used computer programs, but is now more in line with the proceedings of the EPO. The German Patent Office (*Deutsches Patent- und Markenamt* (DPMA)) and lower courts, on the other hand, have not always the strict ruling of the Federal Court of Justice, but followed the more generous approach of the EPO. The Federal Court of Justice initially took the position that software which is used as the solution to operational problems and which solely makes use of a data-processing system whose construction and function is known would not be patentable, as in this scenario the

39 German Federal Court of Justice, Judgment of September 10 2008 – 5 U 114/07 – *Agenda*; Judgment of April 7 2008 – 3 W 30/08 – *Baby-Body-Slogan*.

40 EPA T 1173/97.

solution to the problem would be achieved without the use of controllable natural forces. A different conclusion could be drawn only when a program would require a new, inventive set-up of a data-processing system or if the latter would be used in a new, non-obvious way. For the question of patentability, the Federal Court of Justice found it irrelevant whether the result of the program could be used in the technical field or whether its use was solely or purposely achieved with the help of technical tools.[41] When examining whether an invention has a technical character, the Federal Court of Justice held that only the 'new' and 'inventive' declared core of the solution to a problem will be considered *'Kerntheorie'*.

On the contrary, since 1987 the DPMA has stated in its examination guidelines that when applications which contain data-processing programs or rules are examined with regard to the technical character of the invention, the examiner shall look not at the core of the invention, but at the totality of the invention which underlies the application. Some senates of the Federal Patent Court followed this opinion.[42] Other senates, such as the 17th Senate of the Federal Patent Court, which has subject-matter jurisdiction regarding computers – on the other hand followed the Federal Court of Justice's approach and thus in most cases rejected the technical character of the invention and thus patentability.[43]

In 1991, the Federal Court of Justice again emphasised that its *'Kerntheorie'* would still be in effect.[44] Nevertheless, with a ruling of the same day it followed a more lenient approach and held that questions as to whether the method was new, progressive or inventive were irrelevant when determining the technical character. The court held that the solution to a problem could already qualify as technical when it affects the functionality of a data-processing system.[45]

In 1999, the Federal Court of Justice broadened its definition of an 'invention' with regard to the technical character insofar as it no longer required the immediate use of controllable natural forces in order to speak of an invention, but held that it would suffice that technical knowledge would be used.[46]

In two decisions from 2001 and 2004,[47] the court made clear that a method could not be patented only because it requires the use of a computer. Moreover, it would be necessary that the defining approach of the method would have to address the solution to a specific technical problem. This leads to the result that patent claims which suggest, for the solution to a problem in the common areas of technique, that certain steps in a procedure shall be carried out by a computer, are generally possible. The fact that a claim is directed towards a tangible object such as a data-processing

---

41 German Federal Court of Justice, Judgment of April 21 1977 – X ZB 24/74 – *Straken*; German Federal Court of Justice, Judgment of February 14 1978 – X ZB 3/76 – *Fehlerortung*.

42 Federal Patent Court, Judgment of July 25 1988 – 19 W (pat) 93/87 – *Rollladen-Steuerung*; Judgment of July 10 1990 – 18 W (pat) 135/89 – *Schleifverfahren*.

43 Federal Patent Court, Judgment of March 18 1986 – 17 W (pat) 74/84 – *Elektronisches Übersetzungsgerät*; German Patent Court, Judgment of February 18 1991 – 17 W (pat) 83/89 – *Verfahren und Vorrichtung zur Postgebührenberechnung*.

44 German Federal Court of Justice, Judgment of June 10 1991 – X ZB 24/89 – *Chinesische Schriftzeichen*.

45 German Federal Court of Justice, Judgment of June 11 1991 – X ZB 13/88 – *Seitenpuffer*.

46 German Federal Court of Justice, Judgment of December 13 1999 – X ZB 11/98 – *Logikverifikation*.

47 German Federal Court of Justice, Judgment of October 17 2001 – X ZB 16/00 – *Suche fehlerhafter Zeichenketten*; German Federal Court of Justice, Judgment of May 24 2004 – X ZB 20/03 – *Elektronischer Zahlungsverkehr*.

system or a disk, will not on its own, on the other hand, be sufficient to affirm patentability. Rather, such a device will be of relevance only when the characteristics of the claim would benefit the solution to the problem.

Inventive step: The Federal Court of Justice is reluctant to consider elements which do not possess a technical character when examining the inventive step of an invention.[48] This stands in contrast to a prior decision,[49] where the court had held that when analysing the inventive step, the whole invention must be considered, including rules for computing. The Federal Patent Court concluded from this ruling[50] that an inventive step could only be based on a technical contribution with regard to the state of the art. When examining the technical contribution, the whole claim – including the non-technical parts – must be considered. If there is a technical connection, even non-technical parts can thus be taken into account.

In a recent case the Federal Court of Justice has affirmed its ruling that when determining the question of the patentability of a computer program, as a first step it must be established whether the object of an invention can be said to be within the technical field. For this, it is sufficient if parts of the method solve a technical problem. In a second step it is necessary to determine whether the claimed technical teaching provides specific directions (beyond the mere data-processing operation immanent to any computer program) which serve the purpose of solving a technical problem with technical means.

Such a technical means for the solution of a technical problem exists if:

- components of a device are modified or addressed in a different way;
- the procedure of a data-processing program which is used for the purpose of solving a problem is determined through technical facts outside of the data-processing system; or
- the solution exists just in the fact of organising a data-processing program takes account of in such a way the technical circumstances of the data-processing system.

(b) *Business methods*

According to Section 1 par 3 lit 1, par 4 of the Patent Act, business methods are not patentable, as the connection to the use of controllable natural sources and thus the technical character of an invention is missing.[51] They only give directions to actions which a human being can control without influencing natural procedures. The human understanding alone which is used when putting the business method into action, is not considered a natural source and its use can be characterised as technical.[52] However, if a business method is integrated into a technical system, the method can be patentable under German law.

48 German Federal Court of Justice, Judgment of May 11 2000 – X ZB 15/98 – *Sprachanalyseeinrichtung.*
49 German Federal Court of Justice, Judgment of February 4 1992 – X ZR 43/91 – *Tauchcomputer.*
50 Federal Patent Court, Judgment of April 29 2002 – 20 W (pat) 38/00 – *Elektronischer Zahlungsverkehr.*
51 Federal Patent Court, Judgment of May 7 1998 – 17 W (PAT) 55/96 – *Pflanzenanordnung.*
52 German Federal Court of Justice, Judgment of June 22 1976 – X ZB 23/74 – *Dispositionsprogramm.*

(c) ***Mathematical methods***

Mathematical methods are not patentable according to Section 1 (3) lit 1, (4) of the Patent Act, as the monopolisation of such abstract knowledge would inhibit development. Nevertheless, mathematical methods are considered instructions. It is problematic, however, that mathematical methods cannot be generally assessed as a solution to a specific technical problem, but rather a universal instruction regarding a mathematical proceeding.

According to the Patent Court,[53] this is true even when the method is limited to a technical system. It seems possible, though, to patent mathematical methods but to limit the patent claim to the computerised implementation of the procedure. In this regard, the specific software code constitutes the technical teaching claimed and not the mathematical method as such.[54] In this case, of course, the other requirements for the patentability of computer programs must be fulfilled. If a mathematical method is committed to technical measures, it can be patentable. This is also true if the mathematical method solves a concrete technical problem.

(d) ***Presentation of information***

The presentation of information is not patentable according to Section 1 (3) lit 1, (4) of the Patent Act, as it is defined as a non-technical directive. Here too, compliance with the directive only generates perceptions which do not suffice. But if the claimed tool also has a technical character (ie, if the claimed method consists of directives which serve to solve a specific technical problem), it can be patented.[55]

3.2 Bioinformatics

German law on bioinformatics is influenced by EU law, especially by EU Directive 98/44/EC on the legal protection of biotechnological inventions. Bioinformatics such as a novel DNA sequence or protein structure are generally patentable. Nevertheless, exceptions concerning, for example, the body of a human being or parts of it, plants and animals, as well as cloning, are listed in Sections 1a, 2, 2a of the Patent Act. Special requirements for patents regarding a sequence or the partial sequence of a gene are regulated in Section 1a(3) and (4) of the Patent Act. According to Section 34a of the Patent Act, if an invention is based on biological material of plant or animal origin or if it uses such material, the patent application should, where appropriate, include information on the geographical origin of such material, if known. The scope of a granted bioinformatic patent is governed by Section 9a to c of the Patent Act (implementing Articles 8 to 11 of EU Directive 98/44/EC). Article 9a(1) of the Patent Act provides that the protection conferred by a patent on biological material possessing specific characteristics as a result of the invention will extend to any biological material derived from that biological material through propagation or multiplication in an identical or divergent form and possessing those

---

53 Federal Patent Court, Judgment of July 30 2002 – 17 W (pat) 66/01 – *Fuzzy Clustering.*

54 Federal Patent Court, Judgment of September 18 2004 – 17 W (pat) 31/03 – *Partitionsbaum.*

55 German Federal Court of Justice, Judgment of May 19 2005 – X ZR 188/01 – *Aufzeichnungsträger.*

same characteristics. Corresponding provisions concerning patents on a process or a product can be found in Articles 9a(2) and (3).

Further, it is customary to deposit the bioinformatic material. Details are regulated under the regulation on the deposition of bioinformatic material.

3.3 Issues specific to Germany

(a) Infringement on the Internet

Whether German courts have jurisdiction over patent infringements committed via the Internet is determined according to the general rules and thus in the same way as infringement of any other IP rights via the Internet. The fact that the information is accessible from Germany is insufficient on its own to establish the necessary connection with Germany and thus to establish jurisdiction of the German courts.

In order to establish a sufficient domestic connection, there must be a significant result in the country in which the infringing patent is protected. As this issue relates to exclusive IP rights, there must be a focus on the conditions of the market. There must be a noticeable impact on the market of the country in which patent protection exists. Noticeable impact is significantly more than a simple *de minimis* limit.

Independently of the Internet, the rule is that an offer of a product which is protected by German patent law within Germany is a patent infringement. This is true regardless of the country in which a contract was signed, where the infringing product was delivered from or where the offer was addressed.

(b) Process patents

Whether a process patent can be infringed via the Internet where only a part of the process is carried out in Germany depends on the nature of the contact with Germany. If a process patent is used entirely outside of the territory in which it is protected, there is no domestic patent infringement. If a part of the patented claim is used within the territory in which it is protected, German patent law applies.

3.4 Remedies available for patent infringement

Where there is a patent infringement, German patent law provides the patentee with different claims against the infringer.

(a) Injunction (Patent Act, Section 139(1))

An injunction protects the patentee from future infringements. To get an injunction, the patentee must show that there is a risk of re-offending. This risk can be shown if there is already at least one infringing action, or when the facts indicate that there is a severe risk that an infringement will occur (Patent Act, Section 139(1) sentence 1). A wilful action by the infringer is not necessary. The injunction does not automatically cover the whole scope of protection of the patent, but only the specific infringing act.

(b) Destruction of infringing goods (Patent Act, Section 140a(1))

Any person who uses a patented invention in contravention of German patent law may be sued by the injured party for destruction of those products which the infringer possesses or has in his custody and which infringe the patent. This also applies if such products have been made using a process that is the subject matter of the patent. This also applies to any materials or apparatus in the custody of the infringer. Wilful infringement is not necessary and the claim can be precluded if the claim is disproportionate in the specific circumstances.

(c) ***Recall of products (Patent Act, Section 140a(3))***

Any person who uses a patented invention in contravention of German patent law can be sued by the injured party for recall of the products that are the subject matter of the patent or for their definitive removal from distribution channels. This encompasses scenarios where there are products that have been directly made by a process that is the subject matter of the patent. Again, wilful infringement is not necessary and the claim can be precluded if it is disproportionate in the specific circumstances.

(d) ***Information claim (Patent Act, Section 140b)***

Any person who uses a patented invention in contravention of German patent law may be sued by the injured party for prompt information as to the origin and the distribution channel of the products used. In cases where the infringement is obvious or in cases where the injured party has filed a legal action against the infringer, the claim also applies against any person that, on a commercial scale:

- had infringing products in their possession;
- made use of infringing services;
- provided services used for infringing acts or
- participated, according to the statement of one of the persons referred to in the three bullet points above, in the manufacture, production or distribution of such products or the provision of such services, except if such person is entitled to refuse to give evidence against the infringer in the lawsuit pursuant to Sections 383 to 385 of the Code of Civil Procedure.

The type of information that the person must provide is regulated in Section 140b(3) of the Patent Act. The claim for information may not be disproportionate (Patent Act, Section 140b(4)). Where the person required to provide information intentionally or with gross negligence provides information that is incorrect or incomplete, such person shall be liable to compensate the injured party for any damage incurred as a result.

(e) ***Damages claim (Patent Act, Section 139(2) sentence 1)***

Any person who intentionally or negligently infringes a patent will be liable to compensate the injured party for any losss incurred thereby. When assessing the damages, the profit which the infringer has made by infringing the right may also be taken into account. The claim for damages may also be calculated on the basis of the amount that the infringer would have had to pay as an adequate remuneration had he obtained the authorisation to use the invention.

(f) *Other claims*

Besides the aforementioned claims of German patent law, a patentee might also be entitled to claims provided by the Civil Code. The claims provided by German patent law are not exclusive (Patent Act, Section 141a).

(g) *Entitled persons*

Only the patentee and/or a licensee of an exclusive licence is entitled to claim an injunction and/or a claim for damages. Non-exclusive licensees are not entitled to do so.

(h) *Patent litigation proceeding*

For all legal actions whereby a claim arising from one of the legal relationships regulated by the Patent Act is asserted (ie, patent dispute cases), the civil chambers of the regional courts have exclusive jurisdiction without regard to the value in dispute. The term 'patent dispute' is interpreted broadly. A connection with rights or claims originating in German patent law will suffice.

Before a claim is filed with the court, the infringer should be warned by the plaintiff in order to avoid a quick acknowledgement by the infringer which would shift the burden of cost of the law suit to the plaintiff (Section 93 of the Code of Civil Procedure).

When a legal action has been brought on the basis of the Patent Act, it may be ordered in the judgment that the prevailing party may make the judgment public at the expense of the losing party, if the prevailing party can show a legitimate interest therein. The type and extent of publication are determined in the judgment (Patent Act, Section 140e).

With respect to Section 145 of the Patent Act, it is generally not possible to bring several legal actions against the same infringer. Any person who has brought a legal action pursuant to Section 139 of the Patent Act may bring a further action against the defendant on account of the same or a similar act on the basis of another patent only if, through no fault of his own, such person was unable to assert that patent in the earlier law suit.

The court of the main proceedings also has jurisdiction over preliminary injunction proceedings. The patentee must present *prima facie* evidence for its claim. As the preliminary injunction can be an *ex parte* proceeding in which the potential infringer might not be heard, the potential infringer has the possibility to send a protective letter to the court as soon as it expects the initiation of a preliminary injunction proceeding by the other side. The protective letter enables the potential infringer to argue why it does not infringe the patent. The need to send a protective letter is not so urgent in preliminary patent law proceedings, as decisions without an oral hearing of both sides before a judgment are exceptional.

According to Section 142a of the Patent Act, a product that infringes a patent that is protected by the Patent Act is subject, at the request of the holder of the rights and against its security, to seizure by the customs authorities, on import or export, in those cases where infringement is obvious and if EU Regulation 1383/2003 is not to be applied.

(i) ***Criminal prosecution***

According to Patent Act, Section 142(1) any person who, without the required consent of the patentee or of the owner of a supplementary protection certificate:

- makes or offers, puts on the market, uses or imports or possesses for such purposes a product which is the subject matter of the patent or of the supplementary protection certificate; or
- uses or offers for use within the German territory a process which is the subject matter of the patent or of the supplementary protection certificate,

may be punished by up to three years' imprisonment or a fine.

An attempt to commit such an offence will also be punishable (Patent Act, Section 142(3)). Offences under subsection (1) are prosecuted only on complaint, unless the prosecuting authorities deem that *ex-officio* prosecution is justified in view of the particular public interest (Patent Act, Section 142(4)).

Criminal prosecution does not have much practical relevance in Germany.

4. Disclosure orders against ISPs

4.1 Availability

A disclosure order can be obtained against ISPs requiring them to disclose the identity and contact details of a user of their service who is suspected of infringing an IP right. The relevant provisions are Section 19(2) of the Trademark Act, Section 140b of the Patent Act and Section 101 of the Copyright Act. It is also possible to file a criminal complaint against an alleged infringer who is identified by his IP address and then to request access to the criminal records (Section 406e of the Code of Criminal Procedure), in order to gain information regarding the identity of the infringer. The right of access to criminal records is, however, applied very restrictively.

4.2 Requirements

The requirements the patentee must show in order to obtain such an order are listed in Section 140b of the Patent Act. The patentee must show, among other things, that the infringement is obvious, that it is on a commercial scale and that the disclosure claim is not disproportionate. In some cases additional requirements can apply (Patent Act, Section 140b(9)).

In order to obtain access to criminal records, the patentee must file a criminal complaint against an alleged infringer, criminal investigation proceedings must have been started and the patentee must show a legitimate interest in gaining access to the files.

4.3 'John Doe' injunctions

John Doe injunctions are not common in Germany. According to Section 253(1) of the Code of Civil Procedure, which is also applicable to patent proceedings, the plaintiff must state the name of the defendant in the complaint or describe the defendant so clearly that there is no doubt as to the identity of the person.

Hong Kong

Justin Davidson
Norton Rose Fulbright Hong Kong

1. Copyright, database rights and design rights

1.1 Overview

Putting content on the Internet is no different to the off-line world; IP and other laws will still apply, they just need to be interpreted in the on-line environment.

In Hong Kong, the main protections for IP rights in digital works on the Internet are provided in the Copyright Ordinance. To be protected by copyright, internet content must first fit within one of the prescribed categories of work under the Copyright Ordinance.

(a) Literary and artistic works[1]

Written material such as articles and website content can clearly constitute literary works and in the same way, images and photos can constitute artistic works.

Software and applications are also primarily protected in Hong Kong as literary works. Literary works are defined as works which can be written, spoken or sung. This will include computer programs and preparatory design materials for computer programs.

The Copyright Ordinance does not, however, define what is a 'computer program'. The Hong Kong Court of Appeal in *HKSAR v Chan Tak Tim*[2] recognised as persuasive Australian jurisprudence that machine or object code could not constitute a literary work, since electrical impulses inside a computer cannot be perceived by a human's senses, though object code could be protected as an adaptation of source code (which can itself be a literary work).

(b) Films, sound recordings, and broadcasts[3]

Video and audio content on the Internet will naturally fall within films and sound recordings respectively. It is irrelevant the medium on which the sound recording is made or the methods by which the sounds are produced. Film can be a recording on any medium from which a moving image may by any means be produced.

TV and radio stations can also transmit their content over the Internet. Such material can be protected as television and sound broadcasts.

1 Sections 4 and 5 of Copyright Ordinance (Cap 528).
2 [2004] 3 HKLRD 112.
3 Sections 6, 7 and 8 of the Copyright Ordinance.

(c) ***Typographical arrangement of a published edition***

Copyright only subsists in original works, so it will not subsist in a typographical arrangement if it is a reproduction of the typographical arrangement of a previously published off-line publication.[4]

(d) ***Protection of the user interface***

The user interface may be protected as a literary and/or artistic work, but to the extent it has not been copied substantially, in whole or in significant part, it would be difficult to protect the 'look and feel' of the whole graphical user interface under copyright law.

(e) ***Computer-generated works***

Works created using a computer, applicable to most internet content, will attract copyright in the normal way as the computer is no more than a tool for the creation of the work.

Works generated by a computer can also attract copyright, provided they fall within the prescribed categories of copyright work. In the absence of a human author though, the period of copyright runs for 50 years from the end of the calendar year in which the work was made.[5]

(f) ***Websites protected as databases***

There is no separate protection for a database as an independent right in Hong Kong.

(g) ***Compilations***

Copyright can subsist in compilations. The Hong Kong Court confirmed in the case of *Apple Daily Ltd v Oriental Press Group Ltd*,[6] by refusing to strike out the claims, that there was an arguable case that the plaintiff's articles were protected by copyright as compilations of news and press information, even if there was no copyright in the information itself.

1.2 Infringing acts

The Hong Kong Copyright Ordinance provides the authors of internet content with the exclusive right to copying, performing, broadcasting and making available on the Internet, provided that the work falls under one of the previously described protected categories of work.

(a) ***Copying***

Temporary copies: It can be an act of copying even if the copy is a temporary or transient copy, if it was reproduced in a material form.[7]

In any medium: Copying includes storing the work in any medium by electronic means.[8]

---

4 Section 10 of the Copyright Ordinance.
5 Section 17(6) of the Copyright Ordinance.
6 [2011] 2 HKC 28.
7 Section 26(6) of the Copyright Ordinance.

(b) ***Issuing copies to the public***

In addition to copying, it is an act restricted by copyright to issue copies of a work to the public.[9]

(c) ***Making available of copies***

It is also an act restricted by copyright to make available copies of works through the Internet.[10]

(d) ***Perform, show or play work in public***

The playing or showing of a sound recording, film, broadcast or cable programme in public, which includes by electronic means such as on the Internet, is an act restricted by copyright.[11]

(e) ***Rent or lend the work to the public***

The rental of the original or copies of a film, sound recording or a computer program is an act restricted by copyright.[12]

(f) ***Authorising another person to do any of the above***

Copyright in a work is infringed by a person who without the consent of the copyright owner does, or authorises another to do, any of the above restricted acts.[13]

(g) ***Secondary infringement***

It is an offence for a person to make (for sale or hire), sell, let for hire, import or export infringing copies for a commercial purpose, or distribute infringing copies of any work to the extent that it prejudicially affects the copyright owner.[14]

The scope of 'distributing infringing copies' was considered in the landmark Hong Kong internet-related criminal case *Chan Nai Ming v HKSAR*.[15] In that case, a man named Chan Nai Ming was the first person in the world to receive a custodial sentence for using Bit Torrent software to infringe copyright. Chan had uploaded copies of legally purchased films using a software program called Bit Torrent which 'seeds' the films to allow other Bit Torrent users to download the films onto their computers.

On appeal, Chan's lawyers argued that the magistrate erred in law by ignoring the condition that 'distributing' a 'copy' must include complete copies of the work. The Bit Torrent software operates by allowing users to download files through assembling multiple parts of a shared file from different users, thus there are no users with a complete copy of the shared file, though a complete copy can still be re-created by users transferring different parts of the shared file to each other.

8 Section 23 of the Copyright Ordinance.
9 Section 24 of the Copyright Ordinance.
10 Section 26(2) of the Copyright Ordinance.
11 Section 27 of the Copyright Ordinance.
12 Section 25 of the Copyright Ordinance.
13 Section 22(2) of the Copyright Ordinance.
14 Section 118(1) of the Copyright Ordinance.
15 [2007] 2 HKLRD 489.

Accordingly, it was argued Chan could not have committed an offence because he was only distributing electronic data, rather than distributing a complete copy.

The Hong Kong Court of Final Appeal held that there can be a transfer or distribution of electronic copies without the use of a tangible storage device since an electronic copy of a work can be transmitted through the network of computers and cables making up the Internet. Moreover, the Court found that since 'distribution' is not defined in the Ordinance, it should include distributions in the form of digital information sent to the downloaders and reassembled by their computers. As an aside, the Court also said that it would be an offence to enable others to rent a film by transmitting an electronic copy to another through the Internet and programming it to delete itself after a specific date (infringement by rental of work to the public).

(h) *Infringement by communicating to the public*

The Copyright (Amendment) Bill 2011 seeks to introduce a new restricted act to provide a 'catch-all' which will be particularly relevant to the online environment, though it is framed as technology neutral, so as not to go out of date with future technological developments. It includes any type of electronic communication, including uploading and transmission on the Internet.[16] It will also be criminal infringement, including for non-commercial communication, though in the latter case only if the communication is to such an extent "as to affect prejudicially the copyright owner".[17]

1.3 Test for copyright infringement

A fundamental requirement to constitute copyright infringement is that a substantial part of the plaintiff's work must have been copied. There must be an adequate degree of objective similarity between the plaintiff's and the defendant's work to the extent that the defendant's work must have derived from that of the plaintiff.[18]

In determining whether it is a substantial or an insubstantial part that has been copied, the Hong Kong courts will consider both the quantity and the quality of what has been copied and in particular, the significance of that part in relation to the overall work. In *Chow Wai Man, Vivian & Polygram Records, Ltd v Easy Finder Ltd*[19] the singer's distinctive face (from a photo in which her record label had copyright) had been pasted onto the picture of an unknown woman's nude body.

Repeated copying of insubstantial parts will not necessarily constitute copyright infringement.

1.4 Exemptions/defences to copyright infringement

Under Hong Kong law, there are several exceptions or defences to copyright infringement. In determining whether an act is a permitted under an exception, the

16 New Section 28A.
17 New Section 118(8B).
18 *Fossil Inc v Trimset Ltd & Anor* [2003] 3 HKLRD 11.
19 [1995] HKCFI 402.

primary consideration is that the act does not conflict with a normal exploitation of the work by the copyright owner and does not prejudicially affect the legitimate interests of the copyright owner.[20]

(a) *Personal copying rights*

There is no comprehensive personal right to copy (simply for domestic non-commercial use) and even though the copying of material for personal use in the confines of homes may be widespread and politically and socially acceptable in Hong Kong, it is not technically an exception to infringement unless it falls within one of the other exceptions mentioned below.

(b) *Time shifting*

Domestic copying of a cable programme or a broadcast to be viewed by the person making the copy at a more convenient time is expressly permitted.[21] Time shifting is deemed not to infringe copyright in the broadcast or cable programme or in any work included in it, but the statutory provisions do not define what falls under a 'cable programme' or 'broadcast service'. In a UK case, *Sony Music Entertainment (UK) Ltd v Easyinternetcafe Ltd,*[22] it was remarked (*obiter*) that the Internet can constitute a cable programme service and while this case has not been cited in Hong Kong, if a similar case arose, the Hong Kong courts would likely take guidance from this case.

(c) *Format shifting*

It is not an exception to copyright infringement in Hong Kong for an individual to transfer an authorised copy of a work from one medium to another. It should be noted, though, that the Copyright (Amendment) Bill 2011 seeks to introduce a limited domestic copyright exception for format shifting of sound recordings (eg, copying music from a CD into another format) for private use.[23]

(d) *Fair dealing*

Certain so-called 'fair dealing' exceptions to copyright infringement are specifically permitted in Hong Kong, namely using works in research and private study;[24] for criticism, review or news reporting;[25] and for giving/receiving instruction on a specified course of study provided by an educational establishment.[26] There is no general 'fair use' defence, as in some other jurisdictions, to permit other non-prescribed uses.

In deciding whether an act is 'fair dealing', the Hong Kong court will look at the nature of the conduct, in particular whether it is of a commercial nature and the impact it will have on the market or the value of the work, as well as the amount and significance of the copied portion in question.

For internet news reporting services to fall within this exception, it must be in the

---

20 Section 37(3) of the Copyright Ordinance.
21 Section 79 of the Copyright Ordinance.
22 [2003] FSR 48.
23 New Section 76A.
24 Section 38 of the Copyright Ordinance.
25 Section 39 of the Copyright Ordinance.
26 Section 41A of the Copyright Ordinance.

context of reporting of current events and, except in the case of reporting by means of a sound recording, film, broadcast or cable programme, it must be accompanied by a sufficient acknowledgement of the author of the copyright work.

(e) ***Caching/temporary copies as part of communication process***

The incidental or transient copying of work which is technically required for the viewing of, or listening to, a work is statutorily permitted in Hong Kong.[27] Incidental or temporary cache copies saved on to a computer for improved browsing are regarded as such incidental copies. This excuses only the user using a web browser which temporarily stores copies for viewing a website and not the user specifically downloading films or other content.

(f) ***Hosting***

There is not presently a specific 'hosting defence' as such in Hong Kong, but to date, no internet service providers (ISPs) in Hong Kong have been held liable for the copyright infringing content of their users. The Copyright Ordinance does provide a defence for the "mere provision of physical facilities for enabling the making available of copies of works",[28] which may apply to ISPs, but there must be no actual or constructive knowledge of the copyright infringement.

The Hong Kong government has been consulting on a 'safe harbour' for hosting providers since 2006 and the Copyright (Amendment) Bill 2011 includes proposals to introduce a statutory regime for limiting the liability of ISPs for damages for copyright infringement that has occurred on their platforms. There is also a draft Code of Practice under consultation setting out 'notice & (counter) notice' and 'notice & take down' procedures, to facilitate cooperation between copyright owners and ISPs to combat online infringement.

(g) ***Back-up copies***

It is statutorily permitted to make a back-up copy of a legitimate computer program without infringing the copyright in the software if it is necessary to have the back-up copy for the lawful use of the legitimate programme.[29]

(h) ***Reverse engineering***

Reverse engineering of a work is not prohibited in itself, though it can be an infringement if there is any copying or adaptation of a work. The user of a computer program may, however, copy or adapt a programme if the copying or adapting is necessary for his lawful use, such as for the purpose of correcting errors.

(i) ***Parody defence***

Hong Kong does not have a specific parody defence to copyright infringement, which in some other jurisdictions has been claimed under a broader 'fair use'

---

27 Section 65 of the Copyright Ordinance.
28 Section 26 of the Copyright Ordinance.
29 Section 60 of the Copyright Ordinance.

doctrine. There has been concern about how criminal liability for copyright infringement in respect of political parody might inhibit free speech in Hong Kong, and the Copyright (Amendment) Bill 2011 does include a non-exhaustive list of factors to consider in deciding when criminal liability may arise. These include:

- the purpose of communication;
- the amount and substantiality of the portion copies (in relation to the work as a whole);
- the mode of communication;
- the nature and commercial value of the work; and
- the economic prejudice caused to the copyright owner as a result of the communication.[30]

In July 2013, the Hong Kong government launched a public consultation on the treatment of parody to explore the balance between copyright protection and freedom of expression. The three proposed treatments include clarification of the relevant existing provisions in the Copyright Ordinance, introduction of a criminal exemption and/or the introduction of an express fair dealing exception.

(j) ***Incidental inclusion***

The incidental inclusion of a copyright work in an artistic work, sound recording, film, broadcast or cable programme is an exception to infringement in Hong Kong.[31]

1.5 Remedies available for copyright infringement

Available remedies include injunctions to restrain the infringer from further infringing the copyright, and an order demanding the infringer to destroy or deliver up all infringing copies of the work.

Other remedies include damages or an account of profits based on an amount equivalent to the loss suffered by the copyright owner or the profits made by the infringer. Hong Kong courts also have the power to award what are called 'additional damages'. These are not punitive damages, but the court will consider the flagrancy of the conduct, whether the defendant received any financial benefit from the infringement, and the accuracy and integrity of the defendant's business accounts and records.

Hong Kong Customs and Excise is responsible for criminal investigation and prosecution of copyright infringement. Offenders can be liable for certain copyright offences to a fine of up to HK$500,000 and imprisonment for up to eight years.[32]

1.6 Copyright liability

(a) ***Hosting/cloud computing where infringing content uploaded by user of service***

There is no specific defence at present available to the provider of platform hosting

30 New Section 118(8C).
31 Section 40 of the Copyright Ordinance.
32 Section 119 of the Copyright Ordinance.

services for infringing content put up by a user, other than that the copyright infringement act of 'making available copies of works to the public' will not itself be constituted by the mere provision of physical facilities (cloud computing servers) for enabling the making available of copies, provided there is no actual or constructive knowledge.

(b) ***Hypertext linking***

To a third-party website: Assuming the link itself (words or image) is not a copy of a copyright work, the act of linking to a third-party website does not involve a restricted act under copyright, as the user is simply transported by the link to the website.

To an infringing work: In general, posting a hyperlink that links to infringing content does not automatically amount to an infringement, without control over the infringing content.

Copying of headlines: The general rule in Hong Kong has historically been that there is no copyright in a title; however, headlines could potentially be substantial enough to attract copyright.

(c) ***P2P network***

Supplier of P2P software: There has not been a Napster-style case against a peer-to-peer sharing site in Hong Kong and there would be difficulties, since none of the restricted acts is carried out by the software supplier itself. There could be a possible claim for 'authorising' copyright infringement by its users, but establishing authorisation might be difficult in Hong Kong.

Uploaders/downloaders: In *Cinepoly Records Co Ltd & Others v Hong Kong Broadband Network Ltd & Others*,[33] an online investigation revealed massive online infringement activities. Each of 22 uploaders identified had uploaded more than 100 song titles, some had exceeded 1,000 song titles and some of the songs uploaded had not yet been made commercially available. The Hong Kong court held that the copyright owners had not consented to the uploading of their musical works to the Internet. Accordingly, the unauthorised uploading constituted copyright infringement.

(d) ***Webcasting***

There have been no Hong Kong decisions on the copyright position with regarding to webcasting.

(e) ***Streaming***

Hong Kong does not have any specific laws dealing with streaming and so the streaming of copyright material would likely be treated as the downloading of a transient copy, but it will not fall within the exception to copyright infringement as

33 [2006] 1 HKLRD 255.

a cache copy since it is a specific user-initiated step. The interesting question of delayed streaming, and the availability of a time-shifting defence, has also not been considered in Hong Kong, though the courts would look closely at current developments on this elsewhere, including in Australia.[34]

(f) *Framing*

There have been no cases in Hong Kong concerning framing, but framing that deep-links (allows viewers to enter directly into an inside page without viewing other content, such as a homepage or advertisements which the original website owner intends his/her visitors to see) may be considered an infringement. There may also be an issue with moral rights if there is insufficient attribution.

(g) *Transmission of infringing work across a communications network*

The provider of a communications network in Hong Kong would probably be able successfully to argue that it is not liable for the transmission of infringing work across its network, for example by email, but it will depend on the extent of the provider's own activities.

If also engaged in active control (ie, not just being a 'passive conduit'), or offering other online services and content, then the provider may not be able to avail itself of the statutory defence to copyright infringement as the 'mere provider of physical facilities'.[35]

(h) *Aggregator websites (eg, Google News, price comparison websites)*

There are no Hong Kong decisions on the deep-linking practices of news and other aggregator sites, but it would be perhaps unlikely to be copyright infringement unless content itself is copied.

(i) *Treatment of user-generated content*

Original user-generated content will attract copyright protection in the same way as any other content, though ISPs may, by contract (through their terms of service), require copyright in such content to be assigned, or at least licensed to the ISP and/or the public.

1.7 Joint liability for internet service providers

ISPs are viewed as having substantial control over an infringement, because they can remove public internet access to materials and/or terminate the internet services of the infringing user so they could potentially be jointly liable for acts carried out by users of their services.

There is no specific ISP hosting defence in Hong Kong, though to date no ISP has been found jointly liable for the copyright-infringing content of its users.

The Copyright (Amendment) Bill 2011 proposes introducing a set of conditions that if fulfilled, will protect ISPs from liability in damages for copyright infringement

---

34 *National Rugby League Investments Pty Ltd v Singtel Optus Pty Ltd* [2012] FCAFC 59.

35 Section 26(4) of the Copyright Ordinance.

occurring on their service platforms. The conditions are:

- The ISP takes reasonable steps to limit the infringement as soon as practicable after it becomes aware that any infringement has occurred.
- The ISP is not receiving any financial benefit attributable to the infringement.
- The ISP accommodates and does not interfere with any technical measures set up by the copyright owners to protect their copyright works.
- The ISP has designated an agent to receive notice of alleged infringements by supplying, through its service, the name, address, telephone number and electronic mail address of the agent.

The Secretary for Commerce and Economic Development is presently consulting with the public on a Code of Practice for ISPs. The code involves a set of guidelines for ISPs to follow when they are notified of infringing activities on the services provided by them. The Bill expressly provides that an ISP shall be treated as having satisfied the above conditions if it complies with the provisions in the (to be) published Code of Practice.

1.8 Relief

Even if not liable for damages (when the Copyright (Amendment) Bill 2011 comes into force), injunctive relief will still be available against an ISP.

1.9 Issues specific to Hong Kong

(a) Jurisdiction

In Hong Kong, the court will consider whether it has jurisdiction at the time an action is commenced. The court will have jurisdiction if the potential defendant is an internet user or service provider residing in Hong Kong. If the potential defendant resides outside Hong Kong, the plaintiff will need to convince the court that Hong Kong is the appropriate jurisdiction to hear the dispute. The Rules of the High Court set out the conditions on which a Hong Kong court will grant leave for an action to be served on a defendant outside the jurisdiction. Order 11, Rule 1(1)(f) states that the claim must be founded on a tort and the damage must have been sustained, or resulted from an act committed, within Hong Kong.

The Hong Kong Court of First Instance confirmed in *Shanghai Reeferco Container Co Ltd v Waggonbau Elze Gmbh & Co Besitz Kg*[36] that a patent infringement is considered a tort for these purposes. The case is also suggested as authority for copyright and other IP infringements being considered as torts for the purpose of the jurisdictional rule.

(b) Claim to infringement of foreign copyright

Hong Kong has long been party to the Berne Convention[37] (pre-1997 through

36 [2005] 2 HKLRD 711.

37 Berne Convention for the Protection of Literary and Artistic Works 1886 (revised).

accession by the UK, post-1997 through accession by the People's Republic of China) and most other international IP treaties. Accordingly, Hong Kong courts recognise the foreign copyright of nationals of the other countries who are signatories to the Berne Convention.

(c) *Emission theory*

Hong Kong law recognises that the infringing act in relation to copyright can take place at both the location where the infringing work is uploaded and where it is downloaded.

1.10 Orphan works

There will not be an infringement of copyright in a literary, dramatic, musical or artistic work if it is not possible to ascertain the identity of the author.[38] This exemption does not apply in relation to a work in which government copyright subsists.

1.11 Online piracy measures

The Hong Kong Customs and Excise Department is responsible for taking criminal action for IP rights infringement. They have set up two internet anti-piracy teams to monitor activities on the Internet, including to investigate cases which involve the use of pirated software and copyright works for commercial purposes.

1.12 Electronic infringement of moral rights

Hong Kong has three moral rights that may be infringed in the internet context:

- right to be identified as author or director (paternity right);[39]
- right to object to derogatory treatment (integrity right);[40] and
- false attribution – right to guard against impersonation.[41]

Most digital works have all three moral rights; however, software authors have no right of paternity or integrity, only a right against false attribution (to avoid association with a modified version of an author's software).

2. Trademarks

2.1 Use of a trademark

In Hong Kong, a registered trademark may be revoked on the ground that the trademark has not been genuinely used in Hong Kong by the owner, or with his/her consent, in relation to the goods or services for which it is registered, for a continuous period of at least three years, and there are no valid reasons for non-use.[42]

---

38 Section 66 of the Copyright Ordinance.
39 Section 89 of the Copyright Ordinance.
40 Section 92 of the Copyright Ordinance.
41 Section 96 of the Copyright Ordinance.
42 Section 52 of the Trademarks Ordinance (Cap 559).

The burden of proving use of the registered mark during the relevant period lies with the registered owner.[43]

Revocation of a registered mark for non-use can be avoided through use on an active website that enables transactions to be done from Hong Kong. The mark must be used in the same form as it is registered, or in a form which differs only in elements that do not alter the distinctive character of the mark as registered,[44] and the use should be 'genuine use'.

The assessment of 'genuine use' will take into account all the facts and circumstances relevant to establishing whether such use is aimed at maintaining or creating a share in the market for the goods or services protected by the mark.

Use of a registered trademark on a Hong Kong-based website, or a foreign website for goods/services which can be transacted from Hong Kong through the website, can be trademark infringement in Hong Kong.

Less clear is the Hong Kong law infringement position for more passive foreign websites on which transactions are not carried out. A key factor will be the connections to Hong Kong, but the Hong Kong courts have not gone as far as confirming the test, used in some places, of whether the website is objectively aimed at or intended for consumers in the jurisdiction.[45]

2.2 Infringement

(a) *Metatags*

There have been no decisions in Hong Kong regarding use of metatags; however, the Hong Kong courts are likely to conclude that the unauthorised use of third-party trademarks in metatags in the course of trade will be considered trademark infringement, unless there is some legitimate reason for their use and it is not misleading.

(b) *Keywords*

Hong Kong has not yet had any decided cases on the use of trademarks as keywords. If the use of a reputable trademark as a keyword resulted in a loss of distinctiveness of the trademark, or if an advertiser used the trademark as a keyword to offer for sale imitations, these would likely be found to be trademark infringement.

(c) *Sponsored links*

There are no Hong Kong decisions with regard to trademark infringement for using trademarks in sponsored links. The Hong Kong courts would likely follow the decisions and reasoning in relevant UK and ECJ decisions, and entitle a trademark owner to restrain an online marketplace operator (such as eBay) from advertising (on the basis of a keyword identical to his/her trademark and which has been selected through an internet referencing service (eg, Google AdWords) by that operator)

---

43 Section 82(1) of the Trademarks Ordinance.
44 Section 52(3)(a) of the Trademarks Ordinance.
45 *KK Yakult & others v Yakudo Group Holdings* [2004] HKCFI 156.

goods bearing that trademark which are offered for sale in the marketplace, in circumstances where reasonably well-informed and observant internet users cannot easily discern from the advertising whether the goods in question originate from the trademark proprietor or from a third party.[46]

(d) ***Hidden text***

There are no Hong Kong decisions on whether the incorporation without authorisation of another's trademarks in the hidden text on a website, in order for the website to appear higher in the list of 'organic' results generated by a search engine, is unauthorised use of a trademark; however, the Hong Kong courts would likely conclude that it would be, if there was no legitimate reason for doing so.

(e) ***Internet domain names***

Registration of the domain name itself does not automatically give rise to liability for trademark infringement in Hong Kong, but even passive holding of a domain name could still give rise to a successful complaint for transfer of the domain name under HKDNR's[47] Domain Name Dispute Resolution Policy.

(f) ***Search navigation tools***

A search navigation tool that includes a trademark would likely be treated in the same way as a metatag or keyword that includes a trademark.

(g) ***Hypertext links***

Including a word or image that is a registered trademark as the hypertext link on a website, without the trademark owner's permission, is likely to constitute trademark infringement in Hong Kong.

(h) ***Framing***

There are no Hong Kong decisions on framing, but framing would likely give rise to trademark liability if trademarks from the original website are displayed in such a way as to give the impression that the trademark owner endorsed or consented to association with the framing site, and that framing site is used in the course of business.

2.3 Defences

There are some potential defences available in relation to the above acts:

(a) ***Descriptive (non trademark) use of the mark***

Honest concurrent use of a registered trademark is permitted in Hong Kong.[48]

The following uses also specifically do not amount to infringement:[49]

- own name or address, or the name of the place of business;

46 *L'Oreal SA v eBay* [2011] Case C-324/09.
47 Hong Kong Domain Name Registration Company Limited (the .hk registrar).
48 Section 19 of the Trademarks Ordinance.
49 Section 19(3) of the Trademarks Ordinance.

- name of a predecessor in business or the name of a predecessor's place of business;
- signs that serve to designate the kind, quality, quantity, intended purpose, value, geographical origin, time of production of goods or rendering of services, or other characteristics of goods or services; or
- where use of the trademark is necessary to indicate the intended purpose of goods or services (for example as accessories or spare parts), provided the use is in accordance with honest practices in industrial or commercial matters.

(b) Comparative advertising

It is possible in Hong Kong for a trader to use a competitor's trademark by way of a comparison, for the purpose of identifying the latter's goods or services, provided that such use is in accordance with honest practices in industrial or commercial matters.[50] In determining this, the Hong Kong court may consider any factors it considers relevant, including:

- whether the use takes unfair advantage of the trademark;
- whether the use is detrimental to the distinctive character or repute of the trademark;
- whether the use is such as to deceive the public.

(c) Parodies

Parodies will likely also be exceptions to trademark infringement, provided there is no likelihood of confusion.

2.4 Parallel imports

Hong Kong is a strong proponent of free markets generally and does not restrict consumer choice through prohibiting parallel imports. It is not therefore trademark infringement in Hong Kong to offer genuine branded goods (that have been first placed on the market elsewhere with the trademark owner's consent) for sale in Hong Kong via a website (ie, parallel import or grey import goods).[51]

2.5 Remedies

Injunctions are available to restrain an infringer from further infringing the trademark. A trademark owner can also obtain an order demanding an infringer to deliver up to it, or to dispose of, infringing articles offered on the website.

Other remedies include damages or an account of profits based on an amount equivalent to the loss suffered by the trademark owner or the profits made by the infringer. The courts also have the power to award 'additional damages', depending on the flagrancy of the conduct, whether the defendant received any financial attributions from the infringement, and the accuracy and integrity of the defendant's business accounts and records.

---

50 Section 21 of the Trademarks Ordinance.
51 Section 20 of the Trademarks Ordinance.

2.6 Liability of ISPs

There is no specific hosting defence for ISPs in Hong Kong, though to date no Hong Kong ISP has been found liable for damages for activities carried out by users of its service.

2.7 Advertising law and regulation

There are currently no specific advertising laws or advertising codes of practice in Hong Kong. However, any advertising conducted should still be in compliance with the Trade Descriptions Ordinance (Cap 362) which generally requires that any description of goods in advertisements must be truthful and not misleading.

2.8 Domain name disputes

A complaint against a .hk domain name (administered by HKDNR) may be filed by a complainant with the Hong Kong International Arbitration Centre (HKIAC) under the HKDNR's Domain Name Dispute Resolution Policy.

Three elements must be established in the complaint under the HKDNR Policy:

- the domain name holder has no rights or legitimate interests in respect of the domain name;
- the domain name is identical or confusingly similar to a trademark to which the complainant has rights; and
- the domain name has been registered and is being used in bad faith.

The following examples may be treated as indicative of bad faith:

- the domain name was registered or acquired primarily for the purpose of selling, renting, or otherwise transferring it to the owner of the trademark or to a competitor, for valuable consideration;
- the domain name was registered in order to prevent the owner of the trademark from reflecting the mark in a corresponding domain name;
- the domain name was registered primarily for the purpose of disrupting the business of a competitor; or
- by using the domain name, the registrant has intentionally attempted to attract, for commercial gain, internet users to its website, by creating a likelihood of confusion as to the source, sponsorship, affiliation, or endorsement of its website.

(a) Fees and time frame

The official fees for filing a .hk domain name complaint depend on the number of domain names involved in the complaint and the number of panellists hearing the dispute. For example, the official fees for filing a complaint for one domain name to be heard by one panellist would be US$1,300 and for three panellists would be US$2,800.

Under normal circumstances, a decision can usually be reached in 60 days from the date a complaint is filed with the HKIAC.

2.9 Unfair competition/passing off

If internet content includes unregistered trademarks or a website has a 'look and feel' that passes the site off as that of another, then there may in addition be a common law claim for passing off. In Hong Kong, a passing off claimant must show three elements:

- the goods or services must have acquired goodwill or reputation in the marketplace that distinguishes such goods or services from competitors;
- the defendant misrepresents his/her goods or services, either intentionally or unintentionally, so that the public may have the impression that the offered goods or services are those of the claimant; and
- the claimant may suffer damage because of the misrepresentation.

3. Patents

3.1 Patentability of 'internet' inventions

Under the Hong Kong Patents Ordinance, patent protection may only be awarded where an invention is "susceptible of industrial application, is new and involves an inventive step".[52]

There are a number of specific statutory exclusions:[53]

(2) The following in particular shall not be regarded as inventions:

(a) a discovery, scientific theory or mathematical method;

(b) an aesthetic creation;

(c) a scheme, rule or method for performing a mental act, playing a game or doing business, or a program for a computer;

(d) the presentation of information.

The above exclusions are, however, narrowly interpreted, meaning that only those patent applications that are 'solely characterised' within one of the above excluded categories will be excluded on that basis.[54] In practice, this means that websites and website features that may constitute computer programs, business methods, mathematical methods and the presentation of information, while unable to be patented in themselves, may still potentially be patentable if they form part of an otherwise patentable 'invention'.

3.2 Bioinformatics

The Hong Kong Patent Office does not presently conduct substantive examination of patent applications. (However, this is under review.) Standard patents in Hong Kong are registered on the basis of granted patents in the following designated registries: the Intellectual Property Office of the United Kingdom, the European Patent Office (EPO) and the State Intellectual Property Office of the People's Republic of China. On specific issues such as patentability of novel DNA sequence or protein structure discovered through the use of bioinformatics, Hong Kong generally follows

52 Section 93(1) of the Patents Ordinance.
53 Section 93(2) of the Patents Ordinance.
54 *Koninklijke Philips Electronics NV v Wealthful Technology Ltd* [2002] HKCFI 82.

UK and EPO jurisprudence. Given the acceptance of such DNA sequence patents discovered by bioinformatics under current UK and EPO practice, Hong Kong courts will likely uphold such Hong Kong patents granted based on filings in the United Kingdom and EPO as valid in Hong Kong.

3.3 Issues specific to Hong Kong

(a) Infringement on the Internet

A Hong Kong patent will be infringed on the Internet provided that the particulars of the infringement are performed within the confines of Hong Kong jurisdiction. Whether the infringement falls within Hong Kong depends on whether the acts, as they occurred in Hong Kong, constitute an infringement of the patent under Hong Kong law.

For an overseas defendant, the claim must be founded on a tort and the damage sustained, or result from an act committed, within the jurisdiction.[55] It is accepted that patent infringement constitutes a tort for these purposes.[56]

(b) Process patents

A process patent, infringed via the Internet, where only part of the process is carried out in Hong Kong will not likely be infringement in Hong Kong until all the particulars required for infringement occur in Hong Kong.

3.4 Remedies available for patent infringement

Remedies available in Hong Kong include an injunction, orders for delivery up (the court orders the defendant to deliver up or to destroy any patented product in relation to which the patent is infringed or any article in which the product is inextricably incorporated), damages, or an account of the profits derived from the infringement and a declaration that the patent is valid and has been infringed by the defendant.

4. Disclosure orders against internet service providers

4.1 Availability

Standalone disclosure orders can be obtained in Hong Kong against innocent ISPs, requiring them to disclose the identity and contact details of a user of their service who is suspected of infringing an IP right.[57] These are known in Hong Kong practice as Norwich Pharmacal orders after the original UK decision.[58] The purpose of a Norwich Pharmacal order is to enable a person to discover the identity of a wrongdoer so as to seek appropriate remedies against the infringer directly.

Whether or not a Norwich Pharmacal order will be granted depends on the facts of each case. The court must balance the competing interests of the rights owner, the

---

55 Order 11(1)(1)(f) of the Rules of the High Court of Hong Kong (Cap 4).
56 *Shanghai Reeferco Container Co Ltd v Waggonbau Elze Gmbh & Co Besitz KG* [2005] 2 HKLRD 711.
57 *Cinepoly Records Co Ltd v Hong Kong Broadband* [2006] 2 HKLRD 255.
58 *Norwich Pharmacal Co v Customs & Excise Commissioners* [1974] AC 133.

innocent ISP and the individual's privacy in deciding how to exercise its discretion. Such an order is not made lightly and the court is required to bear in mind the following:

- there must be strong and compelling evidence to show that a serious tortious or wrongful act has been committed (ie, there must at least be a *prima facie* case of a wrong having been committed);
- it must be clearly shown that the order will or will likely result in substantial and worthwhile benefits for the rights owner (eg, it will enable the rights owner to bring an action against the wrongdoer and the ISP has or is likely to have information regarding the identity of the wrongdoer); and
- the discovery sought must not be unduly wide (ie, the order must be specific and restricted only to information that is necessary).

4.2 Requirements

To obtain such an order the IP rights owner must establish that:

- serious tortious or wrongful activities have been committed; and
- the suspected infringer is a person whom the rights owner *bona fide* believes to be infringing his/her rights in the sense that he/she could reasonably be assumed to be the wrongdoer; and
- the innocent ISP, against whom discovery is sought, has become involved or caught up in such infringing activities, thereby facilitating them.

If any of the above elements are not established, the rights owner's application will fail.

On top of establishing the above elements, the rights owner must further show that it is just and convenient in all the circumstances of the case for the Hong Kong court to exercise its discretion and grant the Norwich Pharmacal order.

4.3 Jurisdictional issues

A Norwich Pharmacal order may be sought in Hong Kong against a Hong Kong ISP to aid in potential foreign proceedings.

4.4 'John Doe' injunctions

'John Doe' injunctions can be obtained in Hong Kong to prevent IP rights infringement against persons unknown, so long as the description of the persons against whom the injunction is sought is sufficiently certain to identify those that are included and exclude those that are not.

India

Apar Gupta
Advani & Co

1. Copyright, database rights and design right

1.1 Overview

(a) *Artistic works*

The Indian Copyright Act 1957, Section 2(c) defines an 'artistic work' as including a painting, drawing, engraving or photograph which shows a certain modicum of creativity. It also includes works of architecture and craftsmanship. Thus, pictorial representation and graphics on websites may fall under this definition.

(b) *Literary works*

Section 2(o) of the act defines 'literary works' as these mentioned in the list, without stating any criteria. It covers computer programs and compilations, including databases.[1] Section 13 also states that copyright subsists in artistic and literary works.[5]

(c) *Films, sound recordings, and broadcasts*

According to Section 2(f) of the Copyright Act, the term 'cinematograph' would be defined as any medium through which any moving image is produced by any means and would also include any sound recording in parallel with the visual recording.[2] Section 13(4) states that copyright in cinematography would not affect any separate copyright which is vested in any other work from which a substantial part is taken. Cinematography also includes clips and films hosted on a website or the Internet.

Section 2(xx) of the act defines 'sound recording' as including sounds produced regardless of the medium and method of producing them.

Section 2(dd) of the act defines 'broadcast' as any communication through the medium of wireless or by wire of signs, sounds or images or by wire. It also includes broadcast and internet broadcast rights of various sporting events. Indian law also recognises 'broadcasting reproduction rights' with regard to all broadcasts which subsist for 25 years starting from the beginning of the calendar year following that in which the broadcast is made. This enables the author to obtain protection against third parties in the event of unlicensed acts such as re-broadcasting, the broadcast or

1 The term 'database' was first included in the Amended Copyright Act 1994. Also see the Indian Copyright Act 1957, Section 13(1)(a); and see Alok Kumar Yadav, Protection of Databases in India, in *Copyright in the Digital Era*.

2 See *The South Indian Film Chamber of Commerce v Entertaining Enterprises*, 1995 SCC (2) 462.

making available to the public for payment or where such recording was done without licence or, where licensed, for any purpose not mentioned in the licence, or for selling and hiring any such recording of the broadcast to the public.

(d) *Typographical arrangement of a published edition*

There is no authoritative decision regarding the typographical arrangement of a published edition, and even the Copyright Act does not expressly grant typographical arrangement protection. However, certain elements of typographical arrangements may qualify as artistic works and may be protected by Indian law. In the case of *Bikanervala*[3] the font and style of the vendor's brand name was held by a court to have *prima facie* copyright protection, while in another case, the Intellectual Property Appellate Board rejected the copyright registration of fonts. Headnotes of legal decisions contained in proprietary legal databases have also been held to be entitled to copyright protection.[4]

(e) *Protection of the user interface*

There is no clear ruling on the protection of a user interface under Indian copyright laws. However, in a recent case the Delhi High Court has held that there is no copyright in a physical game board which can be displayed in computer programs since it is a design as per the Designs Act.[5]

(f) *Compilations*

Though Section 2(o) of the Copyright Act contains the term 'compilation', it does not define it. The Indian Supreme Court in the *Eastern Book* case[6] held that databases, which are understood to be a subset of compilations, can be granted protection only if there is some measure of creativity. The court in the case rejected the 'sweat of the brow' doctrine.

1.2 Infringing acts

(a) *Copying*

Temporary copies: Under Section 52(aa), certain acts do not constitute infringement with regard to computer programs, such as the making of copies and the adaptation of computer programs if carried out by a lawful possessor for the purpose of utilising the program. Thus, temporary caching which enhances access to the program and results in a temporary copy does not constitute infringement. Also, making temporary back-up copies for protection against damage and loss for the purpose of utilising the program does not constitute infringement.

In any medium: There is no limitation under copyright law regarding the medium

---

3 *Bikanervala v Bikaner Sweetwala*, IA 588/2004 in CS(OS) 69/2004.
4 *Eastern Book Company v DB Modak*, 101 (2002) DLT 205.
5 *Mattel, Inc v Mr Jayant Agarwalla*, IA No 2532/2008 in CS (OS) 344/2008.
6 *Eastern Book Company v DB Modak*, 101 (2002) DLT 205.

in which a temporary copy is made. However, it is usual practice for software and media to be sold under a user licence which prohibits any change in the medium of storage.

(b) ***Issuing copies to the public***

Under Sections 51(b)(i) and (ii) of the act, if a person sells or hires or by any means of trade displays the material for sale or hire or distributes for the purpose of trade any copyrighted work to the public or any act which prejudicially affects the owner of the copyrighted work, such person will be deemed to have infringed the copyright.

(c) ***Communicating work to the public***

Under Section 51(b)(iii), where any person by way of trade exhibits in public any copies of the work deemed to have infringed the copyright, there will be a prohibition on the exhibition of any copy of the copyrighted work to the public. Any person who carries out such an act will be deemed to have infringed the copyright.

(d) ***Perform, show or play work in public***

Under Section 2(qq), the term 'performer' includes an actor, musician, singer, dancer, juggler etc or any person making any performance. Section 38(1) sets out the 'performer's right', to which every performer is entitled. This right also extends to the Internet. The right is generally available to a performer for 50 years from the beginning of the calendar year following that in which the performance is made.

(e) ***Rent or lend the work to the public***

Section 14(b) of the act grants the author an exclusive right to rent or lend a computer program to the public. By necessary implication, there is a statutory bar to renting or lending a software program. However, the section states that such a rental is allowed when the software program is merely incidental to the rental.

(f) ***Authorising another person to do any of the above***

Under Section 18, the owner of the copyright has the power to assign any copyrighted work to any person, in relation to the existing work or work which will be in existence in future. An assignment of future work takes effect when the work comes into existence and the authorised person is known as the assignee and possesses all rights in relation to the work assigned.

No doubt, this authorisation constitutes a passive infringement. However, in India, the Copyright Act 1957 is silent as to the liability of websites which authorise the exposure of third-party content by their users. Although there is no specific mention, Section 51(a)(ii) imposes liability upon a person who, without a licence from the owner of the copyright or the registrar of copyrights, permits any place to be used for the communication of the work to the public where such a communication constitutes an infringement of the copyright. Thus, internet service providers (ISPs) fall within this category of persons. The only exception is where the person authorising such an infringement does not know of the harm being caused to the copyright owner. Thus, such a person is criminally liable under Section 63 of the Copyright Act if it knowingly allows third-party content to be exposed to the public. This section includes abetment to infringement.

(g) *Secondary infringement*

Indian courts have recognised the principle of secondary infringement in their interpretation of Section 51(a)(ii) of the Copyright Act. Under this provision, if a person allows the use of a place for any work, the communication of which is a violation of copyright, it will also be held liable. In *Super Cassettes Industries Ltd v Myspace Inc*,[7] the Delhi High Court held that secondary infringement extended to ISPs which allowed users to upload infringing copies of songs. In *Microsoft Corporation v Mr Kiran*[8] the High Court expressly noted that the acts mentioned in Section 51(b) may be termed as secondary acts of infringement.

1.3 Test for copyright infringement

(a) *Requirement of substantial reproduction*

The requirement under the Indian Copyright Act for substantial reproduction arises from Section 14, which states that the author has exclusive rights over a work or any substantial part thereof. Having demonstrated that a defendant in an infringement action has substantially copied the plaintiff's work, Indian courts have dispensed with the requirement of demonstrating actual copying by the defendant.[9]

(b) *Repeated copying of insubstantial part*

Indian courts have held that substantial reproduction cannot be precisely defined and is dependent on an inquiry as to the specific and unique facts and circumstances of each case. Here, more than the mere physical amount of the reproduction, the parts that are reproduced will be material to the determination of substantial reproduction.[10] Thus, if enough random original parts are copied which may be individually incapable of constituting copyright infringement, their collective aggregate may constitute copyright infringement.

1.4 Exemptions/defences to copyright infringement

(a) *Format shifting*

The Copyright Act 1957 does not expressly state that format shifting is legal. However, in terms of personal copying under Section 52(1)(ad), a back-up copy, on which no limitation has been placed, would normally involve format shifting.

---

7 *Super Cassettes Industries Ltd v Myspace Inc*, IA No 15781/2008 and IA No 3085/2009 in CS (OS) No 2682/2008.

8 *Microsoft Corporation v Mr Kiran*, 2007, (35) PTC 748 Del.

9 *Barbara Taylor Bradford v Sahara Media Entertainment Ltd*, 2004, (28) PTC 474 Cal.

10 *RG Anand v M/S Delux Films*, 1978 AIR 1613.

(b) ***Personal copying rights***

Under Section 52(1)(ad), a person is allowed to make copies or adaptations of a computer program from a legally obtained copy for non-commercial personal use. Although this does not expressly state that a person is allowed to change the format, this exception would ordinarily allow a user to make a back-up copy from a CD to a CDR. With respect to other artistic and visual works, there is currently no provision that allows digitisation or format shifting.

(c) ***Time shifting***

The Copyright Act 1957 contains no express provision to state that time shifting is legal.

(d) ***Fair use***

Fair use is an exemption available under Section 52 of the act. According to an amendment to the act in 1994, there are specific provisions – including Sections 52(1)(aa), 52(1)(ab), 52(1)(ac) and 52(1)(ad) – which are applicable to computer programs. Beyond this, the fair use provisions under Section 52, when not specifically excepted, also apply.

A person that relies on the defence of fair use must prove that such a use of the copyrighted material is not reasonably likely to have caused any harm to the owner of the copyright.

Fair use is based on a presumed intention of the author to allow certain uses of his work. However, this presumption must pass the test of reasonableness. Another approach is to derive the result from the doctrine of *de minimis non cural lex*. This means the use of minimal amounts of material from the copyrighted work. This flows from the above approach of reasonable presumption. It is presumed that if a substantial part of the work is used, it would cause harm to the author/owner of the copyright. The use of minimal material from his work would not have a harmful effect. However, this doctrine might fail if the author claims the absolute right on every part of his work.

The intention of the legislature is to encourage the production of literary works; therefore, use of copyrighted material may be carried out in a reasonable manner, as it may not be possible to complete a work without reference to previous works in that particular field.[11]

(e) ***Caching/temporary copies as part of communication process***

Temporary copies or 'caching' is permissible under Section 52(aa) of the Copyright Act when the copies so made are part of a communication process and necessary for accessing the program.

(f) ***Hosting***

Hosting of any content when done without knowledge, or selection or modification of the content, by a web host would generally not invite liability as per Section 79 of

---

11 Lal's *Commentary on the Copyright Act 1957*, Delhi Law House, 2006.

the IT Act 2000. However, as per the Delhi High Court judgment in *Super Cassettes Industries v Myspace*,[12] and the proviso under Section 81 of the IT Act, this safe harbour does not extend to copyright infringement. These provisions state that nothing contained in the IT Act 2000 shall restrict any person from exercising any right conferred under the Copyright Act 1957 or the Patent Act 1970. Thus, the IT Act may override any other law, but by way of operation of the proviso to Section 81, the rights of the copyright owner cannot be curtailed by applying any other provision of the IT Act. Hence, web hosts will ordinarily be liable for copyright infringement for hosting infringing copies.

(g) ***Back-up copies***

As per Section 52(1)(ad) of the Copyright Act, making back-up copies is allowed when done from a legally obtained copy for non-commercial personal use.

(h) ***Reverse engineering***

Section 52(1)(ab) of the Copyright Act would allow reverse engineering insofar as it is necessary for obtaining information essential for ensuring the inter-operatibility of software programs, provided it is not otherwise available. Section 52(1)(ac) also allows the observation, study or testing of the functioning of a computer program in order to determine ideas and principles which underlie any elements of the program while performing such acts necessary for the functions for which the computer program was supplied.

(i) ***Parody defence***

A parody defence is not expressly included within Section 52, which contains the fair use defences of the Copyright Act. However, courts have allowed 'criticism' of and 'comment' on artistic and literary works when it does not compete with the original work and does not make improper use of the original. Hence, by implication, even a parody defence could be extended to be included within fair use.

(j) ***Incidental inclusion***

Section 52(1)(u)(ii) states that, with respect to cinematograph films, inclusion that is incidental or by way of background to the principal matter in a film will not constitute copyright infringement. A broader reading is also given as per the judgment of the Indian Supreme Court in *RG Anand v Delux Films*,[13] in which it was held that if the coincidences in a work are clearly incidental, there will be no infringement.

1.5 Remedies available for copyright infringement

Civil and criminal remedies exist for copyright infringement in India. Civil remedies, which are contained in Section 55 of the Copyright Act, include injunctions,

---

12 *Super Cassettes Industries Ltd v Myspace Inc*, IA No 15781/2008 and IA No 3085/2009 in CS (OS) No 2682/2008.

13 *RG Anand v M/S Delux Films*, 1978 AIR 1613.

damages, rendition of accounts and costs. The preferred remedy for most plaintiffs is an *ex parte* injunction.

Criminal remedies, which are included within Section 64 of the act, empower the police to seize infringing copies without warrant. The powers also include the power of search, seizure and arrest without a warrant.

1.6 Copyright liability

(a) *Hosting/cloud computing where infringing content uploaded by user of service*

As explained above, Section 79 of the IT Act 2000 contains a wide safe harbour for internet intermediaries which includes within it hosting and cloud computing providers when the infringing content is uploaded by the users of the service. The Information Technology (Intermediaries) Guidelines 2011 even contemplate a limited notice and takedown process under which this safe harbour is provided. However, as per the Delhi High Court's interpretation of the proviso to Section 81 in the IT Act, in *Super Cassettes v Myspace*,[14] this safe harbour does not extend to cases of copyright infringement.

(b) *Hypertext linking*

To third-party website: There is no express copyright protection regarding hyperlinks under Indian copyright law, but if the underlying work forms part of an artistic or visual work it may be protected under Indian copyright law.

However, courts have prohibited deep linking in the past. In *Info Edge v Bixee*,[15] the plaintiff claimed that the defendant was taking job listings from its database and displaying them as classified advertisements on its website with a hyperlink to the plaintiff's page. The Delhi High Court issued an interim injunction restraining Bixee.com from deep-linking to Naukri.com. By means of this interim order, the Delhi High Court extended protection to the website of Naukri.com and Bixee.com was restrained from copying, downloading and reproducing the content of Naukri.com.

To an infringing work: Though linking to an infringing work has not been expressly prohibited by the Copyright Act, in a recent case the CEO of a website was arrested where the website merely provided links to unauthorised copies of Bollywood songs.[16]

Copying of headlines (when used as hypertext links): At present, there is no legislative guidance contained in the Copyright Act with respect to copyright protection for the copying of headlines, and there have been no reported cases to date. Under Section 52(1)(m) of the act, the reproduction in a newspaper, magazine

---

14 *Super Cassettes Industries Ltd v Myspace Inc*, IA No 15781/2008 and IA No 3085/2009 in CS (OS) No 2682/2008.

15 *Info Edge v Bixee*, Suit No 1633/2005.

16 Anita Iyer, Guruji.com CEO arrested for music piracy, April 30 2010, available at www.radioandmusic.com/content/editorial/news/gurujicom-ceo-arrested-music-piracy (accessed April 8 2012).

or other periodical of an article on current economic, political, social or religious topics does not constitute an act of infringement of copyright under the Copyright Act of 1957, unless the author of such article has expressly reserved the right of such reproduction.

(c) *P2P network*

Supplier of P2P software: There are no rulings as such on the liability of P2P software providers; however, Indian plaintiffs have obtained John Doe orders which have been utilised by them for the blocking of file-sharing websites.

Uploaders/downloaders: The uploading and downloading of any content protected by copyright law without due authorisation falls within the terms of Section 51(a)(i) and constitutes copyright infringement.

(d) *Webcasting*

Webcasting is prohibited, unless authorised by the copyright owner.

(e) *Streaming*

Streaming is prohibited, unless authorised by the copyright owner.

(f) *Framing*

There are no express provisions under Indian law regarding framing of websites. However, if the framing involves modification of the copyrighted work, as it often does, it will be deemed to be infringement.

(g) *Transmission of infringing work across a communications network*

The transmission of an infringing work across a communications network is considered infringement, as it would necessarily result in the creation of a copy or streaming the content.

(h) *Aggregator websites (eg, Google News, price comparison websites)*

There are no express provisions under Indian law regarding website aggregators or protection for such aggregators. Since such content cannot be classified as user-generated content and is made on the basis of an algorithm specifically designed by the website, it falls within the category of use which is carried out without authorisation of the owner and may constitute copyright infringement

(i) *Treatment of user-generated content*

Under the Copyright Act, the author of content will be deemed to be its owner. Hence, the natural copyright with regard to any user-generated content resides with the user and not the ISP. However, it is usual practice that the terms of service of many ISPs mandate that the user licenses the rights in the content to the ISP.

1.7 Joint liability for ISPs

As stated above, the safe harbours under the IT Act 2000 do not extend to cases of copyright infringement. In line with the ruling of the Delhi High Court in *Super Cassette Industries v Myspace,*[17] ISPs are liable for the content uploaded by end users.

1.8 Relief

All reliefs, including interim injunctive reliefs, are available against ISPs.

1.9 Issues specific to India

(a) *Jurisdiction*

In cases of copyright infringement under Section 62(2) of the Copyright Act, the plaintiff may institute proceedings in the forum where it ordinarily resides. Since the section also contains an overriding clause, there are no jurisdictional limitations other than the residence of the plaintiff in the forum in which the suit is filed. This jurisdictional test has been approved in a case of intermediary liability arising in the Delhi High Court.

(b) *Claims to infringement of foreign copyright*

Copyrights of works of the countries mentioned in the International Copyright Order are protected in India, as if such works are Indian works. The courts in India have jurisdiction to hear claims for infringement of a foreign copyright, as any person to whom an order under this act relates is treated as a citizen of India. Moreover, under Section 62 of the Copyright Act, the jurisdictional rules for demonstrating a link to the forum are relaxed. It provides that the institution of the proceedings will be valid if the person instituting the suit or other proceedings or, where there is more than one such person, any of them actually and voluntarily resides or carries on business or personally works for gain. The infringement claims for foreign copyrights are heard by the same courts which heard claims of copyright infringement for local copyrights.

(c) *Emission theory*

There is no express mention of the emission theory in Indian law.

1.10 Orphan works

Orphan works are not defined under the Copyright Act 1957. However, the act does take into account works whose owners are anonymous. Under Section 23 of the act, when a literary, artistic, dramatic or musical work is published anonymously or pseudonymously, the term in respect of such a work is 60 years from the beginning of the calendar year following the year in which the work is published. However, if the identity of the author is disclosed before the expiry of the said period, copyright will subsist until 60 years from the beginning of the calendar year following that in which the author dies.

---

17 *Super Cassettes Industries Ltd v Myspace Inc,* IA No 15781/2008 and IA No 3085/2009 in CS (OS) No 2682/2008.

1.11 Online piracy measures

The Copyright Act does not include any legal provisions specifically aimed at online piracy. However, plaintiffs have recently utilised John Doe orders to have websites which engage in piracy of Indian movies and songs blocked in India. It is also relevant to state that the Intermediaries Guidelines[18] state that an internet intermediary must take down any content within 36 hours of a complaint that the content infringes any copyright.

1.12 Electronic infringement of moral rights

(a) ***Right to object to derogatory treatment***

Under Section 57(1)(b) of the Copyright Act, the author of a work enjoys moral rights which include the right to guard against distortion, mutilation, modification or other act which would be prejudicial to the author's honour or reputation. There are no reported cases of this being extended to the Internet.

(b) ***False attribution – the right to guard against impersonation on the Internet***

Under Section 57(1)(a) of the act, the author of a work also enjoys the right of attribution. This includes the right to guard against false attribution and impersonation on the Internet.

(c) ***Paternity right***

Section 57(1)(A) of the Copyright Act is also understood to include the right to paternity.

2. Trademarks

2.1 Use of a trademark

The Trademarks Act 1999 does not expressly state what constitutes 'use' of a trademark, but courts in India have interpreted the term '*bona fide* use' as 'genuine use'. Genuine use would always denote commercial usage of the mark and not mere usage, and it also protects consumers from confusion as to the originality of the goods and services. According to the act, non-usage for five years or more from the date of registration could be grounds for the cancellation of a trademark. The act does not establish conditions regarding the degree of usage, but it is settled principle that mere usage can be a ground for avoiding cancellation of registration for non-use.

The question of use to demonstrate jurisdiction is not relevant in cases of trademark infringement as Trademarks Act, Section 134(2) allows a plaintiff to file suit for trademark infringement based on where the plaintiff resides.

The Act states that an infringement of a registered trademark takes place when the person uses the goods in course of a trade which is similar to the owner of the mark.[19]

---

18 Information Technology (Intermediaries) Guidelines 2011.
19 Indian Trademarks Act 1999, Section 29(1).

If the usage of goods is similar and is likely to create confusion, it will be regarded as deceptive similarity and will be deemed to be an infringement.[20] The act also touches on the protection of an unregistered trademark on the basis of the common law principle of passing off. A person is entitled to claim compensation for the violation of a trademark if it is carried out without prior permission. The burden lies with the plaintiff to show that he was the prior user and not the defendant.

2.2 Infringement

(a) *Metatags*

There have been increasing numbers of trademark violations in the cyberworld through the use of metatags. The law in India is that if any proprietor of a website uses another person's registered trademark, it will generally be regarded as a violation under the Trademark Act. In *Tata Sons Limited v Bodacious Tatas*,[21] the plaintiff – the registered trademark owner of the name Tata – brought an action to prevent the defendant from using the name Tata in metatags and as a domain name. The Delhi High Court held that Bodacious's use of 'Tata' constituted infringement and prohibited Bodacious from using the name both in metatags and as a domain name. The court in *Samsung Electronics Company v Kapil Wadhwa*[22] held that the use of metatagging by the defendant had led to the infringement of a trademark, as the metatags used by the defendant had deceived consumers by making them believe the relevant products were Samsung products.

(b) *Keywords*

In *Consim Info Pvt Ltd v Google India Pvt Ltd*[23] the Indian High Court stated that the service provider of a keyword should ensure that the registered trademarks of any other party should not be violated or used by others.

(c) *Sponsored links*

In *Tata Sons Limited v Bodacious Tatas*,[24] the court held that if internet users clicked a sponsored link and had reason to think that it was Tata's website when in fact it was not, the advertisers of the sponsored link unfairly exploited the good reputation and goodwill of that website. A joint reading of Section 29(6) and (8) of the Trademarks Act would clearly state that a registered trademark can be used for the purposes of advertising, provided that it does not lead to an unfair advantage or to any act which is detrimental to the character of the mark.

(d) *Hidden text*

Hidden text generally constitutes infringement under the Trademarks Act. There is

---

20 Indian Trademarks Act 1999, Section 29(2).
21 *Tata Sons Limited v Bodacious Tatas*, Suit No 1991/99.
22 *Samsung Electronics Company v Kapil Wadhwa*, IA No 7774/2011 and IA No 10124/2011 in CS (OS). No 1155/2011.
23 *Consim Info Pvt Ltd v Google India Pvt Ltd and Ors*, 2011 (45) PTC575 (Mad).
24 Suit No 1991/99.

specific provision on this issue in the Act,[25] which establishes certain grounds for the infringement specifically where it creates confusion among consumers, or when any other advertising for any product would constitute unfair advantage or would be detrimental to other products.

(e) *Internet domain names*

The Trademarks Act is silent on the issue of whether the mere registration of a domain name would give rise to liability. However, in some reported decisions where domain names have been registered on a plaintiff's registered trademark, the domain name owner has been asked to transfer ownership.

An act of infringement with regard to the registration of a domain name will arise when any person uses the domain name to sell goods and services which are similar to those of a trademark owner who possesses a similar domain name. In *Adobe Systems v Rohit Rathi*,[26] a court held that the use of a website by the defendant had infringed trademark laws, as the defendant was using a similar domain name and this was likely to result in confusion. The intention to deceive is the most important criterion.

(f) *Search navigation tools*

There are no specific provisions and there has been no relevant case law regarding the issue of search navigation tools such as breadcrumb trails. However, the linking of websites or web pages does constitute infringement under the Indian Trademarks Act.

(g) *Hypertext links*

The use of hyper-linking of registered trademarks to promote goods and services to derive a benefit certainly constitutes trademark infringement. In the *Mattel* case,[27] the Delhi High Court restrained RJ Software from making use of hyper links. The company was ordered to remove the infringing links from the website. The court discussed the balance of convenience and the concept of irreparable injury.

(h) *Framing*

Indian trademark law does not provide much guidance as to the legality of framing. The issue can be assessed more directly by reference to the Indian Copyright Act of 1957.

2.3 Defences

(a) *Descriptive (non-trademark) use of the mark*

The defence of descriptive use is available under the Trademarks Act. There is no express provision in this regard. Section 30(1) states that such use should not have a

---

25 Indian Trademarks Act 1999, Section 29.
26 *Adobe Systems v Rohit Rathi* (2008 (37)PTC 523 (Del)).
27 *Mattel, Inc v Mr Jayant Agarwalla*, IA No 2532/2008 in CS (OS) 344/2008.

mala fide intention or be unjust. Under Section 35, such description should have a *bona fide* intention. The use in this context should be for a prolonged period. In *Marico Limited v Agro Tech Foods Limited*,[28] the court held that Marico's use of the trademark for just seven years would not constitute descriptive use. The *Marico* case also laid down the principle that simply because a company registers a trademark which is supposed to be used, it does not acquire distinctiveness by default. Post-registration use to acquire the distinctiveness of the mark will not give rise to infringement.

(b) Comparative advertising

Under Section 29(8) of the Trademarks Act, a trademark is infringed through advertising if such advertising is practised in a dishonest manner and creates an advantage by means of unfair industrial and commercial practices. In *Reckitt & Colman India Limited v MP Ramachandran*,[29] it was held that an advertiser was not barred from advertising and declaring his goods and products of superior quality, even though they may or may not have been the best quality available in the market. The court also held that while claiming to be of superior quality, the advertiser has no right to defame competitors and the court may grant an injunction in this regard.

Comparative advertising is permitted, but with limitations. The advertiser may make untrue statements about its own products and can prove these by comparison with the competitor's product; but this comparison should not be misleading or defamatory. The comparison should comply with the central thrust of the Comparative Advertising Directive.

If the comparison shown is an honest comparison and does not take unfair advantage in commercial or industrial uses, it is permitted.

(c) Parody

The Indian approach to parody as a defence can be ascertained by examination of *Tata Sons Limited v Greenpeace India*.[30] Here the court held that use of a trademark as a tool with regard to comment and also in the case of an attack does not necessarily constitute infringement of the trademark. The court was of the view that Section 29(4) of the Trademarks Act will take effect where a party uses the mark for the purpose of generating profit. In this case the court was of the view that Greenpeace was not a non-profit-making body and was not in competition with Tata. The court held that the materials on record did not constitute defamation.

2.4 Parallel imports

Under Section 30(3) of the act, if consent has been granted to any person who has acquired a mark or to any person entrusted with any goods, the sale of those goods by such person will not constitute an infringement of the trademark. In *Samsung Electronics Company Limited v G Choudhary*,[31] the court held that if a person imports

---

28 *Marico Limited v Agro Tech Foods Limited*, 169 (2010) DLT 325.

29 *Reckitt & Colman India Limited v MP Ramachandran*, 1999 PTC (19) 741.

30 *Tata Sons Limited v Greenpeace India*, IA No 9089/2010 in CS (OS) 1407/2010.

31 *Samsung Electronics Company Limited v G Choudhary*, 2006 (33) PTC 425(Del).

the registered product of the proprietor and changes the original product without the proprietor's consent, this may constitute infringement under the act. Thus, the act prevents trademark owners from restricting the marketing of lawfully acquired goods.

2.5 Liability of ISPs

Section 79 of the IT Act provides an exemption to ISPs against any liability for acts of their users, provided that the ISP acts as an intermediary and does not modify or select information. Where the ISP has knowledge of infringements committed by its users, it must expeditiously remove the information and observe due diligence in line with the Intermediaries Guidelines. In *Super Cassettes Industries v Myspace,*[32] the court held that under Section 81, Section 79 will not extend to copyright infringement actions.

ISPs are often made parties to an action to give effect to the relief which is granted by Indian courts, since the actual users of these online service providers often remain untraceable to the plaintiffs. For instance, there have been trademark infringement cases where the plaintiff has made a search engine a party for storing cached pages which contain the trademark infringement. Though plaintiffs often claim monetary damages in addition to injunctions against ISPs, such cases are not pursued beyond the interim injunctions which are granted against ISPs if the infringers/users cannot be identified.

2.6 Remedies

The Trademarks Act provides remedies to the plaintiff for infringement or passing off. Under Section 135, remedies include damages, injunction or account of profits. The remedy available for infringement is regarded as a statutory remedy, whereas in passing-off cases it is a common law remedy. Interim injunctions may be granted if the plaintiff can show that there is a reasonable likelihood that it will suffer irreparable harm if the order is not granted. In some cases, a local commissioner may be appointed to seize infringing goods which are in the possession of the infringer, and infringement may also lead to a term of imprisonment of not less than six months.

2.7 Advertising law and regulation

India lacks a concrete body of advertising law, with much of it being focused solely on television broadcasting. This is dealt with by Rule 7 of the Cable Television Networks Rules, 1994 (CTNR). This rule contains a list of categories under which advertisements are not allowed. In addition, by an amendment to this law in 2006, the advertising standards prescribed by the Advertising Standards Council of India (ASCI) have been made mandatory for broadcasters.

The ASCI is a self-regulatory voluntary organisation of the advertising industry.

---

32 *Super Cassettes Industries Ltd v Myspace Inc,* IA No 15781/2008 and IA No 3085/2009 in CS (OS) No 2682/2008.

Its main objective is to promote responsible advertising, thereby enhancing the public's confidence in advertising.

For the purposes of the ASCI Code, an 'advertisement' is defined as a paid-for communication, addressed to the public or a section of it, the purpose of which is to influence the opinions or behaviour of those to whom it is addressed. Any communication which in the normal course would be recognised as an advertisement by the general public would be included in this definition, even if it is carried free of charge for any reason.

The ASCI Code set out in Rule 7 of the CTNR does not apply to online advertising and is limited to traditional television broadcasters. Here, it would also extend to television broadcasts which are made by Internet Protocol television.

2.8 Domain name disputes

India's country level domain is '.in.' Under Paragraph 4(iii) of the .IN Domain Name Dispute Resolution Policy (INDRP), a party that wishes to defend a domain name must show that the allegedly offending domain name is similar or identical to that of the complainant and that the offending party has no rights in respect of the domain name, and also the complainant's domain name was registered in good faith.

Under the INDRP Rules of Procedure, the registry must serve notice within three days of receiving a complaint, and the arbitrator must make an award within 60 days and forward a copy to the respondent and to the registry.

The IN Registry's administration fees are set out in the INDRP Rules of Procedure. The fees are subject to a maximum of two hearings.

2.9 Unfair competition/passing off

Indian courts have consistently held that in order to claim for passing off, the plaintiff must demonstrate that it has goodwill associated with the mark and that there has been misrepresentation by the defendant which has resulted in confusion for consumers. If these grounds are established, the plaintiff can claim that the trade dress belongs to the plaintiff. In *Colgate Palmolive Co v Anchor Health & Beauty Care*,[33] the Delhi High Court injuncted the defendant on the basis of use of similar colour combinations in the packaging of toothpaste. In the absence of a similar mark or registered trademark, a claim for passing off can be granted in relation to website layout or colour combinations since these may constitute trade dress.

3. Patents

3.1 Patentability of 'internet' inventions

(a) *Computer programs*

According to Section 3(K) of the Patents Act 1970, computer programs are expressly excluded from patent protection, since they are regarded as inventions. Computer programs are per se not patentable and the invention must represent more than mere

33 *Colgate Palmolive Co v Anchor Health & Beauty Care* (2003 (27) PTC 478 (Del).

'computer software'. According to the Manual of Patent Office Practice and Procedure 2011, software can be patented if it is combined with another patentable invention and forms an integral part of such invention.

(b) *Business methods*

Section 3(K) of the Patents Act bars patentability for business methods as these are also considered to be inventions. Under the manual, business methods claimed in any method are not patentable and this specifically includes inventions claimed for the development of technology related to e-commerce and business-to-business and business-to-consumer transactions.

(c) *Mathematical methods*

Mathematical methods are barred from patentability under Section 3(K) of the act. The provision also bars the granting of a patent to an 'algorithm'. As per the manual, mathematical methods are regarded as an act of mental skill and are deemed to include calculation formulation, equations, finding square roots and any acts involving mathematical methods. The manual also states that mathematical methods include writing algorithms and computer programs.

The presentation of information is barred from patentability under Section 3(n) of the Patents Act 1970.

3.2 Bioinformatics

As per Section 3(c) of the Patents Act, the mere discovery of any scientific principle or discovery with regard to any living thing or non-living substance occurring in nature will not constitute an invention. Thus, the isolation and determination of DNA cannot be patented under the act. Under the draft manuals of the Patent Office 2005 and 2008, the isolation of DNA will be considered as a discovery and not an invention and is not patentable. However, the manual states that in cases of a genetically modified gene sequence/amino acid sequence, claims may be directed to a gene sequence/amino acid sequence. This lends credence to the practice of granting of patents to genetically modified gene sequences.

3.3 Issues specific to India

(a) *Infringement on the Internet*

Under Section 104 of the Patents Act, civil courts have jurisdiction in cases of patent infringement. Such claims are based on the jurisdictional rules which are prescribed by the Code of Civil Procedure 1908. As patents are treated as moveable property, Section 19 of the code applies. This provision stipulates that an action may be pursued in the forum where the infringement occurred or where the defendant resides or carries on business, or personally works for gain.

Since there have been no cases on patent infringement on the Internet to date, the courts have not had occasion to create specific jurisdictional rules beyond the broad mandate of Section 19 of the code.

(b) *Process patents*

The Patents Act also grants both process and product patents. However, for infringements of process patents, the relevant patent should be granted in India. As process patents are not granted for software and business processes, no cases of infringement via the Internet have yet come before the courts in India.

3.4 Remedies available for patent infringement

Under Section 108 of the Patents Act, there are several remedies for patent infringement. These include interim as well as permanent injunctions, damages or account of profits, and seizure, forfeiture or destruction of the infringing articles. Additionally, the patent holder may claim relief with regard to infringement of a partially valid specification, a certificate of validity in terms of a declaratory holding and costs relating to the infringement proceedings.

4. Disclosure orders against ISPs

4.1 Availability

Section 2(1)(w) of the IT Act treats ISPs as intermediaries. Such intermediaries are exempted from liability if they observe proper due diligence and take down any content which may be deemed illegal under Section 79 of the act. Courts may seek to obtain the details of users who are suspected of infringement and may order ISPs to disclose their identity.

The Intermediaries Guidelines Rules define the term 'due diligence' and Section 3(7) of the act empowers the court to seek from the ISP the identity of any users involved in infringing IP rights.

Previously, in cases of defamation, the Bombay High Court[34] and the Delhi High Court[35] have in individual cases asked blog hosting platforms to disclose user sign-up information as well as their logs. To obtain such disclosure, the content owner must specifically demonstrate in its pleadings that it requested from the intermediary the disclosure of the user's identity prior to approaching the court.

4.2 Requirements

Courts may order disclosure by way of interim injunction, if the rights holder alleges that an infringement action will be unable to proceed further unless a disclosure order is made. Interim injunctions are granted under the Code of Civil Procedure 1908[36] and the owner must show that it has suffered irreparable harm and that the balance of convenience is in its favour.

Under the Intermediaries Guidelines, the intermediary must disclose user data that facilitates investigation proceedings. In order to avail of disclosure, the content owner must show that the intermediary's facilities have led to infringement and that the intermediary has refused to disclose the relevant information.

---

34 *Gremach Infrastructure Equipments & Projects Limited v Google India Private Limited*, Suit No 506 of 2008, Bombay High Court (order dated Feburary 26 2008).

35 *Nirmaljit Singh Narula v Indijobs At Hubpages.Com* (CS (OS) No 871/2012) (order dated March 30 2012).

36 The Code of Civil Procedure 1908, Order 39, Rules 1 and 2.

4.3 Jurisdictional issues

The jurisdictional rules relating to the grant of injunctions turns on the nature of the intellectual property that is involved. The jurisdictional rules for copyright infringement and trademark infringement are prescribed under the Copyright Act 1957 and the Trademarks Act 2002 respectively. Beyond the statutes, claims which arise from common law, such as passing off, are on the basis of the jurisdictional limits prescribed under the Code of Civil Procedure 1908.[37]

(a) *Copyright infringement*

Under Section 62(2) of the Copyright Act 1957, in cases of copyright infringement the plaintiff may institute proceedings in the forum where it ordinarily resides. Since the section also contains an overriding clause, there are no jurisdictional limitations other than the residence of the plaintiff in the forum in which the suit is filed. This jurisdictional test has been approved in a case of intermediary liability arising in the Delhi High Court.[38]

(b) *Trademark infringement*

Under Section 134(2) of the Trademarks Act 1999, in cases of trademark infringement the forum within whose territorial jurisdiction the person instituting the suit resides or carries on business or personally works for gain at the time of the institution of the suit will have jurisdiction to try a suit for infringement of a registered trademark.

(c) *Patent Infringement*

Under Section 104 of the Patents Act 1970, the civil courts have jurisdiction in cases of patent infringement. Such claims are based on jurisdictional rules prescribed by the Code of Civil Procedure. As patents are treated as moveable property, Section 19 of the code applies. This provision states that an action may be preferred in the forum where the wrong was done or where the defendant resides or carries on business, or personally works for gain.

(d) *Passing off and other common law actions*

With respect to passing off, the Indian courts seem to have adopted a limited jurisdiction based on the effects test, where the IP owner must demonstrate the specific targeting of the forum by the defendant. This rule has been evolved by the courts in light of Section 20 of the Code of Civil Procedure, which states that the plaintiff can institute an infringement action in a forum where the cause of action arises in whole or in part.[39]

4.4 'John Doe' injunctions

John Doe injunctions are granted by courts in India in cases of IP rights infringement when the plaintiff specifically anticipates widespread and sporadic piracy. The first

---

37 Code of Civil Procedure 1908, Sections 18 to 20.

38 *Super Cassettes Industries Ltd v Myspace Inc,* IA No 15781/2008 and IA No 3085/2009 in CS (OS) No 2682/2008.

39 *Banyan Tree Holdings Limited v A Murali Krishna,* CS (OS) No 894/2008.

instance of the grant of a John Doe injunction was by the Delhi High Court in *Taj Television v Rajan Mandal*,[40] where the injunction restrained local cable operators from illegally airing the FIFA World Cup 2002 for which the telecast rights were exclusively vested in the plaintiff.

John Doe injunctions have gradually been extended to piracy carried out by unauthorised copying and distribution of content online. This has been most visible in cases of Bollywood movies whose low-quality prints are made available on streaming websites soon after their release. One such John Doe injunction which was widely reported for the plaintiff's attempt to apply the John Doe injunction to torrent websites is *Reliance BIG Entertainment v Jyoti Cable Network*.[41]

---

40 *Taj Television v Rajan Mandal*, 2003 FSR (22) 407.

41 *Reliance BIG Entertainment v Jyoti Cable Network* July 20 2011 (Delhi HC) (Unreported).

Italy

Giulio Enrico Sironi
Adriano Vanzetti
Vanzetti e Associati

1. Copyright, database rights and design rights

1.1 Overview

In Italy, the main source of regulation in matters of copyright and related rights is the Copyright Law (hereinafter 'CL') April 22 1941, no 633, and subsequent amendments. Copyright is secured with the creation of a work, without the need for any formal procedures to be conducted. Copyright has an inalienable moral component and a financial component constituted by the rights financially to exploit a work – rights which may be assigned to third parties and which last for the entire life of the author and until the end of the seventieth year after his/her death. The work then comes into the public domain and may be freely used, provided the moral right is respected.

The duration of related rights (a category which covers rights, also regulated by CL, whose contents are in certain respects similar to those of copyright but whose scope is narrower) is more limited and varies according to the individual right. In some cases certain formalities need to be conducted in order to exercise such rights.

Italian copyright law does not contain any *ad hoc* discipline for internet content, save for a number of particular cases. Such content may, however, be protected by copyright law by being brought within the general categories of protected works under Article 2 of CL should it meet the requirements.

(a) *Literary works and artistic works*

Copyright-protected works comprise, firstly, works of literature, including literary, dramatic, scientific, didactic and religious works, whether in written or oral form. The text need not be in a material form; it may also be in digital format. Consequently, if any text published online, including the content of newsgroup messages, possesses sufficient expressive character and meets the requirement of creativity it may in itself be protected by copyright as a work of literature.

Emails can also be protected by the related right provided by Copyright Law in matters of epistolary correspondence (CL, Article 93). This article bars publication, reproduction or dissemination to the public, in any way whatsoever, without the consent of the author and recipient.

Photographs posted online can be protected by copyright when they have creative character and are not the mere documentary reproduction of a certain object or event. Otherwise, they may be protected by a related right provided by Articles

87ff of CL. In this case the right on a photograph lasts 20 years from its production (ie, the moment in which it is taken (CL Article 92)). In order that the related right may be exercised, each photograph needs to indicate: the name of the photographer or the party holding the rights to its financial exploitation; the date of production of the photograph; and, where relevant, the name of the author of the work of art which has been photographed (CL, Article 90). If this information is absent, reproduction of the photograph is not considered unlawful unless the photographer can prove that the party reproducing the photograph acted in bad faith.

The protection of software as an intellectual work was expressly introduced into copyright law by implementation of EC Directive 91/250 on computer programs, which equates software with literary works. Software is therefore protected in any form in which it is expressed, provided it is original in the sense that it is the author's own intellectual creation (CL, Article 2, no 8). The ideas and principles underlying any element of a program, including those underlying its interfaces, cannot be protected. The term program also covers preparatory material for the design of the program itself. Copyright protection of software is regulated by Articles 64*bis* ff of CL.

(b) *Films, sound recordings, and broadcasts*

Copyright-protected works also include musical works and compositions, with or without words, dramatico-musical works and musical variations which in themselves constitute original work (CL, Article 2, no 2). Song lyrics or the libretto of a dramatico-musical work are also copyright-protected works within this category.

The unauthorised online posting of audio files, both in their original version and in new digital formats, including MP3 and WAV, as well as the posting of song lyrics, is an infringement of copyright.

MIDI music files (reproduction only of the bases of certain musical motifs) are elaborations of original work and must, therefore, be authorised by the author of the piece or by the party holding the rights to its financial exploitation.

Save for the rights due to the author of a musical work, producers of phonograms enjoy a related right regulated by Articles 72ff of CL.

All works of cinematographic art, whether silent or in sound form, provided they are not mere documentaries, are protected by copyright (CL, Article 2, no 6). Such works are considered to be collective works and the author of the subject matter, the screenwriter, the composer and the artistic director are considered joint authors of the work (CL, Articles 44ff). Exercising the rights financially to exploit the work belongs to the party which has organised the production of the work itself and concerns the cinematographic exploitation of the work produced (CL, Articles 45 and 46).

Therefore, the unauthorised online use of videos and films, even should they only be clips, constitutes infringement of copyright. Alongside copyright, the law provides a related right for the producer of a cinematographic or audiovisual work which is also enjoyed by a producer of mere sequences of moving images and thus also simple documentaries. This related right is regulated by Article 78*ter* CL.

(c) *Typographical arrangement of a published edition*

The Copyright Law bars (Article 102) the reproduction or imitation in other works of a similar nature of headings, emblems, ornamentation, arrangements of printing signs or characters, or any other particularity of form or colour in the external appearance of an intellectual work, when such reproduction or imitation is capable of creating confusion between works or authors. Under Article 100 of CL "the title of a work, when it uniquely identifies the work, may not be reproduced in connection with any other work without the consent of the author". The bar does not extend to works which are of a kind or nature so far removed as to exclude all possibility of confusion. The reproduction of headings used in periodical publications in such a regular way as to identify the normal or characteristic features appearing therein is also barred subject to the same conditions. The name of a newspaper, magazine or other periodical publication may not be reproduced in other works of the same kind or nature until two years have elapsed since cessation of its publication.

(d) *Protection of the user interface*

With regard to the protection of a graphical user interface (in particular, for example, a look and feel interface), no specific decisions have been issued by the Italian courts. However, it must be observed that, as was stated by the ECJ in its decision of December 22 2010, in C-393/09, an interface which constitutes a creative intellectual work may be protected by copyright (a graphical interface, however, is not protected as a computer program). A graphical interface may also be protected as a registered or unregistered design and possibly as an atypical trademark or distinctive sign.

(e) *Computer-generated works*

Under Italian law a work may be protected by copyright only if it is a creative and original expression of human intellect. Therefore, a prerequisite for a work being protected by copyright is that it have a 'human author'. Consequently, computer-generated works (created in conditions such as to rule out any significant human intervention) cannot be protected by copyright. Computer-aided work can, however, be protected. Such work comes within the general discipline whereby a work will be protected by copyright to the extent that it possesses the legal requirements, and copyright will be enjoyed by its author or co-authors.

(f) *Websites protected as databases*

Databases are understood as all collections of works, data or other independent elements which are systematically or methodically set up and individually accessible by electronic or other means.

Adoption of EC Directive 96/9 saw the introduction at EU level of a double level of protection for databases: copyright for databases which may be considered as creative works according to the criteria of protectability laid down in the Berne Convention and the TRIPs Agreement, and a *sui generis* right for databases which do not possess creativity in the selection or arrangement of material.

The Directive was implemented in Italy with Legislative Decree 169/1999, which amended the CL by adding *ad hoc* provisions for databases.

Creative databases are expressly included in Article 1.2 and Article 2, no 9 of CL among intellectual works if "by reason of the selection or arrangement of their contents (they) constitute intellectual creation on the part of the author".

Decree 169/1999 also inserted Articles 64*quinquies* and 64 *sexies* into the Copyright Law, which respectively regulate the rights financially to exploit the databases and the exceptions to these rights.

The main novelty of the Directive is the provision of a *sui generis* right in the case of non-creative databases, according to the Anglo-Saxon 'sweat of the brow' doctrine. Such databases are now specifically covered by Articles 102*bis* and 102*ter* of CL, introduced by the Decree. Protection applies if the party setting up the database has made "substantial investment in setting up, verifying or presenting the database, committing itself in terms of finance, time and work for that purpose".

Websites are not expressly covered by the CL. Some legal theorists maintain that they are in any case protected as databases. The type of protection (copyright or *sui generis*) will then depend on whether or not a website possesses the requirement of originality, understood as creative effort on the part of the author, in the selection and arrangement of texts, images, sounds, animation and other content which combined give life to the website, without prejudice to any rights on individual elements which compose the work. Other legal theorists, however, maintain that websites fall within the notion of collective works as defined by Article 3 of CL.

(g) *Compilations*

Compilations may be protected by copyright as collective works under Article 3 of CL.

In this case the moral copyright belongs, under Article 7 of CL, to the author 'of the compilation' (ie, to the party which organised and directed the creation of the multimedia work or of the website as a whole), each author however (save for agreement to the contrary) having the right to see his/her name on his/her portion of the work (CL, Article 40). The right to financial exploitation belongs, save for agreement to the contrary, to the publisher of the work (CL, Article 38), without prejudice to the moral right which still belongs to the organiser or director of the creation. Furthermore, the various authors are entitled to extract their articles or portions of articles provided they mention the collective work from which they have been taken and the date of publication (CL, Article 42).

Non-creative compilations can only be protected as databases under Articles 102*bis* and 102*ter* of CL.

Under Recital 19 of EC Directive 96/9 compilations "of several recordings of musical performances on a CD" are not protectable.

1.2 Infringing acts

The rights of financial exploitation awarded to an author and his/her assignees which are relevant in the context of internet include the following rights.

(a) *Copying*

The author has the exclusive right to reproduce the protected work (CL, Article 13), that is, the right to make copies of all or part of the work, by any means or procedure, in any way or form, either directly (from the original) or indirectly (reproducing or copying in turn a previous reproduction). Therefore, both permanent and temporary reproduction by third parties is barred if not authorised by the author or his/her assignee. However, copyright law provides for two exceptions to the bar on temporary reproduction. The first is provided for service providers in order to allow online data transmission between third parties (Article 68*bis* of CL and Article 15 of Legislative Decree 70/2003). Under these articles, temporary reproduction which does not have its own independent economic significance and which is transitory or incidental to or is part and parcel of a technological process, conducted with the sole purpose of allowing online transmission between third parties with the intervention of an intermediary, is exempt from the reproduction right. The second, also provided by Article 68*bis* of CL, concerns temporary reproduction required in order to effect use which is lawful because it is authorised either by the author or by the law (eg, reproduction of a work by a person benefiting from free use, in the memory of his/her computer).

(b) Issuing copies to the public

Another exclusive right is that of distribution, which concerns the right to market, place in circulation or make available to the public, by whatever means and for whatever purpose, the original of the work or copies thereof and also includes the exclusive right to bring copies of a work made in non-EU states into EU member states for the purposes of distribution (CL, Article 17).

(c) Communicating work to the public

The rights to financial exploitation include the exclusive right to communicate a work to the public at a distance (CL, Articles 16 and 16bis), including the right of interactive communication (on-demand exploitation). Copyright law gives authors and their assignees the exclusive right to communicate work to the public by wire or wireless means by one of the methods of tele-dissemination, such as telegraphy, telephony, radio or television broadcasting and other like methods (and thus also internet), by satellite and cable re-transmission as well as encrypted transmission by means of specific conditions of access. It also includes making a work available to the public in such a way that members of the public may access it from a place and at a time individually chosen by them. All activities aimed at reaching a public composed of a certain number of people in different places not necessarily at the same moment are operations of communication to the public which are the preserve of the rights holder. Webcasting, streaming, P2P exchange, posting a work on a company network or online database and video on demand thus all constitute communication to the public and are lawful only if authorised. However, uncertain cases include, for example, the exchange of emails between a certain number of people or unauthorised links to websites or works protected by copyright (in the case of links to websites of infringing works, the prevailing opinion is that this constitutes participation in another's infringement, save for what shall later be stated in relation to internet service provider (ISP) liability).

(d) ***Perform, show or play work in public***

Exclusive rights include the right to perform, show or play in public, in any way whatsoever, either free of charge or upon payment, a musical, dramatic or cinematographic work, or any other work suitable for public showing, and oral works (CL, Article 15).

(e) ***Renting or lending the work to the public***

The author or his/her assignees also have the exclusive right to authorise renting or lending by third parties (CL, Article 18*bis*). The exclusive right to rent covers the making available for use of originals, copies or carriers of copyright works, for a limited time and for direct or indirect financial or commercial benefit. The exclusive right to lend covers the making available for use of originals, copies or carriers of copyright works, by institutions open to the public, for a limited period, for purposes other than obtaining financial or commercial benefit. These rights are not exhausted by sale or distribution in any form of the originals, copies or carriers of the works. Even should an author assign the right to rent to a producer of phonograms or cinematographic or audiovisual works or works comprising sequences of moving images, he/she retains the right to obtain equitable remuneration for a rental contract between the producer and third parties.

(f) ***Authorising another person to do any of the above***

Rights to financial exploitation belong to the author of the work and his/her assignees. Authorisation to exploit the work can be given by the holder to anyone he/she wishes; exploitation without consent constitutes infringement. However, should a third party authorise another party to exploit the work in one of the ways indicated in the preceding points without having the right to do so, both the party exploiting the work and the third party which has authorised this without having the right to do so are guilty of infringement. The party which was 'authorised' by the third party may take action against the latter for the damage it has suffered as a consequence.

(g) ***Secondary infringement***

There is no specific regulation in Italy in this matter. However, on the basis of general principles all those who have, in various ways, participated in or contributed to the infringement are liable.

1.3 Test for copyright infringement

(a) ***Requirement of substantial reproduction***

All portions of the work are protected, provided they are able significantly to identify the creative nature of the work itself. Consequently, copying not only the work as a whole, but also substantial parts of the work constitutes infringement.

(b) ***Repeated copying of insubstantial parts***

As to the copying of insubstantial parts, such parts are in themselves irrelevant.

However, as shall be seen in the next paragraph, there are cases in which the law provides exceptions to the exclusive rights of an author – the so-called free uses. Within the ambit of these free uses and in certain cases (eg, that of databases), the systematic copying of insubstantial parts may be significant, with the result that this use infringes copyright when it is effected in such a way as to compromise the owner of the work's exercise of exclusive rights.

1.4 Exemptions/defences to copyright infringement

Under Italian law there are a number of limitations on the exclusive right of an author of a work financially to exploit the work. These limitations also apply to related rights. Free use derives from the need to harmonise copyright, the expression of the constitutional principle of free economic initiative, with other rights which are also constitutionally guaranteed, such as those of public information and justice.

(a) Format shifting

The exclusive rights of an author and his/her assignees also include the right to amend, transform and adapt a work. Therefore it is, generally speaking, the holder of a work who has the right to format shift, unless it is done within the context of one of the free uses of a work expressly provided by copyright law and examined in the following points.

(b) Personal copying rights

Reproduction of single works or of portions of works for the personal use of readers, when carried out by hand or by a means of reproduction unsuitable for marketing or disseminating the work in public, is permitted (CL, Article 68.1).

With the exception of sheet music, reproduction for personal use of intellectual works carried out by means of photocopying, xerocoping or like means is permitted, limited to 15% of each volume or issue of a magazine, excluding advertising pages. The authors and publishers of the works in question must receive equitable remuneration from those responsible for the premises or copy centres or public libraries where photocopiers, xerocopiers or similar copying systems are used or made available to third parties, even free of charge (CL, Article 68, paragraphs 3 and 4). Sale to the public of copies made for personal use and, in general, any use which competes with an author's right financially to exploit the work is barred (CL, Article 68.6).

Private reproduction of phonograms and videograms (therefore only of musical and audiovisual works) is also permitted on any carrier on condition that it is carried out: by natural persons; for the sole purpose of personal use; without gainful intent or direct or indirect commercial purposes; in compliance with the technological measures applied by the rights holder (CL, Article 71 *sexies*). Free reproduction cannot be carried out by a third party and the supply of services for the purposes of enabling reproduction of phonograms and videograms by natural persons for personal use constitutes an act of reproduction which requires the consent of the rights holder. Rights holders must allow, notwithstanding the application of the technological measures of protection, any natural person who has acquired legal possession of copies of the protected work or material, or has legally accessed them, to make a private copy, which may also be simply an analog copy, for personal use, provided that this does not conflict with the normal exploitation of the work or of other materials and does not unreasonably prejudice rights holders.

However, such free use does not apply to protected works or materials made available to the public in such a way that members of the public may access them from a place and at a time individually chosen by them, when the work is protected by technological measures of protection or when access is permitted on the basis of contractual agreements.

Such free reproduction does not apply to software, for which only free reproduction of back-up copies is permitted.

Authors and producers of phonograms, as well as original producers of audiovisual works, performing artists and executors and producers of videograms, and their assignees, are entitled to receive remuneration for the private reproduction of phonograms and videograms. This remuneration is determined by ministerial decree and is paid by persons who manufacture or import into Italy with gainful intent equipment for the analog or digital recording of phonograms or videograms and blank audio and video recording carriers, such as analog carriers, digital carriers, and fixed and transferable memories intended for the recording of phonograms or videograms. Remuneration is paid to the Italian Society of Authors and Publishers (SIAE), which distributes it among the entitled parties.

There are no specific rules in Italy regarding remuneration within the context of the Internet.

(c) *Time shifting*

In Italy time shifting is not expressly provided as a free use of intellectual works and therefore, unless it comes within the ambit of personal copying under (b) above, the consent of the rights holder is required.

(d) *Fair use*

Other free uses provided by Italian law are described below.

Under Article 65.1 of CL, for reasons of public information, articles of current interest of an economic, political or religious nature, published in magazines or newspapers, or broadcast or made available to the public, and other like materials may be freely reproduced or communicated to the public in other magazines or newspapers, also in broadcast programmes, unless such reproduction or use is expressly reserved (the so-called declaration of reserve), provided the source, the date and the author's name, if quoted, are indicated. A much-disputed point in legal theory and case law is the applicability of this limitation in the case of the reproduction of newspaper articles in electronic press reviews (as could also be the case with Google News) made available to the public online, particularly when reproduction occurs in real time. A number of decisions have ruled online reproduction to be unlawful, including cases of reproduction of radio and television broadcasting on freely accessible websites, when republication is simultaneous with publication by the holder of the right in the article. This is because online press reviews are more damaging to the rights holder due to the rapidity of dissemination, size of the audience and greater ease of access to the information compared to hard copy reproduction. The view is taken that online republication, as opposed to hard copy republication, does not aid the development of public information since it acts as a disincentive to the creation of original articles. However, there are other decisions of the opposite tenor whereby, for the purposes of applying the exemption in question, the type of carrier (hard copy or electronic) on which an article is republished is irrelevant.

Under Article 65.2 of CL, the reproduction or communication to the public of protected work or material used during current events is permitted for the purposes of reporting the events and to the extent justified by the purpose of disseminating information, provided that, unless it is impossible to do so, the source, including the author's name, if quoted, is given.

Under Article 66 of CL speeches on matters of political or administrative interest delivered in public assemblies or in any other public manner, as well as extracts of public conferences, may be freely reproduced or communicated to the public, to the extent justified by the purpose of disseminating information, in magazines or newspapers, as well as broadcast news or news in electronic format, provided that the source, the author's name, the date and the place where the speech was delivered are indicated.

Likewise loans by libraries and music collections of the state and public entities for the sole purpose of promoting culture or private study do not require the rights holder's authorisation. Neither is any remuneration due to the rights holder (CL, Article 69).

Communication or making available to individual members of the public is free if it is for the purposes of research or private study on dedicated terminals on the premises of publicly accessible libraries, educational establishments, museums or archives, limited to the works or other materials contained in their collections that are not subject to limitations imposed by purchase or licensing agreements (CL, Article 71ter).

Article 70 of CL permits, within certain limits, the abridgement, quotation or reproduction of fragments or parts of work and their communication to the public, for the purposes of dissemination of culture.

The freedom to publish online low resolution or degraded images and music for teaching or scientific purposes free of charge was introduced in 2008; but such use must be for non-profit-making purposes (CL, Article 70.1*bis*). However, an implementing decree is due to be issued defining the limits of such teaching and scientific use.

The reproduction of works or portions of works is permitted for the purposes of justice or public security, in parliamentary, judicial or administrative proceedings, provided the source, including where possible the author's name, is indicated (CL, Article 67).

Lastly, for reasons of social solidarity, persons with specific disabilities are permitted, for personal use, to reproduce protected work or material or communicate them to the public provided such reproduction or communication relates directly to their disability, is of a non-commercial nature and is limited to the extent of the requirement of the disability (CL, Article 71*bis*). The reproduction of broadcasts by public hospitals or prisons, for internal use only, is permitted provided rights holders receive equitable remuneration (CL, Article 71*quater*).

(e) ***Caching/temporary copies as part of the communication process***

As mentioned above, under copyright law there are two exceptions to the exclusive right of temporary reproduction: the first is if reproduction is carried out in order to allow online data transmission between third parties with the intervention of an intermediary; and the second is if it is carried out in order to allow lawful use of the work (CL, Article 68*bis*). The exception in the case of temporary reproduction by a provider is also covered by Article 15 of Legislative Decree 70/2003, which implemented Article 13 of EC Directive 2000/31 in Italy.

(f) ***Hosting***

Article 16 of Legislative Decree 70/2003, which implemented Article 14 of EC Directive 2000/31 in Italy, provides for exemption in the case of hosting, on the fulfilment of certain conditions.

(g) ***Back-up copies***

The rules applying to back-up copies are the same as those which apply to private copies examined in (b) above.

(h) ***Reverse engineering***

In software matters, reverse engineering is permitted when necessary for the interoperability of a piece of independently created software with other programs and provided certain conditions, laid down by Article 64*quater* of CL, are met.

(i) ***Parody defence***

Parody, an expression of the constitutional right of freedom of thought and criticism (Article 21 of the Constitution), is, according to Italian case law, a work which is independent of and distinct from the work to which it refers and does not require the consent of the holder of the right to financial exploitation. The work will, therefore, only be attributed to the parodist and not to the author of the parodied work, even in part.

(j) ***Incidental inclusion***

Italian law does not treat incidental inclusion as one of the exceptions and limitations to copyright. It may, however, have some bearing for the purposes of the author of the violation being excluded from liability for damage if he/she cannot even be charged with negligence.

1.5 Remedies available for copyright infringement

In the case of violation of copyright and related rights in civil proceedings a plaintiff may seek:

- as interim measures an injunction and a seizure order;
- as sanctions in an action on the merits a definitive injunction on the unlawful activity, removal or destruction of the results of the unlawful activity, compensation and publication of the decision.

There are also a number of administrative sanctions (eg, suspension of the commercial production activity and financial sanctions) and criminal sanctions for violation of rights to financial exploitation.

1.6 Copyright liability

Defendants in a civil action for copyright violation will be those who have in any way participated in the violation, including those who have facilitated violation by others.

Generally speaking a website proprietor is liable for the content of the website, and thus also fully liable for all copyright violation on or committed through his/her website. Particular problems arise, however, in cases in which the content of the website depends totally or to a certain degree directly on user intervention (ie, on content posted or uploaded online by users), without the website proprietor intervening or mediating in advance in the insertion of the content (eg, social networking sites, forums, newsgroups).

ISP liability is regulated by EC Directive 2000/31, implemented in Italy by Legislative Decree 70/2003. This provides for exemption from liability upon certain conditions for ISPs which perform 'mere conduit' services; temporary memorisation (ie, 'caching'); or hosting. Exemption from liability is conditional upon the fact that the ISP does not play an active role but only performs a 'neutral' service, and also upon the fact that the ISP takes prompt action to put a stop to the unlawful activity as soon as it becomes aware of it. In any case an ISP is not obliged to supervise the information it transmits or memorises; nor is it obliged actively to search out incidents or circumstances indicating unlawful activity. Furthermore, specific measures and procedures protecting copyright with regard to ISPs are provided by the "Rules on copyright protection on electronic communications networks" adopted by the Communications Regulatory Authority on December 12 2013.

Save for the limitations and exceptions under section 1.4, the following activities give rise to copyright liability under current law, as interpreted by the courts:

(a) Hosting/cloud computing where infringing content is uploaded by a user of the service

While a user is always liable for the unlawfulness of the content he/she uploads, a provider which only performs a hosting service is not liable for violations committed directly or independently by a user. A provider which acts as a mere access provider/data transmitter or host provider, without producing its own content, without playing an active role and without being aware of the content uploaded by third parties, is not liable for violations committed by users of its services. In such cases an ISP is a neutral 'intermediary' in the managing and sorting of communications which are in transit or which it hosts. However, it is liable when it becomes aware of the unlawful activity and, upon becoming aware, does not take action to remedy the situation.

Certain recent Italian decisions have found that in the actual cases examined there was still direct contribution on the part of the provider in handling the content of the website uploaded by users, and thus ruled that the host provider was jointly liable with the user for copyright violations and, in general, for IP infringement committed by the latter (Court of Rome, December 16 2009 and Court of Rome, March 22 2011, relating respectively to the liability of YouTube and Yahoo Video for the transmission of videos posted by users).

(b) Hypertext linking

To a third-party website: The Italian courts tend to rule that the mere presence of a link to the web pages of third parties is not unlawful, except in cases in which the link may cause damage to the holder of the linked website. The Competition Authority tends to rule likewise (AGCM 22/12/2010).

To an infringing work: Linking to websites which contain material which is unlawful on the grounds that it violates copyright gives rise to liability if, according to the specific case, it is reasonable to suppose that the manager of the linking website was aware or, in any case, had the possibility of being aware of the illegal content.

According to the above principles an ISP may also be liable.

Copying of headlines: Use of the headline of a protected work as a hypertext link by a search engine or website is not in itself unlawful but could become so if the link causes damage to the holder of the right on the protected work or the holder of the linked website, or in the case above.

(c) P2P network

P2P is a system of file exchanging and sharing, which as such is not unlawful. Nor is the software used for downloading files from the computer of one user to that of another unlawful.

Supplier of P2P software: The liability of a P2P software supplier depends in general on the type of activity conducted by the exchange service provider. In pure P2P systems, in particular, there is no central server which sorts and indexes requests and which has an overall view of the users and files contained in the hard disks of the computers of users. File searching and, above all, file sharing does not go from a central server but takes place directly through the computers of individual users (peers). A P2P software supplier is therefore unlikely to be aware of files possibly illegally exchanged between users and, therefore, to be liable for copyright violation by individual users.

Hybrid client/server systems in which illegal content goes through a central server may be liable but – given that an ISP is not generally obliged to supervise – only to the extent that a provider may be supposed to be aware of the illegal content of files exchanged by users.

Uploaders/downloaders: Both are individually liable for copyright violation.

(d) ***Webcasting***

Sending in real or delayed time audio and video transmissions by means of web technology is the preserve of holders of exclusive rights and is therefore unlawful if not authorised by rights holders.

(e) ***Streaming***

A user who uploads illegal content is individually liable. A website manager is jointly liable to the extent to which it, in some way, participates in the handling of the illegal content uploaded by the user or is or becomes aware of the unlawfulness of the content but takes no action to remove it.

(f) ***Framing***

With framing the content of the framed website is considered to be known to the manager of the framing website, and is therefore handled as if it were part of the framing website. The manager of the framing website is therefore directly individually liable in relation to illegal content.

(g) ***Transmission of infringing work across a communications network***

Transmitting copyright-violating content is unlawful and gives rise to liability, save as stated above regarding mere conduit activity (such as transmission performed by search engines).

(h) ***Aggregator websites (eg, Google News, price comparison websites)***

There are no specific regulations in Italy for aggregator and price comparison websites. With regard to websites whose content is, in turn, constituted by content from other framed websites by virtue of particular software, there could be violation of another's rights of reproduction to the extent that the content of third-party websites is reproduced substantially and is protected content for which no authorisation was given by the holder of the rights to it. In fact, if a substantial part of another's protected work is reproduced, this ends up compromising the legitimate holder's right of financial exploitation. However, if another's information, data, content is reproduced only partially and not substantially it is reasonable to suppose that copyright has not been violated.

In any case, an author is entitled to oppose his/her website or work being framed on another's website if framing is prejudicial to his/her reputation or honour. With regard to news aggregators see also section 1.4(d).

There is no copyright violation if content which is framed, even to a substantial degree, is not protected by copyright. In this case, if requirements hold, it may only be possible to speak of unfair competition.

(i) ***Treatment of user-generated content***

If user-created and uploaded content meets the requirement of creativity it is also protected by copyright and can be exploited only with the consent of the users, unless there is an obligation to assign or share the content under the general terms and conditions of contract of the website onto which the content is uploaded.

1.7 Joint liability for ISPs

As mentioned above, an ISP may be exempt from liability under Article 68*bis* of CL and Legislative Decree 70/2003. If the conditions for exemption do not hold, an ISP may be jointly liable for any of the activities indicated in section 1.6 if carried out by users of its service (see also the "Rules on copyright protection on electronic communications networks" adopted by the Communications Regulatory Authority on December 12 2013).

1.8 Relief

Even should ISPs be exempt from liability they may still be issued with injunctions by the competent administrative and judicial authorities under Articles 14.3, 15.2 and 16.3 of Legislative Decree 70/2003.

Furthermore Article 156.1 of CL stipulates:

Whoever has reason to fear that his/her right to financial exploitation under this law will be violated or intends to impede continuation or repetition of violation which has already been committed either by the author of the violation or by an intermediary whose services are used to commit said violation may take action before the courts to have his/her right upheld and continuation of the violation forbidden.

1.9 Issues specific to Italy

(a) Jurisdiction

If a defendant is domiciled within the European Union, jurisdiction is determined on the basis of EC Regulation 44/2001. Otherwise, on the basis of Article 3 of Law 218/1995, jurisdiction is determined according to the criteria laid down in the 1968 Brussels Convention. For the purposes of the present discussion, the Regulation and the Convention both contain essentially identical provisions. The Italian courts have jurisdiction if a defendant is domiciled or has its seat in Italy. Otherwise, the Italian courts have jurisdiction if Italy is the place in which the harmful event occurred or may occur. Place of the event, according to case law, must be understood not only as the place in which the harm arose but also as the place in which the event generating the harm occurred (ECJ, October 25 2011, joined cases C-509/09 and C-161/10). Therefore, the Italian courts are held to have jurisdiction if Italy is the place in which uploading occurred, or the place in which the unlawful material was disseminated (on dissemination see in similar cases Court of Naples, June 14 2000; Court of Verona, December 18 2000).

(b) Claim to infringement of foreign copyright

Although not common in standard practice, it is theoretically possible for an Italian court to examine a case of infringement of foreign copyright, provided that it has the jurisdiction to do so. This situation arises, according to the above rules, when a defendant is domiciled in Italy and is sued in Italy according to the *forum rei* criterion.

(c) ***Emission theory***

As seen above, if copyright and related rights are violated, the place where the allegedly unlawful material is uploaded and that in which the material is disseminated are considered to have a bearing for the purposes of jurisdiction (eg, the place in which a server is located, or that in which the website containing the allegedly unlawful material is actually managed).

1.10 Orphan works

Within the ambit of the European Union, regulations on orphan works are contained in EU Directive 2012/28 'on certain permitted uses of orphan works'. This Directive, however, has not yet been implemented in Italy. In Italy there is no specific legislation yet in matters of works, protected by copyright, whose authors cannot be identified or traced. As (the necessary) consent cannot be obtained to use these works, their exploitation could give rise to copyright infringement actions.

1.11 Online piracy measures

Online piracy is combated by means of a system of administrative and penal sanctions provided by Articles 171 to 174*quinquies* of CL.

1.12 Electronic infringement of moral rights

Regardless of the exclusive rights financially to exploit a work, and also after assignment of the rights themselves, an author retains his moral rights over the work (CL, Article 20), as these are perpetual, inalienable, indefeasible and non-transferable. The moral rights comprise:

- the right to object to derogatory treatment: an author has the right to oppose any distortion, mutilation, modification or other act causing detriment to the work, if this may be prejudicial to his reputation and honour. However, an author who is aware of and has accepted modification of his work can no longer take action to stop the modification or request that it be cancelled. This right may be exercised for example in the case of 'mashups', provided it can be demonstrated that the framed content is prejudicial to the author's reputation and honour.
- False attribution – the right to guard against impersonation on the Internet: an author may, at any time, claim ownership of a work published or disseminated online and stop others qualifying themselves in any way as authors of the work.
- Paternity right: whoever has created a work has the right to identify himself as the author of the published work, and if the work has been published anonymously or under a masking pseudonym, he may at any time reveal himself as the author of the work.

2. Trademarks

Trademark rules are contained in Articles 7ff of the Code of Industrial Property (CIP) issued with Legislative Decree February 10 2005, no. 30. The rules correspond essentially to those of EC Directive 2008/95 and EC Regulation 207/2009 on the Community Trademark.

2.1 Use of a trademark

Both for the purposes of maintaining a right on a registered trademark, avoiding its lapse through non-use, and in relation to trademark infringement, use of a trademark on a website constitutes use in Italy if it is use in trade (ie, connected to the offer of goods or services on the market and if the site on which use occurs is directed at consumers in Italy). It may be deduced that a site is directed at consumers in Italy from, for example, the fact that it is written in Italian or that it contains offers directed at Italian consumers. The goods offered on the website do not need to be in Italy already. It is sufficient that they may be ordered online by consumers in Italy. However, if the site is merely accessible in, but has no connection with Italy, there is no use in Italy.

Under Articles 20 and 22 of CIP, for there to be infringement it is sufficient that use as described above occurs. However, under Article 24 use in itself does not suffice to avoid lapse through non-use. Use must be genuine (ie, it must reach a threshold of significance) and not be limited in time or relate to an insignificant number of goods, etc.

2.2 Infringement

Italian legal theorists and the courts agree in asserting that certain uses of another's trademark on the Internet may also give rise to infringement under Articles 20 and 22 of CIP. Under these articles there is infringement in the case of use in the course of trade without the consent of the holder of: a sign which is identical to another's trademark for identical goods or services; a sign which is identical or similar to another's trademark for identical or similar goods or services if there is a likelihood of confusion or association for the public; or a sign which is identical or similar to another's trademark with a reputation, where use by the third party without due cause takes unfair advantage of, or is detrimental to, the distinctive character or the repute of the trademark. The courts have mainly dealt with cases of conflict between domain names and earlier trademarks. Other types of cases of internet use have been brought to the courts more rarely and for a number of them there is as yet no precedent.

(a) Metatags

Use of another's trademark as a metatag for the purposes of attracting web surfers to a website is considered an unlawful act in both legal theory and case law. However, in initial decisions the courts held that this was only a question of unfair competition, not trademark infringement. Later decisions ruled that use as a metatag also constituted infringement (Court of Milan, November 14 2005; Court of Milan August 8 2007).

(b) Keywords

Use of another's trademark as a keyword is considered trademark infringement and unfair competition by an advertiser (Court of Milan, March 11 2009). The position of search engines has not as yet been addressed by the Italian courts. However, it may be held that future decisions will follow the principles asserted by the ECJ starting from the March 23 2010 decision in the *Google* case.

(c) ***Sponsored links***

Use of another's trademark in a sponsored link may also constitute infringement and unfair competition. Initial confusion has also, at times, been considered to be a case of likelihood of confusion of a level sufficient to constitute infringement. On the other hand, even those who maintain that initial confusion does not constitute a likelihood of confusion proper state that it still gives rise to free riding on another's trademark, and therefore infringement under rules on the protection of trademarks with reputation.

(d) ***Hidden text***

There is no precedent on this matter, even if it may be equated with use in a metatag, with the consequent probable application by any courts examining the question of the same interpretative criteria. In fact, use in a hidden text could also constitute infringement if, due to network functioning methods, there may be confusion between the trademark holder and the third-party site or the third party may in some way be free riding on the reputation of the trademark holder.

(e) ***Internet domain names***

It is now undisputed (only in the past were there rare decisions finding otherwise) that use of another's trademark as a domain name constitutes trademark infringement if the prerequisites of Articles 20 and 22 of CIP hold, in particular if there may be a likelihood of confusion for the public or if the domain name is identical or similar to a trademark with a reputation and there may be free riding on or harm to the trademark itself.

A number of decisions have stated that registration in itself of a domain name and the ensuing 'occupation' of the sign, as well as its visibility to web surfers, constitutes a form of use which may give rise to infringement even if the website is not yet functioning.

(f) ***Search navigation tools***

There is no precedent. Use in search/navigation tools such as 'breadcrumb trails' on a website may essentially be equated with use of another's trademark in a link, which may give rise to infringement.

(g) ***Hypertext links***

Use of another's trademark in a link connected to the website of a party other than the holder constitutes infringement, provided the prerequisites under Article 20 of CIP hold. Linking to the website of the trademark holder may also be unlawful if it gives rise to confusion (eg, as to the existence of an economic connection), or if the third party draws unfair advantage from the linking or the linking is detrimental to a trademark with a reputation.

(h) ***Framing***

Framing may also constitute trademark infringement due to the presence of another's trademark in the framed page and to the possible erroneous belief on the part of the public that there is a connection with the trademark holder (a connection which does not actually exist) or, in any case, due to free riding on the renown of the trademark.

2.3 Defences

Article 21.1 of the CIP provides for a number of cases of lawful use of another's trademark. In particular, a third party cannot be prevented from using a sign which is identical or similar to another's trademark if the sign corresponds to the name or address of the third party; or if the sign is used to describe the characteristics of goods or services or to indicate the purpose of the goods of the third party as in the case of spare parts intended to be installed in an original product. In any case, use is permitted only if it complies with honest practices in industrial or commercial matters and thus, essentially, only if it does not interfere with the protected functions of the trademark.

(a) Descriptive (non-trademark) use of the mark

Under Article 21.1.b of CIP use for exclusively descriptive purposes which fully complies with honest practices in industrial or commercial matters does not constitute infringement.

(b) Comparative advertising

In Italy a special rule on comparative advertising is contained in Legislative Decree 145/2007. The Decree corresponds exactly to the same rules in EC Directive 114/2006. Use of a trademark in comparative advertising which complies with all the conditions of lawfulness provided by Article 4 of Legislative Decree 145/2007 does not constitute infringement. In any case, use is not lawful, and constitutes infringement, if it gives rise to a likelihood of confusion, if it draws unfair advantage from the renown of the trademark, if it harms the image of the trademark itself or if it is made for goods or services which are presented as imitations or replicas of the original products (Article 4 of Legislative Decree 145/2007).

(c) Parody

Use of another's trademark in a parody which has no commercial significance and which is the simple expression of freedom of thought does not constitute infringement (Court of Milan, September 7 2004). However, if the parody forms part of a trading activity and harms the reputation of the trademark or draws unfair advantage from it, this constitutes infringement (Court of Milan, March 4 1999; Court of Rome, June 23 2008).

2.4 Parallel imports

Under Article 5 of CIP trademark rights are exhausted in relation to goods put on the market by the trademark holder or with his/her consent within the European Economic Area; a holder may oppose further circulation of the goods in Italy only with just cause. Therefore, in theory a holder cannot oppose parallel importation of goods sold by it or with its consent within the European Economic Area. This also applies when the goods are offered for sale in Italy via a website. Conversely, putting goods on the market in non-EEA countries does not lead to exhaustion even if it takes place with the consent of the holder. Parallel importation from non-EEA countries therefore constitutes infringement.

2.5 Remedies

A trademark holder can seek the following sanctions under Articles 124 to 126 of CIP in the case of infringement: injunction on repetition of the unlawful activity, with a fine being imposed for any breach of the injunction; a compensation order and an order to return profits; withdrawal from the market and destruction of the goods and the relative advertising material; handing the goods over to the trademark holder; publication of the decision. At an interim stage, pursuant to Articles 126 and 129 to 131 of CIP he/she can obtain an injunction accompanied by a fine, seizure of the goods and publication of the order providing for the interim measures.

2.6 Liability of an ISP

It is normally held that an ISP cannot be held responsible for making available a service which is then exploited for unlawful purposes. With regard to the liability of ISPs, Italy implemented EC Directive 31/2000 by means of Legislative Decree 70/2003. In all likelihood, the Italian courts will, in applying the Decree, follow the same principles as those expounded by the ECJ in the *Google* decision of March 23 2010 and the *L'Oréal/eBay* decision of July 12 2011.

As to the question of injunctions which may be issued against ISPs to stop infringement by their users, Italy has implemented Article 11 of EC Directive 48/2004 on the Enforcement of IP Rights – including the specific part relating to injunctions against intermediaries which supply a service used by third parties to commit an infringement – by means of Article 124.1 of CIP (which, however, expressly requires, differing here from Article 11 of the Directive, that the ISP be party to the action). In all likelihood, the Italian courts will follow the principles of the ECJ in the *L'Oréal/eBay* decision on this point too.

Furthermore, under Articles 14.3, 15.2 and 16.3 of Legislative Decree 70/2003, the competent administrative and judicial authorities may issue injunctions against ISPs.

2.7 Advertising law and regulation

There are specific rules relating to advertising which are also applicable to internet advertising. Legislative Decree 145/2007 regulates advertising in relations between competitors (or professional practitioners). It bars any form of misleading advertising and makes the lawfulness of comparative advertising conditional upon a series of requirements corresponding to those of EC Directive 114/2006. For what concerns advertising in relation to consumers, the Consumers' Code (Legislative Decree 206/2005) in Articles 21 to 26 bars any form of advertising which is misleading for or aggressive in relation to consumers. In the event of violation of Legislative Decree 145/2007 or the Consumers' Code, the Competition Authority will be competent to examine the matter. The procedure is started simply by any interested party reporting violation and then proceeds *ex officio*.

A private self-regulatory code – the Code for Self-Regulation in Advertising (CSRA) – bars any form of comparative advertising which does not comply with conditions similar to those under the EC Directive as well as any form of misleading, defamatory or aggressive advertising. Upon a report being made by interested parties or by a watchdog committee (set up by the CSRA), the Adjudicating Panel of the Self Regulation in Advertising Institute (also set up by the CSRA) assesses whether or not a piece of advertising complies with the CSRA.

2.8 Domain name disputes

Disputes relating to the allocation and use of domain names within the ambit of the local country code ('.it') may be resolved extra-judicially on the basis of the Regulation for the Resolution of Disputes in the Country Code Top Level Domain.it (now in its 2.0 version of June 19 2009). The Regulation provides, in particular, for an arbitration procedure and an administrative procedure of reallocation. For the latter procedure to succeed, the holder of a distinctive sign which is prior to the domain name for which re-allocation is requested must provide evidence of a number of alternative circumstances, such as a likelihood of confusion between the earlier sign and the domain name, the absence of a 'right' which justifies registration ('right' may simply be the fact that the registrant used or prepared to use, prior to the opposition, the domain name to offer goods or services to the public) and bad faith on the part of the registrant.

The reallocation procedure is conducted by organisations called Providers of the Service of Dispute Resolution (PSRD). Each has its own fee rates which vary according to the number of domain names involved in the procedure and the number of experts called upon to decide. Generally, a procedure involving a single domain name will cost between €1,000 and €4,000, depending on the number of experts called. A decision will be taken within 15 days of the adjudicating panel of experts being set up (30 days if the panel has requested further details or documents from the parties).

2.9 Unfair competition/passing off

Domain names and other distinctive signs which appear on a website (the original layout of a website can also be considered a distinctive sign) may be protected – even if they are not registered as trademarks – as unregistered distinctive signs on the basis of the CIP and unfair competition rules. The basis of this protection is to be found in Articles 1 and 2 of CIP, which state that there is an exclusive IP right on unregistered signs and in Article 2598, no 1 of the Civil Code which bars as an act of unfair competition use of signs which are identical or similar to another's distinctive signs even if they are not registered, if such use gives rise to likelihood of confusion. In both cases, the prerequisite for protection is that use has been made of the unregistered sign and that this use has given rise to 'qualified' renown (ie, renown which is accompanied by a perception on the part of the public of the sign as a distinctive sign). The scope of protection is limited to the product category and territory within which there may be a likelihood of confusion following use of an identical or similar sign by a third party.

The copying of web content which does not give rise to confusion but constitutes free riding on the activity of a competitor is, in turn, an act of unfair competition under Article 2598, no 2 of the Civil Code.

3. Patents

Rules on patents are contained in Articles 45ff of the Code of Industrial Property (CIP) and, as regards biotech patents, Articles 81*bis* ff of CIP. In particular, Articles 45 and 81*quater* CIP deal with the question of which inventions may be patented.

3.1 Patentability of 'internet' inventions

Under Article 45.2 of CIP, computer programs, business methods, mathematical methods and data presentations cannot be patented. However, Article 45.3 of CIP states that this bar on patenting holds only to the extent to which the patent application or the patent concern the above entities 'as such'. Italian legal theory and case law maintain that, since the bar only exists for these entities 'as such', the bar does not apply if programs and methods have an industrial application.

(a) Computer programs

In the application of this principle, in relation to computer programs, defined as 'instructions' which are necessary for the use of a computer for a specific use, according to the prevailing approach in Italy two categories of software inventions are patentable. The first is that of inventions in which the program has a technical effect inside a computer, commanding its method of functioning. This is the case, for example, in software which organises the memory of a computer, allowing the simultaneous execution of a number of programs on one single system, thus reducing waiting times. The second category is that of inventions in which the program manages through the computer an industrial process or a piece of apparatus which is external to the computer (computer-implemented inventions). This is the case, for example, in software which manages a control unit of a piece of radiological apparatus with the aim of optimising exposure of a patient to X rays, protecting him or her from over exposure.

(b) Business methods

The trend in Italy is to admit patentability of business methods only if they allow a technical problem to be overcome and constitute something material inside an industrial product, use of which allows the effect of the principle underlying the business methods 'to be repeated'. The prevailing opinion in Italy is to consider methods concerning a particular way of organising a business or professional activity to be unpatentable. Methods of production, methods aimed at saving energy and methods in general which may be applied in an industrial activity are, on the other hand, considered to be patentable.

(c) Mathematical methods

With regard to mathematical methods, in the application of the general principle whereby the entities listed in Article 45.2 are not patentable only if they do not have an industrial application, an invention which replaced a data transposition and table reference in a perpetual calendar with a particular kind of slide rule has been considered to be patentable.

(d) ***Presentation of information***

In Italy the question of the patentability of the presentation of information has arisen basically in relation to advertising methods. According to the prevailing approach not all new advertising methods are patentable as industrial inventions, but only those which give rise to particular advertising goods or services which may be sold as products of an advertising industry.

3.2 Bioinformatics

In Italy the specific question of the patentability of a novel DNA sequence or protein structure discovered through the use of bioinformatics has yet to be addressed. Under current law there is, however, no doubt that if these inventions possess the requirements provided by patent law in Articles 45ff and 81*bis* ff of CIP, they may be patented no matter how they are obtained, and thus also by means of bioinformatics.

3.3 Issues specific to Italy

(a) ***Infringement on the Internet***

In the case of online infringement, the Italian courts have jurisdiction first and foremost when the defendant is domiciled in Italy, according to the general criterion of *forum rei*. When the defendant is not domiciled in Italy, in cases involving infringing goods offered for sale online, the Italian courts have jurisdiction when goods are directed at Italian consumers, for example when consumers in Italy may purchase the product online; or, in all likelihood, when the server onto which the site managing online sales is uploaded is in Italy; or when the goods are warehoused in Italy and sent from Italy to consumers buying online. Mere visibility in Italy of a foreign website directed at consumers outside Italy does not suffice. However, in cases in which it is the way of functioning of a website which infringes a patent (eg, a software or method patent), there is no certain solution and no precedent: if a defendant is not domiciled in Italy, it may be held that the Italian courts have jurisdiction only if the server on which the website is uploaded is located in Italy; or more broadly that the Italian courts have jurisdiction, even though the server is located in another country, when the website is directed at users in Italy.

(b) ***Process patents***

With process patents infringement may occur online where only part of the process is carried out in Italy, if that part may be considered, in itself, sufficient to constitute implementation of the inventive idea covered by the patent. Otherwise, it may be held that the activity carried out in Italy constitutes contributory infringement. There is, however, no precedent on this point.

3.4 Remedies available for patent infringement

Under Articles 124 to 126 of CIP the main sanctions for infringement are an injunction on repetition of the offences, which may be reinforced by a fine to be paid if the injunction is breached; orders to pay compensation and to hand over profits made; and publication of the decision. Other sanctions provided by the law are destruction or withdrawal from the market of the goods; handing over of the goods to the patent holder and seizure of the goods for the duration of the patent. However, these other sanctions are not usually imposed in standard practice. An injunction accompanied by a fine, seizure of goods and publication of the decision may also be granted as emergency measures under Articles 126 and 129 to 131 of CIP.

4. Disclosure orders against ISPs

4.1 Availability

A number of legal theorists in Italy have maintained that an ISP may be issued with a disclosure order under Article 121*bis* of CIP which states:

> *1) The judicial authority, both in interim proceedings and in an action on the merits, may, upon being presented with a justified and proportionate application, order that information be disclosed as to the origin and to the distribution networks of goods or services infringing a right under this law by the infringer or by any other person who: a) has been found in possession of infringing goods on a commercial scale; has been found to be using infringing services on a commercial scale; b) has been found to be providing on a commercial scale services used in infringing activities; c) has been indicated by persons under a) and b) as being involved in the production, manufacture or distribution of such goods or in the supply of such services. 2) The information under 1) may, inter alia, include the name and address of the producers, manufacturers, distributors, suppliers and of other previous holders of the goods or services, plus wholesalers and retailers, as well as information as to the quantities produced, manufactured, delivered, received or ordered, and the price of the goods or services. 3) Information is obtained through oral examination of the parties in paragraph 1. 4) The applicant must specifically identify those persons who are to be questioned and the matters on which they are each to be questioned.*

Article 121*bis* is applicable in trademark and patent cases. An identical provision in Article 156*ter* of CL is applicable in copyright matters. The Italian courts have, on occasions, granted orders pursuant to Articles 121*bis* of CIP and 156*ter* of CL against service providers (Court of Rome, September 26 2006; Court of Rome, March 1 2007). Some court decisions have, however, ruled (in cases in which information was requested of telephone line managers with regard to user data) that disclosure orders cannot be issued if privacy needs to be protected (Court of Rome, March 17 2008; Court of Rome, July 14 2007).

4.2 Requirements

As indicated in section 4.1, an applicant must demonstrate that its IP right has been infringed, that the petition for information is directed at the infringer or one of the other parties indicated in Article 121*bis* of CIP and Article 156*ter* of CL, and that the petition is justified and proportionate. This final requirement means that the applicant must explain why information needs to be disclosed and that the information requested must be proportionate to the offence and not extend unduly to other aspects of the third party's activity.

4.3 Jurisdictional issues

A request for information must be contained within an application submitted to the IP Division of the territorially competent court. If an application is admitted, information is disclosed by means of oral examination.

4.4 'John Doe' injunctions

John Doe injunctions are not admitted. Measures can only be sought against a party identified in advance.

Japan

Louise Stoupe
Chie Yakura
Morrison & Foerster LLP/Ito & Mitomi

Japan is a civil law country with relatively developed internet-related intellectual property laws. The Japanese regulatory regime generally favours the protection of intellectual property rights through a series of acts including the Copyright Act, the Patent Act, the Trademark Act, the Unfair Competition Act, and Act on the Limitation of Liability for Damages of Specified Telecommunications Service Providers and the Right to Demand Disclosure of Identification Information of the Senders (the 'Provider Liability Limitation Act'). The civil code in some of these areas, such as the Copyright Act, is relatively extensive with detailed regulations and significant case law that assists with the interpretation of the code. In other areas, such as the Trademark Act, the code is less extensive with respect to internet-specific issues.

In order to administer these laws, there are a number of specialised administrative and judicial departments tasked with the management and registration of intellectual property rights. These administrative offices include the Copyright Section of the Agency for Cultural Affairs, which handles the voluntary registration of Japanese copyrights; the Software Information Center (SOFTIC), which handles the voluntary registration of copyrightable computer programs and circuit board layouts; and the Japan Patent Office (JPO), which handles registrations of Japanese patents, design rights, trademarks, and the like. Since April 1 2005, Japan has used an Intellectual Property High Court to hear appeals from JPO decisions and district courts actions related to intellectual property.

In intellectual property cases, Japanese judges are bound by the nation's Constitution and enacted laws. Though non-binding, prior court judgments can influence lower courts. Although the Supreme Court and the Intellectual Property High Court have made various leading decisions, not all cases in Japan are reported and a significant percentage of the cases end in settlement, so intellectual property law in Japan is highly reliant on the plain text of various statutes.[1]

1. Copyright, database rights and design rights

1.1 Overview

Japanese copyright law grants exclusive rights to authors of literary, scientific,

1 This chapter frequently refers to unofficial English translations of statutes provided by the Japanese Ministry of Justice (available at www.japaneselawtranslation.go.jp), but the original Japanese language text of each statute is the actual law.

artistic, and musical works in which "thoughts or sentiments are expressed in a creative way".[2] In determining whether thoughts or sentiments are creatively expressed, courts consider factors such as the manner of expression (eg, the selection of words in a written work) and the extent to which a medium of expression allows a creator a wide variety of choices in preparing a work. Work in a medium where choices are limited is less likely to be deemed creative expression. For example, copyright law does not protect news reports and other "reports having the character of being mere communications of facts".[3]

Japanese copyright law also separately protects performances, phonograms, and broadcasts in addition to any underlying content.[4]

(a) *Literary works and artistic works*

Japanese copyright law can protect any internet or digital literary or artistic content that fits the statutory requirement of creative expression.[5] Indeed, courts have held that even postings to internet message boards are protectable where such postings satisfy that requirement.

Software is protectable as a 'computer program work' (and not as a 'literary work'),[6] but that protection does not extend to programming languages, rules and algorithms which are specifically excluded as protectable works.[7]

(b) *Films, sound recordings, and broadcasts*

Subject to the creative expression requirement, 'cinematographic works' are eligible for copyright protection.[8] In practice, this term captures all film, television, and similar audio/video content, including user-generated content uploaded to video sharing sites such as YouTube.[9]

Phonograms,[10] the performances recorded therein, and underlying musical compositions all receive independent protection.[11]

Broadcasts that involve transmissions made for simultaneous reception (such as online 'webcasts') are protectable as 'broadcasts' in addition to and separately from the content broadcast.[12]

---

2 *Chosakukenhō* [Copyright Act], Law No 48 of 1970, Article 2(1)(i) (hereinafter 'Copyright Act').
3 *Ibid* at Article 10(2).
4 *Ibid* at Article 1. Performances, phonograms, and broadcasts are not 'copyrighted', but rather protected by so-called 'neighbouring right[s]'.
5 *Ibid* at Article 2(1)(i).
6 Note also that software is subject to a special (albeit voluntary) registration process through the Software Information Center (SOFTIC).
7 Copyright Act at Article 10(1)(ix), (3).
8 *Ibid* at Article 10(1)(vii).
9 'Cinematographic works' include any "work which is (i) expressed through a process producing visual or audio-visual effects similar to those of cinematography, and (ii) is fixed in an object" (*ibid* at Article 2(3)). Storage on a hard drive or other medium is generally sufficient to satisfy this and other 'fixation' requirements.
10 'Phonograms' are "fixations of sounds on phonographic discs, recording-tapes and other forms of tangible medium, excluding, however, those fixations [of sound] that are intended to be replayed exclusively with images" (*ibid* at Article 2(1)(v)).
11 *Ibid* at Articles 8, 7(ii).
12 *Ibid* at Articles 1, 2(1)(viii), 9, 9-2.

(c) *Typographical arrangements of a published edition*

Though unlikely, a typographical arrangement could conceivably qualify as an 'artistic work' if it is a sufficiently creative expression of thought or sentiment.[13]

(d) *Protection of the user interface*

Graphical user interfaces (GUIs) have been held protectable as creative works where they meet the creative expression requirement.[14]

(e) *Computer-generated works*

Computer-generated works, such as computer graphics and automated programs, are eligible for protection to the extent that they are the product of human creativity. Where a computer is a mere tool used by a creator to express thoughts and sentiments in a creative way, the resulting work is protectable.[15]

(f) *Websites protected as databases*

Under the Copyright Act, a database is "a collection of information ... which is systematically organised so that such information can be searched by [a] computer".[16] A database may be independently protected where such database constitute an intellectual creation "by reason of the selection or systematic construction of information contained therein".[17] Where a website meets that standard, it would be protectable as a database. Regardless of the effort involved in their creation, databases that lack sufficient creativity are not eligible for protection.

(g) *Compilations*

A compilation, which is any collection that is not a 'database',[18] may be independently protected where it "constitute[s an] intellectual creation [through the] selection or arrangement of [its] contents".[19] Again, only compilations that have sufficient creativity are eligible for protection.

1.2 Infringement

A person infringes Japanese copyright by violating a rights-holder's copyrights, neighbouring rights (which are the rights associated with broadcasting and communicating works and are held, eg, by a broadcaster) or moral rights.[20]

(a) *Copying*

Under the Copyright Act, a rights-holder has the exclusive right to reproduce their

---

13 See *ibid* at Article 2(1)(i).

14 *Tōkyō Chihō Saibansho* [Tokyo Dist Ct] June 13 2001, Hei 13 (yo) no 22014, 131 *Hanrei jihō* 1761; *Ōsaka Chihō Saibansho* [Osaka Dist Ct] March 30 2000, Hei 10 (wa) no 13577.

15 Agency for Cultural Affairs Copyright Comm'n, Ninth Subcomm, Computer Creations Report, ch 3 (1993).

16 Copyright Act at Article 2(1)(x)-3.

17 *Ibid* at Article 12-2 (1).

18 Any work that meets the definition of a 'database' is not additionally or alternatively protectable as a 'compilation' (*ibid* at Article 12(1)).

19 *Ibid* at Article 12(1).

20 See *ibid* at Articles 18-20, 21-50. Moral rights are discussed at section 1.12.

work,[21] which can be infringed upon by the production of digital copies. Thus, unauthorised uploading, downloading, or file sharing can constitute unlawful reproduction.

(b) Issuing copies to the public

Issuing unauthorised reproductions to the public, whether done for profit or not, can infringe on a rights-holder's exclusive right to transfer ownership of reproductions to the public.[22] Nonetheless, authorised owners may sell or transfer their reproductions of a work.[23] Thus, a person infringes copyright where that person uploads a copy of a copyrighted work to a website and allows others freely to download that work without the authorisation of the work's owner.

(c) Communicating the work to the public

Even if no copy is made or transferred, communicating a protected work to the public can infringe the right of public transmission.[24] Moreover, even where no transmission actually occurs, merely making a work transmittable or available for transmission can also infringe.[25] Thus, for example, a user could infringe by making protected content available to stream on demand over the Internet without authorisation.

(d) Perform, show or play the work in public

A rights-holder has the exclusive right to perform, present on screen, recite, or exhibit their work.[26] Accordingly, unauthorised public performance, even online, would likely infringe at least one of these rights.

A rights-holder also has the exclusive rights to make recordings of a performance and to broadcast that performance or recording,[27] meaning that both unauthorised recording and/or streaming can infringe.

(e) Rent or lend the work to the public

A rights-holder has the exclusive right to offer their work to the public for rent.[28] This provision does not apply to cinematographic works[29] or phonographic works,[30] for which special rules apply.

(f) Authorising another person to do any of the above

Though Japanese law does not explicitly contain a provision prohibiting the indirect infringement of copyright, courts punish indirect infringement under a doctrine of

---

21 Copyright Act at Article 21. 'Reproduction' is "reproduction in a tangible form by means of printing, photography, photocopy, sound or visual recording or other methods" (*ibid* at Article 2(1)(xv)). Creating digital copies on a hard disk, CD, or other storage medium qualifies as "reproduction in a tangible form".

22 *Ibid* at Articles 21, 26, 26-2, 26-3.

23 *Ibid* at Article 26-2(2).

24 *Ibid* at Article 23. See *ibid* at Article 2(1)(vii)-2, (ix)-4.

25 *Ibid* at Article 23(1).

26 *Ibid* at Articles 22, 22-2, 24, 25.

27 *Ibid* at Articles 21, 2(1)(xv)(a).

28 Copyright Act at Article 26-3; see also *ibid* at Article 2(8).

29 *Ibid* at Article 26-3.

30 *Ibid* at Article 95-3.

vicarious liability similar to respondent superior. Liability under that theory depends on:

- whether the party in question:
  - manages, or
  - controls a third party committing an infringing act; and
- whether the third party's infringement was profitable to the first party.[31]

(g) ***Secondary infringement***

Distributing, possessing for the purpose of distributing, and exporting infringing objects by a person who is aware of such infringement is itself infringement.[32] Importing goods for the purposes of distribution that were made by an act that would have been infringing if performed within Japan is also infringement.[33]

1.3 The test for copyright infringement

Generally, to state a claim for infringement, a claimant must show that the allegedly infringing work is both: similar to; and 'dependent' upon (ie, actually copied from) the protected work. Under this standard, the essential characteristics of the original work must be copied. Even the extensive copying of unprotected elements of a work, such as facts, ideas, or tropes, does not infringe. Moreover, even where a work is substantially similar to an existing copyrighted work, unless the original work was actually copied, there is no infringement.

1.4 Exceptions and defences to copyright infringement

Japan has the following limited number of statutory exceptions to infringement.

(a) ***Format shifting***

It is untested whether format shifting constitutes infringement, but given the inclination of the courts strictly to interpret creation of a copy, it is likely that format shifting would constitute infringement.

(b) ***Personal copying rights***

The 'private use' exception allows reproduction for "personal use or family use or other equivalent uses within a limited scope" even though such reproduction would otherwise infringe.[34] Nonetheless, if a user downloads (and thereby copies) an infringing work uploaded on the Internet while knowing the downloaded work is infringing, even though such an act would qualify as a personal use, such downloading would be an infringing act.[35]

(c) ***Time shifting***

Recording broadcast content for later use involves reproduction and thus could

---

31 *Saikō Saibansho* [Sup Ct] March 15 1988, *Shōwa* 59 (o) no 1204, 1 *Hanrei jihō* 981. See also *Tōkyo Kōtō Saibansho* [Tokyo High Ct] March 3, 2005, *Heisei* 16 (ne) no 2067; *Tōkyo Kōtō Saibansho* [Tokyo High Ct] March 31, 2005, *Heisei* 16 (ne) no 405.

32 *Ibid* at Article 113(1)(ii).

33 *Ibid* at Article 113(1)(i).

34 *Ibid* at Article 30(1).

35 *Ibid* at Article 30(1)(iii).

infringe; however, as a practical matter, such time shifting would often fall under the private use exception (discussed in section 1.4(b) above).

(d) *Fair use*

Japanese law contains no broad 'fair use' provision, but instead includes a number of narrow statutory exceptions to infringement.

For example, under the quotation exception, it is permissible to "quote from and thereby exploit a work already made public, provided that such quotation is compatible with fair practice and to the extent justified by the purpose of the quotation, such as news reporting, critique or research".[36] In practice, courts further require that the quotation be: distinguishable from the rest of the work; relatively 'subordinate' to the rest of the work; and properly cited.

(e) *Caching/temporary copies as part of communication processes*

Where limited to the extent necessary to prevent communication failure[37] and/or to allow for proper functioning of a computer system,[38] caching and other forms of temporary copying (eg, in RAM) which might otherwise infringe are permitted.

The law also exempts search engines from liability for any allegedly infringing conduct to the extent that such conduct is "for the provision of ... search results".[39]

(f) *Hosting*

Hosting infringing content online and allowing that content to be downloaded by users could each violate, *inter alia*, the right to reproduce and/or to transfer ownership to the public.[40] Hosting user-uploaded content can also result in secondary liability (discussed in section 1.6(a) below).

(g) *Back-up copies*

The Copyright Act contains a special exception for necessary computer program back-up copies created by the user.[41] The same provision also exempts reproduction of computer programs for purposes of installation, debugging, and transplantation.[42] This provision does not authorise or protect the transfer of such copies to third parties.

(h) *Reverse engineering*

Reverse engineering is not infringement insofar as it involves the reproduction of a copyrighted work for the purposes of analysing it with a computer.[43] This definition explicitly includes reverse engineering for the purpose of analysing source code.[44]

---

36 *Ibid* at Article 32(1).
37 *Ibid* at Article 47-5.
38 Copyright Act at Article 47-8.
39 *Ibid* at Article 47-6.
40 *Ibid* at Articles 21, 26, 26-2.
41 *Ibid* at Article 47-8.
42 *Ibid.*
43 Copyright Act at Article 47-7.
44 *Ibid.*

(i) ***Parody defence***

There is no 'parody' defence under Japanese law. In fact, a parody may infringe an author's moral right against derogatory treatment (discussed in section 1.12(a) below), which prohibits acts of exploitation "prejudicial to the honor or reputation of the author"[45] even where such acts are otherwise not infringing. However, parody may be permissible under, *inter alia*, the quotation exception (discussed in section 1.4(d) above).[46]

(j) ***Incidental inclusion***

Though incidental inclusion could be found to infringe before the recent amendment to Copyright Act came into force as of January 1 2013, incidental inclusion is explicitly excluded from infringement so long as such inclusion would not unreasonably harm the interest of a rights-holder with respect to types of copyrighted work, way of use, or manner of copy.[47]

1.5 Remedies

Under the Copyright Act, a rights-holder whose rights have been infringed may be entitled to a preliminary and/or permanent injunction,[48] potentially including the destruction of any infringing materials, machines, or tools used exclusively for infringement.[49] A rights-holder may also seek compensatory damages, damages based upon the infringing party's profits, and, in rare circumstances, damages for mental suffering.

1.6 Copyright liability

(a) ***Hosting/cloud computing where infringing content is uploaded by the user of a service***

A telecommunications service provider may face secondary liability where it passively hosts infringing content uploaded by users. Of course, a provider which actively enables such behaviour through, for example, a P2P network may also be liable.[50]

Nonetheless, the Provider Liability Limitation Act creates a safe harbour that shelters providers from liability for the infringing conduct of their users except where it was "technically possible to take measures to prevent such [infringing information distribution] from being transmitted", and where the service provider knew that the infringement was caused by such information distribution, or it had knowledge of such information distribution and could reasonably have known that the infringement was caused by such information distribution.[51]

---

45 *Ibid* at Article 113(6).
46 *Ibid* at Article 32.
47 That is, the works do not involve actual copying of the copyrighted work (see above section 1.3).
48 Copyright Act at Article 112(1).
49 *Ibid* at Article 112(2).
50 See below, section 1.6(c) regarding P2P networks.
51 Act on the Limitation of Liability for Damages of Specified Telecommunications Service Providers and the Right to Demand Disclosure of Identification Information of the Senders, Law No 137 of 2001, Article 3 (hereinafter 'Provider Liability Limitation Act').

(b) Hypertext linking

To a third-party website: A person does not infringe by merely linking to a third party's website. Insofar as they might infringe, quotations used in the process of such linking would likely be protected by the quotation exception (discussed in section 1.4(d)).[52]

To an infringing work: A person does not infringe by merely linking to an infringing work. This act may, however, make the person liable in tort where, for example, the work's rights-holder is harmed by the link.

Copying of headlines: Although it is unlikely that a headline alone could constitute protectable creative expression, protection is not categorically impossible. However, even if a headline were theoretically protectable, its use in most cases would most likely fall under the quotation exception discussed in section 1.4(d).[53]

Note that even if copying a headline is not copyright infringement, it could violate other laws, including those against unfair competition.

(c) P2P networks

Suppliers of P2P software: Suppliers of P2P software can be held criminally liable for the infringing conduct of their users where: the supplier knew of either actual infringement or a high probability of infringement by the software's user base; the supplier made the software available to the public; and the user base actually committed infringement.[54]

Uploaders and downloaders: A user can infringe by uploading and/or sharing protected content without authorisation.[55] A user can also infringe by downloading infringing content with the knowledge that the content is infringing.[56]

(d) Webcasting

Webcasting can, *inter alia*, violate an owner's reproduction rights.[57] Where webcasting duplicates a broadcast signal, it can also violate the rights of an owner of a broadcast.[58] Accordingly, where a user streams a television channel live, that user potentially infringes both the rights of the owner of the underlying content and the rights of the owner of the broadcast signal.

---

52 Kazuyuki Takahashi, Shigeru Matsui and Hidemi Suzuki, *Internet and the Law* 279 (2010) (original in Japanese).

53 Copyright Act at Article 32.

54 *Saikō Saibansho* [Sup Ct] December 19 2011, *Hei* 21 (a) no 1900 (hereinafter the *Winny Case*). In the *Winny Case*, criminal liability was not found, because the file-sharing program 'Winny' had both legal and illegal uses and because the creators of Winny only knew of a general possibility that Winny would be used for copyright infringement.

55 *Ibid.*

56 See below section 1.11 regarding online piracy.

57 Copyright Act at Articles 21, 26, 26-2.

58 See *ibid* at Articles 2(1)(viii), 9. Note again that these are 'neighbouring rights' and not copyrighted works *per se*.

(e) ***Streaming***

Where a user uploads and makes copyrighted material available for on-demand streaming access without authorisation, that user infringes, *inter alia*, the right of public transmission.

It is less clear whether watching an unauthorised streaming video is infringement. Even though the viewer's computer makes a temporary copy of the work (eg, in RAM), such copying is probably lawful under an exception permitting duplication for the purposes of computer operation.[59]

(f) ***Framing***

'Framing' (the act of placing one website within another) could infringe to the extent that it may appropriate and rewrite the content of another.

(g) ***Transmission of infringing work across a communications network***

As discussed above in the context of P2P networks (section 1.6(c) above), a user infringes by transmitting a protected work on a communications network without the permission of the rights-holder.

(h) ***Aggregator websites (eg, Google News, price comparison websites)***

Aggregators such as Google News are likely protected under the search engine exception (discussed in section 1.4(e) above).

(i) ***Treatment of user-generated content***

While ownership vests in a work's creator by default, ownership of user-generated content also depends on the terms and conditions of agreements between service providers and users.

1.7 Joint liability for ISPs

Under the Provider Liability Limitation Act, a telecommunications service provider cannot be held liable for infringement committed by its users except where:

- it was "technically possible to take measures to prevent such [infringing information distribution] from being transmitted"; and
- where the service provider knew that the infringement was caused by such information distribution, or it had knowledge of such information distribution and could reasonably have known that the infringement was caused by such information distribution.[60]

1.8 Relief

Although not liable for infringing content or conduct of its users where within the safe harbour described in section 1.7, a provider must comply with legitimate disclosure and blocking requests made by rights-holders harmed by such user infringement.

59 *Ibid* at Article 47-8.
60 Provider Liability Limitation Act at Article 3(1).

When a provider discloses information about or blocks a user's transmissions, or when a provider blocks a user's potentially infringing transmissions in response to a request or on its own initiative, the service provider will not be liable to the user so long as such actions have only been taken where necessary to prevent such transmissions and where either the provider had a reasonable belief that infringement was occurring, or the user had failed to contest the provider's actions when notified of the request and the provider's contemplated actions.[61]

1.9 Issues specific to Japan

(a) *Jurisdiction*

Japanese courts have jurisdiction over copyright infringement that occurs within Japan. They do not have jurisdiction where an infringing act outside of Japan causes injury within Japan where such injury was not ordinarily foreseeable.[62] However, if the infringing act outside Japan is committed by a Japanese domiciled person, an action can be brought in Japan based on the domicile of the defendant.[63]

(b) *Claim to infringement of foreign copyright*

Japanese courts will hear claims regarding the alleged infringement of copyrights granted by foreign countries that are signatories to relevant international treaties such as the Berne Convention.[64]

(c) *Emission theory*

In Japan, the 'making available' of an infringing work by uploading that work on the Internet is infringement and takes place only in the location of upload, regardless of whether or not that infringing work is in fact downloaded by a third party.[65] As for unauthorised downloading, please see section 1.11 below.

1.10 Orphan works

When it is not possible to contact the rights-holder despite reasonable efforts to do so, the Commissioner of the Agency for Cultural Affairs may grant a compulsory licence to those who wish to use a work.[66]

1.11 Online piracy

The unauthorised downloading of copyrighted material could be infringement under Japanese copyright law.[67] Additionally, a recently adopted law effective October 1 2012 establishes serious criminal penalties for those who knowingly download

61 *Ibid* at Article 3(2).
62 See Code of Civil Procedure at Article 3-3(viii).
63 See Code of Civil Procedure at Article 3-2(1) and (3).
64 Japan is a signatory to the Berne Convention, which requires Japan to protect the rights of international rights holders. See Berne Convention for the Protection of Literary and Artistic Works, September 9 1886, as last revised at Paris, July 24 1971 (amended October 2 1979), S Treaty Doc No 27 (1986), 828 UNTS 221, at Article 3.
65 Copyright Act at Article 23(1).
66 *Ibid* at Article 67.
67 *Ibid* at Article 30(1)(iii).

infringing content.[68] These criminal penalties include imprisonment not exceeding two years or a fine not exceeding two million yen.[69]

1.12 Electronic infringement of moral rights

Japanese law recognises moral rights, which are rights that protect the personal interests of an author. These rights are personal to an author and thus cannot be transferred.[70] Also, they are subject to the exceptions listed above in section 1.4.

(a) Right to object to derogatory treatment

An author has the right to "maintain the integrity of his work" such that "no distortion, mutilation or other modification thereof shall be made against his intent".[71] Additionally, any use of a work in a manner that is "prejudicial to the honor or reputation of the author" is an infringement of that author's moral rights.[72] These rights apply equally to content on the Internet.

(b) False attribution – the right to guard against impersonation on the Internet

False attributions of authorship may infringe the moral rights of a work's real author under Japanese copyright law.[73] False attributions may also be considered a form of fraud or unfair competition, depending on the circumstances.

(c) Paternity rights

An author has a right of attribution;[74] however, "[i]t is permissible to omit the name of the author where, to the extent compatible with fair practice, it is determined that there is no risk of damage to the interests of the author in his claim to authorship in light of the purpose and the manner of the exploitation of the work".[75]

2. Trademarks

Trademark law in Japan is predominantly set out in two acts: the Trademark Act and the Unfair Competition Prevention Act. Generally speaking, the Trademark Act protects against the infringement of registered trademarks, while the Unfair Competition Prevention Act protects against the infringement of sufficiently well-known but unregistered marks.

2.1 Use of a trademark

Under Japanese law, trademarks are "any character(s), figure(s), sign(s) or three dimensional shape(s), or any combination[s] thereof" that are used in connection with specified goods or services.[76] 'Use' of a trademark includes affixing a trademark

---

68 *Ibid* at Article 119(3).
69 *Ibid*.
70 *Ibid* at Article 59.
71 *Ibid* at Article 20(1).
72 *Ibid* at Article 113(6).
73 Copyright Act at Article 19.
74 *Ibid*.
75 Copyright Act at Article 19(3); see also Copyright Act at Article 19(1).
76 Trademark Act, Law No 127 of 1959, Article 2 (hereinafter 'Trademark Act').

to goods, delivering trademark-affixed goods to others, and distributing materials advertising goods or services upon which a trademark is affixed.[77]

2.2 Infringement

Infringement under the Trademark Act generally entails the use of a mark similar (or identical) to a registered trademark in connection with the designated (or similar) goods or services.[78] Though not explicitly stated in the Trademark Act, the possibility of consumer confusion plays a major part in determining whether or not a trademark has been infringed. The Unfair Competition Prevention Act allows for a finding of infringement under substantially similar circumstances where a trademark is sufficiently well known but unregistered.[79]

(a) Metatags

Japanese courts have held that the use of trademarks in metatags may constitute infringement because metatags are visible to users and can thereby create consumer confusion.[80]

(b) Keywords

Keyword advertising by advertisers (or the search engines who sell such keywords) probably does not constitute trademark infringement due to the low risk of consumer confusion that such advertising entails.[81]

(c) Sponsored links

There are no reported Japanese cases on this issue to date. Nonetheless, where users are confused as to the sponsor or source of a link through the misleading use of a trademark, even when such confusion is temporary 'initial interest confusion', a violation of Japanese trademark law may exist.

(d) Hidden text

This issue has not yet been addressed by Japanese courts. Hidden text may constitute trademark infringement if it causes consumer confusion by, for example, influencing search engine keywords.

(e) Internet domain names

Mere use of a trademarked word or phrase as a domain name cannot constitute trademark infringement without the use of that domain in commerce or in connection with designated or similar goods or services. Thus, 'domain name squatting' does not itself constitute trademark infringement.[82]

Nevertheless, the Japan Network Information Center (JPNIC)[83] has independent

---

77 *Ibid* at Article 2(3).

78 *Ibid* at Article 37. Note that there are numerous other infringement provisions.

79 Unfair Competition Prevention Act, Law No 47 of 1993, Article 2(1) (hereinafter 'Unfair Competition Prevention Act').

80 *Ōsaka Chihō Saibansho* [Osaka Dist Ct] October 20 2005, *Heisei* 16 (wa) no 12032.

81 *Chizai Ken Kiyou* 2010 [Research Bulletin of Intellectual Property 2010] Chapter 17, available at www.iip.or.jp/summary/pdf/detail09j/21_17.pdf (last accessed July 1 2012).

arbitration procedures for domain name disputes that provide aggrieved trademark owners relief (discussed in section 2.8 below). Moreover, domain name squatting may also violate unfair competition laws, which prohibit activities like domain name purchases that are made for the purpose of seeking unfair profits or that are made to cause harm to others.

(f) ***Search navigation tools***

Search navigation tools have also not been addressed by the Japanese courts to date. It is likely, however, that a search navigation tool would be found to infringe where it causes customer confusion regarding the source of goods or services through the misleading use of a trademark.

(g) ***Hypertext links***

There are no reported Japanese cases on this issue. Hyperlinking could potentially constitute trademark infringement if, for example, a company used a competitor's trademark to deceive users into clicking a link that led to its own product.[84]

(h) ***Framing***

Although it has not been addressed directly by the Japanese courts, framing could constitute trademark infringement where use of a mark in the process of framing causes consumer confusion.[85]

2.3 Defences

(a) ***Descriptive (non-trademark) use of the mark***

The legitimately descriptive use of a trademark to reference goods or services properly identified by that trademark is not an infringement and does not cause consumer confusion.[86]

(b) ***Comparative advertising***

As with descriptive use, comparative advertising does not cause customer confusion regarding a trademark, and thus does not infringe.[87]

(c) ***Parody***

There is no absolute or categorical parody defence to a claim of trademark infringement. In fact, Japanese courts have held that parody can infringe a trademark where it creates customer confusion regarding the source of goods/services.[88]

---

82 Kazuyuki Takahashi, Shigenori Matsui & Hidemi Suzuki, *Internet and the Law* 312 (2010) (original in Japanese).

83 The JPNIC is the National Internet Registry of Japan.

84 Aoki Hiromichi, *Brand and Design in Intellectual Property Rights* 189 (2007) (original in Japanese).

85 *Ibid.*

86 *Ibid.*

87 *Ibid.*

88 *Chiteki-zaisan kōtō-saiban-sho* [Japanese Intell Prop High Ct] July 12 2010 (unpublished).

2.4 **Parallel imports**

The parallel importing of genuine goods is permissible where the goods are legally branded with the same trademark, from the same (ultimate) source, and of the same quality as the domestic good such that the trademark owner's reputation is not harmed.[89]

2.5 **Remedies**

A variety of remedies are available in an action for trademark infringement, including a preliminary injunction,[90] a permanent injunction,[91] compensatory damages,[92] unjust enrichment,[93] and remedial advertising and/or public apology.[94]

2.6 **Liability of ISPs**

The Provider Liability Limitation Act (discussed in section 1.6(a) above) shields telecommunications service providers from secondary liability for trademark infringement committed by the service's users where the Act's safe harbour requirements are met.[95]

2.7 **Advertising law and regulation**

The misleading use of another's trademark in connection with offering products or services for sale, such as in the context of online advertising, may constitute unfair competition or false advertising, where, *inter alia*, such use causes customer confusion.[96]

Under certain circumstances, Japanese courts may attempt to assert jurisdiction over foreign advertisers who have directed misleading messages to the Japanese market and to Japanese consumers. Their capacity to do so, however, is currently unclear.

2.8 **Domain name disputes**

According to policy adopted by the Japan Network Information Center (JPNIC), domain name disputes are handled by the Japan Intellectual Property Arbitration Center (JIPAC). In JIPAC arbitrations, a petitioner must demonstrate that a domain name is identical to or confusingly similar to trademarks or other intellectual property rights held by the petitioner; the registrant has no legitimate connection to the domain name; and the registrant is using the domain name(s) in bad faith.[97]

2.9 **Unfair competition/passing off**

Japanese unfair competition law prohibits the "creation of confusion with another person's goods or business by use of a [mark]"[98] where such mark, although not registered under the Trademark Act, is "well known among consumers".[99] Such

---

89 *Saikō Saibansho* [Sup Ct] February 27 2003, 61 *Saikō Saibansho Saibanshū Minji* 3245.
90 Trademark Act at Article 36.
91 *Ibid.*
92 *Ibid* at Article 38.
93 Minp [Civ Ct], Article 703.
94 Trademark Act at Article 39.
95 See Provider Liability Limitation Act at Article 3.
96 Unfair Competition Prevention Act at Article 2(1).
97 Rules for JP Domain Name Dispute Resolution Policy, Japan Network Information Center, www.nic.ad.jp/doc/jpnic-01065.html (last accessed July 3 2012).

limitation on unauthorised use extends to both identical and similar marks.[100] Marks deemed 'famous' receive greater protection.[101]

3. Patents

3.1 Patentability of 'internet inventions'

To be patentable under the Patent Act, an 'invention' must be a "highly advanced creation of technical ideas utilizing the laws of nature".[102]

(a) Computer programs

Computer programs are protectable by both apparatus and method patent claims.[103] In order to be protectable, such programs must process information in a way that is concretely realised by hardware.[104]

(b) Business methods

Simple business ideas are not patentable subject matter to the extent they merely involve economic rules and the like, as such methods do not comprise "technical ideas utilizing the laws of nature".[105] Nevertheless, as with software, certain business methods may be patentable where such methods involve the processing of information in a way that is concretely realised by hardware.[106]

(c) Mathematical methods

Mathematical methods, such as formulae and equations, are not themselves patentable.[107] However, a device or method utilising mathematical methods (like a machine with the ability to improve the performance of a technological means by using data from a mathematical calculation) could be patentable.

(d) Presentation of information

Methods that merely present information cannot be patented because they are not technical ideas and thus are not patentable subject matter.[108] If technical features involve the presentation of information, an invention embodying these technical features could be patented.[109]

---

98 Unfair Competition Prevention Act at Article 2(1)(i).
99 *Ibid.*
100 *Ibid.*
101 *Ibid* at Article 2(1)(ii).
102 *Tokkyoh* [Patent Act], Law No 121 of 1959, Article 2(1) (hereinafter 'Patent Act').
103 *Ibid* at Articles 2(3)(i)(ii), 2(4).
104 See Examination Guidelines for Patent and Utility Model in Japan, Japanese Patent Office Section 2.2.1, www.jpo.go.jp/tetuzuki_e/t_tokkyo_e/Guidelines/7_1.pdf (last accessed July 3 2012).
105 See Patent Act at Article 2(1).
106 See Examination Guidelines for Patent and Utility Model in Japan, Japanese Patent Office Section 2.2.1, www.jpo.go.jp/tetuzuki_e/t_tokkyo_e/Guidelines/7_1.pdf (last accessed July 3 2012).
107 See Examination Guidelines for Patent and Utility Model in Japan, Japanese Patent Office, Section 1.1(4), www.jpo.go.jp/tetuzuki_e/t_tokkyo_e/Guidelines/2_1.pdf (last accessed July 3 2012).
108 See Patent Act at Article 2(1). See also Examination Guidelines for Patent and Utility Model in Japan, Japanese Patent Office, Section 1.1(5), www.jpo.go.jp/tetuzuki_e/t_tokkyo_e/Guidelines/2_1.pdf (last accessed July 3 2012).
109 See Patent Act at Article 2(1).

3.2 Bioinformatics

Bioinformatics technology could be patented where it meets the same standard as for computer programs (discussed in section 3.1(a)).

A novel DNA sequence or protein structure discovered through the use of bioinformatics technology may be patentable as a biological invention.[110] However, a biological invention cannot be patented unless its specification describes its utility as an industrially applicable invention.[111]

3.3 Issues specific to Japan

(a) Infringement on the Internet

Japanese courts have jurisdiction where online patent infringement occurs within Japan. However, they do not have jurisdiction where an infringing act outside of Japan causes injury within Japan where such injury was not ordinarily foreseeable.[112]

(b) Process patents

In order for Japanese courts to have jurisdiction over the alleged infringement of a process patent, all steps of the process covered by the patent must occur within Japan in principle.[113] Therefore, Japanese courts cannot grant an injunction if only part of a patented process is carried out in Japan.

3.4 Remedies

An injured patent owner may seek damages, a preliminary and/or permanent injunction, and the disposal of products constituting such acts of infringement.[114]

4. Disclosure orders against ISPs

4.1 Availability

Under the Provider Liability Limitation Act, any rights-holder may demand that a telecommunications service provider[115] disclose the identifying information of any user who has allegedly utilised the service to infringe the intellectual property rights of the rights-holder.

In practice, tracking down an alleged infringer typically entails making two such disclosure demands: one demand to a website to discover the IP address and timestamp of a specific user; and another demand to the user's ISP to discover the

110 Examination Guidelines for Patent and Utility Model in Japan, Japanese Patent Office, Section 1.1.1, www.jpo.go.jp/tetuzuki_e/t_tokkyo_e/Guidelines/7_2.pdf (last accessed July 3 2012).

111 *Ibid*; see also Patent Act at Article 29(1).

112 Code of Civil Procedure at Article 3-3(viii).

113 See Makiko Takabe, (A) 'Detailed Explanation of Patent Litigation Practice(s)' 251 (2011) (original in Japanese).

114 *Minpō* [Civ Ct], Article 709; Patent Act at Article 100(1).

115 A 'Telecommunications service provider' is "a person who relays others' communications with the use of specified telecommunications facilities, or provides specified telecommunications facilities to be used for others' communications". Provider Liability Limitation Act at Article 2(iii). This definition includes ISPs, websites, and the like.

name, address and e-mail address of the customer who used the particular IP address at the particular date and time.

4.2 Requirements

In order to demand disclosure from a telecommunications service provider, a rights-holder must show that: (1) their rights "were infringed by the distribution of the infringing [communication]", and (2) "there [are] justifiable ground[s] for said person to receive [the] disclosed identification information of the sender [of the communication]", such as where the information demanded "is necessary for the person demanding said disclosure to exercise his or her rights to claim damages".[116]

4.3 Jurisdictional issues

The Provider Liability Limitation Act does not contain jurisdictional provisions. Accordingly, courts having jurisdiction over a service provider's physical address should have jurisdiction to compel that service provider to disclose users' identifying information.[117]

4.4 'John Doe' injunctions

Japanese law does not currently permit injunctions against unnamed persons.[118] Thus, an aggrieved rights-holder must demand identifying information from a telecommunications service provider in order to sue a then-unknown infringer.

116 Provider Liability Limitation Act at Article 4(1).

117 Japanese courts probably do not have jurisdiction over foreign telecommunications service providers which do not have any physical address within Japan.

118 Code of Civil Procedure at Article 133(2)(i).

Netherlands

Wolter Wefers Bettink
Thomas de Weerd
Houthoff Buruma

1. Copyright, database rights and design rights

1.1 Overview

Article 1 of the Dutch Copyright Act (Auteurswet) defines copyright as:

> *"the exclusive right of the author of a literary, scientific or artistic work or his successors in title to communicate that work to the public and to reproduce it, subject to the limitations laid down by law".*

The basic rule of Dutch copyright law is that ideas are not protectable, but the specific expression of an idea is. The threshold for copyright protection is relatively low. In the *Screenoprints* decision,[1] the Supreme Court decided that in order to be protected by copyright, a work should have its own, original character and show the personal choices of the author. The usual question to determine whether a work has its own character is whether it is reasonably possible that two authors have created the same work independently from one another.

In the *Van Dale/Romme* decision,[2] the Supreme Court distinguished two requirements which must be met for a work to attract copyright protection: a work must possess its own original character and bear the personal stamp of its author. The work should be the result of human creation and the personal choices should be apparent from the work itself, not from circumstances outside of the work.

In its *Endstra* decision,[3] the Supreme Court clarified these requirements. According to the court the first requirement implies "that its form is not copied from another work". The second requirement means "that there must be a form that is the result of human creativity and of creative choices, and thus is a product of the human mind. This excludes, in any case, all forms that are so banal or trivial as to not demonstrate any creative labour whatsoever."

The *Infopaq I* decision of the European Court of Justice[4] further specifies that copyright shall only apply in relation to "a subject-matter which is original in the sense that it is its author's own intellectual creation", and that such intellectual creation can be created "through the choice, sequence and combination of those words that the author may express his creativity in an original manner".

1 Dutch Supreme Court, November 29 1985, NJ 1987/880 (*Screenoprints v Citroën*).
2 Dutch Supreme Court, January 4 1991, NJ 1991/608 (*Van Dale v Romme*).
3 Dutch Supreme Court, May 30 2008, NJ 2008/556 (*Endstra*).
4 ECJ, July 16 2009, C-5/08, (*Infopaq International A/S v Danske Dagblades Forening*).
5 Dutch Supreme Court, February 22 2013, LJN BY 1529 (*Stokke v H3*).

It is generally held that this is the same threshold as 'own original character and personal stamp of the author' developed by the Supreme Court.[5]

(a) Literary works and artistic works

Article 10 of the Copyright Act provides a non-exhaustive list of literary, scientific or artistic works eligible for copyright protection, including books and newspapers (sub 1°), musical works (sub 5°), drawings and paintings (sub 6°), photographic works (sub 9°), cinematographic works (sub 10°) and computer programs and preparatory material (sub 12°).

(b) Films, sound recordings, and broadcasts

Article 10 of the Copyright Act specifies musical works (sub 5°), photographic works (sub 9°) and cinematographic works (sub 10°) as literary, scientific or artistic works eligible for copyright protection.

(c) Typographical arrangement of a published edition

Although the Dutch Copyright Act does not explicitly mention the typographical arrangement of a published edition as a work eligible for copyright protection, such works are eligible for copyright protection in the Netherlands if they have their own original character and the personal stamp of the author.

(d) Protection of the user interface

In the *Czech BSA* ruling of the European Court of Justice,[6] the ECJ ruled that a graphical user interface is not a form of expression of a computer program within the meaning of the Software Directive[7] and cannot be protected by copyright as a computer program under that directive. However, a graphical user interface can be protected by copyright if that interface is its author's own intellectual creation.

(e) Computer-generated works

A computer-generated work will generally not be the result of human creation (*Van Dale/Romme*[8]), and will therefore not qualify as a work which is eligible for copyright protection.

A computer-generated work which is not subject to copyright protection may be protected as a 'sweat of the brow' work, pursuant to Article 10 paragraph 4 of the Copyright Act. However, following the *Football Dataco* decision of the European Court of Justice,[9] the Supreme Court has ruled that this form of protection for what essentially is a compilation of data is not allowed under the Database Directive.[10]

---

6 ECJ, December 22 2010, C 393/09 (*Bezpe nostní softwarová asociace – Svaz softwarové ochrany v Ministerstvo kultury*).

7 Directive 91/250/EEC of May 14 1991 on the legal protection of computer programs, OJ L 122, 17/05/1991 pp 42–46.

8 See note 2.

9 ECJ, March 1 2012, C-604/10 (*Football Dataco Ltd v Yahoo! UK Ltd*). In February 2013, the Dutch government published a consultation version of a bill to abolish the *geschriftenbescherming*.

10 Directive 96/9/EC of March 11 1996 on the legal protection of databases, OJ L 077, 27/03/1996 pp 20-28.

(f) *Websites protected as databases*

The Dutch Database Act (*Databankenwet*), which implements the Database Directive,[11] provides for a *sui generis* protection for databases meeting certain requirements. A database is a collection of independent works, data or other materials arranged in a systematic or methodical way and individually accessible by electronic or other means. To be protected, there must have been a substantial investment in obtaining, verifying or presenting the contents of the database (Article 1a of the Database Act). The database owner has the exclusive right to retrieve and reproduce a substantial part of the database which cannot be circumvented by repeatedly and systematically retrieving or reproducing parts of the database by third parties.

Generally, a website and its design will not be eligible for protection under Dutch database right law. However, if the website contains or provides access to a database, certain investments made in the system which forms part of the website may qualify as investments in obtaining, verifying or presenting the contents of the database, and may consequently be counted as investments in determining whether the database is eligible for database rights.

(g) *Compilations*

A compilation is a work consisting of literary, scientific or artistic works of two or more persons. The person under whose guidance and supervision the work as a whole has been made or, if there is no such person, the compiler of the various works, will be deemed the author of the whole work, without prejudice to the copyright in each of the works separately (Article 5, paragraph 1 of the Copyright Act).

A compilation which is not subject to copyright protection can be protected as a 'sweat of the brow' compilation (*geschriftenbescherming*), pursuant to Article 10, paragraph 4 of the Copyright Act. However, it is debatable whether this form of protection is allowed following the *Football Dataco* decision of the European Court of Justice.[12]

1.2 Infringing acts

Copyright is the exclusive right of the author of a literary, scientific or artistic work or his/her successors in title to communicate that work to the public and to reproduce it, subject to the limitations laid down by law (Article 1 of the Copyright Act).

The Copyright Act specifies various acts that qualify as a communication to the public (Article 12 of the Copyright Act) or reproduction (Article 13 of the Copyright Act) against which the rights holder can act.

(a) *Copying*

Temporary copies: See paragraph 1.6(g).

In any medium: The reproduction of a literary, scientific or artistic work includes

---

11 Dutch Supreme Court January 17 2014, ECL:NL:PHR:2013:114 (*RyanAir*).
12 See note 9.

the fixation of the whole or part of the work on an object which is intended to play a work or to show it (Article 14 of the Copyright Act).

(b) ***Issuing copies to the public***

The distribution of the whole or part of a work or of a reproduction thereof, as long as the work has not appeared in print, qualifies as a communication to the public (Article 12, paragraph 1, sub 2° of the Copyright Act).

(c) ***Communicating work to the public***

The communication to the public of a reproduction of the whole or part of a work, (Article 12, paragraph 1, sub 1° of the Copyright Act) includes the making available of that work online, or by any other electronic means.

In *FTD/Eyeworks*[13] the court ruled, citing various ECJ decisions including *SGAE/Rafael Hoteles*,[14] that communicating to the public can be divided into two categories: the right to communicate the work to the public, which entails the transmission of a signal comprising the work, in such manner that it reached the public; and the right to communicate the signal comprising the work to the public in such manner that it is available to the public. The offering of a .nzb file which enabled users to download a copyrighted motion picture from a Usenet server did not qualify as a communication to the public.

(d) ***Perform, show or play work in public***

The recitation, performance or presentation in public of the whole or part of a work or a reproduction thereof qualifies as communication to the public (Article 12, paragraph 1, sub 4° of the Copyright Act).

(e) ***Rent or lend the work to the public***

The rental or lending of the whole or part of a work, with the exception of works of architecture and works of applied art, or of a reproduction thereof which has been brought into circulation by or with the consent of the rights owner, qualifies as a communication to the public (Article 12, paragraph 1, sub 3° of the Copyright Act).

(f) ***Authorising another person to do any of the above***

The owner of a copyright can authorise another person to conduct an act that the copyright holder is exclusively entitled to conduct based on its copyright. Such authorisation can be granted in the form of a licence. The Copyright Act does not include any formal requirements for the granting of a copyright licence. Therefore, licences can be granted in writing, and also orally or implicitly.

(g) ***Secondary infringement***

Secondary infringement does not automatically qualify as an infringement of

13 Appeal Court The Hague, November 15 2010, IER 2011/28 (*FTD v Eyeworks*).

14 ECJ, December 7 2006, C-306/05 (*Sociedad General de Autores y Editores de España (SGAE) v Rafael Hoteles, SA*).

intellectual property rights under Dutch law. However, rights owners can act against secondary infringement. Secondary infringement may qualify as an unlawful act under Article 6:162 Dutch Civil Code.

In *Brein/Mininova*,[15] the court ruled that the offering by torrent-website Mininova of torrent links to infringing materials did not infringe any intellectual property rights, as the relevant copyrighted works were not offered on the Mininova website. However, by providing an opportunity to, and enticing and profiting from the infringement of copyrights of parties represented by, Brein, Mininova acted unlawfully. Mininova was ordered to take such measures as would be necessary to ensure that no torrent links to copyrighted materials were offered on its website.

1.3 Test for copyright infringement

In the *Una voce particulare* case, concerning an alleged copyright infringement in a format for a television programme,[16] the Supreme Court ruled that in determining whether a work infringes the copyright in another work, the assessment should be based on whether the allegedly infringing product contains copyrightable elements of the original product to such an extent that the overall impression of the two products differs too little to consider the allegedly infringing product to be an independent work. In *Stokke/Fikszo*, the Supreme Court confirmed that the overall impression of the works should be considered when deciding on the infringement.[17] In relation to industrial design, non-copyrightable elements may not be disregarded but should be included in the comparison of the overall impression of the relevant products. However, when assessing whether the overall impression is similar, individual unprotected elements can only be taken into account if they form part of a combination of such elements which qualifies as a copyrightable work.

1.4 Exemptions/defences to copyright infringement

(a) Format shifting

Format shifting (ie, the copying of a work from one carrier to another) is allowed under the private copy exemption (described in section 1.4(b) below), if done for private practice, study or use of the person who makes the copy. The private copy exemption does not apply to software (Article 45n of the Copyright Act); the making of a back-up copy of software is allowed (Article 45k of the Copyright Act).

(b) Personal copying rights

The copying of a copyrighted work on a carrier intended to show or play the work recorded on it, is not deemed an infringement if such copy is made without a direct or indirect commercial purpose and for the sole purpose of private practice, study or use of the person who makes the copy (Article 16c, paragraph 1 of the Copyright Act). The carriers used for such private copy exemption are subject to a reasonable

---

15 District Court of Utrecht, August 26 2009, LJN BJ6008, 250077, HA ZA 08-1124 (*Brien v Mininova*).
16 Dutch Supreme Court, November 29 2002, NJ 2003/17 (*Una voce particulare*).
17 Dutch Supreme Court April 12 2013, NJ 2013, 502 (*Stokke v Fikszo*).

compensation for rights owners (Article 16c, paragraph 2 of the Copyright Act). Such compensation is collected from producers and/or importers of such carriers, and is generally included in the consumer purchase price.

The downloading of copyrighted materials from the Internet, whether with consent from the rights owner or from an illegal source, falls under the scope of the private copy exemption.[18] As the private copy exemption does not apply to software (Article 45n of the Copyright Act), downloading of software is not allowed without permission of the rights owner.[19]

Reasonable compensation for rights owners (Article 16c, paragraph 2 of the Copyright Act) is due from producers or importers of certain data carriers, on which the private copies are made. Copyright levies are due on writable DVDs and CDs, some other carriers such as analog video and audio cassette tapes and, since January 1 2013, on computer hard drives, hard disk recorders and portable devices (such as iPods).[20]

(c) Time shifting

Time shifting (ie, the recording of a broadcasted work on a carrier for later viewing) will be allowed under the private copy exemption, as long as the time shift is conducted for private practice, study or use of the person who makes the copy.

(d) Fair use

Dutch copyright law does not include a 'fair use' doctrine. Article 1 of the Copyright Act specifies that copyright is an exclusive right, which is subject to limitations laid down by law. In its implementation of the Copyright Directive,[21] the Dutch government has tried to meet objections that the directive lacks room for a general 'fair use' provision. It has sought to deal with these concerns by implementing a substantial number of the limitations set out in the Copyright Directive in the Dutch Copyright Act.

(e) Caching/temporary copies as part of communication process

Providers of services consisting of caching of (temporary) copies for later use or as part of a communication process are not liable for damages, even if the copying in itself may constitute copyright infringement, provided they meet the conditions of Article 6:196c, paragraph 4 of the Dutch Civil Code. These conditions are based on Article 13 of the e-Commerce Directive[22] and require that:

- the provider does not modify the information;
- the provider complies with conditions on access to the information;

---

18 Appeal Court The Hague, November 15 2010, IER 2011/27 (*ACI v Thuiskopie*).

19 The case is currently pending before the Dutch Supreme Court which has submitted preliminary questions to the ECJ. In his opinion of January 10 2014, the Advocate General has stated that the downloading of unlawful material does not fall under the private copying exemption and therefore constitutes copyright infringement. Opinion Advocate General P Curz Villalón, ECJ 9/1/2014, case no C-435/12 (*CACI/Thuiskopie*).

20 Decree of October 23 2012, Stb 2012, 505.

21 Directive 2001/29/EC of May 22 2001 on the harmonisation of certain aspects of copyright and related rights in the information society, OJ L 167, 22/06/2001, pp 10–19.

22 Directive 2000/31/EC of the European Parliament and of the Council of June 8 2000 on certain legal aspects of information society services, in particular electronic commerce, in the internal market, OJ L 178, 17/7/2000, pp 1–16.

- the provider complies with rules regarding the updating of the information, specified in a manner widely recognised and used by industry;
- the provider does not interfere with the lawful use of technology, widely recognised and used by industry, to obtain data on the use of the information; and
- the provider acts expeditiously to remove or to disable access to the information it has stored upon obtaining actual knowledge of the fact that the information at the initial source of the transmission has been removed from the network, or access to it has been disabled, or that a court or an administrative authority has ordered such removal or disablement.

(f) ***Hosting***

See paragraph 1.6(a).

(g) ***Back-up copies***

A lawful user of a computer program and preparatory material is allowed to create a back-up copy of such materials where this is necessary for the use of such materials and their intended purpose (Article 45k of the Copyright Act). The creation of such copy shall not be deemed an infringement of copyright.

(h) ***Reverse engineering***

Reverse engineering of software by a person who lawfully obtained a copy of the software is permitted if such act is indispensable for obtaining information necessary to achieve the interoperability of an independently created computer program with other programs (Article 45m, paragraph 1 of the Copyright Act).

(i) ***Parody defence***

The publication or reproduction of a literary, scientific or artistic work in the context of a caricature, parody or pastiche will not be regarded as an infringement of copyright in that work, provided the use is in accordance with what would normally be sanctioned under the rules of social custom (Article 18b of the Copyright Act).

In *Mercis/Punt.nl*,[23] the Amsterdam Court of Appeal ruled that the online publication of cartoons in which the child-friendly Miffy (Nijntje) character was depicted in combination with 'rude and aggressive' texts was permitted on the basis of the parody exemption.

(j) ***Incidental inclusion***

The incidental processing of a literary, scientific or artistic work as a component of subordinate significance in another work will not be regarded as an infringement of copyright (Article 18a of the Copyright Act).

1.5 Remedies available for copyright infringement

A copyright holder may obtain an injunction (in urgent cases in summary

---

23 Appeal Court Amsterdam, September 13 2011 IER 2012, 15 (*Mercis v Punt.nl*).

proceedings) backed up by a penalty, which will be forfeited in the event of a violation of the injunction. In full proceedings, the copyright holder may obtain damages or remittance of profit (or, in the event of counterfeit or other intentional infringement, both). In rare cases an advance is awarded in summary proceedings. The copyright holder may also obtain an order against the infringer to provide information identifying the supplier and the manufacturer of the goods, as well as documents evidencing the extent of the infringement and the profit made (certified by a statement of an accountant). In the event of unlawful comparative advertising the court may order a rectification advertisement to be placed.

1.6 Copyright liability

Under Article 26d of the Dutch Copyright Act, rights holders may apply for a cease-and-desist order against intermediaries (such as internet service providers (ISPs)) whose services are used by a third party to infringe copyright.[24] This article implements Article 11 of the Directive on the enforcement of intellectual property rights.[25]

(a) Hosting/cloud computing where infringing content uploaded by user of service

Under Article 6:196c, paragraph 4 of the Dutch Civil Code (DCC),[26] a hosting provider is exempted from liability for infringing content uploaded by a user of the service, if the service provider does not (and should not) have any actual knowledge of the illegal activity or information and, after it has obtained such knowledge, it expeditiously removes or disables access to the information.[27]

Following the *L'Oréal v eBay* ruling,[28] the Court of Appeal of Leeuwarden ruled in *Stokke/Marktplaats*[29] that Marktplaats, an operator of an online marketplace, was not liable for users who were advertising lookalike baby chairs, thereby infringing Stokke's copyright in its 'Tripp Trapp' chairs. The court decided that as Marktplaats played a neutral role and had an effective notice-and-take-down procedure in place, it should be considered as a hosting provider under Article 6:196c, paragraph 4 of the DCC and, as a consequence, was exempted from liability for IP infringements by its users.

The court also decided that providing a platform for classified advertisements is not 'making available to the public' and, therefore, that Marktplaats was not thereby infringing Stokke's copyright.

(b) Hypertext linking

Under Dutch case law, a hypertext link is considered to be a reference to the website

---

24 District Court Utrecht, August 26 2009 IER 2009, 60 (*Mininova*); District Court The Hague, January 11 2012, AMI 2012-3, nr 13 (*BREIN v Ziggo & XS4ALL*).

25 Directive 2004/48/EC of the European Parliament and of the Council of April 29 2004 on the enforcement of intellectual property rights, OJ L 157, 30.4.2004.

26 This implements Article 14 of Directive 2000/31/EC of the European Parliament and of the Council of June 8 2000 on certain legal aspects of information society services, in particular electronic commerce, in the internal market, OJ L 178, 17.7.2000, pp 1–16 (Directive on electronic commerce).

27 *FTD v Eyeworks*, see note 13.

28 ECJ 12 July 2011, IEPT20110712 (*L'Oréal v eBay*).

29 Appeal Court Leeuwarden, May 22 2012, IEPT20120522 (*Stokke v Marktplaats*).

to which it is linked. By placing (deep) links on a website the copyrighted material on that site is not reproduced, nor made available to the public. Therefore, hypertext linking is not considered to constitute copyright infringement.[30]

The publication of a hyperlink to copyrighted material which has been published without the consent of the rights owner may, however, be unlawful if this facilitates the access to the unlawful material, in particular where the medium publishing the hyperlink entices the public to use the hyperlink to view the material.[31]

An embedded link is considered to be a reproduction of the copyrighted work, since the content, after activation of the link, is being viewed within the context of the website providing the link.[32]

(c) ***P2P network***

Supplier of P2P software: In *Kazaa*, the Appeal Court in The Hague decided that a supplier of P2P software cannot be held liable for unlawful use of that software (eg, to exchange music and films without the consent of the rights owners) by its users.[33]

Uploaders/downloaders: Article 16c of the Copyright Act allows the reproduction of works for non-commercial private use. This also applies to the downloading of infringing content. Uploading of copyrighted content involves a reproduction and making available of such content which constitutes copyright infringement if done without consent of the copyright owner.[34]

(d) ***Webcasting***

Webcasting is considered a 'communication to the public', which is not allowed without the permission of the rights holder. The district court of Amsterdam has ruled that radio station Fresh FM was not permitted to webcast music without permission from the rights holders, in this case by obtaining a licence from collecting society Buma/Stemra.[35]

(e) ***Streaming***

Streaming is the reproduction and making available to the public of the material involved. This is not allowed without the permission of the rights holders.[36]

---

30 District Court Rotterdam, August 22 2000, IER 2000, 55 (*Kranten.com v Dagbladen*).

31 Appeal Court Amsterdam, November 19 2013, ECLI:NL:GHAMS:2013:4019 (*Sanoma v Geenstijl*). This concerned nude pictures of a TV personality which had been stored on the Filefactory website (a cloud storage provider) under a specific URL for the Dutch Playboy magazine which was to publish the photos. When blog site Geenstijl became aware of the URL, which was only known to a limited group of people, it published part of one of the pictures and the URL announcing that more photos could be found there.

32 Appeal Court 's-Hertogenbosch, January 12 2010, IEPT2010112 (*C More Entertainment v Myp2p Holding BV*).

33 Appeal Court Amsterdam, March 28 2002 Computerrecht 2002, p 144 (*Buma/Stemra v Kazaa*).

34 See *Mininova and Brein v Ziggo & Xs4all*, note 26.

35 District Court Amsterdam, May 26 2010, IEPT20100526 (*Buma v Scoezh*).

36 District Court Amsterdam (provisional relief court), July 26 2011, IEPT20110702 (*Buma/Stemra v Target Media*); District Court, The Hague March 22 2011, IER 2011/44 (*Premier League v MyP2P*). In the *nederland.fm* decision (see note 38) the presentation of streams in a frame of the nederland.fm website was found to infringe copyright in the music streamed.

(f) ***Framing***

Framing is considered copyright infringement if it creates the impression to the public that the information on the framed website is that of the framing website.[37] A website with hyperlinks to radiostreams was found to infringe the copyright in the music streamed, since the streams were presented in frames (with logos of the radio stations) on the website and thereby made available to a different audience than that of the original streams.[38]

(g) ***Transmission of infringing work across a communications network***

Under Article 6:196c, paragraph 1 of the DCC an ISP is not liable for information transmitted if it complies with the obligations of Article 12 ('mere conduit') of the E-Commerce Directive.

(h) ***Aggregator websites (eg, Google News, price comparison websites)***

The reproduction and making available of (parts of) text and pictures through an aggregator website may be permitted if the requirements of the citation exemption are met (Article 15a of the Copyright Act).[39] However, the press and other media (which includes websites, blogs, etc having the same function) may quote from each other without consent if they meet the requirements of the press and media exemptions (Articles 16 and 16a of the Copyright Act).

(i) ***Treatment of user-generated content***

The copyright on user-generated content is owned by the author. By uploading the content to a public website, the author licenses the website to make the content available to the public subject to the terms and conditions of the website.[40]

1.7 Joint liability for ISPs

An ISP may be jointly liable for copyright infringement by a user of its service if it does not meet the criteria of Article 6:196c, paragraph 4 of the DCC (see section 1.6 above).

1.8 Relief

In its decision concerning the website thepiratebay.com and various related websites, which all offered links enabling the downloading of unlawfully uploaded copyrighted content, the Appeal Court of the Hague ordered several internet providers in the Netherlands to block access to the website for their subscribers.[41] The court based its decision on the fact that a considerable number of subscribers used the service to exchange copyrighted material without the copyright owners' consent.

In *Stokke v Marktplaats*,[42] the Appeal Court Leeuwarden dismissed a request for an

---

37 District Court Leeuwarden, October 30 2003. IER 2004, 25 (*Vriend v Batavus*).
38 District Court The Hague December 19 2012, ECLI:NL:RBSGR:2012:CA0291 (Nederland.fm).
39 Appeal Court Arnhem, July 4 2006 NJ 2006, 497 (*NVM v Zoekallehuizen*).
40 District Court Amsterdam, March 9 2006, IER 2006, 40 (*Curry v Audax*).
41 District Court the Hague, January 11 2012, AMI 2012-3 (*Brein v Ziggo and XS4ALL*).
42 See note 31.

order to the trading platform Marktplaats to remove within 24 hours any advertisement for secondhand chairs infringing Stokke's copyright or its trademark rights. The court ruled that the costs and the damaging effect of such an order for Marktplaats were not reasonable when compared to the limited benefit for Stokke, nor in proportion to the purpose thereof. The Appeal Court also declined to order Marktplaats to require its advertisers to provide full contact details upon registration.

1.9 Issues specific to the Netherlands

(a) *Jurisdiction*

Courts have jurisdiction where the infringement takes place in the territory of the Netherlands. If the infringement is carried out through a website, Dutch courts will have jurisdiction if the website is directed in the Netherlands (or, in the event of infringement of trademark rights or model and design rights, the Benelux countries). Factors to be taken into account include whether goods were ordered through the website by persons residing in the Netherlands (Benelux) and delivered there, and whether the Netherlands (Benelux) appears on a list of countries where goods are delivered, as well as the language used on the website, the currency in which payments can be made, provision of telephone numbers with an international code, the top level domain name used for the website and whether an advertisement with a link to the website features in a Google search conducted from the Netherlands.[43] This case law may change as a consequence of the ECJ decision in *Pinckney*.[44] The ECJ ruled that a court in a member state has jurisdiction to hear a copyright infringement liability action where the infringement occurred through an internet site accessible within the jurisdiction of that court, be it only to determine the damage caused in the member state within which it is situated.

(b) *Claim to infringement of foreign copyright*

A Dutch court will hear a claim for infringement of foreign copyright in conjunction with the claim that the corresponding copyright is infringed in the Netherlands by the same defendant (or a party under his/her direction or control) and the same products or services.

(c) *Emission theory*

The emission theory does not apply, as downloading of unlawful content does not constitute copyright infringement if it falls within the scope of the private copying exemption. Uploading without the copyright owner's consent is an infringement of copyright in the Netherlands if it is carried out by a person or entity located in the Netherlands.

---

43 See also ECJ December 7 2010, cases C-585/08 and C-144/09 (*Pammer* and *Hotel Alpenhof*). Although the cases concerned the question of jurisdiction over a consumer contract concluded with the aid of a website, the same criteria could be applied to determine jurisdiction over a website used in a copyright infringement.

44 ECJ October 3 2013, Case C-170/12 (*Pinckney v Mediatech*).

1.10 Orphan works

The Dutch Copyright Act does not provide an exemption for orphan works. As a consequence, libraries and archives are hesitant to digitise works of which the rights owner is not known. However, the Act will have to be amended to implement Directive 2012/28/EU on orphan works, which *inter alia* requires member states to provide for an exception to the right of reproduction and the right of making available for certain permitted uses of orphan works.[45]

1.11 Online piracy measures

There is no specific legislation against online piracy in the Netherlands.

1.12 Electronic infringement of moral rights

Under the Copyright Act, the author's moral rights also apply in the internet context. Such rights include the right to object to derogatory treatment and false attribution, as well as the paternity right.

2. Trademarks

Trademark rights are protected under the Benelux Convention on Intellectual Property ('the BCIP') which applies to Belgium, the Netherlands and Luxemburg.

2.1 Use of a trademark

Under the BCIP, use of a trademark on a website constitutes 'use' for the purposes of avoiding revocation of a trademark registration for non-use or for the purposes of an infringement claim, if the website is directed at the Benelux countries (see 1.9 above).

2.2 Infringement

(a) Metatags

The use of a third-party trademark in a metatag has been considered to constitute trademark infringement if it takes unfair advantage of or is detrimental to the reputation or distinctiveness of the trademark.[46] This may have been overruled by the ECJ's decision in *Interflora*.[47]

(b) Keywords

The use of a third-party trademark as a keyword (eg, in the Google AdWord service) constitutes 'use' of that trademark. In accordance with ECJ case law, such use would not constitute infringing use if it concerns goods which have been put on the market by or with the consent of the trademark owner.[48] Likewise, use of a keyword to

---

45 Directive 2012/28/EU of the European Parliament and of the Council of October 25 2012 on certain permitted uses of orphan works, OJ L 299/5 of 27.10.2012.

46 District Court The Hague, March 3 2010, LJN BL6449 (*Bodum*).

47 ECJ September 22 2011, case C-323/09 (*Interflora*).

48 ECJ July 8 2010, case C-558/08 (*Portakabin*).

49 See *Interflora*, note 49. See also Appeal Court The Hague November 22 2011, IEPT20111122 (*Tempur v Medicomfort*) and District Court The Hague, January 23 2013, IEF 12276 (*Actifry v Actifryer*) where use of a trademark as an Adword was found not to constitute trademark infringement.

advertise competing goods is allowed, unless that use is liable to have an adverse effect on one of the functions of the trademark.[49]

(c) *Sponsored links*

Use of a third-party trademark in sponsored links may constitute infringement if the advertisement involved creates the impression that the reseller and the trademark owner are economically linked,[50] or otherwise creates confusion as to the origin of the goods or services,[51] or if the advertiser takes unfair advantage of[52] or damages the distinctiveness or reputation of the trademark.[53] No distinction is made between the use of the trademark in the link itself or, after clicking the link, on the website of the advertiser.

(d) *Hidden text*

If the use of the trademark in hidden text takes unfair advantage of or damages the distinctiveness or reputation of the trademark, such use may constitute infringement.

(e) *Internet domain names*

The mere registration of a domain name containing a third-party trademark may constitute infringing use of that trademark, because the registration prevents the trademark owner from registering his/her trademark as a domain name.[54]

(f) *Search navigation tools*

Use of a trademark in search navigation tools, appearing across the top of a web page to indicate the pages the user has navigated, has not been the subject of case law in the Netherlands. It would be allowed unless it takes unfair advantage of or damages the distinctiveness or reputation of the trademark.

(g) *Hypertext links*

The use of a third-party trademark in a hypertext link may constitute infringement if the hyperlink takes unfair advantage of or damages the distinctiveness or reputation of the trademark (eg, by creating the incorrect impression that the infringer is an official dealer of the trademark owner).[55]

(h) *Framing*

Framing may constitute trademark infringement if the trademark is used in a way that may create confusion as to the origin of the framed page.[56]

---

50 ECJ March 23 2010, cases C-236 to 238/08 (*Google France*).

51 See *Portakabin*, note 50.

52 This may be the case where the advertiser "seeks by that use to ride on the coat-tails of the mark with a reputation in order to benefit from the power of attraction, the reputation and the prestige of that mark and to exploit, without paying any financial compensation, the marketing effort expended by the proprietor of the mark in order to create and maintain the mark's image", see ECJ June 18 2009, case C-487/07 (*L'Oréal v Bellure*).

53 See *Interflora*, note 49.

54 Appeal Court Amsterdam, January 11 2001, Computerrecht 2001/2, p 98 (*Elsevier v Gaos*).

55 District Court Leeuwarden, October 30 2003, IER 2004, 25 (*Vriend v Batavus*).

56 See note 39.

2.3 Defences

(a) *Descriptive (non-trademark) use of the mark*

As a rule, there is no trademark infringement if the words used, although constituting or being part of a valid trademark, are descriptive and are used in that manner.[57]

(b) *Comparative advertising*

A trademark may be used in comparative advertising if such use complies with the Comparative Advertising Directive[58] as implemented by Article 6:194a (see paragraph 2.7 below).

(c) *Parody*

Use of a trademark for the purpose of a parody does not constitute infringement.[59]

2.4 Parallel imports

If products have been put on the market in the European Union by or with the consent of the trademark owner, a reseller may use the trademark to advertise the products (eg, on a website directed at the Benelux, see section 1.9), unless use of the trademark creates the incorrect impression that the reseller and the trademark owner are economically linked or if such use takes unfair advantage of or damages the distinctiveness or reputation of the trademark.[60]

2.5 Remedies

A trademark owner may obtain an injunction (in urgent cases in summary proceedings) backed by a penalty, which will be forfeited in the event of violation of the injunction. In full proceedings, the trademark owner may obtain damages or remittance of profit (or, in the event of counterfeit or other intentional infringement, both). In rare cases, an advance is awarded in summary proceedings. The trademark owner may also obtain an order against the infringer to provide information identifying the supplier and the manufacturer of the goods as well as documents evidencing the extent of the infringement and the profit made (certified by a statement of an accountant). In the event of unlawful comparative advertising or other unlawful use of a trademark (eg, sending an unfounded warning letter to customers alleging that a certain product infringes the trademark owner's rights), the court may order a rectification advertisement to be placed.

2.6 Liability of ISPs

Under Article 6:196c, paragraph 4 of the DCC[61] an internet hosting provider is exempted from liability for infringing use of a trademark contained in information

---

57 Appeal Court Amsterdam December 28 2010, IEPT December 28 2010 (*Travelcard v Multicard*).

58 Directive 2006/114/EC of the European Parliament and of the Council of December 12 2006 concerning misleading and comparative advertising.

59 Appeal Court Amsterdam, September 13 2011, IER 2012/15 (*Nijntje v Punt.nl*).

60 See *Portakabin*, note 50.

61 This implements Article 14 of the Directive 2000/31/EC on certain legal aspects of information society services, in particular electronic commerce, in the Internal Market, OJ 17.7.2000, L 178/1.

which has been stored upon request, if the provider does not (and should not) have actual knowledge of the illegal activity or information and, after obtaining such knowledge, expeditiously removes or disables access to the information.[62]

According to Article 6:196c, paragraph 5 of the Civil Code, the exemption from liability does not preclude a trademark owner from obtaining a court order against the hosting provider to stop an infringement by a user of its services. However, the court cannot give a general order to a hosting provider to monitor all traffic in order to prevent intellectual property infringements of specific IP rights.[63]

According to Article 22.2, paragraph 6 of the BCIP, the courts may at the request of the owner of a trademark order cessation of services against intermediaries whose services are being used by a third party to infringe its trademark right.

2.7 Advertising law and regulation

Under Article 6:193b of the DCC,[64] a trader who engages in an unfair commercial practice acts wrongfully towards the consumer. The criteria to establish whether a commercial practice is unlawful are contained in Articles 6:193c to 6:193i of the DCC.

According to Article 6:194 of the DCC,[65] it is unlawful towards a competitor to communicate misleading commercial information with regard, *inter alia*, to nature, composition, quantity, quality, characteristics or possibilities for use.

Article 6:194a of the DCC,[66] provides that comparative advertising (ie, advertising which identifies a competitor or goods or services offered by a competitor) is permitted, if certain conditions are met. For instance, the commercial communication must objectively compare one or more material, relevant, verifiable and representative features of those goods and services, which may include the price.

Article 6:162 of the DCC, the general provision on tort, may be relied upon if an advertisement is otherwise unlawful.

Specific rules apply to advertisements for financial products[67] and to the use of an e-mail address to send unsolicited commercial, idealistic or charitable messages. The latter requires prior consent (opt–in) from the recipient and the opportunity to opt out each time a commercial message is sent.[68]

In addition, the Dutch Advertising Code, adopted by advertisers, communication advisers and media, allows the filing of a complaint with the Advertising Code Committee if an advertisement is misleading or contrary to public morals. The committee's recommendations (eg, to discontinue the advertisement) are usually implemented by the advertiser.[69]

---

62 Appeal Court Leeuwarden, May 22 2012, IEPT20120522 (*Stokke v Marktplaats*).
63 ECJ February 16 2012, C 360/10 (*Netlog v Sabam*).
64 This implements Directive 2005/29/EC concerning unfair business-to-consumer commercial practices in the internal market. L 149/22.
65 This implements Directive 84/450/EEC concerning misleading advertising, OJ L 250, 19/09/1984 P 0017 – 0020.
66 This implements Directive 97/55/EC concerning misleading advertising so as to include comparative advertising. L290/18, OJ L 194, 10.7.1998, pp 54–54.
67 See for example the Financial Supervision Act (*Wet op het financieel toezicht*).
68 See Article 11.7 of the Dutch Telecommunications Act.
69 For more information, see www.reclamecode.nl/bijlagen/20120112_NRC_Engels.pdf.

2.8 Domain name disputes

An alternative dispute resolution procedure exists for disputes about .nl domain names.[70] Disputes are first submitted to mediation and if this is unsuccessful decided by an independent domain name panel. The procedure is administered by WIPO which also appoints the panel.

The complainant has to pay an administrative fee (a minimum of €1,500). There is no costs award. A decision can usually be obtained in a period of around two months.

A complaint may be filed by the holder of rights in a trademark, trade name, personal name or a name of a Dutch public organisation to which the domain name is confusingly similar. The complainant must show that the registrant has no right to or legitimate interest in the domain name and that the domain name has been registered or is being used in bad faith.

Participating in a procedure does not prevent either party from referring the same dispute to a court of law, before, during or after that procedure.

2.9 Unfair competition/passing off

The BCIP has a first to file system and unregistered trademark rights are therefore not protected. Company names are protected under the Trade Names Act. Unregistered signs, such as domain names, and websites with a certain layout which is otherwise unprotected, may be protected against unfair competition.

3. Patents

3.1 Patentability of 'internet' inventions

Patents are regulated in the Dutch Patent Act 1995 ('DPA 1995'). There are two ways to obtain patent protection in the Netherlands. An applicant can file an application for a Dutch patent or an application for a European patent.[71] As soon as the European patent has been granted, it will fall apart in a bundle of national patents that can be validated in the designated countries chosen by the applicant. As soon as the European patent is validated in the Netherlands, the DPA applies to the Dutch part of the European patent.

According to Article 2 of the DPA 1995, for an invention to be patentable it must be new, involve an inventive step and be susceptible to industrial application.

An invention is new if it does not form part of the state of the art. This comprises everything that has been made available to the public, orally or in writing, before the filing date of the application or, if the priority of an earlier invention is claimed, of the application for the latter invention.

An invention comprises an inventive step if the invention, having regard to the state of the art, is not obvious to a person skilled in the art.

The Dutch Patent Office does not *ex officio* assess whether the invention claimed fulfils the requirements of novelty, inventive step and industrial applicability. The validity of a patent will ultimately be assessed by the court in patent litigation

---

70 For more information, see www.sidn.nl/en/about-nl/disputes-and-complaints/infringement-of-rights.
71 Convention on the Grant of European Patents, www.epo.org/law-practice/legal-texts/epc.

proceedings. If the court is of the opinion that the patent does not meet the requirements of patentability, the patent will be revoked.

In order to be patentable, an invention must have a technical character. Article 2, section 2 of the DPA 1995 contains a list of subject matter that is as such excluded from patent protection, which includes business methods, computer programs and presentations of data. However, it is possible to obtain patent protection for a combination of technical and excluded subject matter.

Thus, computer programs can be patented in so far as they have a technical character. As there are no specific provisions relating to the patentability of software, this is assessed on a case-by-case basis. Generally, a computer program can be patented if it is combined with a technical product or a technical process. The same would seem to apply for business methods, mathematical methods and presentation of information.

3.2 Bioinformatics

Under Dutch patent law, it is possible to obtain patent protection for a DNA sequence or protein structure, provided that the DNA sequence or protein structure is claimed in combination with its function. Furthermore, the requirements of novelty and inventive step will have to be met.[72] The exclusive right of the holder of a patent relating to a product that consists of or contains genetic information, includes any material in which the product is incorporated and in which the genetic information is included and performs its function.[73] It is not relevant how the DNA sequences or protein structures have been discovered. DNA sequences and protein structures that have been discovered through the use of bioinformatics can be patented, provided the aforementioned requirements have been met.

3.3 Issues specific to the Netherlands

(a) Infringement on the Internet

Based on Article 53 of the DPA 1995, the patent holder has the exclusive right to make, use, put on the market or resell, hire out or deliver the patented product, or otherwise deal in it in or for its business, or to offer, import or stock it for any of those purposes. If the patent relates to a process, the patent holder has the exclusive right to use the patented process in or for its business or to use in or for its business, put on the market or resell, hire out or deliver the product directly obtained as a result of the use of that process, or to offer, import or stock it for any of those purposes. The patent holder can enforce its patent against third parties that perform any of the aforementioned activities without its permission.

The scope of protection of a Dutch patent (and the Dutch part of a European patent) is limited to the Netherlands territory. This means that the patent holder can only enforce its patent if the patent is infringed in the Netherlands.

In the event that infringing products are offered for sale on a website, the

72 For an extensive analysis of the patentability of proteins and DNA sequences, see for example "Enabling SJR Bosteyn, *Biotechnical inventions in Europe and the United States*, European Patent Office, 2001.

73 ECJ, March 9 2010, C-428/08, (*Monsanto v Cefetra*).

products are considered to be offered for sale in the Netherlands if the design of the website is directed at the Netherlands (see 1.9 above). Circumstances where it is assumed that the website is not directed to the Netherlands are, for example, that there is no '.nl' top-level extension, the website is in a foreign language, there are no language options for the Dutch language and there are no other references to the Netherlands on the website.[74] The District Court of The Hague has exclusive jurisdiction in respect of claims relating to the infringement of a Dutch patent (or the Dutch part of a European patent).[75]

(b) *Process patents*

A process patent is infringed in the event that the claimed process is applied in the Netherlands. If only part of the claimed process is applied in the Netherlands, the patent is not infringed, unless infringing activities are performed in the Netherlands with respect to the product directly obtained from the patented process.

Moreover, under Article 73 of the DPA, the patent holder can enforce its patent against parties that offer or supply in the Netherlands or Netherlands Antilles, in or for their business, to parties that are not authorised to use the patented invention, the means for the application of the patented invention in the Netherlands or Netherlands Antilles in respect of an essential part of the invention, provided such parties know, or it is evident in view of the circumstances, that those means are suitable and intended for application of the patented invention in the Netherlands or Netherlands Antilles.

3.4 Remedies available for patent infringement

In the event of patent infringement, the patent holder can request the court to prohibit the infringing party from performing any infringing act, such as applying the patented process or producing the patented product (section 3.3(a) above). In addition to an infringement injunction, the patent holder can claim damages or surrender of profits derived from infringing activities and the rendering of an account of such profits. Furthermore, the patent holder can file various ancillary claims such as a recall and destruction of the infringing products, and rectification (eg, a publication on a website or a letter to customers); and can request the provision of information regarding the origin of the products and the distribution chain, including names and contact details of suppliers and customers and the amount of sales and profit generated by the infringing activities.

The party that has lost the proceedings will be ordered to pay the legal costs incurred by the other party to the extent that these costs are considered reasonable. Generally, in patent litigation proceedings compensation for all lawyer and patent attorney fees will be awarded, provided that these costs are sufficiently and timely specified.

Apart from regular patent infringement proceedings, the patent holder can start

---

74 District Court The Hague, November 26 2008, IEPT 20081126 (*Glaxo Group v Cipla*).

75 In *Glaxo v Cipla* (note 76), the District Court held that in this respect one single sale instigated by the patent holder cannot be qualified as an infringing delivery.

accelerated patent proceedings in The Netherlands. Under the accelerated regime, the court determines the dates for filing the written submissions and the oral hearing beforehand. A judgment is rendered within approximately 10 months. In very urgent matters, the patent holder can claim an infringement injunction in preliminary proceedings, provided the case is not too complex from a technical or factual perspective.

4. Disclosure orders against ISPs

4.1 Availability

From Dutch case law it appears that, provided certain conditions are met, a disclosure order can be obtained against an ISP to disclose the identity and contact details of a user of the service who is suspected of unlawful behaviour, including infringement of intellectual property rights. For such an order to be granted, the plaintiff should establish a reasonable case that the information is unlawful and damaging towards him or her; that he or she has a valid interest in obtaining the contact details; that it is reasonably likely that there is no less intrusive manner to obtain those details; and that, after weighing up the interests of the third party, the service provider and the website owner, the interest of the plaintiff should prevail.[76]

In practice, the proportionality requirement implies that the plaintiff must show that it was not possible to obtain the contact details directly from the website owner or through publicly available resources. Filing a criminal complaint and using criminal procedure to obtain the contact details has been judged not to be a less intrusive way of obtaining that information.

In a case where a rights owner organisation demanded a disclosure order for a bank providing payment services for a website which had already been found to infringe copyright, the order was refused *inter alia* on the ground that the role of a bank in internet commerce is decidedly different from that of an ISP, as it is not instrumental in facilitating the infringement.[77]

4.2 Requirements

See section 4.1.

4.3 Jurisdictional issues

A court order may be obtained only if the website containing the unlawful content was directed at the Netherlands or (in case of trademarks) the Benelux (see paragraph 1.9 above).

4.4 'John Doe' injunctions

The code of civil procedure does not provide a basis for granting an injunction where the defendant is unknown.

---

76 Dutch Supreme Court, November 25 2005, NJ 2009, 550 (*Lycos v Pessers*).

77 District Court Amsterdam, May 15 2013, ECLI:NL:RBAMS:2013:CA0350 (*Brein v ING*).

Russia

Ekaterina Tilling
Baker Botts LLP

1. Copyright, database rights and design rights

1.1 Overview

Currently, all general legal issues relating to the treatment of intellectual property on the Internet are governed by the Fourth Part of the Civil Code of the Russian Federation (the 'Russian Civil Code'). In addition, this chapter will refer to the acts of two high-level courts – the Supreme Court and the Supreme Commercial Court[1] – whose interpretation of the intellectual property legislation affects law enforcement practice.

The changing market environment reflects in case law, which in its turn reveals gaps in intellectual property legislation, and all this has led to the necessity to change the existing laws. As a result, on February 25 2014, the amendments to the Russian Civil Code[2] ('Amendments') were adopted in the third reading by the Russian Parliament and are expected to come into force on October 1 2014.

Some of these amendments, particularly those regarding the liability of internet service providers (ISPs), have already been enacted[3] by the so-called 'Anti-Piracy Law', which came into force on August 1 2013. Accordingly, in this chapter we will be also guided by those amendments.

Thus, a website is treated as a composite work which includes internet content and software. As a rule, internet content consists of such intellectual property (IP) as databases, trademarks, copyright works (eg, user interface), etc. The Amendments provide the following definition of a website: "... a set of independent materials presented in an objective form and systematized so that they could be placed on the Internet".

It is important to note that although, as a general rule, the website as a whole is protected by copyright law as a composite work, different elements of internet content can be protected separately. Consequently, internet content may be divided into different categories:

- Software (a computer program) is protected by copyright law as a literary work (Article 1259 of the Russian Civil Code).

1 Joint Decree of the Plenum of the Supreme Court of the Russian Federation and the Supreme Commercial Court of the Russian Federation No 5/29 dated March 26 2009.
2 Federal Law 'On Amendments to Parts 1, 2 and 4 of Russian Civil Code and separate legal acts of the Russian Federation' No 47538-6/7.
3 Federal Law 'On Amendments to Legal Acts on Intellectual Property Rights Protection in Informational-Telecommunications Networks' dated July 2 2013 No 187-FZ (the 'Russian Anti-Piracy Law').

- Other internet content placed on a website such as films, sound recordings, and broadcasts are also protected by copyright law as copyright works.
- Typographical arrangement of a published edition is usually not protected by copyright law or by design law. However, if such an arrangement is a result of a creative work in terms of selection or arrangement of materials, it can be considered as a composite copyright work.[4]
- The design of a website interface may be protected by copyright law if it meets the requirements of a creative work.
- Computer-generated works are protected by copyright law, since any scientific, literary and artistic works are treated as copyright work irrespective of the merit and significance of the work or the method whereby it is expressed.
- The website will be protected as a database if it meets the requirements of a database (ie, as a collection, presented in an objective form, of independent materials (articles, calculations, normative acts, court decisions and other similar materials) which are systematised so that these materials can be found and processed by means of a computer).

There are two types of database protection in Russia.

If a database can be considered to be the result of creative work (in terms of selection or arrangement of materials), it will be protected by copyright law as a composite copyright work.

If the creation of a database requires substantial financial, economic, organisational or other investment, the database will be protected by the related rights law: the creator of the database will have a special exclusive right to the database, which is very similar to the *sui generis* database right in the European Union. This right lasts 15 years and may exist independently (if the database cannot be considered as a copyright work), or in addition to copyright.

If a compilation cannot be considered as a database protected by copyright or related rights law, it will not be protected in Russia.

1.2 Infringing acts

According to Article 1270 of the Russian Civil Code, actions committed without the consent of the rights holder are deemed to infringe the exclusive right to a work. The following actions relevant to the Internet constitute infringements:

- the reproduction of a work (ie, making of one or more copies of the work or a part thereof);
- distribution of a work by sale or other alienation of its original or copies;
- importation of the original or a copy of a work for the purposes of distribution;
- communicating a work to the public (eg, by radio or television);
- performing, showing or playing a work in public;
- renting or lending the original or a copy of a work;

---

4 A composite copyright work is one that consists of other copyright works or parts of works where their selection and arrangement can be regarded as the result of a creative work.

- translation or other reworking of a work;
- disseminating a work to the general public.

1.3 Test for copyright infringement

Under Part 2 of Article 1270 of the Russian Civil Code, the use of a work without the consent of the rights holder is deemed to be an infringement if it constitutes a reproduction of the work (ie, the making of one or more copies of the work or a part thereof[5] in any material form, including the form of a sound or video recording, the making of one or more three-dimensional copies of a two-dimensional work and of one or more two-dimensional copies of a three-dimensional work). There is no requirement in Russian legislation that a reproduction must be substantial to constitute an infringement.

1.4 Exemptions/defences to copyright infringement

The law stipulates the following cases where the use of a copyright work is allowed without the copyright owner's consent:

- reproduction for personal purposes (except for cases established by law);
- use of a work for information, scientific, educational or cultural purposes;
- use of a work by reproduction – that is, a reproduction of one copy of a work by all technical means – not for commercial or publication purposes (eg, reproduction of works by libraries and archives for recovery, replacing lost or damaged copies of the work and provision of other libraries with these copies). Such reproduction does not include reproduction or keeping of these copies in an electronic form, except for temporary copies for the purposes of reproduction (Article 1275 of the Russian Civil Code);
- use of a work permanently located in a place open to the public;
- reproduction of a work for law enforcement purposes.

It is also permissible to make temporary copies if they are an integral and substantial part of the technological process solely intended for the legal use of a record or legally making the work known to the public.

It is important to note that reproduction of software without the copyright owner's consent is not allowed even for personal purposes, except for cases established by law.

Thus, under Article 1280 of the Russian Civil Code, a person, who lawfully possesses a copy of a computer program or a database, has the right to perform the following actions without the consent of the author or the rights holder and without the payment of additional compensation:

- making changes to the computer program or database exclusively for the purpose of its functioning for the technical purposes of the user and taking actions necessary for the functioning of such computer program or database

5 Russian law does not stipulate that an infringement occurs only if a 'substantial part' is reproduced. However, in cases where a citation is allowed (in scientific, polemical, critical and informational contents), the scope of such a citation should be consistent with its purpose (ie, it should not be excessive).

in accordance with its purpose, including recording and storing in the memory of a computer (one computer or one user of a network) and also correcting obvious errors;
- preparing a copy of a computer program or database on the condition that this copy is meant only for archival purposes or for replacement of a lawfully obtained copy in cases when such a copy has been lost, destroyed, or has become unsuitable for use.

Such person also has the right to reproduce and transform the object code into source text (ie, to decompile the computer program), provided the following conditions are met:
- the information necessary for achieving the capability for interaction was not previously accessible to this person from other sources;
- these actions are carried out with respect only to those parts of the decompiled computer program that are necessary for the achievement of the capability for interaction.

However, the law stipulates some restrictions on the use of the information obtained as a result of decompilation.

Russian IP legislation does not contain any direct provisions regarding format shifting, but some general provisions of copyright law should be used for determining whether format shifting can be treated as an infringement.

Accordingly, format shifting in relation to copyright works will be treated as an infringement of an exclusive right, if it leads to making copies or changing the computer program. Making copies of media files without the permission of a rights holder is considered to be an infringement.

In this case, recording of the work on an electronic medium, including saving in a computer memory, will also be deemed to be reproduction, except for cases when such saving is temporary and is an integral and significant part of a technological process solely intended for legally using a record or legally making the work known to the public.

Thus, if format shifting may result in making copies or changing the program, it is not allowed unless these actions fall within the exceptions set out in Article 1280 of the Russian Civil Code, as discussed above.

1.5 Remedies available for copyright infringement

In Russia, the following general remedies are available for a rights holder in the event of intellectual property infringement:
- recognition of the right;
- injunction against activities infringing the right or creating a threat of its infringement;
- damages;
- seizure of infringing articles;
- destruction of materials and equipment used or designated for the commission of the offence;

- publication of the court decision regarding the infringement committed, together with an indication of the actual rights holder.

In cases of copyright infringement the rights holder may claim payment of compensation instead of recovery of damages:

- in the amount of Rb10,000 to Rb5,000,000 (ie, approximately US$300 to US$150,000) at the discretion of the court depending on the nature of the infringement;
- in an amount equivalent to twice the value of counterfeit copies of the work;
- of twice the value of the right of use of the work determined on the basis of the price normally charged in comparable circumstances for the illegal use of the work.

1.6 Copyright liability

Russian legislation has recently been amended by provisions establishing the liability of ISPs. These amendments were implemented by the Russian Anti-Piracy Law which came into force on August 1 2013; however, they resulted from recent case law.

Thus, initially, the grounds for exempting ISPs from liability were established by case law (eg, the *Masterhost*[6] and *Agava-Soft*[7] cases). These grounds were that the provider:

- does not initiate the transfer, does not choose the recipient of the information, and does not affect the integrity of information;
- takes preventive measures to avoid an infringement;
- has technical tools for controlling and changing information as well as to undertake action to prevent the unlawful use of IP rights; and
- does not obtain a profit from the activity relating to the use of IP rights of third parties.

The first three grounds above were considered as the main criteria for courts to establish whether an ISP is to be deemed liable for IP rights infringement which takes place on a relevant social media source.

When all three of these criteria are established by the court, liability will be imposed on a relevant social media source. If any of the criteria are missing, the court will decide that the an ISP should bear liability for the IP rights infringement.

For example, a social media source V kontakte (In Touch) has been deemed liable for unlawful use of songs of Russian singers posted by a social media user.[8] The court established that this service provider duly notified its users of possible violation of third-party IP rights, by placing a relevant policy on its internet site. Moreover, the court found that the social media source derived no profits from its activities.

---

6 Resolution of Plenary session of the Supreme Commercial Court of the Russian Federation under the case No 10962/08 dated December 23 2008.

7 Resolution of Plenary session of the Supreme Commercial Court of the Russian Federation under the case No 6672/11 dated November 1 2011.

8 Ruling of the Federal Arbitrazh Court of the Northern-West District dated August 20 2012, case No A56-57884/2010.

However, the court took the view that upon receiving written notice from IP rights holders regarding a violation of their rights, the provider did not undertake sufficient measures to eliminate the IP rights infringement.

As noted above, as a result of this case law, the Russian Civil Code was amended by a new Article 1253.1, which came into force on August 1 2013 as part of the Russian Anti-Piracy Law. This new Article 1253.1 introduces the concept of 'information intermediaries' – ISPs and operators – and establishes criteria to determine when they will be liable for IP rights infringement, as follows:

- the ISP transmits the information via the Internet (eg, Google, Yandex);
- the operator provides a platform (source) for placing the information on the Internet (eg, social networks).

Consequently, ISPs will not be deemed liable for infringement of IP rights if they:

- do not initiate transfer of the information and do not determine its recipients;
- do not change the information being transmitted except for changes performed for technical purposes of such transmission; and
- did not know or should not have known about any infringement that has taken place.

Operators will not be liable for infringement of IP rights provided that:

- they did not know and could not have known about the infringement; and
- upon receipt of a written notice from the IP rights owner, they undertake necessary and sufficient measures to stop the infringement in a timely manner.

Thus, if these criteria are not met, the relevant ISP or operator will be liable for the copyright infringement.

1.7 Joint liability for ISPs

Under Russian law, joint liability may arise where an infringement is the result of the actions of several parties. There is no special regulation on this issue in Russian law, but there have been benchmark cases where several ISPs were found jointly liable.

1.8 Relief

The Digital Millennium Copyright Act is not applied in the Russian Federation, so that relief can be granted against an ISP only at the request of law enforcement agencies in the court decisions.

Thus, under the Russian Anti-Piracy Law, when a copyright owner discovers that a video has been placed illegally on the Internet, he/she is entitled to apply to the Moscow City Court seeking a preliminary injunction against the website owner. After the injunction is granted the copyright owner should file a lawsuit within 15 days, otherwise the preliminary injunction will be revoked by the same court.

The Federal Service for Supervision of Communications, Information Technology, and Mass Media will execute the court injunction. In particular, it must identify the ISP and officially notify it within three working days. Following receipt of the notification, the ISP has one day to contact the owner of the informational source where the illegal content was placed with a request to delete the content or to limit access to the content. If the website owner does not delete the content within one day of the notification, the ISP will be obliged to block access to the illegally placed content.

It should be noted that the Russian Anti-Piracy Law provides for the protection mainly of copyrights for movies and films. However, it is expected that it may be extended to include illegally placed music, literature and computer programs. Amendments to this effect were introduced in the Parliament on September 17 2013, and it is hoped that they will be enacted soon.

1.9 Issues specific to Russia

(a) Jurisdiction

In cases where copyright infringement has taken place in the territory of the Russian Federation, Russian courts have jurisdiction to hear copyright infringement claims. If the copyright infringement is committed overseas, jurisdiction shall be determined in accordance with the law of the country where the infringement took place. However, if there is any connection between such infringement and Russia (eg, through the defendant's residence or the location of his/her property (assets)), Russian courts will have jurisdiction to hear the case and Russian law will apply.

At present, IP disputes in Russia are considered by state courts, in particular, civil courts (ie, courts of general jurisdiction) and state *arbitrazh* courts, depending on the parties to a particular dispute, and by the recently established Intellectual Property Court.

The general rule is that civil courts will deal with disputes involving individuals. State *arbitrazh* courts handle disputes between companies and/or individual entrepreneurs. These courts are an integral part of the Russian state judicial system and should not be confused with commercial arbitration courts. The confusion between two different kinds of bodies usually originates from the English translation that often fails to distinguish between them. For the purposes of this chapter, state *arbitrazh* courts are Russian state courts which handle disputes involving legal entities and entrepreneurs.

The Intellectual Property Court commenced its work on July 3 2013 and is intended to deal with cases concerning protection of IP rights. As a court of first instance, it deals for example with cases on challenges to regulatory acts, disputes regarding the grant and termination of IP rights, and cases on the infringement of IP rights. The Intellectual Property Court is set up within the system of Russia's state *arbitrazh* courts and will handle disputes falling within its competence, both between companies and involving individuals.

Decisions made by the Intellectual Property Court as a court of cassation are subject to judicial review by the Supreme Commercial Court of the Russian Federation.

Details on consideration of IP disputes by the Russian state courts following the creation of the Intellectual Property Court are summarised in Table 1.

It should be mentioned that at the time of writing, the Russian Parliament is considering amendments to the Constitution which will introduce substantive changes relating to the merger of two court systems – the civil courts and the state *arbitrazh* courts – making them a unified civil court system.

(b) *Claim to infringement of foreign copyright*

Russian courts have jurisdiction to hear claims for infringement of foreign copyright if an infringement takes place in the territory of the Russian Federation (*lex loci actus*). If a defendant infringes copyright overseas, Russian courts may have jurisdiction based on the Russian residence of the alleged infringer.

(c) *Emission theory*

Russian law does not contain any direct provisions regarding application of the 'emission theory'; however, it stipulates that the country where the infringement took place shall be determined irrespective of where the illegal content has been uploaded. The main criterion for determining where an infringement has taken place is a connection between the website where the illegal content is placed and the territory of a particular country. Such connection can be determined on the basis of the following conditions:

- the website in question targets the internet users of a particular country – the evidence for this may be, for example, the fact that the website domain name is registered under a particular country domain zone code;
- the owner (administrator) of a domain name is a resident of the particular country; in some cases an owner of the internet content (the web page owner and/or IP address owner) can be also involved as a co-defendant.

1.10 Orphan works

Russian law does not contain any provisions on orphan works, but in accordance with law enforcement practice these are copyright works for which a copyright owner (author) cannot be contacted. The copyright liability of a person who uses an orphan work without the consent of a copyright owner (author) might be reduced if he/she uses this work in good faith. This means that if a user takes all necessary measures to find the author (copyright owner), or his/her successors and ensures payment of royalties for the use of such work to the author in the future, his/her liability for any copyright infringement can be reduced.

1.11 Online piracy measures

As noted in sections 1.6 and 1.8 above, specific measures against online piracy in Russia have recently been established by the Russian Anti-Piracy Law. In addition, prosecution and investigation authorities may obtain a disclosure order against innocent ISPs, requiring them to disclose the identity and contact details of a user of their service who is suspected of infringing an intellectual property right (IPR). For further information see section 4.1 below.

Table 1: IP disputes in state courts following creation of the Intellectual Property Court in Russia

Criteria for determining jurisdiction	Category of disputes and parties ↓	↓	↓
Category of dispute	Challenges to regulatory acts Disputes on grant and termination of IP rights, except copyright, allied rights and integrated circuit masks +	Infringement of IP rights, including copyright-related rights and integrated circuit masks +	Infringement of IP rights, including copyright-related rights and integrated circuit masks +
Parties	Legal entities, individual entrepreneurs and/or individuals ↓	Legal entities and/or individual entrepreneurs ↓	Individuals ↓
Court of first instance	Intellectual Property Court ↓	State *arbitrazh* courts ↓	Civil courts ↓
Court of second instance	N/A ↓	State *arbitrazh* courts of appeal ↓	Civil courts of appeal ↓
Court of third instance	Intellectual Property Court	Intellectual Property Court	Civil courts of cassation

1.12 Electronic infringement of moral rights

Under Russian legislation, an author has the following moral rights:

- a right of authorship – a right to be recognised as the author of a copyright work;
- a right to one's own name – a right of using or permitting the use of a work under the author's name, a pseudonym or without an indication of a name (ie, anonymously);
- a right to the integrity of the work;
- a right to publish the work;

- a right of withdrawal – a right to rescind a previously adopted decision to make a work public (withdrawal right) on the condition of compensation for losses caused by such a decision. If the work has already been made public the author will also have the right to give public notice of its withdrawal.

The following moral rights may be infringed on the Internet:

(a) ***Right to object to derogatory treatment (ie, a right to integrity of the work)***

Without the author's consent it is prohibited to make modifications, cuts or addenda to a work, or to attach illustrations, a preface, afterword, comments or any explanations (ie, the right of integrity of the work).

When a work is used after the author's death, the person owning the exclusive right to the work is entitled to permit modifications, cuts or addenda to the work, provided the author's idea is not distorted, the integrity of perception remains intact, and it does not conflict with the author's preferences expressly stated in a will, letters, diaries or other written form. A perversion, distortion or another modification of a work that denigrates the honour, dignity or business reputation of the author, and equally an attempt at committing such actions authorises the author or his/her successor to claim protection of his/her honour, dignity or business reputation in accordance with the rules of Article 152 of the Russian Civil Code.

(b) ***False attribution – right to guard against impersonation on the Internet***

The right of authorship and the right to one's own name may be infringed, for example, where the author's name is not indicated or indicated incorrectly. These rights are inalienable and non-transferable – for instance, in situations where the exclusive right to the work is assigned to another person or transferred to another person, and where the right of using the work is granted to another person. The waiver of these rights is deemed to be null and void.

When a work is published anonymously or pseudonymously (except for cases when the author's pseudonym leaves no doubt as to his/her identity), the publisher (Item 1 of Article 1287 of the Russian Civil Code) whose name is indicated on the work shall be deemed the author's representative, unless otherwise proven. In this capacity the publisher is entitled to protect the author's rights and ensure the exercise of such rights. This provision remains effective until the author of the work discloses his/her identity or announces his/her authorship.

(c) ***Paternity rights***

There is no time limit for the protection of the authorship, the name of the author or the integrity of a work. In the procedure set out for designating the executor of a will (Article 1134 of the Russian Civil Code), the author may indicate the person in whom he/she vests the duty to protect authorship, the name of the author and the integrity of a work (paragraph 2 of Item 1 of Article 1266 of the Russian Civil Code) upon the author's death. The person must execute his/her duties for life. If there is no such indication or if the person designated by the author has refused to execute these powers, then after the death of the person the protection of the authorship, the name of the author and the integrity of the work must be maintained by the author's heirs, their successors and other persons concerned.

2. Trademarks

2.1 Use of a trademark

The use of a trademark on a website will be treated as sufficient 'use' for the purposes of avoiding revocation of the trademark registration for non-use, if such trademark is used on the website for goods and services for which it was registered.

To avoid revocation, the trademark owner should use the trademark for the purposes of introducing goods/services into commerce. If a trademark is used for this purpose under the licence contract or under the control of a trademark owner and goods labelled with this trademark are introduced for sale or sold, it should also be considered as 'use'. In this case evidence of using such trademark would include licence contracts, distribution contracts, franchise contracts and sales receipts or invoices.

2.2 Infringement

A trademark owner (ie, an individual entrepreneur or a legal entity in whose name the trademark is registered[9] – a rights holder) has the exclusive right to use a trademark in any manner that is not contrary to the law. The exclusive right to a trademark allows the identification of goods, work or services with respect to which the trademark has been registered, in particular by using a trademark:

- on goods including labels and packaging of goods, that are produced, offered for sale, sold, displayed at exhibitions and fairs, or otherwise introduced into civil circulation within the territory of the Russian Federation, or are kept or transported for this purpose, or imported into the territory of the Russian Federation;
- while performing work or rendering services;
- on documents introducing goods into civil circulation;
- while offering goods for sale, work for performance, and services for rendering as well as in announcements, on signs, and in advertising;
- on the Internet, including in a domain name and for other means of address.

According to Russian case law, if a trademark is used on a website such use is deemed to be use in Russia if either of the following conditions is met:

- a website is targeted at Russian internet users – the evidence of this may be:
  - the fact that the website is registered in domain zones '.ru', '.рф' or '.su' (or any other relating to Russia);
  - the fact that the website is registered in another domain zone (eg, '.org' or '.com'), but directed at Russian consumers (eg, offers goods/services in the Russian language);
- an owner of a domain name is a Russian citizen or it is a legal entity registered in the Russian Federation.

---

9 Under Russian law, the right to a trademark arises only after the trademark is properly registered.

Under Article 1484 of the Russian Civil Code, no one is permitted without the permission of the trademark owner to use designations similar to a trademark belonging to the owner in relation to the goods for which the trademark is registered, or in relation to similar goods, if the result of such a use is that there is a likelihood that confusion will arise. Consequently, such use constitutes infringement of an exclusive right to a trademark.

Under Russian legislation, the main grounds for deeming the unauthorised use of a trademark to be an infringement arise where:

- a designation is used for the distribution of goods and services for which such trademark was registered or for similar goods/services;
- a designation is identical or similar to the trademark.

When both of these grounds arise, the use of the trademark will be deemed as an infringement of the exclusive right of a trademark owner.

Russian legislation provides for three types of liability for trademark infringement: civil, administrative and criminal liability.

(a) *Civil liability*

Primary rules on civil liability for illegal use of a trademark are set out in Article 1515 of the Russian Civil Code:

- Goods, labels and packages on which a trademark or a designation confusingly similar to a trademark has been illegally placed are deemed to be counterfeit.
- Trademark owners may request the withdrawal of counterfeit goods, labels and packages of goods (on which an illegally used trademark or a confusingly similar designation is placed) from the market, and their destruction at the expense of the infringer.
- Trademark owners may also claim damages or compensation instead of reimbursement of losses:
  - in the amount of Rb10,000 to Rb5,000,000 (ie, approximately US$300 to US$149,838) at the court's discretion depending on the nature of the infringement;
  - in an amount equal to twice the value of the goods on which the trademark has been illegally placed, or twice the value of a right to use the trademark, assessed on the basis of the price normally charged in comparable circumstances for the legal use of the trademark.

The final amount to be paid by the infringer will be determined by the court in accordance with the relevant circumstances.

(b) *Administrative liability*

Under Article 14.10 of the Code of Administrative Offences, illegal use of another person's trademark or a confusingly similar designation will lead to the confiscation of the counterfeit goods and:

- for citizens: the imposition of a fine of Rb1,500 to Rb2,000 (ie, approximately US$45 to US$60);

- for officials: a fine of Rb10,000 to Rb20,000 (ie, approximately US$300 to US$600);
- for legal entities: a fine of Rb30,000 to Rb40,000 (ie, approximately US$900 to US$1,200).

In addition, Article 14.33 of the Code of Administrative Offences stipulates liability for unfair competition as follows:

- for officials: a fine of Rb12,000 to Rb20,000 (ie, approximately US$350 to US$600);
- for legal entities: a fine of Rb100,000 to Rb500,000 (ie, approximately US$3,000 to US$15,500).

Placing on the market goods which make illegal use of intellectual property constitutes unfair competition. Such unfair competition will be punishable by a fine on public officials in an amount of Rb20,000 (ie, approximately US$600), or disqualification for a period of up to three years; and on legal entities of 1% to 15% of the revenue obtained by the infringer from the infringing commodity, work or service on whose market the infringement has been committed but not less than Rb100,000 (ie, approximately US$3,000).

(c) Criminal liability

Under Article 180 of the Criminal Code of the Russian Federation, where there has been illegal use of a trademark or where such use has caused substantial damage, this offence will be punishable by a fine of up to Rb200,000 (ie, approximately US$6,000); or an amount equivalent to up to 18 months' wages or salary, or any other income of the convicted person; or by compulsory work for a term of up to 480 hours; or by corrective labour for a term of up to two years.

If such actions are carried out by a group of persons by previous concert or by an organised group, such persons will be punishable by a fine of Rb500,000 to Rb1,000,000 (ie, approximately US$15,500 to US$31,000); or an amount equivalent to three to five years' wages/salary or other income of the convicted person; or by compulsory labour for a term of up to five years; or by imprisonment for a period of up to six years with a fine of up to Rb500,000 (ie, approximately US$15,500); or the amount of a wage/salary or other income of the convicted person for a period of up to three years without such fine.

Russian legislation does not include any specific provisions on the use of trademarks in metatags, keywords, sponsored links, hidden text, search navigation tools, hypertext links or framing. However, as a general rule, such use can be treated as trademark infringement if the mark is used for the identification of goods and services for which such trademark was registered (or similar/goods, services) and is identical or similar to the trademark, and there is a likelihood of confusion as a result of such use.

2.3 Defences

(a) *Descriptive (non-trademark) use of the mark*

Under Russian court practice, if a mark is used for descriptive purposes (ie, it is used for non-commercial purposes and is not aimed at identifying the same goods and services), it will not constitute trademark infringement even if such a use may cause a likelihood of confusion.

(b) *Comparative advertising*

Under Russian legislation, an advertisement is deemed unfair if it contains incorrect comparisons between advertised goods and goods manufactured by other manufacturers or sold by other sellers. Thus, comparative advertising can be treated as unfair if it contains incorrect comparisons. In this case, trademark owners, whose goods are labelled with a trademark and incorrectly compared with goods of another company, may object that such advertising is unfair and seek to prohibit it.

(c) *Parody*

The treatment of a trademark which is used as a parody will depend on the nature of such use. If a trademark is used within a composite work which can be treated as parody, and is used for non-commercial purposes, such use will not constitute infringement. On the other hand, if a trademark is used as a part of a parodic work, but is aimed at distributing goods and services labelled with such trademark, this use will constitute infringement.

2.4 Parallel imports

Branded goods offered for sale in Russia via a website where those goods have not first been placed on the Russian market by the trademark owner or with its consent will not be treated as parallel imports, but will be deemed to be trademark infringement on the Internet (ie, the sale of branded goods via a website without the consent of a trademark owner).

Parallel imports can be defined as imports of lawfully trademarked goods without the permission of the rights holder, or imports by an unauthorised importer. As Russian law has set out the national principle of exhaustion of exclusive rights to a trademark, the exclusive right to a trademark will not be deemed infringed if the trademark is used by other persons in respect of goods that have been introduced in civil law transactions on the territory of the Russian Federation directly by the rights holder or with his/her consent.

In settling civil law disputes relating to the import of goods into Russia which have not been sanctioned by the rights holder, the courts will be guided primarily by whether the rights holder consented to the goods being placed on the Russian market (eg, by entering into a relevant licence agreement).

If goods are imported for sale through official distributors, such imports are deemed to be legitimate even if there is no licence agreement between the distributor and the rights holder. If goods are imported by someone other than the rights holder or someone who has not been licensed by it, or without its consent, such imports are deemed to be illegal, regardless of whether the holder's rights have been infringed during the production or distribution of such goods outside Russia. This follows directly from Article 1484 of the Russian Civil Code. Thus, from the civil law perspective, unless the rights holder consents, such import of goods will constitute infringement, even when such goods have been legally marked and released onto the market outside Russia.

The Customs Register records trademarks, authorised importers and those permitted by the rights holder to place its goods on a specific market. If importers are not listed on the register and try to import trademarked products into Russia, Customs will treat these goods as counterfeit and seize them. The Customs Register is an effective way of preventing the import of counterfeit products into Russia, since the Authorised Importer List on the Customs IP Register testifies as to whether imports of goods is sanctioned.

Trademarked goods imported by individuals or delivered by international mail in small quantities for personal, family, household or any other non-business purposes are not affected by this. Administrative law allows Customs to suspend imports and apply penalties, including the confiscation of illegally trademarked items (Article 14.10 of the Code of Administrative Offences). A court decision to hold an infringer liable will be based on a lawsuit filed by the relevant customs officials.

Until recently, this administrative procedure appeared to be effective in preventing parallel imports, among other things, owing to a prompt response by Customs to communications from rights holders and a willingness to seize unsanctioned imports at the border. In considering customs lawsuits, the courts have been guided by the rule that the import of goods into Russia is a separate use of a trademark. Thus, should goods be imported without the rights holder's permission or by an unauthorised importer, they will be subject to seizure, even if the trademark was placed on the goods lawfully during manufacture.

However, on February 3 2009, the Presidium of the Supreme Commercial Court examined,[10] by way of supervision, the unsanctioned import into Russia of a Porsche Cayenne S car in an unroadworthy condition by the company Genesis (which is not an official Porsche Cayenne S dealer). This case set a judicial precedent that has changed the approach taken by the courts to imposing the administrative liability contemplated in Article 14.10 of the Code of Administrative Offences when considering customs cases. LLC Porsche Cayenne Russland, which was licensed to use the Porsche and Cayenne marks in Russia, reported the infringement in question to Central Excise Customs. This office in turn applied to the Moscow Arbitrazh Court, which ruled against Genesis, imposed a fine and ordered the vehicle to be confiscated on charges of administrative violation. Subsequently, Genesis filed a complaint with the Supreme Commercial Court, which overturned the rulings of the lower instance courts and held that the confiscation was illegal on the grounds that the vehicle was not counterfeit. The court held that as the Porsche Cayenne S car had been manufactured by the holder of the relevant trademark and bore no signs of

10 Ruling of the Supreme Commercial Court No 10458/08, case No A40-9281/08-145-28 dated February 3 2009.

illegitimate trademark reproduction, there were no legal grounds for holding Genesis liable for importing the vehicle into Russia under Article 14.10 of the Code of Administrative Offences.

The courts have thus assumed a position that the liability envisaged in Article 14.10 of the Code of Administrative Offences does not apply to the import of goods that are not counterfeit within the meaning of Article 1515 of the Civil Code. Specifically, liability does not apply to goods on which the trademark has been placed legitimately by the rights holder itself, even if the import of such goods was not authorised by the rights holder.

In spite of these judicial precedents, a rights holder can independently seek judicial protection of its exclusive rights in civil court proceedings claiming the unsanctioned import of goods into Russia. Although civil proceedings take much longer than administrative proceedings, the civil law procedure might prove to be quite an effective instrument for preventing parallel imports. Exclusive remedies allow the rights holder to combat unauthorised imports by third parties, including by banning the use of trademarks during the import into Russia of goods bearing such trademarks. These judicial precedents have made parallel imports the subject of heated debate in business circles and there is some disagreement as to the potential legislative solutions.

2.5 Remedies

In the event of a trademark infringement, trademark owners may use the following general remedies:

- recognition of the right;
- injunction against activities infringing the right or creating a threat of infringement;
- damages;
- seizure of the infringing articles;
- destruction of materials and implements used or designated for the commission of the offence;
- publication of the court decision on the infringement committed, with an indication of the actual rights holder.

Under Article 1515 of the Russian Civil Code, the trademark owner is entitled to demand that the infringer pays compensation instead of reimbursement of losses:

- of Rb10,000 to Rb5,000,000 (ie, approximately US$300 to US$150,000) at the court's discretion, based on the nature of the infringement;
- in an amount equivalent to twice the value of the goods on which the trademark has been illegally placed, or twice the value of the right of using the trademark assessed on the basis of the price normally charged in comparable circumstances for the legal use of the trademark.

The final amount will be determined by the court according to the circumstances of the particular case.

2.6 Liability of ISP

The general provisions discussed in section 1.6 above can also be applied in relation to ISPs in the event of trademark infringement.

2.7 Advertising law and regulation

The exclusive right to a trademark may be used for the identification of the goods, work or services with respect to which the trademark has been registered, in particular by using a trademark in advertising.

Advertising will be deemed to be unfair and will infringe the exclusive right under a trademark if:

- it contains incorrect comparisons of advertised goods with goods manufactured by other manufacturers or sold by other sellers; or
- it constitutes unfair competition in accordance with the competition law.[11]

It is important to note that if the trademarks are used by third parties in advertising for the purpose of identification of their goods, such use will constitute infringement. The judgment of the Federal *Arbitrazh* Court of Moscow District, No KG-A41/4778-09 dated August 5 2009, established that the use of bags, which were labelled with a name similar to the trademark of Louis Vuitton, in the advertisement video of a company Nidan Juices could mislead consumers regarding the advertised goods and cause confusion with accessories and goods of the plaintiff.

However, if registered trademarks are used by a third party without any intention of identifying its goods/services (eg, they are to describe a product or service sold by the third party involving the trademark owner or its goods and services) and such use is not likely to lead to confusion as to origin of goods (or their manufacturer), or to a relationship between the trademark owner and the third party, such use will be permitted.[12]

There is no specific regulatory regime in the Russian Advertising Law relating to internet advertising, but general provisions of advertising law are applicable to advertising on the Internet.

2.8 Domain name disputes

The main grounds for treating the unauthorised use of a trademark in a domain name as a trademark infringement are:

- where the website with the disputed domain name is used for the distribution of goods and services for which such trademark was registered or for similar goods;
- where the domain name is identical or similar to the trademark where such use of the domain name would result in a likelihood of confusion.

When both of these grounds exist, the use of the domain name will constitute infringement of the exclusive right of the trademark owner.

---

11 Federal Law 'On Advertising' dated March 13 2006 No 38-FZ.

12 Ruling of the Presidium the Supreme Commercial Court of the Russian Federation No 14685/03 dated April 6 2004.

It is important to note that court practice has moved from the trademark owner having to prove the use of the domain name for activities that are the same as those for which the trademark is registered, to a simpler criterion of having a legitimate interest in domain ownership. In other words, the fact of registration of a domain can be considered as an infringement, even if a website is not used and does not distribute similar goods.

For example, in a case regarding the infringement of a trademark – *Tissot*[13] – the domain name owner had not used the domain name having received a right of administration of the domain name 'tissot.ru'. The court considered this as a trademark infringement, as it interfered with the right of the trademark owner to use its trademark in a domain name and was therefore an abuse of rights.

In the *MUMM* case considered by the Supreme Commercial Court,[14] the above-mentioned criteria were also extended to the Russian domain zone. In this case the court ruled that the right of administration of a domain name creates a threat of the infringement of the exclusive right to a trademark and it is an obstacle for the use of such trademark in a domain name. So the levels of protection for trademark owners against infringements of domain names and prosecutions of domain name registrants are high, regardless of the similarity of goods and services.

However, courts may apply another approach in defining the infringement of exclusive rights. For instance, the court[15] took into account the similarity of goods distributed on the website 'swatch.ru' (watches), and goods for which the trademark 'Swatch' was registered. Accordingly, the court satisfied the claims of the trademark owner to recognise the trademark infringement, prohibit the use of the trademark in a domain name of the defendant and award the compensation.

2.9 Unfair competition/passing off

The main legal issues relating to unfair competition are regulated by the Federal Law on Protection of Competition. This defines unfair competition as "any actions of economic entities (groups of persons) aimed at obtaining a benefit while carrying out business activity, in contravention of the legislation of the Russian Federation, business traditions, requirements of respectability, rationality and equity and which have inflicted or may inflict losses upon other economic entities/competitors or have harmed or may harm their business reputation".

Competitors are entities which produce similar or substitutable goods, or act within one market. It is important to note that unfair competition is possible only where a competitive relationship exists. Otherwise, liability for trademark infringement can be imposed only on the basis of civil law provisions and only by judicial procedure.

Under Article 14 of the Federal Law on Protection of Competition, the main forms of unfair competition in relation to IP are:

---

13 Ruling of the Federal *Arbitrazh* Court of Moscow District under the case No 40-4514/11-12-38 dated August 8 2012.

14 Ruling of the Presidium of the Supreme Commercial Court of the Russian Federation No 18012/10, case No A40-47499/10-27-380 dated May 18 2011 (the legal proceeding regarding the trademark 'MUMM').

15 Ruling of the Federal *Arbitrazh* Court of Moscow District No KG-A41/4373-11, case No A41-22989/10 dated May 30 2011.

- the sale or exchange of, or any other means of placing, a commodity in circulation where there has been illegal use of the results of intellectual activity and it is likely that the commodity will be identified with a legal entity, production, works or services, and such use causes confusion between the goods, works and services;
- the unauthorised acquisition and use of the exclusive right to means of identification of production, works or services.

In order to qualify as an act of unfair competition, the infringer must actually introduce goods into circulation. If this is not the case, there will be no infringement. In most cases relating to unfair competition with the use of trademarks, the main ground for the imposition of liability is the confusing similarity between trademarks. For example, a court[16] established that as the packaging of the confectionary 'ESFERO Crema' (CJSC *KONTI-RUS*) was confusingly similar to the bulk trademarks and figurative trademark of Ferrero SPA and these companies were competitors, the defendant committed an act of unfair competition. Moreover, placing goods into circulation must provide an opportunity to receive profits, thereby damaging competitors and creating a likelihood of confusion.

The unfair acquisition of exclusive rights to means of identification may be expressed in the following ways:

- registration of a trademark or service mark;
- registration of a company (with a company name) and its use in real commercial activity or in activity involving interference with the business of competitors.

The law prohibits unfair competition relating to the acquisition and use of exclusive trademark rights. In addition, the Russian legislation on protection of competition prohibits unfair competition in the form of misrepresentation regarding the nature, method and place of production, consumer characteristics, or quality and quantity of goods, or in relation to its producers. Although this rule is not specific to trademarks, it may in some cases be used by trademark holders to protect against acts defined as 'erosion' of the trademark. in which these actions give rise to confusion among consumers regarding the manufacturer of the goods. However, the Federal Law on Protection of Competition directly identifies as a form of unfair competition only the unlawful use of a trademark with the introduction of goods in circulation.

Liability for unfair competition is set out in Article 14.33 of the Code of Administrative Offences (see 'Administrative liability' in section 2.2. above).

16 Ruling of the Ninth *Arbitrazh* Appeal Court No 09AP-34420/2010-AK, case No A40-69684/10 dated November 12 2010.

3. Patents

3.1 Patentability of 'internet' inventions

Under Article 1350 of the Russian Civil Code, business methods, mathematical methods and presentation of information cannot be patented as inventions.

Under Article 1259 of the Russian Civil Code, computer programs are protected as literal works and are, therefore, copyrightable objects. They cannot be patented as inventions. However, an algorithm of the program can be protected as a method for the invention, if it has the potential to cause a 'further technical effect', which must go beyond the inherent technical interactions between hardware and software.

In this case, the algorithm of the program that can provide this further technical effect can be patentable, subject to the other patentability requirements, such as novelty, inventive step and industrial applicability. It means that it would be recognised as providing a technical solution to a technical problem.

3.2 Bioinformatics

There is no practice for obtaining a patent for a novel DNA sequence or protein structure discovered through the use of bioinformatics in Russia, but it is possible to obtain a patent for a novel DNA sequence or protein structure.

3.3 Issues specific to Russia

(a) Infringement on the Internet

The infringement of patent rights takes place when all the essential features of the independent claim of a patent are used in goods posted on a website and this website is closely related to the Russian Federation. This means that because a patent is protected in the territory for which it was registered, in order to prove patent infringement there must be a link between the website and Russia.

According to relevant case law, Russian courts have jurisdiction to consider cases on patent infringement committed via the Internet in cases where:

- a website on which goods are placed containing a patented invention, or operated by means of a process patent, is registered in local Russian zones such as '.ru', '.рФ' or '.su' and others, if there is a link with the territory from which the website operates;
- an owner of a domain is a Russian citizen, or is a legal entity registered in the Russian Federation.

(b) Process patents

If a part of the algorithm of a program or invention used on a website is covered by a patent, the unauthorised use of this part will deemed to be an infringement if either a domain name is registered in a local domain name zone, or a special part of a website or a process is developed or specially designed for Russia or for Russian consumers.

3.4 Remedies available for patent infringement

Where the infringement of a patent right occurs in Russia, the patentee may claim:

- recognition of the right;
- an injunction against the activities infringing the right or creating a threat of its infringement;
- damages;
- seizure of the infringing articles;
- destruction of materials and implements used or designated for the commission of the infringement;
- publication of the court decision relating to the infringement, with an indication of the actual rights holder.

The most common remedies are injunction and compensation for loss.

4. Disclosure orders against ISPs

4.1 Availability

A disclosure order can be obtained against innocent ISPs, requiring them to disclose the identity and contact details of a user of their service who is suspected of infringing an IPR in cases prescribed by law. In Russian law, such disclosure orders may be made only by the prosecuting or investigating authorities on the basis of court decisions, if there are sufficient grounds for such orders (eg, criminal prosecution of a user).

4.2 Requirements

See section 4.1 above.

4.3 Jurisdictional issues

See section 4.1 above.

4.4 'John Doe' injunctions

Under Russian law 'John Doe' injunctions may not be obtained to prevent IPR infringement against persons unknown.

Singapore

Kelvin Tan
Drew & Napier LLC

1. Copyright, database rights and design rights

1.1 Overview

In Singapore, internet content is generally protected by the law of copyright.

(a) *Literary works and artistic works*

Computer programs: The Copyright Act[1] protects original literary works,[2] and a computer program is deemed to be a literary work.[3]

To qualify as a 'computer program' under the Copyright Act, the material must be: *an expression, in any language, code or notation, of a set of instructions (whether with or without related information) intended, either directly or after either or both of the following: (a) conversion to another language, code or notation; (b) reproduction in a different material form, to cause a device having information processing capabilities to perform a particular function.*[4]

Website content: Website content may variously be protected under the Copyright Act as literary and artistic works.

While there is no statutory definition of what constitutes a 'literary work', the High Court has defined a literary work as one which is written down and contains information which can be read by somebody, as opposed to being appreciated simply with the eye.[5]

An 'artistic work' is defined by the Copyright Act to mean:

- a painting, sculpture, drawing, engraving or photograph, whether the work is of artistic quality or not;
- a building or model of a building, whether the building or model is of artistic quality or not; or
- a work of artistic craftsmanship to which neither of the preceding bullet points applies.[6]

1 Cap 63, 2006 Rev Ed. This first came into force on April 10 1987.
2 Section 27 of the Copyright Act.
3 Section 7A(1)(b) of the Copyright Act provides that 'literary work' includes 'a computer program'.
4 Section 7(1) of the Copyright Act.
5 *Real Electronics Industries Singapore (Pte) Ltd v Nimrod Engineering Pte Ltd* [1995] 3 SLR(R) 909.
6 Section 7(1) of the Copyright Act.

The various constituents of a web page may enjoy separate copyright as literary and artistic works.

(b) *Films, sound recordings and broadcasts*

Cinematograph films[7] and sound recordings[8] that are embedded in web content are also protected by copyright. A 'broadcast', however, must take place by wireless telegraphy.[9] Therefore, the communication of content on the Internet may not be a copyrightable broadcast.

(c) *Typographical arrangement of a published edition*

There is copyright in a published edition of a work.[10] This is in addition to and independent of any copyright in the authors' works from which the published edition is derived.[11] Therefore, the presentation and arrangement of a work on a web page may qualify for protection as a published edition of that work.[12]

(d) *Protection of the user interface*

To the extent that the operation of a computer program involves a user interface, the latter may be protected as a literary work. The words and graphics appearing on a user interface are literary and artistic works, respectively, which may enjoy copyright if they are original.

A computer program may not be registered as a 'design' under the Registered Designs Act.[13] This raises doubt over whether the aesthetic appearance of a user interface is registrable.

(e) *Computer-generated works*

Where a computer program is used to generate a work, the copyright in the work will belong to the author, who would usually be the person using the computer program.

(f) *Websites protected as databases*

There is no specific provision for the copyright protection of databases. However, a database may be protected as a compilation.

(g) *Compilations*

Compilations are protected as literary works.[14] However, to constitute a 'compilation' for the purposes of the Copyright Act, it must amount to an 'intellectual creation',

---

7 Section 88 of the Copyright Act.
8 Section 87 of the Copyright Act.
9 Section 7(1) of the Copyright Act.
10 'Works' comprise literary, dramatic, musical and artistic works. Their scope and protection are set out in Sections 26 and 27 of the Copyright Act.
11 Section 117(1) of the Copyright Act.
12 Note, however, where newspapers are concerned, it seems that copyright does not subsist in each individual news item or article, but the typographical arrangement of the paper as a whole (*Newspaper Licensing Agency Ltd v Marks & Spencer plc* [2003] 1 AC 551).
13 Section 7(1) of the Registered Designs Act (Cap 266, 2005 Rev Ed). A 'design' is defined as "features of shape, configuration, pattern or ornament applied to an article by any industrial process ..." (Section 2(1) of the Registered Designs Act).
14 Section 7A(1)(a) of the Copyright Act.

by reason of 'the selection or arrangement of its contents'.[15] Thus, 'sweat of the brow' compilations would not be protected. The Court of Appeal has held that the test of originality applies (ie, there must be sufficient amount of skill, labour and judgement involved in the creative process). With the proliferation of computers and the ready availability of computer software, a court will consider the ease and convenience that computers bring to the process of compiling.[16]

1.2 Infringing acts

(a) Copying

Temporary copies: The unauthorised reproduction of a work may be an infringing act even if the copy is transient in nature.[17]

However, the Copyright Act provides specific defences to copyright infringement when transient copies are made, which are discussed below.

In any medium: There is no requirement that a work be copied onto any particular medium before infringement would arise.

(b) Issuing copies of unpublished works to the public

One of the exclusive rights of copyright in an unpublished work is publication.[18] A work is deemed to be published if reproductions of the work have been supplied (whether by sale or otherwise) to the public.[19]

Copyright in a sound recording includes the exclusive right to publish an unpublished sound recording,[20] and a sound recording is deemed to have been published if records embodying the recording have been supplied (whether by sale or otherwise) to the public.[21]

The unauthorised issue of copies of unpublished works and sound recordings on the Internet may therefore constitute infringing acts.

(c) Communicating published works to the public

The unauthorised communication of published works on the Internet may constitute infringing acts.

A copyright owner of a work has the exclusive right to communicate his/her work to the public.[22] A copyright owner of a sound recording has the exclusive right to make the sound recording available to the public by means of a digital audio

---

15 Section 7A(3) of the Copyright Act.

16 *Asia Pacific Publishing Pte Ltd v Pioneers & Leaders (Publishers) Pte Ltd* [2011] 4 SLR 381.

17 Section 15(1A) of the Copyright Act. A work is also reproduced if "it is converted into or from a digital or other electronic machine-readable form, and any article embodying the work in such a form is taken to be a reproduction of the work" (Section 15(1B) of the Copyright Act).

18 Sections 26(1)(a)(ii), 26(1)(b)(ii) and 82(1)(c) of the Copyright Act.

19 Section 24(1)(a) of the Copyright Act.

20 Section 82 of the Copyright Act.

21 Section 24(1)(c) of the Copyright Act.

22 Section 26(1)(a)(iv) and 26(1)(b)(iii) of the Copyright Act.

23 Section 82(1)(d) of the Copyright Act.

transmission.[23] Copyright owners of cinematograph films,[24] television and sound broadcasts,[25] and cable programmes[26] have the exclusive right to communicate the relevant subject matter to the public.

Communication would take place when there is "the making available of a work or other subject-matter (on a network or otherwise) in such a way that the work or subject-matter may be accessed by any person from a place and at a time chosen by him".[27] Parliament's intention behind the enactment of the exclusive right of communication to the public was to address the indiscriminate dissemination of copyrighted work on the Internet.[28]

Where a work is only available to subscribers to an internet service, the subscribers will be considered as 'the public'.[29]

(d) *Performing, showing or playing works in public*

An owner of copyright in a literary, dramatic or musical work has the exclusive right to perform the work in public.[30] The broad definition of 'performance'[31] to include "reference to any visual or aural presentation, whether the presentation is by the use of any receiving apparatus, exhibition of a cinematograph film, by the use of a record or by any other means" means that any presentation of works transmitted over the Internet may be an infringing act.

(e) *Renting or lending works to the public*

The renting or lending of the authorised copies of a work to the public is not an infringing act.

(f) *Authorising another person to do any of the above*

A party, who is not the copyright owner or his/her licensee, may be liable for copyright infringement for 'authorising' a third party to do an infringing act.[32]

However, 'authorisation' can only come from somebody having or purporting to have authority. An act is not authorised by somebody who merely enabled, possibly assisted or even encouraged another to do that act, but did not purport to have any authority which he/she could grant to justify the doing of that act.[33]

In determining whether authorisation to do an act comprised in a copyright has been granted illegitimately, the court will consider:

- whether the alleged authoriser had control over the means by which copyright infringement was committed;
- the nature of any relationship between the alleged authoriser and the actual infringer;

---

24 Section 83(c) of the Copyright Act.
25 Section 84(1)(d) of the Copyright Act.
26 Section 85(1)(d) of the Copyright Act.
27 Section 7(1)(c) of the Copyright Act.
28 Second Reading of the Copyright (Amendment) Bill 2004 on November 16 2004.
29 *Record TV Pte Ltd v Mediacorp TV Singapore Pte Ltd* [2011] 1 SLR 830.
30 Section 26(1)(a)(iii) of the Copyright Act.
31 Section 22 of the Copyright Act.
32 Sections 31(1) and 103 of the Copyright Act.
33 *Ong Seow Pheng v Lotus Development Corp* [1997] 2 SLR(R) 113.

- whether the alleged authoriser took reasonable steps to prevent the infringement; and
- whether the alleged authoriser had actual or constructive knowledge of the occurrence and/or likelihood of infringement.[34]

(g) *Secondary infringement*

Secondary infringement may be committed where a person engages in the commercial exploitation of an infringing product, without the licence of the owner of the copyright, where the person knows or ought to know that it is an infringing product.

There are two main types of secondary infringement:

- the act of selling or otherwise trading in the article (whether imported or not);[35] and
- the act of importing the article for the purpose of sale or other dealings.[36]

Infringing articles are those made without the consent of the relevant owner of the copyright. The identity of the relevant owner depends on whether the article is made in Singapore or overseas.[37]

The Copyright Act also contains criminal offences for secondary infringement.[38]

1.3 Test for copyright infringement

(a) *Requirement of substantial reproduction*

In order to establish primary infringement of copyright, the following must be shown:[39]

- the infringing act must be done in Singapore;
- the defendant must have copied the plaintiff's copyright work; and
- the infringing act must relate to at least a substantial part of the work.

In deciding whether there is copying of a substantial part of a work, a court would assess the quality of the part that is copied, rather than the quantity of the part that is copied in relation to the entire work.

(b) *Repeated copying of insubstantial part*

Correspondingly, there would be no infringement by the mere repeated copying of an insubstantial part of a work.

---

34 *RecordTV Pte Ltd v Mediacorp TV Singapore Pte Ltd* [2011] 1 SLR 830.
35 Section 33 of the Copyright Act.
36 Section 32 of the Copyright Act.
37 Sections 25(2) and (3) of the Copyright Act.
38 Section 136 of the Copyright Act.
39 Section 31 (authors' works) and Section 103(1) (entrepreneurial works) of the Copyright Act.

1.4 Exemptions/defences to copyright infringement

(a) Format shifting

The copying of work into a different format for private and domestic use is probably exempted from being an infringing act by fair dealing provisions of the Copyright Act.[40] This exemption applies, for example, when a person who owns a legitimate music CD copies it onto his/her MP3 player.

(b) Personal copying rights

Certain instances of personal copying are exempted by the general fair dealing defence, which is discussed below.

(c) Time shifting

Time shifting is a defence – when a recording of a television broadcast or a cable programme, or a sound recording of a sound broadcast, television broadcast or a cable programme is made for 'private and domestic use', the relevant copyright is not infringed.[41]

(d) Fair dealing

The Copyright Act provides a general defence of fair dealing,[42] which is not limited to purposes of 'research and study'.[43] In determining whether there is fair dealing, the matters that would be taken into account include:[44]

- the purpose and character of the dealing, including whether such dealing is of a commercial nature or is for non-profit educational purposes;
- the nature of the work or adaptation;
- the amount and substantiality of the part copied taken in relation to the whole work or adaptation;
- the effect of the dealing upon the potential market for, or value of, the work or adaptation; and
- the possibility of obtaining the work or adaptation within a reasonable time at an ordinary commercial price.

Two specific purposes, criticism or review[45] and reporting current events,[46] are excluded from the general fair dealing defence and have their own fair dealing provisions.

(e) Caching/temporary copies as part of communication process

A user caching defence[47] was introduced in 1999 to provide that no infringement

40 Section 35 of the Copyright Act.
41 Section 114 (authors' works) and Section 116 (published editions of works) of the Copyright Act.
42 Section 35(1) of the Copyright Act.
43 Section 35(1A) of the Copyright Act.
44 Section 35(2) of the Copyright Act.
45 Section 36 (authors' works) and Section 110 (entrepreneurial works) of the Copyright Act.
46 Section 37 (authors' works) and Section 111 (entrepreneurial works) of the Copyright Act.
47 Sections 193E and 252D of the Copyright Act. See also Section 38A of the Copyright Act.

occurs by the making of transient and incidental copies of copyrighted material and recordings of performances that are available on a network, if the making of the first-mentioned copy is needed to view, listen or utilise the material or performances by the network user. This defence contemplates communication processes that are involved during internet surfing.

(f) *Hosting*

Part IXA of the Copyright Act[48] deals with the activities of network service providers,[49] for example, transmission, routing and provision of connections,[50] system caching,[51] and storage and information location.[52]

Generally, network service providers are not liable and/or need not pay compensation if they satisfy certain 'safe harbour' conditions.[53]

Network service providers are also protected against liability to third parties (eg their customers), if they remove or disable access to materials on their networks because of prescribed notices from the copyright owner.[54]

(g) *Back-up copies*

The copyright in a literary work that is a computer program is not infringed by making a reproduction of the work if:

- the reproduction is made by, or on behalf of the owner of the copy from which the reproduction is made; and
- the reproduction is made for the purpose only of being used by the owner of the original copy, in lieu of the original copy in the event that the original copy is lost, destroyed or rendered unusable.[55]

However, this defence will not apply if a copy is made from an infringing copy of the computer program.[56]

(h) *Reverse engineering*

Decompilation or disassembly of computer programs is permitted under the Copyright Act provided that:

- it is necessary to do so in order to obtain necessary information to create an independent computer program; and
- the information obtained is not used for any other purpose.[57]

---

48 Sections 193A to 193F of the Copyright Act. Corresponding provisions for performers' rights are found in Sections 252A to 252D of the Copyright Act.
49 A 'network service provider' is defined in Section 193A of the Copyright Act.
50 Section 193B of the Copyright Act.
51 Section 193C(1) of the Copyright Act.
52 Section 193D(1) of the Copyright Act.
53 Section 193B(2) (for transmission, routing and provision of connections); Section 193C(2) (for system caching); Section 193D(2) (for storage and information location) of the Copyright Act.
54 Section 193C(2)(b), Section 193D(2)(b)(iii), and Section 193D(4)(b)(iii) of the Copyright Act.
55 Section 39(1) of the Copyright Act.
56 Section 39(2) of the Copyright Act.
57 Section 39A of the Copyright Act.

(i) *Parody defence*

A parody may be exempted under the general fair dealing defence. In addition, a parody may in some cases not constitute infringement, in that it does not reproduce a substantial part of the parodied work.

(j) *Incidental inclusion*

Incidental inclusion may, in an appropriate case, be justified under the general fair dealing defence.

1.5 Remedies available for copyright infringement

The remedies under the Copyright Act include any of the following: an injunction; a monetary award (damages, account of profits, statutory damages);[58] and an order for delivery up and disposal of the infringing copies.[59]

Regarding the monetary remedies, if the defendant was not aware, and had no reasonable grounds for suspecting that the act constituting an infringement was an infringement of the copyright in question, the plaintiff will be entitled to an account of profits in respect of the infringement and not damages.[60]

1.6 Copyright liability

(a) *Hosting/cloud computing where infringing content uploaded by user of service*

A user who uploads infringing content may be liable for copyright infringement. However, network service providers may avoid liability if they satisfy the 'safe harbour' conditions in the Copyright Act.

(b) *Hypertext linking*

To third-party website: It appears unlikely that mere hyperlinking to a third-party website involves any infringing act.

To an infringing work: To establish copyright infringement, a copyright owner must show that the user who provided the hyperlink to an infringing work has authorised the copying of the infringing work. However, the Court of Appeal has held that, in order to for there to be authorisation, a defendant must have or be purported to have the authority to grant the right to do the act complained of, and must have an element of control over the end user's actions.[61] Hyperlinking to an infringing work will therefore not constitute authorising infringement if the user who provided the hyperlink did not have or demonstrate authority to grant the right to copy or deal with the infringing work and did not control whether a user would copy or deal with the infringing work.

---

58 Section 119(2) of the Copyright Act.
59 Section 120 of the Copyright Act.
60 Section 119(3) of the Copyright Act.
61 *Ong Seow Pheng v Lotus Development Corp* [1997] 2 SLR(R) 113.

Copying of headlines: The copying of headlines that are used as hyperlinks would ordinarily not, on the above analysis, appear to be infringing, unless the headline itself enjoys copyright as a literary work. Having said this, it is possible to postulate an exceptional case where a headline constitutes a substantial part of the literary work, in which event it is arguable that the copying of a headline infringes.

(c) P2P network

Supplier of P2P software: A supplier of P2P software may be liable for authorising infringement. Whether authorisation of infringement is committed depends on the factors set out in section 1.2(f) above.

Uploaders/downloaders: An uploader of an infringing copy of a work would be liable for primary infringement because he/she would have created a substantial copy of the work in his/her upload. Likewise, the downloader of an infringing copy of a work would be liable for primary infringement.

(d) Webcasting

See 'Streaming' below.

(e) Streaming

The High Court has, in *dicta*, opined that the end-user who receives a streaming broadcast for private and domestic use, would not be liable for copyright infringement.[62]

(f) Framing

It is arguable that no infringing act is committed in the course of framing, since there is no copying.

(g) Transmission of infringing work across a communications network

It appears that the transmission of an infringing work across a network would involve several infringing acts when transient reproductions of the infringing work are made. However, network service providers are exempted from infringement if they satisfy the stipulated safe harbour conditions.[63]

(h) Aggregator websites (eg, Google News, price comparison websites)

The aggregation of third-party works may infringe copyright in those works on the usual test for copyright infringement (ie, whether the aggregation reproduces substantial parts of the aggregated works).

The fair dealing defence may apply to a news aggregator if it makes a sufficient acknowledgement of the work it aggregates.[64]

---

62 *RecordTV Pte Ltd v Mediacorp TV Singapore Pte Ltd* [2009] 4 SLR(R) 43 and Section 114 of the Copyright Act; see also Section 38A of the Copyright Act which exempts transient reproduction of an authorised copy in the course of making or receiving a communication.

63 Section 193A-DA of the Copyright Act.

64 Section 37(a) of the Copyright Act.

1.7 Joint liability for ISPs

Since an internet service provider (ISP) does not have control over the actions of its users, it is unlikely to authorise infringement. It is also unlikely to be a joint tortfeasor with a user who used its network to commit acts of infringement because joint tortfeasorship requires proof that the defendant (the ISP) had acted in concert with the primary infringer (the user) pursuant to a common design to commit the tort.

1.8 Relief

Depending on the infringing act complained of, the court may grant one or more of the following reliefs against a network service provider:

- an order requiring the network service provider to take reasonable steps to disable access to an online location that is physically situated outside Singapore;
- an order requiring the network service provider to terminate a specified account;
- an order requiring the network service provider to remove or disable access to an infringing electronic copy of the material from the network service provider's primary network; and
- such other order or orders as may be necessary, if that order is the least burdensome to the network service provider among comparatively effective non-monetary orders.[65]

1.9 Issues specific to Singapore

(a) *Jurisdiction*

An action for infringement under the Copyright Act can only be brought in respect of an infringing act that is done in Singapore.[66]

(b) *Claim for infringement of foreign copyright*

If the foreign copyrighted work originates from a jurisdiction named in the Copyright (International Protection) Regulations, the work is protected as if the work originated from Singapore.[67]

(c) *Emission theory*

There has been no judicial discussion of the emission theory.

1.10 Orphan works

Where publication of a work is anonymous or pseudonymous, copyright subsists in the work until the expiration of 70 years after the expiration of the calendar year in which the work was first published.[68] However, the ordinary duration of copyright would apply if, during the aforesaid period, the identity of the author of the work was generally known or could be ascertained by reasonable inquiry.[69]

---

65 Section 193DB of the Copyright Act.
66 Section 31 (authors' works) and Section 103(1) (entrepreneurial works) of the Copyright Act.
67 Section 184 of the Copyright Act.
68 Section 29(1) of the Copyright Act.

1.11 Online piracy measures

Under the Copyright (Amendment) Act 2004, Section 136(3A) of the Copyright Act was enacted to criminalise the 'wilful' and 'significant' infringement of copyrighted works.

Parliament's intention behind the enactment of the offence was to target movie and music piracy on the Internet and criminalise illegal exploitation of copyrighted works by internet users even where such exploitation was for non-profit or non-commercial purposes.

Other than resorting to prosecutions to deter and punish infringers, there have been education campaigns by both the Intellectual Property Office of Singapore and the affected industries to discourage online piracy.

1.12 Electronic infringement of moral rights

The Copyright Act allows an author of a work to prevent a third party from falsely representing an altered work as being the unaltered work of the author, and from falsely attributing the authorship of reproductions of artistic works.[70]

2. Trademarks

This section considers the law of trademarks in the context of their use on the Internet.

2.1 Use of a trademark

The Trademarks Act provides that references to 'use' include use 'otherwise than by means of a graphic representation'.[71] This would include the verbal use of a trademark or a sign.

However, not every online use of a trademark would constitute use for the purposes of the Trademarks Act. The test as to whether the online use is use within the jurisdiction is whether a reasonable trader would regard the use concerned as in the course of trade in relation to goods or services within the jurisdiction.[72]

The High Court has also held that, for the purpose of determining if there is use of a registered trademark in Singapore that could defeat an application to revoke the mark on the ground of non-use, it must be determined whether the proprietor took active steps apart from putting the trademark on the Internet.[73] An example of an active step is for the proprietor actively to offer the sale of products bearing the trademark, instead of merely placing these products on the Internet and facilitating or inviting access and/or enquiries from other parties.

For the purposes of determining whether there is infringement, the Trademarks Act states that a person uses a sign if he/she:

- applies it to goods or the packaging thereof;
- offers or exposes goods for sale, puts them on the market or stocks them for those purposes under the sign, or offers or supplies services under the sign;

---

69 Section 29(2) of the Copyright Act.

70 Sections 189 and 190 of the Copyright Act.

71 Section 2(4) of the Trademarks Act (Cap 322, 2005 Rev Ed). The first piece of trademark legislation in Singapore was the Trademarks Ordinance 1938.

72 *Euromarket Designs Inc v Peters* [2000] IP & T 1290.

73 *Weir Warman Ltd v Research & Development Pty Ltd* [2007] 2 SLR(R) 1073.

- imports or exports goods under the sign;
- uses the sign on an invoice, wine list, catalogue, business letter, business paper, price list or other commercial document, including any such document in any medium; or
- uses the sign in advertising.[74]

Therefore, it would not be every type of use on the Internet that would give rise to infringement, as will be discussed below.

2.2 Infringement

(a) Metatags

There is no decision on whether metatags can constitute infringement of a trademark. However, since the public would not see the metatag for a webpage, the metatag is unlikely to raise the likelihood of confusion on the part of the public.

(b) Keywords

There is no authority on whether keyword search results would infringe a trademark, but it would appear that this would not give rise to a likelihood of confusion on the part of the public.

(c) Sponsored links

The same analysis as keywords above would apply.

(d) Hidden text

The same analysis as metatags above would apply.

(e) Internet domain names

The mere registration of a domain name would not give rise to liability, as there would not be the necessary use. The Court of Appeal has held that:

> *evidence of the existence per se of domain names and websites featuring the name in which goodwill is said to exist will ordinarily be insufficient as proof of exposure of that name; something in addition to proof of the mere existence of such domain names and websites must be shown in order to establish that there has been sufficient exposure of the name in question.*[75]

(f) Search navigation tools

There has been no judicial consideration of how search navigation tools such as 'breadcrumb trails' may infringe trademarks. However, considering that such tools are merely aids to navigation, it seems unlikely that any confusion would be caused to the user.

---

74 Section 27(4) of the Trademarks Act.

75 *Novelty Pte Ltd v Amanresorts Ltd* [2009] 3 SLR(R) 316 at [54].

(g) ***Hypertext links***

There is no decision on whether hyperlinks would give rise to infringement.

(h) ***Framing***

No Singapore decision has dealt with framing. However, if framing gives the public the false impression that a website is associated with a trademark on the framed page, a case may be made that there is infringement.

2.3 Defences

(a) ***Descriptive (non-trademark) use of the mark***

The Trademarks Act permits descriptive uses of the mark, if they are done in accordance with honest practices in industrial or commercial matters.[76]

(b) ***Comparative advertising***

The Trademarks Act permits the use of a registered trademark which constitutes fair use in comparative commercial advertising or promotion.[77]

However, where the use of the established brand involves some falsehood, the established brand proprietor may have recourse in the common law action for malicious or injurious falsehood.[78]

(c) ***Parody***

The Trademarks Act permits the use of a registered trademark where the use is for a non-commercial purpose.[79]

2.4 Parallel imports

Parallel imports are allowed under the Trademarks Act.[80]

2.5 Remedies

In an action for infringement of a registered trademark, the possible remedies include: an injunction; a monetary award (damages; account of profits; statutory damages);[81] an order for erasure of the offending sign;[82] and an order for delivery up and disposal of the infringing goods.[83]

In an action for infringement of a well-known trademark,[84] the only remedy available is an injunction.[85] However, where the action is to restrain use of the well-known trademark as a 'business identifier',[86] the court may also make an order to

76 Section 28 of the Trademarks Act.
77 Section 28(4)(a) and Section 55A(3)(a) of the Trademarks Act.
78 *Integrated Information Pte Ltd v CD-Biz Directories Pte Ltd* [1998] SGHC 356.
79 Sections 28(4)(b) and 55A(3)(b) of the Trademarks Act.
80 Section 29 of the Trademarks Act.
81 Section 31 of the Trademarks Act.
82 Section 32 of the Trademarks Act.
83 Sections 33 and 34 of the Trademarks Act.
84 Section 2(1), (7), (8) and (9) of the Trademarks Act. A well-known trademark may be registered or unregistered.
85 Section 55(2) and (3) of the Trademarks Act.

cancel registration of the offending entry in any record maintained[87] (eg, in the Registry of Companies).

It may also be possible to bring a common law action for passing off in respect of unregistered marks,[88] if the plaintiff can show:[89]

- the plaintiff has acquired goodwill in its goods or services provided by it;
- the defendant had misrepresented to the public, leading to or likely to lead to the public believing that goods or services provided by the defendant are those of the plaintiffs; and
- there is damage or likelihood of damage to the plaintiff's goodwill as a result of the misrepresentation.

2.6 Liability of ISP

Under the Electronic Transactions Act,[90] network service providers enjoy immunity from civil or criminal liability for third-party content to which they merely provide access, if the liability is founded on the infringement of any rights in relation to such content.[91]

2.7 Advertising law and policy

The Advertising Standards Authority of Singapore (ASAS) has published the Singapore Code of Advertising Practice ('the Code'), which "seeks to promote a high standard of ethics in advertising by self-regulation against the background of national law and international law and practice, including the International Code of Advertising Practice published by the International Chamber of Commerce". The Code applies to internet advertising.[92]

Regulation 12 of the Code provides for the following in respect of trademarks:

12.1 Advertisements should not make unjustifiable use of the name, initials, logo and/or trade and service marks of any firm, company or institution.

12.2 Advertisements should not take unfair advantage of another firm, person or institution's goodwill in its name, trade name or other intellectual property, or the goodwill earned by others' advertising and promotion campaigns.

The Code applies to all parties concerned with advertising whether as "advertisers, advertising practitioners, sales promoters, agencies, or the media". The Code further provides that it shall be complied with "for all advertisements appearing in Singapore regardless of their place of origin".

The ASAS has the power to ask an advertiser or advertising agency to amend or withdraw any advertisement which is, in the ASAS' opinion, contrary to the Code.

---

86 Section 2(1) of the Trademarks Act defines the term as "any sign capable of being represented graphically which is used to identify any business".

87 Section 55(5) of the Trademarks Act.

88 See eg, *CDL Hotels International Ltd v Pontiac Marina Pte Ltd* [1998] 1 SLR(R) 975.

89 *Tessensohn Denyse Bernadette (t/a Clea Professional Image Consultants) v John Robert Powers School Inc* [1994] 1 SLR(R) 470.

90 Cap 88, 2011 Rev Ed.

91 Section 26(1)(b) of the Electronic Transactions Act.

92 Regulation 2.2 provides that the Code shall apply to "advertisements in information network services, electronic bulletin boards, on-line databases and internet services".

2.8 Domain name disputes

The Singapore Network Information Centre is responsible for the registration and administration of the .sg domain names in Singapore.

In the event of competing claims or disputes over any domain name registrations, administrative proceedings will be conducted according to the rules for the Singapore Domain Name Dispute Resolution Policy (SDRP) and the supplemental rules for the SDRP issued jointly by the Singapore Mediation Centre and the Singapore International Arbitration Centre as the joint operators of the secretariat established to provide the administrative dispute resolution service under the policy.

Under the SDRP, a registrant of a .sg domain name is required to submit to a mandatory administrative proceeding when a complainant asserts that:

- the registrant's domain name is identical or confusingly similar to a name, trademark or service mark in which the complainant has rights;
- the registrant has no rights or legitimate interests in respect of the domain name; and
- the registrant's domain name has been registered or is being used in bad faith.

2.9 Unfair competition/passing off

The law of passing off is unlikely to provide advantages over the provisions of the Trademarks Act in the context of internet use of trademarks, except that protection extends to goodwill in unregistered marks.

3. Patents

This section examines issues of patent law in relation to the Internet.

3.1 Patentability of 'internet' inventions

(a) Computer programs

A computer program can be patented if it fulfils the requirements for patentability under the Patents Act,[93] as follows:

- it is new;
- it involves an inventive step;
- it is capable of industrial application; and
- its publication or exploitation would not encourage offensive, immoral or anti-social behaviour.[94]

(b) Business methods

The Court of Appeal has recognised that business methods can be patented.[95]

(c) Mathematical methods

Mathematical methods can be patented.

---

93 Cap 221, 2005 Rev Ed.

94 Section 13 of the Patents Act.

(d) *Presentation of information*

It is arguable that a certain manner of presentation of information can be patented if it satisfies the requirements for patentability, although it would appear that protection is more appropriately sought under the law of copyright and registered designs.

3.2 Bioinformatics

Bioinformatics can be patented. In *Genelabs Diagnostics Pte Ltd v Institut Pasteur,*[96] the Court of Appeal upheld a patent for, *inter alia,* the HIV-2 retrovirus, antigens of HIV-2, assay methods and diagnostic kits based on such antigens for the *in vitro* detection of HIV-2 antibodies.

3.3 Issues specific to Singapore

(a) *Infringement on the Internet*

The court may assume jurisdiction where, under the Patents Act,[97] the defendant prima facie infringes the patented product or process by doing any of the listed acts in Singapore without the consent of the patent proprietor, including disposing of the product and offering to dispose of the product.

Territoriality issues arise when the defendant's disposal or offer to dispose of the infringing products is made via the Internet. In *Trek Technology (Singapore) Pte Ltd v FE Global Electronics Pte Ltd,*[98] the defendant was the manufacturer of the infringing products. The manufacture took place outside of Singapore. The defendant sold the infringing products to another party who imported the products into Singapore. The plaintiff's complaint was based on the defendant's advertisements for the infringing products appearing on its website.

The High Court assessed the purpose and effect of the defendant's online advertisements and held that a reasonable user of the Internet would understand that the defendant's online advertisements were targeted at the Singapore market. The defendant's website had 'Singapore' on its list of countries where its products were sold. There were also links to the defendant's website placed through the Singapore importer's website. Therefore, the defendant was held to be liable for offering to dispose of the infringing product in Singapore.

(b) *Process patents*

Where the process used by a defendant is not identical to the plaintiff's process, it is a matter of construction of the patent to determine whether the defendant's process falls within the scope of the patented process.[99]

---

95 *First Currency Choice Pte Ltd v Main-Line Corporate Holdings Ltd* [2008] 1 SLR(R) 335.

96 [2000] 3 SLR(R) 530.

97 Section 66(1)(a) (product patents) and (1)(b) and (c) (process patents) of the Patents Act.

98 [2005] 3 SLR(R) 389.

99 There is no Singapore case dealing with culpability in a situation where only some parts of an entire patented process are carried out in Singapore.

3.4 Remedies available for patent infringement

Under the Patents Act, the following remedies may be ordered:[100]

- an injunction;
- a monetary award in the form of damages or account of profits;
- a declaration that the patent is valid and has been infringed by the defendant; and
- an order for delivery up or for destruction of the infringing product, or any article in which the product is inextricably comprised, or any material or implement the predominant use of which has been in the creation of the infringing product.

4. Disclosure orders against ISPs

4.1 Availability

A copyright owner or exclusive licensee[101] may apply for an order against an ISP for third-party discovery and/or third-party interrogatories under the Rules of Court,[102] compelling the ISP to disclose the identity and contact details of a user of their service who is suspected of infringing intellectual property rights.

4.2 Requirements

The court will consider the relevance of the documents or interrogatories sought, whether the ISP has possession, custody or power of documents, and whether the discovery or interrogatories are necessary for the fair disposal of the case or for saving costs.[103]

4.3 Jurisdictional issues

Since intellectual property rights are territorial in nature, relief would not be granted where the infringing acts are performed outside Singapore.

Conversely, if infringing acts are performed within Singapore by parties situated outside Singapore, service out of jurisdiction on those parties may be permitted such that a Singapore court can exercise its jurisdiction over them.[104]

4.4 'John Doe' injunctions

'John Doe' injunctions are not granted by the Singapore courts.

---

100 Section 67(1) of the Patents Act.

101 But not a person representing the owner of a copyright, even if he/she is the latter's authorised agent (*Odex Pte Ltd v Pacific Internet Ltd* [2008] 3 SLR(R) 18).

102 Cap 322, R 5, 2006 Rev Ed.

103 Order 24, rule 7 of the Rules of Court.

104 Section 16(1) of the Supreme Court of Judicature Act (Cap 322, 2007 Rev Ed); Sections 19(2) and 52(1) of the Subordinate Courts Act (Cap 321, 2007 Rev Ed); Order 11 of the Rules of Court.

South Korea

DuckSoon Chang
Chang-Hwan Shin
Kim & Chang

1. Copyright, database rights and design rights

1.1 Overview

Article 2 of the Copyright Act ('CA', No 11110, amended on December 2 2011, effective as of March 15 2012) defines the term 'work' as an 'original' as well as 'a creative production' that expresses some human idea or feeling, and an 'author' as a person who 'creates' such a work. Thus, to be protected by copyright, a work must be original, creative, and expressive. Mere ideas, as opposed to original expression, will not be protected.

The CA non-exhaustively lists examples of categories of protected works according to the forms they take. If a type of work is not included in this list, it may still be protected under the CA if it is a subject matter that falls under the general definition provided in Article 2. The list of categories of protected works includes literature, music, plays, visual art, architecture, photography, motion pictures, figures and diagrams, computer programs, compilations, etc.

Among these categories, the following are noteworthy:

(a) *Literary works and artistic works*

Literary and dramatic works include novels, poems, theses, lectures, recitations, plays, computer programs, etc.

Artistic works include paintings, calligraphic works, sculptures, crafts, and works of applied art etc. Among others things, the CA defines 'works of applied art' as an artistic work which can be reproduced in the same shape, for example, as industrially made products, but which possesses some originality that may be recognised separately from the goods in which the work might be embodied (Article 2(15)). This provision seems to codify a prior decision of the Korean Supreme Court which, in cases of industrial designs of mass produced products, had held that copyright protection is available only in the exceptional case where the industrial design at issue has some independent artistic value or characteristics considered separately from the function of the products made according to the design.[1] Accordingly, copyright will protect artistic aspects or elements of a work of applied art that can be independently recognised from the functional, physical, or conceptual aspects of embodiments of the work.

1 *State v Daehan Textile, Ltd,* Case No 94Do3266 (Supreme Court, February 23 1996).

(b) *Films, sound recordings, and broadcasts*

Films may be protected by copyright under the label of 'cinematographic works'. Special rules will be applied to cinematographic works, such as terms of protection or transference of rights of individual contributors.

On the other hand, performances, sound recordings, and broadcasts may be protected by neighbouring rights. As a safeguard, the CA provides that its provisions with respect to neighbouring rights shall not be construed as having effects on copyright (Article 65).

(c) *Typographical arrangement of a published edition*

The Korean copyright system does not recognise the independent protection of typographical arrangements, but if a typographical arrangement has sufficient originality and creativity, then it may be protected by copyright in principle.

(d) *Protection of the user interface*

In principle, the look and feel of a graphical user interface may be copyrightable if it has sufficient originality and creativity. Similarly, works that express human ideas and emotions in an original manner are copyrightable, in principle.

(e) *Computer-generated works*

As noted above, works that express human ideas and emotions in an original manner are copyrightable in principle. Thus, it is debateable as to whether purely computer-generated works may be copyrightable, in that they may not manifest human expression. However, there is no court precedent on point.

(f) *Websites protected as databases*

A database is a compilation that arranges or composes subject matter systematically so that such subject matter may be accessed or searched individually.

Regardless of whether a database as a whole is protected by copyright, a *sui generis* right may be available in its content not protected by copyright. For this right to arise, the maker of the database must have invested substantial human capital or financial resources in the verification, renewal, or supplementing of database content.

Although there is no court precedent on this point, websites may theoretically be protected by the *sui generis* right granted over databases.

(g) *Compilations*

A compilation is any compilation that, by reason of the selection or arrangement of its subject matter, constitutes an intellectual creation. A compilation is protected under the Copyright Act, provided that it displays creativity in the selection, arrangement, or composition of its materials.

1.2 Infringing acts

(a) *Copying*

Temporary copies: The newly amended Copyright Act incorporates temporary fixing into the concept of reproduction by defining the term 'reproduction' as "fixing onto, or re-producing into, a tangible object, whether temporarily or permanently, through such methods as printing, photographing, photocopying, audio recording, and video recording, among others". However, it also provides an exception that in the event of using works on a computer, the works may be reproduced temporarily on the computer to the extent necessary for efficient data processing.

In any medium: Reproduction is defined as fixation on, or remaking "... by means of printing, photographing, duplicating, sound or visual recording, or other means". In the case of an architectural work, it also means "construction in accordance with the relevant models or plans". In the case of a play, musical score, and any other similar work, it includes 'recording' a performance or broadcast. Thus, reproduction encompasses reproduction in any medium.

(b) *Issuing copies to the public*

The author of a work has the right to distribute the embodiment of his/her work or copies thereof. Distribution is defined as the 'transfer or rental' of original embodiments or copies to the general public, whether for a price or free of charge. The distribution right is limited by the 'first sale' or 'exhaustion' doctrine: if an embodiment or copy of a work is delivered to the general trade for sale with the consent of the author, it may be distributed successively thereafter without such consent; however, the rights holder retains the right to authorise the rental of commercial phonograms or computer programs even after such sale.

(c) *Communicating work to the public*

This right includes the making available of protected materials to members of the public via wireless or wired communications and it comprises broadcasting, transmission, and digital-audio transmission, defined as follows:

- *Broadcasting* is defined as the "transmission of voices, sounds, or images by wire or wireless communications intended for a concurrent reception by the public".
- *Transmission* is, alternatively, defined as comparable acts "so as to have the public receive or use [transmitted content] at individually selected times and places". Accordingly, it includes on-demand network access but excludes digital-audio transmission.
- *Digital-audio transmission* is any digital transmission of sounds commenced at the request of members of the public for the purpose of enabling them to receive the sounds simultaneously. It thus includes webcasting.

(d) ***Perform, show or play work in public***

The author of a work has the right to perform his/her work publicly. Public performance means the "presentation of the work to the public by acting, musical playing, singing, reciting, screening, or by other means" and also publicly playing or showing 'reproductions', notably recordings, and includes any 'transmission made in a connected place' possessed by the same party. The author also has the right to exhibit the embodiment or copies of his/her work publicly.

(e) ***Rent or lend the work to the public***

See section 1.2(b) above.

(f) ***Secondary infringement***

Korean courts recognise indirect liability (eg, vicarious and contributory liability). In respect of the online environment, courts often hold that the failure of the defendant (ie, the online service provider) to take reasonable measures to cease or to prevent illegal transmission of copyrighted works by direct infringers makes the defendant indirectly liable.

1.3 Test for copyright infringement

There is little Korean jurisprudence indicating how substantial a taking should be in order for it to constitute infringement.

A special provision of the Copyright Act governing computer programs provides some guidance for analysing takings. It excludes the following from protection: programming languages, conventions on the usage of programming languages, and algorithms, such that taking any of these from a program does not necessarily infringe copyright in the program.

1.4 Exemptions/defences to copyright infringement

(a) ***Private use***

For the purpose of his/her personal, family, or other similar uses within a limited circle, a user may reproduce a work already made public. However, copying by publicly available reproduction or recording equipment does not fall within the exception of private use.

(b) ***Fair use***

The Copyright Act as amended on December 2 2011 newly incorporates a complementary catch-all provision for fair use of works. This expressly allows use of copyrighted works for the purposes of reporting, criticism, education and research, etc to the extent that such use does not conflict with the ordinary use of the works, if such use does not unfairly adversely affect the authors' reasonable profit. The provision includes a list of the factors to be considered in determining whether a specific use falls under the fair use provision (CA, Article 35-3).

(c) ***Caching/temporary copies as part of communication process, hosting and information searching***

The amended Copyright Act, effective as of July 1 2011, provides a clear and detailed list of the requirements for the exemption from liability of an online service provider under each of four types of conduct (ie, mere conduit, caching, hosting or information searching). On meeting the aforementioned requirements, an online service provider will not be held responsible for monitoring whether or not an infringing act occurs within the scope of the service that it provides, or for actively investigating the infringing act.

More specifically, an online service provider will not be liable for such infringement if the following requirements are met:

- With respect to an act of transmitting a copyrighted work without modifying the content thereof or designating a route, or an act of storing the work automatically, intermediately and temporarily within a time period reasonably required for such transmission:
  - if the online service provider does not commence the transmission of the copyrighted work; and
  - if the online service provider does not select the work or recipients.
- With respect to an act of storing a copyrighted work automatically, intermediately and temporarily for the purpose of enabling a user effectively to access or receive the work that has been transmitted upon the user's request:
  - if the online service provider does not commence the transmission of the copyrighted work;
  - if the online service provider does not select the work or recipients;
  - if the online service provider does not amend the work;
  - (in the case where there are preconditions to meet to have access to the work) if only users who satisfy the conditions are allowed to have access to the work that is stored temporarily;
  - if the rules on updating of copyrighted works under the regulations on data communication regarding computers or information and communication networks that are generally accepted in the relevant industry, which is stipulated by a person who reproduces and transmits a work, are complied with;
  - if the use of technology that is applied on the site where the copyrighted work is originally located so as to obtain information on the use of the work and that is generally recognised in the relevant industry, is not interrupted; and
  - if the online service provider immediately deletes or blocks access to the copyrighted work upon receiving a request for suspension of reproduction or transmission of the work, if the work is deleted from the site where it was located originally or it becomes impossible to access the work, or upon learning that a court or the head of relevant central administrative authorities has issued an order to delete or block access to the work.

- With respect to an act of storing a copyrighted work in the computer of an online service provider upon request of a person who has reproduced and transmitted the work:
  - if the online service provider does not commence the transmission of the copyrighted work;
  - if the online service provider does not select the work or recipients;
  - if the online service provider does not obtain monetary profit directly from an infringing act by the user because it has the authority and ability to control such infringing act;
  - if the reproduction or transmission of the work is suspended immediately upon actually learning or becoming aware of facts or circumstances through a user's suspension request that there is a clear infringement; and
  - if a specific person who will receive requests for suspension of the reproduction or transmission of the work is appointed and publicly announced.
- With respect to an act of enabling users to know the location of a copyrighted work on the information and communication network or connect the same through an information retrieval tool:
  - if the online service provider does not commence the transmission of the copyrighted work;
  - if the online service provider does not select the work or recipients;
  - if the online service provider does not obtain monetary profit directly from an infringing act by the user because it has the authority and ability to control such infringing act;
  - if the reproduction or transmission of the work is suspended immediately upon actually learning or becoming aware of facts or circumstances, through a user's suspension request, that there is a clear infringement; and
  - if a specific person who will receive requests for suspension of the reproduction or transmission of the work is appointed and publicly announced.

(d) Back-up copies

An end-user may make a back-up copy of software as long as he/she retains legal control over the initial copy.

1.5 Remedies available for copyright infringement

In civil cases, a copyright holder can seek an injunction, damages, or both against copyright infringers. If an urgent injunction is necessary, the owner can seek a preliminary injunction order. In criminal cases, copyright infringers may be sentenced to imprisonment for up to five years, a fine up to 50 million Korean Won, or both. The Customs Office may temporarily seize copyright-infringing products.

1.6 Copyright liability

(a) *Hosting/cloud computing where infringing content uploaded by user of service*

See the comments in section 1.4(c) above.

(b) *Hypertext linking*

Acts facilitating links to infringing materials online may, but do not necessarily, lead to liability for infringement. The Supreme Court has had to rule on a case in which a songwriter had sued online services: users had set up websites that featured links to sites of the defendant's services, from which illegally uploaded files, including the plaintiff's songs, were downloaded or played. It was argued, *inter alia*, that the defendants should be held liable for the resulting infringement because they had provided tags to their users that had facilitated the posting of links to their own sites, from which the songs were made available without the plaintiff's authorisation. On the one hand, the Supreme Court held that the defendants' acts of thus facilitating links, albeit to their own websites which enabled infringing reproductions or transmissions, did not suffice to trigger liability. On the other hand, it held these defendants liable for providing services that allowed users to download and play the plaintiff's songs.[2]

(c) *P2P network*

Suppliers of P2P software: Suppliers of P2P software may be liable for copyright infringement. The popular P2P software Soribada (which means 'sea of sound' in Korean), did incur criminal liability. The Supreme Court, setting aside the defence of the substantial possibility of non-infringing uses, specifically held that "the crime of aiding and abetting copyright infringement includes all direct and indirect acts of facilitating or accommodating the illegal reproduction activities (that is, the direct infringement) and does not require actual or specific knowledge of the timing, location or identity of the wrongdoer of the direct infringement".[3] On that basis and on remand, the lower court found Soribada guilty of participation in criminal infringement.[4] In civil cases, Soribada had already been enjoined from disseminating its file-sharing software.[5]

Uploaders/downloaders: While the liability of uploaders has been recognised in finding the liability of suppliers of P2P software, the liability of downloaders has been a controversial issue and it has not yet been settled.

---

2 *Yong-Soo Cho v Danal*, Case No 2008Da77405 (Supreme Court, November 26 2009). This writer would caution against reading this controversial decision broadly, since it was rendered in a case with rather specific facts involving acts 'of facilitating the posting of links' rather than acts 'of providing links'.

3 Case No 2005Do872 (Supreme Court, December 14 2007).

4 Case No 2007No4374 (Seoul Central District Court, May 9 2008).

5 Compare Case No 2002Kahap284 (Suwon District Court, February 14 2003) (where software enabled users to download files stored in each others' personal computers; injunction issued against Soribada even if it "did not directly infringe the copyrights in operating its Internet service", given "the extent of its participation"), and Case No 2004Kahap3491 (Seoul Central District Court, August 29 2005) (where software enabled sharing via some end-users' 'super peer' computers; software developers were held liable because they knew or should have known of users' infringing activities and offered various user-friendly tools to encourage file sharing).

(d) *Streaming*

In one case, the defendant, who operated a website where users could exchange music recordings by way of streaming, was held liable for aiding and abetting reproduction and transmission of copyrighted recordings by its website members (Seoul District Court 2004KaHap3965, May 30 2005).

In another case, the Bugs Company, operating an internet website for music and other sales services, was found liable for infringing neighbouring rights in recordings when it saved recordings in the process of streaming the music to end-users (Suwon District Court 2002Kahap280, June 25 2003).

(e) *Treatment of user-generated content*

The Seoul High Court ruled that a copyright holder was liable for compensation for losses (rendered on October 13 2010, Seoul High Court 2010Na35260). In this case, the plaintiff created a video file of user-generated content which contained a recording of his daughter singing a musical work of a popular singer, and posted this on his blog. The defendant, a copyright trust management company, requested the suspension of the reproduction and transmission of the plaintiff's video file, claiming that the postings infringed copyrights with which the defendant was entrusted. Accordingly, the operators of the relevant internet portal site removed the postings. The plaintiff then brought a lawsuit against the defendant, claiming compensation for the losses that the plaintiff had incurred as a result of the defendant's request to suspend the reproduction and transmission of the works. The court ruled that the plaintiff's video file fell under the copyright exception for fair use of published works (Article 28 of the Copyright Act), and awarded damages to the plaintiff in accordance with Article 103(6) of the Copyright Act, which provides that a person that has requested an online service provider to suspend the reproduction and transmission of a copyrighted work without any legitimate rights should compensate for any losses caused.

1.7 Joint liability for ISPs

In theory, joint liability may be recognised for direct infringers and internet service providers (ISPs). However, in practice, rights holders have a tendency to pursue only ISPs, because going after the direct infringer is not considered to be an easy task and with little to recover.

1.8 Relief

There is no relief that can be granted if the ISP is not held indirectly liable for copyright infringement.

1.9 Issues specific to Korea

(a) *Jurisdiction*

Pursuant to the Berne Convention, Korean courts have jurisdiction over copyright infringement cases if the infringement at issue occurred in Korea.

(b) *Claim to infringement of foreign copyright*

Works of foreigners are entitled to protection:

- under treaties to which Korea has acceded;
- if such works are first published in Korea or published in Korea within 30 days of first being published elsewhere; or
- if the author resides in Korea.

Foreign works that are protectable under the Copyright Act will enjoy the same terms of protection as domestic works, if they satisfy any of the above conditions.

1.10 Orphan works

Where a person who wishes to use a certain work has been unable to obtain a licence or authorisation from the rights holder because he/she has not been able to identify or contact the holder of the economic rights, in spite of having made reasonable efforts, a party who wishes to use protected content may obtain a licence through an approval from the Minister of Culture, Sports and Tourism upon the payment or deposit of compensation in the amount determined by that minister. However, with effect from June 29 2007, foreign orphan works are not subject to this non-voluntary licence.

1.11 Online piracy measures

A rights holder may avail itself of a notice-and-takedown procedure with an online service provider who enables the internet reproduction or transmission of protected subject matter, notably works, phonograms, or databases. The rights holder may also request an online service provider to take technical measures to prevent infringing activities such as file-sharing. In either case, in complying, the service provider may avoid or limit its liability for infringement.

1.12 Electronic infringement of moral rights

(a) *False attribution – right to guard against impersonation on the Internet*

The author has the right to have his/her name or pseudonym indicated on embodiments and copies of the work and in making it public. This right also entitles the author contractually to require assignees or licensees to indicate his/her name or pseudonym. Absent the author's declaration to the contrary, it suffices to follow his/her prior manner of indicating his/her authorship. However, omission may be excused where it is unavoidable due to both the nature and use of the work.

(b) *Paternity right*

An author has the right to maintain the identity of his/her work, notably the integrity of its content, format, and title. Nonetheless, the author's objection to a modification may not be given effect if the modification at issue is not to a substantial part of the work. This will be the case where the modification:

- relates to expansion, remodelling, or other forms of alteration of a work of architecture;

- involves any other modifications within the limits found unavoidable in the light of the nature of the work or the purpose and manner of its exploitation; or
- if the work is used for school or other educational purposes under the appropriate exception and if the modification at issue is made within the scope deemed unavoidable for such purposes.

2. Trademarks

2.1 Use of a trademark

Generally, in order to satisfy trademark use requirements for defending a non-use claim in Korea, the use of a trademark must be within the Korean market and geared towards Korean consumers. Thus, the use of a trademark on a website will constitute valid 'use' if it is conducted in Korea.

For example, advertising and promoting a trademark, or selling goods bearing a trademark on a Korean website will all be considered valid 'use'. This also means that advertising and sales on a foreign website operated by a foreign entity would not likely be deemed valid trademark use, since Korean courts will likely consider such use as occurring outside of Korea. Although there is an Intellectual Property Tribunal decision ruling that trademark use on a foreign website may be considered sufficient as long as Korean consumers can access the website and make purchases (Case No 2007Dang344, decided on July 31 2007), this is not a mainstream decision.

In order to claim trademark infringement, the alleged infringer's 'use' of the trademark must be in commerce, for business purposes, and as a source identifier.

2.2 Infringement

Aside from internet domain names, there are a few Korean cases on point covering the following issues.

(a) Metatags and hidden text

One district court decision held that solely based on the fact that a trademark is used in a search engine, it is difficult to recognise a likelihood of consumer confusion between the owner of the mark and the operator of a website that can be found as a result of an internet search using the mark (Seoul Southern District Court Case No 2002Kahap14533, decided on April 29 2004). Although this decision did not explicitly mention the terms 'keyword' and/or 'hidden text', it is related to these issues.

(b) Keywords and sponsored links

The Supreme Court has ruled that whether use of a term as a keyword also constitutes use as a source identifier should be determined on a case-by-case basis, and such determinations should depend on the content of the advertisement in which the mark is used and how the mark is used (Supreme Court Case No 2010Hu3073, decided on May 24 2012). In this case, the defendant purchased the keyword from a website providing an online search engine, and when internet users typed the keyword in the search engine, the defendant's advertisement was shown as a sponsored link with the title including the keyword. In addition, the defendant's products and company website address were indicated underneath and users could be forwarded to the defendant's company site by clicking the sponsored link. The court found that in this case the keyword was used by the defendant as a source identifier and such use was infringing the trademark owner's rights.

(c) *Internet domain names*

The Supreme Court ruled that in deciding whether use of a domain name incorporating a trademark of another constitutes trademark infringement, the court must consider the totality of circumstances, including how the domain name was used, the content of the website linked to the domain name etc, and that if the domain name in question indicates the source of product and functions as the source identifier of the domain name owner's product, which distinguishes it from the products of others, trademark infringement liability should be imposed (Supreme Court Case No 2010Do7088, decided on August 25 2011).

However, a cybersquatter's mere registration of a famous trademark may be regulated under Korea's Unfair Competition Prevention and Trade Secret Protection Act (UCPA) and the Internet Address Resource Act (IARA). If the domain name is not used for a functioning website, the rightful trademark owner may have a claim under the anti-cybersquatting provision of the UCPA or the IARA, because the domain name registrant is interfering with the rightful owner's registration and use of the domain name.

2.3 Defences

As discussed above, case law in connection with trademark infringement on the Internet has room to be further developed in Korea, but if cases were to arise, we would expect that the defences available against offline infringement would be applicable in this area. Some of the available defences are as follows:

- descriptive use;
- comparative advertising;
- use of a trade name which has been used without any unfair competitive purpose prior to the registration of the subject trademark.

2.4 Parallel imports

As long as the goods are authentic, sales of parallel imports via a website are not considered to be trademark infringement in Korea. However, if the parallel importer's 'use' of the trademark goes beyond the scope necessary for selling its parallel imported goods and such 'use' causes consumer confusion regarding a business relationship with the trademark owner, then there may be a UCPA violation. For instance, the UCPA may restrict the parallel importer's 'use' of the mark on business cards, exterior signboards, shopping bags etc, because it causes consumer confusion that the parallel importer is the trademark owner's authorised distributor.

2.5 Remedies

The civil remedies available to a trademark owner for trademark infringement include a preliminary or permanent injunction, and compensatory damages, including compensation for injury to the trademark owner's reputation. The criminal penalties for trademark infringement are up to seven years' imprisonment and a fine of up to 100 million Korean Won.

2.6 Liability of ISPs

There are no cases on point relating to ISPs, but in the case of open market sites (ie, online marketplaces linking a variety of sellers and buyers), the Supreme Court ruled that an open market operator is required to take appropriate measures, if the listing on the open market site is clearly infringing, the trademark owner requested that the specific listing be removed or blocked, or it is apparent that the open market operator could have easily recognised the infringement from the appearance of the listing even without notice from the trademark owner; and the open market operator has the technological and economical means to manage and control the listings. If an open market operator neglects its duty, and thus facilitates the individual seller's infringement, the open market operator will be jointly liable for abetting the individual seller's infringing activities. However, an open market operator does not have a duty to provide the trademark owner with the seller's personal information or other sales information connected with the infringing listing (Supreme Court Case No 2010Ma817, decided on December 4 2012).

2.7 Advertising law and regulation

The Fair Labelling and Advertising Act of Korea is applicable to internet advertising and the regulation states that false or exaggerated, deceptive, unlawful comparative, or slanderous labelling and advertising is unlawful, and the representative of the responsible company would be subject to civil liability, as well as up to two years' imprisonment or a fine of up to 150 million Korean Won. Administrative sanctions, such as corrective measures, temporary business suspension, fines etc may also be imposed.

However, in a case where an open market site operator used a banner advertisement on its site but there was a discrepancy between the advertisement and the actual product as to the product details, and as a result, the Korean Fair Trade Commission issued a corrective order to rectify it, the Supreme Court held that the banner advertisement in question constituted a false advertisement under Article 21(1)(i) of the Act on Consumer Protection in Electronic Commerce Transactions, etc (Supreme Court Case No 2010Du24371, decided on June 28 2012).

2.8 Domain name disputes

An administrative proceeding before the Internet Address Dispute Resolution Committee is available in Korea for the transfer or de-registration of .kr-level domain names, which is similar to a UDRP action. The trademark owner must file various objective evidentiary materials as to the well-known status of the trademark within Korea. Aside from attorney's fees, the official fees are 800,000 Korean Won for one arbitrator and 1,600,000 Korean Won for a three-member panel, exclusive of VAT. It generally takes two to three months from the filing date to obtain a final decision. However, the proceedings could take longer if the registrant were to file response and rebuttal briefs.

2.9 Unfair competition/passing off

Website content may be protected under copyright law, if the content is sufficiently original. Further, the 'look and feel' of a website may be protected under unfair competition law, provided that such look and feel is well known in Korea as a source identifier, and there is a likelihood of consumer confusion and/or dilution due to the use of a similar look and feel.

3. Patents

3.1 Patentability of 'internet' inventions

(a) Computer programs

According to the Examination Guidelines issued by the Korean Intellectual Property Office (KIPO), software or a computer program per se is not a patentable subject matter. However, computer-related inventions can be claimed and patented in the form of a 'method', 'apparatus' or 'computer readable medium' (having a recorded computer program).

(b) Business methods

To qualify as a complete Business Method (BM) invention, a claim should not merely describe a simple idea or a pure method, but concretely and clearly describe all the elements needed to achieve the specific purpose. In this regard, a Korean Supreme Court decision regarding the patentability requirement for a BM invention holds that a claim belonging to the invention category of a business method should describe how the operation or processing of information is executed by specific means using the coordination of software and hardware in each of the steps, and specifically realise the information processing by software on a computer in association with hardware (Supreme Court Case No 2007Hu494, decided on December 11 2008).

(c) Mathematical methods

According to the KIPO Examination Guidelines, if a claimed invention utilises any law other than a law of nature, such as mathematical methods, the claimed invention is not considered to be statutory. However, in a case where a claimed invention is not directed to mathematical principles or a method directly using them, but involves technical devices or a method which gives a useful, concrete and tangible result by increasing or controlling the performance of a certain technical tool with the data, which is converted using mathematical manipulations, if the technical devices or technical methods are considered to be universal, repetitive and objective, they are deemed a statutory invention.

(d) *Presentation of information*

A mere presentation of information where the feature resides solely in the content of the information and its main objective is to present the information, is not considered as a statutory invention (eg, an audio compact disc where the feature resides solely in the music recorded thereon). However, if the technical feature resides in the presentation of information, the presenting itself, the means for presentation and the method for presentation might be considered a statutory invention. For example, the KIPO Examination Guidelines state that a plastic card on which information is recorded with letters, numbers and signs embossed on it can be patentable, since there is a technical feature in the means for presentation of information.

3.2 Bioinformatics

Under Korean patent practice, a novel DNA sequence or protein structure is not patentable for lack of industrial applicability under Article 29 of the Korean Patent Act (KPA) unless its specific, substantial, and credible utility is described in (or can be inferred from) the specification.

For example, even if a novel DNA is likely to be a gene coding for a specific protein based on a homology search using a public database, a description of such a utility alone without any other confirming description is not recognised as satisfying the above requirement. Further, when the specification describes the sequence of a claimed protein only and does not indicate the physical, chemical, and biological properties thereof, the utility of the novel protein is not recognised. For a novel DNA fragment or SNP (single nucleotide polymorphism), describing its possible use in obtaining a full DNA sequence or in forensic detection is insufficient to satisfy the utility requirement; rather, the relationship between the claimed DNA fragment or SNP and a specific disease should be confirmed and demonstrated by experiments and the results showing the relationship should be described in the specification.

3.3 Issues specific to Korea

(a) *Infringement on the Internet*

If all of the steps, as recited in a claim of a Korean patent, are practised in Korea, it is considered a patent infringement under the KPA. In this case, a Korean court has jurisdiction over the patent infringement claim. However, when each step recited in the patent is practised outside Korea via the Internet, it is generally not regarded as infringing the Korean patent.

(b) *Process patents*

In general, when some of the steps, as recited in a claim of a Korean patent, are carried out in a country other than Korea, it is not regarded as infringing a Korean patent based on the all-element rule. However, if the essential step of the invention is carried out in Korea, it may be determined to be a patent infringement for the Korean patent even though some steps are practised in a foreign country. Thus, as regards a case in which the defendant's server is located in a foreign country and the service is provided in Korea, a Korean district court holds that the defendant is carrying out the corresponding service in Korea. This is on the grounds that the main steps of the service are provided through the website on a user's computer located in Korea, the defendant's website provides the service in Korea and its domain address is registered on the Korea Internet & Security Agency, the defendant makes a profit from advertisements through the defendant's website, and the main objective of the service is related to increasing users in Korea and improving advertising revenue (Seoul Central Court Case No 2006 GaHap 73442, decided on September 7 2007).

3.4 Remedies available for patent infringement

(a) *Civil remedies*

For infringement of a patent right, the KPA provides the following three types of civil remedies: injunctive relief (both preliminary and permanent); compensation for loss; and restoration of injured business goodwill or reputation.

An infringement action may be initiated at a district court, and any or all of the civil remedies may be sought in one action. As for actions seeking injunctive relief, there are two proceedings: one for a preliminary injunction and the other for a permanent injunction. While other civil remedies may not be sought together in an action for a preliminary injunction, they can be claimed in a main action together with permanent injunction.

The amount of damages can be presumed to be the number of infringing goods multiplied by the estimated amount of profit per unit that the patentee could have obtained by selling the products if there had been no infringing activity.

If the facts relevant to the amount of damages in an infringement action cannot be proven, the court may decide at its own discretion the amount of damages after considering all the arguments and evidence submitted by the parties.

(b) *Criminal sanctions*

A person who has infringed a patent right or an exclusive licence may be criminally prosecuted, irrespective of the filing of a civil action. However, the criminal prosecution of a patent infringer may not be initiated *ex officio* unless the patentee or his/her exclusive licensee files a criminal complaint.

The maximum penalty for infringement is up to seven years' imprisonment, or a fine of up to 100 million Korean Won.

4. Disclosure orders against ISPs

4.1 Availability

The Act on Promotion of Information and Communications Network Utilization and Information Protection (the PICNU) and the CA provided for such disclosure order.

Under the PICNU, a person who alleges that publishing or circulating information by a specific user has violated his/her rights may file a claim with the defamation dispute conciliation division of the Korea Communications Standards Commission to demand that the relevant ISP furnishes any information it possesses regarding the alleged offender (referring to minimum information including the name, address and contact information necessary for filing a civil or criminal complaint), along with materials supporting his/her allegation of the violation, so that he/she can file a civil or criminal complaint against the alleged offender (Article 44-6).

Under the CA, if a person who alleges that reproduction and/or transmission by a specific user of the service offered by the ISP has violated his/her copyright demands that the relevant ISP furnishes the minimum information it possesses regarding the alleged offender in order to file a civil or criminal complaint, but the ISP rejects such demands, that person may file a claim with the Minister of Culture and Sports to order the relevant ISP to furnish such information (Article 103-3).

According to the PICNU, the Korea Communications Standards Commission (particularly the defamation dispute conciliation division) has dealt reasonably with such claims. In principle, the Korea Communications Standards Commission should issue a decision within 30 days after the receipt of a claim filed by the rights holder according to the internal regulations of the Korea Communications Standards Commission.

4.2 Requirements

The IPR owner should prepare and submit a claim form including: his/her name, address, telephone number and e-mail address; the kind of complaint to be filed (civil or criminal complaint) and the tenor of the claim; the rights infringed by a specific user and the facts relevant to the alleged infringement; information on the relevant ISP such as trade name and contact information; and the fact that he/she has demanded that the relevant ISP should furnish the minimum information possessed by it regarding the alleged offender but that it has rejected such demands (in case of the CA) along with evidentiary documents.

4.3 Jurisdictional issues

The likelihood that the PICNU/the CA will apply to foreign ISPs would depend on various circumstantial factors such as location of the server for the subject website, whether or not the subject website offers its services to users mainly to Korean nationals and so on.

4.4 'John Doe' injunctions

In civil actions, 'John Doe' injunctions against persons unknown are not permitted under Korean law.

Spain

Juan Cuerva de Cañas
Montserrat López-Bellosta
Josep Montefusco Monferrer
Sonia Sebé Marín
Clifford Chance SL

1. Copyright, database rights and design rights

1.1 Overview

Generally, according to the Spanish Copyright Act (SCA) any content, including that of a website, is protected by copyright 'by virtue of the mere creation thereof', when: it is the creation of a human being; is expressed in a medium; and is 'original' (SCA, Article 10).

The first requirement automatically means that only natural persons are authors (SCA, Article 5) and, as such, any computer-generated work, such as drawings, music or translations, would not be considered copyrightable work. In those cases, the computer program containing all of the elements required for the computer to obtain the creative results would be copyrightable.[1] Secondly, the work must be expressed or externalised in a medium or format, where a digital format is perfectly valid to afford a work copyright protection. Finally, the Spanish Supreme Court has opted for an objective interpretation of the requirement of originality. Thus, originality

> *consists of having created something new, something that did not exist before, ie, the creation that contributes and constitutes an objective novelty compared to any other pre-existing one: a novel creation is original, and this objective novelty is what determines its recognition as a work and the copyright protection attributed to it by its creator.*[2]

Therefore, any internet content meeting these three requirements will be considered copyrightable work and will be protected by SCA.

Article 10 of the SCA contains a list of examples of different categories of works, including, *inter alia*, works constituting standard content on the Internet:

- texts, such as definitions, descriptions, narratives, press articles, poetry, in any format (ASCII, DOC, DOCX, HTML, PDF, TRF, TXT, etc), are protected as literary works (SPA, Article 10.1(a));
- musical compositions with or without lyrics, in any format (AUDIO FILES, BEATNIK, MIDI, MP3, REAL AUDIO, QUICKTIME, WAVE, SHOCKWAVE), are protected as musical works (SCA, Article 10.1(b));
- cinematographic works, films, videos, broadcasts and any other audiovisual works, in any format (AVI, MOV, MPEG, REALVIDEO, MKV, SHOCKWAVE,

1 Bercovitz, R, *Manual de Propiedad Intelectual*, Tirant Lo Blanch, Valencia, 2006, page 53.
2 Spanish Supreme Court Judgment, of June 24 2004.

etc) are considered audiovisual works, subject to a specific legal regime in SCA (SCA, Articles 86 *et seq*);

- photographs of persons, products, animals, buildings and monuments, landscapes, etc., in any format (GIF, JPEG, BMP, PNG, TIF, etc.), are considered "photographic works and works expressed by a process analogous to photography" (Article 10.1(h) SCA);[3]
- works of painting, illustrations, drawings, picture stories, cartoons or comics, maps, drawings of architectural works and works of engineering, outlines, diagrams, statistical graphs, etc, in any format (CGM, GIF, JPEG, PNG, SVG, etc), are considered plastic works (SCA, Article 10.1(e), (f) and (g)); and
- pursuant to the provisions of Article 1 of Council Directive 91/250/EEC, software and computer programs are protected as literary works,[4] and are subject to specific SCA regulations (Articles 95 *et seq*).

Collections of independent works, data or other materials arranged in a systematic or methodical way and individually accessible by electronic or other means are deemed to be databases. Databases are also eligible for copyright protection provided that, by reason of their structure, or the selection or arrangement of their contents, they constitute original[5] creations (SCA, Article 12). It is important to clarify, for the avoidance of doubt, that database protection does not affect the content thereof and such protection is compatible with the protection that may exist over the data/content of the database.[6]

Together with databases, SCA, implementing Directive 96/9/EC, also protects those other databases that, not being original, have entailed for the manufacturer:

a substantial investment, evaluated either qualitatively or quantitatively in the form of the deployment of financial resources and/or the expending of time, effort and energy or other such means in either the obtaining, verification or presentation of the contents.

The *sui generis* right in databases (SCA, Articles 133 *et seq*) does not grant the manufacturer traditional exploitation rights (ie, reproduction, distribution, communication to the public and transformation). However, it does grant the manufacturer the right to prevent third parties from:

- the extracting and/or re-utilising "the whole or a substantial part, evaluated

---

3 Photographs that simply reproduce everyday scenes are not considered photographic works, but ordinary photographs. The author of ordinary photographs has the exclusive right to license the reproduction, distribution and communication thereof to the public for a term of 25 years as of January 1 in the year subsequent to the date on which the photograph was taken or the reproduction made (SCA, Article 128).

4 The Spanish Supreme Court Judgment of December 17 2004 declared that computer programs and software are protected as literary works.

5 The Spanish Supreme Court judgment of October 17 2007 found that a list of companies prepared by the Chamber of Commerce containing tax, labour and commercial data obtained from the public registries was not original. Meanwhile, in the judgments dated January 30 2008, July 8 2008 and December 18 2008, the Spanish Supreme Court found that originality did exist and, therefore, the database was protected. On the treatment of databases in recent Supreme Court case law, see Marín Lopez, JJ, *'La protección de las bases de datos por el derecho de propiedad intelectual en la praxis reciente del Tribunal Supremo'*, *Comunicaciones en Propiedad Industrial y Derecho de la Competencia*, CEFI, nº 53, January–March 2009, pages 49 to 70.

6 Esteve Pardo, Ma A, *Propiedad Intelectual. Doctrina y jurisprudencia*, Tirant lo Blanch, Valencia, 2009, pages 523 *et seq*. Bercovitz, R, *'La protección jurídica de las bases de datos'*, *Pe.I*, nº 1, 1999, pages 11 *et seq*.

qualitatively and/or quantitatively, of the contents of that database, provided that the obtaining, verification or presentation of the contents represents a qualitatively or quantitatively substantial investment"; and/or
- the "repeated and systematic extraction and/or re-utilisation of insubstantial parts of the contents of a database implying acts which conflict with a normal exploitation of that database or which unreasonably prejudice the legitimate interests of the maker of the database".

As far as websites are concerned, SCA contains no specific regulations. This has been conducive to authors posing the question as to whether a website can per se constitute a copyrightable work, or whether copyright protection can only be obtained for the different elements comprising it. Since a website is a complex computer product combining on the one hand a computer program (back-end), and on the other hand its visual presentation (front-end), composed of different elements, such as texts, videos, photographs, music, etc, the majority of authors[7] consider that websites, as such, are copyrightable works protected as a whole. This does not prevent the works comprising the website from being exploited separately and, precisely depending on the most significant element of the website, it can be classified as:
- a literary work, in those cases in which the website contains text only or text with some accessory images;
- an audiovisual work, when the website mainly consists of a collection of related images, in some sort of sequential order; or
- a database, when the originality of the website resides in the structure, selection or arrangement of its contents. This applies to the majority of websites and web pages, pursuant to the provisions of SCA, Article 12, where: they consist of 'works, data or other materials'; the materials comprising the contents of the web page or website are 'independent' (ie, they can be separated from each other without affecting their informative, artistic or other value); such materials are 'individually accessible' because, by accessing the web 'homepage', the user does not display all of the contents, but generally finds a menu, which can be deployed by clicking on the corresponding buttons; and all of the materials are 'systematically or methodically arranged'.

The interaction between the website and the user is achieved by means of the graphical user interface. As the European Court of Justice ruled in its judgment dated December 22 2010,[8] the graphical user interface "does not enable the reproduction of that computer program, but merely constitutes one element of that program". Thus, the graphical user interface does not constitute a computer program and "it cannot be

7 Garrote Fernández-Déz, I and González Gonzalo, A, '*La protección de las páginas y sitios web a través de la propiedad intelectual*'. *Pe.I*, nº 8, 2001, pages 85 to 90; Minero Alejandre, G, '*Reflexiones acerca de la protección jurídica de las páginas web y la potencial capacidad del derecho de autor y del derecho sui generis sobre bases de datos para adaptarse a las peculiaridades técnicas de las primeras*', *Pe.I*, nº 39, 2011, pages 37 to 114.

8 Case C-393/09.

specifically protected by copyright in computer programs". However, "the graphic user interface can, as a work, be protected by copyright if it is its author's own intellectual creation". Thus, from the perspective of the SCA, 'originality' will have to be decided in accordance with the interpretation given by the Spanish Supreme Court.

1.2 Infringing acts

Under the SCA, the author has the exclusive exploitation rights in any form, especially rights of reproduction, distribution, communication to the public (including the right of making available to the public) and transformation, which rights may not be exercised without its authorisation, except where the SCA stipulates an exemption or limitation. Therefore, any of these acts, including the rental and lending of the works, requires the author's prior consent, without which a copyright infringing act will have been committed. Since the Spanish civil liability system is based on the attribution of fault, it can be said, in general, that third parties that authorise or provide the necessary means for a person to perform acts of infringement do not incur civil liability, except in the specific cases provided for in Law 34/2002[9] (LSSI) with regard to internet service providers (ISPs).

In the digital environment (ie, the Internet) the reproduction right is the most important right because reproduction is an essential first step for the communication of online content. The reproduction right is defined in SCA, Article 18:

Reproduction is construed as the direct or indirect, temporary or permanent, fixation, by any means and in any form, of the work in whole or in part, in such a way as to permit the communication and copying thereof.

Although the reproduction right was traditionally linked to the idea of the copying of the work, with the current definition following the implementation of Directive 2001/29/EC, the reproduction right would appear to emphasise the fixation of the work, albeit temporary or permanent, the subsequent copying of the work being secondary. Therefore, from this perspective, reproduction is not so much the copying of the work as its fixation in any form. Nevertheless, it is accepted that the global concept of the reproduction right includes both the fixation of the work and the obtaining of copies thereof.[10]

However, the legislator has not stipulated the means or procedures for obtaining copies, where any medium suitable for disseminating the work is valid. Thus, copies made on the Internet are deemed to be reproductions for the purposes of SCA, Article 18. Therefore, reproduction exists when the online user saves a work on the hard disk of his/her computer or on a USB device, or when he/she prints it, as well as when he/she receives a temporary copy in the memory of his/her computer.[11]

In short, for reproduction to exist under the SCA, the following prerequisites must be met:

---

9 Law 34/2002, of July 11 on Information Society Services and E-Commerce.

10 López Maza, S, *Límites del derecho de reproducción en el entorno de internet*, Comares, Granada, 2009, pages 16 to 19.

11 Garrote, I, *La reforma de la copia privada en la legislación de propiedad intelectual*, Comares, Granada, 2005, page 128; Bercovitz Rodríguez-Cano, R *et al*, *Las reformas de la Ley de Propiedad Intelectual*, Tirant lo Blanch, Valencia, 2006, pages 42 and 43.

- the fixation of the work must be in a tangible or intangible medium, such reproduction being temporary or permanent; and
- the medium in which the work is fixed must allow for communication to the public and for the obtaining of copies thereof.

So, what acts in the internet context are acts of reproduction?

- For analogue content created off-line to be exploited on the Internet, it must first be digitalised. Digitalisation consists of converting content into a series of bits and then storing it in digital format, in any electronic medium, tangible (CDR, DVD, USB, etc) or intangible (computer memory). Insofar as digitalisation gives rise to a new fixation (reproduction) of content in a medium that makes it possible to communicate it and obtain copies, it is considered an act of reproduction fully covered by the copyright holder's *ius prohibendi*.[12] Digitalisation does not represent a transformation of the work from the point of view of the transformation exploitation right (SCA, Article 21) because the digitalised work is not a different work.[13] It is the same work, having the same degree of originality and all its characteristics. The only thing that has changed is the format.
- Once the digitalisation has been implemented (digitalised works), or if the content was originally in digital format (digital works), the works can be exploited via an open digital network (internet) or a closed digital network (intranet). To that end, they must first be stored on a server (uploading). Uploading is also considered an act of reproduction, which only copyright holders are entitled to perform.[14]
- Downloading content protected by copyright, accessible over the Internet (or an intranet) also constitutes an act of reproduction, which only copyright holders are entitled to perform.[15] This applies when the copies are made on tangible digital media (CD, CDR, DVD, USB, etc), intangible digital media (computer memory) or analogue media (paper). Whether, under certain circumstances, such reproduction falls within the scope of the limitation of copy for private use is an entirely different matter.

---

12 Barcelona Provincial Court Judgment (Section 15) of June 27 2002 [AC 2002/1551] and Baylina, M, *Novedades en la Ley de Propiedad Intelectual*, Bosch, Barcelona, 2007, pages 20 and 21; López Maza, S, *op cit*, pages 16 to 19; Massaguer, J, *'Los derechos de propiedad intelectual en internet'*, in *Comunicaciones y estudios universitarios*, nº 7, 1997, page 63.

13 Garrote, I, *El derecho de autor en internet*, Comares, Granada, 2003 (2nd edition), page 490.

14 Barcelona Provincial Court Judgment (Section 15) of June 27 2002 [AC 2002/1551] and Madrid Provincial Court Judgment (Section 25) of November 16 2005 [JUR 2005/1298]. We have already discussed this matter in Cuerva de Cañas, JA and Baylina, M, *'Comentario a la Sentencia de la Audiencia Provincial de Alicante (Sección 8ª) de 9 de enero de 2007 (Editorial Reus, SA c Universidad de Alicante y Fundación Biblioteca Virtual Miguel de Cervantes Saavedra)'*, in *Comunicaciones en Propiedad Industrial y Derecho de la Competencia*, nº 45, 2005, pages 55 to 85.

15 Note that, according to the Judgment of July 3 2012 of the European Court of Justice (*Usedsoft*; case C-128/11), the distribution right over a computer program is exhausted by downloading the same from the Internet and subsequently storing it on digital hardware, when the download is carried out under a perpetual use licence for an upfront fee to the rights holder of the computer program. For comments on this issue, see Cuerva de Cañas, JA and Baylina, M, *'¿(Ab)used soft? Comentario a la Sentencia del Tribunal de Justicia (Gran Sala) de la Unión Europea de 3 de julio de 2012 (caso Oracle c Usedsoft)'*, in *Comunicaciones en Propiedad Industrial y Derecho de la Competencia*, nº 67, 2012, pages 111 to 145.

Finally, we examine publishing as part of the acts of exploitation that take place on the Internet. Uploading content onto a server connected to a network (publishing) allows an indefinite number of persons to access protected content from the location and at the time they choose.[16] From the point of view of copyright, the main doubt raised by publishing is whether it should be considered an act of distribution or an act of communication to the public (SCA, Article 20). However, on the grounds of Article 3 of Directive 2001/29/EEC and Articles 8, 10 and 14 of the 1996 WIPO Treaties, this doubt has been dispelled in Spain by discarding publishing as an act of distribution because publishing does not entail the distribution of works 'included in a tangible medium'. As a result, when implementing Directive 2001/29/EEC, the Spanish legislator decided to clarify this subject expressly, by adding a new section (i) to SCA, Article 20.2 (right of communication to the public) as follows: "In particular, the following are acts of communication to the public: [...] (i) making works available to the public, by wire or over the air, in such a way that any person can access them from any location and at any time." This means that, at present, it is unanimously accepted that publishing constitutes an act of communication to the public, which only copyright holders are entitled to perform, and without whose consent copyright infringement will have been committed.[17]

1.3 Test for copyright infringement

In all cases involving unauthorised online exploitation, the exclusive rights of reproduction and/or communication to the public will be infringed. In general, it can be affirmed that the Spanish courts do not apply any standardised test to ascertain whether copyright infringement exists.

With regard to the reproduction right, which also applies to a certain extent to the right of communication to the public, it has been asserted that the quantitative aspect does not alter the value of the reproduction: the reproduction of the work may be partial or complete. If the whole of a work is reproduced, it is clear that the reproduction right will be infringed; the same can be said if the work is made available to the public *in integrum*. However, when the reproduction (or communication to the public) only involves part of the work, for infringement to exist, there must be a certain degree of identity between the original and the reproduction to be able to speak of copying. However, for that partial reproduction to be deemed a copy, certain conditions must be met: there must be a certain degree or extent of reproduction compared to the global original work, but a more extensive but insubstantial reproduction will not be considered a real reproduction; and there must be a degree of identity that makes it possible to recognise the original work.[18]

With regard to the number of copies, SCA, Article 18 makes no reference to the number of copies required to be able to speak of reproduction. Notwithstanding the foregoing, the fact that SCA, Article 31, which refers to private copies, uses 'copy' and

16 This is also applicable for intranets.
17 Madrid Provincial Court Judgment (Section 10) of November 13 2003 [JUR 2004/88888].
18 Erdozain López, JC, *Derechos de autor y propiedad intelectual en Internet*, Tecnos, Madrid, 2002, page 125.
19 López Maza, S, *op cit*, page 15; Bercovitz Álvarez, G, *Obra plástica y derechos patrimoniales de su autor*, Tecnos, Madrid, 1997, page 21.

'reproduction' in the singular, has led authors to conclude that one single copy is sufficient to infringe the right of reproduction.[19]

For its part, SCA, Article 133 confers upon the database owner the right to prohibit:

- the extraction and/or re-utilisation of: all or a substantial part of the contents thereof, evaluated *qualitatively* or *quantitatively*; and
- the repeated and/or systematic extraction and/or re-utilisation of insubstantial parts of the contents of the database, implying acts which conflict with a normal exploitation of that database or which unreasonably prejudice the legitimate interests of the maker of the database.

According to the doctrine laid down in the Judgment delivered by the European Court of Justice on November 9 2004,[20] the court found that the *quantitative* evaluation of a substantial part of the contents of the database refers to "the volume of data extracted from the database and/or re-utilised and must be assessed in relation to the total volume of the contents of the database". And, the analysis of the *qualitative* evaluation – ascertaining whether or not the part is substantial – must be made depending on the "scale of the investment in the obtaining, verification or presentation of the contents of the subject of the act of extraction and/or re-utilisation, regardless of whether that subject represents a quantitatively substantial part of the general contents of the protected database". In that respect, authors find that the extraction and/or re-utilisation of a small amount of data could constitute an infringement, provided that it is proven that a substantial investment was made to obtain, verify or present that minimum amount of data.[21]

1.4 Exemptions/defences to copyright infringement

SCA contains a closed list (*numerus clausus*) of limitations or exceptions to copyright (Articles 31 to 40*bis*) where no copyright infringement will exist.

(a) Personal copying rights

As previously stated, a website is a complex computer product combining: a computer program (back-end); and its visual presentation (front-end), comprising different elements, such as text, videos, photographs, music, etc.

With regard to a website computer program, SCA, Article 99(a) prohibits permanent copying for private purposes.[22] This also applies when a visual presentation of a website constitutes a database.

However, a limitation of reproduction for private use may apply to copies of other components of the website front-end (text, videos, photographs, music, etc), provided that all the prerequisites required under SCA, Article 31.2 are met:

---

20 Case C-6/06.

21 Esteve Pardo, Ma A, *op cit*, page 536.

22 *"Without prejudice to the provisions of Article 100 of this Law, the exclusive rights in the exploitation of a computer program by the person who is the owner thereof in terms of Article 97 shall include the right to do or authorize the following: (a) total or partial reproduction, including for personal use, of a computer program by any means and in any form, whether permanent or temporary."*

- the copy is made by a natural person;
- the copy is made for private use, meaning the "use of the copy within the private sphere of the party making the copy";[23]
- the copy is made from a work obtained by legal means;[24] and
- the copy is for non-financial/non-commercial purposes.[25]

Even though there is no specific limitation in SCA with regard to time shifting, in practice, any copies made by a natural person for time shifting purposes will only be authorised if they fall within the scope of limitation of reproduction for private use.

(b) *Format shifting*

The digitalisation of analogue content is not regarded as an act of transformation (SCA, Article 21), given that the digitalised work is not a different work.[26] It is construed as the same work, having the same degree of originality and all its characteristics, the only difference being the format. If this line of reasoning is applied to format shifting, it cannot be maintained, either, that the right of transformation has been infringed when one digital format (CD) is transformed into another (MP3). A change of format is an act of reproduction, which would only be authorised if it falls within the scope of limitation of reproduction for private use.

(c) *Caching and temporary copies as part of the communication process*

The transmission of works over the Internet entails the creation of copies, often temporary or fleeting, but essential to execute the technical data transmission process correctly. These copies, many of which are of a technical nature, are

---

23 Spanish Supreme Court Judgment of June 8 2007.

24 This means that the individual making the copy must have gained access to the work being copied legally (ie, with the author or copyright holder's consent).

25 In these cases, the necessary equipment, devices and materials to make the copy were subject to the payment of private copying levies. See the judgment delivered by the European Court of Justice on October 21 2010 (*Padawan*; case C-467/03) and Barcelona Provincial Court Judgment (Section 15) of March 2 2011 [JUR 2011/68191]. However, in December 2011, the Spanish government decided, through Royal Decree-Law 20/2011, of December 30, on urgent budgetary, tax and financial measures to remedy the public deficit, to abolish the so-called 'private copying levy' or – as it was referred to in the SCA – 'equitable remuneration for private copying'. According to Final Provision Number 23 of Royal Decree-Law 20/2011, the abolition of the private copying levy became effective on January 1 2012 and was not retroactive. Following the abolition of the private copying levy, as of January 1 2012 there is no longer any legal obligation in Spain for the manufacturers, importers and distributors of equipment, devices and materials that make reproductions to pay the collecting entities any amount whatsoever as a private copying levy and the private copying levy is now charged against the General State Budget. In November 2013, the Spanish government approved Order ECD/2128/2013, of November 14, which determines the amount of equitable remuneration for private copying corresponding to 2012 charged against the General State Budget and its distribution among the three manners of making reproductions referred to in law (Official State Gazette nº 275, of November 16 2013, Sec III, page 91797). The amount of the compensation to be assigned to the collecting entities, corresponding to 2012 and charged against the General State Budget, was determined to be €8,636,728.09, to be distributed according to the following percentages: books and publications assimilated by regulation to books: 40.79%, phonograms: 34.43% and videograms: 24.78%.

26 Barcelona Provincial Court Judgment (Section 15) of June 27 2002 [AC 2002/1551]; Garrote Fernández-Díez, I, *El derecho de autor en internet*, Comares, Granada, 2003 (2nd edition), page 490; Baylina, M, *Novedades en la Ley de Propiedad Intelectual*, Bosch, Barcelona, 2007, pages 20 and 21; López Maza, S, *op cit*, pages 16 to 19; and Massaguer, J, '*Los derechos de propiedad intelectual en internet*', *Comunicaciones y estudios universitarios*, nº 7, 1997, page 63.

instrumental with regard to the main act of communication to the public.

For an act of reproduction to be exempt from the reproduction right protection regime, it must fall within the limitation established in SCA, Article 31.1 (Article 5.1 of Directive 2001/29/EC). This occurs when the act of reproduction meets three requirements:

- the copy is transient or incidental. Therefore, permanent reproductions are excluded from the limitation established in SCA, Article 31.1;
- the copy is an integral and essential part of a technological process whose sole purpose is to enable a transmission in a network between third parties by an intermediary, or a lawful use of a work or other subject matter to be made; and
- the copy has no independent economic significance per se.

It is possible to distinguish between different types of provisional reproductions: transient copies, cached copies (caching), RAM copies and temporary reproductions *strictu sensu.*

Transient copies are those made in intermediate points of the network whilst transmitting the works from one point to another. Authors agree that transient copies do not require the copyright holder's consent and are subject to the limitation established in SCA, Article 31.1 because: they are not considered an act of reproduction according to SCA, Article 18 (Article 2 Directive 2001/29/EC), as their function is not the ulterior use of the work; their function is to facilitate the definitive reproduction of the work; and due to their instrumental nature, they have no independent economic significance.[27]

RAM copies are those made in the user's computer memory when he/she displays or reproduces a work, and are deleted when the content disappears from the screen or when the computer is switched off. In other words, these copies only exist when the computer is switched on. From the doctrine of the European Court of Justice (Grand Chamber), it may be concluded that RAM copies are covered by the limitation on exempt temporary reproductions (Article 5(1) of Directive 2001/29/EC and SCA, Article 31.1) because, although they do have 'economic significance', such economic significance is not – as required by Directive and SCA –'independent', insofar as RAM copies "are not capable of generating an additional economic advantage derived from mere"[28] display of web content.[29] This conclusion is also supported by the objective pursued by the limitation on exempt temporary reproductions that "should include acts which enable browsing as well as acts of caching to take place, including those which enable transmission systems to function efficiently".[30] If RAM copies were not considered to comply with the conditions set by Article 5(1) of Directive 2001/29/EC and SCA, Article 31.1 internet

27 Garrote, I, *op cit*, page 125; Carbajo, F, *Publicaciones electrónicas y propiedad intelectual*, Colex, Madrid, 2002, page 126; López Maza, S, *op cit*, page 160.

28 Judgment dated October 4 2011 (Case C-403/2008).

29 It is important to note that there are no precedents in Spain in relation to this issue and the opinion of authors is divided.

30 Recital 33 of Directive 2001/29/EC.

users would be prevented from accessing the web content in the absence of an authorisation from copyright holders. For this reason, some scholars in Spain, prior to the Judgment of the European Court of Justice dated October 4 2011, proposed a solution according to which in the case of content uploaded to the Internet without any kind of control over access, it could be assumed – a *iuris tantum* presumption – that the author was authorising the free display thereof and, therefore, the creation of RAM copies (ie, a kind of implied licence). Meanwhile, when a website or other internet content is made accessible to the public but protected by a password or access control, the RAM copy derived from browsing would not have been authorised for the public as a whole (except for those subjects that were in fact authorised).[31]

Cached copies are reproductions of web pages and websites, which are made when users visit them and which the servers store automatically, so that the user can access the work more rapidly, without having to make a new request to the host servers.[32] When a request for information is made, the caching takes the request, searches the cache to see whether it is available and, if so, recovers it directly from the cache. If it is not in the cache, the file is recovered directly from the source and a copy is stored in the cache memory. There are two kinds of cached copies:

- local cached copies: made automatically in the user's computer by the browser, and stored in the RAM memory, on the hard disk or in a combination of both;[33] and
- proxy copies: when performed automatically on the hard disks of the servers.

Local cached copies, if enduring, do not comply with the requirements established in SCA, Article 31.1 because they are not transient copies and have independent economic significance. If, on the other hand, they are non-enduring, the *iuris tantum* presumption already discussed in relation to RAM copies will apply.

It is true that proxy copies are accessory to internet transmission and are essential to facilitate it. However, it is clear that they have extremely important independent economic significance. Moreover, as they are reproductions for collective and remunerative use, they cannot be included in the limitation of copy for private use established in SCA, Article 31.1. Since proxy copies can only be made by ISPs, the regime of exemptions of liability under LSSI, Article 15 (Article 13 Directive 2000/31/EC)[34] will apply. This means that the ISP will not be liable when the proxy copies are made to transmit information to users more easily and efficiently, and when the other requirements set out in LSSI, Article 15 are met.

Temporary copies *strictu sensu* are those that allow the work to be enjoyed online over a certain period of time. They are stored on the user's hard disk or on the servers, making it possible to access the content. This kind of copy is not protected under the

---

31 Garrote, I, *op cit*, page 351: Garrote, I, '*Comentario al artículo 31 de la Ley de Propiedad Intelectual*' in Bercovitz, R (Dir), *Comentarios a la Ley de Propiedad Intelectual*, Tecnos, Madrid, 2007 (3rd edition), pages 542 to 545: and López Maza, S, *op cit*, page 163.

32 Ribas, J, *Aspectos jurídicos del comercio electrónico en Internet*, Aranzadi, Pamplona, 1999, page 35.

33 López Maza, S, *op cit*, page 141.

34 Barcelona Provincial Court Judgment (Section 15) of September 17 2009 [JUR 2008/336805].

limitation provided for in SCA, Article 31.1. It would be worth analysing whether they fall under the scope of the limitation of copy for private use.

(d) *Back-up copies*

We recall that the back-end of every website consists of a computer program. The possibility of making back-up copies is provided for in the SCA with regard to computer programs. The SCA allows the lawful user of a computer program to make a back-up copy of the program insofar as such a copy is necessary for the use of the program (SCA, Article 100.2). It is therefore a limitation on the reproduction right. It should be pointed out that the SCA does not allow back-up copies to be made in any case, but subjects the application of this limitation to two requirements: the back-up copy can only be made by the person authorised to use the computer program; and such back-up copy must be necessary for the use of the computer program. Therefore, this limitation, applicable to computer programs, would not appear to apply to internet users, in relation to the websites they visit, because it is not necessary to make a back-up copy to access a website. However, the limitation of reproduction for private use may apply to copies of other components of the website front-end.

(e) *Reverse engineering*

Pursuant to the provisions of SCA, Article 100.3 the lawful user of a program is entitled to observe, study or verify the operation thereof, without the owner's prior consent, for the purposes of ascertaining the ideas and principles underlying any element of the program, provided that this is implemented during the course of any program loading, display, operation, transmission or storage operation he/she is entitled to perform. Therefore, it rules out the lawful user accessing the computer program source code in any other situation different from those specifically stated.

(f) *Parody*

The only parody permitted by SCA is the so-called 'target parody', the sole purpose of which is to 'criticise' or joke about a particular work. SCA does not define the concept of parody or the requirements for treating a work as a parody. However, in the majority of cases, parody will be a transformation of a work or a derived work. The parody excludes the need to obtain the website owner's consent to be able to transform, for the purposes of parody, content that is accessible to the public on the website or the website itself. The only limits that SCA, Article 39 establishes for parody are that: the parody must not entail a likelihood of confusion with the original work, or of the author of the parody with the author of the parodied work;[35] and the parody must not cause damage to the original work or its author (ie, it must not constitute slander or libel).[36]

---

35 Garrote, I, *op cit*, page 497; Bercovitz, R, *Manual de Propiedad Intelectual*, Tirant Lo Blanch, Valencia, 2006, pages 116 and 117.

36 Díaz Alabart, S, *"Artículo 39"* in Bercovitz, R (Coord), *Comentarios a la Ley de Propiedad Intelectual*, Tecnos, Madrid (2nd edition), 1997, page 677.

(g) *Quotations*

SCA, Article 32 permits the inclusion of a fragment of a website or of part of its content, in a different website or in another medium outside of the Internet only when the following cumulative requirements are met: the work in question has already been disclosed; the source and the name of the author of the work are stated; the work is included by way of quotation or for analysis, comment or critical assessment; and the use is only made for teaching or research purposes and to the extent justified by the purpose of the inclusion. This means that, if one of the requirements established in Article 32 is not met, this limitation will not be available. Thus, the possibilities of applying this limitation to the exclusive reproduction right are drastically reduced because in the majority of cases, rather than being for teaching or research purposes, websites are commercial or exist purely for entertainment purposes.

1.5 Remedies available for copyright infringement

As well as the right to apply for interim injunctions against the infringer (SCA, Article 141), the SCA confers upon the copyright holder the right to take: a wide-ranging action for the cessation of the acts of infringement (SCA, Article 139); an action for compensation for damages (SCA, Article 140); and an action for the publication of the judgment at the infringer's expense (SCA, Article 138).

The copyright holder can seek the cessation of the infringer's unlawful acts (SCA, Article 139). This cessation may entail: the suspension of the infringing exploitation or activity; a prohibition on the infringer resuming the infringing exploitation or activity; the withdrawal from trade and destruction of unlawful copies; the withdrawal from commercial circuits, disablement and, where necessary, the destruction of the material elements, equipment or instruments used for the reproduction, creation or manufacture of unlawful copies; the removal or sealing off of the equipment used in the unauthorised public communication of works or services; the removal or sealing off of the equipment used in the unauthorised public communication of works accessed by avoiding their technological protection; the confiscation, disablement and destruction of instruments whose only use is to facilitate the unauthorised suppression or neutralisation of any technical device used to protect a computer program; the removal or sealing off of the instruments used to facilitate the unauthorised suppression or neutralisation of any technical device used to protect works or services, even if it were not its only use; and the suspension of the services rendered by ISPs for third parties who use them to infringe copyright rights.

Following the amendment of the SCA by Law 19/2006, the copyright holder whose rights have been infringed can claim compensation for losses, covering not only the value of the loss sustained (consequential damage), but also the income not obtained as a result of the infringement of its rights (loss of profit). The quantum of compensation may also include any investigation expenses incurred to obtain reasonable evidence of the infringement of the copyright.

The loss of profit will be fixed, at the rights holder's discretion, in accordance with one of the following criteria:

- the negative economic consequences, including the loss of profit sustained by the copyright holder, and the profits obtained by the infringer from the unlawful exploitation;[37] or
- the royalty that the rights holder would have received if the infringer had sought authorisation to exploit the right in question.[38]

In addition to financial damage, it is also possible to claim for pain and suffering, as an independent category of compensation,[39] in the event of the infringement of moral rights.[40]

Actions for damages are available by statute of limitation for five years after the party in question could file them.

1.6 Copyright liability

As a general rule, infringement will be deemed to be committed by users whenever they upload or download content that was available on the Internet, without having been authorised by the author or copyright holders to do so. As previously stated, the two exploitation rights infringed by unauthorised acts performed by internet users will be the right of reproduction (SCA, Article 20) and the right of communication to the public (SCA, Article 20).

ISPs are subject to a specific liability regime regulated in LSSI (Articles 13 to 17), which implemented Directive 2000/31/EC in Spanish law. The starting point in LSSI is that ISPs are liable (LSSI, Article 2). Nevertheless, they may be exempt from this liability if they meet certain conditions, confirming that they had not participated in or have any 'actual knowledge' of the unlawful acts performed by the users of their services.

(a) Hosting/cloud computing

Online providers of a mediation service consisting of hosting data provided by a recipient of the service (hosting) will not be liable for the information stored at the request of a recipient, on condition that (LSSI, Article 16):

- they had no actual knowledge of illegal activity or information that it infringes indemnifiable third-party assets or rights; or

---

37 The new wording of SCA, Article 2(a) has given rise to a heated debate among learned writers, which will have to be settled by the courts because, by including both loss of profit 'and' the 'profits that the infringer may have obtained from the unlawful exploitation' as compensation headings, there would appear to be a duplication of the amounts eligible for compensation. 26 of Directive 2004/48/EC does not provide a solution either because, instead of using the conjunction 'and' it opts for the disjunctive 'or'. On this point, see Carrasco Perera, A '*Comentario a los artículos 138 a 141 LPI*', in Bercovitz, R (Coord), *Comentarios a la Ley de Propiedad Intelectual*, Madrid, Tecnos (3rd edition), 2007, pages 1691 *et seq;* Clemente Meoro, M '*Comentario al artículo 140 de la LPI*', in Rodríguez Tapia, JM (Dir), *Comentarios a la Ley de Propiedad Intelectual*, Navarra, Aranzadi, 2007, pages 805 *et seq*.

38 The difficulty inherent in opting for this criterion is proving what royalty the infringer should pay – something the Supreme Court has insisted on (Judgments dated April 5 2000 and May 31 2002).

39 Rodríguez Tapia, JM and Bondía Román, F, *Comentarios a la Ley de Propiedad Intelectual*, Madrid, Civitas, 1997, page 514.

40 Barcelona Provincial Court Judgments of June 23 2005 [AC 2006\117] and March 5 2004 [AC 2004\479]. On compensation for pain and suffering and the quantum of such compensation, see Cuerva de Cañas, JA and Castellví, L, '*Arquitectura de autor: un análisis de ciertos problemas suscitados en torno a la obra arquitectónica y la propiedad intellectual*', *Pe.I*, nº 36, 2010, pages 54 to 67.

- upon obtaining such knowledge, they acted expeditiously to remove or to disable access to the information.

Liability will be incurred by a hosting service provider that does not meet these conditions. It is construed that a service provider has actual knowledge when a competent authority has declared the unlawfulness of the data, has ordered the removal thereof or has disabled access thereto, or a court has declared the infringement and the provider is aware of such decision, without prejudice to any other procedures to detect and remove the content applied by the provider by virtue of voluntary agreements and other means that may be established to obtain actual knowledge.

The above exemption from liability for a hosting service provider does not apply in the event that the recipient of the service acts under the instructions, authority or control of the service provider.

(b) Caching

Any caching service providers that transfer through a telecommunications network data provided by a recipient of the service; and for the sole purpose of rendering more effective the subsequent transfer thereof to other recipients on request, store such data in their systems in an automatic, provisional and temporary manner, will not be liable for the content of such data or for the temporary reproduction thereof, if:

- the information is not amended;
- access is only provided to recipients that meet the conditions imposed to that end by the recipient whose information is requested;
- they comply with generally accepted rules applied to update the information;
- they do not interfere with the lawful exploitation of generally accepted technology used in the sector, in order to obtain data on the use of the information; and
- they remove any information they have stored, or disable access thereto, as soon as they have actual knowledge that:
  - it has been removed from its original location in the network;
  - access thereto has been disabled; or
  - a court or competent authority has ordered the removal thereof or disabled access thereto.

Liability will be incurred when a caching service provider does not meet these conditions. In particular, liability will be incurred if the user-generated content is amended.[41]

(c) Hypertext linking

The current situation in Spain regarding linking remains largely uncertain.

There is near unanimity among the courts and scholars in considering that, for the time being, any surface links through which a website is linked to another

---

41 Barcelona Provincial Court Judgment (Section 15), of September 17 2008 [AC 2008/1773].

website's home page, even when the latter hosts infringing works, do not constitute copyright infringement.[42]

However, it remains controversial whether deep links redirecting the user to an internal page of a website (without going through its home page) could infringe the right of communication to the public (SCA, Article 20) and the integrity right (SCA, Article 14(4)), in the latter case because the display order established by the site author is not met.[43]

Finally, in-line or embedded links are links in respect of which copyright infringement is much clearer. These links 'capture' a work from another website, in principle, without the author's consent. Use of these links may also infringe the right of reproduction, because the website containing the link reproduces therein a work (text, photograph, video, etc) that formed part of another website. Likewise, these links may amount to an act of infringement of the right of communication to the public due to the unauthorised communication of part of a third party's work. And, insofar as a website is divided up, they may also infringe the moral right to integrity.

The most effective solution to clarify this situation would be for the Spanish Parliament to amend the Spanish Intellectual Property Act expressly to clarify whether or not different kinds of links to copyrighted content constitute a public act of communication (SCA, Article 20). However, at the time of writing, the preliminary draft reform of the SCA (the 'Preliminary Draft') that has been made available to the public fails to amend Article 20. Neither does it contain an express reference to the right of communication to the public, in relation to linking activities on the Internet. Notwithstanding the above, as the legislative process is still underway and new amendments may be made to the Preliminary Draft, the possibility that Article 20 could be amended at a later stage cannot be completely ruled out.

Moreover, it must be pointed out that the Preliminary Draft is being processed in parallel to the preliminary questions referred to the European Court of Justice and in which the European Court of Justice is to rule on whether setting a hyperlink to a copyright-protected work amounts to 'communication to the public' within the meaning of Article 3(1) of the Information Society Directive.[44] If the European Court of Justice answers this question in the affirmative and the legislative process in Spain has not concluded, the Preliminary Draft would most likely be amended to echo ECJ doctrine. However, if the legislative process in Spain has concluded without any amendment regarding the right of communication to the public, the Spanish courts would be obliged to change their opinion regarding linking to infringing content, in order to come into line with ECJ doctrine.

In these linking cases mentioned above, those who have created this type of link may be liable. The same applies to service providers in the circumstances established in LSSI, Article 17. According to this rule, any information society service providers providing links to other content or including menus or content search engines will

---

42 Barcelona Provincial Court Judgments (Section 15) of February 24 2011 [AC 2011/86] and July 7 2011 [AC 2011/1505].

43 Ortega Díaz, JF, *Los enlaces en Internet*, Aranzadi, Navarra, 2006, pages 126 to 130; Garrote Fernández-Díez, I, *El derecho de autor en internet*, Comares, Granada, 2003 (2nd edition), page 66.

44 See case C-466/12, case C-348/13 and case C-279/13.

not be liable for any information addressed to their service recipients, provided: they had no actual knowledge of illegal activity or information or that it infringe indemnifiable third-party assets or rights; or upon obtaining such knowledge, they acted expeditiously to remove or to disable the link in question.

It is construed that a service provider has actual knowledge in the same scenarios established for hosting services.

(d) *Framing*

The author of a website can divide it up into several windows, and include a third party's website in one of them. This activity, referred to as framing, raises two issues from a copyright point of view. On the one hand, some authors believe that, by modifying a website's appearance with a frame, a derived work would arise, which would require the transformation right-holder's prior consent (SCA, Article 21), without which copyright infringement[45] would be committed. For others, the creator of the link would infringe the right of communication to the public by reproducing a website without its author's consent. In any case, framing undoubtedly infringes the moral right to integrity of the work, given that the website is communicated to the public in a different context from the one conceived by its author.[46]

(e) *P2P network*

One controversial issue is whether a P2P software supplier may be held liable as a result of 'indirect infringements' caused by the acts of P2P system users. The reason for this discussion is that the Spanish Civil Code (CC) only allows liability to be claimed for a third party's acts in a series of events (CC, Article 1,903), which the Spanish courts have traditionally interpreted restrictively. Nevertheless, opinions exist in favour of holding P2P software suppliers liable under CC, Article 1,903.[47] However there are no court precedents in Spain in this regard.

From the point of view of P2P software users, authors[48] agree that:

- any copy of a work made by a user in a shared file is an act of reproduction. This act of reproduction is not covered by a limitation of reproduction for private use because the copy is subject to collective, not private, use;
- the act whereby a P2P system user makes a work accessible to all other P2P system users exceeds a strictly domestic sphere (SCA, Article 20.1).[49]

---

45 Garrote Fernández-Díez, I, *El derecho de autor en internet, op cit*, page 40.

46 Ortega Díaz, JF, *Los enlaces en Internet, op cit*, page 135.

47 Bercovitz, R, *Manual de Propiedad Intelectual*, Tirant Lo Blanch, Valencia, 2006, pages 116 and 117.

48 Casas, R, *"La lucha por el derecho en las redes peer-to-peer: el caso Grokster ante el Tribunal Supremo de los EE.UU", Revista jurídica del deporte y entretenimiento*, nº 15, 2005; González de Alaiza, J, *'"Napster": copias robadas, responsabilidad de los intermediarios y otros interrogantes para el derecho de autor en internet', Pe. I*, nº 6, 2000; *idem, 'La lucha contra los titulares de derechos de autor contra las redes "peer to peer"', Pe. I*, nº 18, 2004; Serrano Gómez, E, *'Napster y la propiedad intelectual: ¿una relación imposible?', Actualidad civil*, nº 3, 2001; Ruz, F *'Kazaa y el fin de la revolución. Comentario sobre la sentencia del Tribunal Federal de Australia de 5 de septiembre de 2005: Universal Music Australia Pty versus Sharman License Holdings Ltd (2005) FCA 1242', Pe. I*, nº 21, 2005; Garrote Fernández-Díez, I *La reforma de la copia privada en la Ley de la Propiedad Intelectual*, Comares, Granada, 2005.

49 For a definition of the 'strictly domestic sphere' established in SCA, Article 20.1 see Pérez de Ontiveros, C, *'Aproximación al significado de la expresión 'ámbito estrictamente doméstico' en la regulación legal de la facultad patrimonial de comunicación pública', Pe. I*, nº 12, 2002, pages 25 to 52.

Consequently, it amounts to an act of infringement of the exclusive right of communication to the public; and

- any copy made by a P2P system user when downloading a work amounts to an unauthorised act of reproduction, which is not protected by a limitation of reproduction for private use because the user has not legally gained access to the work being copied.[50]

(f) ***Webcasting/streaming***

Any webcasting or streaming of a third party's works or services, without the author or copyright holder's consent, constitutes an act of infringement by the party uploading the content, of: the right of reproduction; and the right of communication to the public, given that the work is made accessible to the public.[51]

1.7 Joint liability for ISPs

In all of the cases referred to in the previous section, any ISPs that do not meet the requirements established in LSSI, Articles 14 to 17, will be held jointly liable with internet users.[52]

As regards the 'actual knowledge' requirement, it is important to note that it has been subject to two interpretations, one broad and the other restrictive. If interpreted restrictively, 'actual knowledge' will only exist when a competent authority has declared the unlawfulness of the data, in the absence of regulatory provisions as to other means of actual knowledge.[53] However, a broader interpretation of when a service provider acquires 'actual knowledge' suggests that the list established in LSSI is not exhaustive and, therefore, other channels exist, through which a provider may acquire 'actual knowledge', such as official notice from the copyright holder.[54] This latter interpretation would appear to be more in keeping with the spirit of Directive 2000/31/EC and would appear to be the interpretation adopted by the Spanish Supreme Court in its recent decisions.[55]

---

50 Garrote Fernández-Díez, I, *La reforma de la copia privada en la Ley de Propiedad Intelectual*, Comares, Granada, 2010, pages 214 to 218.

51 Barcelona Provincial Court Judgments (Section 15) of February 24 2011 [AC 2011/86] and July 7 2011 [AC 2011/1505].

52 See Cavanillas Múgica, S, *Responsabilidades de los proveedores de información en internet*, Comares, Granada, 2007; Busto Lago, JM in Reglero Campos, LF (Coord), *Tratado de Responsabilidad Civil*, Aranzadi, Navarra, 2006.

53 See Madrid Provincial Court Judgment (Section 14) of December 20 2005 [AC2006\233], Madrid Provincial Court Judgment (Section 12) of April 17 2008 [JUR 2008\179170] and Madrid Provincial Court Judgment (Section 9) of February 19 2010 [JUR 2010\133011].

54 See Badajoz Provincial Court Judgment (Section 3) of September 17 2010 [AC 2010\1375]. According to Barcelona Provincial Court Judgment (Section 19) of March 3 2010 [JUR 2010/177852], 'actual knowledge' will be deemed to exist with the mere receipt of a bureaufax sent by the rights holder, reporting the existence of the infringement, as we shall see below.

55 Spanish Supreme Court Judgments of March 4 2013, February 26 2013, December 4 2012 [RJ 2013/195], February 10 2011 [RJ 2011/313], May 18 2010 [RJ 2010/2319] and December 9 2009 [RJ 2010\131]. On this subject, see Cuerva de Cañas, JA and Borras Pieri, X, 'To avoid liability: please broadcast yourself! *Un comentario a la Sentencia del Juzgado de lo Mercantil número 7 de Madrid de 20 de septiembre de 2010 (Caso TELECINCO vs. YOUTUBE)', Comunicaciones en Propiedad Industrial y Derecho de la Competencia*, nº 61, January–March 2011, pages 105 to 140.

1.8 Relief

Following the emergence of new forms of infringement – in particular, peer-to-peer systems (P2P) – Law 19/2006 amended SCA Article 138 with a view specifically to strengthening intellectual property rights against infringements committed on the Internet. Thus, under SCA, Article 138.3, copyright holders who take action against infringers of their rights can apply for: interim injunctions; and cessation measures against the ISPs "whose services a third party uses in order to infringe copyright" even though the mediation acts performed by the ISPs "do not per se constitute an infringement". Thus, the ISP must accept the cessation measures (eg, cutting off the infringer's internet access service or the infringing content hosting service), even if it is not responsible for the infringement.[56] The liability that ISPs could incur is regulated by Law 34/2002, referred to above.

1.9 Issues specific to Spain

When a person makes content available on the Internet, it becomes accessible and can be downloaded from a computer connected to the Internet anywhere in the world. That is why, in disputes on infringements committed on the Internet, there are often elements connected to jurisdictions different from that of the court where the complaint is filed.

(a) Jurisdiction

In the case of copyright infringement actions, when the defendant is domiciled in a member state of the European Community, Spanish courts will determine their jurisdiction by applying European Regulation 44/2001.[57] However, if the defendant is domiciled in Iceland, Switzerland or Norway, the Lugano Convention applies.[58] Finally, in those cases in which the defendant is domiciled in a third country, Regulation 44/2001 refers the court before which the complaint is filed to its domestic legislation, which for Spain is Article 22 of the Judiciary Act (LOPJ).[59]

Generally speaking, for copyright infringement actions the above rules establish two alternative jurisdictions based on which the Spanish courts can declare themselves competent: the general jurisdiction of the defendant's domicile; and the *forum delicti comissi*, which attributes jurisdiction to the courts where the damaging act took place (ie, where the copyright infringement occurred) (Article 5.3 of Regulation 44/2001, Article 5.3 of the Lugano Convention and Article 22.3 of LOPJ).[60]

Albeit not always apparent, the application of the jurisdiction of the defendant's

---

56 Bercovitz, R (Coord), *Manual de Propiedad Intelectual*, Tirant lo Blanch, Valencia, 2006, pages 297 and 303.

57 Council Regulation (EC) No 44/2001 of December 22 2000, on jurisdiction and the recognition and enforcement of judgments in civil and commercial matters.

58 The Lugano Convention (2007) (OJ L 339 of December 21 2007) in force since January 1 2010 – which replaced the Lugano Convention of 1998 – applies to relations between the European Community and Switzerland, Norway and Iceland.

59 Organic Law 6/1985, of July 1 1985.

60 López-Tarruella, A, *'Criterio de Focalización y Forum Delicti Comissi en las infracciones de propiedad industrial e intelectual en internet'*, *Pe.I.*, nº 31, January–April 2009, pages 16 and 17; Calvo Caravaca, LA and Carrascosa, J, *'Conflictos de leyes y conflictos de jurisdicción en internet'*, Colex, Madrid, 2001, pages 106 and 107.

domicile does in fact create problems in those cases where, for example, there is more than one defendant,[61] or where the claimant files an action for infringement committed by a parent company before the Spanish courts, where the subsidiaries are domiciled.[62] However, it is the application of *forum delicti comissi* that creates the biggest problems where copyright infringement on the Internet is concerned.

Notwithstanding the foregoing, it is important to point out that the Spanish courts have declared that they have jurisdiction when *forum delicti comissi* attributes it to them, in actions seeking to prevent imminent acts of infringement[63] and, unlike in some decisions given by the courts in neighbouring countries (such as the Dutch, French, Italian or Belgian Courts), in declaratory actions for non-infringement.[64]

(b) Theories for attributing jurisdiction to Spanish courts when forum delicti comissi *applies*

In order to determine the jurisdiction of the Spanish courts when the rule *forum delicti comissi* (Article 5.3 of Regulation 44/2001, Article 5.3 of the Lugano Convention and Article 22.3 of LOPJ) applies, two different theories have been proposed and the question cannot yet be considered as closed.

The first theory proposed is based on the European Court of Justice case law in the *Fiona Shevill* case,[65] which must be completed with the case law from the *Pinckney* case. According to this theory, an infringer of copyright can be sued before the Spanish courts when:

- his/her domicile or establishment is in Spain (general rule, Article 2 of Regulation 44/2001);
- the contents were uploaded in Spain (Article 5.3, the place where the event giving rise to the damage occurred); and
- it is possible to access the website from Spain or the contents have been downloaded in Spain (Article 5.3, the 'place where the harmful event' occurs).[66]

In the first case, the Spanish courts could hear an action for cessation and compensation for damages referring to all the damage caused in all states (global damages). However, in the third case, only actions for cessation and compensation for damages generated on Spanish territory could be heard (local damages).[67] The issue that remains unresolved according to the doctrine laid down in the *Fiona Shevill*

61 When they are all domiciled in EU member states, Article 6.1 of Regulation 44/2001 allows for the joinder of all the actions before the courts in any of these states, provided that they are interrelated, making it advisable for them to be heard jointly in order to avoid contradictory decisions. See the judgment delivered by the European Court of Justice on July 13 2006 (case C-539/03) and the Rulings given by Madrid Provincial Court on March 27 2008 [JUR 2008/151443] and October 25 2006 [JUR 2006/176059].

62 Spanish Supreme Court Judgment of January 28 1994 [RJ 1994/572].

63 Barcelona Provincial Court Judgment of April 26 2007 [JUR 2007/270652].

64 Navarra Provincial Court Judgment of May 19 2006 [AC 2006/394].

65 Judgment of March 7 1995 (case C-68/93).

66 In the *Pinckney* case (Judgment of October 3 2013; case C-170/12), the European Court of Justice concluded that the national court of the claimant (France) had jurisdiction because there was "the possibility of obtaining a reproduction of the work to which the rights relied on by the defendant pertain from an internet site accessible within the jurisdiction of the court seised".

and *Pinckney* cases, is whether the Spanish courts would have jurisdiction to hear an action for global damages when the contents were uploaded in Spain and the defendant does not have a domicile or establishment in Spain. The authors of ALI Principles (Section 204) and Max Planck Group Principles (Article 2:203) have supported this solution in two exceptional, specific scenarios: when the infringement does not have substantial effects in the state where the infringer has its domicile or establishment; or when the substantial activities for committing the infringement were entirely performed in Spain or the damage caused by the infringement in Spain is substantial in relation to the infringement as a whole. However, there is no record of the Spanish courts having yet pronounced on this matter.

According to a second theory, the Spanish courts would have jurisdiction in the first and second scenarios, but not in the third, because the 'place where the harmful event' occurs (Article 5.3) cannot rank as equivalent to the place where it is possible to access the website or where the content has been downloaded. According to this second theory, the 'accessibility criterion' for the website and the contents must be rejected[68] and replaced by the criterion of the 'focused web'.

Under the 'focused web' criterion, for Spanish courts to be declared competent, it is necessary to prove the existence of a sufficient, substantial and significant link between the infringement and the damage caused in Spain. In other words, it is necessary to prove, taking into account the elements surrounding a particular case, that the website or infringing content is targeted at Spain.[69] Some of the elements to be taken into account in order to ascertain whether a website is 'focused' on Spain, include:[70]

- the active (ie, allowing Spanish users to place orders for goods or services) or passive (ie, only offering information, without permitting interaction) nature of the website;
- the use of access limiters. Websites can be designed in such a way that they only allow users on computers located in certain states to gain access to them. If Spain does not rank among those states, it cannot be construed that the defendant targets its activities at Spain;
- the presence of disclaimers in which the provider makes it clear at which countries, including Spain, the products or content offered on the website are targeted;
- the language used on the website is Spanish and the currency indicated for goods and services is the euro; and

---

67 This has been confirmed, for the case of France, by the European Court of Justice that in judgment of October 3 2013 (*Pinckney*; case C-170/12) limited the jurisdiction of the French court only to the damage caused in France: "45. However, if the protection granted by the Member State of the place of the court seised is applicable only in that Member State, the court seised only has jurisdiction to determine the damage caused within the Member State in which it is situated."

68 Calvo Caravaca, LA and Carrascosa, J, *Derecho Internacional Privado*, Comares, Granada, 2008 (9th edition), Volume II, pages 784 and 785, have declared in favour of the accessibility criterion, while López-Tarruella, A, *op cit*, pages 40 and 41, has declared against it.

69 This criterion was followed in Barcelona Provincial Court Judgment of April 26 2007 [JUR 2007/270652] and Valencia Provincial Court Judgment of November 29 2002 [JUR 2003/32505].

70 López-Tarruella, A, *op cit*, pages 45 to 50.

- the results that appear in internet search engines are identified with the ccTLD corresponding to Spain (eg, google.es, yahoo.es, etc).

Nevertheless, the fact is that, following the Judgment of the European Court of Justice of October 3 2013 (*Pinckney*; case C-170/12), it could be considered that the 'focused web' criterion should be rejected as the European Court of Justice expressly ruled that "Article 5(3) thereof [Regulation 44/2001] does not require, in particular, that the activity concerned be 'directed to' the Member State in which the court seised is situated". However, there is no record of the Spanish courts having applied the case law in the *Pinckney* case to date.

(c) ***Claim for infringement of foreign copyright***

Article 8.1 of Regulation Rome II[71] establishes that "the law applicable to a non-contractual obligation arising from an infringement of a copyright right shall be the law of the country for which protection is claimed". Consequently, when the Spanish courts are competent to hear a copyright infringement, the SCA will apply (*lex loci protectionis*).[72] In order to determine the scope of protection of foreign works and authors, the SCA applies two criteria:

Subjects connected to Spain: According to the SCA (Article 163), all foreign works and authors shall enjoy the same rights provided for in the SCA if the foreign authors are: nationals of other member states of the European Union; nationals of other countries ordinarily resident in Spain; nationals of other countries not ordinarily resident in Spain, for any of their works published in Spanish territory for the first time or within 30 days following their publication in another country.[73]

Subjects not connected to Spain: In all cases, nationals of other countries shall enjoy the protection available under any international conventions and treaties to which Spain is party and, failing that, shall be treated in the same way as Spanish authors when Spanish authors are themselves treated in the same way as nationals in the country in question.

In addition and specifically with regard to databases, they will enjoy protection under the SCA if the copyright holders are: nationals of an EU member state; ordinarily reside in an EU territory; or are companies and enterprises incorporated under the laws of a member state, whose head office, central administration or main activity centre is located in the European Union. If the company or enterprise only

71 Regulation (EC) No 864/2007 of the European Parliament and of the Council of July 11 2007 on the law applicable to non-contractual obligations.

72 See Amores Conradi, MA and Heredia Cervantes, I in Bercovitz, R (Coord), *"Artículo 167"*, *Comentarios a la Ley de Propiedad Intelectual*, Tecnos, Madrid, 2007, pages 2127 to 2185; Baylina, M and Cuerva de Cañas, JA *'Popeye: del dominio de Olivia al dominio público – Un paseo por las revueltas aguas normativas en las que le ha tocado navegar al célebre marino'*, *Comunicaciones en Propiedad Industrial y Derecho de la Competencia*, CEFI, nº 53, January–March 2009, pages 71 to 99; González Gonzalo, A, *'La ley aplicable para la protección de los derechos de propiedad intelectual, con especial referencia a su determinación en los entornos en línea'*, *Pe. I*, nº 11, 2002, pages 71 to 119.

73 Nevertheless, the government may restrict the scope of this principle in the case of nationals of states that do not confer sufficient protection for the works of Spanish authors in comparable circumstances.

has its registered office in the said territory, its operations must be effectively and continuously linked to the economy of a member state.

The author's moral rights must always be recognised, irrespective of his/her nationality.

1.10 Orphan works

There is currently no regulation in Spain concerning orphan works. However, authors have expressed their concern on this matter. In the European arena, in 2006 a group of experts on digital libraries was set up, with representatives from the different sectors affected by digitalisation and online content, including orphan works.[74] The group of experts approved the Final Report on Digital Preservation, Orphan Works and Out-of-Print Works.[75] Moreover, representatives of libraries, archives and holders of rights have signed the Memorandum of Understanding on Diligent Search Guidelines for Orphan Works.[76] All of these reports, together with the Green Paper on copyright in the knowledge economy,[77] gave rise to the Proposal for a Directive of the European Parliament and of the Council on certain permitted uses of orphan works,[78] and the subsequent Directive of the European Parliament and of the Council on certain permitted uses of orphan works,[79] which has not yet been transposed into the Spanish national legal system.

1.11 Online piracy measures

On March 4 2011, Law 2/2011 on Sustainable Economy[80] was passed. Widely known as the 'Ley Sinde' (the 'Sinde Act'), it was named after Ángeles González Sinde, the Minister of Culture of the 2008 Administration. Final Provision 43 of this law introduced several mechanisms to strengthen the legal protection of copyright on the Internet. *Inter alia*, it amended the SCA (Article 158) creating the Second Section of the Copyright Commission, the duty of which is to "safeguard copyright rights against infringement by those responsible for information society services".

In particular the Second Section of the Copyright Commission is entitled to adopt "measures to interrupt the provision of an information society service which infringes copyright rights or in order to remove content that infringes said rights, provided the provider is acting, directly or indirectly, for profit or has caused, or is liable to cause, financial damage". In that respect, a procedure for the removal of content or the interruption of information society services was established begun at the request of the copyright holder.

Once the procedure has commenced, the Copyright Commission issues a first warning to the alleged infringer, allowing it either: voluntarily to remove the content

74 Commission Decision of February 27 2006 setting up a high-level expert group on digital libraries, OJ L 63, 4.3.2006, pages 25–27. The group was subsequently renewed in Commission Decision of March 25 2009, DO 82, 28.3.2009, pages 9 to 11.
75 See http://ec.europa.eu/information_society/activities/digital_libraries/experts/hleg/index_en.htm.
76 See http://ec.europa.eu/information_society/activities/digital_libraries/doc/hleg/orphan/guidelines.pdf.
77 COM(2008) 466.
78 COM(2011) 289.
79 Directive 2012/28/EU of October 25 2012 (OJ L 299/5 of October 27 2012).
80 Spanish Official Gazette nº 55, of March 5 2011, Section I, page 25033.

within a period of 48 hours; or to make allegations and propose evidence. If the alleged infringer removes the content, the procedure ends. Otherwise, evidence is heard within a period of two days and the parties are given a period of five days to present their conclusions. Thereafter, the Commission will issue a Decision within a maximum period of three days. The enforcement of the Decision issued by the Second Section of the Copyright Commission requires prior judicial authorisation from the Central Contentious-Administrative Courts.[81] However, the Contentious-Administrative Court is not able to consider the merits of the case (ie, whether there is indeed a violation of copyright). Rather, the court must only take into account whether the measure in question is detrimental to the freedom of speech established in Article 20 of the Spanish Constitution. Moreover, the court's decision must be limited to either granting or denying the authorisation – it cannot modify or amend the measure.

This peculiar system has raised some major concerns, not the least of which is that it appears to craft an administrative procedure in the hope of achieving something that the courts have been denying so far – deeming that websites that provide links to copyrighted material located in peer-to-peer networks or on public servers, whether for downloading or streaming, engage in copyright infringement and closing them down. This is certainly unusual, as it is difficult to see how an administrative body could find those websites to be infringing, when some courts have found that they are not.

The Sinde Act has been largely unsuccessful in combating piracy. Although the main purpose of the act was to allow rights holders to act against websites linking users to infringing content, and thus indirectly benefiting from copyright infringements (ie, through advertising revenues), its poor drafting did not accurately identify these types of sites. More particularly, the Sinde Act did not properly draw the line between mere 'intermediate' service providers, which are bound only to a general 'duty of cooperation', and illegitimate link and stream aggregators. In practice, this meant that the Sinde Act's provisions led to legal uncertainty which was often ineffective against the internet services that it was initially meant to tackle.

During the first year of the Sinde Act, the Second Section of the Copyright Commission removed fewer than 40 illegal works from the Internet and was able to shut down only about 15 websites linking to infringing content. Consequently, it has come under heavy criticism from stakeholders in the culture sector. In essence, the main practical shortcomings of the Sinde Act are the following:

- Its inability to impose sufficiently stringent sanctions (ie, fines). Under the current regime, an infringer can just 'reboot' its activities with a new website.
- The current regime only allows one application before the Intellectual Property Commission per infringing work. This makes the whole system inefficient and cumbersome, since it does not allow a large number of copyright infringements to be dealt with simultaneously.
- Very rigorous formal requirements make the system highly unmanageable (ie, numerous applications are dismissed for purely formal reasons).

81 On this subject, see Durán Rivacoba, R, *'La protección de la propiedad intelectual en el ámbito de la sociedad de la información y de comercio electrónico'*, *Aranzadi Civil*, nº 2, 2011 [westlaw BIB 2011/467].

- The current regime does not provide an efficient system for properly identifying the individuals and/or companies that are actually operating the websites. This frequently represents a practical obstacle which renders the system ineffective.
- The whole procedure is very time-consuming (ie, applications can remain in the pipeline for many months or even over a year). Furthermore, the Second Section of the Copyright Commission has not established an effective mechanism for the service of documents on foreign individuals and/or companies.

However, it is expected that the Preliminary Draft reform of the SCA – if enacted in its current wording – will address at least some of the shortcomings of the current regime. In this regard, the current Preliminary Draft significantly overhauls the powers of the Second Section of the Copyright Commission. The Preliminary Draft's most significant improvements are the following:

- It will allow the Second Section of the Copyright Commission to act effectively against service providers, even if their participation in copyright infringement is largely indirect. The new wording of the Preliminary Draft aims squarely at streaming, linking and peer-to-peer websites, limiting previous legal safe havens for these types of websites and thus allowing more stringent enforcement. In principle, this overhaul will allow rights holders easily to combat new business models and infringement schemes.
- The current targeted 'work-by-work' approach is abandoned, in favour of a more efficient and flexible 'wide-sweep' system. This will allow a single applicant to either: enforce its rights in respect of any number of different works by means of a single application; or enforce rights in respect of generic subcategories of works (ie, movies, albums, etc) by means of a single application, covering not only its own rights, but also third-parties' rights. This is a key point of the reform which addresses a major shortcoming of the present system and will allow rights holders to combat piracy more efficiently.
- The timeline of the whole administrative process is shorter.
- For the first time, economic sanctions ranging from €30,000 to €300,000 can be imposed upon reoffending infringers.
- The Preliminary Draft also provides revamped mechanisms for fully shutting down internet domains.

The Preliminary Draft reform of the SCA must still undergo the regular legislative approval process. Although this is difficult to predict, in light of previous reform on the occasion of the Sinde Act, it is likely that the Preliminary Draft will be watered down somewhat by the Spanish Parliament.

1.12 Electronic infringement of moral rights

When addressing the question of the infringement of moral rights on websites, we should take into account the moral rights of the author of the site and the moral rights of the works contained therein.

Authors who authorise the inclusion of their work on a website preserve the moral rights *in integrum*. Basically, the paternity right must be recognised in the terms established in the SCA and the work cannot be amended unless strictly necessary. (The sound and image quality must respect the standard parameters for works exploited on the Internet.)[82] Otherwise, the moral rights would be infringed.

The authors of a website also preserve their moral rights (SCA, Article 14). They are entitled to: decide when and where their site is disclosed; have a name appear on the site (ie, paternity right); have the integrity of their work respected (ie, integrity right); modify the site; and remove it from trade. In those cases in which these rights are harmed, the rights are infringed.

(a) ***Proxy copies***

Moral rights can be infringed in relation to the proxy copies made by the servers that provide users with internet access. If the author of a website modifies the site and the server fails to update the proxy copy of the site with sufficient frequency, users may be accessing non-updated versions of such website, in which case they would be infringing the moral rights of the website author.[83]

(b) ***Filtering***

Filtering consists of screening the contents of a website using a computer program according to criteria predetermined by the user (eg, screening for sexual content, explicit violence, etc). If the filtering denies access to the website, no infringement of moral rights has been committed. However, if it permits access to the site but suppresses certain site elements (eg, pornographic images), this could infringe the integrity right, provided that the filtering is not implemented in the user's strictly private environment (ie, in the case of public communications sent from the distorted website).[84]

(c) ***Linking and framing***

When the link redirects the user to the home page of a website and the URL of the target website appears in the address bar of the search engine (ordinary link), this would not infringe moral rights. However, deep links redirecting to a specific page within a website could infringe the integrity right in cases where the website is fragmented/divided into sections or any part thereof is taken out of context, in such a way that it is detrimental to the legitimate interests of the author or discredits the author's reputation. Framing, in turn, is the practice which potentially raises more problems, as it could infringe: the paternity right, if it does not clearly indicate who the website's author is; and the integrity right, if the decontextualisation of the target page harms the legitimate interests or discredits the reputation of the website author.

---

82 Garrote Fernández-Díez, I and González Gonzalo, A, *'La protección de las páginas y sitios web a través de la propiedad intelectual'*, *op cit* page 113.

83 Martínez Espín, P, *"Artículo 14"* in Bercovitz, R (Coord), *Comentarios a la Ley de Propiedad Intelectual*, Tecnos, Madrid, 2007, pages 209 to 237.

84 Garrote Fernández-Díez, I and González Gonzalo, A, *'La protección de las páginas y sitios web a través de la propiedad intelectual'*, *op cit* page 115; Garrote Fernández-Díez, I, *El derecho de autor en internet*, Comares, Granada (2nd edition), pages 163 to 169.

2. Trademarks

2.1 Use of a trademark

Article 39 of the Spanish Trademark Act[85] (STMA) establishes the obligation for the holder of a trademark to use it on the market, either directly or through an authorised third party, for the registered goods or services. Failure to do so may lead to the expiry of the trademark. The legal requirement is that there is an effective and actual use of the trademark in Spain.

Spanish case law has defined the concept of effective use as public and external, not merely symbolic, and with a presence on the market.

For the use of a distinctive sign on a website to be considered effective use in Spain, it will be necessary, first, that the use of the distinctive sign has effects in Spain.[86]

In that respect, the website containing the distinctive sign must first be accessible and operational for the public;[87] this should be construed as meaning not just that the website can be displayed by the public in the territory in which the trademark is valid, but also that such page must be targeted at said public and be valid in that territory. In addition, the use of the sign on the website must consist of a use in the context of trade and an effective use of the trademark for distinguishing the goods or services registered by the trademark.

For the use of a distinctive sign on a website to be considered relevant for the purposes of a national trademark infringement action, the website will have to have effects in Spain and the use of such sign must meet the following requirements: the use must be in the context of Spanish trade; it must be for the purpose of distinguishing goods or services; and it must fall under one of the categories established in STMA, Article 34.2.

Under STMA, Article 34.2 the holder of a registered trademark may prohibit third parties from using, without its consent and in trade:

- any sign identical to the trademark for goods or services that are identical to those for which the trademark is registered;
- any sign that, being identical or similar to the trademark and for identical or similar goods or services, is likely to confuse the public; this likelihood of confusion includes the likelihood of association between the sign and the trademark; and
- any identical or similar sign for goods or services that are not similar to those for which the trademark is registered, when the trademark is well known in Spain and when the use of the sign without just cause may suggest a

---

85 Law 17/2001, of December 7, on Trademarks.

86 The Joint Recommendation of the Paris Union and the World Intellectual Property Organization (WIPO) Regarding the Protection of Marks and Other Industrial Property Rights on Signs on the Internet, approved by the Paris Union Assembly and the General Assembly of the WIPO during the thirty-sixth series of meetings of the Assemblies of Member States of the WIPO, held from September 24 to October 3 2001, establishes that the use of a sign on the Internet will be relevant for, *inter alia*, its maintenance in a specific territory, when said use has commercial effects in said territory, establishing reference criteria to be voluntarily followed by the member states to determine when said use has commercial effects.

87 Madrid Provincial Court Judgment (Section 28) of April 24 2008 [AC 2008/1412].

connection between the said goods or services and the trademark holder or, in general, when that use may take undue advantage or discredit the distinctive or well-known nature of the registered trademark.

2.2 Infringement

(a) Metatags

Conflicts between metatags and trademark rights could arise in situations where a third party's trademark is included in the information of a website's metatag so that when a search is performed on the trademark, the website in question ranks among the results.

For the use of a third party's trademark as a metatag to constitute trademark infringement, such use must comprise use in the normal course of business (ie, the website that includes the metatag must be a website with a market presence, and must be for the purposes of distinguishing the site's goods and services). Such use must also fall under one of the scenarios established in STMA, Article 34.2: the identical nature between the trademark and the metatag and between the goods and/or services; a similarity creating the likelihood of confusion; or similarity or identity of a well-known trademark and the metatag even when the goods or services are not similar.

Although Spanish case law on these issues is not very common, it is possible to cite a few cases. Thus, Alicante Commercial Court nº 1 handed down a ruling on January 31 2011,[88] in a complaint for the infringement of trademark rights and application for interim injunctions filed by three companies that owned several magazines, against the owners of the website www.youkioske.com, for having included as metatags the identifying trademarks of several magazines owned by the plaintiffs. When the name of the magazine was entered into the search engines, the defendants' website appeared. Alicante Mercantile Court granted the interim injunctions as a result of having found that there was evidence to prove that such use consisted of the unauthorised use of a sign identical to the trademark, in the course of business, to identify goods and services identical to those registered by the trademark, which, in turn, damaged the trademark.

In another case, the Provincial Court of Barcelona handed down a judgment dated July 24 2013[89] concluding that the use of a third party's trademark as a metatag to direct searches to the defendants' website would constitute a trademark infringement if the requirements of Article 34.2 of the STMA were met. In that case, the court considered that the use of the words 'Dalí', 'Salvador Dalí', 'Daum Dalí' and 'Dalí theather museum' as metatags in order to direct the search to the defendants' website, which contained the official web page of the defendants' painting exposition, involved trademark infringement. In the same judgment, the court rejected the existence of a trademark infringement in relation to other words also

---

88 [AC 2011/83].

89 [JUR/2013/293085]. Another judgment relating to the use of metatags is the judgment of the Burgos Provincial Court dated January 11 2013 [AC/2013/469].

used as metatags on the grounds that the requirements of STMA, Article 34.2 were not met. In relation to these latter uses, the court indicated that they could constitute acts of unfair competition, although it did not consider them as such since the plaintiff did not allege that possibility in the complaint.

(b) Keywords

Use of a third party's trademark as a keyword by an advertiser for the sake of publicity, such as through the appearance of a banner, could entail trademark infringement in certain cases.

In order to assess whether infringement exists, it would be necessary to ascertain whether the keyword is used in the course of business and to distinguish goods or services. In addition, it should be ascertained whether such keyword is identical or similar to the third party's trademark and used to distinguish identical or similar goods or services, creating a likelihood of confusion.

Although determining whether infringement exists depends on each specific case, the use of a trademark as a keyword could constitute infringement when, after selecting the word in a search engine, the third party's trademark is used in the resulting advertising of the banner to distinguish the advertiser's goods or services (although in this case the infringement would derive from the use of the trademark on the banner); or also in those cases where the resulting advertising does not use any trademark and could give the impression of association between the selected third-party trademark and the goods or services contained in the advertising. Otherwise, it would not appear that the use of a third-party trademark as a keyword could constitute trademark infringement in those cases where the advertiser uses its own trademark in the resulting advertising to distinguish the promoted goods or services.

In this respect, the Provincial Court of Alicante, in its Judgment of June 27 2013,[90] in accordance with the conclusions reached by the European Court of Justice in its Judgment of March 23 2010 (case C-236/08 to C-238/08 – *Google and Google France*), concluded that there was no trademark infringement for the use of a third party's trademark as a keyword, since none of the trademark's functions were affected. According to the judgment, the trademark used as a keyword did not appear in the relevant advertisement resulting from the search, and the manner in which the advert was presented (in particular, on the right-hand side of the screen under the title 'adverts') allowed the public to determine that the advertised products came from a third party and not from the trademark owner.

In those cases where trademark infringement exists, in general, that would be attributable to the advertiser which selects the keyword. As regards the search engine with which the advertising is contracted, although, in principle, it would not appear that such company is committing trademark infringement as a result of using the third-party trademark as a keyword (because, in theory, it would not entail use for distinctive purposes), it could be held liable, in certain circumstances, under LSSI.

90 [JUR/2013/278456].

(c) *Sponsored links*

Conflicts in relation to trademark rights due to contracting sponsored links could arise when the key word, which is the subject matter of the agreement between the advertiser and the search engine, consists of a third-party trademark.

For such use to constitute trademark infringement, the use of the third-party trademark should be carried out in the course of business and for distinctive purposes, as well as falling under one of the scenarios established in STMA, Article 34.2.

As some authorities have argued,[91] in situations where a third-party trademark is used as a keyword, but does not appear in the text of the advertisement, and, on the contrary, the advertiser's trademark does appear, it would be extremely difficult to allege trademark use in relation to the third-party trademark due to the fact that it would be highly unlikely that the user would confuse or establish a link between the offered goods or services and the third-party trademark. In these situations, no trademark infringement would exist.

The foregoing would not, however, prevent such acts from potentially constituting unfair competition, as some learned writers claim (if the requirements are met), because it could entail a means of winning over customers from the competition, who are drawn as a result of an 'initial interest confusion' (ie, the initial curiosity of someone who is looking for one product but comes across another). In any event, each situation must be analysed on a case-by-case basis.

In this respect, the Commercial Court of Madrid, in its Judgment of December 22 2011,[92] in accordance with the conclusions of the European Court of Justice in its Judgments of March 23 2010 (case C-236/08 to C-238/08 – *Google and Google France*) and July 12 2011 (C-324/09), concluded that the use of a third party's trademark as a keyword in order to advertise the defendant's web page (a direct competitor) where the third party's trademark was also used, entailed the existence of a trademark infringement, since the activity affected the trademark's function regarding the determination of the origin.

In another case, the Provincial Court of Granada, in its Judgment of March 16 2012,[93] in a case where the defendant had used a competitor's trademark as a keyword, concluded that, although there was no confusion among the public between the trademark's owner and the advertised web page by means of that keyword, such activity entailed an act of unfair competition since it involved taking advantage of the trademark owner's reputation. The court, in accordance with the conclusions of the European Court of Justice in its Judgment of September 22 2011 (case C-323/09 *Interflora*) rejected the possibility of a trademark infringement, since that activity did not affect the trademark's function regarding the determination of the origin.

---

91 Among others, Nuñez García, JL, *'Enlaces patrocinados y derecho de marcas: una nueva ciberocupación'*, *Revista Aranzadi de Derecho y Nuevas Tecnologías*, nº 11/2006 2, page 20.

92 [AC/2012/441].

93 [JUR/2012/347387].

(d) *Hidden text*

The 'word stuffing' technique consists of using a word in the structure of a website which has the same colour as the page's background, thereby rendering it invisible to users. However, it is detected by search engines and could conflict with trademark rights in those cases where a third party's distinctive sign is used as a hidden word in a website, with the intention of having that website appear in the list of search results on the third-party trademark.

For that use to constitute an infringement, as in the case of metatags, it is necessary to assess whether the use is in the course of business for distinctive purposes, and whether any of the scenarios established in STMA, Article 34.2 apply.

(e) *Internet domain names*

As regards the registration of a domain name, in general, case law[94] indicates that the mere registration of a domain name, alone, without any use, does not constitute the use of the sign on the market as a trademark. In that respect, learned writers are of the opinion that not just any use of a website will entail infringement. Rather, some commercial use must derive from its content.

If such commercial use is thus derived, it must be assessed whether distinctive use exists and whether any of the scenarios established in STMA, Article 34.2 apply.

(f) *Search navigation tools*

The possibility of search navigation tools, such as breadcrumb trails, entailing trademark infringement will depend on how such tools are used. In that respect, for the use of a third-party trademark as breadcrumbs to entail an infringement, such use must comply with the aforementioned requirements (ie, it must be used in the course of business for the purposes of distinguishing goods or services and it must fall under one of the scenarios established in STMA, Article 34.2).

(g) *Hypertext links*

The unauthorised use of a third-party distinctive sign, as a hyperlink on a website, does not always constitute trademark infringement. For such use to be considered as infringing, the third-party trademark as a link must be used in such a way that it convinces consumers that the third-party trademark used is not a link, but rather a sign distinguishing the goods or services of the website containing the link; or when it gives the impression that an economic relationship exists between the owner of the website where the link appears and the trademark used, although the rest of the requirements referred to above must also be met.

Trademark rights could also be infringed when the use of a third-party trademark as a hyperlink takes the consumer to a website not displaying the trademark holder's goods or services, but rather those of a third party.

Determining whether infringement exists will obviously depend on how the specific case is assessed, provided that the requirements established in the aforementioned trademark legislation have been met.

---

94 Vizcaya Provincial Court Judgment (Section 4) of September 6 2002 [JUR 2002/280275].

Lastly, when a third party's trademark is used as a hyperlink with all precautions in place, so that no relationship can be deduced between the website owner and the third-party trademark and when the page to which the link directs is not that of a competitor, such use may constitute a descriptive use, not deemed as a trademark infringement.[95]

(h) ***Framing***

The use of the technique known as 'framing' could entail trademark infringement. This will result in the liability of the owner of the website displaying the frame, in cases where consumers could construe that the goods and services identified by the third party's trademark which are captured or 'framed' on the website originate from the owner of the website displaying the frame, or another company with which it is economically associated. Trademark infringement could also exist, even when no third-party trademark is displayed in the framed website, if the website owner's trademark appears in the window of the website that displays the frame, and consumers could be led to believe that the goods or services appearing on the framed website are offered by the owner of the website displaying the frame, thereby causing confusion as to the company origin thereof. Obviously, ascertaining whether infringement exists will depend on how each specific case is evaluated and on the measures taken (eg, the use of disclaimers in the website that displays the frame).

2.3 Defences

(a) ***Descriptive (non-trademark) use of the mark***

Using a trademark for descriptive purposes, as opposed to a distinctive use, may not entail a trademark infringement, according to Article 37 of the STMA, which establishes limits on trademark rights.

In this regard, and in relation to some of the above-mentioned activities, when a third party's trademark is used as a key word in a referencing system or as a metatag, in order to show a website or advertisement offering spare parts or accessories to complement the products identified by the third party's trademark (ie, indicating the product's allocation) and where the advertiser's trademark was also used, such use may be considered a use of a descriptive (ie, not distinctive) nature and may not entail an infringement. This may also be the case when the third party's trademark is used to indicate the components or raw materials. However, it will be necessary to assess each situation on a case-by-case basis.

(b) ***Comparative advertising***

The use of a third party's trademark as a metatag or as a key word in a referencing system could also be considered as not constituting infringement, if the result obtained is a website or an advertisement where the third party's trademark is used

95 This is acknowledged by Ortega Díaz, JF, *op cit*, pages 226 *et seq*. However, the fact that they do not constitute trademark infringement does not mean that they cannot constitute acts of unfair competition, such as acts taking undue advantage of a third party's reputation.

for the purposes of comparative advertising between the advertiser's products and those of the other trademark, provided that no confusion is created as to the origin of the products and that comparative advertising regulations are met.

2.4 Parallel imports

The parallel import of products and their sale through a website could occasionally entail trademark infringement.

When the products offered, marketed or advertised in Spain on a website and, therefore, not only seen in Spain but also targeted at the Spanish population, consist of products which have not been previously launched on the market within the European Economic Area by the trademark holder or by a third party with its consent, the trademark holder would be authorised to invoke its trademark right against such actions because, in principle, the exhaustion of the trademark right would not apply.

If the marketing or advertising of products refers to products previously launched by the trademark holder within the European Economic Area, or by a third party with its consent, the exhaustion of the trademark right established in STMA, Article 36 would apply and the trademark holder would not, in principle, be able to prevent the marketing and advertising of the products, unless there were legitimate reasons for doing so, in particular, where the products had been modified after the marketing.

With regard to cases involving so-called grey sales, as referred to in some court judgments,[96] the trademark holder could oppose such sales, as an exception to the exhaustion of the trademark right, in those cases in which the third-party distribution of the products discredits the trademark's reputation, for example, by using a sales channel different from the one used by the trademark holder through its authorised distributors.

2.5 Remedies

Under STMA, Article 40 the trademark holder is entitled to take civil and criminal actions against anyone infringing its trademark rights, and to seek the corresponding measures to protect such rights.

Article 41 of the same law establishes the civil actions that trademark holders may take in the event of trademark infringement.

Among such actions, the trademark holder can seek: cessation of the acts infringing its right; compensation for damages sustained; measures required to prevent the infringement from continuing; or publication of the judgment at the infringer's expense, through announcements and notices served on interested parties.

In addition, the trademark holder can request, when appropriate, the adoption of the first and third of the above-mentioned measures against the intermediaries to which a third party turns in order to infringe trademark rights, even though the acts performed by the intermediary do not constitute a trademark infringement,

96 For instance, Madrid Provincial Court Judgment (Section 28) of October 5 2006 of [JUR 2007/54756].

notwithstanding the provisions stated in LSSI. These measures must be objective, proportionate and non-discriminatory.

2.6 Liability of ISPs

In Spain the liability of ISPs is mainly governed by LSSI, implementing European Directive 2000/31/EC.[97] LSSI contains several articles regulating ISPs' liability, depending on the activity performed.

With regard to ISPs, construed as those parties which provide links to content or search instruments, LSSI Article 17.1 states that they will not be liable for the information to which their users are directed, if: they have no actual knowledge of illegal information or activity or that it damages third parties rights or assets, susceptible to be indemnified; or upon obtaining such knowledge, they act expeditiously to remove or to disable the corresponding link.

According to this article, the service provider has 'actual knowledge' when a competent authority has declared the information unlawful, ordering its removal or disabling access thereto, or if the existence of damage has been declared and the service provider is aware of that decision, notwithstanding the procedures for the detection and removal of content that the service providers voluntarily apply, and other means of actual knowledge which could be established. In relation to the concept of the service provider's 'actual knowledge', recent Spanish Supreme Court judgments have provided a broader interpretation, stating that this actual knowledge would also exist in those situations where the service provider could be aware of the activity in question, notwithstanding the decision referred to above.

The exemption from liability established in section 1 of Article 17 will not apply in the event that the content supplier to which the link leads or whose location is supplied is acting on the instructions or authority or under the control of the provider who supplies the location of such content.

In addition, the STMA establishes the possibility for the trademark holder in appropriate circumstances to request from intermediaries (although not themselves liable for trademark infringement), the cessation of infringing activities or the adoption of measures to prevent infringement from continuing, notwithstanding the provisions stated in LSSI.

2.7 Advertising law and regulations

Internet advertising activities are also governed by the General Law on Advertising[98] (GLA) and the Unfair Competition Act[99] (UCA).

The GLA regulates advertising activities which have effects in Spain, and defines advertising as any form of communication implemented by an individual or a company in the context of a commercial, industrial, professional or craft activity, aimed at directly or indirectly promoting the acquisition of movable or immovable property, services, rights or obligations. Therefore, internet advertising would fall

---

97 Directive 2000/31/EC of the European Parliament and of the Council of June 8 2000 on certain legal aspects of information society services, in particular electronic commerce, in the Internal Market.

98 General Law 34/1988, of November 11, on Advertising.

99 Law 3/1991, of January 10, on Unfair Competition.

under this definition. This law also defines what is to be construed as unlawful advertising; however, it does not provide for specific action against unlawful advertising. Since unlawful advertising is also considered unfair competition, any action for unlawful advertising will be governed by the UCA.

The UCA prohibits unfair competition, including unlawful advertising. The law applies to those activities performed on the market for competitive purposes, including internet advertising activities. An activity is deemed to be for competitive purposes when it is suitable for promoting or guaranteeing the diffusion on the market of one's own or a third party's services. For this law to apply, the activity in question must have an effect on the Spanish market, irrespective of the place where the activity is performed and the address of the individual performing the activity.

As the European Court of Justice ruled in its Judgment of July 11 2013,[100] the term 'advertising' covers the use of a domain name and that of metatags in a website's metadata. The use of metatags, consisting of keywords (keyword metatags), which are read by the search engines when they scan the Internet to carry out referencing of the many sites there, constitutes one of the factors enabling those engines to rank the sites according to their relevance to the search term entered by the internet user. Accordingly, the use of such tags corresponding to the names of a competitor's goods and its trade name will, in general, have the effect that, when an internet user looking for the goods of that competitor enters one of these names or that trade name in a search engine, the natural result displayed by it will be changed to the advantage of the user of those metatags and the link to its website will be included in the list of those results, in some cases directly next to the link to that competitor's website.

In the majority of cases, an internet user entering the name of a company's product or that company's name as a search term is looking for information or offers on that specific product or that company and its range of products. Accordingly, when links to sites offering the goods of a competitor of that company are displayed, in the list of natural results, the internet user may perceive those links as offering an alternative to the goods of that company or think that they lead to sites offering its goods. According to the European Court of Justice, in so far as the use of metatags corresponding to the names of a competitor's goods and its trade name in the programming code of a website has the consequence that it is suggested to the internet user who enters one of those names or that trade name as a search term that that site is related to his/her search, such use must be considered as a form of representation within the meaning of Article 2(1) of Directive 84/450 and Article 2(a) of Directive 2006/114.[101] There is no doubt for the European Court of Justice that such use of metatags is a promotional strategy in that it aims to encourage the internet user to visit the site of the metatag user and to take an interest in its goods or services.

In addition, industry codes of conduct would also apply, establishing certain

100 Case C-657/11.

101 Article 2 of Council Directive 84/450/EEC of September 10 1984 concerning misleading and comparative advertising (OJ 1984 L 250, p 17), as amended by Directive 2005/29/EC of the European Parliament and of the Council of May 11 2005 (OJ 2005 L 149, p 22) ('Directive 84/450') and Article 2 of Directive 2006/114/EC of the European Parliament and of the Council of December 12 2006 concerning misleading and comparative advertising (OJ 2006 L 376, p 21).

principles on advertising activities. The *Asociación para la Autorregulación de la Comunicación Commercial* (Autocontrol) has issued the Code of Advertising Conduct which, albeit only binding on its members, establishes certain principles for engaging in advertising activities (including internet advertising activities).[102]

Furthermore, the Code of Online Ethics and Conduct (*Código de Confianza Online*) applies to advertising activities performed by remote electronic means. This code contains certain ethical principles for engaging in advertising activities and is only binding on its members.[103]

2.8 Domain name disputes

The Assignment Authority for '.es' domain names, Red.es, establishes a system for settling, out of court, any conflicts or disputes arising with regard to the registration of an '.es' domain name between the owner of the domain name and a third party allegedly holding a prior right, such as a trademark right. This procedure is governed by the Regulation on the extrajudicial dispute settlement procedure regarding domain names under the country code for Spain.

The procedure commences with the filing of a complaint before a provider accredited by Red.es, in which the plaintiff holding the prior right must prove: that the domain name is similar or identical to its prior right, to the extent that it creates a likelihood of confusion; that the domain name owner has no legitimate rights or interests over said domain name; and that the domain name has been registered or used in bad faith.

Complaints are resolved by an out-of-court dispute settlement expert, appointed by the provider, within two months of the date on which the complaint is filed.

2.9 Unfair competition/passing off

The STMA affords no protection for unregistered trademarks, except in the case of well-known unregistered trademarks, according to CUP, Article *6bis*.[104] However, holders of unregistered trademarks may seek protection under the UCA, provided they meet the relevant requirements.

The existence of a registered trademark does not, however, prevent the potential application of the UCA in certain situations, if the relevant requirements are met.

The STMA and the UCA are complementary systems whereby conduct protected under the former would not be protected under the latter, because the STMA is the special law on the subject. However, certain conduct not covered under the STMA may be covered under the UCA, if the relevant requirements are met.

By way of example, and provided that the requirements are met, it may be that certain conduct, such as the use of a third party's trademark as a metatag, infringes a trademark right because it could create a likelihood of confusion as to the origin of the products, and also be deemed an act of unfair competition, if such use constitutes unfair obstruction or taking undue advantage of a third party's reputation.

---

102 See http://www.autocontrol.es.

103 See http://www.confianzaonline.es.

104 Paris Convention for the Protection of Industrial Property of March 20 1883.

3. Patents

3.1 Patentability of 'internet' inventions

Articles 4.4 and 4.5 of the Spanish Patent Act[105] (SPA) mirror Articles 52.2 and 52.3 of the European Patent Convention[106] (EPC).

Article 4.4 of the SPA provides that, for patentability purposes, mathematical methods, business methods, computer programs and presentations of information are not regarded as inventions.

However, SPA, Article 4.5 makes it clear that mathematical methods, business methods, computer programs and presentations of information cannot be patented if the patent application relates to such subject matter or activities as such. Thus, inventions comprising (as opposed to consisting of) or relying on mathematical methods, business methods, computer programs and presentations of information may be patented if the patented subject matter, considered as a whole, entails some technical element (eg, computer-implemented inventions involving a technical process controlled by a program).

3.2 Bioinformatics

Mirroring Article 5.1 of Directive 98/44/EC,[107] Article 5.4 of the SPA provides that the simple discovery of a part of the human body, for instance, a novel DNA sequence (or a partial sequence) or a protein structure, is excluded from patentability. However, an element isolated from the human body or otherwise produced by means of a technical process may be patented. In the case of a novel DNA sequence, patentability further requires that its industrial application be explicitly disclosed in the patent application.

Thus, in the case of a novel DNA sequence (in whole or in part), or a protein structure, patentability will not depend on whether or not they were discovered through the use of bioinformatics, but on whether or not: such novel DNA sequence and protein may be isolated from the human body or otherwise produced by means of a technical process; and at least one industrial application for the novel DNA sequence may be identified in the patent application.

The degree of detail of the industrial application for the novel DNA sequence or protein that must be disclosed in the patent application to meet this patentability requirement is uncertain. Since there are no court precedents in Spain in this regard, it is likely that Spanish courts would seek guidance from the EPO Technical Boards of Appeal case law whenever they are called to rule on this matter.

3.3 Issues specific to Spain

(a) Infringement on the Internet

With regard to patent infringement committed via the Internet, Spanish courts will

105 Law 11/1986, of March 20, on Patents.
106 Convention on the Grant of European Patents of October 5 1973.
107 Directive 98/44/EC of the European Parliament and of the Council of July 6 1998 on the legal protection of biotechnological inventions ('Directive 98/44').

typically have jurisdiction when: the infringer-defendant is domiciled in Spain (Article 2 of EC Regulation 44/2001; Article 22.2 of Organic Law 1/1985 of July 6, on the Judiciary); or when the infringement of a valid Spanish patent (or of a national validation of a European Patent) has occurred or may occur in Spain (Article 5 of EC Regulation 44/2001; Article 22.3 of Organic Law 1/1985).

Barcelona Provincial Court (Fifteenth Chamber) (a specialist IP court since 1993) found in Ruling nº 122/2007, dated April 26 2007, that the universality of the Internet does not exclude the jurisdiction of Spanish courts when the infringing act also occurs in Spain and there is a valid intellectual property right in place in Spain. Although this case dealt with trademarks, this finding may be applied to patents by analogy. Therefore, in addition to cases where the defendant might be domiciled in Spain, Spanish courts would also typically find that they have jurisdiction over patent infringement cases committed via the Internet if it can plausibly be argued that infringement via the Internet affects the Spanish territory (albeit not substantially) and the claimant is invoking a valid Spanish patent (or a national validation of a European Patent). In other words, Spanish courts will only refuse jurisdiction to hear patent cases where there is no evidence disclosing an intention on the part of the person performing the allegedly infringing act to target the Spanish territory.

(b) Links to websites where patented products are offered for sale

Barcelona Provincial Court (Fifteenth Chamber) found in Judgment nº 446/2010, dated December 13 2010, that placing in a website a link to a different website where infringing products are actually offered for sale, cannot be considered as an infringing act (offer) when, by placing such a link, the owner of the website had no intention of marketing the patented products, but simply provided information on the existence of a different company offering the products. It is worth mentioning that this finding was made in spite of the undisputed relationship between the companies owning the two different websites (ie, they belonged to the same group).

(c) Process patents

With regard to cases involving process patents infringed via the Internet where only part of the process is executed in Spain, unlike in other jurisdictions (eg, the United Kingdom (see *Menashe v William Hill*))[108] there is no case law to shed any light on how Spanish courts would rule on infringement (either direct or contributory).

In principle, it might be expected that Spanish courts would reject direct infringement if the patented process is not executed entirely in Spain. However, if a third party has supplied or offered to supply means to work the patented process, regarding an essential element of the process, to persons not authorised to put it into practice, when that third party knew or it was clear from the circumstances that such means were suitable to put the invention into practice and were intended for that purpose, it should not be ruled out that Spanish courts will find contributory infringement, even if part of the patented process was not executed in Spain.

108 2002EWCA CIV 1702.

Although Spanish courts would be likely to apply the 'double-territorial' test,[109] they might adopt a teleological approach and find contributory infringement if the part of the process not executed in Spain is not material and the technical effect or result of working the patent is available for the user of the process in Spain.

3.4 Remedies available for patent infringement

A patent holder is entitled to take civil and criminal action against anyone infringing its patent rights and to seek corresponding measures to protect such rights.

With regard to civil action, SPA Article 63 includes an illustrative list of the types of relief that may be sought in the main proceedings by a patent holder whose rights have been infringed:

- an order for the cessation of the infringing acts (ie, an injunction);
- an award of damages;
- an order for the seizure of the infringing items and the means exclusively used for the production thereof or for executing the patented process;
- an order for assignment of the ownership of infringing items seized under the above bullet point to the patent holder, where possible, in which case the value thereof will be deducted from the amount of damages awarded and, if the value exceeds the amount of damages awarded, the patent holder will pay the excess amount to the infringer;
- the adoption of any other measures required to prevent the patent infringement from continuing and, in particular, the alteration or destruction of infringing items when this is essential to prevent the patent infringement; and
- the publication of the judgment against the patent infringer, at the infringer's expense, by means of announcements and notices served on interested parties.

4. Disclosure orders against ISPs

4.1 Availability

Under Spanish law, disclosure orders can be obtained against ISPs, requiring them to disclose the identity and contact details of a user of their service who is suspected of infringing intellectual property rights (IPR).

In the context of a civil action, pursuant to the provisions of Article 256.1.7 of the Spanish Law on Civil Procedure (SCPA), an IPR owner who intends to file a claim

109 First, the supply or offer of the essential element of the invention would have to take place in Spain. Secondly, the essential means provided should be also suitable and intended for putting the invention into effect in Spain.

110 In Barcelona Provincial Court Rulings (Section 15) of December 10 and 15 2009 [JUR 2010\117525 and JUR 2010\117178], the court set aside applications filed by IPR owners for ISPs to disclose details of certain internet protocol users who were exchanging protected works in peer-to-peer networks, but not on a commercial scale. Along the same lines, Madrid Provincial Court Ruling (Section 28) of November 12 2010 [AC 2010\2305] confirmed a first instance ruling, which stated that the fact that internet users were using peer-to-peer networks to make unauthorised copies of protected works for personal use, but not to transfer them to third parties for profit, was insufficient to grant Preliminary Procedures in a civil action.

for the infringement of its IPR committed through acts performed on a commercial scale can request, in 'Preliminary Procedures', details of the origin of the goods or services infringing its IPR, including "the names and addresses of the producers, manufacturers, distributors, suppliers and providers of the goods and services, as well as of those who, for commercial purposes, have been in possession of the goods". The exhibition of the bank, financial, commercial or customs documents issued within a specific period of time and assumed to be in possession of the person to be sued and held liable, can also be requested (SCPA, Article 256.1.8).

It is important to stress that it is the commercial level of the infringement of the IPR, together with the degree of the infringement, which justifies a Spanish court making an order to impose the obligation on ISPs to disclose the identity and contact details of a suspected infringer in the framework of civil proceedings. SCPA establishes that 'acts performed on a commercial scale' should be construed as acts performed to obtain direct or indirect financial or commercial profit. In practice, it is extremely difficult to obtain this type of disclosure order from civil courts in cases where users solely share documents without obtaining profits, even though the conduct per se infringes IPR. In recent years, the Barcelona and Madrid Provincial Courts have set aside applications filed by IPR owners for ISPs to disclose details of the identity of users of their services, on the grounds that the activities performed by those unidentified users were not performed on a commercial scale.[110]

In the context of criminal action, a disclosure order can be obtained against ISPs, requiring them to disclose the identity and contact details of any user of their service suspected of infringing an IPR, irrespective of whether or not the infringing acts are performed on a commercial scale. In particular, Spanish Law 25/2007, of October 18, on the Retention of Data Related to Electronic Communications and Public Communications Networks, implementing Directive 2006/24/EC of the European Parliament and of the Council of March 15 2006 on the retention of data generated or processed in connection with the provision of publicly available electronic communications services or of public communications networks, and amending Directive 2002/58/EC, imposes an obligation upon ISPs to retain data generated or processed in the framework of services rendered by way of electronic communications and public communications networks, as well as an obligation to provide such data to authorised agents, whenever they are required to do so in a court order, in order to detect, investigate and prosecute the criminal offences established in the Spanish Criminal Code.

Finally, LSSI Article 8 establishes a further mechanism whereby the Copyright Commission, a body under the authority of the Ministry of Culture,[111] may request ISPs to disclose data so that anyone infringing copyright works can be identified and can appear in the proceedings. The Copyright Commission can only make such a request with prior judicial authorisation.

111 Law 2/2011, of March 4, of Sustainable Economy, created the Second Section of the Copyright Commission, a national collegiate committee, one of the functions of which is to protect copyright.

4.2 Requirements

To obtain a disclosure order, the IPR owner applying for a Preliminary Procedure must file an application at court, stating the grounds that would in its opinion justify the grant of the Preliminary Procedure or pre-trial examination of the potential defendant, with a detailed reference to the subject matter of the legal action that the applicant intends to prepare. The IPR owner must also adduce evidence of the ownership of the IPR. Finally, if the exhibition of documents is requested, the application must be accompanied by *prima facie* evidence of the existence of the infringement.

Should the court find that the application is suitable for the applicant's purposes, and that both just cause and legitimate interest exist, it will grant the application, fixing the security to be furnished by the IPR holder to cover any damage that might be caused to the defendant.

4.3 Jurisdictional issues

Preliminary Procedures must be filed before the Mercantile Courts, specialising in the civil jurisdiction and created in 2004. In addition, jurisdiction must correspond to the court with which the complaint is to be filed. If a new procedure is applied for in view of the outcome of the previous procedure, such new procedure may be applied for before the same court or before the court which, based on the facts ascertained in the previous procedure, has competence to hear the same plea or any new pleas that may be joined thereto.

4.4 'John Doe' injunctions

To date, 'John Doe' injunctions have not been obtained in Spain to prevent IPR infringement, against unknown persons. None the less, SCPA Article 256.1.1 provides for the possibility of applying for Preliminary Procedures against the person against whom a potential future complaint may be filed, so that that person can declare on facts concerning his/her capacity, representation or legal competence, required for filing the IPR infringement complaint.

Sweden

Monique Wadsted
MAQS Law Firm

General

Swedish courts are, in general, loyal to and find it important to rule in conformity with Sweden's international obligations. In this respect EU law and the case law of the Court of Justice of the European Union (CJEU) is of specific importance. Normally, Swedish courts will apply and interpret Swedish law in conformity with EU law and the case law of the CJEU, unless it is obviously contrary to Swedish law. EU law and case law of the CJEU, therefore, have specific importance as legal sources in Sweden in the intellectual property (IP) field.

1. Copyright, database rights and design rights

1.1 Overview

(a) Literary works and artistic works

Literary works and artistic works are protected under Chapter 1, Section 1 of the Swedish Copyright Act (1960:729) ('the Copyright Act'). Copyright includes the right to reproduction and communication to the public, including making available on-demand, public performance, public display and distribution to the public. Further, communication to the public and public performance carried out for profit embrace those made to a closed large group of individuals (eg, communication via an intranet).

The exclusive rights include exploitation of the original or an altered form, in translation or adaptation, in another literary or artistic form, or in another technical manner.

The reproduction right includes any direct or indirect, temporary or permanent reproduction regardless of the form or method by which this is carried out and regardless of whether it concerns the work in whole or in part.

Swedish copyright law is technology neutral. Thus, digital reproductions may attract protection if they are sufficiently original. Further, communication to the public including direct transmission and making available on demand via the Internet is included in the exclusive right of the rights holder.

Software may attract protection as a literary work if it is sufficiently original. Computer programs are not defined in the Copyright Act, but the definition provided by the World Intellectual Property Organization (WIPO) at the start of the 1970s has frequently been applied over the years. According to this definition a computer program is "a set of instructions capable, when incorporated in a machine-readable medium, of causing a machine having information-processing capabilities to indicate, perform or achieve a particular function, task or result". The software protection in the Copyright Act includes all these stages, and also all preparatory design material to computer programs.[1]

(b) ***Films, sound recordings, and broadcasts***

Besides copyright protection (see (a) above) the producer of a film or sound recording has a neighbouring right under Chapter 5, Section 46 of the Copyright Act to the fixation of the film or sound, even if it is not protected by copyright.

The provision provides the same protection for fixations of films and sounds as for copyright, but is limited to producers within the European Economic Area.

Producers of sound recordings have the same rights as producers of films. However, public performances and transmissions of the fixation of a sound recording are permitted without specific authorisation provided the rights holders are compensated for the use. However, making sound recordings available on demand will require authorisation.

Radio and TV broadcasters have a neighbouring right under Chapter 5, Section 48 of the Copyright Act. Under this provision, a broadcaster has an exclusive so-called signal right. The signal right is dependent on the fact that the communication is a 'broadcast'. An on-demand transmission of a TV programme is not considered to be a broadcast under Swedish law and is thus not covered by the 'signal right'.

However, the exclusive right does include the making available on demand by wire or wireless means of a fixation of broadcast.

(c) ***Typographical arrangement of a published edition***

A typographical arrangement may attract copyright protection, provided it is sufficiently original.

(d) ***Protection of the user interface***

The look and feel of a graphical user interface may attract copyright protection as a literary or artistic work on the condition that it is sufficiently original; however, probably not as a computer program after the CJEU held that a graphical user interface is not a form of expression of a computer program.[2]

The look and feel of a graphical user interface can also be protected under the Swedish Design Act.[3] Protection arises if the design is registered. The requirement for registration is that the design is new and has a distinctive character.[4] Application for registration is made to the Patent and Registration Office. Design and copyright protection can exist simultaneously and the two forms of protection are not mutually exclusive.[5]

(e) ***Computer-generated works***

---

1 Olsson, *Upphovsrättslagstiftningen, En kommentar,* Norstedts Juridik, 2009, 3rd edition, p 40.
2 CJEU, Case No C-393/09. Cf Supreme Court judgment NJA 2000, s 580 (*Nintendo*).
3 Prop 2001/02:121, p 47.
4 Chapter 1, Section 2 of the Design Act.
5 Chapter 1, Section 10 of the Copyright Act.

In order to attract copyright protection a creation must be made by a natural person. Thus, works that are created by computers are not protected by copyright in Sweden.

(f) *Websites protected as databases*

The *sui generis* right in the Database Directive (96/9EC) has been implemented in Chapter 5, Section 49 of the Copyright Act. This provision also includes a protection for compilations, such as tables or other similar products, including a large number of information items (ie, the so-called Nordic catalogue rule).

It has been questioned whether the Nordic catalogue rule is still applicable after the implementation of the Database Directive. Websites may be protected under the *sui generis* protection provided that the requirements of substantial investment etc are fulfilled. Further, websites may attract protection under the Nordic catalogue rule if they contain a large number of items of information and if the rule would still be considered applicable. A website may also be protected by copyright if it is sufficiently original and a product of the author's own intellectual creation.

(g) *Compilations*

Chapter 1, Section 5 of the Copyright Act provides that a person who, by combining works or parts of works, creates a literary or artistic compilation shall have copyright therein, but such right will be without prejudice to the rights to the separate parts of the compilation. The fundamental requirement in order for a creation to attract copyright under Swedish law is that that it has "risen to a degree of independence and originality".[6] Thus, a compilation that is sufficiently original may be protected by copyright in Sweden. This is also consistent with the judgment of the CJEU in *Football Dataco and others v Yahoo! and others*.[7]

Sweden does not apply the sweat of the brow doctrine.

1.2 Infringing acts

(a) *Copying*

Temporary copies: Temporary forms of copies of works may be made, if the copying forms an integral and essential part of a technological process and if the copies are transient or have only a secondary importance in that process. However, the following conditions apply: the copies may not have any independent economic importance; or the sole purpose is to enable a transmission in a network between third parties by an intermediary; or the use is lawful (ie, a use that is made with the authorisation of the rights holder or permitted by law). The exception for temporary copies does not apply to production of copies of computer programs or compilations.

(b) *Issuing copies to the public*

The exclusive distribution right covers only physical copies of a work. Transmitting

6 See eg, Supreme Court Judgment NJA 2004 page 149.
7 Case C-604/10.

or making a work available on demand for download by wire or wireless means is included in the exclusive right of communication to the public.

(c) ***Communicating work to the public***

'Communication to the public' includes transmission to the public by wire or by wireless means that occurs from a place other than where the public may enjoy the work. Communicating to the public also includes acts of communication that occur in such a way that members of the public may access the work from a place and at a time individually chosen by them (ie, on demand).[8]

(d) ***Perform, show or play work in public***

The exclusive right of performance to the public includes performances made at the same place where the public may enjoy the work, even if technical devices are used.[9]

(e) ***Rent or lend the work to the public***

Renting or lending to the public covers only physical copies. If a work is rented etc to the public via wire or wireless means, it is included in the exclusive right of communication to the public.

(f) ***Authorising another person to do any of the above***

Only the rights holder may authorise another person's use of the work. The transfer or licence must be clear and precise. A transfer of copyright will only include a right been specifically agreed. However, no specific authorisation is required if more or less all assets of a business are transferred including copyrights; but the transferor will not be relieved from his/her obligations vis-à-vis the previous rights holder.

A transfer of the right to communicate and perform a work to the public is non-exclusive unless exclusivity is specifically agreed. Even if exclusivity is agreed the transfer of the right to communication or performance to the public will become non-exclusive if the acquirer has not utilised its right within three years from the date of the transfer. This does not, however, apply to audiovisual works.

Unless otherwise agreed, an agreement including the transfer of a right to record a literary or artistic work into an audiovisual work as well as a film that is not in itself protected by copyright includes a right to communicate the works to the public, through the film, in cinemas, on television or in other form and to communicate spoken parts of the film in writing and translation (dubbing and subtitles). This right of the acquirer does not extend to musical works.

(g) ***Secondary infringement***

The concept of secondary infringement, or secondary liability, is provided for in Chapter 7, Sections 53 and 53b of the Copyright Act and is based on the principles laid down in Chapter 23, Section 4 of the Swedish Penal Code ('Penal Code').[10]

The Penal Code states that punishment shall be imposed on anyone who has

---

8 Chapter 1, Section 2 of the Copyright Act.
9 Chapter 1, Section 2 of the Copyright Act.

furthered an act by advice or deed. The liability applies also to contributory copyright infringements. The Copyright Act states that punishment shall be imposed on anyone who, in relation to a literary or artistic work, commits an act which infringes the copyright enjoyed in the work. Furthermore, under the Copyright Act, the courts may order an injunction against a person who commits an infringement or contributes to such act of infringement even if such infringement is not made by gross negligence or intent.

In the *Pirate Bay* case[11] the Swedish Court of Appeal held that the defendants, who were the founders of The Pirate Bay, had contributed to copyright infringement by providing a website with well-developed search functions, easy upload and storing capabilities and by conveying contacts between individual file sharers. Also the provision of internet access to The Pirate Bay was considered to be a contribution to the infringements taking place via The Pirate Bay. Thus, the copyright infringements of others were deemed to have been illegally furthered by the activities of the defendants. In other words, the Pirate Bay founders were found to have 'secondary liability'.

Despite this outcome, the infringing activity on the Pirate Bay website continued. As a result, several rights holders applied for an interim injunction against three of the founders and the internet access provider of The Pirate Bay, in order to stop the ongoing infringement. In 2010, the Svea Court of Appeal ordered the founders of The Pirate Bay to stop participating in making certain works available via the website 'piratebay.org'. Furthermore, it ordered the internet access provider to stop providing internet access to the website.[12] A final injunction on the merits with essentially the same content was awarded by the District Court of Stockholm in a judgment of October 2012. The judgment was not appealed and is thus final.

In the case, the plaintiffs applied reasoning based on cause and effect and argued that the services provided by Black Internet were essential for The Pirate Bay being able to provide its services, and thereby contributed to the infringing activities on the site. According to the preparatory works of the Copyright Act, secondary liability is applicable when the intermediary has knowledge, or comes across indications that the server space is being used in a manner which infringes protected material. Black Internet was aware of the fact that copyright-protected material was transmitted within its services and was therefore liable for secondary infringement.

In a third case, the *Portlane* case, a number of rights holders successfully demanded an injunction against the internet service provider (ISP), Portlane, in order to stop it from contributory copyright infringement by providing internet access to trackers related to The Pirate Bay.[13] The Court of Appeal held that Portlane had been informed of the fact that the tracker to which it provided internet access was used by users to file-share movies etc illegally. Moreover, the Court of Appeal found that Portlane was able to prevent further illegal file sharing. Such measures, for instance by completely ceasing to provide internet access to the tracker, were considered proportionate.

10 The Swedish Penal Code (1962:700).

11 Judgment November 26 2010 by Svea Court of Appeal, case No B 4041-09.

12 Decision May 21 2010 by Svea Court of Appeal, cases No Ö 7131-09 and T Ö 8773-09.

13 Decision May 21 2010, Svea Court of Appeal, case No Ö 10146-09.

1.3 Test for copyright infringement

(a) *Requirement of substantial reproduction*

Swedish law does not include any requirement of substantial reproduction. An infringement can thus relate to only one unauthorised reproduction. However, it is not an offence to reproduce computer software and digital copies of compilations that have been published or distributed to the public with the authorisation of the rights holder, provided that the reproduction is made for private use and on the condition that the reproduction is a reproduction of a master copy that is not used in a business or in an operation of a public authority.

Further, an individual that has reproduced an illegal copy of a work for private use will be liable to pay reasonable compensation and damages for this use only if the reproduction was made intentionally or by grossly negligent conduct.

(b) *Repeated copying of insubstantial part*

Whether or not a copy is reproduced by repeated copying of insubstantial parts will not affect the infringement test. As long as the repeated copying results in the whole or an essential part of the work being reproduced, this will be deemed an infringement of the exclusive reproduction right. The same applies to databases.

1.4 Exemptions/defences to copyright infringement

(a) *Format shifting*

Format shifting (ie, when a work is adapted or adjusted into another technological format), is allowed for certain archives and libraries and for specified purposes as stated in Chapter 2, Section 16 of the Copyright Act.

The right for archives and libraries to reproduce works for the purposes mentioned above includes all types of works, except computer programs.[14]

(b) *Personal copying rights*

The Copyright Act includes a private copy exception. This exception is not applicable if the master copy used for the private reproduction has been reproduced or communicated to the public without authorisation of the rights holder. Further, the private copy exception does not permit construction of works of architecture, reproduction of computer programs and digital copies of compilations. Moreover, the provisions do not confer a right to engage another party to make copies for private use, of musical works, cinematographic works, design works or sculptures, or copy another person's work of fine art by means of artistic reproduction.

Copyright levies are payable in Sweden in order to compensate authors, performers and producers to some extent for the production of private copies.

(c) *Time shifting*

Time shifting requires authorisation from all relevant rights holders. From November

---

14 Chapter 2, Section 16 of the Copyright Act.

1 2013, it may be possible for an operator of a time shifting service to mass-license the right to provide such service to its customers through an extended collective licence provided for in Chapter 3a, Section 42h of the Copyright Act.

(d) ***Fair use***

Swedish law does not include a general 'fair use' exception, but specified exceptions (eg, the quotation right that includes a right to quote published works in accordance with proper usage and to the extent necessary for the purpose).

(e) ***Caching/temporary copies as part of communication process***

Temporary forms of copies of works may be made, if the making of the copies forms an integral and essential part of a technical process and if the copies are transient or have only a secondary importance in that process[15] (see further above, section 1.2(a)).

(f) ***Hosting***

Under the Copyright Act, hosting may be a contributory infringement for hosting infringing content. The requirement is that the hosting has been carried out intentionally or by gross negligence. An injunction requires neither intent nor negligence, but that the hosting provider has been informed in one way or another that it hosts infringing content.

The limitations on criminal liability for hosting in the E-commerce Act were invoked by the founders of The Pirate Bay in the *Pirate Bay* criminal case.[16] However, the court held that since they had acted intentionally, the limitation did not apply.

Further, the Act on Responsibility for Electronic Bulletin Boards provides that the operator of an electronic bulletin board is obliged to supervise the service to an extent that is reasonable considering the extent and objective of the service. If it is obvious that a user by uploading something to an electronic bulletin board infringes copyright or a related right, the operator will be obliged to remove the infringing content or in some other way make it inaccessible. (The act is applicable to, for example, web hotels, chats and blogs.)

(g) ***Back-up copies***

Anyone who has the right to use a computer program is entitled make such back-up copies of the program as are necessary in order for the user to use the program within the scope of its intended use.[17] The copies may be used only for this purpose and only during the period that the user has the right to use the program.

(h) ***Reverse engineering***

Anyone who has the right to use a computer program is entitled to observe, study or test the function of the program in order to ascertain the ideas and principles which underlie the various details of the program. This applies provided that it is made in

15 Chapter 2, Section 11a of the Copyright Act.

16 Judgment November 26 2010 by Svea Court of Appeal, case No B 4041-09, cf section 1.2(g) above.

17 Chapter 2, Section 26g of the Copyright Act.

connection with such loading, on-screen display, processing, transmission or storing of the program that the user is entitled to make.[18]

(i) *Parody defence*

There is no specific parody defence under Swedish law. However, anyone may create a new work inspired by or developed from another work provided the new work is an independent creation. If the new creation is sufficiently original, it may attract its own copyright which is not dependant on the copyright to the original work. A work adapted into a parody may thus be considered to be a new independent creation. The Supreme Court has tried a case where a radio channel was accused of copyright infringement by an author.[19] The author claimed that her moral rights as an author had been infringed by the parody. The court held the parody was a new creation that included a comic effect that was not in the original work. However, the court stated that even though a parody may be considered to be an independent new work, it may present the original work in a manner that is insulting to the author, and thereby infringe the author's moral rights. Nevertheless, the Supreme Court found that the feature aired by the radio channel did not infringe the author's moral rights.

(j) *Incidental inclusion*

Under the Copyright Act, anyone is entitled, by means of a film or a television program, to prepare and distribute copies of works of fine art, publicly perform works of fine art and communicate works of fine art to the public, if the exploitation of the work is incidental in relation to the content of the film or the television program. The same applies to works of fine art that appear in the background, or otherwise form an insignificant part, of a picture.[20] This exception requires that the rightholder has published or transferred the original to the public.

1.5 Remedies available for copyright infringement

The criminal sanction for copyright infringement or contributory copyright infringement is a fine or a maximum of two years' imprisonment.[21] Moreover, property in relation to which a violation of the Copyright Act has occurred, or its value, may be declared forfeit.

Rights holders may also claim both civil interim injunctions and final injunctions on the merit on pain of a fine against infringers and contributors. Furthermore, the rights holder will be entitled to reasonable compensation for the exploitation, irrespective of intent or gross negligence on the part of the infringer. If the exploitation is carried out intentionally or by negligence, the rights holder will also be entitled to damages. When assessing the amount of damages the following must specifically be addressed: lost profits; the profits made by the infringer; damage

---

18 Chapter 2, Section 26g of the Copyright Act.
19 Judgment December 23 2005, Supreme Court, Case No T 4739-04 (NJA 2005 p 905).
20 Chapter 2, Section 20a of the Copyright Act.
21 Chapter 7, Section 53 of the Copyright Act.
22 Chapter 7, Section 54 of the Copyright Act.
23 Cf the *Pirate Bay* case, Judgment November 26 2010 by Svea Court of Appeal, case No B 4041-09; section 1.2(g) above.

caused to the reputation of the work; other moral damage; and the interests of the rights holder that infringements are not committed.[22]

1.6 Copyright liability

(a) *Hosting/cloud computing where infringing content uploaded by user of service*

Uploading which includes reproduction and/or communication to the public constitutes an infringing act. The service provider may be held liable for contributory infringement and an injunction order to prevent further infringement may be issued by a court upon petition by the rights holder.[23] Further, where the host has exploited the relevant works on a commercial basis, it may be liable to pay reasonable compensation for the use, and damages.

(b) *Hypertext linking*

The CJEU rendered its judgment on February 13 2014.[24] The case was referred to the CJEU by the Swedish Appellate Court, Svea Court of Appeal, which asked the following questions:

> *If anyone other than the holder of copyright in a certain work supplies a clickable link to the work on his website, does that constitute communication to the public within the meaning of Article 3(1) of Directive 2001/29/EC of the European Parliament and of the Council of 22 May 2001 on the harmonisation of certain aspects of copyright and related rights in the information society?*
>
> *Is the assessment under question 1 affected if the work to which the link refers is on a website on the Internet which can be accessed by anyone without restrictions or if access is restricted in some way?*
>
> *When making the assessment under question 1, should any distinction be drawn between a case where the work, after the user has clicked on the link, is shown on another website and one where the work, after the user has clicked on the link, is shown in such a way as to give the impression that it is appearing on* the same website?
>
> Based on the judgment of the CJEU in this case the following applies in Sweden.

To third-party website: Linking is included in the right of communication to the public in Article 3.1 in the Copyright Directive (2001/29). Linking requires the authorisation of the rights holder in all cases, apart from those where the work has been made available freely via the Internet with the rights holder's authorisation – but only as long as the work is available to the public on the site on which it was initially communicated with the authorisation of the rights holder.

It is not permitted to link to protected works on a website that is available only to a restricted public.

To an infringing work: It is not permitted to link to works that have been made available freely via the Internet, without the authorisation of the rights holder.

---

24 Case C-466-12 *Svensson et al.*

Copying of headlines (when used as hypertext links): This issue has not been tried in Sweden.

(c) ***P2P network***

Supplier of P2P software: Supply of P2P (peer-to-peer) software in itself is not subject to liability for infringement. However, in the *Pirate Bay* case, the founders were found guilty of contributory copyright infringement by providing a website with well-developed search functions, easy upload- and storing capabilities and by conveying contacts between individual file sharers of protected works without authorisation from the rights holders.[25]

Uploaders/downloaders: Uploading and downloading a file without authorisation from the rights holder constitutes infringement.

(d) ***Webcasting***

Communication of a webcast to the public without the authorisation of the rights holders also constitutes an infringing act under Swedish law

(e) ***Streaming***

The dominant opinion in Sweden is that temporary copies produced by the receiver of streamed content are exempted from liability under the temporary copy exception. However, the UK Supreme Court has recently referred a case to the CJEU that will hopefully shed some light on this issue. The case will probably be tried during 2014.[26]

The provision of access to streamed content is, however, a clear infringing act if it is made to the public or to a large group of individuals for profit and without authorisation from the rights holders. Furthermore, downloading of streamed content is included in the exclusive right of reproduction.[27]

(f) ***Framing***

In *Svensson et al*,[28] the CJEU held that 'communication to the public' is not affected by framing. However, it could well be an infringement of moral rights.

(g) ***Transmission of infringing work across a communications network***

See section 1.2(a) above regarding temporary copies.[29]

(h) ***Aggregator websites***

In a judgment of December 19 2013, the CJEU held that a dedicated meta search engine could infringe database protection under certain conditions.[30] This case law is applicable in Sweden.

---

25 Cf section 1.2(g) above, judgment November 26 2010 by Svea Court of Appeal, case No B 4041-09.
26 Case C 360/13 *Public Relations Consultants Association.*
27 Prop 2004/05:110 p 382.
28 Case C-466-12.
29 Olsson, *Upphovsrättslagstiftningen. En kommentar*, Norstedts, 3rd edition, p 65.
30 Case C-202/12, *Innoweb.*

(i) *Treatment of user-generated content*

The exclusive right of communication to the public is also applicable to user-generated content. Under Swedish law it is not permitted to communicate protected works without the authorisation of the rights holder. This applies even if the communication is made for non-commercial purposes.

1.7 Joint liability for internet service providers

Neither Article 8(3) of Directive 2001/29, nor Article 11 of the Enforcement Directive 2004/48 have been directly implemented in Sweden. Instead contributory liability applies. Under Swedish law, both the infringer and any contributors to an infringement may be held jointly or independently liable for relevant infringements. An ISP that contributes to an infringement may thus be punished, may be prohibited from continuing its contributory acts and may be liable to pay reasonable compensation as well as damages. It is not a requirement under Swedish law that both the infringer and the contributors are addressed. The contributor is independently liable for its own actions.

The threshold for contributory liability under Swedish law is low. For example, the Swedish Supreme Court found that a person who held a coat that an assailant had handed over to him before starting to beat the victim was liable for contributing to the assault. This was because he must have realised that the assailant had intended to assault him.[31] In another case the Supreme Court found the driver of a car guilty of contributing to assault because he stopped his car a second time and let out the passengers/assailants at their request, when they saw the victims they had just beaten and were now afforded the possibility of beating them again.[32]

Further, the provision regarding contributory liability in Chapter 23, Section 4 of the Penal Code does not require the contributors to enable the relevant crime. Contributory liability may be imposed even if it was not a necessary condition in order for the criminal act to take place. Contributory liability can also be imposed on a person who only contributes to the crime in an insignificant manner.

Furthermore, persons who have committed acts only briefly associated with the main offence may incur criminal liability as contributors.

However, according to the government, civil contributory liability for an ISP would require something more than the actual provision and operation of the ISP's services. The government has stated that contributory liability at least in an objective sense could be at hand if someone concludes an agreement with an intermediary and "receives concrete indications that the server space is being used in a manner which constitutes copyright infringement".[33]

This statement in the Government Bill has been disputed by professor emerita in Swedish Criminal Law Suzanne Wennberg who, in a legal opinion, clarified her view of the statement as follows (translated short version):

It can be noted initially that there is an objective facilitation of copyright infringement

---

31 NJA 1963, p 574.
32 NJA 1984, p 922.
33 See Government Bill 2001/02:150, p 89 *et seq* and Government Bill 2004/05:110 p 340.

when anyone continuously provides a connection to a particular service which directly enables copyright infringement.

An objective facilitation would normally not require insight into the criminal use or, in other words, any subjective coverage. It is said that intermediaries may not be made liable, on the grounds that they started and conducted the business in question. The operation of such a business, in light of the societal interest in a well-functioning information technology infrastructure, must be deemed socially justifiable. The risks which are associated with conducting the business are such that the risk-taking must be designated as permissible. In other words, it is not possible to hold the intermediary liable for facilitation of access to illegal material solely on the grounds that it started and conducted the business as such.

I interpret the statement in the bill that the concrete indications of the copyright infringement entail that the original permissible risk-taking becomes an impermissible risk-taking. In point of fact, the issue is one of liability for a failure to act when the point of departure for the reasoning is that the intermediary does something active.

The ISP facilitates the user's copyright infringement when it continues to offer connection to the specific service notwithstanding that it has obtained indications that the users use the service to commit copyright infringement. The risk of the uncontrolled consequences, in both qualitative and quantitative terms, has been so great that there has been reason to refrain from this action. Since this constitutes an impermissible risk-taking, a release from liability on the grounds of social justification cannot be asserted. The objective facilitation remains therefore unchanged.

This interpretation of the contributory liability of ISPs has been adopted by several Swedish courts. See section 1.2(g) above regarding ISP liability, and regarding linking see the section 1.6(b) above.

1.8 Relief

As noted, Article 11 of the Enforcement Directive has not been implemented in Sweden. However, in order for a court to issue an injunction it is enough for it to find that the ISP contributes to the infringement in an objective sense. In the *Pirate Bay, Black Internet* and *Portlane* cases injunctions were ordered since the parties were considered, at least objectively, to be contributing to infringing acts (see section 1.2(g) above).

1.9 Issues specific to Sweden

(a) Jurisdiction

In order for Sweden to have jurisdiction to hear a copyright infringement claim, the act must be a criminal offence under Swedish law. Chapter 2 of the Penal Code states the conditions under which Swedish law is applicable. The general principle in Chapter 2, Section 1 of the Penal Code is that crimes committed in Sweden shall be tried in accordance with Swedish law and by a Swedish court (the 'territoriality principle'). The same applies when it is uncertain where the crime was committed, but grounds exist for assuming that it was committed in Sweden. Additionally, Swedish law can be applied to acts which have been committed abroad, if for example an infringement claim concerns works of Swedish nationals or of persons who have their habitual residence in Sweden. The same goes for infringing acts in respect of works that are first published in Sweden or simultaneously published in Sweden.

(b) *Claim to infringement of foreign copyright*

Swedish courts may try claims for infringement in respect of works protected in other countries, provided there is a reciprocal agreement with the relevant country or with an intergovernmental organisation which has been approved by the Parliament.

(c) *Emission theory*

In the *Pirate Bay* case, the Swedish Court of Appeal made it quite clear that a copyright infringement is deemed to have been committed both where the criminal act was carried out and where the crime was completed.[34] The Court of Appeal stated that the principal offences involved making films, games and music available to the public in Sweden. The court dismissed the 'country of effect principle', since it could lead to colliding criminal claims and an extremely far-reaching investigatory obligation for police and prosecutors. The court stated that the fact that it was possible for the public to obtain access to the works in Sweden (as well as in almost all of the other countries of the world) was not enough to form the basis for the conclusion that the principal offences were deemed to have been committed in Sweden. However, it stated that a crime can be located in Sweden as soon as a part of the criminal act has been undertaken within the country's borders. The court came to the conclusion that the placing of the torrent files in Pirate Bay's database constituted an essential element of the main perpetrators' infringements. Since it was found that Pirate Bay's servers were located in Sweden, the crimes were considered to have been committed in Sweden. As a consequence, Swedish law was applicable and the Swedish courts were considered to have jurisdiction.

1.10 Orphan works

In Sweden, orphan works have partly been dealt with by introducing the possibility of extended collective licences under Chapter 3a, Section 42g of the Copyright Act. Under this provision, radio and television companies may make works available to the public, provided they have previously been published, that they are part of the company's own production catalogue and that they have been previously broadcast before July 1 2005. The reason for the government's proposed implementation was that many orphan works were stored in different state-owned facilities without being accessible to the public. The government argued that the works were an important part of Swedish cultural heritage and should therefore be accessible to the public. Because this kind of 're-use' encountered a number of problems attached to copyright, the government suggested the implementation of extended collective licences.[35]

On May 24 2011, the EU Commission presented a proposal for a directive concerning orphan works. The general purpose of such a directive would be to make

---

34 Judgment November 26 2010 case No B 4041-09, cf section 1.2(g) above.
35 Prop 2010/11:33, p 26.

it easier for institutions such as archives and libraries to make orphan works available on the Internet.

1.11 Online piracy measures

Besides the measures described above a court may order an ISP to provide information regarding particular infringers. An order may be issued only if the rightholder can show probable cause that an infringement has taken place and if it can be assumed that the information would facilitate an investigation of the infringement.[36]

1.12 Electronic infringement of moral rights

(a) *Right to object to derogatory treatment*

The Copyright Act protects the intellectual, emotional or personal connection between the author and his/her work. This protection contains two elements: to acknowledge or credit the author of a work in accordance with proper usage; and to give due recognition to the author for the work (ie, not to change the original creation or communicate the creation to the public in such a manner, form or context as is prejudicial to the author's literary or artistic reputation or to his individuality). These rights exist for all types of works and any attempt to transfer them is limited. The author is only bound by transfers of moral rights that are limited to specific uses and areas. Moral rights can also be allocated in the electronic environment.

In the case NJA 2008 s 309 commercial interruptions in motion pictures were considered to interrupt the film's continuity and dramaturgy and thus constituted a violation of the author's moral right.

A mashup that is a new independent work does not require authorisation of the original authors (see section 1.4(i) above regarding the parody defence). If the mashup is considered to be an adaptation or a compilation of the original music, the authorisation of the original authors is required and prejudicial use of their creations is not permitted but protected by their moral rights.

If a literary or artistic work is performed or reproduced in a manner which violates cultural interests, a court may, upon petition by an authority appointed by the government, issue an injunction prohibiting such use, under penalty of a fine.

(b) *False attribution – right to guard against impersonation on the Internet*

When a work is communicated via the Internet, the name of the author must be stated to the extent and in the manner required by proper usage.[37] The exact definition of the concept of 'proper usage' will differ depending on the situation.[38] The name of a well-known author must in principle always be presented in connection with any publishing of his/her works and to present another person as the author is a violation of the author's moral rights. However, in most cases it is not a requirement to present the name of the copywriter in connection with the

36 Chapter 7, Section 53c of the Copyright Act.
37 Chapter 1, Section 3 of the Copyright Act.
38 Prop 1960:17, s 65.

publishing of an ad, but may be a violation of the copywriter's moral rights if another person is presented as the author.

(c) *Paternity right*

See (b) above.

2. Trademarks

2.1 Use of a trademark

Sweden enacted a new Trademark Act in 2011. The wording of the new Act is closer to the wordings of the Trademark Directive than the previous Act. Under the Trademark Act, the following examples of uses that are covered by the protection are mentioned:

- affixing a sign to goods or to the packaging thereof;
- offering goods, putting them on the market, stocking them for these purposes or offering or supplying services under a sign;
- importing or exporting goods under a sign; or
- using a mark in business papers and in advertising (see Article 5(3) of the Trademark Directive).

In order for a use to be an infringement it is required that the sign is used in the course of trade and for goods or services. The use of a trademark on a website may constitute trademark infringement if, for example, it is used to advertise or offer goods or services. A use that creates the impression that the infringer offers goods under a certain trademark may also constitute infringement.[39]

Under Swedish law, a domain name is not in itself considered to be a trademark and there is no legislation specifically regulating the right to domain names. A domain name is considered to have a different function than a trademark or a trade name and the view is that it is not evident that the use of a domain name that is identical or similar to a trademark or a trade name constitutes an infringement. However, if the domain name that is identical or similar to a trademark is used as an address for a website where the alleged infringer markets and sells products that are similar to the ones offered by the proprietor under the trademark, it may constitute an infringement. Further, it may constitute trademark infringement if a domain name that is similar to a trademark is used to refer internet users to the alleged infringer's website.[40]

In order for the use to be infringing, the alleged infringer must direct its goods or services towards the Swedish market or the web page must otherwise be intended to have a commercial effect in Sweden. An indicator of such intention is, for example, that the web page is in Swedish, it has commercial effect in Sweden, the price of goods or services are presented in Swedish currency, there is a reference to a Swedish retailer, or there is contact information such as a telephone number or similar to a Swedish contact person.

In order to prevent revocation of a trademark registration, the proprietor must

---

39 See judgment of Court of Appeal of Västra Sverige, October 13, 2013, case No T 4304-12.
40 See judgment of the Court of Appeal of Skåne and Malmå, April 22 2013, case No B 3113-12.

make genuine use of the trademark. The principles laid down in CJEU case law apply when interpreting genuine use.[41]

2.2 Infringement

(a) *Metatags*

The Stockholm District Court has ruled on this matter in one particular case.[42] The court held that the use of a third party's trademark as a metatag may constitute a trademark infringement. However, as the ruling is more than 10 years old and made by a District Court it does not have strong value as a precedent. More interesting is the judgment of July 11 2013 where the CJEU held that the use of metatags can include misleading advertising.[43]

(b) *Keywords*

In 2012, the Swedish Market Court tried a case where one party had purchased from Google its competitor's trademark as a search word (AdWord). Internet users that used the trademark as a search word were presented with a list of ads in a specific section on their computers. The ad of the alleged infringer was placed on top of this list, but did not include the trademark. The Market Court referred to the CJEU case law and held that a reasonably well-informed and reasonably observant internet user must understand that the ad and the service that the search word, including the trademark that it was connected to did not originate from the proprietor. The Market Court, therefore, held that the use had no adverse effect on the function of indicating origin of the trademark. Further, the Market Court held that since the alleged infringer only offered the consumers an alternative through the use of the trademark, the use did not adversely effect the advertising and investment function of the trademark. Finally, the Market Court held that the goodwill of the trademark was not transferred to the alleged infringer. All in all, the Market Court found that the use by the alleged infringer was not an infringement under the Trademark Act and thus did not constitute improper marketing.[44]

(c) *Sponsored links*

See (b) above.

(d) *Hidden text*

In 2010, the Swedish Market Court tried a case where a party had included an ad in the source code of its website. When internet users searched for 'easy credit' via Google, the ad became visible to users. The Market Court held that this activity constituted advertising, and because it found that the ad was improper, prohibited the defendant from continuing to communicate the ad under penalty of a fine of SEK1 million (judgment of the Market Court, MD 2010:30).

---

41 See Supreme Court judgement NJA 2005, page 643.
42 Stockholm District Court, Case No T 5066-00.
43 See judgment of 11 July 2013 in case C-657/11 (*Belgian Electronic Sorting Technology NV*).
44 MD 2012:15.

(e) *Internet domain names*

The mere registration of a domain name does not give rise to liability in Sweden. However, the Swedish Registry '.SE' has its own alternative dispute resolution (ADR). Under the rules of the ADR a domain name that is identical or similar to a trademark may be transferred to the trademark proprietor, provided that:

- the proprietor can show that it has a right to the trademark that is valid in Sweden;
- the holder of the domain name has acted in bad faith when it registered or used the domain name;
- the holder cannot show that it has any right or justified interest in the domain name.

See section 2.1 above and section 2.8 below regarding domain names and trademarks.

(f) *Search navigation tools*

Breadcrumb trails (ie, links back to each previous page the user has navigated through to get to the current page) probably do not result in trademark infringement under Swedish law, even if the links include a trademark.

(g) *Hypertext links*

The provision of a link to a website that includes trademark infringing activities may constitute trademark infringement under Swedish law (see further above under section 2.1).

(h) *Framing*

Where a frame is used in order to create the impression that there exists a connection between the proprietor of a trademark and the alleged infringer, this may constitute trademark infringement. The same applies if the inclusion of a trademark in a frame uses the good-will associated with that mark. An alternative is for the proprietor to take action against the alleged infringer under the Marketing Act. The Marketing Act includes more extensive protection against improper or misleading advertising by use of other parties' good-will than the Trademark Act.

2.3 Defences

(a) *Descriptive (non-trademark) use of the mark*

Since a trademark owner can only prohibit use that affects his/her own interests as a proprietor of the mark in regard to the trademark's functions, merely using a descriptive term to describe the goods and services does not constitute a trademark use.[45]

45 CJEU C-206/01.

(b) *Comparative advertising*

Comparative advertising is allowed under the Marketing Act.[46] However, the comparative advertising may not take undue advantage of the reputation of another trader's trademark, business name or other distinguishing marks or their designation of origin.

(c) *Parody*

The Swedish Supreme Court has held that the mere use of a trademark that is a parody of another party's trademark is not sufficient to constitute an infringement if the marks are not confusingly similar.[47]

2.4 Parallel imports

To offer branded goods for sale in Sweden via a website when the goods have not first been placed on the Swedish market may constitute trademark infringement, but it depends on whether the goods have first been placed on the market of an EU country or a country outside the European Union. Under Article 13 of Council Regulation 207/2009 on the Community trademark, and Chapter 1, Section 12 of the Trademarks Act, goods that have been released in a member state of the European Union shall be considered rightfully released on the EU market with the consequence that the rightful owner cannot hinder the goods from being parallel-imported into another EU country. The CJEU has stated that the exhaustion of a trademark right is regional within the European Union and, therefore, any release of goods outside the EU does not impact the owner's right to release goods within the EU.[48]

2.5 Remedies

The Trademarks Act stipulates fines or a maximum of two years' imprisonment for intentional or grossly negligent trademark infringement and attempt and preparation of an infringement. Contributors to the infringement may also be punished. The infringing goods can be declared forfeit by the court. A court may also order the infringer to recall all infringing goods from the market or to destroy the goods. Upon a petition by the rights holder, the court may issue an injunction to prohibit further infringing action. Failure to observe the terms of the injunction may lead to the imposition of a fine. Finally, the infringer and/or the contributor may be liable to pay reasonable compensation for the use of the trademark and also damages if the infringement has been carried out intentionally or by negligent conduct.[49]

2.6 Liability of ISPs

In essence, the same principles apply as those in relation to copyright (see section 1.7 above). Sweden has not implemented Article 11 in the Enforcement Directive; thus, only an ISP that contributes to an infringement may be held liable for its activities.

---

46 Article 18 of the Swedish Marketing Act.
47 See Supreme Court judgment in NJA 1992 p 633.
48 CJEU C-355/96.
49 Chapter 8 of the Trademarks Act.

2.7 Advertising law and regulation

The Swedish Marketing Act[50] is applicable for all kinds of advertising, including internet advertising. Additionally, special statutes and regulations are used where it is necessary to specify or clarify certain legal questions. These include the E-commerce Act (2002:562),[51] the Distance and Doorstep Sales Act (2005:59),[52] and the Marketing and Advertising Code of the International Chamber of Commerce.

The Nordic consumer ombudsmen have presented a joint opinion regarding marketing via the Internet in 2010. The opinion includes the following:

a *A trader is generally responsible for all material presented on its website, even if the material has been provided by others.*

b *A trader should not link to sites or materials that are not consistent with legislation.*

c *When a website includes links to other websites it should be clear to the consumer when it leaves the first site.*

In 2012, the Nordic consumer ombudsmen presented their joint position regarding marketing via social media – specifically Facebook. The position includes the following of specific interest.

(a) Messages to inbox and timeline (profile)

On Facebook, it is possible to send messages to users' inboxes (messages) or to post notices on users' timelines. In the opinion of the consumer ombudsmen, such messages from traders fall within the definition of electronic mail and therefore require prior consent.

(b) Banner advertisements

Banner advertisements, such as those shown under 'Sponsored', probably cannot be considered electronic mail as the messages are hardly stored until collected by the recipient, nor are they normally considered sent to a specific recipient. Accordingly, the Nordic consumer ombudsmen do not consider banner advertisements to be other unsolicited communications for purposes of direct marketing as defined in Article 13(3) of the Directive on Privacy and Electronic Communications. This means that no consent is required, and no possibility of opting out of banner advertisements is required.

(c) 'News Feed'

Messages appearing to a Facebook user under 'News Feed' may include 'status updates' from traders whom the user has 'liked'. They may also include messages indicating that the user's friends 'like' a particular trader, information received because one of the user's friends has 'shared' information about a trader, or messages indicating that a friend has participated in a competition.

It is uncertain whether messages from traders appearing under a Facebook user's News Feed fall within the definition of electronic mail. Until greater clarity has been achieved on this matter, the Nordic consumer ombudsmen are of the opinion that

---

50 *Marknadsföringslagen* (2008:486).

51 *Lag om elektronisk handel och andra informationssamhällets tjänster* (2002:562).

52 *Distans- och hemförsäljningslag* (2005:59).

such communications must be considered 'other unsolicited communications' as defined by Article 13(3) of the Directive on Privacy and Electronic Communications, and that recipients must be able to opt out of receiving such communications if their purpose is marketing. The Nordic consumer ombudsmen will discuss with the European Commission and the European enforcement authorities how these rules are to be interpreted.

If a trader rewards a user or creates a particular incentive for the user to share or spread commercial messages, the consumer ombudsmen would consider such messages to be sent from the trader, and the user's friends must therefore be able to opt out of receiving such messages. If the spreading or sharing depends solely on the user's own decision, the consumer ombudsmen would not consider the message to fall within the rules on unsolicited communications.

If participation in a competition makes a commercial message appear on a user's wall and subsequently on his/her friends' start pages ('Home') under 'News Feed', the user's friends must be able to opt out of receiving future communications from the trader.

2.8 Domain name disputes

When a dispute arises concerning a domain name, a party may consider Alternative Dispute Resolution (ADR) as an alternative to litigation. The Swedish Registry '.SE' has its own ADR. Under the rules of the ADR a domain name that is identical or similar to a trademark may be transferred to the trademark proprietor provided that:

- the proprietor can show that it has a right to the trademark that is valid in Sweden;
- the holder of the domain name has acted in bad faith when it registered or used the domain name;
- the holder cannot show that it has any right or justified interest in the domain name.

All three prerequisites must be met in order for the petitioning party to succeed.

An ADR proceeding should be decided within 30 days (with one arbitrator), or 60 days (with three arbitrators) after it has been submitted to the arbitrators. The application fee of an ADR proceeding is normally SEK10,000 if it is to be tried by one arbitrator and SEK20,000 if it is to be tried by three arbitrators. However, half of the fee will be repaid if the applicant wins. The application fees are lower for individuals and smaller enterprises.

An expedited proceeding is possible if the counter-party does not respond to the ADR application. In an expedited proceeding the arbitral tribunal always consists of a sole arbitrator who will decide on the case within 10 working days. The application fee for this kind of proceeding is SEK 2,000.

2.9 Unfair competition/passing off

(a) Passing off

The passing-off doctrine is not applicable in Sweden.

(b) ***Unregistered trademarks***

Under Chapter 1, Section 7 of the Trademarks Act, an exclusive right to a trademark may be acquired by becoming established on the market. A trademark is considered to be established on the market when it has become known to a significant part of the relevant public as an indication for the goods or services being offered under it in the country where it has been established. If the trademark has only been established in a part of a country the exclusive rights apply only within that territory.

(c) ***Unfair competition***

The purpose of the Swedish Marketing Act is mainly to protect consumers from improper marketing. However, it also offers protection against unfair competition. An improper use of a trademark in marketing on a website that does not amount to a trademark infringement may well be considered to be an unfair use of the goodwill associated with a trademark. The requirement is that the trader takes unfair advantage of the reputation associated with another trader's trademark, business name, or other distinctive marks or the designation of origin of the goods.

3. Patents

3.1 Patentability of 'internet' inventions

(a) ***Computer programs***

Under Section 1, p 3 of the Swedish Patent Act (1967:837) (the 'Patent Act'), the code of a computer program cannot be patented, as there is a requirement of a technical character. However, if a computer program is a part of a technical solution it can be patentable, for example, if a machine is using the computer program. The same requirements for what constitutes patentable subject matter apply for (b), (c) and (d) below.

(b) ***Business methods***

Under Section 1, p 3 of the Patent Act, business methods per se are not patentable in Sweden.

(c) ***Mathematical methods***

In accordance with Section 1, p 1 of the Patent Act, mathematical methods per se are not patentable in Sweden.

(d) ***Presentation of information***

Under Section 1, p 4, the Patent Act, the presentation of information is not patentable in Sweden.

3.2 Bioinformatics

A novel DNA sequence or a protein structure that is discovered separately from its natural environment or produced through a technical procedure is patentable in Sweden under Section 1b of the Patent Act. Plain discoveries of nature, however, are not patentable.

3.3 Issues specific to Sweden

(a) Infringement on the Internet

Swedish courts have jurisdiction over infringement of a Swedish patent if the infringement takes place in Sweden. The principal rule is that a crime is deemed to have been committed both where the criminal act was carried out, in whole or in part, and where the crime was completed. If the infringement takes place via the Internet (eg, using servers placed in Sweden), the infringement is considered to take place in Sweden, and Swedish courts will have jurisdiction.

(b) Process patents

It is sufficient that a crime is carried out only partly in Sweden, in order to be deemed to be committed in Sweden.[53]

3.4 Remedies available for patent infringement

The Patent Act states fines or a maximum of two years' imprisonment for intentional or grossly negligent patent infringement. Attempts or preparations for the crime are also sanctioned under the Penal Code. The infringing goods can be declared forfeit by the court. A court may also order the infringer to recall all infringing goods from the market or to destroy the goods. Upon petition by the rights holder, the court may issue an injunction prohibiting further infringing action. Failure to comply with the terms of an injunction will result in a fine. Lastly, the infringer may be liable to pay reasonable compensation for the exploitation and further damages, if the exploitation was made intentionally or by negligent conduct.[54] An action for reasonable compensation and damages will be limited to losses which have occurred during the five years preceding the filing of the action.

4. Disclosure orders against ISPs

4.1 Availability

The European Parliament and the Council has issued Directive 2004/48/EC on the enforcement of intellectual property rights (IPRED). The Directive has been implemented in Sweden in the Copyright Act, the Trademarks Act, the Swedish Designs Act, and the Swedish Patents Act. Under these provisions a court may issue an information order including information on the origin and distribution networks of the goods or services which infringe an intellectual property right. An information order may be issued against anyone who, on a commercial basis, has provided an electronic communication service which has been used in the infringement (ie, against an ISP).

The rights holder must show probable cause that someone has infringed or contributed to the infringement. It is not required that the infringer or contributor is identified. Furthermore, it is not a requirement that the infringement has been carried out intentionally or through negligent conduct. It is sufficient that there is

53 NJA 1993 s 292 and RH 2000:84.
54 Chapter 9 of the Patent Act.

probable cause that an infringement has been carried out in an objective sense. However, an information order may only be issued if it can be assumed that it will facilitate the investigation of an infringement.

The courts also take into consideration the principle of proportionality. Thus, an information order may only be issued if the reasons for the order outweigh the detriment that it may cause to the ISP or any other opposing interest. In each individual case an evaluation must be made as to whether the measure needs to be taken, or whether the purpose can be met through a less intrusive measure. Generally, making works available through uploading or file-sharing via the Internet, will typically result in major damage for the rights holder, and as a consequence the above-mentioned requirement will be met. The same applies to extensive extraction of protected works, such as downloading. In cases of file-sharing or downloading on a smaller scale, the balancing of interests may end up in favour of the privacy interest, meaning that the rights holder is not entitled to the information.

Application of the law was, however, put on hold when the Supreme Court referred a case regarding a disclosure order in *Bonnier Audio AB and others v Perfect Communication Sweden AB (ePhone)* to the CJEU.[55] The question referred to the CJEU was whether a new interpretation of the law, as established in the *Promusicae* case[56] and the LSG decision,[57] would be needed due to the enactment of Directive 2006/24/EC (the Data Retention Directive).[58] The CJEU issued its judgment on April 19 2012 and held that the Data Retention Directive must be interpreted as not precluding the possibility of a disclosure order, since that legislation does not fall within the material scope of Directive 2006/24. Based on the findings of the CJEU, the Supreme Court in December 2012 ordered the ISP to provide the requested information under penalty of a fine.

4.2 Requirements

The rights holder must show probable cause that an infringement or violation has occurred. Moreover, an information order may only be issued if it can be assumed that it will facilitate the investigation of an infringement and that it is a proportionate response.

4.3 Jurisdictional issues

The court where an action for infringement has been filed will be authorised to try information orders. If an action for infringement has not been filed, the rights holder may file its application with the Stockholm District Court.

4.4 'John Doe' injunctions

The rightholder must show probable cause that someone has infringed or contributed to the infringement. It is not required that the infringer or contributor is identified.

---

55 C-461/10.

56 ECJ Judgment January 29 2008, case No C-275/06.

57 REG 2009, p I-1227.

58 Directive 2006/24/EC on the retention of data generated or processed in connection with the provision of publicly available electronic communications services or of public communications networks, and amending Directive 2002/58/EC.

Switzerland

Martin Steiger
Steiger Legal

1. Copyright, database rights and design rights

1.1 Overview

Internet content can be protected by copyright law in Switzerland; however, there are almost no specific provisions for internet content.

In summary, copyright law in Switzerland covers two objects of protection: works (ie, creations of the mind that possess an individual character and pass the threshold of originality); and neighbouring rights for certain content-related activities and results of such activities without any further threshold that must be passed (ie, activities and results of activities by broadcasters, performers and other relevant parties in relation to content with and without copyright protection).

Works in Swiss copyright law are legally defined as literary and artistic creations of the mind – irrespective of their declared purpose or economic value – that possess an individual character (ie, that are original). Originality is used as a threshold for copyright protection with the statistical uniqueness of a work often used as a practical test. Any content that passes the threshold of originality – including internet content – is covered by copyright protection in Switzerland. Trivial creations on the other hand remain in the public domain. In practice, the threshold is low with higher requirements only for certain categories of works. For visual works for example, a distinction is made between copyright-protected photographs and snapshots without copyright protection; however, even the case law thereto is inconsistent.

As a rule of thumb in legal practice, internet content can be considered copyright protected under Swiss copyright law if the threshold of originality is not obviously missed or no copyright exemption applies. Only a small number of works are excluded from copyright protection, in particular court decisions, legislative texts such as laws and ordinances, patent documentation and published patent applications, and administrative and official texts such as minutes and reports by public authorities.

A work is protected under Swiss copyright law as soon as it has been created. The copyright owner is the creator, who can assign his/her intellectual property rights to third parties.

Switzerland has no official register for copyrighted works, nor is it mandatory publicly to declare copyrighted works as such. Copyright notations such as © do not affect copyright protection in Switzerland, although they might be useful as deterring information to third parties, in particular abroad.

In assessing copyright law in Switzerland, it is important to consider that although the German term *Urheberrecht* is translated as copyright in English, copyright stands for a predominantly common law concept with many essential differences to the concept of *Urheberrecht* in the German legal sphere.

(a) *Literary works and artistic works*

Swiss copyright law does not have a *numerus clausus* of works protected by copyright. Common categories of literary and artistic works – including literary, scientific and other works of language, works of music and other acoustic works, works of visual art, works with scientific or technical content, architectural works, works of applied art and visual or audio-visual works – are listed as examples.

Copyright protection does not depend on the communication or publishing medium used to create works and internet content is therefore copyright protected if it meets the general requirements for copyright protection in Switzerland. In addition, computer programs (ie, software), are explicitly mentioned as copyright protected and Swiss copyright law contains several special provisions on copyrighted software. The first sale doctrine is applicable to computer programs while the right to rent software out remains exclusively with the software creator.

Software under Swiss copyright law must meet the threshold of originality for copyright protection. In practice, this threshold is met by novelty or absence of triviality in comparison to existing software. Software copyright covers source code and the object code, but not the underlying ideas and principles. Algorithms, formulas and ideas used in and for software for example are not copyright protected in Switzerland.

(b) *Films, sound recordings and broadcasts*

Copyright protection in Switzerland applies to films, sound recordings and broadcasts on the Internet. Neighbouring rights are in particular relevant in this context. Performers, for example, have the moral right of recognition for their status as performers and the right to make their performances perceivable in other places than those in which they were performed (eg, through download and streaming platforms such as Google's YouTube or internet television offers by Swiss internet providers).

(c) *Typographical arrangement of a published edition*

Swiss copyright law does not protect the typographical arrangement of a published edition; nor are typefaces specifically protected by copyright. Swiss courts have been very reluctant to grant copyright, design or any other legal protection to typefaces. The name of a typeface, however, can be protected as a trademark and the typographical arrangement of a published edition might in theory be protected under unfair competition law.

(d) *Protection of the user interface*

The look and feel of graphical user interfaces (GUI) of any kind of software including web applications can be protected under Swiss copyright law if the threshold of originality is met. An alternative or cumulative intellectual property protection under Swiss design law is possible if the design law-specific requirements are met, in particular the requirements of originality and novelty. In addition, only registered designs are protected while copyright protection does not require a registration. GUI registered and protected as designs are rare in Switzerland.

(e) *Computer-generated works*

Computer-generated works are protected under Swiss copyright law if the threshold of originality is met. Such works must in particular be the results of creative human activity, for example computer-generated music by a composer. Randomly computer-generated works – for example paintings – are copyright protected if randomness was explicitly used by the creator.

(f) *Websites protected as databases*

Swiss copyright law does not provide for *sui generis* database protection, unlike for example the European Union and its member states; therefore, a legal definition of 'database' does not exist. Databases might be copyright protected as compilations if the selection and presentation of the data used is particularly individual and original. Protection might in theory also be provided under Swiss unfair competition law.

(g) *Compilations*

Compilations are protected under Swiss copyright law if the selection and presentation of the data used results from a creation of the mind that possesses an individual or original character. The data compiled does not need to consist of protected works. 'Sweat of the brow' compilations are not known in Swiss copyright law. Swiss intellectual property law in general does not use a sweat of the brow criterion as a threshold for protection.

1.2 Infringing acts

Swiss copyright law grants the creator of a copyrighted work or the copyright holder the exclusive right to decide whether, when and how a copyrighted work may be used. Common uses of copyrighted works such as reproduction, translation, editing, distribution, sale, performance, broadcast and transfer of works are listed in Swiss copyright legislation without the copyright protection being limited thereon.

Any use of copyrighted works by third parties without permission by the creator or the copyright holder constitutes an infringing act if no copyright exemption or defence is applicable. Specific infringing acts listed in Swiss copyright law include using a work under a false designation or a designation that differs from that decided by the creator, publishing a work, altering a work, using a work to create a derivative work, manufacturing copies of a work in any matter, selling or otherwise distributing copies of a work, making a work perceivable in any way either directly or with the help of any type of means, broadcasting a work by radio, television or a similar process, making a broadcast or rebroadcast perceivable, hiring out software and omitting to state the source of a work.

The concept of secondary infringement – for example by file hosting services – is possible under Swiss copyright law while there exists no legal definition of 'secondary infringement'. The case law on secondary infringement is rare and inconsistent. From a criminal copyright law perspective, secondary infringement results from complicity in copyright–infringing acts such as listed above with knowledge and intent on the part of the secondary infringer.

1.3 Test for copyright infringement

The *de facto* test for copyright infringement under Swiss copyright law is to assess the originality of a work (ie, any infringing act with regard to a work that passes the threshold of originality and is therefore a copyrighted work, constitutes a copyright infringement). A copyright infringement under Swiss copyright law requires neither substantial reproduction nor repeated copying of an insubstantial part of copyright-protected works. Any infringing act with regard to a copyrighted work constitutes a copyright infringement if no copyright exemption or defence is applicable.

1.4 Exemptions/defences to copyright infringement

(a) Format shifting

Format shifting of licensed copyrighted works – with the exception of copyrighted works with technological protection measures (TPM) such as digital rights management (DRM) for software – is not considered a copyright infringement under Swiss copyright law. The circumvention of TPM is prohibited in principle; however, there is a notable exception as the prohibition does not apply to circumventing TPM for the purpose of lawful use (eg, back-up copies of computer programs or within the broad exemption of personal use). Providing knowledge and services on the circumvention of TPM on the other hand is prohibited.

(b) Personal copying rights

The Swiss copyright law exemption relating to personal use grants various mandatory use permissions for any copyrighted content with the exception of computer programs. Any use of copyrighted content except for software is permitted as personal use in the personal sphere and among closely related persons – for example, among friends or relatives – including such use through the Internet. The same exemption applies for educational purposes such as teaching in class. In companies as well as in the public administration and in similar institutions, the reproduction of copyrighted works for internal documentation and information is permitted.

Third parties are allowed to act on behalf of beneficiaries of personal use permissions. Such third parties include, for example, companies and libraries providing copy machines for use by their customers and visitors, or online service providers that enable digital variants of personal use permissions as long as such variants are limited to partial reproductions.

The use of copyrighted content for personal use is free in principle; however, indirect (and therefore hidden) copyright levies often apply. Third parties acting on behalf of beneficiaries of personal use permissions are subject to copyright levies, for example on copy machines, printers and computer networks. Also subject to copyright levies are manufacturers and importers of so-called blank recording mediums as required for most personal use. The definition for blank recording mediums applies not only to traditional storage mediums such as compact discs and hard disk drives, but also to mobile phones and tablets capable of playing music and other content. Copyright levies are collected by five private collective administration societies under federal supervision.

(c) ***Time shifting***

Time shifting directly by consumers – for example with a digital video recorder (DVR) at home – is considered personal use under Swiss copyright law. Manufacturers and importers of DVRs and similar devices with digital storage capacity, or other blank recording mediums, are subject to copyright levies.

Time shifting offered by third-party providers – in Switzerland predominantly by telecommunications providers such as UPC Cablecom (cable television) and Swisscom (internet television) or internet streaming providers such as Wilmaa and Zattoo – is subject to copyright levies and limited to seven days according to a recent decision of the Swiss Federal Arbitration Commission on Copyright. Representatives of the US entertainment industry had originally argued for single licence agreements, but finally accepted the arbitration commission's decision.

(d) ***Fair use***

Fair use, or an equivalent doctrine, does not exist in Swiss copyright law. Personal copying rights are more comprehensive but limited to certain environments such as the personal sphere for personal use.

News aggregators such as Google News operate in Switzerland mainly under the right of quotation and a copyright exemption for media reports on current events. In addition, many news articles – in particular headlines and intros – do not reach the threshold of originality for protection under Swiss copyright law. A dedicated neighbouring right for print publishers such as exists in Germany has not been implemented in Switzerland to date.

(e) ***Caching/temporary copies as part of communication process***

Temporary caching and non-permanent reproduction of licensed copyrighted works are explicitly permitted under Swiss copyright law if necessary as part of communication processes in electronic networks and if they do not have any independent economic significance. Examples are a user's browser cache, random access memory (RAM) in a computer or a proxy server in a network.

(f) ***Hosting***

There are no specific provisions in Swiss law regarding hosting. There are accordingly no exemptions, safe harbours or defences to copyright infringement for hosting (and other) internet providers in Switzerland. General administrative, civil and criminal Swiss law provisions are applicable to hosting.

(g) Back-up copies

One back-up copy of a published copyrighted work is permitted under Swiss copyright law if such copy is clearly designated as a back-up copy and stored in an archive that is not publicly accessible. In a digital context, more than one copy is considered lawful, for example through versioning or the necessity of backups on-site as well as off-site. Back-up copies are also permitted for software and the right to create a back-up copy of a computer program cannot be excluded by contract.

Libraries, archives, educational institutions and museums are permitted to make copies of published copyrighted works if necessary to maintain and secure their stocks and if they do not pursue an economic or commercial interest.

(h) Reverse engineering

Lawful owners of a computer program in Switzerland are granted the right to obtain information on the computer program's interfaces by reverse engineering of the computer program's source code themselves or by commissioning a third party to obtain such information. The use of information obtained by reverse engineering is legally limited to the development, maintenance and use of interoperable (ie, interactive) computer programs and must not affect the normal exploitation of the computer program, or the legitimate interests of the intellectual property rights owners in the computer program.

(i) Parody defence

Published copyrighted works may be used to create parodies or comparable variations of works.

(j) Incidental inclusion

The defence of incidental inclusion does not formally exist under Swiss copyright law. From a criminal copyright law perspective, only intentional acts of copyright infringement are punishable. Civil actions for damages due to copyright infringements are mostly based on actual loss for the rights holder – in lieu of reasonable royalties (licence analogy) – and profits by the infringer. Incidental inclusion might therefore *de facto* be used as a defence to copyright infringement claims.

1.5 Remedies available for copyright infringement

Swiss intellectual property law offers various administrative, civil and criminal actions against copyright infringers and relevant third parties such as internet access, content and hosting providers. The remedies available are identical or very similar for copyright, design, patent and trademark infringements.

Civil actions include actions for declaratory judgment on whether a copyright claim or a legal relationship with regard to copyright subsist under Swiss copyright law, actions for execution such as cease and desist orders for imminent or existing copyright infringements, and actions for information on copyright infringements such as their duration in order to assess damages. Swiss intellectual property law further refers to general Swiss civil law to institute proceedings for the compensation of losses (ie, actions for damages including moral damages and profits gained by the infringing party). Swiss intellectual property law also allows for preliminary injunctions, for example to enable pre-litigation discovery or for the grant of immediately effective cease and desist orders. The burden of proof for preliminary injunctions lies with the claimant, and it is necessary to show that there is a reasonable likelihood that a copyright infringement is likely to have occurred or is likely to occur in the near future.

Most criminal actions require a formal complaint by the holders of the allegedly infringed copyrights and only intentional acts of infringements are punishable. The criminal sanctions are imprisonment up to one year or a fine; fines are based on the daily disposable income of the defendant up to CHF3,000 per day and for up to 360 days. For copyright infringements deemed a commercial practice, a complaint by the copyright holders is in theory not required and the sanctions are up to five years' imprisonment together with a fine.

Administrative actions are within the competence of Swiss customs authorities or may be requested by copyright holders. In the context of the Internet, they are mainly relevant with regard to the retention of imported physical goods ordered via e-commerce and other online channels.

1.6 Copyright liability

(a) Hosting/cloud computing where infringing content uploaded by user of service

Swiss law does not contain any specific provisions on hosting or cloud computing. Copyright liability with regard to hosting and cloud computing must therefore be assessed by general administrative, civil and criminal Swiss law provisions. Specific exemptions, safe harbours or defences to copyright infringement do not exist for hosting and cloud computing providers in Switzerland.

Case law on copyright liability of hosting and cloud computing providers is rare and inconsistent, and parts of such case law date back to the pre-internet age. Internet providers try to avoid liability by seriously assessing copyright claims and usually react promptly on obvious copyright infringements, often based on respective provisions in their terms and conditions of use. In any other case, they will usually refer claimants to administrative, civil or criminal legal actions in order to remain impartial between their customers and third parties as well as to avoid liability to their customers.

The Swiss Internet Industry Association (SIMSA) published a code of conduct for hosting providers in spring 2013 and this has been incorporated into the terms and conditions of most major Swiss hosting providers. The code of conduct has not been tested in court to date.

(b) Hypertext linking

To third-party website: Links to publicly accessible third-party websites and web pages do not amount to copyright infringement under Swiss copyright law. From a Swiss legal perspective, links to third-party websites are considered essential for the world wide web part of the Internet to function.

To an infringing work: Known links to obviously copyright infringing works can amount to copyright infringement. Content publishers and providers can be held liable if they do not act appropriately (ie, upon sufficient knowledge, for example through copyright notices). Several 'Pirate Bay'-style websites in Switzerland linking almost exclusively to torrents sharing allegedly copyright-infringing works were shut down and their Swiss-based operators faced civil actions and criminal sanctions. Such websites are no longer present in Switzerland today. File hosting providers on the other hand can operate legally in Switzerland (eg, Rapidshare).

Copying of headlines: Copying of headlines when used as hypertext links does not amount to copyright infringement under Swiss copyright law. As far as such headlines are protected by copyright at all, copying such headlines usually falls under right of quotations.

(c) P2P networks

Suppliers of P2P software: Suppliers of P2P software have not been held liable for copyright infringement in Switzerland. Since P2P software can be, and is, used for various purposes including many and probably mostly legal purposes, liability of P2P software suppliers without a business model primarily or exclusively related to obvious copyright infringement would be unreasonable.

Uploaders/downloaders: Downloading protected works except for computer programs from P2P networks and other sources – independent of the presumed legal nature of such sources – is considered personal use in Switzerland and therefore fully legal. Copyright levies are applicable to blank storage mediums used to store such works. Uploading on the other hand is not covered as personal use and therefore unlawful.

The Swiss exemption of downloads to copyright infringement independent of the source is often criticised by representatives of the US entertainment industry. In a report published in 2011, the Swiss Federal Council – Switzerland's federal government – deemed that a legal intervention with regard to lawful downloads for private use is not necessary, in particular due to the substantial copyright levies already applicable and the missing proof of significant damage to Switzerland's cultural landscape. Criminalising a considerable share of Switzerland's population for personal use downloads could also reduce the political acceptance of copyright law in general and would make it more difficult for law enforcement authorities to assign appropriate priorities.

(d) Webcasting

Webcasting – including radio and television programmes – is lawful under Swiss copyright law if all necessary intellectual property rights have been secured. Copyright levies might be applicable. Streaming without the necessary intellectual property rights constitutes a copyright infringement. Internet access providers are not liable for webcasting from third parties to their users over their network.

(e) Streaming

Streaming – including simulcasting of radio and television channels – is lawful under Swiss copyright law if all necessary intellectual property rights have been secured. Copyright levies might be applicable. Streaming without the necessary intellectual property rights constitutes a copyright infringement. Internet access providers are not liable for streaming from third parties to their users over their network.

(f) Framing

Framing is lawful if all necessary intellectual property rights have been secured. Framing without the necessary intellectual property rights constitutes a copyright infringement.

(g) Transmission of infringing work across a communications network

Communications network providers are not liable for the transmission of infringing works under Swiss copyright law. The sender of such transmission – for example the uploader in a P2P network – commits a copyright infringement if no copyright exemption or defence is applicable.

Some internet providers in Switzerland had to block access to internet content based on occasional court decisions with regard to the violation of personal rights. Many Swiss internet providers further block child pornography-related internet content on a voluntary basis in cooperation with public authorities.

Providers have no obligation to monitor their communications networks for copyright and other intellectual property law infringements.

(h) Aggregator websites (eg, Google News, price comparison websites)

Aggregator websites such as Google News can lawfully operate under Swiss copyright law. They operate mainly under the right of quotation and a copyright exemption for media reports on current events. In addition, the content aggregated might not even be copyright protected in Switzerland due to a lack of originality, and a *sui generis* protection for databases does not exist either. News aggregation or price comparison might constitute unfair competition, but the relevant case law is rather liberal in favour of aggregator websites.

(i) Treatment of user-generated content

Swiss law does not contain any specific provisions on the treatment of user-generated content. Copyright liability with regard to user-generated content and its treatment, in particular by internet providers, must therefore be assessed according to general administrative, civil and criminal Swiss law provisions. Specific exemptions, safe harbours or defences to copyright infringement do not exist with regard to the treatment of user-generated content.

Case law on copyright liability of internet providers for user-generated content is rare and inconsistent. As noted in section 1.6(a) above, internet providers strive to avoid liability by seriously assessing copyright claims and they are usually quick to react in relation to obvious copyright infringements, often based on respective provisions in their terms and conditions of use. In practice, liability exists mainly for user-generated content moderated by providers, similar to traditional media and their responsibilities. In any other case, however, internet providers will usually refer claimants to administrative, civil or criminal legal actions in order to remain impartial between their customers and third parties.

1.7 Joint liability for ISPs

Swiss law does not contain any specific provisions on joint liability for internet service providers (ISPs). Joint liability for ISPs therefore needs to be assessed according to general administrative, civil and criminal Swiss law provisions; however, relevant case law is rare and inconsistent.

1.8 Relief

Swiss law does not contain any specific provisions on relief against ISPs in the case of copyright infringements. Swiss intellectual property law on the other hand allows, among other things, legal actions for preliminary injunctions, for example to obtain an immediately effective cease and desist order against an ISP. The various administrative, civil and criminal actions against copyright infringers and relevant third parties such as ISPs as discussed above are also available.

1.9 Issues specific to Switzerland

(a) Jurisdiction

Swiss courts have jurisdiction over copyright infringement claims under the so-called Brussels Regime on the jurisdiction of courts and the recognition and enforcement of judgments in civil and commercial matters (ie, under European Council Regulation (EC) No 44/2001 and the Lugano Convention). An alleged copyright infringer can be sued at his/her domicile or his/her usual place of residence in Switzerland, as well as at the places in Switzerland where the copyright infringements occurred or had adverse effects. Swiss international private law also gives jurisdiction to the Swiss court where a copyright infringement is claimed. Exceptions are valid choices of jurisdiction between the relevant parties, for example in a licence agreement.

(b) Claim to infringement of foreign copyright

Courts in Switzerland are competent to hear foreign copyright claims in the event of claims against a defendant with any kind of domicile in Switzerland. Court decisions on such copyright claims will be made based on the applicable foreign copyright law, although the relevant parties might have to provide respective support to the court. In addition, the parties may agree that Swiss copyright law is to apply.

(c) Emission theory

Swiss copyright law does not use the emission theory to define the location where copyright–infringing acts take place. A copyright infringement might take place at various locations, for example in the case of copyright infringing P2P file sharing of computer programs at the locations of the uploaders, the listing website's administrators, the hosting provider of such a website and the downloaders.

1.10 Orphan works

Orphan works are only regulated with regard to audiograms and videograms in Swiss copyright law. The assertion of specific rights to works where the copyright owners are unknown or untraceable, the respective works were created more than 10 years ago and the works are in publicly accessible archives is reserved to collective administration societies under federal supervision. This regulation has no practical importance due to the many restrictions and the limitation to audiograms and videograms.

Any other orphan works with copyright protection cannot be lawfully used without the copyright owner's permission.

1.11 Online piracy measures

In a report published in 2011, the Swiss Federal Council deemed a legal intervention to establish online piracy measures to be unnecessary, in particular due to the substantial copyright levies already applicable in Switzerland and because there was no proof of significant damage to Switzerland's cultural landscape. Thus, Swiss copyright law does not currently provide for any specific measures against online piracy.

In 2012, mounting economic and political pressure by representatives of the US entertainment industry led to the formation of two ad-hoc forums to discuss the implementation of online piracy measures in Switzerland:

- In the working group on the optimisation of the collective management of copyright and related rights (so-called AGUR12 in German), representatives of artists – mostly collective administration societies – producers, commercial users, consumers and the federal administration discussed various copyright-related issues and possible amendments to Swiss copyright law. In spite of the working group's official name and original mandate, the focus mostly shifted to restrictive online piracy measures.

The working group's final report with recommendations for the attention of the Swiss Federal Council and the Swiss Federal Assembly was published in December 2013. Only a small number of the various issues discussed resulted in recommendations, and the working group reached consensus for these recommendations only as an overall package and not for all individual recommendations (ie, there was actually no consensus within the working group). Most of the published recommendations focus on online copyright enforcement including blocking access to websites, take-down and stay-down notices to internet providers, internet surveillance for the collection of IP addresses and other personal data of alleged copyright infringers, copyright notices to internet users and more efficient civil and criminal proceedings against copyright infringements in P2P networks. In addition, a safe harbour regime for internet providers cooperating with copyright holders was recommended.

The recommendations were widely criticised, especially by civil rights organisations, the ICT industry association and internet providers. Internet providers in particular were not members of the working group and they clearly stated their opposition to policing the Internet. It remains unclear if and in what time frame the working group's recommendations could lead to any amendments of Swiss copyright law. Amendments to Swiss copyright law in the past have taken years if not decades, and the current Swiss copyright law was only amended a few years ago after many challenges to reach the necessary political consensus. Further online piracy measures are also very controversial, not only in Switzerland but also in a European context.

- At the same time, US–Swiss discussions on online piracy measures take place in the form of a round table. This round table has always met in secret to date, and it is therefore unclear if it will produce any results with regard to Swiss copyright law.

1.12 Electronic infringements of moral rights

In addition to strictly property-based copyrights, Swiss copyright law includes a number of moral rights to protect a creator's personality. Such rights include: the right to the integrity of works (ie, the right to object to derogatory treatment); the right to object to false attribution; and the right to be recognised as creator (right of paternity). With the exception of parodies, a creator might even oppose contractually agreed or legally permitted uses of his/her copyrighted works if such uses violate his/her personal rights.

2. Trademarks

2.1 Use of a trademark

Maintaining trademark protection requires actual use of the relevant trademark in Switzerland. Use on the Internet clearly related to the goods and services listed for a protected trademark and with focus on consumers in Switzerland is generally considered sufficient to avoid revocation for non-use. As a notable exception, use limited to a domain name is insufficient. Trademark infringement claims on the other hand require that the allegedly infringing party uses an identical or confusingly similar trademark for identical or similar products or services in a way clearly related to Switzerland – in particular with focus on Swiss consumers – and for an economic purpose.

2.2 Infringement

(a) Metatags

Using a trademark registered by another trademark holder within the metatags of a website does not constitute a trademark infringement if there is an objective link between the trademark in the metatags and the goods or services offered on the website. The use of such trademark is unlawful if there is no objective link to the goods and services offered (eg, where there is no reference to branded goods and services offered, but solely the use of the trademark of a competitor which thereby potentially confuses or misleads the general public).

(b) *Keywords*

The use of a registered trademark as a keyword by a search engine or by an advertiser does not constitute a trademark infringement if there is an objective link between the trademark and the goods and services listed by a search engine or advertised by an advertiser. The use of such a trademark is, however, unlawful without an objective link to the goods and services listed or advertised, with the potential to confuse or mislead the general public.

(c) *Sponsored links*

Initial interest confusion through registered trademarks used in sponsored links suffices for trademark infringement since a sufficient distinction from registered trademarks must be maintained to prevent confusion. It is, however, lawful to use a registered trademark where there is an objective link between the trademark and the goods and services mentioned in sponsored links, as long as the sponsored links do not have the potential to confuse or mislead the general public.

(d) *Hidden text*

Using a registered trademark within the hidden text of a website (eg, within metatags or in HTML comments), does not constitute a trademark infringement if there is an objective link between the trademark and the goods or services offered on the website. The use of such a trademark is unlawful if there is no objective link to the goods and services offered (eg, where there is no reference to branded goods and services offered, but solely the use of the trademark of a competitor which thereby potentially confuses or misleads the general public).

(e) *Internet domain names*

The registration of an internet domain name which is confusingly similar or identical to a registered trademark may give rise to liability, although relevant case law has to date been inconsistent. Some inactive domain names were not considered relevant use against a registered trademark while others were, sometimes in connection with other intellectual property rights and unfair competition law claims.

(f) *Search navigation tools*

The use of a registered trademark within search or navigation tools such as 'breadcrumb trails' on a website does not constitute a trademark infringement given an objective link between the trademark and the goods and services listed in the search or navigation tools. It is unlawful to use a trademark, without an objective link to the goods and services listed in the search or navigation tools, with the potential to confuse or mislead the general public.

(g) *Hypertext links*

Registered trademarks can be used in hypertext links if an objective link to the linked content is given without the potential to confuse or mislead the general public. A link to the website of branded goods or services, for example, can contain the respective registered trademark.

(h) ***Framing***

Content using registered trademarks shown through framing becomes part of the website on which it is visible to visitors. Framing does therefore not constitute a trademark infringement if the same content directly published on a website would be a lawful use of a trademark.

2.3 Defences

(a) ***Descriptive (non trademark) use of the mark***

The concept of a descriptive use defence is not formally known in Swiss trademark law. Case law, however, similarly allows for descriptive references to registered trademarks for informational use and use in the media, for use in works of reference and for decorative purposes. Descriptive references are also allowed for comparative advertising and the description of goods and services if an objective link exist as between the offered goods and services and the respective registered trademark, for example in a hypertext link or sign leading to an independent provider of goods and services with the respective trademark. In addition, the principle of good faith is applicable (ie, a registered trademark is not infringed if the description including a registered trademark is limited to suitable, necessary and appropriate use for the respective purpose).

(b) ***Comparative advertising***

Registered trademarks may be used for comparative advertising if their use is not potentially confusing or misleading to the general public. Trademark disparagement in comparative advertising on the other hand might constitute unfair competition.

(c) ***Parody***

A parody using registered trademarks does not constitute a trademark infringement under Swiss trademark law if the parody is recognisable or if the parodied trademark is not used for an economic purpose.

2.4 Parallel imports

In Switzerland, the principle of international exhaustion applies to protected trademarks. It is therefore not considered a trademark infringement to offer branded goods or services in Switzerland via a website, even if those goods or services have not first been placed on the market in Switzerland by the trademark owner or by a third party with the trademark owner's consent. It is legally sufficient for parallel imports or grey import goods if such goods are already available in a foreign market and consumers as well as the general public in Switzerland are not potentially being confused or misled.

2.5 Remedies

Swiss intellectual property law offers various administrative, civil and criminal actions against trademark infringers and relevant third parties such as internet access, content and hosting providers. As noted above, the remedies available are identical or very similar for copyright, design, patent and trademark infringements.

Civil actions include actions for declaratory judgment on whether a registered trademark or a legal relationship with regard to intellectual property subsists under Swiss trademark law, actions for transfer of trademarks and actions for execution such as cease and desist orders for imminent or existing trademark infringements. Swiss intellectual property law further refers to general Swiss civil law to institute proceedings to compensate for losses (ie, by an action for damages including moral damages and profits gained through a trademark infringement). Swiss intellectual property law also allows for preliminary injunctions (eg, to enable pre-litigation discovery or to obtain an immediately effective cease and desist order). The burden of proof lies with the claimant, and it is necessary show that there is a reasonable likelihood that a trademark infringement has occurred or is likely to occur in the near future.

Most criminal actions require a formal criminal complaint by the holders of the allegedly infringed trademarks and only intentional acts of infringements are punishable. The criminal sanctions are usually up to one year's imprisonment or a fine. Fines are based on the daily disposable income of the defendant up to CHF3,000 per day and for up to 360 days. For copyright infringements which are deemed to be a commercial practice, a complaint by the copyright holders is in theory not required and the sanctions are up to five years' imprisonment together with a fine.

Administrative actions are within the competence of Swiss customs authorities or may be requested by trademark holders. In the context of the Internet, they are mainly relevant with regard to the temporary seizure of imported physical goods ordered via e-commerce and other online channels.

2.6 Liability of ISP

Swiss law does not contain any specific provisions on the liability of ISPs for trademark infringing activities carried out by their customers. Possible joint liability for ISPs therefore needs to be assessed by general administrative, civil and criminal Swiss law provisions. In Swiss trademark law, ISPs are usually not liable since a trademark infringement by their customers does not constitute trademark use by themselves.

Among other legal actions, Swiss intellectual property law allows for preliminary injunctions, for example to obtain an immediately effective cease and desist order against an ISP.

2.7 Advertising law and regulation

General advertising in Switzerland including advertising on the Internet and to a Swiss online audience is governed by Swiss unfair competition law (ie, the regulatory regime for advertising is relatively liberal as long as advertising does not constitute unfair competition). In addition to the respective case law, the legally non-binding 'Principles on Fair Competition in Commercial Communications' of the private Swiss Fair Commission provides for self-regulation within the Swiss advertising industry based on Swiss unfair competition law practice.

A stricter regulatory regime exists for certain goods such as alcohol and tobacco, certain activities such as gambling, and certain services such as legal or medical services. On the Internet, mass advertising by e-mail is only lawful if advertisers follow the opt-in principle and make it easy to unsubscribe from newsletters and other mass e-mailings; other mass advertising by e-mail is considered unsolicited (ie, spam) and therefore punishable as unfair competition.

2.8 Domain name disputes

An alternative dispute resolution procedure with the Arbitration and Mediation Center of the Word Intellectual Property Organization (WIPO) is available for domain names under the Swiss country top-level domain '.ch'.

The procedure consists of two stages: an attempt at conciliation; and an expert's decision. The first stage lasts a maximum of 60 days from the payment of the fees, and the second stage a maximum of 20 days. The fees for an attempt at conciliation are CHF600, and CHF2,000 for an expert's decision. The expert's decision will be implemented by SWITCH, the official .ch domain name registry, if the domain holder has not instituted civil proceedings within 20 working days upon the expert's decision.

The trademark owner must show a clear infringement of Swiss trademark law or any other intellectual property rights including distinctive signs and actions under the Swiss Federal Act on Unfair Competition. The trademark owner is not limited to trademark-related claims.

2.9 Unfair competition/passing off

Passing off is considered unfair competition according to Swiss unfair competition law and offers protection for website content independent of any registered trademarks (ie, resulting in additional or cumulative legal protection for trademark owners). Swiss unfair competition law in particular prohibits deceptive or misleading statements on the link between one's own goods and services and the goods and services offered by others under registered trademarks, unregistered marks, domain names, trade names and other names used in business and for an economic purpose.

3. Patents

3.1 Patentability of 'internet' inventions

Switzerland is a member state of the European Patent Convention (EPC). National patents according to Swiss patent law, as well as European patents, are therefore granted only for inventions in all fields of technology. To qualify, such inventions must be new, involve an inventive step and be susceptible of industrial application. 'Internet' inventions are not patentable as a rule of thumb.

(a) Computer programs

Computer programs 'as such' are not patentable in Switzerland. Inventions based on computer programs, however, might be patentable if they contain further technical elements (ie, if they make non-obvious technical contributions or solve a technical problem in a non-obvious way by running computer programs).

(b) ***Business methods***

Business methods 'as such' are not patentable in Switzerland.

(c) ***Mathematical methods***

Mathematical methods 'as such' are not patentable in Switzerland.

(d) ***Presentations of information***

Presentations of information 'as such' are not patentable in Switzerland.

3.2 Bioinformatics

Patents for a novel DNA sequence or a protein structure discovered through the use of bioinformatics can be obtained in Switzerland if such discoveries are produced by means of a technical process, their function is specifically indicated and the general requirements for patentability are met. Swiss and European case law explicitly dealing with aspects of bioinformatics is rare and bioinformatics patents are still a somewhat controversial legal and political issue. The existing decisions attempted to apply the established case law on computer programs and in particular so-called computer-implemented inventions to inventions in bioinformatics.

3.3 Issues specific to Switzerland

(a) ***Infringement on the Internet***

Swiss courts have jurisdiction over patent infringements committed via the Internet and in Switzerland, if the so-called Brussels Regime on the jurisdiction of courts and the recognition and enforcement of judgements in civil and commercial matters is applicable (European Council Regulation (EC) No 44/2001 and Lugano Convention). In this case, a patent infringer in Switzerland can be sued at his/her domicile before a single court (ie, the Swiss Federal Patent Court established in January 2012). Under Swiss international private law, Swiss courts further have jurisdiction at the Swiss domicile or at the usual place of residence of a patent infringer as well as at the places in Switzerland where the patent infringements occurred or had adverse effect. The latter provision in particular gives Swiss courts broad jurisdiction over patent infringements.

(b) ***Process patents***

Process patents can be infringed via the Internet when only part of the process is carried out in Switzerland given that the respective process – on the Internet often a business method – is patented in Switzerland.

3.4 Remedies available for patent infringements

Swiss intellectual property law offers various administrative, civil and criminal actions against patent infringers and relevant third parties such as internet access, content and hosting providers. The remedies available are identical or very similar for copyright, design, patent and trademark infringements.

Civil actions include actions for declaratory judgment on whether a patent or a legal relationship with regard to patents subsist under Swiss intellectual property law, actions for execution such as cease and desist orders for imminent or existing patent infringements and actions for description of a process used by a third party allegedly infringing a patent. Swiss intellectual property law further refers to general Swiss civil law to institute proceedings to compensate for losses (ie, action for damages including moral damages and profits gained through a trademark infringement). Swiss intellectual property law also allows for preliminary injunctions, for example to enable pre-litigation discovery or obtain immediately effective cease and desist orders. The burden of proof lies with the claimant, who must show that there is a reasonable likelihood that a patent infringement has occurred or is likely to occur in the near future.

Most criminal actions require a formal criminal complaint by the holders of the allegedly infringed patents and only intentional acts of infringements are punishable. The criminal sanctions usually include up to one year's imprisonment or a fine. Fines are based on the daily disposable income of the defendant up to CHF3,000 per day and for up to 360 days. For patent infringements that are deemed to constitute a commercial practice, a complaint by the patent holders will, in theory, not be required and the sanctions are increased to up to five years' imprisonment together with a fine.

Administrative actions are within the competence of Swiss customs authorities or may be requested by patent holders. In the context of the Internet, they are mainly relevant with regard to the temporary seizure of imported physical goods ordered via e-commerce and other online channels.

4. Disclosure orders against ISPs

4.1 Availability

Disclosure orders for the identity and contact details of users who are suspected of infringing intellectual property rights can in principle be obtained against innocent ISPs in Switzerland. ISPs follow only disclosure orders by courts or other competent authorities such as law enforcement authorities. In practice, disclosure orders can only be obtained through criminal proceedings, and law enforcement authorities are reluctant to grant disclosure orders if not for substantial intellectual property infringements since data privacy as a fundamental personal right is often valued with priority against intellectual property rights as mostly property rights.

4.2 Requirements

Disclosure orders against ISPs require the filing of a criminal complaint against an unknown person accused of an intellectual property infringement. The criminal complaint should include as much information as possible on the unknown accused person and the alleged intellectual property infringement. Criminal complaints solely based on collected IP addresses of P2P network users as evidence to be used in civil proceedings are considered a violation of Switzerland's relatively strict data privacy legislation and courts or law enforcement authorities will therefore refuse to issue disclosure orders based solely on such evidence.

4.3 Jurisdictional issues

Swiss courts and law enforcement authorities have jurisdiction at the place in Switzerland where an intellectual property infringement occurred or had effect. Swiss courts and law enforcement authorities offer legal assistance to courts and law enforcement authorities abroad.

4.4 'John Doe' injunctions

'John Doe' injunctions or equivalent legal actions are not available in Swiss law.

United Kingdom

Persephone Bridgman Baker
Neville Cordell
Allen & Overy LLP

1. Copyright, database rights and design rights

1.1 Overview

In UK law, copyright exists as a property right, giving authors the right to control the exploitation of a variety of different works. UK copyright law, currently enshrined in the Copyright, Designs and Patents Act 1988 (CDPA), has taken account of many historical changes since the first copyright statute in 1709. The Internet and digitisation are the latest challenges posed to the system. The ease of replication and transmission of works, transitory works, online liability, location and laws that pertain to infringing acts are all areas covered by recent UK case law.

The function of copyright – to protect listed categories of works against copying – is to protect the expression of ideas, whether or not such expressions are online or offline, digital or tangible. However, with structured categories of 'expressions' that copyright protects, and with the variations on infringement that are possible online, the United Kingdom has a system of protection that is not always a natural fit in the online context.

(a) *Literary works and artistic works*

'Literary works' are defined as:

> *any work, other than a dramatic or musical work, which is written, spoken or sung, and accordingly includes –*
> *(a) a table or compilation other than a database;*
> *(b) a computer program;*
> *(c) preparatory design material for a computer program; and*
> *(d) a database.*[1]

This definition specifically includes compilations, databases and computer programs (notably undefined in the legislation). The preparatory design for computer programs is also included within this definition, and 'writing' is defined as including any form of notation or code and literary material on screen displays in computer programs. The CDPA implements the EU Software Directive,[2] which provides that a 'computer program', including any preparatory design material, is protected in itself by copyright as a literary work.[3] Digital literary works therefore

1 Copyrights, Designs and Patents Act 1988, Section 3.
2 Directive 2009/24/EC on the legal protection of computer programs (Software Directive).
3 Software Directive, Article 1.

include software, text stored in electronic form, titles of web pages or hypertext links, or databases.

Artistic works,[4] including works of artistic craftsmanship, are interpreted as requiring a material object, manifesting properties of visual significance. While works on the Internet can be protected by copyright under this category, some may fall short due to lack of artistic intent. Digital artistic works include still electronic images, graphics on a website or parts of computer games.[5]

(b) *Films, sound recordings and broadcasts*

Audio and visual works will be protected on the Internet in the same way as offline content. Sound recordings are protected regardless of the medium or method used to make or play the recording.

The definition of 'broadcast' is an electronic transmission of visual images, sounds or other information, transmitted either for simultaneous reception or at a time determined solely by the person making the transmission. Internet transmissions are expressly included.

(c) *Typographical arrangement of a published edition*

A 'published edition' is a "published edition of the whole or any part of one or more literary, dramatic or musical works".[6] This could be used to protect the design and layout of a web page.

(d) *Protection of the user interface*

The Software Directive provides that protection shall apply to "the expression in any form of a computer program". However, "ideas and principles which underlie any element of a computer program, including those which underlie its interfaces, are not protected by copyright under this [Software] Directive".[7]

European case law has ruled that a graphical user interface, typically consisting of icons, drop-down menus and windows, cannot be protected as a computer program, but could be protected by the ordinary law of copyright as an artistic work or typographical arrangement.[8]

In practice, the most difficult question that arises regarding infringement of copyright in software relates to non-literal copying of the 'look and feel' of the visible parts of a program. The structure, appearance or operation of a computer program can be copied without accessing or copying the source code or object code. This 'look and feel' infringement is a difficult issue, given that it is possible for two programs to produce the same results even if they are completely different in terms of structure or program code.

---

4 CDPA, Section 4.

5 *Nova Productions Limited v Mazooma Games Limited* [2007] EWCA Civ 219.

6 *Navitaire Inc v Easyjet Airline Company* [2004] EWHC 1725 (Ch).

7 Software Directive, Article 1(2).

8 *Bezpe nostní softwarová asociace – Svaz softwarové ochrany v Ministerstvo kultury*, Case C-393/09, December 22 2010; *SAS Institute Inc v World Programming Ltd*, Case C-406/10, May 2 2012.

(e) *Websites protected as databases*

Databases enjoy dual protection in the United Kingdom. Databases are protected by the CDPA as a literary work, and defined as a "collection of independent works, data, or other material which (i) are arranged in a systematic or methodical way, and (ii) are individually accessible by electronic or other means".[9] Copyright protection for databases is subject to a higher originality test than that for other literary works: the database must be the author's own intellectual creation "by reason of the selection or arrangement of the contents of the database".[10] Databases are also, since January 1 1998, protected as a *sui generis* right under the Database Directive,[11] where there must have been a substantial investment in obtaining, verifying or presenting the contents of the database.[12]

Due to the broad protection of databases applying to both copyright and the *sui generis* database right, a website could be protected as a digital database. Online databases expressed on websites are, subject to the originality test, protectable by copyright or the *sui generis* database right.

Elements of a computer program may also constitute a database.

(f) *Compilations*

Tables and compilations, other than databases, are protected as literary works under the CDPA.[13] A 'compilation' is not defined in the CDPA, but case law has indicated that a compilation should be a collection of material representing a single exercise of taste and judgment,[14] and planned with overall design.[15] Where a compilation of data or other materials falls within the statutory definition of a 'database' it is also protectable via both copyright and the *sui generis* database right. In such cases, the higher test of originality would apply, as outlined above.

Elements of software are protectable as compilations: where a computer program consists of smaller related programs, the collection can be protected as a compilation where sufficient skill and effort has gone into the selection of works included.

1.2 Infringing acts

(a) *Copying*

The copyright owner has the exclusive right to reproduce the protected work,[16] and this protects against copying of the whole or a substantial part of the protected work in any medium, applying online as for any other context. This also includes the storing of the work by electronic means.[17]

---

9 CDPA, Section 3(d), defined in Section 3A, as inserted by the Copyright and Right in Databases Regulations 1997, SI 1997/3032, regulation 6.

10 CDPA, Section 3A(2).

11 Directive 96/9/EC on the legal protection of databases (Database Directive).

12 Copyright and Right in Databases Regulations 1997, Regulation 13(1).

13 CDPA, Section 3(1)(a).

14 6, *ibid.*

15 *Forensic Telecommunications Services Ltd v West Yorkshire Police* [2011] EWHC 2892 (Ch).

16 CDPA, Section 17.

17 CDPA, Section 17(2).

Exceptions apply where the copies are transient or incidental to another legitimate use of the work[18] (see section 1.4(e) for further details).

(b) ***Issuing copies to the public, communicating work to the public, performing, showing or playing work in public***

The copyright owner has the exclusive right to do each of the above-listed acts. The exclusive right of the copyright owner to issue copies to the public[19] or communicate the protected work to the public[20] includes broadcasts and on-demand transmissions. Case law demonstrates that this includes the running of peer-to-peer (P2P) software and the sharing of music files on the Internet: the uploader commits an infringing act.[21]

An internet service provider (ISP) may be liable for the issuing of copies of a work to the public if it allows users to download or make copies of copyright material. If an ISP provides a platform on which copyright work can be viewed (eg, a video streaming service), it could be found to have communicated the work to the public.

Internet transmissions can also be infringing where communication to the public includes the broadcasting of a work or the making available of a work in such a way that members of the public may access it from a place and at a time chosen by them (on-demand transmission).[22] These developments are a result of changes made to the CDPA by the Copyright and Related Rights Regulations 2003.[23]

Where copyright in a work is infringed by its being performed, played or shown in public by means of apparatus for receiving visual images or sounds conveyed by electronic means, the person by whom the visual images or sounds are sent, and in the case of a performance, the performers, shall not be regarded as being responsible for the infringement.[24]

(c) ***Renting or lending the work to the public***

It is an infringement to rent or lend copies of a literary, dramatic or musical work, artistic works in the online context, or a film or sound recording.[25]

(d) ***Authorising another person to do any of the above***

It is an act of infringement to authorise any of the restricted acts set out in (a) to (c) above. With regard to copyright in the digital context, this includes the facilitation or enablement of copying via the Internet, where no person operates the numerous servers and supporting networks. ISP liability is addressed at section 1.7 below.

(e) ***Secondary infringement***

Secondary infringement occurs where a person imports, possesses or deals with an

---

18 CDPA, Section 17(6).
19 CDPA, Section 18.
20 CDPA, Section 20.
21 *Polydor Limited v Brown* [2005] EWHC 3191 (Ch).
22 CDPA, Section 20(2); *ITV Broadcasting Ltds v TV Catchup Ltd* (No 2) Case C-607/11 [2013] Bus LR 1020.
23 The Copyright and Related Rights Regulations 2003.
24 CDPA, Section 19(4).
25 CDPA, Section 18A.

infringing copy in the course of business, or provides the means for making infringing copies, and has the requisite knowledge or belief (eg, that he knows or has reason to believe he is dealing in an infringing copy of the work). As above, a key question in the digital context is whether an ISP can be held liable for infringement and if so, what knowledge is required for liability. ISP liability is addressed at section 1.7 below.

1.3 Test for copyright infringement

The test for copyright infringement requires that an infringing act (see sections 1.2(a) to 1.2(e) above) is undertaken in relation to the whole or a substantial part of a protected work.

(a) *Requirement of substantial reproduction*

The 'substantial part' is not a statutorily defined term. That it is a matter of quality, not quantity is a concept enshrined in UK case law, no less applicable to the digital context than with regard to tangible works.[26]

In *Newspaper Licensing Agency Ltd (NLA) v Marks & Spencer*[27] it was held that the typographical arrangement of a newspaper constituted the published edition as a whole. 'Quality', it was noted, is adjudged by reference to the reason that the work is protected by copyright, supported by the European Court of Justice (ECJ) ruling in *Infopaq I*[28] and applied by the UK courts in *NLA v Meltwater.*[29] The key question in UK law therefore is: do the reproduced elements constitute 'the expression of the intellectual creation of the author' as opposed to any quantitative test?

(b) *Repeated copying of an insubstantial part*

Repeated copying of smaller parts of a copyright work on a regular basis is a more problematic area in copyright,[30] but has not been expressly ruled against by the UK courts.

With regard to database right infringement, it is expressly provided that the repeated and systematic extraction or utilisation of insubstantial parts of the contents of a database may amount to the extraction or utilisation of a substantial part of those contents, thereby amalgamating to constitute infringement. This was confirmed in *British Horseracing Board v William Hill.*[31]

1.4 Exemptions/defences to copyright infringement

(a) *Format shifting*

Currently, format shifting constitutes copyright infringement in the United

---

26 *Ladbroke v William Hill* [1964] 1WLR 273; *Designers Guild Limited v Russell Williams (Textiles) Limited* [2000] 1 WLR 2416, HL.

27 [2001] 3 WLR 290, paragraph 19.

28 *Infopaq International A/S v Danske Dagblades Forening* (Case C-5/08) July 2009.

29 *The Newspaper Licensing Agency Ltd v Meltwater Holding BV* [2010] EWHC 3099 (Ch); *The Newspaper Licensing Agency Ltd v Meltwater* [2011] EWCA Civ 890.

30 *Electronic Techniques (Anglia) Ltd v Critchley Components Ltd* [1997] FSR 401.

31 [2001] RPC 612.

Kingdom. However, in practice, millions of people undertake format shifting on a daily basis, although to date no action has been brought against an individual.

The Hargreaves Review, published in May 2011, proposed changes to introduce a narrow private copying exception applying equally to all types of private storage and copyright works. This exception would allow a lawful owner or buyer of a copy of a work to reproduce that copy for personal use, but not to permit the sharing of copies. The new legislation is predicted to come into force in 2014.

(b) Personal copying rights

Prompted by the proposals for a format-shifting exception, music companies proposed a levy, licence or tax on copying devices, voicing concerns that the format-shifting private copying exception will adversely affect music sales. This proposal was rejected.

(c) Time-shifting

A time-shifting exception exists that allows for a recording of a broadcast at home for private use in order that it can be viewed or listened to at a more convenient time.[32] This exception does not enable legitimate users of place-shifting technology, where broadcast signals are transmitted outside of domestic premises for non-domestic use.

(d) Fair use

'Fair dealing' with certain types of copyright work is permissible for the purposes of research and private study,[33] criticism or review,[34] or reporting current events[35] with sufficient acknowledgement of the original copyright work. Fair dealing is not otherwise defined.

In *Meltwater*[36] the court rejected the defendant's argument that viewing by end users of extracts from, and links to, newspaper articles provided by an online news monitoring service could amount to fair dealing for the purpose of criticism or review. This was justified on the basis that the users did not apply their critical faculties at all to the work, whether the article or the text extracts. The purpose of the news monitoring service was merely to enable users to decide whether they wanted to see the full content of the newspaper articles. The Court of Appeal rejected the appeal on the point of the narrow interpretation of what constituted 'criticism or review'.

(e) Caching/temporary copies as part of communication process

A temporary copy, transient or incidental, which is an integral and essential part of a technological process, the sole purpose of which is to enable either a transmission of the work between third parties by an intermediary or a lawful use of the work, and

---

32 CDPA, Section 70.
33 CDPA, Section 29.
34 CDPA, Section 30.
35 CDPA, Section 30.
36 29, *ibid*.

which has no economic significance, does not infringe copyright.[37] Notably, this does not apply to computer programs or databases.

This exception was introduced in the Digital Copyright Directive[38] to cover caching while browsing a website. The exception is narrowly drawn and should be considered in connection with the broader exceptions to liability for acting as a 'mere conduit', caching, and hosting, as set out in the E-commerce Directive.[39]

(f) ***Hosting***

The E-commerce Directive provides safe harbours from liability for ISPs. Article 14 provides for an exception for ISPs where information is stored at the request of a recipient of the service. The ISP must not have actual or constructive knowledge of this illegal activity. The ISP, on obtaining any such knowledge, must act expeditiously to remove the information.

This exception has not prevented the UK court from issuing injunctions under Section 97A of the CDPA ordering ISPs to block access to IP addresses, as exampled in the *Pirate Bay* peer-to-peer (P2P) case.[40]

(g) ***Back-up copies***

With regard to computer programs, specific exceptions are in place to allow for lawful users of a computer program to make back-up copies necessary for the purposes of lawful use. It is irrelevant whether there exists any term or condition in a user agreement purporting to prohibit such act.[41]

See also (b) above (personal copying rights).

(h) ***Reverse engineering***

With regard to computer programs, specific exceptions are in place to allow for observation, studying and testing or decompilation by a lawful user if done while performing any of the lawful acts of loading, displaying, running, transmitting or storing the program. The purpose of such reverse engineering can even be in order to determine the ideas and principles which underlie an element of the program.

Decompilation should be interpreted strictly and cannot take place where the user does not have access to the source.[42] The information obtained may not be used for any other purpose[43] outside of those specified in the statute. Additionally, the derogation will not apply if the lawful user:

- has the information necessary to achieve the permitted objective 'readily available to him';
- does not confine the decompiling to what is necessary to achieve the

37 CDPA, Section 28A.

38 Directive 2001/29/EC of the European Parliament and of the Council on the harmonisation of certain aspects of copyright and related rights in the information society, Article 5 (Digital Copyright Directive).

39 Directive 2004/48/EC of the European Parliament and of the Council of April 29 2004 on the enforcement of intellectual property rights (E-commerce Directive).

40 *Dramatico Entertainment Ltd v British Sky Broadcasting Ltd* [2012] EWHC 1152 (Ch).

41 CDPA, Section 50A.

42 *SAS Institute Inc v World Programming Ltd* (Case C-406/10).

43 CDPA, Section 50B(2)(b).

permitted objective;

- supplies the information obtained to anyone to whom it is not necessary to supply it in order to achieve the permitted objective; or
- uses the information to create a program which is substantially similar in expression to the program decompiled or to do any other act which is restricted by copyright.

(i) ***Parody defence***

The Hargreaves Review suggested the introduction of a parody defence, noting that video parody in particular is becoming more common with the increase in popularity of YouTube and social networking sites: the economic and cultural importance of parody was cited as justifying an exception. A new exception for parody is expected to be included in the legislation expected to come into force in 2014.

(j) ***Incidental inclusion***

Copyright is not infringed by the incidental inclusion of a protected work in an artistic work, sound recording, film or broadcast.[44] This incidental inclusion exception does not include the deliberate inclusion of such works. The leading case law relates to the inclusion of the Football Association's logo in photographs of footballers for collectors' stickers.[45] The key question is why the work has been incidentally included, and in this case, the importance of featuring players wearing authentic club strips meant that the inclusion of the logo was not merely incidental.

1.5 Remedies available for copyright infringement

The same civil remedies are available for copyright infringement as those in respect of infringement of any other IP right.[46] Civil remedies include interim relief (Norwich Pharmacal disclosure orders,[47] search orders, freezing orders and interim injunctions) and final relief (orders for delivery-up, seizure of infringing copies, final injunctions and damages, or account of profits).

Criminal sanctions are also available for copyright infringement, with the remedies for the online offence[48] currently carrying a lesser penalty than for the offences concerning physical infringement. Additional provisions create criminal offences regarding the circumvention of copy-protection technology measures.[49]

1.6 Copyright liability

(a) ***Hosting/cloud computing where infringing content is uploaded by user of service***

The primary liability for copyright infringement rests with the user or uploader of

---

44 CDPA, Section 31(1).
45 *Football Association Premier League Ltd v Panini UK Ltd* [2003] EWCA Civ 995.
46 CDPA, Section 96(2).
47 *Norwich Pharmacal Co v Customs and Excise Commissioners* [1974] AC 133.
48 CDPA, Section 107(2A).
49 CDPA, Sections 296 to 296ZG.

the infringing content. However, ISPs can be liable for failing to take down infringing content, and the line between public and private networks becomes less distinct when considering liability for infringing content in cloud computing applications.

Article 14 of the E-commerce Directive provides a safe harbour for ISPs where information is hosted at the request of a recipient of the service. The ISP must not have actual or constructive knowledge of this illegal activity. The ISP, on obtaining any such knowledge, must act expeditiously to remove the information. In other words, the ISP must operate a notice and takedown procedure.

(b) Hypertext linking

Further clarity is expected after the ECJ decision of *Svensson*,[50] in which the question of whether hypertext linking constitutes a communication to the public has been referred to the ECJ.

The issue also came up in a recent High Court case before Justice Arnold, in which he held as follows:[51]

> *I acknowledge that it is arguable that the mere provision of a hyperlink is not enough to constitute communication to the public (particularly if the hyperlink is not directly to a source of the copyright work). I also acknowledge that it is arguable that it makes no difference whether or not the source of the copyright work to which the hyperlink links is licensed by the copyright owner. I also acknowledge that it is arguable that it makes no difference whether clicking on the links results in framing (ie the work being presented within the frame of the operator's website) or not.*

However, in the *Paramount* case the defendants' acts went beyond the mere provision of hyperlinks linking (directly) to (unlicensed) sources of copyright works (which were framed). They were intervening in a highly material way to make the copyright works available to a new audience, and hence their acts did constitute a communication to the public.

Hypertext linking to an online database can also constitute database right infringement, as the provision of the data to the public, even by hyperlinking, is protected.

(c) P2P network

Supplier of P2P software: While not engaging directly in the reproduction of protected material, the suppliers of P2P services can still be liable for copyright infringement as authorisers of infringement,[52] secondary infringers[53] or potentially as a joint tortfeasor, although this requires a common design by the parties to infringe.

Uploaders/downloaders: In the running of P2P software and the sharing of media files on the Internet, both the uploader and the downloader may commit an infringing act.

---

50 C-466/12.
51 *Paramount Home Entertainment International Limited v BSkyB* [2013] EWHC 3479(Ch).
52 CDPA, Section 16(2).
53 CDPA, Section 24.

(d) *Webcasting*

Webcasting constitutes a communication to the public, which is an act restricted by copyright under UK law.

(e) *Streaming*

Addressed in 2013 by the ECJ, the distribution of copyright-protected works by live streaming is an infringement and requires the authorisation of the rights holder.[54] Streaming constitutes a means of communication to the public.

(f) *Framing*

The issue of whether framing constitutes an act restricted by copyright has also been referred to the ECJ in the cases of *Svensson*[55] and *BestWater International GmbH v Mebes*.[56] As noted above in (b) above, in the recent *Paramount* decision, Arnold commented that:

> *I also acknowledge that it is arguable that it makes no difference [to the question of infringement] whether clicking on the links results in framing (ie the work being presented within the frame of the operator's website) or not.*

(g) *Transmission of infringing work across a communications network*

Copyright in a work is infringed by a person who, without the licence of the copyright owner, transmits the work by means of a telecommunications system (otherwise than by communication to the public), knowing or having reason to believe that infringing copies of the work will be made by means of the reception of the transmission in the United Kingdom or elsewhere.[57]

(h) *Aggregator websites*

Aggregator websites potentially infringe copyright through a communication to the public.

A recent High Court decision[58] concerned FirstRow, which is a website operating as an indexing and aggregation portal to streamed broadcasts of sporting events. A visitor to the FirstRow website is presented with lists of links, organised by sport and time of the day, to streams containing live coverage of a wide range of sporting events, including in particular Premier League matches. Upon clicking on one of those links, the user is taken to a new page, which features a 'frame' or window in which that live coverage then appears, accompanied by advertising.

The streams which are indexed on FirstRow are provided by third-party streamers using one of a number of user-generated content (UGC) websites. The captured broadcast may be one that the streamer is watching on his television or computer legally (eg, via a legitimate subscription), or it may be an illegal stream. FirstRow has moderators who vet and index these submissions. The user clicks on the link, thereby

---

54 *ITV Broadcasting Ltd v TV Catchup Ltd* C-607/11.
55 C-466/12.
56 Case C-348/13.
57 CDPA, Section 24(2).
58 *The FA Premier League Limited v BSkyB Limited* [2013] EWHC 2058 (Ch).

enabling the user to watch the stream. FirstRow itself does not itself transmit any of the streams. Rather, the streams emanate from the UGC sites.

Arnold held that FirstRow was liable for communicating the works to the public. FirstRow aggregates a large number of streams from a variety of streamers, indexes them for the convenience of the user and provides a simple link for the user to click on in order to access a specific stream. While it was true that the technical effect of clicking on the link was to direct the stream from the UCG site to the user's computer, the stream was presented in a frame provided by FirstRow. Further, FirstRow was liable as a joint tortfeasor together with the UGC sites.

1.7 Joint liability for ISPs

In the case of *L'Oreal v eBay*,[59] Arnold held that eBay was not jointly liable for any infringements of eBay sellers given that eBay is under no legal duty to prevent infringement; and facilitation with knowledge and an intention to profit is not enough. This establishes the text applicable under English law to the issue of whether internet intermediaries are jointly liable for infringements committed by users of the service.

Further, even where an ISP would otherwise be liable under English law, there are various defences provided in the E-commerce Directive. The immunities are aimed at 'intermediary service providers' whose activities are of a 'mere technical, automatic and passive nature'.

Articles 12, 13 and 14 of the directive provide defences for ISPs and information society service providers where their acts consist of being a mere conduit, caching or hosting respectively. However, these exceptions do not result in complete immunity for ISPs; for example in the case of the hosting defence, they must operate a notice and takedown procedure or else they may be forced to remove the infringing content via an injunction.

Additionally, Article 15 of the E-commerce Directive provides that EU member states may not impose a general obligation on ISPs to monitor information which they transmit or store, nor actively to seek facts or circumstances indicating illegal activity.

1.8 Relief

The relief available for copyright infringement includes interim injunctions, final injunctions, delivery up of infringing copies, damages (both compensatory and additional damages) or an account of profits, declarations and publication of the decision at the cost of the infringer.

Relief can also be granted against intermediaries whose services are used to infringe, namely an injunction under Section 97A of the CDPA. This power has been used extensively by the English High Court to grant blocking injunctions, requiring the UK ISPs to block access to websites which were illegally communicating copies of works to the public.

---

59 [2009] EWHC 1094 (Ch).

1.9 Issues specific to the United Kingdom

(a) *Jurisdiction*

The UK courts have jurisdiction to hear copyright infringement claims:[60]

- if the defendant is domiciled or established in the United Kingdom, or is a UK national; or
- if the harmful event occurred in the United Kingdom, comprising both the location of the act causing the harm and the location where the harm was suffered. This is not always simple in online copyright infringement cases, not least due to the ability to locate servers outside the jurisdiction.

Notably, infringement by authorisation can occur even if the act of authorisation takes place in another jurisdiction.[61]

(b) *Claim to infringement of foreign copyright*

The UK courts can exercise jurisdiction based on foreign copyright, and the Supreme Court has held that this favours the modern trend of enforcement of IP rights, whether foreign or domestic.

Accordingly, where the defendant is domiciled in the United Kingdom, the UK courts have jurisdiction to hear claims of infringement of foreign copyright, at least so long as subsistence of copyright is not in issue.[62]

(c) *Emission theory*

In a recent High Court decision,[63] Arnold held that there is a communication to the public in the United Kingdom even where a server is hosted overseas, provided there is an intention on the part of the operators of the relevant website to target the public in the United Kingdom.

1.10 Orphan works

Where it is not possible by reasonable enquiry to identify the author of a work, or it is reasonable to assume that the copyright has expired in a work, it is not infringing to deal with that work in a way that would infringe a protected work.[64] These works have been the subject of recent government consultations regarding the definition of 'orphan works', the diligence required in searching for a rights owner and how to protect absent rights holders. The Enterprise and Regulatory Reform Act 2013 inserted new provisions into the CDPA to allow for secondary legislation in this area to implement a licensing scheme.

The Orphan Works Directive[65] entered into force in October 2012, intending to facilitate the digitisation of and cross-border access to orphan works. A single

---

60 EU Regulation 44/2001 on jurisdiction and the recognition and enforcement of judgments in civil and commercial matters (Brussels Regulation), Articles 2 and 5.

61 *ABKCO Music v Music Collection International Ltd* [1995] RPC 657.

62 *Lucasfilm v Ainsworth* [2011] UKSC 39.

63 *The FA Premier League Limited v BSkyB Limited* [2013] EWHC 2058 (Ch).

64 CDPA, Section 57(1).

65 Directive 2012/28/EU on certain permitted uses of orphan works (Orphan Works Directive).

publicly accessible EU-wide database will be compiled containing information relating to works defined as orphan.

1.11 Online piracy measures

The Digital Economy Act 2010 contains provisions aimed at tackling copyright infringement caused by online file sharing. Examples of the provisions include the imposition of various obligations on ISPs to notify subscribers if IP addresses are reported in copyright infringement reports by rights holders, and to provide rights holders with anonymised copyright infringement lists (the 'three strikes' notification rules). This opens the ISP to Norwich Pharmacal disclosure orders being sought by the rights holders to obtain names and addresses of potential infringers.

None of the provisions of the act relating to online piracy are yet in force.

1.12 Electronic infringement of moral rights

The CDPA incorporated the moral rights of paternity and integrity into UK law, and added the right to object to false attribution. All moral rights subsist as long as copyright subsists, except for the right to false attribution, which subsists for 20 years after a rights holder's death.

The paternity and integrity rights do not apply to certain digital works such as computer programs or computer-generated works.

(a) *Right to object to derogatory treatment*[66]

Where treatment amounts to distortion or mutilation of the work or is otherwise prejudicial to the honour or reputation of the author, this integrity right is infringed.

(b) *False attribution – right to guard against impersonation on the Internet*[67]

Infringement of this right occurs if a person exhibits in public, performs, communicates or issues to the public a work which has been falsely attributed. Examples from case law include the publication of spoof diaries in *Clark v Associated Newspapers Ltd.*[68]

(c) *Paternity right*

If an author has asserted a right of paternity, then the author of any literary, dramatic, musical or artistic work, and directors of films, have the right to be identified whenever the work is published commercially or copies are issued or communicated to the public. Commercial publication includes the making available of the work by means of an electronic retrieval system[69] such as the Internet.

2. Trademarks

The UK registered trademark legislation is set out in the Trademarks Act 1994,[70]

---

66 CDPA, Section 80.
67 CDPA, Section 84.
68 [1998] 1 All ER 959.
69 CDPA, Section 175(2).
70 Trademarks Act 1994.

which implements the EU Trademarks Directive.[71] Provisions relating to Community trademarks are contained in the Community Trademark Regulation.[72]

The UK and EU legislation sets out fundamental principles that are as applicable to online use and infringement as they are to offline use. The effect of multinational business transacted via the Internet is that case law has supplemented this legislation, with metatags and keyword advertising featuring prominently in recent ECJ case law.

2.1 Use of a trademark

(a) Use

The grounds for revocation of a registered trademark can be found in Section 46 of the Trademark Act. Subsection (1)(a) concerns the non-use of a registered trademark within the period of five years following registration. The use must be in the United Kingdom. There is extensive case law on what constitutes 'genuine use', supplementing Section 46.

The basic starting point for what constitutes 'genuine use' is from *Ansul,*[73] which ruled that 'genuine use' arises where the mark is used in accordance with its essential function, guaranteeing the origin of the goods or services for which it is registered. Token use will not constitute genuine use, but any use serving a real commercial purpose will suffice. The ECJ has declined to rule on further matters of the threshold of what constitutes genuine use.

An offer for sale online would constitute genuine use as long as the requirement of real commercial purpose is fulfilled. For a UK trademark, the genuine use must take place in the United Kingdom. With regard to online offers for sale, these would therefore have to be directed at UK consumers (ie, in pounds sterling and for delivery and shipping in the United Kingdom). The lack of international mail order availability on a trademark owner's website has been held to indicate a realistic prospect of the UK trademark being revoked for non-use.[74]

(b) Infringement

Trademark infringement occurs where a registered trademark is used in the course of trade without the proprietor's consent in any of the following circumstances:

- The sign used is identical to the registered trademark and is used in relation to goods or services which are identical to those for which the trademark is registered;[75]
- The sign used by the infringer is:
  - identical to the registered trademark, and used in relation to goods or services which are similar to those for which the trademark is registered; or

---

71 Directive 2008/95/EC (TMD).
72 Formerly 40/94/EEC, but replaced as of April 13 2009 by consolidated Regulation 207/2009/EC (CTMR).
73 *Ansul BV v Ajax Brandbeveiliging BV* Case C-40/01.
74 *Euromarket Designs Inc v Peters and Crate & Barrel* [2001] FSR 20.
75 TMA, Section 10(1); TMD, Article 5(1)(a); CTMR, Article 9(1)(a).

  - similar to the registered trademark, and used in relation to goods or services which are identical or similar to those for which the trademark is registered;

  and, in each case, there exists a likelihood of confusion on the part of the public;[76] or

- The sign used by the infringer is identical or similar to the registered trademark, the trademark has a reputation in the United Kingdom, and use of the sign without due cause takes unfair advantage of, or is detrimental to, the distinctive character or repute of the trademark.[77]

Online use in the course of trade that is covered by the first to the third bullets above will be infringing. However, use must be of a sign in a third party's own commercial communication, thereby largely excluding from infringement websites such as Google which do not 'use' the sign on their own behalf.

As regards use of a trademark on a foreign website, this will constitute use of the mark in the United Kingdom for the purposes of infringement if the website is targeted at UK consumers.[78]

2.2 Infringement

(a) Metatags

Metatags consist of text embedded in the HTML of a webpage, invisible to the end user but locatable by search engines using the metatags to list sites. Metatags are therefore essential for this indexation process and key for attracting web traffic to a site. The use of metatags is mostly lawful, but there are examples of UK cases where website owners have diverted traffic to their site through the unauthorised use of a third-party trademark.

Initial cases found that metatag use of a third-party trademark would constitute trademark infringement. There has since been a shift away from this decision and the Court of Appeal has ruled that such use of metatags is non-infringing where, even in the case of similar marks for similar services, there is no confusion caused by a web search resulting in listings for both companies.[79]

(b) Keywords and sponsored links

Infringement: Use of a sign as a keyword to trigger advertisements has been established by the ECJ to be potentially infringing use. These judgments have been pivotal in recent trademark law development.[80]

Internet search engines: Keywords are sold by internet search engines which are not themselves advertising. Following references to the ECJ in three sets of proceedings

76 TMA, Section 10(2); TMD, Article 5(1)(b); CTMR, Article 9(1)(b).
77 TMA, Section 10(3); TMD, Article 5(2); CTMR Article 9(1)(c).
78 *Euromarket Designs Inc v Peters and Crate & Barrel* [2001] FSR 20.
79 *Reed Executive plc and Another v Reed Business Information* [2004] EWCA Civ 159.
80 79 *ibid.*

brought by trademark owners against Google, guidance was given on the liability of internet search engines and advertisers for the use of others' trademarks as advertising keywords.[81]

The ECJ ruled that the search engine (Google) was not liable for infringement through the storing of the keyword and its use in its search optimisation tool.

Advertisers: A trademark owner can prevent advertisers from using its trademark as a keyword where the resultant advertisement fails to make it clear that the goods or services emanate from someone other than the trademark owner. In order to avoid infringement, advertisements resulting from the use of keywords must enable the reasonably well-informed and reasonably attentive internet user to ascertain whether the service referred to in the advertisements originated from the trademark owner or an economically connected undertaking, or originated from a third party.

Initial interest: A claimant need not show any actual confusion at the point of sale to establish a likelihood of confusion under Trademark Act, Section 10(2). 'Initial interest' confusion is sufficient and occurs where a consumer mistakenly believes that a product originates from a different source, but this is corrected before the point of sale.[82]

In *Interflora*,[83] initial interest confusion was also held to be relevant in showing an adverse effect on the origin function of the trademark for the purposes of Section 10(1) infringement.

(c) Hidden text

See section at 2.2(a) above; the position is likely to be the same for hidden text.

(d) Internet domain names

Use of a registered trademark in the registration of a domain name can constitute trademark infringement and passing off.[84] Trademark owners are able to seek the transfer of a domain name to themselves where that domain name is identical or confusingly similar to their own and there is an element of bad faith in the use or registration of that name.

Mere registration of a domain name incorporating the well-known trademark of a third party can amount to the creation of an instrument of fraud on the basis that any realistic use of them as domain names would result in passing off.[85]

(e) Search navigation tools

Use of a sign as part of a so-called 'breadcrumb trail' on a website or in a hypertext link can constitute use in a trademark sense (to denote origin), rather than being regarded merely as a navigational tool,[86] and hence give rise to trademark infringement.

---

81 82, *ibid.*
82 *Interflora Inc v Marks and Spencer Plc* [2013] EWHC 1291 (Ch).
83 80, *ibid.*
84 *BT plc v One In A Million Limited* [1999] 1 WLR 903.
85 *BT plc v One In A Million Limited* [1999] 1 WLR 903.
86 *Datacard Corporation v Eagle Technologies Ltd* [2011] EWHC 244 (Pat).

(f) ***Framing***

Where framing suggests a link between the two framed sites, there is a potential claim for passing off. Framing inherently involves a seamless transition between sites, thereby incurring a greater risk of confusion between the sites.

2.3 Defences

The various defences to trademark infringement[87] are subject to the proviso that the use is in accordance with honest practices in industrial or commercial matters.

(a) ***Own name***

A trademark owner cannot prohibit the use by a person of his own name.[88] This has been held to extend to the use by a company of its own name, in accordance with honest practices as above.

(b) ***Descriptive (non-trademark) use of the mark***

A trademark owner cannot prevent third parties from using indications concerning the kind, quality, quantity, intended purpose, value, geographical origin, time of production of the goods or of rendering of the service, or other characteristics of the goods or service, as long as the use is in accordance with honest practices in industrial or commercial matters.[89]

(c) ***Comparative advertising***

The Comparative Advertising Directive[90] was implemented in the United Kingdom by the Business Protection from Misleading Marketing Regulations 2008.[91]

A comparative advertisement is one that identifies a competitor or goods or services offered by a competitor.[92] A comparative advertisement is permitted under the Comparative Advertising Directive if the following conditions are fulfilled:

- It is not 'misleading';[93]
- It compares goods and services intended for the same purpose;[94]
- It objectively compares one or more material, relevant, verifiable and representative features of those goods and services;[95]
- It does not discredit or denigrate the trademark, trade names, other distinguishing marks, goods, services, activities or circumstances of the competitor;[96]
- For products with designation of origin it relates to products with the same designation;[97]

87 TMA, Section 11, Section 12; TMD, Article 6; CTMR, Article 12.
88 TMA, Section 11(2)(a); TMD, Article 6(1)(a); CTMR, Article 12(a).
89 TMA Section 11(2)(b); TMD, Article 6(1)(b); CTMR, Article 12(b).
90 EU Directive 2006/114/EC concerning misleading and comparative advertising (Comparative Advertising Directive).
91 SI 2008/1276.
92 Comparative Advertising Directive, Article 2(c).
93 Comparative Advertising Directive, Article 4(a).
94 Comparative Advertising Directive, Article 4(b).
95 Comparative Advertising Directive, Article 4(c).
96 Comparative Advertising Directive, Article 4(d).

- It does not take unfair advantage of the reputation of a trademark, trade name or other distinguishing marks of a competitor or of the designation of origin of competing products;[98]
- It does not present goods or services as imitations or replicas of goods or services bearing a protected trademark or trade name;[99] and
- It does not create confusion among traders, between the advertiser and a competitor or between the advertiser's trademarks, trade names, other distinguishing marks, goods or services and those of the competitor.[100]

Accordingly, case law has ruled that use of a third-party mark in these circumstances is legitimate so long as it does not cause confusion.[101] Third-party marks can be used freely for comparative purposes as long as it is clear whose mark is whose. The ECJ has ruled that, within the natural reading of the legislation, the term 'advertising' in the Comparative Advertising Directive covers the use of a domain name and metatags but not the registration of a domain name.[102]

(d) *Parody*

No parody defence as such exists in the United Kingdom,[103] although cases have indicated that parody trademarks may be permissible, so long as confusion or detriment is not caused to the original trademark.[104]

2.4 Parallel imports

A registered trademark is not infringed by the use of the mark on goods that have been put on the market in the European Economic Area under that trademark by the proprietor or with its consent.[105] This principle of exhaustion allows for the free movement of goods within the European Economic Area (EEA) by providing that goods which are placed on the market in one EEA state can be freely exported by third-party distributors and sold in other member states.

Conversely, it is an infringement to sell or to offer for sale genuine goods in the United Kingdom if those goods have not been put on the market in the EEA by the trademark owner or with its consent. Accordingly an offer to sell genuine non-EEA goods on a website, where that website is targeted at UK consumers, is likely to infringe the relevant UK or Community trademarks.

---

97 Comparative Advertising Directive, Article 4(e).

98 Comparative Advertising Directive, Article 4(f).

99 Comparative Advertising Directive, Article 4(g).

100 Comparative Advertising Directive, Article 4(h).

101 *O2 Holdings Limited (formerly O2 Limited), O2 (UK) Limited v Hutchison 3G Limited* [2006] EWCA 1656.

102 *Belgian Electronic Sorting Technology NV v Peelaers* Case C-657/11.

103 *Ate My Heart Inc v Mind Candy Ltd* [2011] EWHC 2741 (Ch).

104 Application No 2281390 by the National Canine Defence League to Register a Trademark in Classes 16, 36, 41 and 42 and Opposition under No 90127 by Geoffrey, Inc, July 29 2003; *Specsavers International Healthcare Ltd, Specsavers BV, Specsavers Optical Group Ltd, Specsavers Optical Superstores Ltd v Asda Stores Ltd* [2012] EWCA Civ 24.

105 TMA Section 12; TMD Article 7; CTMR Article 13.

2.5 Remedies

The remedies available in the United Kingdom for trademark infringement include:

- injunctions (interim and final);
- damages or an account of profits;
- orders for erasure, removal or obliteration of offending signs from infringing goods, materials or articles; and
- orders for delivery-up and destruction of infringing goods, materials or articles.

Criminal penalties are also available. Sanctions for breach of the criminal provisions of the Trademark Act include fines and imprisonment.

2.6 Liability of ISPs

Under UK law, website hosts, ISPs and search engine providers can be responsible for trademark infringement. However, the E-commerce Directive provides safe harbours for information society services. A website host, ISP or search engine provider will not be liable for information placed on its service by third parties unless it fails to act expeditiously after being made aware of illegality. There will not be, via injunctive relief or otherwise, any obligation imposed on information society services to monitor information or actively to seek out infringing material.[106] However, failure to act on becoming aware, or taking an active role, may give rise to liability.

The safe harbours apply only where activities are of a mere technical, automatic and passive nature. An information society service provider, such as an online marketplace provider, that stores and uses a sign identical to a trademark to organise the display of adverts on the basis of that keyword does not make infringing use of that sign.[107]

However, infringing use may occur if an active role is taken in the drafting and publication of the advertisement[108] or if it provides assistance in optimising presentation of offers for sale or promotion of those offers.[109]

The law in relation to accessory liability is governed by UK law rather than EU harmonised provisions. Under UK law, a party will be liable as a joint tortfeasor only where it intends, procures and shares a common design in the infringement.[110]

Recent case law shows that even if a website host facilitated infringement, knew that such infringements occurred and were likely to keep occurring, and profited from such infringements, this was still not sufficient to establish a common design.[111]

Article 11 of the Enforcement Directive[112] requires EU member states to ensure that, where an IP right is infringed, an injunction should be issued to prohibit the continuation of the infringement. It also requires EU member states to ensure that rights holders can apply for an injunction against intermediaries whose services are used for such infringement.

---

106 79 *ibid.*
107 79 *ibid.*
108 *L'Oréal SA v eBay International AG* (Case C-324/09).
109 111, *ibid.*
110 *CBS Songs Limited v Amstrad Consumer Electronics Plc* [1988] AC 1013.
111 *L'Oréal v eBay* [2009] EWHC 1094 (Ch).
112 Directive 2004/48/EC on the enforcement of intellectual property rights (Enforcement Directive).

Injunctions must be 'effective, proportionate and dissuasive'.[113] Any requirement actively to monitor is incompatible with Article 3 of the Enforcement Directive, which requires measures to be fair, proportionate and not excessively costly. Furthermore, the Enforcement Directive should not be interpreted so as to affect Articles 14 and 15 of the E-commerce Directive.

2.7 Advertising law and regulation

The main enforcement body in the United Kingdom is the Advertising Standards Authority (ASA), which enforces rules for all advertising, both broadcast and non-broadcast. The ASA is an independent body, outside of government and the advertising industry, funded by an industry-wide levy on advertising space.

The current non-broadcast code of practice is the 12th edition of the UK Code of Non-broadcast Advertising, Sales Promotion and Direct Marketing (the CAP Code). All the main trade and professional bodies that represent those involved in advertising (advertisers, agencies and media owners) are members of CAP and agree not to accept any advertising which contravenes the CAP Code. The CAP Code is enforced by the ASA.

The CAP Code and the ASA's remit for online advertising covers the following:

- editorial content on websites;
- ads in paid-for space (eg, banner advertisements, pop-ups);
- advertising content in commercial emails;
- sales promotions;
- commercial text messages;
- viral marketing emails;
- paid-for entries in search engine results;
- advertisements on electronic billboards;
- advertisements in electronic games; and
- use of email addresses for marketing purposes (eg, spam).

The CAP Code sets out a number of important general principles. Advertising should be legal, decent, honest and truthful, be prepared with a sense of responsibility to consumers and society, and respect the principles of fair competition generally accepted in business.[114]

If the ASA finds that an online advertisement breaches the CAP Code, the ASA will ask the advertiser to withdraw or change it. The ASA does not have the ability to impose fines, but does have a number of other sanctions, which it can use to ensure compliance. These include refusal of further advertising space, adverse publicity via publication of rulings on its website, and withdrawal of trading privileges. As a last resort, the ASA can refer the matter to the Office of Fair Trading to pursue the matter in court.

In addition, for online advertising within the control of the advertiser, such as on the advertiser's own website, the ASA may remove paid-for search advertisements

---

113 111, *ibid.*
114 CAP Code, Rule 1.

that link directly to the non-compliant advertisement. The cooperation of search engines is required to implement this.

2.8 Domain name disputes

The Internet Corporation for Assigned Names and Numbers (ICANN) has a system for settling domain name disputes, through the Uniform Domain Name Dispute Resolution Policy (UDRP), for global top-level domain names.

Nominet runs an arbitration system for disputes concerning UK country-code domain names. Under its dispute resolution policy, a domain name complaint can be filed where a UK domain name meets the following criteria:

- The complainant has trademark rights in respect of a name or mark which is identical or similar to the domain name; and
- The domain name, in the hands of the respondent, is an abusive registration.

'Abusive registration' means a domain name which either:

- was registered or otherwise acquired in a manner which, at the time when the registration or acquisition took place, took unfair advantage of or was unfairly detrimental to the complainant's rights; or
- has been used in a manner which has taken unfair advantage of or has been unfairly detrimental to the complainant's rights.

2.9 Unfair competition/passing off

The UK tort of passing off protects the goodwill associated with a mark or get-up, allowing for the protection of unregistered marks.

Although similarities exist between passing off and unfair competition in the continental or US sense, a claim for passing off is narrower in scope and more difficult to prove. The Court of Appeal has emphatically rejected that passing off might be capable of developing into the tort of unfair competition.[115] A claim for passing off is as available for infringement online as it would be offline.

The basic principle at the foundation of the tort of passing off is that "a man is not to sell his own goods under the pretence that they are the goods of another man".[116] There is no statutory basis for the claim; instead it has developed through case law.

For a name, mark or get-up to be protected by an action in passing off, the public must recognise the features as denoting the quality or character of the goods originating from a particular trader. This 'goodwill' forms the basis of the claim and is that which is protectable by the action. Passing off has traditionally concerned the use of a name, mark or get-up but has developed to encompass branding or marketing techniques such as slogans or visual images from advertisements, more relevant to the online context.

The use of metatags[117] and domain names[118] has given rise to claims in passing off;

---

115 *L'Oréal v Bellure* [2007] EWCA 968.
116 *Perry v Truefitt* (1842) 5 Beav 66 at 73.
117 83 *ibid.*
118 88, *ibid.*

for the latter, the mere registration of a mark has been held to be sufficient to give rise to an action in passing off.

3. Patents

3.1 Patentability of 'internet' inventions

(a) Computer programs

Computer programs are expressly excluded from patentability under the Patents Act[119] where the patent relates to a computer program 'as such'. The same is provided under the European Patent Convention (EPC), but it is well established that the application of a computer program may be patentable if it possesses technical character, although there is a divergence between the UK and European Patent Office (EPO) approach.

The UK approach to assessing the patentability of computer-implemented inventions is now set out in two Court of Appeal judgments, *Aerotel*[120] and *Symbian*.[121] If the claimed invention makes a technical contribution which in itself is not a computer program, it will not be precluded from registration. The *AT&T/Cvon*[122] case provides signposts to what constitutes the 'relevant technical effect'.

(b) Business methods

Business methods are expressly excluded from patentability under the Patents Act[123] where the patent relates to a business method 'as such'. This exclusion tends to prevent patent applications seeking protection for carrying out a business method over the Internet from being granted (eg, a patent application for a means of carrying out an Internet auction).

(c) Mathematical methods

Mathematical methods are expressly excluded from patentability under the Patents Act[124] where the patent relates to a mathematical method 'as such'.

However, as for computer programs, where the technical contribution is not, in itself, a mathematical method, it will not be precluded from patentability.

(d) Presentation of information

A presentation of information is expressly excluded from patentability under the Patents Act[125] where the patent relates to a presentation of information 'as such'. As for computer programs, despite the explicit exclusion of presentations of information from patentability, protection may be obtained where the technical contribution goes further than being a presentation of information.

---

119 Patents Act 1977 (PA), Section 1(2)(c).
120 *Aerotel Ltd v Telco Holdings Ltd* [2006] EWCA Civ 1371.
121 *Symbian Ltd v Comptroller General of Patents* [2008] EWCA Civ 1066.
122 *AT&T Knowledge Ventures LP v Comptroller General of Patents Designs and Trademarks* [2009] EWHC 343 (Pat).
123 PA, Section 1(2)(c).
124 PA, Section 1(2)(a).
125 PA, Section 1(2)(d).

3.2 Bioinformatics

Bioinformatics relies upon the considerable increase in the amount of DNA and amino acid sequence data created and stored in publicly accessible databases and a parallel increase in the power of computers. Bioinformatics enables researchers to identify genes (and the proteins for which they encode) by comparing their sequences with previously identified and characterised genes. It is not a bar to patentability that an invention has been found using bioinformatics techniques.

The main issue with inventions discovered through bioinformatics is the industrial applicability of the information obtained.[126] The requirement of industrial applicability of an invention is one of the fundamental requirements for patentability in the United Kingdom.[127]

Additionally, the Biotech Directive[128] provides that "an element isolated from the human body or otherwise produced by means of a technical process, including the sequence or partial sequence of a gene, may constitute a patentable invention, even if the structure of that element is identical to that of a natural element". However, "the industrial application of a sequence or partial sequence of a gene must be disclosed in the patent application".[129]

The principles to be applied in determining industrial applicability and sufficiency of an invention discovered through bioinformatics are as follows:

- The patent must disclose "a practical application" and "some profitable use" for the claimed substance, so that the ensuing monopoly "can be expected [to lead to] some ... commercial benefit".
- A "concrete benefit", namely the invention's "use ... in industrial practice" must be "derivable directly from the description", coupled with common general knowledge.
- A merely "speculative" use will not suffice, so "a vague and speculative indication of possible objectives that might or might not be achievable" will not do.
- The patent and common general knowledge must enable the skilled person to "reproduce" or "exploit" the claimed invention without "undue burden", or having to carry out "a research programme".

Where a patent discloses a new protein and its encoding gene:

- The patent, when taken with common general knowledge, must demonstrate "a real as opposed to a purely theoretical possibility of exploitation".
- Merely identifying the structure of a protein, without attributing to it a "clear role", or "suggest[ing]" any "practical use" for it, or suggesting "a vague and speculative indication of possible objectives that might be achieved", is not enough.

---

126 *Human Genome Sciences Inc v Eli Lilly and Co* [2011] UKSC 51.

127 PA, Section 1(1)(c).

128 Directive 98/44/EC of the European Parliament and of the Council of July 6 1998 on the legal protection of biotechnological inventions (Biotech Directive).

129 Biotech Directive, Article 5.

- The absence of any experimental or wet lab evidence of activity of the claimed protein is not fatal.
- A "plausible" or "reasonably credible" claimed use, or an "educated guess", can suffice.
- Such plausibility can be assisted by being confirmed by "later evidence", although later evidence on its own will not do.
- The requirements of a plausible and specific possibility of exploitation can be at the biochemical, the cellular or the biological level.

Where the protein is said to be a family or superfamily member:

- If all known members have a "role in the proliferation, differentiation and/or activation of immune cells" or "function in controlling physiology, development and differentiation of mammalian cells", assigning a similar role to the protein may suffice; So "the problem to be solved" in such a case can be "isolating a further member of the [family]".
- If the disclosure is "important to the pharmaceutical industry", the disclosure of the sequences of the protein and its gene may suffice, even though its role has not "been clearly defined".
- The position may be different if there is evidence, either in the patent or elsewhere, which calls the claimed role or membership of the family into question;
- The position may also be different if the known members have different activities, although they need not always be "precisely interchangeable in terms of their biological action", and it may be acceptable if "most" of them have a common role.

3.3 Issues specific to the United Kingdom

(a) Infringement on the Internet

The Patents Act states that patent infringement occurs when a person undertakes one of the following infringing acts in relation to a valid UK patent. The act must take place in the United Kingdom.

(1) Subject to the provisions of this section, a person infringes a patent for an invention if, but only if, while the patent is in force, he does any of the following things in the United Kingdom in relation to the invention without the consent of the proprietor of the patent, that is to say:

(a) where the invention is a product, he makes, disposes of, offers to dispose of, uses or imports the product or keeps it whether for disposal or otherwise;

(b) where the invention is a process, he uses the process or he offers it for use in the United Kingdom when he knows, or it is obvious to a reasonable person in the circumstances, that its use there without the consent of the proprietor would be an infringement of the patent;

(c) where the invention is a process, he disposes of, offers to dispose of, uses or imports any product obtained directly by means of that process or keeps any such product whether for disposal or otherwise.

(2) *Subject to the following provisions of this section, a person (other than the proprietor of the patent) also infringes a patent for an invention if, while the patent is in force and without the consent of the proprietor, he supplies or offers to supply in the United Kingdom a person other than a licensee or other person entitled to work the invention with any of the means, relating to an essential element of the invention, for putting the invention into effect when he knows, or it is obvious to a reasonable person in the circumstances, that those means are suitable for putting, and are intended to put, the invention into effect in the United Kingdom.*[130]

The UK courts will have jurisdiction over patent infringement that occurs where one of these acts of primary or contributory infringement takes place within the United Kingdom (see also section 1.9 for general jurisdiction of the UK courts).

Primary infringement can often occur online where offers for disposal or disposals are made online. Contributory infringement can occur online where an offer to supply or supply of a means essential to the patented invention is made in the United Kingdom, where it is known or obvious to the reasonable person that this means will put the invention into effect in the United Kingdom.

It has been held that a website of a foreign company not directed specifically to the United Kingdom was not sufficient evidence of an offer to supply.[131] Online offers would have to be made to UK customers, with shipping availability into the United Kingdom or offers for sale in pounds sterling. Under the aforementioned circumstances, infringement could occur even from a website hosted in or a defendant located in another jurisdiction.

(b) Parts of system claimed in patent located outside the United Kingdom

The case of *Menashe v William Hill* concerned a patent entitled "Interactive, computerised gaming system with remote control".[132] Claim 1 claimed "a gaming system for playing an interactive casino game comprising a host computer, at least one terminal computer forming a player station, communication means for connecting the terminal computer to the host computer and the program means for operating the terminal computer, the host computer and the communication means ... characterised in that the terminal computer is situated at a location remote from the host computer".

The defendant alleged it did not infringe on the basis that the gaming system did not have means relating to an essential element of the invention for putting that invention into effect in the United Kingdom, as the host computer was situated outside the United Kingdom in Antigua or Curacao.

The Court of Appeal found that there was contributory infringement pursuant to Section 60(2) of the Patents Act 1977. While the claimed invention required there to be a host computer, it did not matter where the host computer was situated. A person who was situated in the United Kingdom who obtained in the United Kingdom a CD and then used his terminal to address a host computer would not be bothered where

130 PA, Section 60.

131 *Boegli-Gravures SA v Darsail-ASP Ltd* [2009] EWHC 2690 (Pat).

132 [2002] EWCA Civ 1702.

the host computer was located. The punter uses his terminal in the United Kingdom and accordingly he effectively uses the host computer in the United Kingdom too. In those circumstances the UK punter will use the claimed gaming system in the United Kingdom, even if the host computer is situated in Antigua. Thus, the supply of the CD in the United Kingdom to the UK punter was intended to put the invention into effect in the United Kingdom.

In the more recent case of *Research in Motion UK Limited v Motorola Inc*,[133] Arnold applied the *Menashe* decision and said the relevant test is to ask: who uses the system and where is it used?

3.4 Remedies available for patent infringement

The remedies available for patent infringement in the United Kingdom include:

- injunction (interim and final);
- order for delivery-up or destruction of any patented product;
- damages; and
- an account of profits.

4. Disclosure orders against internet service providers

4.1 Availability

The UK courts are able to make a disclosure order against anyone who, even innocently, becomes involved in the wrongful act of another.[134] Where an applicant has evidence that an ISP user has infringed an IP right but requires disclosure as to the identity of that infringer, a Norwich Pharmacal order may be available against the ISP.

The courts must conduct a balancing exercise in assessing whether the interests of justice are served by the subjection of an innocent party to such an order. Costs will be borne by the applicant on the granting of such an order.

4.2 Requirements

In order to obtain a Norwich Pharmacal order against a third party, the applicant must have evidence to show the following:

- A wrong has been committed;
- An order for disclosure is required in order to take action against the wrongdoer; and
- The respondent is involved in the wrongdoing (albeit perhaps innocently) and is able to provide the necessary information.

Norwich Pharmacal relief is not suitable where the respondent is likely to become a party to the main proceedings. In such situations, disclosure of this sort is available under the Civil Procedure Rules.

A Norwich Pharmacal order is a discretionary remedy. The court will grant such

---

133 [2010] EWHC 288 (Pat).
134 47, *ibid*.

an order only where it is necessary and proportionate, and there are other competing rights that must be accounted for. In addition, the court will have to be satisfied that there is a good arguable case that there has been a wrongdoing, as the Norwich Pharmacal hearing will take place commonly prior to and separately from main proceedings.

Norwich Pharmacal relief has been granted in a number of IP cases including online copyright infringement, illegal downloading and P2P file sharing.

4.3 Jurisdictional issues

Where the ISP is based in the United Kingdom, an application is straightforward. However, many ISPs are based in the United States (eg, Facebook, Google) and while they may not oppose applications for Norwich Pharmacal relief, they do not submit to the jurisdiction of the UK courts.[135] We believe that in the case of foreign respondents, the appropriate course is for the applicant to serve a letter of request under an international treaty such as the Brussels Regulation, rather than applying for Norwich Pharmacal relief.

A Norwich Pharmacal order may be used to obtain information subsequently used in foreign proceedings, but cannot be used to obtain evidence where there is an alternative statutory regime for obtaining such evidence.[136]

4.4 'John Doe' injunctions

There is no prohibition in the United Kingdom against the granting of a 'John Doe' injunction, with no named defendant, so long as there is a defendant the identity of which is unknown. If the identity of a 'John Doe' defendant is subsequently exposed, the injunction will bite on the infringer.

Such injunctions have only recently been applied to IP rights, and will only be available where the defendants are clearly identifiable by description if not by name.[137]

135 *Lockton Companies International v Persons Unknown* [2009] EWHC 3423 (QB).
136 *Omar v Omar* [1995] 1 WLR 1429.
137 *Bloomsbury Publishing Ltd v News Group Newspapers Ltds* [2003] 3 All ER 736.

United States

David B Adler
Quinn Emanuel Urquhart & Sullivan LLP
James P Barabas
Budd Larner
Laura R Hall
Paul Keller
Allen & Overy
Reggie Schafer
Cohen & Gresser

1. Copyright, database rights and design rights

1.1 Overview

Copyright is a form of protection provided under US laws to internet content that consists of original works of authorship – the originality requirement does not mean that work must be novel, merely that it must have been created by the author rather than copied from another. In addition, the work must be 'fixed in a tangible medium'; as discussed below, electronic media, including the Internet, meet this requirement. Although copyright does not protect facts, ideas, systems or methods of operation, it may in certain instances protect the way these things are expressed.

US copyright laws are codified at Title 17 of the United States Code (USC). For works created in the United States after January 1 1978, copyright protection is automatic upon creation of the work and expires 70 years after the death of the author or, for work of corporate authorship or a work whose author is not known, the earlier of 95 years from publication or 120 years from creation (17 USC § 301). Registration is not a prerequisite to copyright protection, but is generally a prerequisite to bringing suit on the copyright. Determining when copyright protection expires for works created prior to 1978 requires consideration of the copyright law in effect at the dates of creation and publication of the work, including any requirements then in force that a copyright notice be affixed or that the work be registered. US copyright protection for works first published outside the United States is governed by international treaties.

(a) Literary works and artistic works

Literary and certain artistic works are protected under US copyright laws (17 USC § 102). In a landmark decision, *Apple Computer, Inc v Franklin Computer Corp*,[1] the Court of Appeals for the Third Circuit held that "a computer program, whether in object code or source code, is a 'literary work' and is protected from unauthorized copying, whether from its object or source code version".[2] The term 'computer program' is

1 714 F 2d 1240 (3d Cir 1983).
2 714 F 2d at 1249.

defined in 17 USC § 101 as "a set of statements or instructions to be used directly or indirectly in a computer in order to bring about a certain result".

(b) ***Films, sound recordings and broadcasts***

Films, sound recordings and broadcasts are protected under US copyright laws (17 USC § 102).

(c) ***Typographical arrangement of a published edition***

US laws do not specifically afford protection for 'the typographical agreement of a published edition', but do provide protection for compilations (discussed at section 1.1(g) below).

(d) ***Protection of the user interface***

If an audiovisual display is copyrighted separately as an audiovisual work and apart from the computer program that generates it, the display may be protectable regardless of the underlying program's copyright status.[3] Nonetheless, copyright protection does not extend to any idea, procedure, process, system, method of operation, concept, principle or discovery with respect to software or websites, regardless of the form in which it is described, explained, illustrated, or embodied (17 USC § 102). For this reason, in *Lotus Development Corp v Borland Int'l, Inc*,[4] the court found Lotus's menu command hierarchy was an unprotectable method of operation given that the Lotus menu command hierarchy provided the means for users to control and operate Lotus 1-2-3.

(e) ***Computer-generated works***

US copyright statutes are silent with respect to whether computer-generated works are protected works, and there appears to be very little case law on the topic. One court has noted in *dicta* that "copyright laws, of course, do not expressly require 'human' authorship".[5] Given the lack of guidance from courts, secondary literature remains divided on whether computer-generated works are protected.[6]

(f) ***Websites protected as databases***

Databases may be protected by copyright as compilations (discussed below).

(g) ***Compilations***

17 USC § 101 defines a 'compilation' as "a work formed by the collection and assembling of pre-existing materials or of data that are selected, coordinated, or arranged in such a way that the resulting work as a whole constitutes an original work of authorship". The US Supreme Court has rejected the 'sweat of the brow'

---

3 See *Computer Assocs Int'l, Inc v Altai, Inc*, 982 F.2d 693 (2d Cir 1992).

4 49 F.3d 807 (1st Cir 1995).

5 *Urantia Foundation v Maaherra*, 114 F.3d 955, 958 (9th Cir 1997) (finding that copyright protection applied to a dispute between parties who believed the copyrighted work was authored by 'celestial beings' but transcribed, compiled and collected by human authors).

6 See Melville B Nimmer and David Nimmer, *Nimmer on Copyright* (§ 5.01[A] (2011).

doctrine and has ruled on compilations as follows:

Factual compilations ... may possess the requisite originality. The compilation author typically chooses which facts to include, in what order to place them, and how to arrange the collected data so that they may be used effectively by readers. These choices as to selection and arrangement, so long as they are made independently by the compiler and entail a minimal degree of creativity, are sufficiently original that Congress may protect such compilations through the copyright laws.[7]

A copyright in a compilation extends only to the material contributed by the author of the compilation. Including pre-existing material created by others does not give the author of the compilation any exclusive right to the pre-existing material, which may be used by others in accordance with whatever copyright protection applies to that pre-existing material.

1.2 Infringing acts

(a) *Copying*

Temporary copies: Some courts have held that infringement can occur when a temporary copy is made in a computer's random access memory (RAM) ("The law also supports the conclusion that [defendant's] loading of copyrighted software into RAM creates a 'copy' of that software in violation of the Copyright Act.")[8] However, the inquiry is fact-specific, and other courts, relying on the Copyright Act's statement that, for a copy to be 'fixed', and therefore for copying to occur, the work must be held in some medium 'for a period more than a transitory duration', have found that brief copying incident to use of computer technology is not an infringement ("Given that the data reside in no buffer for more than 1.2 seconds before being automatically overwritten, ... we believe that the copyrighted works here are not 'embodied' ... for a period of more than transitory duration, and are therefore not 'fixed' ... .")[9] The Second Circuit noted that the parties in *MAI* appear not to have disputed that the Copyright Act's duration requirement was met under the factual circumstances of that case, in which the copyrighted software program, once initiated, remained in the computer's RAM until the computer was turned off.[10]

In any medium: An unauthorised reproduction of a copyrighted work in another medium still constitutes copyright infringement.[11]

(b) *Issuing copies to the public*

Distribution of copies of copyrighted works to the public constitutes copyright infringement.[12]

---

7 *Feist Publ'ns, Inc v Rural Tel Serv Co, Inc* (499 US 340, 348 (1991).
8 *MAI Sys Corp v Peak Computer, Inc*, 991 F 2d 511, 518 (9th Cir 1993).
9 *Cartoon Network LP, LLP v CSC Holdings, Inc*, 536 F 3d 121, 131 (2d Cir 2008).
10 *Ibid* at 128 to 131.
11 See *Rogers v Koons*, 960 F 2d 301 (2d Cir 1992).
12 See 17 USC § 106; 17 USC § 501(a).

(c) ***Communicating work to the public***

Display of copyrighted works to the public constitutes copyright infringement.[13]

(d) ***Performing, showing or playing work in public***

Public display and performance of copyrighted works constitutes copyright infringement.[14]

(e) ***Renting or lending the work to the public***

Distribution of copyrighted works by rental, lease or lending constitutes copyright infringement.[15]

(f) ***Authorising another person to do any of the above***

The United States recognises secondary infringement (discussed below).

(g) ***Secondary infringement***

One who distributes a device with the object of promoting its use to infringe copyright, as shown by clear expression or other affirmative steps taken to foster infringement, is liable for the resulting acts of infringement by third parties.[16]

1.3 Test for copyright infringement

(a) ***Requirement of substantial reproduction***

Substantial similarity is a required element of actionable copyright infringement. US courts have employed different tests to determine whether there is substantial similarity between works. A common test for determining substantial similarity is the 'ordinary observer' test, which relates to whether the average lay observer would overlook any dissimilarities between the works and would conclude that one was copied from the other.[17] However, other tests are applied by courts, including the 'total concept and feel' test.[18]

(b) ***Repeated copying of insubstantial part***

Although 'repeated copying of an insubstantial part' is not an established infringement test in the United States, courts have found infringement where a party copies segments of a work.[19]

---

13 See 17 USC § 106; 17 USC § 501(a).

14 See 17 USC § 106; 17 USC § 501(a).

15 See 17 USC § 106; 17 USC § 501(a).

16 See *Metro-Goldwyn-Mayer Studios Inc v Grokster, Ltd*, 545 US 913 (2005) (holding that the distributors of popular peer-to-peer 'file sharing' software could be secondarily liable for copyright infringement committed by their users if the companies took active steps to induce infringement).

17 See *Nihon Keizai Shimbun, Inc v Comline Bus Data, Inc*, 166 F 3d 65 (2d Cir 1999).

18 See *Boisson v Banian, Ltd*, 273 F 3d 262 (2d Cir 2001).

19 See *Iowa State University Research Foundation, Inc v American*, 463 F Supp 902 (SDNY 1978) (finding infringement for network's broadcast of "a seven or twelve second segment ... and a two-and-a-half minute segment [of a film]").

1.4 Exemptions/defences to copyright infringement

(a) Format shifting

Although the US Copyright Act does not have an explicit 'format-shifting' exception, courts have expressed approval of it as a type of fair use. For instance, in a case involving the Rio media player, the Court of Appeals for the Ninth Circuit stated that the "Rio merely makes copies in order to render portable, or 'space-shift,' those files that already reside on a user's hard drive ... . Such copying is paradigmatic non-commercial personal use entirely consistent with the purposes of the Act".[20]

(b) Personal copying rights

In 1992, Congress enacted the Audio Home Recording Act, which places a levy on those who "import into and distribute, or manufacture and distribute, any digital audio recording device or digital audio recording medium", and bars copyright holders from pursuing infringement actions against such manufacturers, importers or distributors or against a consumer who uses such a device to make digital or analogue musical recordings for non-commercial purposes.[21] The levy (or royalty) is 2% of the transfer price of recording devices and 3% of the transfer price of recording media.[22] Such royalties have much more limited application in the internet context, as the statute does not extend to electronic data copying.[23]

(c) Time shifting

Time shifting is a recognised exception to copyright infringement.[24]

(d) Fair use

The fair use of copyrighted work for purposes such as criticism, comment, news reporting, teaching, scholarship or research is permissible.[25] Factors to be considered to determine fair use include:

- the purpose and character of the use, including whether such use is of a commercial nature or is for non-profit educational purposes;
- the nature of the copyrighted work;

---

20 *Recording Industry Ass'n of Am v Diamond Multimedia Sys, Inc*, 180 F 3d 1072 (9th Cir 1999); see also Christopher T Wheatley, "Overreaching Technological Means for Protection of Copyright: Identifying the Limits of Copyright in Works in Digital Form in the United States and the United Kingdom", 7 *Wash U Global Studies L Rev* 353 (2008) ("Under the United Kingdom's copyright law, there is no format shifting exception to the exclusive rights of the copyright owner. In the United States, however, such activities constitute fair use").

21 17 USC §§ 1003(a), 1008.

22 17 USC § 1004.

23 See *Recording Industry Ass'n of Am v Diamond Multimedia Sys, Inc*, 180 F 3d 1072 (9th Cir 1999) (finding that a portable music player was not subject to the levy because "a hard drive is excluded from the definition of digital music recordings under AHRA [and the portable music player] d[id] not record 'directly' from 'digital music recordings,' and therefore could not be a digital audio recording device unless it makes copies 'from transmissions'").

24 See *Sony Corp of America v Universal City Studios, Inc*, 464 US 417 (1984) (finding time shifting of free broadcast programming by private individuals in their homes to be fair use).

25 See 17 USC § 107.

26 See *ibid.*

- the amount and substantiality of the portion used in relation to the copyrighted work as a whole; and
- the effect of the use upon the potential market for or value of the copyrighted work.[26]

The Court of Appeals for the Ninth Circuit recently ruled on fair use in the internet context in *Perfect 10, Inc v Amazon.com, Inc*,[27] which involved a lawsuit against Google and Amazon.com by an adult magazine whose images were widely available without authorisation. The plaintiff argued that the defendants' visual search engines made unauthorised thumbnail reproductions of infringing copies of their works that were displayed with search results. The court rejected the plaintiff's arguments and concluded, among other things, that "the significantly transformative nature of Google's search engine, particularly in light of its public benefit, outweighs Google's superseding and commercial uses of the thumbnails in this case".[28]

(e) Caching/temporary copies as part of communication process

Caching can be considered fair use. In *Field v Google, Inc*,[29] the court noted that caching websites is "socially important", and held that to the extent that Google itself copied or distributed the plaintiff's copyrighted works by allowing access to them through 'cached' links, Google engaged in fair use of those copyrighted works.

(f) Hosting

See discussion in sections 1.6(a) and 1.7 below.

(g) Back-up copies

The owner of a copy of a computer program may make another copy of that computer program if the new copy created is an essential step in the utilisation of the computer program in conjunction with a machine and is used in no other manner, or if the new copy is for archival purposes only.[30]

(h) Reverse engineering

A person who has lawfully obtained the right to use a copy of a computer program may reverse engineer to identify and analyse the program's elements.[31]

(i) Parody defence

Parody is a defence to copyright infringement. For purposes of determining whether parody of copyrighted work is 'fair use', the inquiry focuses on whether the work merely supersedes the object of original creation or whether and to what extent it is 'transformative' and alters the original work with new expression, meaning or message.[32]

---

27 508 F 3d 1146 (9th Cir 2007).
28 *Ibid* at 1166.
29 412 F Supp 2d 1106 (D Nev 2006).
30 See 17 USC § 117.
31 See 17 USC § 1201(f).
32 See *Campbell v Acuff-Rose Music, Inc*, 510 US 569 (1994).

(j) *Incidental inclusion*

Courts have dismissed claims of copyright infringement where the use of copyrighted material is incidental.[33]

1.5 Remedies available for copyright infringement

A wide range of remedies are available for copyright infringement, including temporary and permanent injunctive relief, impound and disposition of infringing articles, recovery of the copyright owner's actual losses and any additional profits of the infringer, and recovery of litigation costs and attorneys' fees.

1.6 Copyright liability

(a) *Hosting cloud computing where infringing content uploaded by user of service*

Service providers are not held liable for material stored on their website or system at the direction of users if they have no actual knowledge of infringement or awareness "of facts or circumstances from which the infringing activity is apparent", and, if they have the right or ability to control the infringing activity, do not receive a direct financial benefit from it, so long as they maintain designated agents to receive notifications of copyright infringement and act expeditiously to remove or disable access to infringing material upon receiving such notifications.[34]

(b) *Hypertext linking*

To third-party website: Service providers are not held liable for copyright infringement for "referring or linking users to an online location containing infringing material or infringing activity, by using information location tools, including a directory, index, reference, pointer, or hypertext link", if they have no actual knowledge of infringement or awareness "of facts or circumstances from which the infringing activity is apparent", and, if they have the right or ability to control the infringing activity, do not receive a direct financial benefit from it, so long as they maintain designated agents to receive notifications of copyright infringement and act expeditiously to remove or disable access to infringing references or links upon receiving such notifications.[35]

To an infringing work: Service providers are not held liable for copyright infringement for "referring or linking users to an online location containing infringing material or infringing activity, by using information location tools, including a directory, index, reference, pointer or hypertext link", if they have no actual knowledge of infringement or awareness "of facts or circumstances from

---

33 See *Italian Book v American Broad Cos*, 458 F Supp 65, 68 (SDNY 1978) ("The filming and recording of the song as part of the television news report was wholly fortuitous, entirely uncomplicated by any prior intent on ABC's part to film that particular song. The resulting news broadcast in no manner constituted a subterfuge or cover for private or commercial exploitation. Use of the song was incidental to the overall, informative purpose of the newscast").

34 See 17 USC § 512(c).

35 17 USC § 512(d).

which the infringing activity is apparent", and, if they have the right or ability to control the infringing activity, do not receive a direct financial benefit from it, so long as they maintain designated agents to receive notifications of copyright infringement and act expeditiously to remove or disable access to infringing references or links upon receiving such notifications.[36]

Copying of headlines: Although US courts do not appear to have ruled on the propriety of the copying of headlines for hyperlinks, generally speaking, titles are a special category of short writing that is excluded from copyright protection "as a matter of statutory construction" and regardless of creativity.[37]

(c) ***P2P network***

Supplier of P2P software: Suppliers of peer-to-peer software may be held liable under theories of vicarious or contributory infringement for the infringement of copyrights by users of their software if they distribute the software "with the object of promoting its use to infringe copyright, as shown by clear expression or other affirmative steps taken to foster infringement".[38]

Uploaders/downloaders: Users of peer-to peer networks may be held liable for copyright infringement because, when a user requests the download of a shared file from the network, a copy of the file is created on the requesting user's computer.[39]

(d) ***Webcasting***

Webcasting copyrighted material may constitute copyright infringement.[40]

(e) ***Streaming***

Streaming can constitute infringement by infringing on a copyright holder's exclusive right to public performance.[41]

(f) ***Framing***

US courts do not appear to have specifically addressed whether framing may constitute infringement, but secondary sources suggest that framing would not constitute infringement.[42]

---

36 17 USC § 512(d).

37 See 1 Melville B Nimmer and David Nimmer, *Nimmer on Copyright* § 2.16 (2011).

38 See *Metro-Goldwyn-Mayer Studios Inc v Grokster, Ltd*, 545 US 913, 919 (2005).

39 See *Metro-Goldwyn-Mayer Studios Inc v Grokster, Ltd*, 545 US 913, 921 (2005).

40 See *Live Nation Motor Sports, Inc v Davis*, No 3:06-CV-276-L, 2007 WL 79311 (ND Tex Jan 9 2007) ("[Defendant] has violated [plaintiff's] copyrights by providing a link of its webcasts without authorization, and not for a protected 'fair use' purpose under the Copyright Act").

41 See *US v American Soc'y of Composers, Authors, Publishers*, 627 F.3d 64 (2d Cir 2010) ("A stream is an electronic transmission that renders the musical work audible as it is received by the client-computer's temporary memory. This transmission, like a television or radio broadcast, is a performance because there is a playing of the song that is perceived simultaneously with the transmission")

42 See Ian C Ballon 1 "E-Commerce and Internet Law" 9.04[1] (2011) ("So long as a party configures its site so that there is no confusion or mistake about the origin of particular content, the mere existence of a frame should not expose a party to liability").

(g) ***Transmission of infringing work across a communications network***

Transmission across a communications network may constitute infringement.[43]

(h) ***Aggregator websites (eg, Google News, price comparison websites)***

Aggregator websites do not infringe if they limit information posted to non-protected facts. In one such case, a court held that the use by a defendant, an online ticket seller, of Ticketmaster's website for Ticketmaster information and data and the defendant's subsequent posting on its own website was fair use and not actionable.[44]

(i) ***Treatment of user-generated content***

The Digital Millennium Copyright Act provides for certain 'safe harbour' protections against direct and secondary infringement claims for internet service providers (ISPs) that have insufficient notice of infringing user-generated content.[45]

1.7 Joint liability for ISPs

Under the Online Copyright Infringement Liability Limitation Act, ISPs cannot be held liable for the activities of their users if they have no actual knowledge of infringement or awareness "of facts or circumstances from which the infringing activity is apparent", and, if they have the right or ability to control the infringing activity, do not receive a direct financial benefit from it, so long as they maintain designated agents to receive notifications of copyright infringement and act expeditiously to remove or disable access to infringing content upon receiving such notifications.[46] Under the same act, ISPs are not liable for copyright infringement for the creation of transitory copies of copyrighted works on their systems through the user-initiated automatic operation of their transmitting, routing or communication technologies.[47]

1.8 Relief

Injunctive relief can be granted against an ISP in the form of:

- an order restraining the ISP from providing access to infringing material or activity residing at a particular online site on the provider's system or network;
- an order restraining the service provider from providing access to a subscriber or account holder of the ISP's system or network; or
- such other injunctive relief as the court may consider necessary.[48]

---

43 See, for example, 37 CFR Part 201 (2000) ("The Copyright Office is amending its regulatory definition of a 'Service' for purposes of the statutory license governing the public performance of sound recordings by means of digital audio transmissions in order to clarify that transmissions of a broadcast signal over a digital communications network, such as the Internet, are not exempt from copyright liability under section 114(d)(1)(A) of the Copyright Act").

44 See *Ticketmaster Corp v Tickets.com, Inc*, No CV997654HLHVBKX, 2003 WL 21406289 (CD Cal 2003).

45 See 17 USC § 512.

46 See 17 USC § 512.

47 See 17 USC § 512(a).

48 See 17 USC § 512(f).

1.9 Issues specific to the United States

(a) *Jurisdiction*

Generally speaking, US copyright law does not extend to acts of infringement that take place entirely abroad.[49] Instead, for US copyright law to apply, "at least one alleged infringement must be completed entirely within the United States".[50]

(b) *Claim to infringement of foreign copyright*

Courts have heard claims for infringement of foreign copyright in certain instances. For instance, in one case, the court refused to dismiss the plaintiff's case even though it arose from infringement of the plaintiff's UK copyright and did not involve any US copyrights.[51] Nonetheless, courts will decline to hear such cases for various reasons, including under general principles of comity or on *forum non conveniens* grounds[52] – notably, the *London Film* case, in which the New York federal court retained jurisdiction concerning claims against a New York resident corporation that potentially was not subject to personal jurisdiction in the United Kingdom.

(c) *Emission theory*

Courts have found digital reproduction to occur at the time of both upload and download.[53]

1.10 Orphan works

US copyright laws do not provide for any special treatment with respect to orphan works.

1.11 Online piracy measures

In 2011, the US Senate and the US House of Representatives introduced two bills: the Preventing Real Online Threats to Economic Creativity and Theft of Intellectual Property Act and the Stop Online Piracy Act. Following intense internal protests, neither bill has been signed into law.

1.12 Electronic infringement of moral rights

(a) *Right to object to derogatory treatment*

Authors of 'visual art' – defined as a painting, drawing, print or sculpture that exists in a single copy or in a limited edition – have the right to prevent any intentional distortion, mutilation or other modification of that work that would be prejudicial

---

49 See *Subafilms, Ltd v MGM-Pathe Commc'ns Co*, 24 F.3d 1088 (9th Cir 1994).

50 *Allarcom Pay Television, Ltd v Gen Instrument Corp*, 69 F 3d 381, 387 (9th Cir 1995).

51 *London Film Prods Ltd v Intercontinental Commc'ns*, 580 F Supp 47 (SDNY 1984).

52 See *Murray v British Broad Corp*, 906 F Supp 858 (SDNY 1995) (dismissing the plaintiff's action on forum non conveniens grounds where the plaintiff's "claim for copyright infringement under English law require[d] application of English intellectual property law, which differ[ed] from American intellectual property law in several respects").

53 See *Playboy Enters, Inc v Sanfilippo*, No 97–0670–IEG. 1998 WL 207856 (SD Cal Mar 25 1998) (finding infringement for uploading copyrighted photographs); *Marobie-FL, Inc v Nat'l Ass'n of Fire Equip Distribs*, 983 F Supp 1167, 1172 (ND Ill 1997) (finding infringement for downloading of copyrighted materials).

to his honour or reputation.[54] However, databases, electronic information services and electronic publications are excluded from the definition of 'visual art'.[55]

(b) ***False attribution – right to guard against impersonation on the Internet***

An author of 'visual art' – defined as a painting, drawing, print or sculpture that exists in a single copy or in a limited edition – has the right to prevent the use of his name as the author of any work of visual art that he did not create. However, databases, electronic information services and electronic publications are excluded from the definition of 'visual art'.[57]

(c) ***Paternity right***

Authors of 'visual art' – defined as a painting, drawing, print or sculpture that exists in a single copy or in a limited edition – have the right to claim authorship to that work.[58] However, databases, electronic information services and electronic publications are excluded from the definition of 'visual art'.[59]

2. Trademarks

2.1 Use of a trademark

To prevail in a trademark infringement claim for a registered trademark, a plaintiff must establish that: it has a valid mark that is entitled to protection under the Lanham Act, and that the defendant used the mark in commerce; "in connection with the sale, distribution or advertising of goods or services", without the plaintiff's consent.[60] A mark is used in commerce if it is placed on goods, their containers, displays, labels, or documents associated with the goods and sold in commerce.[61] The term 'use' serves as a threshold requirement in evaluating this prong of the test. While any number of activities may be 'in commerce', no such activity is actionable under the Lanham Act absent the 'use' of a trademark.

A trademark dilution claim is available only to holders of 'famous' marks. To qualify as a famous mark, the trademark must be "widely recognized by the general consuming public of the United States as a designation of source of the goods or services of the mark's owner".[62] Dilution claims may be based on theories of 'blurring' or 'tarnishment'. The holder of a famous mark can bring a claim for dilution by blurring when the use of a trade name or trademark by another threatens to lessen the distinctiveness of the famous mark.[63] A dilution by tarnishment claim may be brought when the "association arising from the similarity between a mark or

54 USC § 106A(a).
55 17 USC § 101.
56 17 USC § 106A(a).
57 17 USC § 101.
58 USC § 106A(a).
59 17 USC § 101.
60 15 USC § 1114(1)(a).
61 15 USC § 1127.
62 15 USC § 1125(c)(2)(A).
63 15 USC § 1125(c)(2)(B).

trade name and a famous mark that harms the reputation of the famous mark".[64] The statutory remedy for either type of dilution is an injunction against the use of diluting trade name or mark, and the holder of the famous mark need not prove "actual or likely confusion, [] competition, or [] actual economic injury".[65]

Usage of trademarks on the Internet faces different scenarios, which arediscussed below.

2.2 Applicability of US trademark law

Although a common law or federally registered US trademark generally gives trademark holders rights only within US territory, mark holders have been held to have rights under US law even when the putative infringer of the mark is located outside of the United States. In determining whether US trademark law applies, courts consider whether the infringing use has "a significant effect on United States commerce" and whether asserting US jurisdiction would offend the trademark law and policy of the foreign state in which the use is occurring.[66] The court looks to whether the trademark in question is owned by either party in the jurisdiction where the use is occurring; and the citizenship of the user may be relevant – a foreign citizen with no ties to the United States may be deemed a less appropriate subject of US jurisdiction and, indeed, the court may be unable to obtain personal jurisdiction in that case.

The connection to US commerce is essential because use of the trademark in commerce is one of the elements of the trademark infringement cause of action.[67] A significant effect on US commerce is determined based on consideration of whether the user intends to reach a US audience, whether the user is targeting the market in which the trademark is used by its owner and whether there is customer confusion.[68]

2.3 Infringement and dilution

(a) Metatags

Using metatags is a way to direct traffic to a website that may infringe trademark rights. A metatag is HTML code not visible to the user that is read by web browsers and search engines and that describes the contents of a website or lists keywords relevant to the site. Several courts of appeal have held that using trademarks in a website's metatag is actionable under the initial interest confusion theory of liability, as customer confusion that creates initial interest in a competitor's product.[69] The court in *Brookfield* held that "[u]sing another's trademark in one's meta tag is much

---

64 15 USC § 1125(c)(2)(C).

65 15 USC § 1125(c)(1).

66 See *Basis Int'l Ltd v Research in Motion Ltd*, 827 F Supp 2d 1302, 1306-07 (DNM 2011) (finding jurisdiction over a Canadian company's proposed use of a US trademarked term in Singapore technology convention).

67 15 USC § 1114(1).

68 Basis Int'l, 827 F Supp 2d at 1306.

69 See *North American Med Corp v Axiom Worldwide, Inc*, 522 F.3d 1211 (11th Cir 2008); *Australian Gold, Inc v Hatfield*, 436 F.3d 1228 (10th Cir 2006); *Century 21 Real Estate Corp v Lendingtree, Inc*, 425 F.3d 211 (3d Cir 2005); *Promatek Indus, Ltd v Equitrac Corp*, 300 F.3d 808 (7th Cir 2002); *Brookfield Commc'n v West Coast Entm't Corp*, 174 F.3d 1036 (9th Cir 1999)).

like posting a sign with another's trademark in front of one's store".[70] The court in *Playboy Enters v Netscape Commc'ns Corp*,[71] added:

> *Although dispelled before an actual sale occurs, initial interest confusion impermissibly capitalizes on the goodwill associated with a mark and is therefore actionable trademark infringement. [...] Even if [Internet users] realize immediately upon accessing the competitor's site that they have reached a site wholly unrelated to [the plaintiff's], the damage has been done: through initial consumer confusion, the competitor will still have gained a customer by appropriating the goodwill that [the plaintiff] has developed in its mark.*

However, the Second Circuit exercised caution in examining initial interest confusion in the internet context in *Savin Corp v Savin Group*.[72] The court stated that internet initial confusion is quite different from the usual initial interest confusion: "because consumers diverted on the Internet can more readily get back on track than those in actual space, thus minimizing the harm to the owner of the searched-for site from consumers becoming trapped in a competing site, Internet initial interest confusion requires a showing of intentional deception." Not only may this higher standard protect defendants in internet cases, but nominative fair use may also serve as a defence, depending on the facts of the case.

(b) Keywords

The main issues of trademark law regarding the Internet are connected with keyword advertising, which is a vital method to reach users and has caused a fair amount of litigation, brought by trademark holders, seeking to deter competitors from bidding on their trademarks, deceiving consumers and taking them away from their own sites in violation of the Lanham Act. Google's AdWords service, for example, allows a business to nominate certain words to trigger the display of a link to that website when a user conducts a search using those words. A sponsored link is displayed separately from the results, and typically consists of a hyperlink to the advertiser's website and a short description. The advertiser pays Google for each 'click' to its website from the sponsored link. Keywords are not sold on an exclusive basis; this is why advertisers can use the same keyword, and thus a variety of sponsored links may stand to be triggered by a given search. In order to rank the links, priority is given to those links with the highest per-click price. The higher the per click price the advertiser is willing to pay, the more likely it is that its sponsored link will appear.

The US courts have consistently held that the purchase of a trademark as a keyword is a 'use in commerce' under the Lanham Act.[73] Courts have yet to fully address the question of whether 'use in commerce' actually leads to trademark infringement. In more than a decade since the first keyword advertisement decision there have only been a few cases that can actually shed light on the issue of whether

---

70 174 F.3d at 1062.

71 354 F.3d 1020, 1025 (9th Cir 2000).

72 391 F.3d 439 (2d Cir 2004).

73 See *Network Automation, Inc v Advanced Sys Concepts*, 638 F 3d 1137 (9th Cir 2011); *Fair Isaac Corp v Experian Info Solutions Inc*, 645 F Supp 2d 734 (D Minn 2009); *Buying for the Home, LLC v Humble Abode, LLC*, 459 F Supp 2d 310 (DNJ 2006).

keyword advertising is a violation of the Lanham Act. In view of this situation, some plaintiffs try to prove trademark infringement not only by relying on the likelihood of confusion theory but also by relying on the concept of initial interest confusion to argue that search engines violate their trademark rights.[74]

Whether keyword advertising is a violation of the Lanham Act is still unsettled, a decade after the first key word advertising case.[75]

The court in *Hearts on Fire Co v Blue Nile, Inc*[76] established a bright-line test under which the 'indexing function' of generating keyword ads was deemed essentially no different from permitted natural search results and found no liability. However, the US District Court for the Central District of California in *Binder v Disability Group Inc*[77] ruled that a law firm's use of a competitor's trademark in keyword advertising constituted trademark infringement based on a finding of likelihood of confusion.

In *Network Automation Inc, v Advanced Sys Concepts Inc,*[78] the Court of Appeals for the Ninth Circuit held that a software company's purchase of a competitor's trademark as a search engine keyword did not cause likely consumer confusion and thus did not likely cause trademark infringement. The court held that "it would be wrong to expand the initial interest confusion theory of infringement beyond the realm of the misleading and deceptive to the context of legitimate comparative and contextual advertising".[79] The court further emphasised that the trademark owner "must demonstrate likely confusion, not mere diversion" in order to prove an infringement claim. Finally, the court held that the most relevant factors in a keyword advertising case are:

- the strength of the mark;
- the evidence of actual confusion; the type of goods and degree of care likely to be exercised by the purchaser; and
- the labelling and appearance of the advertisement and the surrounding context in the screen displaying the results page.

Despite the unsettled question surrounding whether keyword advertising is in accordance with the Lanham Act, ISPs such as Google and Yahoo! are willing to perform a limited investigation and respect reasonable requests to remove trademark terms from the bidding process, and thus are willing to provide a trademark owner with a minimum of protection.

(c) ***Sponsored links***

Sponsored links, also known as pay-per-click ads, are links to websites that pay for placement next to a search engine's search results. They are usually clearly labelled as sponsored links and are targeted to the topic and location of a search. These listings are generally purchased by companies to have their business or websites

---

74 See *Hearts on Fire Co, LLC v Blue Nile, Inc,* 603 F Supp 2d 274 (D Mass 2009).
75 *Playboy Ent, Inc v Netscape Commc'ns Corp,* 55 F Supp 2d 1070 (CD Cal 1999).
76 603 F Supp 2d 274 (D Mass 2009).
77 97 USPQ 2d 1629 (2011).
78 638 F 3d 1137 (9th Cir 2011).
79 *Ibid* at 1148.

appear for a specific search term related to their services. As the usage of sponsored links is simply another form of keyword advertising, the aforementioned rules apply.

(d) Hidden text

The usage of trademarked terms in hidden text or in page text for purposes of gaining a higher ranking from search engines can constitute trademark infringement or unfair competition. The rules for keyword advertising and especially the rules regarding initial interest confusion apply accordingly.

(e) Internet domain names

Beginning in the mid-1990s, entrepreneurs registered thousands of domain names containing the trademarks of famous companies in the hopes of selling them back for a higher price. Since then, courts have found that a defendant's registration of a domain name containing a federal trademark constituted infringement or dilution.[80] This is especially so when cybersquatters incorporate a trademark owner's mark. In 1998 the Ninth Circuit became the first federal appellate court to treat cybersquatting as 'commercial use' in the *Panavision Int'l, LP v Toeppen* decision.[81] Since then, numerous decisions have followed that holding.

More recent issues, such as the trend of individuals to reserve or 'jack' usernames of famous companies with trademark protection on social networking sites such as Facebook and Twitter, have caused new problems and may give rise to trademark infringement and dilution claims.[82]

(f) Search navigation tools

A 'breadcrumb trail' is a navigational tool used to display the path to the current website. One can distinguish different types of breadcrumb trail. The path breadcrumb trail, for example, shows the actual route taken by a user to reach the current page. The location breadcrumb trail displays the route from the home page of the user to the current page, no matter how the user got there. At the time of writing, trademark infringement has not been addressed within this context in the United States.

(g) Hypertext links

Usage of a third party's trademark as a link to a different website presents the potential for trademark disputes, as this practice can be infringing when the usage is without the consent of the trademark owner and the linking site is offensive to the mark owner. In *Ticketmaster Corp v Microsoft Corp*, filed in the Central District of California on April 28 1997, a website linked directly to Ticketmaster pages, bypassing the home page. Ticketmaster alleged that this form of linking constituted trademark dilution and unfair competition. Although the case was settled and thus

---

80 See, for example, *Nissan Motors v Nissan Computers Corp*, 378 F.3d 1002 (9th Cir 2004).

81 141 F 3d 1316 (9th Cir 1998).

82 See Dan Malachowski, "Comment: 'Username Jacking' in Social Media: Should Celebrities and Brand Owners Recover from Social Networking Sites when their Social Media Usernames are Stolen?", 60 *DePaul L Rev* 223 (2010).

cannot function as a precedent, it made internet users aware that linking can cause trademark infringement. Thus, many websites include in their sites appropriate disclaimers and disavowals, for example, by explaining the ownership of trademarks used on a website and disavowing any affiliation or endorsement by the trademark owners or by operators of a linked site. Such disclaimers can play a significant role in trademark infringement disputes. In *The Playboy Enters, Inc v Welles*,[83] the court stated that the use of disclaimers "indicates good faith in the use of the trademarks and weights in favor of defendant".

(h) Framing

Framing is another way a trademark can be infringed on the Internet. Framing occurs when one internet site displaces another site's content by surrounding or framing it with a portion of its own site. The question of trademark infringement due to framing has not been resolved, because the major disputes arising from framing have been settled out of court. For example in *Washington Post v Total News*, filed in the Southern District of New York on February 20 1997, a group of online news organisations sued Total News, in part, on grounds of trademark infringement based on the defendant's use of framing. Specifically, content was imported from plaintiffs' sites within the frame of the defendant's website. The plaintiffs alleged that the defendant consequently unfairly attracted advertisers and users, and thus claimed that the actions constituted misappropriation, trademark dilution, trademark infringement, false designation of origin and unfair competition. The plaintiffs argued that the defendant took the entire commercial value of the material located on the plaintiffs' websites and sold it to others for the defendant's own profit. They also argued that the defendant's unauthorised use of their trademarks in connection with unauthorised advertisements was likely to cause confusion and to deceive consumers as to the source of origin of the advertisements.

The case settled with the defendant, Total News, agreeing not to frame without the permission of the plaintiff news organisations, and thus does not serve as a judicial precedent.

2.4 Defences

(a) Descriptive (non trademark) use of the mark

The right to control use of a trademark is not absolute. The Lanham Act provides fair use limitations to the protection granted to trademarks. The fair use defence is crucial in scenarios in which a third party uses the owner's trademark in domain names, websites and HTML meta tags. This is true not only in classic fair use cases, in which the defendant has used the plaintiff's mark to describe the defendant's own product (eg, see *Playboy Enterprises Inc v Welles*),[84] but also in nominative fair use cases, in which the defendant uses the plaintiff's trademark to describe the plaintiff's product, even if the defendant's ultimate goal is to describe its own product (eg, see *Mattel Inc*

83 7 F Supp 2d 1098, 1104 (SD Cal 1998).
84 279 F 3d 796 (9th Cir 2002).

v Walking Mountain Prod);[85] in either case, the fair use doctrine is applicable. In both cases the defence requires that the infringing term is used not as a trademark, but fairly and in good faith to describe the goods and services; and the defendant especially does not have the burden of showing unlikely confusion in order successfully to rely on the fair use defence.[86]

Nominative users – third parties that make use of a foreign trademark solely to describe not their own product, but the products of the trademark owner – may rely on the fair use doctrine. A former Playboy playmate was thus allowed to use the terms 'Playboy' and 'playmate' to describe herself as such on her personal website. The court in *Playboy Enterprises Inc v Welles* held that such use of the marks both on the website and in the website's metatags was purely nominative and therefore fair use. The court reasoned that the metatags are not visible to the web surfer.

(b) *Comparative advertising*

Comparative advertising is subject to regulation through a combination of federal, state and local laws, as well as self-regulatory codes of conduct. These include the Federal Trade Commission Act (FTC) and Section 43(a) of the Lanham Act (15 USC § 1125(a)). The FTC, an independent agency of the US government, has taken the position that industry self-regulation should not limit the use of comparative advertising, including brand comparisons, where the comparisons are clearly identified, truthful and non-deceptive, and can provide consumers with useful and important information to help them make rational purchasing decisions. Moreover, under the Lanham Act the use of visual comparative advertising is valid so long as it does not contain misrepresentations or contain missing information intended to mislead the consumer. In addition, the use of another's trademark cannot suggest endorsement or some sort of affiliation with the competitor. Careful use is necessary because any inaccuracies will be exposed by the competitor in a claim that use of its trademark is an attempt to cause confusion, and thus could result in allegations of false advertising and trademark infringement.

(c) *Parody*

Another valuable defence is the First Amendment to the US Constitution, which protects criticism and parody. There is abundant case law, beginning prior to the popularity of the Internet, that such parodies are protected under the First Amendment to the US Constitution. In *Bally Total Fitness v Faber*,[87] the court transferred this defence into the context of domain name registration. The plaintiff, which owned the federally registered marks 'Bally' and 'Bally Total Fitness', sued the defendant, who operated a 'Bally Sucks' website dedicated to complaints and commentaries about Bally's health-club business practices. The plaintiff claimed infringement of its trademarks. Although the court held that the defendant did not 'use' the trademarks in commerce, it nevertheless addressed the issue of likelihood of

85 353 F 3d 792 (9th Cir 2002).

86 See *KP Permanent Make-up, Inc v Lasting Impression I, Inc*, 543 US 111 (2004).

87 29 F Supp 2d 1161 (CD Cal 1998).

confusion and dilution. In its reasoning the court emphasised that the defendant merely used his 'Bally Sucks' web page to demonstrate and market his website design skills, which was akin to an online resumé, not use in commerce. Furthermore, the court stressed the First Amendment implications and held that the plaintiff could not stifle the defendant's right to free expression. If the plaintiff wished to respond to the defendant's contentions, it could likewise use the Internet to do so. Other decisions show a similar line of reasoning (eg, *Ford Motor Co v 2600 Enters*,[88] in which the court held that the gripe domain 'fuckgeneralmotors.com', which automatically transferred visitors to 'ford.com', did not harm Ford Motor's commercial success).

2.5 Parallel imports

Under the exhaustion doctrine, the first unrestricted sale of a trademarked item exhausts the trademark owner's control over that particular item. There are two prevailing theories regarding exhaustion – namely, that once goods bearing a trademark have been placed into commerce by, or with the consent of, the trademark owner either:

- the owner cannot use its trademark rights to prevent the further distribution of such goods anywhere – the so-called 'international exhaustion' rule; or
- it cannot use its trademark rights to prevent further distribution of such goods in the same country, but may prevent such distribution in other countries, the so-called 'national exhaustion' rule. The US laws have long considered that the nature of trademark rights, at least with respect to parallel imports, is universal and thus in the United States the international exhaustion doctrine is followed.

If a trademarked item is offered for sale in the United States via a website without the consent of the trademark owner, the trademark owner has three different ways to prevent parallel imports: the Tariff Act § 526; the Lanham Act § 42; and the Lanham Act § 32(a) for registered marks and § 43(b) for unregistered marks. The Tariff Act § 526(a) prohibits absolutely the importation of a product of foreign manufacture "that bears a trademark owned by a citizen of ... the United States and is registered in the US Patent and Trademark Office". Section 526(a) is the only means by which a US company can use its US trademark to prevent importation of truly genuine goods manufactured abroad. It requires no proof of a likelihood of confusion, but is exclusively available for domestic US trademark owners that have no corporate affiliation with the foreign manufacturer (ie, they must not be owned by the same parent corporation or be in a parent-subsidiary relationship). A purely economic relationship, such as a trademark licence, does not amount to affiliation and renders the goods subject to the Tariff Act. Section 32(a) of the Lanham Act provides the general remedy for trademark infringement and proscribes the use in commerce of any reproduction, counterfeit, copy or colourable imitation of a registered trademark which is likely to cause confusion. Section 42 bars the importation of goods bearing a mark which shall 'copy or simulate' a registered

88 177 F Supp 2d 661, 664 (ED Mich 2001).

trademark, enabling the registered owner of a trademark to have counterfeit products seized by Customs at the border. However, the plain language of Section 42 does not bar importation if the goods are genuine, but bars such importation only if they copy or simulate a trademark. From a trademark infringement perspective, the question arises that if grey market goods are in fact genuine, how does their sale in the United States deceive consumers as to source? The leading case is *A Bourjois & Compel v Katzel*,[89] in which the Supreme Court held that the importation of the competing grey market goods infringed Bourjois' trademark rights because the US public understood that the trademark in the United States signified that the goods came from the plaintiff, not the French defendant. Therefore, the importation and sale of genuine goods from the French company entitled to use that trademark in France would be likely to cause confusion as to source because consumers familiar with the US trademark holder would believe that it, and not the French company, was the source of the product. The defendant's use of the trademark misrepresented the origin of the goods in the United States and therefore constituted trademark infringement.

2.6 Remedies

There are several remedies available to the owner of a trademark in the event of infringement. Remedies are provided under the Lanham Act (15 USC §§ 1116 to 1121) and the Trademark Counterfeiting Act of 1984 (18 USC § 2320). However, relief may also be obtained under the common law of certain states. These remedies include monetary relief, equitable relief, seizures and costs and attorneys' fees. The Lanham Act provides for the recovery of monetary relief: actual damages; lost profits resulting from the infringement; accounting for infringer's profits; and treble damages for wilful infringement. Actual losses incurred, including any profits lost as a result of the infringement, are commonly awarded. Damages may be increased threefold in cases of wilful infringement. Additionally, in cases of wilful infringement, the infringer's profits may be recovered. Punitive damages are generally not awarded in federal trademark infringement cases, but may sometimes be available under state unfair competition laws. As equitable relief, the trademark owner can seek a preliminary or permanent injunction. A preliminary injunction is an order of a court made in the early stages of a lawsuit which prohibits the parties from doing an act which is in dispute (eg, using the trademark). A permanent injunction is a final order of a court that a person or entity discontinue doing certain activities permanently or take certain actions. Preliminary injunctive relief is granted if the trademark owner can demonstrate a probability of winning the case and if it can show a permanent injury sustained in the absence of injunctive relief. The courts will also take into account the hardships that an injunction imposes on the parties and any public interest involved. It is within the court's discretion whether to grant permanent injunctive relief, although it is often awarded to the prevailing trademark owner. The court may also issue an order allowing the trademark owner's seizure of the counterfeit goods and the infringer's business records. Finally, a trademark owner

89 260 US 689 (1923).

may recover its costs and, in extraordinary cases of wilful infringement, reasonable attorneys' fees.

2.7 Liability of ISPs

The question whether ISPs have the ability to control illegitimate trademark usage through their services, and may therefore be held liable for trademark infringements on their web pages, is rather new. Since ISPs do not themselves perform the infringing activity, the basis for liability would be contributory infringement. Unlike the statutory provisions in copyright law on secondary liability, the theory of secondary liability in the trademark context evolved through case law over the last century.[90] Because courts have just recently found that companies may be directly liable for utilising competitors' trademarks in internet advertising campaigns, the possibility arises that a court could find an ISP contributorily or vicariously liable for enabling those uses. *Rosetta Stone v Google Inc*,[91] is one of the first cases decided on the merits after the Second Circuit's landmark decision in *Rescuecom Corp v Google Inc*,[92] which held that ISPs such as Google or Yahoo! 'use' trademarks in commerce in conjunction with their advertising services. In *Rosetta Stone* the district court granted summary judgment for Google after determining that Google's online advertising programme AdWords did not violate the Lanham Act. In its complaint, Rosetta Stone alleged that Google should be liable for vicarious or contributory trademark infringement for the sale and display of sponsored links containing trademark terms, which third parties purchased and formulated. The court disagreed and held that the sponsored links containing the plaintiff's marks were unlikely to cause consumer confusion, and emphasised that Google did not actively attempt to influence or encourage third parties to bid on trademarked terms in keyword auctions.

2.8 Advertising law and regulation

The Lanham Act's prohibition against false advertising is found in 15 USC § 1125(a)(1). This section specifically prohibits a person from using a false or misleading description of fact, or false or misleading representation of fact, in commercial advertising or promotion, which misrepresents the nature, characteristics, qualities or geographic origin of its or another person's goods, services or commercial activities. To establish a cause of action for false advertising under The Lanham Act, the plaintiff must show that the challenged statement is literally false or, even though the statement is not literally false, that it is likely to deceive or confuse customers. In addition to this first showing, the plaintiff must also show that the defendant's false or misleading representation was material in the sense that it would have some effect on the consumers who are making the purchasing decision. This requirement helps to prevent frivolous claims by ensuring that the plaintiff's cause of action for federal false advertising is properly based on a likelihood of being damaged by the defendant's representations.

---

90 See *Inwood Labs, Inc v Ives Labs, Inc*, 456 US 844 (1982).
91 730 F Supp 2d 531, 534–35 (ED Va 2010).
92 562 F 3d 123 (2d Cir 2009).

Additionally, to ensure that products and services are described truthfully in online ads and that consumers get what they pay for, the Digital Advertising Alliance (DAA) published a Self-Regulatory Programme for Online Behavioural Advertising in 2009. It gives consumers a better understanding of and greater control over ads that are customised based on their online behaviour (also called 'interest-based' advertising). The FTC published Dot Com Disclosure guidelines in 2000 and has addressed the unique issues that arise from the fast-paced, interactive advertising environment on the Internet. Continuing to work alongside the FTC, in 2011 the DAA expanded the scope of the self-regulatory programme beyond OBA with the Self-Regulatory Principles for Multi-Site Data, which established a clear framework governing the collection of online data from a particular computer or device regarding web viewing over time and across non-affiliated websites; and has launched the 'Your AdChoices' public education advertising campaign designed to inform consumers about interest-based advertising and how they could take greater control of their online privacy through the 'AdChoices' icon. In addition to pre-existing laws, the US Congress has enacted several new laws that govern internet advertising and privacy. The most important of these is HR 29, more commonly known as the Securely Protect Yourself Against Cyber Trespass Act, which came into effect on March 5 2005. The Act prohibits specific types of internet advertisements and methods for manipulating users' computers, including advertisements that cannot be closed without undue effort or knowledge by the user or that can be closed only by turning off the computer or closing all sessions of the internet browser for the computer.

The FTC has enforced and will continue to enforce its consumer protection laws, and thus its guidance should be followed closely by businesses and consumers advertising on the web. The FTC itself can enforce its guidelines (and its more generalised rules governing all advertising) through its regulatory power, obtaining far-reaching discovery and imposing a consent decree. And private litigants may use the guidelines to gain an advantage. For example, several state unfair competition laws prohibit 'unfair', 'fraudulent' or 'false' advertising. The FTC's guidelines can be crucial in determining whether an ad violates these standards.

2.9 Domain name disputes

Congress enacted the Anti-cybersquatting Consumer Protection Act of 1999 to prohibit bad-faith and abusive registration of distinctive marks as internet domain names. A trademark holder may bring an *in personam* action against the party that registered the domain (subject to obtaining personal jurisdiction over that person or company) or may bring an *in rem* action in the jurisdiction of the registrar which registered the domain name at issue. The act enables an owner of US trademarks to file suit against a 'cybersquatter' that:

- has a bad-faith intent to profit from the mark; and
- registers, traffics in or uses a domain name that is:
  - identical or confusingly similar to a distinctive mark;
  - identical or confusingly similar to or dilutive of a famous mark; or
  - a trademark protected by 18 USC § 706 (marks involving the Red Cross) or 36 USC § 220506 (marks relating to the Olympics).

Nevertheless, some cases have held that merely reserving a domain name with another's trademark does not infringe the mark as long as the domain name is not used in commerce and thus does not rise to the level of civil liability.[93]

The year 1999 also marked the release of the World Intellectual Property (WIPO) Internet Domain Name Process, which it titled the Uniform Dispute Resolution Procedure (UDRP). Congress further has amended the Lanham Act to deter the practice of bad-faith selling of domain names.[94] Finally, the Internet Corporation for Assigned Names and Numbers Uniform Domain Name Dispute Resolution Policy enables trademark owners to obtain through arbitration domain names that third parties are utilising that infringe upon their marks.

2.10 Unfair competition/passing off

A website's content can also be protected by unfair competition law. A federal cause of action for unfair competition derives from 15 USC § 1125(a), commonly known as Section 43(a) of the Lanham Act. Different categories of federal unfair competition exist under the Lanham Act, including passing off and false advertising. The Lanham Act's prohibition against passing off specifically prohibits a person from using a "false or misleading description of fact, or false or misleading representation of fact" in commerce, which "is likely to cause confusion, or to cause mistake, or to deceive as to the affiliation, connection, or association of such person with another person, or as to the origin, sponsorship, or approval of his or her goods, services, or commercial activities by another person". This provision provides a cause of action for unfair competition even though the plaintiff's goods are not the subject of federal registrations. The requirements for a passing off claim for federal unfair competition are an association of origin by the consumer between the mark and the first user, and a likelihood of consumer confusion when the mark is applied to the second user's good. Apart from the federal law, there are also individual unfair competition law regulations on the state level.

3. Patents

3.1 Patentability of 'internet' inventions

In the United States, as a general matter, internet-related inventions are patentable. The general rule governing the patentability of inventions, 35 USC § 101, provides in relevant part as follows:

> *Whoever invents or discovers any new and useful process, machine, manufacture, or composition of matter, or any new and useful improvement thereof, may obtain a patent therefore, subject to the conditions and requirements of this title.*

In addition to having utility, patentable inventions must also be novel, non-obvious and fully and particularly described.[95] In contrast, laws of nature, natural phenomena and abstract ideas are not patentable.[96] As the Federal Circuit recently

---

93 See *HQM, Ltd v Hatfield*, 71 F Supp 2d 500 (D Md 1999).
94 See, for example, *Sporty's Farm LLC v Sportsman's Market, Inc*, 202 F 3d 489, 495 (2d Cir 2000).
95 35 USC §§ 101, 102, 103, and 112.
96 See *Diamond v Chakrabarty*, 447 US 303, 309 (1980).

explained, "[i]t therefore generally follows that any invention within the broad statutory categories of § 101 that is made by man, not directed to a law of nature or physical phenomenon, and not so manifestly abstract as to pre-empt a fundamental concept or idea is patent eligible".[97]

(a) *Computer programs*

Computer programs may be patentable. As the Supreme Court explained in its *Bilski* decision, while it was once argued that well-established principles of patent law probably would have prevented the issuance of a valid patent on any conceivable computer program, "this fact does not mean that unforeseen innovations such as computer programs are always unpatentable".[98] In *Diamond v Diehr*, the Supreme Court held that a procedure for moulding rubber that included a computer program was within the realm of patentable subject matter.[99]

(b) *Business methods*

Business methods may be patentable, as long as they satisfy the various conditions for patentability set forth above, including utility, novelty and non-obviousness. The Supreme Court's *Bilski* decision provides a framework for determining when a business method is and is not patent eligible. In its decision, the Supreme Court ruled that the Federal Circuit's 'machine or transformation' test is not the sole test to be used for determining the patentability of a 'process' under the Patent Act, 35 USC § 101. Pursuant to this test, formulated by the Court of Appeals for the Federal Circuit, an invention is a process only if "it is tied to a particular machine or apparatus", or "it transforms a particular article into a different state or thing".[100] Instead, the machine-or-transformation test is "a useful or important clue, an investigative tool, for determining whether some claimed inventions are processes under § 101".[101]

In explaining that Section 101 precludes the broad contention that the term 'process' excludes business methods, the Supreme Court found support in other US patent law statutes. In particular, "[t]he argument that business methods are categorically outside of § 101's scope is further undermined by the fact that federal law explicitly contemplates the existence of at least some business method patents".[102]

The Federal Circuit continues to struggle with explaining the exact contours of when business method claims are patent eligible under Section 101, as evidenced by the recent decision in *CLS Bank International v Alice Corp Pty Ltd*,[103] involving patents relating to the use of an escrow system to minimise risk in settling financial transactions. In *CLS Bank*, a one-page *per curium* decision followed by six conflicting opinions, the Federal Circuit ruled that a computerised platform for reducing risk in financial transactions was an abstract concept that was ineligible for financial

97 *Dealertrack, Inc v Huber*, 674 F 3d 1315 (Fed Cir Jan 20 2012).
98 *Bilski v Kappos*, 130 SCt 3218, 3227 (2010).
99 450 US 175 (1981).
100 *Bilski*, 130 SCt at 3225 (citations omitted).
101 *Ibid* at 3227.
102 *Ibid* at 3228.
103 717 F 3d 1269 (Fed Cir 2013) (*en banc*).

protection. At the time of writing, the US Supreme Court has granted CLS Bank's petition for writ of *certiorari* to review the Federal Circuit's decision.

(c) *Mathematical methods*

Mathematical methods, in and of themselves, are not patentable. Even if a mathematical formula's reach is limited to a particular technological use, it is not patentable.[104]

(d) *Presentation of information*

While information in and of itself is not patentable, information technology-related patents are very common in the United States, and such patents may be granted as long as they meet the above-listed requirements for patentability. Such patents must be useful, novel, non-obvious and fully and particularly described.[105]

3.2 Bioinformatics

Bioinformatics-related inventions are patentable in the United States, as long as they meet the statutory requirements for patentability. Such patents must be useful, novel, non-obvious and fully and particularly described.[106]

In *Association for Molecular Pathology v Myriad Genetics*,[107] the Supreme Court held that a naturally occurring DNA segment is a product of nature and not patent eligible merely because it has been isolated, but that cDNA is patent eligible because it is not naturally occurring.

Similarly, protein structures are also patentable, whether they are discovered through the use of bioinformatics or some other technique. The requirements for patentability of protein structures which are amino acid sequences are similar to the requirements for patentability of nucleic acids which are nucleotide sequences. The USPTO has special requirements in its Manual of Patent Examination Procedure for patenting both types of sequences, including the requirements set forth in § 1.821, "Nucleotide and/or amino acid sequence disclosures in patent applications".

3.3 Issues specific to the United States

(a) *Infringement on the Internet*

In the United States, two types of jurisdiction must be established in a patent case – subject-matter jurisdiction and personal jurisdiction.

Subject-matter jurisdiction in patent cases is straightforward – federal courts, not state courts, have jurisdiction over all cases in which infringement of a patent is asserted.

Establishing personal jurisdiction is more complicated. The Federal Circuit's decision in *Trintec Industries* describes the two types of personal jurisdiction, and the

104 See *Diamond v Diehr*, 450 US 175, 192 n 14 ("A mathematical formula does not suddenly become patentable subject matter simply by having the applicant acquiesce to limiting the reach of the patent for the formula to a particular technological use").

105 35 USC §§ 101, 102, 103, and 112.

106 35 USC §§ 101, 102, 103, and 112.

107 133 SCt 2107, 2111 (2013).

requirements for establishing personal jurisdiction, in this case under the District of Columbia's statutes, as follows:

> *There are two types of personal jurisdiction – specific and general. 'Specific jurisdiction "arises out of" or "relates to" the cause of action even if those contacts are "isolated and sporadic." ... General jurisdiction arises when a defendant maintains "continuous and systematic" contacts with the forum state even when the cause of action has no relation to those contacts.' (citations omitted). The District of Columbia permits courts to exercise general jurisdiction over a foreign corporation for claims that do not arise from the corporation's conduct within the District, if the corporation is 'doing business' in the District and its business contacts are 'continuous and systematic'* (citations omitted). *The reach of general jurisdiction in the District of Columbia ... is 'coextensive with the reach of constitutional due process'.* (citations omitted).[108]

The District of Columbia's personal jurisdiction statute is representative of those of many US states and provides in relevant part as follows:

> *(a) A District of Columbia court may exercise personal jurisdiction over a person, who acts directly or by an agent, as to a claim for relief arising from the person's –*
> *(1) transacting any business in the District of Columbia;*
> ...
> *(3) causing tortious injury in the District of Columbia by an act or omission in the District of Columbia;*
> *(4) causing tortious injury in the District of Columbia by an act or omission outside the District of Columbia if he regularly does or solicits business, engages in any other persistent course of conduct, or derives substantial revenue from goods used or consumed, or services rendered, in the District of Columbia.*[109]

Courts have held that merely operating a website is insufficient to establish personal jurisdiction.[110]

In particular, courts have distinguished between active websites, allowing for order placement, and passive websites, which merely provide information.[111] In *ESAB Group, Inc v Centricut LLC*,[112] a court declined to find personal jurisdiction where it found that the patent infringement defendant conducted no commercial activity in South Carolina and thus was not subject to general personal jurisdiction in South Carolina based on the maintenance of a web page viewable in the state.

In contrast, an Illinois court held that an interactive website directed at the United States established minimum contacts with Illinois, where it noted that the operation of the website itself allegedly constituted patent infringement.[113]

---

108 *Trintec Indus v Pedre Promotional Products, Inc*, 395 F.3d 1275, 1279 (Fed Cir 2005).

109 *Trintec*, 395 F 3d at 1280.

110 See *Pebble Beach Co v Caddy*, 453 F 3d 1151, 1156 (9th Cir 2006) (holding that defendant's use of 'Pebble Beach' in passive website advertising his services and in the website's domain name were not acts aimed at the state of California, and thus were insufficient to subject him to personal jurisdiction there, and that defendant's acts were insufficient to subject him to personal jurisdiction under the federal long arm rule).

111 See *Agar Corp, Inc v Multi-Fluid Inc*, 45 USPQ 2d 1444 (SD Tex 1997) (dismissing lawsuit for lack of personal jurisdiction, where website was mostly passive and not directed specifically to Texas residents).

112 49 USPQ 2d 1822 (DSC 1999).

113 See *CoolSavings.Com Inc v IQ.Commerce Corp*, 51 USPQ 2d 1136 (ND Ill 1999).

The recent US Supreme Court decision in *Daimler v Bauman*,[114] which limits where a corporation is subject to general personal jurisdiction to its principal place of business and its place of incorporation except in exceptional circumstances, may alter the jurisdictional analysis applicable to websites.

In summary, establishing personal jurisdiction is very fact specific, and to the extent that a plaintiff can establish purposeful contacts with the state, as opposed to only a passive connection (eg, the operation of a website), a court will be more likely to exercise personal jurisdiction.

(b) Process patents

A process, or method, patent cannot be infringed via the Internet where only part of the process is carried out in the United States. The Federal Circuit explained in *NTP v RIM* as follows:

> *Because a process is nothing more than the sequence of actions of which it is comprised, the use of a process necessarily involves doing or performing each of the steps recited. This is unlike use of a system as a whole, in which the components are used collectively, not individually. We therefore hold that a process cannot be used 'within' the United States as required by section 271(a) unless each of the steps is performed within this country. In the present case, each of the asserted method claims of the '960, '172, and '451 patents recites a step that utilizes an 'interface' or 'interface switch,' which is only satisfied by the use of RIM's Relay located in Canada. Therefore, as a matter of law, these claimed methods could not be infringed by the use of RIM's system. See Eli Lilly & Co v Am Cyanamid Co, 82 F.3d 1568, 1571 (Fed Cir 1996) (discussing the enactment of section 271(g) and stating that '[p]rior to the enactment of the [Process Patents Amendments Act of 1988], a patentee holding a process patent could sue for infringement if others used the process in this country, but had no cause of action if such persons used the patented process abroad to manufacture products, and then imported, used, or sold the products in this country'); see also Zoltek Corp v United States, 51 Fed Cl 829, 836 (2002) (stating that 'if a private party practiced even one step of a patented process outside the United States, it avoided infringement liability, as [section 271(a)] was limited to acts committed within the United States').*
>
> *Thus, we agree with RIM that a finding of direct infringement by RIM's customers under section 271(a) of the method claims reciting an 'interface switch' or an 'interface' is precluded by the location of RIM's Relay in Canada. As a consequence, RIM cannot be liable for induced or contributory infringement of the asserted method claims, as a matter of law.*[115]

3.4 Remedies available for patent infringement

Two basic types of remedy are available for patent infringement: damages and injunctive relief. With respect to damages, 35 USC § 284, entitled "Damages", provides in relevant part as follows:

---

114 134 SCt 746 (2014).

115 *NTP, Inc v Research in Motion, Ltd*, 418 F 3d 1282, 1318 (Fed Cir 2005).

116 See *Panduit Corp v Stahlin Bros Fibre Works, Inc*, 575 F 2d 1152, 1157 (6th Cir 1978) ("When actual damages, eg, lost profits, cannot be proved, the patent owner is entitled to a reasonable royalty").

Upon finding for the claimant the court shall award the claimant damages adequate to compensate for the infringement, but in no event less than a reasonable royalty for the use made of the invention by the infringer, together with interest and costs as fixed by the court.

When the damages are not found by the jury, the court shall assess them. In either event the court may increase the damages up to three times the amount found or assessed ….

The court may receive expert testimony as an aid to the determination of damages or of what royalty would be reasonable under the circumstances.

Patent law damages come in two forms: a reasonable royalty and lost profits.[116]

With respect to injunctive relief, 35 USC § 283, entitled "Injunction", provides as follows:

The several courts having jurisdiction of cases under this title may grant injunctions in accordance with the principles of equity to prevent the violation of any right secured by patent, on such terms as the court deems reasonable.

The Supreme Court's *eBay* decision makes clear that to obtain an injunction, a plaintiff in a patent case must satisfy the same four-factor test as plaintiffs in any other type of litigation:

The test requires a plaintiff to demonstrate: (1) that it has suffered an irreparable injury; (2) that remedies available at law are inadequate to compensate for that injury; (3) that considering the balance of hardships between the plaintiff and the defendant, a remedy in equity is warranted; and (4) that the public interest would not be disserved by a permanent injunction. The decision to grant or deny relief is an act of equitable discretion by the district court, reviewable on appeal for abuse of discretion.[117]

As a practical matter, since this decision, it has become much more difficult to obtain injunctive relief in district court patent litigations, whereas prior to this decision, such relief was essentially automatic upon a finding of patent infringement.

4. Disclosure orders against ISPs

4.1 Availability

Disclosure orders can be obtained against innocent ISPs, requiring them to disclose the identity and contact details of a user of their service who is suspected of infringing an IP right. As long as the requisite showings can be made, such orders are not unduly difficult to obtain in practice.

4.2 Requirements

In the subpoena context, federal and state courts have applied various standards before granting disclosure orders against ISPs requiring that an anonymous online speaker be identified, including the summary judgment standard, the motion to dismiss standard and the good-faith standard.

In *Doe v Cahill*,[118] applying the summary judgment standard, the Delaware

117 *eBay v MercExchange, LLC*, 547 US 388, 391 (2006).
118 884 A 2d 451, 460 (Del 2005).

Supreme Court ruled that "before a defamation plaintiff can obtain the identity of an anonymous defendant through the compulsory discovery process he must support his defamation claim with facts sufficient to dismiss a summary judgment motion".

In *Columbia Insurance Co v Seescandy.com*,[119] applying the motion to dismiss standard, the district court in the Northern District of California held that "plaintiff has made a satisfactory showing that there is an actual person behind the [allegedly infringing] acts who would be amenable to suit in federal court", where the plaintiff provided specific evidence that the listed defendants remaining in the case appeared to be aliases for a person known as Ravi or Robby Kumar, including e-mails with a person named 'Ravi'.

In *Krinsky v Doe 6*,[120] applying the good-faith standard, the California court required "a prima facie showing of the elements of libel in order to overcome a defendant's motion to quash a subpoena seeking his or her identity", and reversed the order denying the motion to quash the subpoena, where the court held that the *prima facie* tort showing was not made.

In summary, in the subpoena context, courts have applied various standards to determine whether a disclosure order can be obtained to disclose the identity and contact details of a user of an ISP suspected of infringing an IP right.

4.3 Jurisdictional issues

Discovery on third parties can be obtained through the use of subpoenas pursuant to Federal Rule of Civil Procedure 45.

In the United States, subpoenas seeking information, such as the identification of the identity and contact details of users of their services, are often issued on technology companies. If the ISP objects to the subpoena, whether on the merits or on jurisdictional grounds, it can move to quash the subpoena, and a court will then have to rule on whether the ISP will be required to provide the requested information.

4.4 'John Doe' injunctions

'John Doe' injunctions, or injunctions against unnamed individuals or entities, are permissible in the United States. The type of injunctive relief available depends on the particular facts at hand, but US courts have enjoined, for example, named and unnamed defendants from selling or offering to sell, without authorisation or licence, merchandise bearing the photograph, name, likeness, image, tour information and/or logo of a musician within the United States.[121] In the trademark context, various other US courts have granted injunctive relief against unknown defendants.[122] In *SKS Merch*, the preliminary and permanent injunctions became binding on the named and unnamed defendants upon service of the court's order

---

119 185 FRD 573, 579 (ND Cal 1999).

120 159 Cal App 4th 1154 (Cal Ct App 2008).

121 See *SKS Merch, LLC, v Barry*, 233 F Supp 2d 841, 852 (ED Ky 2002) (entering nationwide injunction against unnamed defendants).

122 See, for example, *NBA Properties v Various John Does*, 113 F 3d 1246 (10th Cir 1997) (unpublished decision overturning district court's denial of *ex parte* TRO against unnamed parties); *Brockum Int'l, Inc v Various John Does*, 551 F Supp 1054 (ED Wis 1982) (prospectively enjoining unknown trademark violators); *Joel v Various John Does*, 499 F Supp 791 (ED Wis 1980) (same).

upon them, and were to be enforced by the seizure of any merchandise covered by the court's order, consistent with any other applicable laws or ordinances. Under federal law, to obtain injunctive relief, whether preliminary or permanent, courts apply a four-factor test:

- likelihood of irreparable harm to the plaintiff in the absence of an injunction;
- whether the likelihood of that harm is outweighed by the likelihood of harm to the defendant if the injunction were granted;
- the success of the plaintiff on the merits (or the likelihood of success in the case of a preliminary injunction); and
- the general public interest.[123]

123 *Metro-Goldwyn Mayer, Inc v 007 Safety Products, Inc*, 183 F 3d 10, 15 n 2 (1st Cir 1999)).

About the authors

David B Adler
Associate, Quinn Emanuel Urquhart & Sullivan, LLP
davidadler@quinnemanuel.com

David B Adler is an associate in Quinn Emanuel's IP department. Working in Hamburg and New York, Dr Adler focuses on contentious and non-contentious IP litigation. His expertise includes patent, design, trademark, unfair competition, and copyright proceedings. He regularly handles lawsuits in multiple jurisdictions.

Dr Adler is both a German-qualified attorney and an attorney at law (New York). He earned his Ph.D. in law from Albert Ludwigs University of Freiburg, Germany and the Max Planck Institute for Intellecutal Property Law in Munich, Germany (*magna cum laude*), and his LLM from Fordham University, New York (*cum laude*). He also holds a degree in law and economics from the University of Bayreuth, Germany. He is a lecturer on various aspects of IP law at the University of Hamburg.

James P Barabas
Associate, Budd Larner
jbarabas@buddlarner.com

Jim Barabas focuses on patent litigation, as well as IP due diligence and transactional matters. In particular, he has significant experience representing clients in patent litigation in the chemical, pharmaceutical and biotechnology industries. In the pharmaceutical area, he represents clients in Hatch-Waxman litigations. In the chemical and biotech areas, he has represented clients in litigations concerning DNA microarrays, labelling reagents and immunochemical detection systems. He also has significant experience litigating patent cases in the electrical engineering and computer science area. Such cases have involved, among others, redirection software, laptop computers and mobile phones. His practice is international in scope, and he has litigated in courts across the country, and in international arbitrations in Switzerland and Germany. Mr Barabas has significant experience in litigation in popular patent forums, including Delaware, New Jersey, the Eastern District of Texas, the Western District of Wisconsin, and the International Trade Commission (ITC). In the transactional area, his experience includes advising investment banks, private equity firms and corporations on the IP aspects of mergers, acquisitions, and other corporate transactions. As part of this transactional work, he has reviewed patent portfolios and outstanding patent litigations for leveraged buy-out and takeover candidates.

Persephone Bridgman Baker
Associate, Allen & Overy LLP
persephone.bridgmanbaker@allenovery.com

Persephone Bridgman Baker is an IP litigation associate in Allen & Overy's international IP team, based at the firm's London office. She graduated in law from the University of Cambridge, where she specialised in intellectual property, before completing her training contract at Allen & Overy. She specialises in cross-border and online IP enforcement work, and has worked in house on secondment to develop these practice areas. She acts for prominent pharmaceutical and online retail companies, working on both hard and soft IP disputes and advice. Ms Bridgman Baker works closely with Allen & Overy's corporate and dispute resolution teams on litigious and commercial IP matters in Hong Kong and the Middle East, having been seconded to Allen & Overy's offices in both. Ms Bridgman Baker is a regular contributor to the Allen & Overy Litigation Review and has recently written for *Intellectual Property Magazine*. She also holds a postgraduate diploma in IP law and practice from Oxford University and is an active member of the International Association for the Protection of Intellectual Property (AIPPI).

Juan Cuerva de Cañas
Associate, Clifford Chance
juan.cuerva@cliffordchance.com

Juan Cuerva is a member of both the IP and litigation and dispute resolution (L&DR) teams of Clifford Chance, Barcelona. He holds a law degree, procedural and civil law postgraduate degrees and a diploma of advanced studies in intellectual property. Since joining Clifford Chance in 2005, he has advised international pharmaceutical, publishing, IT and online companies and handled litigation involving IP and IT rights, with special emphasis on copyright and patents. Mr Cuerva is an associate lecturer on copyright, personality rights and advertising law at the Open University of Catalonia and at Ramon Llull University. He regularly lectures in copyright law at the LLM on intellectual property organised by the Barcelona Bar Association. Mr Cuerva is author of several articles on copyright for numerous publications, including Pe I, and often participates in seminars on copyright. He is member of ALADDA (the Spanish group of the *Association Littéraire et Artistique Internationale*).

DuckSoon Chang
Partner, Kim & Chang
ducksoon.chang@kimchang.com

DuckSoon Chang's principal practice areas include IP litigation, technology licensing, antitrust and international arbitration.

Mr Chang is currently the head of the IP Training Institute of the Seoul Bar Association, a committee member of the Korea Internet Address Dispute Resolution Committee, and an adviser to the Korea Fair Trade Commission on IP-related policies. He also served as an advisor to the Korea Trade Commission (an equivalent to the US ITC) on IP matters. Mr Chang is recommended as a band 1 IP attorney for Korea by Chambers Asia and selected among the world's pre-eminent patent lawyers by the *International Who's Who Legal* every year.

Mr Chang graduated from Seoul National University with an LLB degree and received an LLM degree from Harvard Law School. He is admitted to the Korean Bar and the Bars in the states of New York and California. He was a foreign attorney at Latham & Watkins from 1999 to 2000.

Neville Cordell
Partner, Allen & Overy LLP
neville.cordell@allenovery.com

Neville Cordell is a partner in Allen & Overy LLP's London office specialising in IP litigation and advisory work. He has 20 years' experience of acting for some of the world's leading technology companies and brands in patent, trademark, design, breach of confidence and copyright disputes. He is highly technically qualified, having graduated with a B Eng (first class honours) in aerospace systems engineering and an MSc (with distinction) in structural molecular biology. He also has been LLM with distinction in IP law.

Chambers ranks Mr Cordell as one of the United Kingdom's leading IP litigation lawyers, describing him as "very clever" and "well-organised" and states that he "has distinguished himself in IP disputes of all types, including both patents and soft IP". Uniquely, he is ranked both as one of the world's leading trademark lawyers by *WTR 1000* and as one of the world's leading patent lawyers by *IAM Patent 1000*.

Justin Davidson
Partner, Norton Rose Fulbright
justin.davidson@nortonrosefulbright.com

Justin Davidson is an IP and technology partner with Norton Rose Fulbright based in Hong Kong. He is admitted to practise in Hong Kong and in England & Wales. He was born in Asia and has worked in both London and Hong Kong.

Mr Davidson specialises in IP law and has a strong record advising both multinational and Asian businesses on a wide range of contentious and non-contentious IP and technology law issues across Asia. He regularly assists clients in protecting and exploiting their IP portfolios and with the growing sophistication of the Chinese legal system, has been increasingly active in China, in particular with patent litigation. His practice also includes advising on the IP aspects of acquisitions, spin-offs, joint ventures and initial public offerings.

Mr Davidson has regularly been acknowledged as a leading IP lawyer in Hong Kong and China by Asialaw and he is also named by Chambers Asia as a leading individual in the area of intellectual property. In 2010, *Asian Legal Business* named Mr Davidson as one of Asia's Hot 100 Lawyers and in 2014 *Managing Intellectual Property* picked him as an 'IP Star'.

Carlos Eduardo Eliziário de Lima
Partner, Dannemann Siemsen Advogados/Dannemann Siemsen Bigler & Ipanema Moreira
carlos.eduardo@dannemann.com.br

Carlos Eduardo Eliziário de Lima is a partner of Dannemann Siemsen Advogados and Dannemann Siemsen Bigler & Ipanema Moreira. He holds a law degree from Universidade Presbiteriana Mackenzie and a post graduate degree (LLM equivalent) in business contracts from the law school of Fundação Getúlio Vargas in Sao Paulo, Brazil. He is one of the co-authors of the Brazilian chapter of the books *2009 Licensing Update, 2010 Licensing Update* and *2011 Licensing Update* (Aspen Publishers) and author of a number of articles on intellectual property, innovation and business contracts. His practice focuses, among other things, on business contracts, including technology transfer agreements, IP licences, franchise and joint ventures. He has represented clients in local and cross-border transactions and has provided consultation on all aspects of business contracts, including tax issues.

Daniel Avila Failla
Attorney, Dannemann Siemsen Advogados/Industrial Property Agent at Dannemann Siemsen Bigler & Ipanema Moreira
dfailla@dannemann.com.br

Daniel Avila Failla is an attorney at law at Dannemann Siemsen Advogados and an industrial property agent at Dannemann Siemsen Bigler & Ipanema Moreira. He holds a law degree from Pontifícia Universidade Católica de São Paulo (PUC-SP). He is author of a number of articles on business contracts. His practice focuses, among other things, on contracts, antitrust and compliance.

Apar Gupta
Partner, Advani & Co
apar.gupta@advaniandco.com

Apar Gupta is a partner at Advani & Co's New Delhi office where he is a part of the general commercial advisory and litigation practice groups. He works closely with internet and technology companies, advising them on corporate structuring, business growth and financing, IP strategy, protection and enforcement, privacy and data protection, and outsourcing and service-level agreements. Mr Gupta is also retained by the Government of India on a panel of experts to advise the root certifying authority for digital certificates in India.

Mr Gupta is regularly quoted in the press on issues of internet regulation. His past media mentions include the *Wall Street Journal*, CNN International, National Public Radio (NPR), the *Times of India* and the *Hindustan Times*. He has also authored a book on the Information Technology Act, the primary enactment governing electronic commerce in India.

Laura R Hall
Associate, Allen & Overy
laura.hall@allenovery.com

Laura R Hall is an associate in the litigation practice in Allen & Overy's New York office, focusing on intellectual property and bankruptcy litigation. She has represented clients in trademark, trade secret, copyright and patent matters, as well as adversary proceedings in Chapter 11 proceedings and cross-border proceedings under Chapter 15 of the US Bankruptcy Code. Her matters have covered a wide range of technologies, including specialised insurance products, telecommunications devices, servers, operating systems and software. Ms Hall also has experience in complex commercial litigation at the trial and appellate level, including the drafting of complaints and answers, briefing motions to dismiss, preparing and responding to discovery requests and defending fact and expert depositions, as well as writing motions for summary judgment.

Nadine Herrmann
Partner, Quinn Emanuel Urquhart
& Sullivan, LLP
NadineHerrmann@quinnemanuel.com

Nadine Herrmann is managing partner of the Hamburg office of Quinn Emanuel Urquhart & Sullivan, LLP. She is both a German-qualified attorney and a solicitor (England and Wales).

Dr Herrmann specialises in IP and antitrust litigation. Her IP practice focuses on design, unfair competition, copyright and trade secret cases. In antitrust matters, her practice centres on the intersection of intellectual property and antitrust law (eg, FRAND licensing, including compulsory licences and their enforcement), covering all aspects of German and European competition law. She has significant expertise representing clients in the high-tech and life sciences industries. The author of a textbook on EU antitrust and German unfair competition law, Dr Herrmann has been internationally recognised as an expert in IP and antitrust matters. She has practised in Germany, the United States, and the United Kingdom.

Before joining Quinn Emanuel in 2012, Dr Herrmann was a partner at Allen & Overy LLP for three years, where she headed the firm's German IP practice. She earned her PhD in law from Philipps-Universität Marburg (*summa cum laude*), and her LLM from the University of Sydney.

Mimiao Hu
Associate, Orrick, Herrington & Sutcliffe LLP
mhu@orrick.com

Mimiao Hu is a managing associate in Orrick's IP group and resident attorney in the firm's Beijing office. She advises regional and international clients on China-related IP issues in both disputes and transactional matters.

Her work includes trademark, trade dress and copyright strategies, IP litigation, unfair competition, IP due diligence, cybersquatting and related technology issues.

Ms Hu has represented major clients including: a global fashion company in trademark and domain name disputes in China; a leading Japanese optics and imaging company in trademark disputes through which its brand was recognised as a well-known trademark in China; a leading Italian luxury company in a trademark licence in China; a leading video game company in copyright protection; and a leading US bank in investment in a large Chinese pharmaceuticals group (IP due diligence).

Prior to joining Orrick, Ms Hu was a senior associate in the Beijing and Shanghai offices of a major Chinese law firm.

Yali Hu
Managing associate, Orrick, Herrington & Sutcliffe LLP
yhu@orrick.com

Yali Hu is a managing associate in Orrick's Beijing office and a member of the IP group. She assists local- and foreign-based companies with all aspects of their IP rights in China, Europe and the United States, including Section 337 US ITC litigation. She has extensive experience in patent, trademark, domain name, copyright and trade secret matters.

Ms Hu's IP-related services include drafting application documents (claims, specification, abstract and drawings) and advising on the proper scope of protection based on the technical disclosure provided by clients; correcting application documents in preliminary examination procedures; transferring and responding to office actions in substantive examination procedures; requesting re-examination with respect to decisions of final rejection, communicating with examiners and amending application documents in pre-reexamination and re-examination procedures; requesting invalidation, searching for and analysing evidence; and analysing and assisting patent infringement disputes.

Paul Keller
Partner, Allen & Overy
paul.keller@allenovery.com

Paul Keller is a partner in Allen & Overy's litigation practice, focusing on patent litigation as well as IP due diligence and transactional matters. He has represented a wide range of clients in all stages of lawsuits from pre-suit investigation to final disposition of jury and bench trials and ITC investigations, including the presentation of arguments at Markman, discovery-dispute hearings, and direct and cross-examination of witnesses. His notable litigation experience includes co-managing and directing the defence in a patent infringement lawsuit in the Eastern District of Texas in which, for the first time in that district's history, a jury verdict of non-infringement and invalidity was successfully obtained.

In addition to his litigation work, Mr Keller has expertise in transactional IP issues, such as advising clients regarding the licensing of their intellectual property and active involvement in due diligence investigations and counselling in numerous acquisitions, potential acquisitions, and other investments.

Martin PJ Kratz
Partner, Bennett Jones LLP
KratzM@bennettjones.com

Martin Kratz, QC leads the IP practice and co-leads the e-commerce practice for Bennett Jones LLP. His practice focuses primarily on technology transactions, protection and commercialisation of intellectual property, information and privacy law, outsourcing and IT procurement. Mr Kratz is national co-director of Osgoode Hall Law School's national IP LLM programme and teaches courses in that programme, as well as at Concordia University College. He is widely acknowledged as a leading lawyer in the fields of intellectual property, internet law and technology law. He has written more than 280 publications including the following books: *Canadian Internet Law; Canadian Intellectual Property Law*, 2nd edition; *Trademarks and Industrial Designs; Internet Law; Obtaining Patents,* 2nd edition; *Protection of Copyright and Industrial Design,* 2nd edition; *Information Systems Security*, 2nd edition; *The Computer Virus Crisis*, 2nd edition. He has also written chapters in *IP&IT Handbook*: Data Protection – Canada; *Outsourcing* (Canada); *Licensing; Intellectual Property Disputes*; and *Electronic Commerce Law.*

Joachim Lehnhardt
Of counsel, Quinn Emanuel Urquhart & Sullivan, LLP
JoachimLehnhardt@quinnemanuel.com

Joachim Lehnhardt is a German-qualified attorney specialising in contentious IP matters with a particular focus on copyright and patent law. He has deep technical expertise in a variety of fields, principally relating to software and other computer technologies. Prior to joining the firm, Mr Lehnhardt worked with Allen & Overy LLP in Hamburg for six years, and as a research assistant at the Institute for Information, Telecommunications and Media Law in Münster before that. He regularly lectures on media and IT law.

Montserrat López-Bellosta
Partner, Clifford Chance
Montserrat.lopez-bellosta@cliffordchance.com

Montserrat López-Bellosta is a partner in the litigation, dispute resolution and IP department at Clifford Chance's Barcelona office and has over 15 years' experience in IP, regulatory, litigation and arbitration matters. She is sector leader for Spain for Clifford Chance's global consumer goods and retail sector group, as well as global head of the regulatory legal product group in Clifford Chance's healthcare, life sciences and chemical sector. Her recent relevant experience includes: defending litigation cases involving patents, design rights, copyrights, trademarks, commercial matters and unfair competition; customs seizures in order to prevent the import of counterfeit products and liaising with law enforcement and customs authorities to detect and respond to counterfeit activities; representing innovative companies in criminal court proceedings in relation to offences against public health and against IP rights; advising on licence, research, agency and distribution agreements and advising pharmaceutical, medical device and consumer goods and retail companies regarding several regulatory aspects such as pharmacovigilance, marketing authorisation procedures, EU paediatric regulation, advertising, promotion and compliance. She regularly publishes articles in specialist journals and participates in seminars, conferences and courses on private international law, regulatory, litigation and IP topics.

Josep Montefusco Monferrer
Senior associate, Clifford Chance
josep.montefusco@cliffordchance.com

Josep Montefusco is a member of both the IP and L&DR teams of Clifford Chance, Barcelona. He has degrees in law and economics from Universitat Pompeu Fabra of Barcelona. Since he joined Clifford Chance in 2000, he has advised on, and handled litigation involving unfair competition and advertising and infringement and validity of a wide range of IP rights such as patents, utility models, trademarks and designs. Mr Montefusco specialises in the pharmaceutical and automotive sectors, in which he has extensive experience representing leading multinational corporations. Mr Montefusco regularly gives lectures on IP, unfair competition/advertising and procedural law at some of the most highly reputed masters programmes in Barcelona, such as the IP&IT ESADE's LLM; the *Master de Abogacía* and *Master de Abogacía Internacional Instituto Superior de Derecho y Economía's* LLM; and the *Master de Derecho de los Negocios* and *Master de Derecho de Propiedad Industrial e Intelectual* organised by the Barcelona Bar Association.

Gustavo de Freitas Morais
Partner, Dannemann Siemsen
gustavo@dannemann.com.br

Gustavo de Freitas Morais is an engineer and attorney at law licensed in Brazil, with a specialisation in intellectual property at the Franklin Pierce Law Centre in the United States. He is a law professor for the Lato Sensu Post-Graduation Course of Law at the *Escola de Direito de São Paulo – Fundação Getúlio Vargas* and at the *Centro de Extensão Universitária* on intellectual property. Mr Morais is experienced in litigation, IP negotiations, patents, industrial designs, copyright, software protection, technology transfer, unfair competition, trademarks, biodiversity and traditional knowledge. He has a diverse international IP practice and represents a large number of companies based in Brazil, North America and Latin America, Europe, Africa and Asia. Mr Morais advises clients in numerous industries, including agrochemicals, automotive, biotechnology, chemical and petrochemical manufacturing, electronics and technology, foods, beverages and tobacco and pharmaceuticals.

Alexandra Neri
Partner, Herbert Smith Freehills Paris
alexandra.neri@herbertsmith.com

Alexandra Neri heads Herbert Smith Freehills' Paris IP technology, media and telecommunications group. She is an expert in contentious and non-contentious IP issues and is both a mediator and an arbitrator for the World Intellectual Property Organisation.

Ms Neri advises clients on matters including trademark and patent issues, IP rights in the digital economy, domain name litigation and cybersquatting, international data protection and cross-border data flows, online contracts and digital signatures. She has also represented clients in litigation against counterfeiters and advised on the values and indemnities involved. In the context of mergers and acquisitions, she advises on due diligence in relation to intellectual property.

Ms Neri was voted IP/IT Woman of the Year in 2010 by *Option Droit & Affaires* and won the Europe Women in Business Law Awards 2011.

Reggie Schafer
Associate, Cohen & Gresser
rschafer@cohengresser.com

Reggie Schafer is an associate in the litigation practice at Cohen & Gresser. He has broad-based experience in general commercial and IP litigation and has represented leading technology companies, investment and commercial banks, multinational corporations and individual directors and officers. In addition to his litigation work, Mr Schafer has advised corporate and banking clients in mergers and acquisitions, financing, litigation due diligence, and bankruptcy proceedings.

Sonia Sebé Marín
Associate, Clifford Chance
sonia.sebe@cliffordchance.com

Sonia Sebé is a member of both the IP and L&DR teams of Clifford Chance in Barcelona. She holds a degree in law from the Pompeu Fabra University of Barcelona and an LLM in IP law from ESADE Law School.

Since joining Clifford Chance in 2005, she has advised international companies in matters such as IP rights, data protection, publicity and compliance, and also handled litigation proceedings involving IP rights, with special emphasis on trademarks and patents. She lectures on intellectual property at the master's programme on intellectual and industrial property law (*Master de Derecho de Propiedad Industrial e Intelectual*) organised by the Barcelona Bar Association.

Chang Hwan Shin
Foreign attorney, Kim & Chang
chshin@kimchang.com

Chang Hwan Shin is a member of both the IP and entertainment department of Kim & Chang, specialising in copyright, media, film, music, business software and entertainment software laws, and so on. Prior to joining the firm, Mr Shin gained extensive experience serving as the deputy director of the Copyright Division and Publication and Newspaper Division of the Ministry of Culture and Tourism for nine years. He is a member of the Korea Copyright Commission and Contents Dispute Resolution Committee. Previously, he had served as a policy advisor to the Office of the President, a non-executive director of Korea Music Copyright Association, and a member of Game Rating Board. Mr Shin has written as a co-author for numerous publications, including P Geller, *et al, International Copyright Law and Practice* (Matthew Bender, 2012 and 2013 editions).

Giulio Enrico Sironi
Partner, Avv Prof Adriano Vanzetti e Associati
g.sironi@vanzettieassociati.it

Giulio Enrico Sironi is a partner of the law firm Avv Prof Adriano Vanzetti e Associati in Milan. He deals with all fields of intellectual property, in particular patents, trademarks, appellations of origin and geographical indications, copyright, designs and models and unfair competition.

He has a research doctorate in IP law. Since the 2005/2006 academic year he has been a lecturer on a patent legislation course at the University of Parma, and since the 2012/2013 academic year he has been a lecturer in IP law in the economics faculty of the Catholic University of Milan.

Mr Sironi is the author of numerous publications in the IP field, including a monograph and commentaries, and is a member of the editorial board of the reviews *Giurisprudenza Annotata di Diritto Industriale* and *The Trademark Reporter*. He is also a member of the AIPPI, the International Trademarks Association (INTA) and the Licensing Executives Society. He regularly gives papers at conferences and on master's courses.

Martin Steiger
Managing partner, Steiger Legal
steiger@steigerlegal.ch

Martin Steiger is founding and managing partner of Zurich-based boutique law firm Steiger Legal. He specialises in advising private clients and small to mid-cap companies on IP/IT law, media law and aviation law, as well as related litigation. His practice includes copyright, data privacy, social media, unfair competition and trademarks including IP/IT/media aspects of general commercial matters. Mr Steiger worked for the Zürich offices of major international law firms in IP/IT and mergers and acquisitions. He is a regular contributor of articles on IP/IT-related topics and co-publisher of the leading Swiss compilation on IP/IT law. Mr Steiger has extensive experience in representing principals from the internet industry and is often quoted as a legal expert in major media.

Louise Stoupe
Partner, Morrison & Foerster LLP/Ito & Mitomi
lstoupe@mofo.com

Louise Stoupe is a partner in the litigation department of Morrison & Foerster's Tokyo office. Her practice focuses on intellectual property and complex commercial transactions. Ms Stoupe is a trial lawyer, a recognised expert in e-discovery and international IP law, and a highly regarded counsellor on IP issues to some of the largest technology companies in the world. In 2008, *IP Law & Business*, a sibling publication of *The American Lawyer*, named Ms Stoupe to its first-ever Top 50 Under 45 list of IP lawyers. Ms Stoupe is recognised as a leading lawyer in dispute resolution in Japan by *Chambers Asia*. She is licensed to practise law in the state of California, England and Wales, and New Zealand.

Kelvin Tan
Director, Drew & Napier LLC
kelvin.tan@drewnapier.com

Kelvin Tan joined Drew & Napier in 1995, and is a director in the disputes department. Mr Tan has an active practice in intellectual property, and regularly handles copyright, designs, patents, trademarks and confidential information matters. He has extensive experience advising the owners of well-known brands and leading technologies in various spheres of business, including luxury goods, consumer goods, food and beverage, advertising and education. Some of his recent cases have involved complex technology such as semiconductor manufacturing, multiplayer online games and software development. Apart from IP matters, Mr Tan handles civil and commercial disputes in the Singapore courts and in international arbitration.

Ekaterina Tilling
Special counsel, Baker Botts LLP
ekaterina.tilling@bakerbotts.com

Ekaterina Tilling is recognised in the field of intellectual property, with significant experience in complex investment projects involving different IP assets, as well as in negotiating and advising on various IP/IT transactions (eg, software development, franchising, IP assignment and licensing). She is also highly skilled in solving IP disputes in Russian courts of all levels.

Ms Tilling is qualified as a mediator in international and community conflicts by the Conflict Resolution, Research and Resource Institute, Inc. She has been recommended among the European leading experts for IP matters by professional ratings such as *Legal 500* and Chambers since 2007. She is the author of many IP publications in Russia and abroad (eg *IP Review 2006, The World IP Review 2007* and *IP Value 2008–2011*) including commentaries on Russia's key legislative acts.

Adriano Vanzetti
Founding partner, Avv Prof Adriano Vanzetti e Associati
studio@vanzettieassociati.it

Professor Adriano Vanzetti is the founding partner of the law firm Avv Prof Adriano Vanzetti e Associati in Milan, which operates principally in the IP field, and especially in the sector of trademarks and other distinctive signs, appellations of origin and geographical indications, patents, designs and models, unfair competition, antitrust law and copyright.

Professor Vanzetti handles judicial and extra-judicial cases in all IP sectors. He has managed and coordinated important national and transnational disputes, often involving cross-border problems. In the patent field, he has vast experience in the mechanics, energy, electronics, chemical, pharmaceutical and biotechnology sectors. In the area of trademarks he has protected – before the ordinary courts, before the European Court of Justice and in domestic and international arbitration proceedings – the trademarks and names of leading fashion houses, food and beverage companies, car manufacturers and wine producers.

He is emeritus professor of IP law in the faculty of law of the Catholic University of Milan and president of the Italian Society for the Study of Intellectual Property. In 1972, he launched the IP legal review *Giurisprudenza Annotata di Diritto Industriale* and has been its editor since then. He is the author of numerous articles, monographs and commentaries in the field of IP law, including the most widely used Italian handbook on IP law, and has been a member of numerous ministerial expert commissions appointed by the Italian government for the reform of Italian laws in the field of IP law. He regularly organises, chairs and is a speaker at conferences in the IP field.

Monique Wadsted
Partner, MAQS Law Firm
Monique.wadsted@se.maqs.com

Monique Wadsted has been a partner at MAQS Law Firm since 1997 and is head of intellectual property in the firm's Stockholm office. She specialises in IP and IT law, marketing, media, privacy and e-commerce, entertainment and arbitration and litigation. She is well known for her work as counsel for Hollywood studios in both the criminal and civil law cases related to The Pirate Bay. *Legal 500* ranks Ms Wadsted as a Leading Individual in IP and media.

Xiang Wang
Partner, Orrick, Herrington & Sutcliffe LLP
xiangwang@orrick.com

Xiang Wang is the Asia managing partner and the lead partner for Orrick's China-focused IP practice, and is also the managing partner of the firm's Beijing office. He assists local and foreign companies with all aspects of IP rights in China, Hong Kong and the United States.

Dr Wang has developed the region's premier IP practice. Due to its success in patent disputes in both litigation and arbitration in China, the Orrick China IP team was exclusively featured in a 30-minute documentary film *Patent Wars* by China Central Television in 2011.

Dr Wang has been interviewed by numerous news media on IP issues, including *The New York Times, The Wall Street Journal, Reuters, Bloomberg, International Herald Tribune, Financial Times, Law360, Asian Legal Business, Managing Intellectual Property*, China Central Television, Caixin Media, China Radio International, *China Business Law Journal, Chinese Lawyer, Chicago Herald, Managing Intellectual Property, Asia IP, CFO Innovations* and the Swedish Broadcasting Corporation.

Thomas de Weerd
Partner, Houthoff Buruma
t.de.weerd@houthoff.com

Thomas de Weerd is a partner in the IT and IP team of Houthoff Buruma. He specialises in IT and internet law, e-commerce, outsourcing, IP and technology-related contracts and transactions as well as privacy law. Mr De Weerd is co-author of a Dutch handbook on IT agreements and several other publications on IT and internet-related subjects. He is a member of the board of the Netherlands Association for Information Technology and Law, and chair of the e-commerce, technology, outsourcing and privacy practice group of international law firm network Lex Mundi.

Wolter Wefer Bettink
Partner, Houthoff Buruma
w.bettink@houthoff.com

Wolter Wefers Bettink has been a partner since 1993. He specialises in IP, IT law, e-commerce and privacy law. As an IP litigator he concentrates on technology-related disputes and non-contentious matters (including patents and breeders' rights), trademarks and copyright. He litigates and advises on internet-related matters with a focus on IP-related disputes, electronic contract formation, and online gambling. He advises clients on complex IT agreements (including enterprise resource planning and outsourcing), and on the resolution of disputes arising from failed IT projects. He provides advice on data protection under both EU and national privacy legislation, including on privacy issues related to e-discovery, cross-border civil litigation and corporate investigations. Mr Wefers Bettink is an arbitrator for the Netherlands Arbitration Institute and a mediator for the International Chamber of Commerce on IT and IP disputes. He is also a domain name panelist for the World Intellectual Property Organisation and the Czech Arbitration Court. Mr Wefers Bettink is co-author of the chapter on the Netherlands in *International Design Protection (A Global Handbook)* and a contributor to *Commentaries on the Community Trademark Regulation and the Community Design Regulation* (to be published in 2014 by CH Beck Hart Nomos). He is a member of INTA, iTechlaw and the AIPPI.

Michael Williams
Partner, Gilbert + Tobin
mwilliams@gtlaw.com.au

Michael Williams heads up the IP group at Gilbert + Tobin. He is well known for his strategic skills, subject matter knowledge and robust approach to high-stakes IP litigation. Mr Williams practises across the spectrum of IP issues, including copyright, patents, trademarks, false advertising, breach of confidence, product liability and anti-counterfeiting. He is recognised as a leading IP practitioner in Australia with a band 1 ranking in intellectual property in *Chambers Asia Pacific*, and he has been described as "a major force in copyright litigation". He is also ranked as a Leading Individual in *Asia Pacific Legal 500*. He acts for a wide range of Australian and international clients in fields as diverse as consumer electronics, content, entertainment, software, fast-moving consumer goods, mining and financial services in federal, state and appellate courts, including the High Court of Australia. He has written for many legal publications including Halsbury's Laws of Australia (Patents and Copyright) and *Lahore's Patents, Trademarks and Related Rights* (Unfair competition). Mr Williams is also vice president of the Copyright Society of Australia.

Jibo Wu
Patent attorney, Orrick, Herrington & Sutcliffe LLP
jibu.wu@orrick.com

Jibo Wu is a contract patent attorney at Orrick's Beijing office, focusing on IP issues. He holds a bachelors degree in electrical engineering, two master's degrees in systems engineering and computer sciences and has a strong engineering background to support his legal practice in intellectual property. Mr Wu has more than 20 years' experience in the fields of electrical engineering and information technology. He is now engaged in cross-border patent prosecution and patent litigation, particularly between China and other countries.

Chie Yakura
Partner, Morrison & Foerster LLP/Ito & Mitomi
cyakura@mofo.com

Chie Yakura is a partner in the litigation department of Morrison & Foerster's Tokyo office. She represents both non-Japanese and Japanese corporations on a wide range of litigation matters with an emphasis on intellectual property, technology transactions, and trade secrets as well as cross-border contractual and commercial disputes. Ms Yakura has also advised on product liability, real estate, licensing, antitrust/competition law and corporate restructuring matters. She has handled cases in a variety of industries including software, hardware, consumer electronics, pharmaceutical, biotechnology, transportation, real estate and manufacturing. Ms Yakura is a *Bengoshi*, admitted to practice in Japan. She is also a patent attorney (*Benrishi*) in Japan and a qualified lawyer in the state of New York.

Carol Yan
Managing associate, Orrick, Herrington & Sutcliffe LLP
cyan@orrick.com

Carol W Yan is a senior associate in Orrick's Beijing office and a member of the IP group. Her practice focuses on patent filing and prosecution as well as patent litigation in multiple industries, including chemicals, materials science, pharmaceuticals, biotechnology, medical devices, semiconductors and auto mechanics. She has extensive experience in patent, trademark, domain name, copyright and trade secret matters.

Ms Yan has handled more than 500 Chinese patent applications and has extensive experience in drafting and filing responses to office actions, re-examination and invalidation.

Ms Yan's recent experience includes: representing multinational chemical, pharmaceutical, biotechnology, semiconductor and auto parts companies; proposing advice for multinational chemical and auto mechanical companies regarding operating in China, including assessment of potential patent infringement risks; and providing advice for multinational pharmaceutical and semiconductor companies regarding IP litigation in China, including trial preparation, trial and post-trial counselling on patent lawsuits.

Shelley Zhang
Senior associate, Orrick, Herrington & Sutcliffe LLP
szhang@orrick.com

Shelley Zhang is of counsel in Orrick's Beijing office and a member of the IP group. Her practice focuses on IP prosecution and enforcement. She has extensive experience in patent, trademark, domain name, copyright and trade secret matters.

Ms Zhang's related IP experience includes: prosecution of patents and trademarks, including application preparation, office actions/oppositions procedures and re-examination procedures; enforcement and technology transfer/licensing arrangements for substantial patent and trademark portfolios for companies doing business in China; patent invalidation proceedings, patent infringement suits, anti-counterfeiting, anti-piracy efforts and patent and trademark enforcement dispute strategy planning in China; advising on IP protection strategies; assisting Chinese companies in Section 337 US ITC investigations, patent infringement litigations and product liability litigations in the United States; IP due diligence and portfolio counselling; and customs registration and enforcement for patent, trademark and copyright.